# Time Out

# Andalucía

**timeout.com/andalucia**

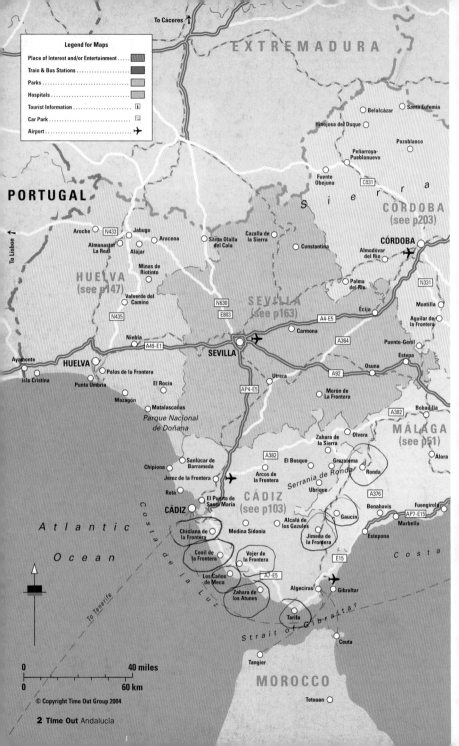

**Legend for Maps**

Place of Interest and/or Entertainment . . . . .
Train & Bus Stations . . . . . . . . . . . . . . . . . . . . . .
Parks . . . . . . . . . . . . . . . . . . . . . . . . . . . . . . . . . . . . .
Hospitals . . . . . . . . . . . . . . . . . . . . . . . . . . . . . . . . .
Tourist Information . . . . . . . . . . . . . . . . . . . . . . . 🛈
Car Park . . . . . . . . . . . . . . . . . . . . . . . . . . . . . . . . . 🅿
Airport . . . . . . . . . . . . . . . . . . . . . . . . . . . . . . . . . . ✈

To Cáceres ↑

**EXTREMADURA**

**PORTUGAL**

To Lisbon ↑

Belalcázar
Santa Eufemia
Hinojosa del Duque
Pozoblanco
Peñarroya-Pueblonuevo
Fuente Obejuna
C031

S i e r r a

**CÓRDOBA**
(see p203)

**CÓRDOBA**

Aroche  N433
Jabugo
Almonaster La Real
Aracena
Alájar
Santa Olalla del Cala
Cazalla de la Sierra
Almodóvar del Río
Minas de Riotinto
Constantina
Palma del Río
N331

**HUELVA**
(see p147)

Valverde del Camino

**SEVILLA**
(see p163)

Montilla
Aguilar de la Frontera

N435
N630
E803
A4-E5
Écija

Niebla
A49-E1
**SEVILLA**
Carmona
A364
Puente-Genil
Estepa

Ayamonte
**HUELVA**
Palos de la Frontera
Utrera
A92
Osuna

Isla Cristina
Punta Umbría
El Rocío
AP4-E5
Morón de La Frontera

Mazagón
Matalascañas
A382
Bobadilla

**Parque Nacional de Doñana**

Zahara de la Sierra
Olvera
**MÁLAGA**
(see p51)

Chipiona
Sanlúcar de Barrameda
A382
El Bosque
Grazalema
Álora

Jerez de la Frontera
Arcos de la Frontera
Ronda

Rota
Ubrique
Serranía de Ronda
A376

El Puerto de Santa María
**CÁDIZ**
(see p103)
Benahavís
Fuengirola
AP7-E15

**CÁDIZ**
Alcalá de los Gazules
Gaucín
Marbella

Chiclana de la Frontera
Medina Sidonia
Jimena de la Frontera
Estepona

Conil de la Frontera
Vejer de la Frontera
E15
C o s t a

**Atlantic**
Los Caños de Meca
A7-E5

**Ocean**
Zahara de los Atunes
Algeciras
Gibraltar

C o s t a   d e   l a   L u z
Tarifa

To Tenerife
Strait of Gibraltar
Ceuta

0 _____ 40 miles
0 _____ 60 km
Tangier

© Copyright Time Out Group 2004

**MOROCCO**

Tetouan

**2** Time Out Andalucía

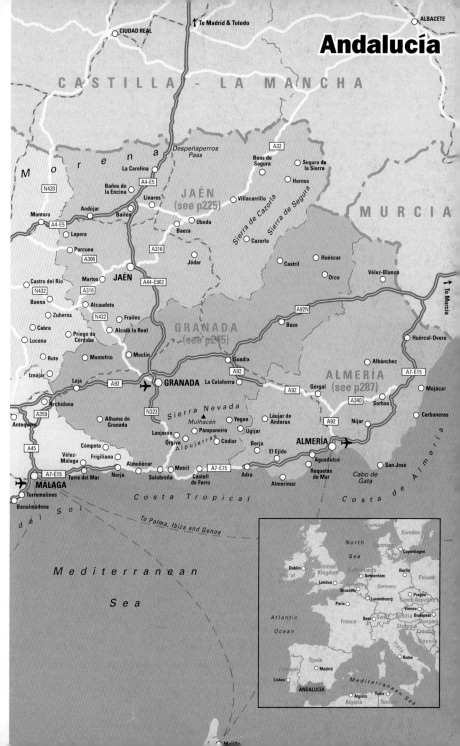

**Published by Time Out Guides Ltd,** a wholly owned subsidiary of Time Out Group Ltd.
Time Out and the Time Out logo are trademarks of Time Out Group Ltd.

**© Time Out Group Ltd 2004**
Previous edition 2002

10 9 8 7 6 5 4 3 2 1

**This edition first published in Great Britain in 2004 by Ebury**
Ebury is a division of The Random House Group Ltd,
20 Vauxhall Bridge Road, London SW1V 2SA

Random House Australia Pty Limited, 20 Alfred Street, Milsons Point, Sydney, New South Wales 2061, Australia
Random House New Zealand Limited, 18 Poland Road, Glenfield, Auckland 10, New Zealand
Random House South Africa (Pty) Limited, Endulini, 5A Jubilee Road, Parktown 2193, South Africa

Random House UK Limited Reg. No. 954009

**Distributed in USA by Publishers Group West**
1700 Fourth Street, Berkeley, California 94710

**Distributed in Canada by Penguin Canada Ltd**
10 Alcorn Avenue, Toronto, Ontario, Canada M4V 3B2

For further distribution details, see www.timeout.com

ISBN 1-904978-25-8

A CIP catalogue record for this book is available from the British Library

Colour reprographics by Icon, Crowne House, 56-58 Southwark Street, London SE1 1UN

Printed and bound by Cayfosa-Quebecor, Ctra. De Caldes, KM 3 08 130 Sta, Perpètua de Mogoda, Barcelona, Spain

**Time Out Guides Limited**
**Universal House**
**251 Tottenham Court Road**
**London W1T 7AB**
**Tel + 44 (0)20 7813 3000**
**Fax + 44 (0)20 7813 6001**
**Email guides@timeout.com**
**www.timeout.com**

## Editorial

**Editor** Jonathan Cox
**Consultant Editor** Michael Jacobs
**Deputy Editor** Jenny Piening
**Listings Checkers** Alix Leveugle, Alex Phillips, Cecily Doyle
**Proofreader** John Watson
**Indexer** Selena Cox

**Editorial/Managing Director** Peter Fiennes
**Series Editor** Ruth Jarvis
**Deputy Series Editor** Lesley McCave
**Business Manager** Gareth Garner
**Editorial Co-ordinator** Anna Norman
**Accountants** Sarah Bostock, Abdus Sadique

## Design

**Art Director** Mandy Martin
**Deputy Art Director** Scott Moore
**Senior Designer** Tracey Ridgewell
**Designer** Oliver Knight
**Junior Designer** Chrissy Mouncey
**Digital Imaging** Dan Conway
**Ad Make-up** Charlotte Blythe

## Picture Desk

**Picture Editor** Jael Marschner
**Deputy Picture Editor** Tracey Kerrigan
**Picture Researcher** Ivy Lahon
**Picture Desk Assistant/Librarian** Laura Lord

## Advertising

**Sales Director** Mark Phillips
**International Sales Manager** Ross Canadé
**International Sales Executive** James Tuson
**Advertising Sales (Andalucía)** The Broadsheet
**Advertising Assistant** Lucy Butler

## Marketing

**Marketing Director, Guides** Mandy Martinez
**US Publicity & Marketing Associate** Rosella Albanese

## Production

**Production Director** Mark Lamond
**Production Controller** Samantha Furniss

## Time Out Group

**Chairman** Tony Elliott
**Managing Director** Mike Hardwick
**Group Financial Director** Richard Waterlow
**Group Commercial Director** Lesley Gill
**Group General Manager** Nichola Coulthard
**Group Circulation Director** Jim Heinemann
**Group Art Director** John Oakey
**Online Managing Director** David Pepper
**Group Production Director** Steve Proctor
**Group IT Director** Simon Chappell

## Contributors

**Introduction** Jonathan Cox. **History** Adam Coulter (*Cliché: Paradise Lost?* Jonathan Cox). **Andalucía Today** Adam Coulter.
**Architecture** Helen Crawshaw, Jonathan Cox. **Literary Andalucía** Michael Jacobs. **Food & Drink** Adam Coulter, Jonathan Cox.
**Festivals & Events** Adam Coulter. **Province Introductions** Jonathan Cox. **Walks** Guy Hunter-Watts. **Málaga City** Tara Stevens.
**Costa del Sol** Tara Stevens. **East of Málaga** Tara Stevens. **North of Málaga** Helen Crawshaw, Jonathan Cox (*Top five: Birding spots* Jonathan Cox). **West of Málaga** Jonathan Cox, Rupert Eden, Guy Hunter-Watts (*Cliché: Bandits* Jonathan Cox). **Cádiz City** Adam Coulter, Martin Hastings (*Carnaval* Adam Coulter). **North of Cádiz** Adam Coulter, Martin Hastings (*Cliché: Sherry & brandy* Susan Low; *Flamenco puro* Adam Coulter; *Sea horses* Martin Hastings). **East of Cádiz** Jonathan Cox, Rupert Eden, Guy Hunter-Watts. **Costa de la Luz** Tara Stevens. **Gibraltar** Tara Stevens. **Huelva City & the Coast** Kirsten Foster, Joanne Williams (*The last wilderness* Kirsten Foster). **North of Huelva** Kirsten Foster, Joanne Williams (*Hang 'em high* Joanne Williams). **Sevilla City** Adam Coulter, Chris Moss (*Cliché: Bullfighting* Adam Coulter; *Cliché: Flamenco* Chris Moss; *Extreme unction* Jonathan Cox; *NO-8-DO* Adam Coulter; *Sacred and profane celebrations* Adam Coulter). **East of Sevilla** Kirsten Foster, Martin Hastings. **North of Sevilla** Kirsten Foster. **Córdoba City** Kirsten Foster, Amanda White (*The lost city* Amanda White; *Cliché: Julio Romero de Torres* Kirsten Foster). **The Guadalquivir Valley & North of Córdoba** Amanda White. **South of Córdoba** Martin Hastings, Amanda White. **Jaén City** Adam Coulter, Jonathan Cox. **South of Jaén** Jonathan Cox. **North of Jaén** Jonathan Cox (*Echoes of war* Michael Jacobs). **East of Jaén** Adam Coulter, Jonathan Cox. **Granada City** Jonathan Cox, Nadia Feddo, Kirsten Foster. **West of Granada** Sophie Blacksell. **East of Granada** Jonathan Cox. **Sierra Nevada & the Alpujarras** Sophie Blacksell, Tara Stevens (*Being Chris Stewart* Tara Stevens). **Almería City** Adam Coulter, Jonathan Cox (*Let me take you down...* & *Almería 2005* Jonathan Cox). **Costa de Almería** Adam Coulter, Jonathan Cox (*Tent city* Jonathan Cox). **Almería Interior** Adam Coulter, Jonathan Cox. **Directory** Adam Coulter, Jonathan Cox.

**The Editor would like to thank:**
Karen Abrahams (Casas Karen), Barry Branham, Daniel Busturia (Hacienda Benazuza), Colette & Glen (Casas Cinco), Warren Dyer, Giles & Tara, Penny Jarret, Ingunn Kroken & Ana Raczkowski, Jane Richards (Hertz), Antonio Martín Machuca (Andalucía Tourist Board), Carolina Oficialdegui (Hotel Larios), Matt Osborne, Paco, Ali Rigby (GB Airways), Kjell Sporrong, Rune Vik & Eva Lindblom (The Beach House), Paco Ruiz, Chris Stewart, and especially Michael Jacobs, and Selena and Joseph James Cox.

**Maps** JS Graphics (john@jsgraphics.co.uk).

**Photography** Jonathan Cox, except: page 34 akg images; page 34 Corbis; pages 45, 112 Spanish Tourist Office; page 185 PA; page 210 The Art Archive/Museo Romero de Torres/Joseph Martin; page 274 Skishoot Offshoot. The following image was provided by the featured establishment/artist: page 277.

# Contents

# Introduction

For many northern Europeans, Andalucía is a second (and, increasingly frequently, a first) home. The Brits and the Germans, in particular, have had a love affair with southern Spain for more than 40 years. Yet the waves of holidaymakers and expats of the last few decades are but the latest in almost three millennia of foreign invasions.

Since ancient times this immense and immensely varied region has held an allure, a mystique, a whiff of the exotic. Nowhere does Europe come closer to Africa – literally and metaphorically. Many aspects of its flora and fauna, its history, culture and architecture span two continents, and it's this unique blending that has long given the region its distinctive flavour. Educated travellers have, for the last two centuries, been seduced by this exoticism, and particularly the legacy of the Moors, whose 700-year presence in Spain remains etched in stone and stucco across the region.

Another major draw today is that Andalucía is popularly seen as the quintessence of Spain. Here is the home of virtually everything perceived of as stereotypically Spanish – the blood and machismo of the bullfight, the fire and passion of flamenco, fragrant orange blossom, wild-eyed gypsies, tapas, sherry… Clichéd these images may be, but they remain defining features of the region.

And then there's Andalucía extraordinary natural beauty and diversity. It's perfectly possible to ski in pristine alpine scenery in the morning, and then drive through a multi-hued desert to reach unspoiled beaches in time for a late afternoon swim.

Of course, it's not all light and loveliness. The region has no shortage of problems – severe rural poverty, racial tensions, a coastline that has, in large part, been irredeemably ruined by overdevelopment – but, as a visitor, the former two issues will rarely be encountered and the latter can easily be avoided.

For a tourist, Andalucía really has got it all. Whatever type of holiday you seek, you can find it somewhere here. Bucket-and-spaders can soak up the rays, swig sangría and party all night long on the Costa del Sol; more individualistic sun-seekers choose to head for the Costa de la Luz or the Cabo de Gata for low-key resorts and endless white-sand beaches. Urban sophisticates can bar-hop the hip hangouts of Granada, Málaga, Córdoba and Sevilla, while more tradition-minded folk might prefer to crawl classic trapped-in-amber tapas bars in the very same cities. The culturally inclined can follow in the footsteps of the Moors, via extraordinary castles, palaces and mosques; those who favour physical over cerebral pleasures can windsurf off Tarifa's famed beaches, scuba dive off Gibraltar or hike and ski among Spain's highest peaks, the Sierra Nevada.

But be warned: this place is a drug. Once visited, you'll find yourself wistfully enquiring after local property prices, and dreaming of that perfect place in the sun.

## ABOUT TIME OUT GUIDES

*Time Out Andalucía* is one of an expanding series of travel guides produced by the people behind London and New York's successful listings magazines. Our guides are all written and updated by local experts who have striven to provide you with all the most up-to-date information you'll need to explore the region, whether you're a regular or a first-time visitor.

## THE LOWDOWN ON THE LISTINGS

Above all, we've tried to make this book as useful as possible. Websites, telephone numbers, transport information, opening times, admission prices and credit card details have all been checked and were correct at the time we went to press. However, owners and managers can change their arrangements at any time. Before you go out of your way, we'd strongly advise you to call and check opening times and other particulars. While every effort has been made to ensure the accuracy of the information contained in this guide, the publishers cannot accept responsibility for any errors it may contain.

## PRICES AND PAYMENT

We have noted whether venues such as hotels and restaurants in major towns and cities accept the following major cards: American Express (AmEx), Diners Club (DC), MasterCard (MC) – also known as EuroCard – and Visa (V). Many businesses will also accept other cards, such as Switch/Maestro and Delta, and travellers' cheques.

The prices we've supplied should be treated as guidelines, not gospel. All were correct at the time this guide went to press, but be aware that fluctuating exchange rates, inflation and price increases will result in changes.

### THE LIE OF THE LAND AND MAPS

In order to make this guide as easy to navigate as possible, we have divided it into sections corresponding to the eight provinces that make up Andalucía. Each section starts with a map of the region and a summary of the province's major features and attractions. Detailed maps of the cities and towns are included in the chapters that follow, all with full grid referencing. A map of the entire region can be found at the front of the guide.

### TELEPHONE NUMBERS

All telephone numbers in this guide include the relevant three-figure provincial code, which must always be dialled, regardless of whether you are within or outside the province in question. The international dialling code for Spain is 34.

To dial numbers as given in this book from abroad, use your country's exit code (00 in the UK, 011 in the US), followed by 34 (the country code for Spain) and then the number as printed. For more details of phone codes and charges, *see p322.*

### ESSENTIAL INFORMATION

For all the practical information you might need for visiting the city – including visa and customs information, disabled access, emergency telephone numbers, a list of useful websites and the lowdown on the local transport network – turn to the Directory chapter at the back of this guide. It starts on p308.

### LET US KNOW WHAT YOU THINK

We hope you enjoy *Time Out Andalucía*, and we'd like to know what you think of it. We welcome tips for places that you consider we should include in future editions and take notice of your criticism of our choices. You can email us on guides@timeout.com.

There is an online version of this book, along with guides to over 45 other international cities, at **www.timeout.com**.

# Prices in restaurants

Within this guide you will see that we have denoted the price range of each restaurant we mention with between one and four euro symbols. These correspond approximately to the following price brackets for a full meal with drinks per person (in Gibraltar, £ = under £15, etc):

| € | = under €15 |
|---|---|
| €€ | = €15-€25 |
| €€€ | = €25-€35 |
| €€€€ | = over €35 |

# Advertisers

We would like to stress that no establishment has been included in this guide because it has advertised in any of our publications and no payment of any kind has influenced any review. The opinions given in this book are those of Time Out writers and entirely independent.

# In Context

## Features

The pivotal **Battle of Las Navas de Tolosa**, 1212. See p15.

# History

After three millennia the lure of southern Spain remains irresistible.

Andalucía has always had a character distinct from the rest of Spain. Invaders – trekking through the emptiness of the Castilian plains, or across from the deserts of North Africa, or sailing to the Mediterranean's westernmost reaches – saw it as a kind of paradise. Rolling hills, lush forests, fertile plains, bountiful seas and a mild climate have attracted everyone from the Greeks and Phoenicians of antiquity to the package tourists of today. The concept of Andalucía as a geographical area is most popularly attributed to the Moors. Although the name 'al-Andalus' was used freely to refer to the entire Moorish kingdom, which stretched as far north as the Pyrenees at one time, it is most strongly associated with the geographical area we know today, which the Moors singled out as 'Yesira al-andalus' ('the Island of al-Andalus').

Andalucía's shape is dictated by geography – it is largely cut off from the rest of Spain by a mountain range, the Sierra Morena, and for centuries there was only one entry point by land from the north: the Despeñaperros Pass,

a dramatic gorge through the otherwise impenetrable sierra. To the west the River Guadiana provides the logical border with Portugal, while to the east the Sierra de los Filabres separates Andalucía from Murcia. Only in the far north-west, where the province of Huelva meets Extremadura, has the border been more fluid.

## PREHISTORIC ANDALUCÍA (60,000 BC-1,100 BC)

The region has a rich prehistory, and is scattered with early archaeological sites and artefact-packed local museums to prove it. The earliest evidence of human habitation in Spain is Neanderthal Man, or, rather, Woman – a 60,000-year-old female skeleton that was uncovered on Gibraltar.

Andalucía also abounds in cave paintings. Perhaps the most impressive are those in the Cueva de la Pileta, in the Serranía de Ronda, which date from c25,000 BC; images of animals, fish and magic symbols are etched in charcoal, yellow and red on the walls. Skeletons of

Palaeolithic Man and pottery fragments have also been discovered here. The paintings in the Cueva de Nerja in Málaga province, and the Cueva de Tajo de las Figueras, near Benalup de Sidonia in Cádiz province, date from a similar period and contain Neolithic artefacts.

Southern Spain boasts the oldest dolmens in western Europe, on the outskirts of Antequera in Málaga province. These enormous megalithic tombs date back as far as 4500 BC; their interiors are covered with etchings and paintings.

The Bronze Age in Andalucía (from c2600 BC) is best represented by the settlement at Los Millares in Almería province, one of the most important of its kind in Europe. Finds from the area reveal a people who made bronze and stone weapons and tools, grew crops, and hunted as well as bred animals. The culture lasted some 800 years, but, despite its apparent sophistication, appears to have had little lasting influence on the region. Instead, it was the arrival of the Phoenicians that would mark out a new era of development in southern Spain.

## TARTESSUS, PHOENICIANS AND CARTHAGINIANS (1,100 BC-201 BC)

The Phoenicians are popularly said to have first landed in Andalucia at Cádiz (Gadir, as they knew it) in about 1100 BC. Originating in what is now Lebanon, these bold seafarers were interested in trade with the native Iberians rather than conquest, and were especially keen to get their hands on the region's great mineral wealth. In exchange, they, and subsequent Greek traders, brought with them two crops that have done more to shape Andalucía's landscape and subsequent history than any others – the grape and the olive.

The period of Phoenician influence in the region (during which they founded a series of coastal towns such as Málaga, Almuñecar and Adra) coincided with the golden age of the kingdom of Tartessus. This most mysterious and least documented of Andalucian civilisations supposedly covered all or most of the region at this time. Yet no definitive archaeological proof has been found to attest to the existence of Tartessus as a city – the only evidence is literary, and much of that is contradictory.

For the Greeks, who first made landfall near Málaga in 636 BC, Tartessus was a promised land in the west, overflowing with natural wealth and ruled over by a powerful king called Arganthonius. Although some archaeological finds associated with the Tartessians have been discovered (including the treasure of Carambola, now in the Museo Arqueológico in Sevilla), historians and archaeologists are still struggling to establish details of the dominion and culture of this legendary kingdom.

What is known is that during this period native Iberians prospered from trade with the Phoenicians and began to develop a parallel inland culture in hilltop settlements, found primarily in the east of the region. Towns, like Porcuna in Jaén province, were mainly residential and contained few public buildings. Two terracotta sculptures of women, the Dama de Baza and the Dama de Elche, represent a high point of the Iberian cultural legacy. Both pieces date from about 400 BC and were found in Granada province, although they are now on display in Madrid. The best collection of fifth-century BC Iberian sculptures in all Spain, though, was unearthed at Obulco (near Porcuna) and now rests in the Museo Provincial in Jaén.

The decline of Tartessus from about 550 BC had a detrimental effect on the Phoenicians, with whom the Tartessians had enjoyed an excellent trading relationship, and many Phoenician colonies disappeared at this time. Those that survived expanded under the rule of Carthage, a former Phoenician colony in modern-day Tunisia, whose dominion spread throughout the western Mediterranean.

Carthage appears to have crushed the power of Tartessus, but its aggressive expansionist policies were to be its undoing. The newly powerful Romans became increasingly concerned about events in the west, leading to the First Punic War of 264-241 BC, and the subsequent loss to the Carthaginians of many of their possessions in the western Mediterranean. Despite this setback, Carthage continued to expand across the Iberian Peninsula from a new capital at Cartegena in Murcia. By 237 it had gained military control over most of Spain.

The Second Punic War was precipitated by Hannibal, the Carthaginian commander in Spain, who in 219 BC attacked Saguntum (now Sagunto, near Valencia), a Roman ally, before marching on to invade Italy. In retaliation, the Romans landed at modern Tarragona in Catalonia, with an army of 15,000 troops and headed south, conquering successive coastal towns. Two decisive battles – at Bailén in 208 BC and Ilipa (Alcalá del Río) in 207 BC – signalled the demise of Carthaginian rule and the start of six centuries of Roman occupation on the Iberian Peninsula.

## THE ROMANS (201 BC-AD 409)

By 201 BC, Rome was in control of most of present-day Spain. The Romans divided the Peninsula into two parts: Hispania Citerior, stretching from the Sierra Morena to the Pyrenees, and Hispania Ulterior, covering the western half of the Guadalquivir valley.

Occupation was not easy, however; guerrilla warfare was widespread across the Peninsula (though less so in Andalucía), with frequent struggles between rival factions and challenges to Roman rule in both provinces. It was not until Julius Caesar's decisive victory against the supporters of Pompey at Munda near Bailén in 45 BC that an uneasy peace was established.

## 'Baetica played a key role in the development and prosperity of the Roman Empire, both commercially and culturally.'

There followed a period of colonisation in which Roman towns, populated by Roman citizens, were established. Under the Emperor Augustus the Peninsula was divided again, this time into three provinces: Lusitania, encompassing modern Portugal; Hispania Citerior, covering the centre and Catalonia; and Baetica, roughly equivalent to modern Andalucia and part of Extremadura. The capital of Baetica was Córdoba.

Baetica played a key role in the development and prosperity of the Roman Empire, both commercially and culturally. Thanks to their long history of interaction with other cultures, the native inhabitants of the south took far more readily to Roman rule than elsewhere in Spain. Baetica was also the richest of the three provinces, producing olive oil, minerals from the Sierra Morena, wool and wine. The well-preserved town of Baelo Claudio, in Cádiz province, was the Peninsula's major centre for production of *garum* (a fishy relish made from tuna, which was exported all over the Empire).

The emperors Trajan, Hadrian and Theodosius were born in Itálica (the first Roman city in Spain and now the region's most famous Roman ruins) and the intellectuals Seneca and Lucan were from Córdoba.

Roman bridges at Córdoba and Andújar, amphitheatres at Ronda la Vieja and Cádiz, and city walls and a necropolis at Carmona all testify to the Romans' lasting impact on Andalucia. They provided the region with a good transport infrastructure, developed a strong agricultural base, and established Latin as the foundation of the Spanish language, thus linking the Peninsula to the rest of Europe.

### VANDALS AND VISIGOTHS (AD 409-711)
However, as civil war wracked Italy in the late fourth and early fifth centuries, so decline set in across the Empire. In 409 tribes from northern Europe – the Vandals, Alans and Sueves – sensing an opportunity for plunder and colonisation, poured over the Pyrenees and settled in Spain and Portugal.

The Vandals quickly established themselves in Baetica, and although they left little in the way of monuments, they may have lent their name to the region – Vandalusia. In AD 416, while the rest of Spain fell to the semi-Romanised Visigoths from Gaul, the Vandals consolidated their power in the south, stubbornly refusing to budge until 429 when they headed south to North Africa. A treaty between Rome and the Visigoths in 456 led to a second invasion by the latter, and by the 470s the whole peninsula was under direct Visigoth rule.

The Visigoths were military men first and foremost, statesmen a poor second. They kept the majority of their subjects servile and relied on support from landowners in times of war. Despite frequent plots, counterplots and regicides, the Visigoths muddled along for three centuries under a succession of kings who varied in their ability to bind the country together.

Among the most significant rulers were Athanagild (554-67), who moved the capital from Sevilla to Toledo in central Spain, and his successor Leovigild (569-86), who reconquered much of the land around the Guadalquivir valley, which had been lost to Byzantine forces earlier in the sixth century. The zenith of Visigothic culture in Andalucia was the scholarship of St Isidore (560-636) from Sevilla.

The death of Leovigild's Catholic son Recared in 601 led to a century of political instability in the kingdom, culminating in civil war in 710, when Roderic, Duke of Baetica, usurped the Visigoth throne. Opponents of Roderic gained the support of Muslims from North Africa, and the new king was defeated by an Arab army in 711.

### THE MOORS (711-1212)
It is hard to overstate the profound influence and lasting legacy of the Moorish occupation of Spain on Andalucia. The architecture and the landscape, the language and the food – all were shaped by more than 700 years of Islamic culture. At times, the Moors controlled almost the whole of the Iberian Peninsula, but it is Andalucia, or al-Andalus as they knew it, which carries their mark most strongly.

Islam had spread remarkably fast following Mohammed's death in the early seventh century, fanning out across the Middle East and North Africa to reach Morocco by 701. It is no surprise, then, that nine years later a Moroccan officer called Tarif made his first excursion across the Straits to the tip of land that now bears his name, Tarifa.

In 711 an army of 7,000 men led by Tariq ibn-Zayad made the same crossing, and, with the help of Visigoths opposed to King Roderic, won a historic battle at Barbate, on the River

Guadelete. They went on to conquer the rest of the Peninsula (apart from the mountains of Asturias in northern Spain) with remarkable ease within five years.

Historians still debate whether the word 'conquer' is the correct way to describe the Moorish occupation. It is not improbable that much of the population welcomed these relatively enlightened invaders, who tolerated both the Jewish and the Christian religions, encouraged cross-faith marriages and gave areas limited autonomy in return for taxes.

## 'By the time of Abd al-Rahman's death in 788 al-Andalus stretched from the Mediterranean to the Pyrenees.'

Power shifted between Tariq and his governor, Musa Ibn Nusayr, during the early years, finally settling on Musa's son, Abd al-Aziz, in 714. He promptly made Sevilla the capital of the Emirate in Spain, but after his assassination in 716, the capital moved to Córdoba, where it remained until the 11th century. For several decades, warring factions of Berbers, Syrians, Egyptians and Yemenis threatened to tear the fragile state apart. However, the arrival in 756 of a young prince from the Umayyad dynasty in Damascus, Abd al-Rahman, united these disparate elements and brought peace and prosperity to the region.

By the time of Abd al-Rahman's death in 788, al-Andalus stretched from the Mediterranean to the Pyrenees. His successors consolidated this power, and in 929 Abd al-Rahman III proclaimed himself the legitimate descendant of Mohammed, and ruler of an autonomous Caliphate, independent of Baghdad.

Andalucía now entered its greatest period of cultural, philosophical, scientific and artistic innovation. Urban life boomed and Córdoba soon became the largest city in Europe, a centre for study and for trade. Universities, mosques and palaces were built, including the Mezquita and the royal city of Medina Azahara. The countryside, too, underwent something of a renaissance, thanks to advanced irrigation techniques that made full use of the land.

The Moorish Golden Age was not to last. By 1008 al-Andalus was on the point of collapse, riven by financial, military and political crises. Much of the blame can be pinned on Abu al-Mansur, or Almanzor, who seized power from the boy Caliph Hisham II and led a series of

bloody and ultimately fruitless military campaigns that squandered the wealth, and diluted the power, of the state. He spent profligately, rewarding his friends, paying off his enemies and dramatically increasing the size of the army.

On his death in 1002, al-Mansur was succeeded briefly by his son Abd al-Malik, who held the Caliphate together despite rising tensions until 1008. After this date, though, the disintegration of al-Andalus was swift. By 1031, when the Caliphate was abolished, the region had fragmented into 30 separate states, or *taifas*, run by different princes all jostling for political power, and Sevilla had replaced Córdoba as the most important city. Civil disobedience and riots were rife, and the once-subdued Christian kingdoms to the north were making ever-more daring raids into al-Andalus.

In 1085 the King of Castilla and León, Alfonso VI, with the help of the warrior El Cid, captured Toledo. It was a significant loss for the *taifa* kings, who requested assistance from Morocco to defend their rapidly shrinking state. Enter the Almoravids, a fundamentalist fighting force, made up mainly of fanatical Berber tribesmen. By 1110, under the leadership of Yusuf ibn-Tashufin, al-Andalus was reunited, but this time under strict Islamic rule: Christianity was suppressed, and wine and poetry banned; tensions rose and civil strife again became the norm.

The Almoravid era was brought to a swift end some 50 years later by the invasion of the Almohads from Morocco. Led by a Muslim preacher named ibn-Tumart, the Almohads, whose name means 'the Upholders of the Divine Unity', were even more fundamentalist than their predecessors. After several forays across the Straits and years of political turmoil, they had gained control of the whole of al-Andalus by 1173.

The following years saw an extension of the Almohad state as far as Lisbon in the west, Madrid in the north and the Balearic Islands in the Mediterranean. It was also a period of cultural and literary activity, which saw the building of the Giralda in Sevilla and the emergence of two great philosophers, Ibn Rushd, better known as Averroës, and Maimonides, both of whom lived in Córdoba.

However, Christian forces were massing in the north, and by 1212 were in position to launch an attack on the Almohads. Under the leadership of Alfonso VIII, the Christian armies secured a decisive victory on the plains of Las Navas de Tolosa, just to the south of the Despeñaperros Pass, thus opening the gateway to Andalucía, and signalling the beginning of the end for Moorish rule in Spain.

# Cliché Paradise lost?

For more than 3,000 years Andalucía has been mythologised. From the time the first Phoenician traders landed at what is now Cádiz, drawn by rumours of fabulous mineral wealth, to the purple prose of present-day tourist brochures and travel writers, southern Spain has been perceived as a demi-Eden, a balmy, fecund land, rich in natural resources and tinged with African exoticism.

And no period in the region's history has been romanticised more than when Africans were dominant on the Iberian Peninsula. Today, it's easy to believe that the 800-year presence of the Moors in Europe was a utopian golden age of exquisite art and poetry, of religious tolerance and scientific enquiry, of agricultural plenty and contented citizenry, particularly when seen in contrast to the stereotypical view of early medieval Europe as a time of brutality and ignorance, rapacious warlords and draughty castles, subsistence farming and serfdom.

The French, British and American Romantic travellers who 'rediscovered' Andalucía in the early 1800s (see p36) must take much of the credit/blame for perpetuating this nostalgic view of southern Spain (though the wretchedly backward condition of the civil war-wracked country they encountered in the 19th century might excuse some of this longing for more glamorous times). And it's a view that continues to be espoused today.

Yet it is no recent phenomenon. The Moors themselves were as susceptible to the charms of Andalucía. One mid eighth-century chronicler referred to it as 'abundant with every good thing... and filled with beauty, so that you could say it was like an August pomegranate.'

There's no doubt that the West owes a huge debt to the scholars of al-Andalus – polymaths such as Averroës and Maimonides, who kept alive classical learning by translating and commenting upon Greek works that would undoubtedly otherwise have been lost. Equally, the legacy of Moorish architecture, art and design is still powerful today. Their mosques, castles and palaces – from the martial might of Almería's Alcazaba, to the imaginative eclecticism of the Mezquita, to the delicate intimacy of the Alhambra – are irresistible draws for today's visitors, Moorish-inspired tiles, courtyards and gardens regularly appear in contemporary design magazines, and neo-Moorish buildings continue to be built across the region, and further afield. There's truth, too, in the picture of the period as a time of agricultural and

## THE RECONQUISTA (1212-1492)

Under the crusading zeal of Iago (James) I of Aragón (1213-76), Fernando III of Castilla (1217-52) and Sancho II of Portugal (1223-48), the next 40 years saw almost the whole of al-Andalus fall into Christian hands during the early stages of the controversially named *reconquista* (Reconquest): the Balearics and Badajoz in 1230; Córdoba in 1236; Valencia in 1238 and, in 1248, the big prize of Sevilla.

It was during this period that the word 'Mudéjar' ('persons allowed to remain') was first used to refer to Muslims living under Christian rule. As the Christians' grip on the region tightened, so did their religious bigotry: forced conversions and expulsions became commonplace, and the status of resident Moors was gradually eroded.

Conquered land was parcelled out in huge swathes to victorious noblemen, imposing a socially and economically ruinous system of immense estates (known as *'latifundia'*), absentee landlords and dispossesed masses. Incredibly, the pattern of land ownership in Andalucia is not greatly different today, and continues to be a major source of economic and (to a lesser extent) political instability.

> **'On 1 January 1492 Boabdil handed over the keys of Granada to Fernando and Isabel, surrendering Moorish rule on the Peninsula once and for all.'**

By 1248 just one Muslim state remained. The Nasrid Kingdom of Granada was founded by Mohammed ibn Yusuf ibn Nasr (known as Mohammed I) in 1237, and, amazingly, managed to survive (though often precariously) for a further 250 years. Stretching from the Mediterranean coast of Almeria to Gibraltar, it repelled Christian invaders with a chain of castles along its borders, and with military back-up from Morocco. Most of the time, however, skilful diplomacy kept the infidels at economic progress. Irrigation techniques (largely adapted from the Romans) succeeded in making the region's fertile but dry earth highly productive.

However, it's the vision of Islamic Spain as a land of peace and tolerance that is perhaps the most misleading of the Moorish myths. War, not peace, was the norm for much of the period. The initial Berber submission of Spain was fast and brutal and was followed by decades of factional fighting before the emergence of the Umayyads; later came the feuding of the 11th-century taifa states, two further Berber conquests and the constant rumblings of Arab-Christian warfare during almost the entire period.

Some historians have come to see the initial invasion as a liberation from the incumbent Visigoths, but it was as much a conquest and colonisation as the Christian *reconquista*. The Moors were, though, certainly smarter than the later Christians in not letting religious dogma override practical consideration and absorbing any pliant existing communities and hierarchies. (One of the *reconquista*'s most disastrous results was the loss of agricultural knowledge and depopulation as Moors and *moriscos* fled or were expelled.)

As fellow 'peoples of the book', Jews and Christians were allowed to practise their religions by Islamic law, and, compared to elsewhere in contemporary Europe, life was certainly easier in al-Andalus for minority faiths. Christians and Jews could on occasion rise to prominence, yet they were always second-class citizens. It was true that the talented Samuel ibn Naghrila, and his son Joseph after him, became formidable powers in 11th-century Granada. But, just as anti-Jewish pogroms scarred much of medieval Europe, so al-Andalus was far from immune from outbreaks of religious bigotry. Joseph was killed along with many other Granadan Jews by their fellow townsfolk in 1066. Christians also suffered; there was a major deportation of Christians to Morocco in 1126. Such extreme events may have been relatively rare, but there's plenty of evidence that religious freedom was countered by widespread everyday discrimination and prejudice against non-Muslims.

Particularly in the light of 9/11 and the threat to the West posed by al-Qaeda (which supposedly has its European HQ in Andalucía) and Islamic extremism, it is tempting to look back on Moorish Spain as a model of mutual tolerance and enlightenment. It's tempting, but it's overly simplistic.

bay. Life inside this tiny kingdom recalled the Golden Age of al-Andalus: the arts flourished and construction began on the most beautiful Moorish monument in the world, the Alhambra.

Granada's fate was sealed by the marriage of Fernando II of Aragón and Isabel of Castilla in 1469 (who became known collectively as *Los Reyes Católicos* – literally, 'the Catholic Kings'), resulting in the union of the two most powerful Christian kingdoms in Spain. Fernando and Isabel's fundamentalist Catholic views would not tolerate religious diversity, and so they set about conquering the Moorish kingdom.

Málaga fell to Christian forces in 1487, followed by Baeza and Almería in 1489. In 1491 the Christians began an eight-month siege of Granada that culminated in its surrender. On 1 January 1492 Boabdil, last king of the Nasrid dynasty, handed over the keys of Granada to Fernando and Isabel, surrendering Moorish rule on the Peninsula once and for all. As he left the outskirts he turned for one last look at his beloved city, at a spot now known as El Suspiro del Moro, 'the Moor's Sigh'.

## THE SPANISH EMPIRE (1492-1700)

The two centuries following the taking of Granada are traditionally known as Spain's Golden Age – a period of unparalleled Christian wealth, expansionism and artistic achievement.

In 1492 Cristóbal Colón (Christopher Columbus) set sail across the Atlantic from the coast of Huelva province and discovered the Americas. Within ten years the *conquistadores* had conquered much of the continent and established an enormous empire for their rulers in Spain. Gold, silver and precious stones poured into the region via Cádiz and up the Guadalquivir to Sevilla, which became one of the wealthiest and fastest-growing metropolises in Europe. By 1570 it was the largest city in Europe after Venice and Rome.

Meanwhile, Boabdil and his followers had decamped to the Alpujarras (in the Sierra Nevada mountains, south of Granada) to set up a small community of about 250,000 people. The terms of surrender had guaranteed religious rights to Granada's former citizens, but this policy was soon reversed. Fernando and

Isabel unleashed a wave of religious persecution across the country, including the establishment of the Inquisition. Some 40,000 Jews fled the country after an edict in 1492, and in 1499 the fanatical Cardinal Cisneros ordered the forced baptism of 60,000 Muslims in Granada, resulting in a two-year revolt in the Alpujarras.

The Spanish reacted by sailing across the Straits and capturing the towns of Ceuta and Melilla on the Moroccan coast (both of which Spain still possesses), in an attempt to ensure no Muslim invasions could take place. Moorish clothing and speech were banned in Spain and unconverted Muslims were expelled; the Moors who remained became known as *moriscos*.

Carlos I (1516-56; more commonly known as Carlos V, or Charles V, the Holy Roman Emperor) spent most of his reign squandering Spain's new-found wealth in defence of his vast empire, which included the Low Countries and large chunks of France, as well as the Americas. Wars, poor governance and inflation took their toll, and by the time his son Felipe II (1556-98) succeeded to the throne, the country was almost bankrupt. Wealth continued to be concentrated in the hands of a few nobles whose enormous estates were worked by serf-like peasants who had no rights to the land.

In 1568 Felipe II determined to extinguish the last vestiges of Moorish culture in Spain. His decision sparked a revolt in the Alpujarras that was finally quashed in 1571, with the expulsion of a huge number of *moriscos* to North Africa. (It is said there are houses in Morocco that still contain the keys to the owners' 16th-century homes in Granada.) Felipe III (1598-1621) went one better, ordering the expulsion from Spain of all descendants of the Moors.

The consequences were not just personally disastrous for those exiled unfortunates, but also for the *vegas* (plains) that they had irrigated so skilfully and kept so productive. What had once been one of the wealthiest and most cultured corners of Europe now became one of its poorest and most backward. In hardship the country turned to religion and developed many of the Catholic festivals and celebrations that are such a feature of the Andalucian calendar today.

By the 1620s money from the Americas was drying up and Spaniards were getting tired of financing profligate monarchs. Plagues devastated populations across Spain, particularly in Sevilla, and uprisings and skirmishes by disenchanted subjects broke out across the country, leading to the loss of Portugal in 1640. (The Netherlands and Spanish possessions in France were also lost.) Yet despite economic and political decline, Andalucía was the cradle for some of the

A liberal constitution is proclaimed in Cádiz in 1812. *See p19.*

finest Spanish artists of the century – Velázquez, Zurbarán and Murillo were all born in the region.

When Felipe IV (1621-65) died, he left a bitterly divided country under the leadership of the weak Carlos II. The French launched a series of raids in the 1690s and put increasing pressure on Carlos to appoint a French successor to the Spanish throne. Just before his death in 1700 Carlos complied, naming the Bourbon Duke of Anjou as the future king of Spain, Felipe V (1700-46).

## REVIVAL (1700-92)

During the 18th century Spain appeared to rally under Bourbon rule; some cities in Andalucía, particularly Cádiz, even prospered as trade with the Americas revived. However, the reign of Felipe V was to have dire consequences for the Spanish succession and to lead to French occupation of Spain in the following century.

Soon after Felipe became king, war broke out between Spain and Archduke Charles of Austria, who had a rival claim to the Spanish throne. Charles was supported by Dutch and British forces, which captured Gibraltar in 1704. The Treaty of Utrecht (1713) ended the War of the Spanish Succession and recognised Felipe as the legitimate King of Spain, but at the expense of the Spanish Empire: Austria took the Spanish Netherlands and Spanish possessions in Italy, while the British claimed Menorca and broke Spain's monopoly on the slave trade to the Americas.

Fernando VI (1746-59) built up the Spanish navy, which took part in a brief war with the British in 1748 over American trade. This was followed by Spain's involvement in the Seven Years War (1761-63) and the War of American Independence (1779-83), during which Menorca and Florida were recaptured from the British, and Gibraltar lay under siege for a year.

The succession of Carlos III (1759-88) signalled an upturn in the fortunes of Andalucía, with wide-scale resettlement in the deserted countryside and the founding of new planned immigrant towns, among them La Carolina, La Louisiana and Olivares, just south of the Sierra Morena. A new age of enlightenment saw the emergence of various groups dedicated to improved farming techniques and mass education. Carlos also attempted to reform local government, particularly in Andalucía, where he ordered common lands to be redistributed as smallholdings to the poor and landless. He also oversaw a road-building programme to link disparate parts of the country, and exercised a more tolerant attitude towards the gypsies.

Peace with Britain in 1783 saw Spain's fortunes revive further: trade between Andalucía and the Americas was booming and the economy experienced ten years of sustained growth.

## A DIVIDED COUNTRY (1792-1931)

The upheaval following the French Revolution was to bring development and progress within Spain to a halt. The weak Carlos IV (1788-1808) presided over a rapidly disintegrating Empire and a poverty-stricken country, with effective power in the hands of his chief minister Manuel Godoy. Godoy compromised with the French, attracting the enmity of the British, who blockaded the coast, effectively cutting off trade between Spain and the Americas and leading to a sharp decline in Cádiz's fortunes.

When the joint Spanish and French fleets were decisively defeated by Nelson at the Battle of Trafalgar off the coast of Cádiz province in 1805, Godoy was blamed for the defeat and was overthrown. Carlos abdicated in 1808, and the Emperor of France, Napoleon Bonaparte, seized the opportunity to gain control of Spain. Carlos and his son Fernando were escorted out of the country by French troops, and the Spanish crown was given to Napoleon's brother Joseph.

## 'The liberal constitution created by the Cortes in Cádiz in 1812 was to become a talisman of democratic Spain'

French rule was hugely unpopular with the Spanish populace: spontaneous riots broke out across the country on 2 May 1808 (vividly portayed in Goya's painting of the same name) and were brutally suppressed by French troops. Meanwhile, local administrators raised armies against the French occupiers. The British could not accept French hegemony in Spain, and landed in Portugal, starting the Peninsular War. The first major battle took place at Bailén in Córdoba province in 1808, where a Spanish army unexpectedly defeated the French.

The Spanish court and what remained of its government fled to Cádiz, where in 1812 it established a parliament (*Cortes*) and published a liberal Spanish constitution that was to become a talisman of democratic Spain. A year later, Spanish, Portuguese and British forces,

led by the Duke of Wellington, forced Joseph back into France, and Fernando VII (1814-33) returned as king. In the meantime, most of Spain's American colonies had broken free of colonial rule, and the last Spanish pretence of playing a world role evaporated.

Although a fledgling Spanish democracy had been born during the French occupation, too many non-liberal pro-monarchist factions remained powerful around the country for it to survive: the *Cortes* was abolished and its leading liberals were put to death – acts of conservative despotism that sowed the seeds for the eventual Civil War.

A succession crisis led to the First Carlist War (1833-39), a civil war that was repeated in 1872-76 in the Second Carlist War, during which time (1873-74) Spain briefly experienced its First Republic.

Andalucía, at the vanguard of the political reforms of the early 19th century, was left more backward and impoverished than ever by their suppression: peasants continued to struggle to eke an existence from land they did not own; foreigners ran the agriculture and mining operations; and Cádiz was again reduced to an insignificant port. It was perhaps inevitable, then, that the region would be open to new political ideas, among them anarchism, which came to Andalucía in 1870. The backwardness of the region contributed to its political radicalism, and led in 1910 to the establishment of the anarcho-syndicalist union, the CNT.

Violence in the shape of terrorism and banditry continued unchecked, particularly in the lawless mountain areas. This atmosphere contributed to the modern view of Andalucía as a land of romance, exoticism and danger. Foreign writers, among them Washington Irving and Richard Ford, were attracted to the region and helped perpetuate this image.

Meanwhile, the last fragments of the Spanish Empire were slipping away. By the end of the 19th century Spain had lost Cuba, its last American colony, and was faced with political unrest at home, despite the introduction of universal male suffrage in 1892.

Political strife was compounded by the lack of continuity in government, with no fewer than 34 administrations holding power between 1902 and 1923. General Primo de Rivera attempted to assert stability on the country by carrying out a military coup in 1923.

For a brief period, prosperity seemed to be returning. Spain still had international pretensions, as the 1929 Expo in Sevilla was intended to prove, but the fair left the city bankrupt and political and economic tensions re-emerged. Primo de Rivera's dictatorship collapsed and Alfonso XIII abdicated in 1931.

A dangerous precedent had been set – conservative forces increasingly saw military might and dictatorship as the solution to Spain's problems.

## FROM REPUBLIC TO CIVIL WAR (1931-39)

The Second Republic was established on 14 April 1931. It was Spain's first genuine democracy and was greeted with widespread celebrations in the street. In Andalucía it was met with jubilation by the poor labourers, who for the first time could look forward to a landowning future, and horror by landowners.

Expectations were high – too high for the new government to deliver. Caught between the hopes of the deprived and the fears of the conservatives, the nation again began to fray. Strikes were called, unemployment soared and divisions occurred within the Republican movement, foreshadowing the split in the Civil War between the anarchists and the socialists. The Right, meanwhile, was divided between traditional conservatives and the fascist Falangist party, established in 1933 by José Antonio Primo de Rivera. Elections in 1934 saw the Republicans replaced by a radical right-wing government. Peasant unrest grew, and whispers of an army coup were rife.

The 1936 election was won by the left-wing Popular Front alliance, but this only caused the violence to esculate, with assassinations and bloody reprisals on both sides. The scene was set for outright civil war.

The Civil War (1936-39) was the most divisive, bloody and bitter episode in modern Spanish history, involving not simply Nationalists versus Republicans, but also landowners versus peasants, anarchists versus communists, and the Catholic Church versus libertarians. It is also widely regarded as a prelude to World War II, since the non-intervention of both Britain and France and an embargo on arms imports from the United States allowed Hitler, Mussolini and Stalin to use Spain as a testing ground for their latest aircraft and military equipment. Foreign troops gained combat experience in the field, and modern military techniques such as *Blitzkrieg* bombing were first employed. (The most infamous example of the latter being the destruction of Guernica.)

The war was also the last 'romantic', idealised war in Europe. It was popularly regarded the world over as a fight against fascism and attracted hundreds of foreign volunteers, known as the International Brigades, to join the left-wing Republican cause.

Although subsequently many historians regarded the outbreak of war as inevitable, its scale and scope were unexpected at the time. In fact, when General Francisco Franco launched his Nationalist military uprising in Spanish Morocco on 17 July 1936 he did not expect the coup to last more than a few days, so confident was he of success. Preliminary signs were good for the Nationalists, with Ceuta and Melilla secured by that evening, allowing safe passage by German transport planes from Africa to the ports of Andalucía the following morning.

On 18 July the rebel forces captured Cádiz, Jeréz, Algeciras and La Línea, encouraged in no small part by landowners of the huge Andalucian estates. Sevilla, Huelva and Granada – where rebel troops razed the Albaicín district to the ground – all fell a few days later.

Granada was the scene of one of the most infamous episodes of the war, which galvanised intellectuals and artists in France and Britain to oppose the Nationalist rebels. Federico García Lorca, who had returned to his home town just a few days before the uprising, was arrested by Nationalist forces and taken to the village of Viznar, where he was shot. His body was never found and his death remained a forbidden topic in Spain until after Franco's death.

The Nationalists' initial swift progress through Andalucía met with firm resistance at Málaga and all points east. Elsewhere in Spain, Galicia and most of Castilla and León had fallen, but the rest of the country, including Madrid, Barcelona and Valencia, remained loyal to the Republicans.

In the second week of August, however, the Nationalists began to head east, capturing Córdoba and most of Granada province, before heading south to Ronda, where they exacted swift and bloody retribution on its citizens, throwing many into the town's gorge, as recreated in Ernest Hemingway's *For Whom the Bell Tolls*. By the end of September the Nationalists had pressed deep into eastern Andalucía and now controlled the provinces of Huelva, Cádiz, Sevilla and Córdoba and large parts of Granada and Málaga. Only Almería and Jaén remained under Republican command.

Málaga held out until February 1937, when Nationalist forces were joined by 10,000 Italian fascist troops and air cover from the Legionary Air Force. They attacked from all sides, including a naval bombardment by the Nazi warship *Admiral Graf Spee*, and within three days were at the city's outskirts. The Republican force of 12,000 militia, a third of whom had no rifles, was powerless to defend the city. The Nationalist atrocities committed in Málaga were some of the most horrific in the whole war: 3,500 people were killed in the first six days and a further 16,500 over the next seven years. By 1938 it is estimated that 150,000 people in Andalucía had been murdered by the Nationalists.

Loading torpedoes in Málaga during the Civil War.

The fall of Málaga signalled the end of the war proper in the south, and the two provinces which had held out against the Nationalists – Jaén and Almería – remained largely unaffected by the fighting in the north of the country until the end of the war.

Elsewhere in Spain the Republicans were gradually losing territory in a series of bitter, bloody battles, and both sides suffered terrible losses during the winter of 1937, which was one of the coldest on record. Thoroughly demoralised, the Republicans offered little resistance when the Nationalists advanced east towards the Mediterranean coast in spring 1938. They did, however, launch one last disastrous counter-offensive at the Battle of the Ebro on 25 July 1938, resulting by November in the loss of 70,000 Republican troops and a large part of the Republican air defences.

On 26 January 1939 the Nationalists triumphantly entered Barcelona, and on 27 March the Republican frontline spontaneously disappeared as the Nationalists took Madrid, thereby gaining control of the whole country.

### REPRESSION AND REFORM (1939-75)

The Civil War was followed by a brutal and bloody period of retribution. Franco did not just want to defeat the Republicans, he wanted to destroy them. Anyone with left-wing sympathies was targeted, resulting in mass arrests, imprisonments, show trials and executions across the country. Many Republicans fled to refugee camps in France; towns and cities were left in ruins, and the remaining citizens were reduced to near-starvation. Andalucía in particular saw mass emigration that decimated the population of the countryside.

Franco became chief of state and head of government in September 1939 and declared his shattered country neutral when hostilities broke out in the rest of Europe later that month. He then set about eradicating everything he believed had 'infected' the country during its experiment with democracy and liberalism. Strikes were banned on penalty of death, wages were reduced to 1936 levels and all the land that had been redistributed under the agrarian reforms of the early 1930s was given back to its original owners. Democrats, atheists, liberals, communists, Jews, anarchists, Freemasons – all were targeted and persecuted. The Catholic Church, in contrast, was elevated to an unprecedented level of importance, playing a part in almost every aspect of public life.

## 'The development of the Costa del Sol led to the rediscovery of Spain by foreigners.'

Spain became insular and isolated during the 1940s, choosing to stay clear of the world stage. However, Franco's attempts at national self-sufficiency didn't work, and by the end of the decade it became obvious that the economy had to be liberalised. In 1953 Franco handed over Spanish land to the USA in exchange for US$625 million. The US used the land to establish a number of military bases, among them Rota in Cádiz province. Two years later Spain rejoined the United Nations.

By the mid 1950s the Spanish economy had still not improved, inflation was rife and a series of strikes spread across the country. The government reacted with further liberal economic reforms, including the introduction of industrial programmes in the major cities and a dam project in Andalucía, intended to stop the crippling cycle of floods and famine.

The key initiative, however, was the development of the Costa del Sol as a first experiment in mass tourism. It led to the rediscovery of Spain by foreigners, and increased prosperity for Andalucia – at least for those who lived along the coast. Throughout the 1960s Spain enjoyed growth rates twice as high as other countries in the European Economic Community. Annual tourist numbers increased from four million to 14 million during that decade, and tourist spending leapt from less than £80 million to more than £500 million.

By the early 1970s Spain was industrially and economically on a par with the rest of western Europe. Politically and culturally, however, it was still lagging behind. Renewed regionalism and a rediscovery of officially forbidden customs and languages became widespread. Student riots broke out and were brutally suppressed by the authorities, and the Basque separatist group ETA was formed.

The last two years of Franco's rule were characterised by social unrest and the dictator's gradual descent into Parkinson's disease. Finally, the king-in-waiting, Juan Carlos, was nominated by Franco as his successor.

Tourism on the **Costa del Sol** in the 1960s.

## MODERN ANDALUCÍA (FROM 1975)

Franco died in November 1975 and Juan Carlos was crowned king two days later. The educated monarch, who had spent time abroad, was committed to democracy, but was aware that the country was still riven by rival factions. He successfully manoeuvred to replace the old Francoist Prime Minister Carlos Arrias Navarro with Adolfo Suárez, who was equally committed to reform. After victory in the 1977 elections, Suárez steered the country towards democracy and drafted a modern constitution, which was approved by 88 per cent of voters in December 1978.

Just three years after the dictator's death, the Franco regime had been dismantled and replaced with a modern democracy. The only fly in the ointment was the army, which was still fiercely loyal to Franco's memory, and unhappy at the pace of change. On 23 February 1981, Lieutenant Colonel Antonio Tejero led an attempted coup on the parliament. Fortunately, miscalculations by Tejero and the intervention of the King as commander-in-chief of the armed forces meant that the coup failed, but its consequences were far-reaching.

Spaniards, outraged at Tejero's actions, made their disapproval felt in the elections of 1982, when the left-wing PSOE, led by the Sevillian Felipe González, swept to victory. The pace of change following the elections was rapid, and with a *sevillano* in charge of the government, Andalucia returned to the forefront of Spanish

policy and politics. In 1986 Spain joined the European Community and NATO, regional autonomy was granted, democracy was consolidated and the arts flourished.

In 1992 the quincentenary of Columbus's discovery of the Americas was marked by high-profile celebrations all over Spain: Sevilla put on another hugely expensive Expo; a high-speed train link, known as the Alta Velocidad España (AVE), was constructed between Andalucia and Madrid; Barcelona got ready to host the Olympic Games; and Madrid was made European City of Culture.

This enormous national spending spree led to a recession and a loss of support for the PSOE, which was compounded by damaging stories about high-level corruption. The 1996 elections saw victory for the first right-wing government since Franco's death, the Partido Popular led by José María Aznar. Spain's complex labour laws were revised and the economy was further liberalised under the conservatives, who won a second term in 2000. With an absolute majority the PP set Spain firmly on the path to monetary union with the rest of Europe, culminating in the adoption of the euro on 1 January 2002.

In Andalucía there has been a general swing to the right since the mid 1990s. The PP made substantial gains in the municipal elections of 2003, despite huge opposition across Spain to the Iraq War, and would almost certainly have remained in power had is not been for the Madrid bombing of 11 March 2003. Instead, the PSOE's José Luis Rodríguez Zapatero became the new prime minister. Never has terrorism so definitively influenced a European election.

# Key events

## PREHISTORY TO THE PHOENICIANS

**c60,000 BC** Evidence of Neanderthal Man on Gibraltar.
**c25,000 BC** Prehistoric man occupies caves in Málaga province.
**2600 BC** Copper Age settlement at Los Millares in Almería.
**1100 BC** Phoenicians land at Cádiz.
**c1500-550 BC** Kingdom of Tartessus dominant in the Guadalquivir valley.
**500-400 BC** Carthage colonises south Spain.
**241-201 BC** Iberian Peninsula falls to the Romans in the Punic Wars.

## ROMANS, VANDALS AND VISIGOTHS

**205 BC** Founding of Itálica, first Roman city on the Iberian Peninsula.
**27 BC** Southern Iberia becomes Roman province of Baetica; Córdoba is its capital; start of Golden Age of Roman Empire in Spain.
**409** Vandals invade Spain from the north and settle in Baetica.
**456-711** Second Visigoth invasion leads to colonisation of the Peninsula.

## THE MOORS

**710** Tarif crosses the Straits from Morocco to the Andalucían coast at Tarifa.
**711-16** Tariq ibn-Zayad defeats Visigoths and goes on to conquer the rest of the Peninsula.
**716** Córdoba becomes capital of al-Andalus.
**756** Abd al-Rahman unites al-Andalus heralding the Moorish Golden Age in Spain; construction of Córdoba's Mezquita begun.
**929** Abd al-Rahman III establishes the Córdoban Caliphate.
**1031** Caliphate abolished; al-Andalus is divided into 30 *taifa* kingdoms.
**1085** Loss of Toledo to Alfonso VI.
**1110** Al-Andalus reunited under the Almoravids from North Africa.
**1160** Almohad invasion.
**1173-1211** Expansion and consolidation of Almohad kingdom; Sevilla's Giralda is built.
**1212** Alfonso VIII defeats the Almohads at Las Navas de Tolosa.

## THE RECONQUISTA

**1214-48** Christian forces take control of major cities in Andalucía; Sevilla falls in 1248.
**1237-1492** Nasrid Kingdom of Granada. Moorish arts flourish; the Alhambra is built.
**1487-92** Fernando and Isabel take control of major cities in the Nasrid kingdom, culminating in the surrender of Granada.

## THE SPANISH EMPIRE

**1492** Columbus discovers the Americas; Spanish Empire is established.
**1499-1501** First Alpujarran uprising.
**1520** Carlos I becomes Holy Roman Emperor Carlos V. Start of Spanish Golden Age.
**1568-71** Second Alpujarran uprising.
**1609** Expulsion of *moriscos* from Spain.
**1649** Great plague in Sevilla.
**1700** Succession of Bourbon Duke of Anjou as Felipe V of Spain, triggering the War of the Spanish Succession.
**1704** British forces capture Gibraltar.
**1713** Spain loses territory to Britain and Austria by the Treaty of Utrecht.
**1759** Succession of Carlos III heralds an age of enlightened despotism in Spain.

## A DIVIDED COUNTRY

**1805** Battle of Trafalgar.
**1808** Napoleon seizes power and gives the Spanish crown to his brother Joseph, precipitating the Peninsular War.
**1812** The *Cortes* in Cadíz produces the first Spanish constitution.
**1813-14** French driven from Spain by British and Dutch forces, ending the Peninsular War; Fernando VII is restored to the throne.
**1833-36** First Carlist War.
**1834** Andalucía divided into eight provinces.
**1872-76** Second Carlist War.
**1873-74** First Republic.
**1892** Universal male suffrage introduced.
**1929** Expo in Sevilla.

## FROM REPUBLIC TO DICTATORSHIP

**1931** Second Republic established.
**1936-39** Civil War.
**1939** General Franco becomes chief of state and head of government.
**1953** Spanish land sold to USA for use as military bases.
**1950s-60s** Development of the Costa del Sol begins. Economic revival in Spain.

## MODERN ANDALUCÍA

**1975** Franco dies; Juan Carlos becomes king.
**1981** Attempted army coup leads to victory for socialist Sevillian Felipe González in the 1982 elections.
**1992** Quincentenary of Columbus's discovery of the Americas; Expo in Sevilla.
**2002** Euro replaces the peseta.
**2003** Madrid bombings; socialist José Luis Rodríguez Zapatero wins elections.

# Andalucía Today

The sun shines on, but clouds of economic uncertainty are gathering.

Arriving at Málaga airport, and driving west along the Costa del Sol, most first-time visitors to Andalucía are overwhelmed by the scale of development. Mile upon mile of hotels, apartment complexes, resorts, holiday villas, golf courses, marinas, amusement parks and casinos stretch monotonously back from the beach and into the hills. And the construction shows little sign of slowing down – just count the number of cranes visible from any one spot. Most Andalucians don't see a problem: tourism is the industry that transformed this region in the 1960s from poverty-ravaged rural backwater to Europe's cheap 'n' cheerful summer playground, and tourism is the industry that, by and large, keeps it alive today.

### THE TOURISTS

Annually, Spain attracts 50 million visitors (16 million are British), 14% of whom choose to holiday in Andalucía. Add to these seven million foreigners the 13 million Spaniards who head south for their holidays every year and the scale and importance of tourism to Andalucía is immediately apparent.

But package tourists are becoming increasingly discerning and, as a result, many coastal towns are smartening themselves up. Once dirty beaches are being cleaned, swish promenades are being built and ugly tower blocks torn down. The result is that the Costa del Sol is no longer a cheap destination. Ironically this investment – combined with a rising euro, so-called 'destination fatigue' and

stiff competition from emerging markets such as Turkey and Bulgaria – could price it out of the cheap sun and beach market.

Yet the developers build on, and no one with the power to do so seems inclined to say 'enough'. The days of unchecked building might be over, but the trend now for creating land-hungry low-rise *urbanizaciones*, five-star resorts, golf courses and luxury marinas has resulted in just as much, if not more, ecological damage.

Few of the lessons that should have been learned from the wholesale concreting over of the Costa del Sol seem to have been absorbed, and the region's few remaining stretches of unspoiled coastline – such as the once-pristine Costa de la Luz, and parts of the supposedly protected Cabo de Gata in Almería – seem likely to fall before the regiment of bulldozers.

There is some dawning realisation in the regional government, the Junta de Andalucía, that it is not economically or socially healthy for the region that so great a proportion of tourist euros go to the coast while much of the interior remains poor and underdeveloped. It is now pushing for upmarket tourists to spend their euros inland; *turismo rural* is the buzz-phrase, with an increasing number of visitors seeking out *fincas* and villas away from the coast.

### THE FARMERS

Head inland, far from the coast and the cities, and you'll see little evidence of prosperity. Unemployment stands at a hefty 17.2 per cent across the region, and much of the work is still seasonal, relying primarily on the olive harvest (November to February); outside of this period the unemployment rate in many areas runs at more than twice that of the rest of Spain (and at up to 40 per cent in the case of Jerez and Cádiz). And as more young people are drawn to the coast for employment, the villages continue to empty out.

Andalucía is not wholly dependent on tourism, though – farming is also a key pillar of the regional economy. Spain has the third-largest grape harvest in the world; in Andalucía this is centred on wine and sherry production, mainly in Cádiz province. Production has, though, suffered in recent years due to a fall in exports to the UK, the biggest sherry market, and consequently Jerez and other towns heavily reliant upon sherry production have seen a sharp rise in unemployment.

Jaén and southern Córdoba provinces form the world's largest olive-producing area, but the dangers of relying on an economic monoculture are becoming apparent. Competition from North Africa has badly affected production; EU subsidies are due to be slashed; and health fears regarding the chemicals used to treat the trees might soon affect sales.

The key issue afflicting many farmers is the almost feudal system of land ownership that still continues through much of the region. A handful of landowners control vast swathes of land, meaning that most workers are employed on day rates and discarded outside harvest times – rural poverty haunts much of the interior.

The one undoubted boom area in farming is in Almería province, where the *plasticultura* industry (growing produce under plastic), which supplies most of the year-round fruit and veg to northern Europe, is thriving. Yet this too has plenty of adverse environmental and social consequences caused by the demands on natural resources and the influx of foreign workers – not to mention the aesthetic horrors of an entire coastline under plastic (*see p297* **Tent city**).

Livestock farming continues to be important – Andalucía supports almost a million cattle, including cows for meat and milk, and, of course, fighting bulls (*toros bravos*). Pig breeding is also huge, but the market for pork products is confined mainly to Spain. Fish stocks, as everywhere in Europe, have been severely depleted, and even staples like tuna, which traditionally kept entire villages along the Costa de la Luz employed, are becoming scarce.

There is little heavy industry in the region today. Mining in Huelva (location of the famed Río Tinto Mines) is minimal now, oil refining is confined to Algeciras and ship-building to San Fernando, near Cádiz. Salt mining remains big business, however, around Cádiz and Almería.

Andalucía is also pioneering a number of renewable energy projects – wind farming in Tarifa (which has spread to the Alpujarras and the Sierra Sur de Jaén, scarring the countryside without lessening the need to build nuclear power stations), hydro-electricity in Málaga and solar power in Almería.

## THE TERRORISTS

The Basque separatist group ETA's campaign to deliberately target tourists along the Costas was overshadowed by the al-Qaeda train bombings in Madrid on 11 March 2004. Although the majority of suspects involved in 11-M (as the Spanish refer to it) were based in Madrid, it was inevitable that, with its large North African population and proximity to Morocco, attention would soon turn to Andalucía.

Since the Casablanca bombings and the foiled attempt to launch a suicide attack on British ships in the Strait of Gibraltar, it has been suspected that an al-Qaeda cell, or at least groups sympathetic to bin Laden's cause, were based in Andalucía. And a couple of months after the 11-M attacks a Moroccan man was arrested in El Ejido in Almería province. He was a brother of one of the suspects and possibly involved in the organisation of the bombings.

The hasty withdrawal of Spanish troops from Iraq may save Andalucía from future terrorist attacks, but the region remains on the frontline.

As for ETA, it's not clear where it stands in the post-11-M political landscape. It has long exhausted any public sympathy and, now that there is a new government in power that has indicated it is more willing to open a dialogue, it may adopt a different approach.

## *LOS INMIGRANTES*

Despite an imperial past, Spain, unlike almost the whole of the rest of western Europe, has never assimilated a non-Spanish population, largely because the country was pretty much a closed shop until the late '60s. Even now the majority of non-whites in Spain are illegal immigrants, either hawking stuff on the streets or working in the *plasticultura* farms.

Andalucía's proximity to Africa means that, after Madrid and Catalunya, it has the highest number of illegal immigrants in the country. The previous government's response was predictably tough: repealing a law that would have led to the naturalisation of many immigrants; denying work or residency permits to anyone already working; and tightening up external border controls. A couple of months after the Madrid train bombings the new government announced further controls, including the compilation of a register of mosques and clerics to ensure they are not used as terrorist recruitment centres.

But, despite this, boat-loads of hopefuls continue to arrive in Andalucian ports every day; news stories about bodies being washed up on the beaches of Tarifa, or groups of people being rounded up to be returned to Morocco or Senegal are a regular occurence.

## 'It is estimated that there are half a million foreign homeowners in Andalucia.'

The re-emergence and revitalisation of Islamic culture in certain towns – chiefly Granada and Córdoba, where small Arab populations have settled – was dealt a blow by the 11-M terror attacks. Though the resident Islamic community quickly distanced itself from extremism, the damage was done, and it's likely that anyone of North African or Arab appearance will continue to be regarded with suspicion by many Spaniards for some time.

At the other end of the spectrum is immigration of another kind – northern Europeans buying up properties for second homes. It is estimated that there are some half a million foreign homeowners in Andalucia alone. Once confined to the coast, it now seems that no part of Andalucia is out of bounds for Brits and Germans trying to get away from it all. Although locals benefit from the original sale, non-property-owners and young people are increasingly unable to afford to buy, and it's not uncommon to find some villages almost entirely populated by foreigners.

### THE ROCK

The continuing saga of Gibraltar's future has been put on the back burner once again after a fraught period a couple of years ago. In 2002 Tony Blair and the then Spanish Prime Minister José María Aznar tried to sew up a quick solution with a joint sovereignty deal. But no deal can go ahead without agreement from the inhabitants of the Rock, and that is not going to happen in a hurry: a referendum in November 2002 resulted in a 99 per cent 'No' vote.

The British government knows that for a joint sovereignty deal to have any chance of returning a 'Yes' vote, it must be seen as a permanent agreement and not as a stepping-stone to full Spanish sovereignty.

Aznar was always reluctant to grant Gibraltar too much autonomy, feeling it would send out the wrong signal to the Basque country. It remains to be seen how the new Prime Minister approaches the issue. The irony of the continued existence of Ceuta and Melilla, the Spanish protectorates in Morocco, seems lost on Spain, however.

### THE POLITICAL LANDSCAPE

President Manuel Chaves secured a fifth term for himself and the socialist PSOE in the 2004 regional elections, creating history in the process by forming the first regional government in Spain with more women than men (eight to six). One of his first declarations was a pledge to improve the 'quality of democracy' in the region by creating a register of MPs' wealth and interests, and improving communications with senior cabinet members and the public. It's perhaps the first public recognition that politics in Andalucía has been scarred by nepotism and backhanders, and a canny way to tell the populace that he has no intention, after so long in power, of becoming complacent.

Chaves also pledged to both improve relations with Madrid and keep up the pressure to ensure Andalucia is high on the central government's agenda – improving the region's infrastructure is his main priority. The past eight years with the PP in power in Madrid have been tough on the region, with tight restrictions on funding for major projects. He's also identified the creation of new companies and investment in innovation as two other key priorities and, to that end, has created a new Department of Equality and Innovation.

### THE FUTURE

The terrorist attacks in Madrid in March 2004 played a major role in securing the election of the PSOE's José Luis Rodríguez Zapatero as Prime Minister. A new central government and a reinvigorated provincial government of the same political hue should work well for the region.

Many of the big infrastructure projects, such as the extension of the AVE high-speed train link from Sevilla to Málaga (due by 2007) and a metro service in Sevilla, as well as ongoing road-building schemes, will be given a boost.

Communications with the rest of the world have also improved: budget airlines fly to Jerez and Málaga, and GB Airways has direct flights from London to Almería and Sevilla. The type of tourist may be changing, but the numbers stay the same, and the new, more upmarket visitors spend more money – talk of the death of tourism in Andalucía is certainly premature.

Andalucia retains a cultural identity that sets it apart from the rest of Spain, yet it is also being drawn ever-closer to the rest of the country. The region may still celebrate its romantic roots with wild abandon, but it is now also aware of its role within the national story. Sadly, the spectre of global terrorism now hangs heavy over the region. But a renewed political will and an ongoing modernisation drive could see Andalucía regain its historical position as a major player in Europe.

The Roman theatre of **Ronda La Vieja/Acinipo**, near Ronda.

# Architecture

A dazzling Moorish heritage, and a treasury of Gothic, Renaissance and baroque treats.

The legacy of the Moors has bewitched so many writers on Andalucía that it is easy believe that nothing worthwhile existed in southern Spain before their arrival at Tarifa in 711. Yet Andalucía is one of the archaeologically richest regions on the continent, and there's plenty of evidence left of the succession of civilisations that have sought to control this strategically important, mineral-rich land.

There are stunning late-palaeolithic cave paintings at **La Pileta**, near Ronda, neolithic dolmens at **Antequera** (among the most impressive to be found anywhere in the world), an outstanding Bronze Age settlement at **Los Millares** in Almería province and Phoenician tombs at **Almuñécar**, but, unsurprisingly, it was the Romans who left the greatest number of ancient remains.

The most significant Roman site is **Itálica**, just outside Sevilla, which was founded in 205 BC as the first Roman town in Spain. It grew to become a sizeable port and city (birthplace of Hadrian and Trajan) and was lavishly endowed with grand public buildings, such as an amphitheatre, bathhouse and theatre. The site hasn't fared well over the years, and is curiously lacking in atmosphere, though the amphitheatre has now been restored. Other important Roman settlements have been uncovered at **Baelo Claudia**, near Tarifa, and **Ronda la Vieja/**

**Acinipo**, close to Ronda. At **Carmona** there's one of the most important Roman necropolises outside Italy, **Córdoba**'s Roman bridge still spans the Guadalquivir, **Cádiz** has an impressive amphitheatre. The list goes on…

### SENSE AND SENSUALITY: THE MOORS

There is no doubt, however, that the biggest architectural draws in Andalucía are the mosques, castles and palaces built by the Moors during their more than 700 years in southern Spain.

In both architectural and artistic terms, Andalucía's most important Moorish dynasty were the **Umayyads**. Originally from Damascus, the old capital of Islam, they were ousted by a new faction called the Abbasids. The Umayyads then fled to Córdoba in 756, whereupon their leader, Abd al-Rahman, proclaimed himself the first ruler of the independent emirate of al-Andalus. Apart from relative social stability and economic prosperity, the invaders brought with them the best traditions of Islamic architecture and decoration, and quickly set about building in an imposing, confident manner now broadly known as the Umayyad (or Caliphal) style.

One of the great triumphs of this essentially unintellectual style was to fuse classical and Islamic elements, while bringing a new sensuality into architecture – a direct reflection of society at the time, which, according to contemporary literature and poetry, eschewed serious religious contemplation in favour of music, drinking, games of chess and making love. This sensuality manifested itself in a rejection of strict rules of proportion and space in favour of more intangible structures, and in mysterious plays on light and shadow and intricate decorative effects on a grand scale.

## 'The Mezquita is packed with imaginative borrowings and inspired innovation.'

The Umayyad style is exemplified *par excellence* by the **Mezquita**, Córdoba's Great Mosque, which was started around 780, and enlarged and embellished over the next 200 years. It's packed with imaginative borrowings and inspired innovation. Of the former, the Visigothic horseshoe arch is everywhere, as are re-used Roman and Visigothic capitals; the mosaics are strongly Byzantine-influenced; and the arcading (one row of arches on top of another), which was unprecedented in a mosque, was inspired by Roman aqueducts.

But there are also plenty of novel and distinctly Islamic elements – the alternating bands of brick and ashlar masonry, the use of calligraphy as the principal decorative element, employing stone rather than stucco, and the highly suggestive (rather than hierarchic) use of space.

By the mid tenth century, a period known as the '**Umayyad baroque**', architectural complexity was reaching a peak, and the Mezquita's features from this time (in the royal gallery of the Caliph) include elaborate decorative arcading, with interlaced arches, arches with semi-circular segments cut out of them and the earliest use of 'honeycomb' effects. The decoration around the *mihrab* (prayer niche) is spectacularly ornate – star-shaped vaulting, mosaics, and a stunning dome. The blurring between where structure ends and decoration begins was to be immensely influential on Muslim architecture in the coming centuries.

Another good example of the Umayyad style lies just east of Córdoba on the peaceful lower slopes of the Sierra Morena: the ruined **Medina Azahara** palace-city. Originally intended as a summer palace for Abd al-Rahman III, the complex consisted of several palaces, extensive gardens, a zoo, an aviary, a weapons production site and a mosque – it was inspired by monumental Roman constructions, particularly the palace-city of Diocletian at Split. Building started in 936

at huge expense: engraved basins were imported from Constantinople and Syria; marble was brought from Almería and Carthage; and – the most lavish touch of all – the roof tiles were covered in gold and silver, a decadent symbol of Arabic glory.

Unfortunately, the city was largely destroyed when the Umayyads were ousted from Córdoba in 1009, and for centuries the plundered site was left to disintegrate. In recent years, however, an extensive reconstruction and restoration programme has put Medina Azahara back on the map. The centrepiece is an ornately decorated hall that gives visitors an excellent idea of the scale and style of the various buildings that made up this important complex. The carvings are some of the finest of the period, and are notable for their bird and Tree of Life forms, rather than for their scripts.

After the collapse of Umayyad al-Andalus in the early 11th century, the power vacuum was eventually filled by the **Almoravids**, and then the **Almohads**, both strict, morally rigid Berber tribes from North Africa, who between them ruled until the early 13th century. Initially, they had a far more severe, simple view of what architecture should be, and reacted against the decorative excesses of the Umayyads. They were superb military architects – much of the **Alcazaba** in Almería, the most impressive Moorish fortress in Spain after the Alhambra, dates from the Almohad period, as does Sevilla's **Torre del Oro**.

Yet even these austere rulers seemed to have eventually softened to some degree, as can be seen in the exquisite **Giralda minaret** in Sevilla, now incorporated into the cathedral. Completed by the Almohads in 1195, it is a wonderful example of Maghreb architecture, the second movement associated with Islamic constructions in southern Spain, yet is far more ornate than any comparable Almohad structure in North Africa. The tower is a breathtaking display of graceful proportions, trellis-like brick patterning and elegant arabesques. In typical Maghreb style, which became increasingly elaborate as time went on, the square form (the shape of all minarets in Andalucia) is awash with decoration and colour, the latter changing subtly according to the light.

The last stage of Muslim architecture in Andalucia came with the founding of the **Nasrid dynasty** in Granada in the early 13th century, by which time much of al-Andalus had already been lost to the Christians. That a Moorish state survived at all for the next 250 years is remarkable; that its major architectural legacy was the extraordinary **Alhambra** palace is astonishing.

Part private residence, part bureaucratic offices, the halls and courtyards of the Alhambra contain none of the architectural innovations that mark out the Mezquita, but, instead, are a brilliant recapitulation of all that went before. Times being far harder than in the days of the Umayyads, however, it is the cheaper material of stucco (a slow-setting plaster) that is largely employed. The use of stucco reached new heights of complexity, particularly during the period of the so-called 'Nasrid baroque' under Mohammed V in the mid 14th century, when designs fused Kufic (old Islamic script) and Neskhi (modern Islamic). Another development was remarkable stucco *muqarnas* ceilings (sometimes known as stalactite or honeycomb ceilings) – that in the Alhambra's **Sala de las Dos Hermanas** (Hall of the Two Sisters) is the most elaborate of its kind in the Islamic world (there are also fine examples in Sevilla's Alcázar).

Granada itself was the only purpose-built Islamic town in Andalucía (Córdoba was built on Roman foundations), and the maze of alleyways and whitewashed houses swarming over the Albaicín hill below the Alhambra are the most perfectly preserved Moorish quarter in the region. At the foot of the hill is **El Bañuelo**, the 11th-century Arab baths, the oldest civic building in Granada and most complete Moorish bathhouse in Spain. Another remarkable survival, not far from the cathedral, is the 14th-century **Casa del Carbón**, the only surviving wheat exchange of its period in Spain.

Outside of the big cities, there are plenty of other relics from Moorish times. One outstanding example can be found in northern Huelva province, where the village of **Almonaster La Real** possesses a perfect gem of Islamic architecture in the form of a tenth-century mosque. The building was turned into a church by conquering Castilians in the 13th century (as were countless other mosques), but the original Arabic structure was left intact, including incorporated bits of an earlier Visigothic church and Roman stonework.

### TRIUMPHALISM AND SYNTHESIS: THE GOTHIC

The 500-year Moorish domination of Andalucia came to an end in 1212 at the Battle of Las Navas de Tolosa where a Christian army under Alfonso VII defeated the Almohads. And with the new conquerors came fresh architectural ideas and energy. The **Gothic** style, which originated in France, reached Andalucia in the 13th century. Its progress was slow, but once it had gained a foothold, it remained the dominant architectural form until the 16th century, and a defiant statement of the triumph of Christianity.

Thanks to some important technical innovations, the new Gothic constructions tended to be much larger than their Moorish predecessors. Like most significant European buildings of this period, they were characterised by flying buttresses, intricate window tracery, ribbed ceilings and pointed arches, but they differed from their contemporaries in several

---

**Don't miss** Architecture

### Roman

The remains of the city of **Itálica** (see p179), birthplace of Hadrian and Trajan, lie just outside Sevilla. Other important Roman sites include **Baelo Claudia** (see p133), near Tarifa, and the theatre at **Ronda La Vieja** (see p99), not far from Ronda.

### Moorish

**Córdoba**'s astonishing **Mezquita** (see p208) is the prime example of Umayyad period architecture. The later Almohads were masters of military building, as seen in the **Alcazaba** in **Almería** (see p290). Andalucía's most iconic structure is undoubtedly **Granada**'s **Alhambra** (see p249), whose stucco splendours are the greatest legacy of the last Moorish dynasty, the Nasrids.

### Gothic

**Sevilla**'s 15th-century **Catedral** (see p167) is the region's finest Gothic building. In **Granada**, Enrique de Egas's **Capilla Real** (see p259) showcases the flamboyant late Isabelline Gothic style.

### Renaissance

The **Palacio de Carlos V** (see p253) in **Granada** exemplifies the unadorned classical harmony of the pure Renaissance style. More dramatic and theatrical is Diego de Siloé's towering **Catedral** (see p259) in **Granada**. The exquisite towns of **Úbeda** (see p238) and **Baeza** (see p236) contain possibly the finest ensembles of Renaissance architecture in Spain.

### Baroque

The **Monasterio de la Cartuja** (see p261) in **Granada** drips with some of the most extraordinary examples of baroque exuberance in the country. A clutch of fine churches and a remarkable fountain have earned **Priego de Córdoba** (see p223) the title of capital of Andalucían baroque.

ways. The cathedrals, for example, tended to be wider than others in Europe because they were often built on the sites of square mosques.

Furthermore, the choir and chapel containing the high altar could often be found in the middle of the church rather than at one end. New cathedrals were designed with lots of side chapels and, uniquely, contained *retablos*, three-part sculptural altarpieces that frequently filled the whole width of the nave behind the altar. The point of the *retablo*, a purely Spanish invention, was to illustrate Christ's teachings and stories with elaborately carved or painted biblical scenes. The best Gothic example is in Sevilla's cathedral, a masterpiece created by the Flemish sculptor Pieter Dancart in 1482 with more than 1,000 gilded and painted biblical figures.

## 'The best example of Gothic architecture in Andalucía is the cathedral in Sevilla, the largest in the world.'

The Christian conquerors may have found the Moors' religion intolerable, but they had far more time for their artistic and architectural traditions, which strongly influenced the incoming Gothic style. Obvious Muslim borrowings included profusely decorated surfaces and lashings of rich furnishings, as well as the use of decorative strips of lettering. The most popular ceilings – known as *artesonado* ceilings – were also borrowed directly from the Moors, and the Christians continued to use skilled Arab artisans to build them. The employment of Muslims to decorate Christian structures in Islamic style became known as the **Mudéjar** tradition. Their work was characterised by elaborately carved wooden inlays imitating traditional Muslim leatherwork, and remained fashionable until the 17th century.

The best example of Gothic architecture in Andalucía is the **cathedral** in **Sevilla**. Built on the site of the great Almohad mosque, it was completed in 1504, and is the largest cathedral in the world. Its impressive exterior features a great rose window, double buttresses and a 'fence' of Roman columns joined by chains. Inside, the key quality is size rather than grace or beauty, although it does contain some impressive tombs, including those of Alfonso the Wise, Pedro the Cruel and Christopher Columbus.

There are dozens of other Gothic churches throughout the region. One of the most charming is the simple, unambitious church

**La Cartuja** monastery, near Jerez. *See p32.*

of **Santa Ana** in Sevilla, built under Pedro the Cruel. Elsewhere, the straightforward, elegant parish churches of **Córdoba** are well worth a visit, as are the cathedrals at **Jerez de la Frontera** and **Málaga**, both of which combine Gothic, Renaissance and baroque styles.

Andalucía's Gothic period moved into its final and most extravagant phase under Fernando and Isabel, who finally completed the *reconquista* when they took Granada in 1492. The style that developed under their patronage is known as **Isabelline Gothic** or **Gothic Plateresque**, a highly decorative (*platero* means 'silversmith' in Spanish), exuberant extension of the early Gothic form. The movement roughly corresponded with the French Flamboyant and English Perpendicular styles, and was characterised by lace-like ornament, low-relief sculptures, sinuously curved arches and tracery, and playful, naturalistic detail. For supreme examples of this late Gothic flamboyance, see the façade of the **Palacio de Jabalquinto** in Baeza in Jaén province, or, better still, Fernando and Isabel's own burial chapel, the **Capilla Real** in Granada. Here, the greatest architect of the time, **Enrique de Egas** (1445-1534), gave his passion for unrestrained Gothicism a free rein, perfectly illustrated by the splendid north portal, which now stands inside the adjacent cathedral. The chapel, which wasn't completed until 1527, is made all the more interesting by the fact that the men working with Egas favoured a more measured, classical style usually associated with the later Renaissance period. The result is a building that skilfully balances fantastical, late Gothic elements with more restrained features such as the classical archway through which you enter the building from the street.

## HARMONY AND PURITY: THE RENAISSANCE

The Gothic movement proved remarkably resilient in Andalucia, overlapping with the new ideas of the Italian-born **Renaissance** in the early 16th century. The latter brought about a return to the ancient Roman and Greek ideals of harmony and proportion. Columns, arcaded interior courtyards and classical shapes (squares, circles, triangles) made a big come-back although, as in the Gothic period, many new buildings were still imbued with geometric Muslim-style decorative effects.

Spanish Renaissance architecture can be roughly divided into three periods: classical Plateresque, purist Renaissance and Herreresque (though the latter only had a very limited impact in Andalucía). As the name suggests, the **classical Plateresque** movement was a continuation and development of the Gothic Plateresque style. Decorative rather than structural (another legacy of the region's Islamic past), the movement endowed buildings with highly intricate designs resembling those of silverware, and façades were given round-arch portals bordered by columns and stone sculpture.

In contrast, the **purist Renaissance** style steered clear of excessive ornamentation in favour of simple, classical harmony, as exemplified in the **Palacio de Carlos V** in the **Alhambra**. Here, architect **Pedro Machuca**, who had trained in Italy, created an imposing square block notable for its deliberate lack of ornamentation and the unprecedented classical severity of its design.

However, it was the last phase, called **Herreresque** after the architect **Juan de Herrera** (1530-97), that was the plainest of the three – as shown by Herrera's austere **San Lorenzo de El Escorial** monastery complex near Madrid. De Herrera's only work in the region is **La Lonja** in Sevilla.

Just as there were several different periods of Renaissance architecture in Andalucía, so there were several big-name architects associated with the movement. The first was **Diego de Siloé** (1495-1563) who, with the Italian Jacopo Florentino, designed the enormous **Monasterio de San Jerónimo** in Granada, combining Gothic proportions with classical detailing. De Siloé was also ultimately responsible for **Granada**'s **cathedral**, the first plans for which were drawn up by the Gothicist Enrique de Egas. Deemed too old-fashioned

by Carlos V, Egas's design was cast aside in favour of de Siloé's, who set about building an uncompromisingly classical structure that contrasted sharply with Egas's homely chapel next door. Inside, the effect is one of intense drama, created not only by the vast size of the space and towering circular chancel, but also by a giant order of classical columns intended to support barrel vaulting that was, in the end, changed to Gothic vaulting in the late 16th century. The sense of theatre is further emphasised by the fact that the whole place is painted white. In **Almería** there's another cathedral partially designed by de Siloé, and a third in **Guadix**, the latter an austere, grey reminder of one's Christian duty.

> **'The Italian influence was felt in town planning, military architecture and garden design, as well as in individual *palacios* and churches.'**

De Siloé's successor, **Andrés de Vandelvira** (1509-75), quickly established himself as a worthy heir. His **cathedral** at **Málaga** has all the drama of that in Granada, while its counterpart in **Jaén** is a giant construction that dwarfs the town below. Vandelvira was a prolific builder who spanned all three phases of Renaissance architecture, particularly in the neighbouring towns of Úbeda and Baeza in Jaén province, where he constructed some of the finest ensembles of Renaissance architecture in the country. Thanks to a thriving textile industry and the fact that it was home to Carlos V's secretary, Francisco de los Cobos y Molina (who all but ruled Spain during the first half of the 16th century), Úbeda was chosen as the site for Vandelvira's best work: the **Sacra Capilla del Salvador del Mundo**, where de los Cobos y Molina is buried. The chapel was started by de Siloé but executed by Vandelvira and, unusually, remains close to its original state to this day, including most of its 16th-century furnishings and an awesome *retablo* by **Alonso Berruguete**, Spain's leading Renaissance sculptor and a pupil of Michelangelo. The chapel stands on what is undoubtedly one of Andalucía's most beautiful squares, **Plaza de Vázquez de Molina**, lined on every side by remarkable Renaissance buildings.

Nearby, **Baeza** doesn't possess quite the quantity of Renaissance treasures as Úbeda, but the influence of Vandelvira's delicate classicism makes itself felt in its immaculately preserved streets. The tiny **Plaza del Pópulo** is a tiny Renaissance gem of a square.

Another Renaissance masterpiece is the **Colegiata de Santa María de la Asunción** in the beautifully preserved town of **Osuna** in eastern Sevilla province. It was begun in 1534 and, though not finally completed until the 18th century, remains a coherent and essentially early-16th-century structure. The airy interior houses exquisite 16th- and 17th-century furnishings and a staggering 16th-century pantheon of the Dukes of Osuna, itself a miniature church complete with tiny choir stalls and Renaissance decoration.

The Italian influence was felt in town planning, military architecture and garden design, as well as in individual *palacios* and churches. During the 16th century, **Granada**'s **Plaza Nueva** was constructed and the lower city took on a completely new identity as an Italianate Renaissance town. Italian architects and craftsmen were responsible for two of Andalucía's finest castles: **La Calahorra** in Granada province and **Vélez Blanco** in Almería province, both built in the early 16th century and the first important examples of Italian Renaissance design outside Italy. La Calahorra houses a magnificent (if crumbling) Italian Renaissance courtyard. In **Sevilla**, the Moorish gardens of the **Alcázar** acquired new Italian-style features including classical statues, grottoes and the perfectly balanced arcaded pavilion known as the **Pabellón de Carlos V**.

## EXUBERANCE AND EXCESS: THE BAROQUE

If the Renaissance period was largely characterised by sober, restrained design, the **baroque** movement that followed was precisely the opposite. Typically flamboyant and naturalistic in approach, it was a direct reaction against the classical Renaissance form and made extensive use of colour, ornament and decoration. However, while Italian baroque architecture was defined by innovations such as dynamic ground plans, the Spanish version was really only 'baroque' in the sense of being exuberantly ornamental. The structures of the buildings remained remarkably conventional.

Gathering steam in the 17th century, and reaching a peak of opulence in the 18th century with the so-called **churrigueresque** style (named after a family of sculptors and architects from Salamanca called Churriguera, who were, ironically, the least 'churrigueresque' of the churrigueresque architects), Andalucía became one of the European centres of the baroque style. The Spanish movement affected

the look of present-day Andalucía as much as the Muslim period, reaching even the most isolated villages and endowing rural areas with unexpectedly lavish buildings. In the parish church of **San Mateo** in **Lucena** (in southern Córdoba province), for example, there is a Sagrario chapel decorated with an intricacy on a par with the best baroque buildings in Granada and Sevilla. The overall result was a plethora of delightful constructions displaying unprecedented decorative freedom in a uniquely Spanish mode that also incorporated diverse references to previous architectural styles.

One of the most memorable exponents of the new style was **Alonso Cano** (1601-67). Known as the 'Spanish Michelangelo' for his remarkable ability to paint, sculpt and design buildings, he was responsible for the unique 17th-century façade of **Granada**'s **cathedral**. This early baroque construction, with its three tall arches, illustrates the stylistic transition from classical Renaissance to the new Spanish approach, simultaneously displaying elements of baroque ornamentation over firm Renaissance roots. Cano also provided some of the sculptures for the extraordinary baroque façade of the monastery of **La Cartuja** outside **Jerez**.

In Sevilla, **Leonardo de Figueroa** (1650-1730) was responsible for the churches of **El Salvador** and **San Luis**, the **Colegio San Telmo** and what is now the **Museo de Bellas Artes** (the latter being a very early and restrained version of baroque). Others, like **Vicente Acero**, developed the baroque style into rococo forms, with conspicuous constructions such as the façade of the **cathedral** at **Guadix** and José de Bada's church of **San Juan de Dios** in Granada.

Visitors to Granada can admire one of the most sumptuous creations of the period in all Spain: the dazzling gold and marble chancel by **Francisco Hurtado Izquierdo** (1669-1725) in the **Monasterio de la Cartuja**. The sacristy, where not a single bit of the wall is left undecorated, is also an exhilarating experience, as is the nearby **Charterhouse**, which achieves astonishing levels of architectural flamboyance.

Other buildings of note include the **Palacio del Marqués de la Gomera** in Osuna with its strange, asymmetrical skyline, inspired by German rococo illustrations, and the wedding cake-like Sagrario chapel in the delightful town of **Priego de Córdoba**, a soaring, circular construction with plaster-coated balconies that have now been restored to their original sparkling white. The same town possesses another rather surprising baroque structure: a public fountain with mythological statues showered by over 100 jets of water.

**In Context**

## REVIVALISM AND ECLECTICISM: TO THE PRESENT

After the excitement of the baroque movement came a period of relative, neo-classical calm and a return to the cleaner, more serene architectural principles of Ancient Greece and Rome. Thanks to a general economic decline in Andalucía, however, the style, which arrived in the mid 18th century and lasted until the early 19th century, did not take hold with anything like the same force as previous movements. **Cádiz** has the biggest neo-classical heritage in Andalucía: apart from its huge, ungainly cathedral, which was completed in 1856, there are scores of houses and churches bearing testament to this short-lived, under-funded architectural period.

The 19th and 20th centuries witnessed further serious economic decline in the region and a concomitant lack of architectural development. Displaying a yearning for the glory of days gone by, the tendency in recent years has been to revive almost every historical style, particularly that of the Moors.

**Sevilla**'s Ibero-American Exhibition of 1929 left the city with a number of grandiose neo-Moorish/neo-Renaissance buildings, most notably the majestic **Hotel Alfonso XIII** and the extraordinary **Plaza de España**, with its huge sweep of tiles depicting the 40 regions of Spain. A more recent example of neo-Moorish is the city's former **Estación de Córdoba**, a 19th-century railway station that was converted into an exhibition venue in 1992. Other neo-Moorish structures include the **Alhambra Palace Hotel** in **Granada** and the **Palacio de Orleans y Borbón** in **Sanlúcar de Barrameda**, but little splashes of Islamicism, often in the form of decorative tile-work, are found everywhere, from railway stations and markets to bus stations and cottages.

One of Andalucía's rare 20th-century buildings worthy of note is the **Fondación de Rodríguez-Acosta** in **Granada**, an extraordinarily original construction (dating from the second and third decades of the century) that anticipated postmodernism and has been admired by many leading architects of today, such as Rafael Moneo.

The buildings erected for **Sevilla**'s **1992 Expo** were rather less permanent than those built for the 1929 exhibition – most were demolished or removed afterwards – though some were genuinely forward-looking (such as Nicholas Grimshaw's British Pavilion). The Expo's greatest architectural legacy was the two bridges contructed by **Santiago Calatrava**: the crossbow-shaped **Puente de la Barqueta** and the lyre-like **Puente del Alamillo**. The former has become a symbol of the 'new Andalucía', as eloquent as the Giralda was of the old region.

Exciting contemporary buildings continue to be a rarity in Andalucía. Probably the most notable of recent years the long-awaited opening in 2003 of the **Museo Picasso Málaga**, which skilfully fuses a 16th-century palace with a sleek, modern gallery space. Elsewhere, urban regeneration is given a greater priority than new building – Córdoba's Plaza de la Corredera and the Alameda de Hercules in Sevilla, for instance, have been transformed in recent years.

Granada's neo-Moorish **Alhambra Palace Hotel**.

Federico García Lorca. *See p37.*

# Literary Andalucía

Poetry and travel writing are the twin pillars of southern Spain's literary tradition.

Andalucía, a land encapsulating all the romantic clichés of Spain, has inspired some of the greatest foreign writings on the country. But it is also a place whose seductive beauty has nurtured many of Spain's finest poets…

## THE POETS OF AL-ANDALUS

The first of the major Andalucían writers were the poets of the Islamic period, beginning with those from the intensely competitive *taifa* kingdoms. The intellectual giant of this period was **Ibn Hazm** (994-1064), a Córdoba-born polymath who moved to Almería at the time of the collapse of the Caliphate, and wrote one of the most translated works from Muslim Spain, *The Ring of the Dove.* This extraordinary book, which is partly a Neo-Platonic treatise on love, partly an autobiography, and partly a collection of the author's own poems, offers a penetrating psychological portrait of the human heart, as well as interesting titbits about the sexual customs and preferences of the time. Córdoban men, for instance, really did prefer blondes.

Love was a major preoccupation of the other Islamic poets of the 11th century, including, most famously, **Ibn Zaydun** (1003-70), a Córdoban writer whose life and work were dominated

by his passion for the daughter of Caliph al-Mustakfi, Princess Walladah, herself a poetess. When she abandoned him for a wealthier and more influential lover, he wrote a vituperative piece about his rival (a man as 'worthless as a fly or mosquito') that had him thrown briefly into jail. A more positive outcome of his rejection was a poem in which the unending anguish of his loss was expressed through constant repetition of the same rhyme. It has since become one of most famous love poems in the Arab language.

Another celebrated love affair of this time was the relationship between the poet ruler of Sevilla, **al-Mutamid** (reigned 1069-91), and a woman called Itimad. His feverish love poems addressed to her ('I am pining because of being separated from you/Inebriated with the wine of my longing for you') were succeeded in later life by works conveying a general nostalgia for the past and for Andalucía. By then he had been exiled to the remote Moroccan village of Agmat, where his mausoleum is still a place of pilgrimage for sentimental *sevillanos*.

The 11th and 12th centuries also saw the emergence of some of the finest of Spain's Jewish poets (an excellent English anthology is David Goldstein's *The Jewish Poets of Spain 900-1250*, Harmondsworth, 1971), who, though writing in Hebrew, followed classical Arabic forms of verse. **Samuel Ha-Nagrid**, who was born in Córdoba in 993, and rose to become vizier to the Zirids in Granada, was a master of martial verse, and the only Jew ever to lead a Muslim army. Whereas he evoked the *taifa* kingdoms at their height, the collapse of these kingdoms after 1089 was brilliantly conveyed by **Judah Ha-Levi**, who, after long stays in Lucena, Sevilla and Granada, set off to the Middle East, where, according to legend, he was killed at the moment of reaching the gates to Jerusalem.

## 'Ibn Zamrak turned the Alhambra into what has been called the most sumptuous book of verse ever produced.'

The last phase in the history of al-Andalus, the period of the Nasrids, was marked in literature by poets whose verse is inscribed in plaster all over the walls of the Alhambra. Among these writers the Loja-born **Ibn al-Khatib** (1313-71), a vizier to both Yusuf I and Muhammad V, and whose varied and prolific output included the historical work *The Shining Rays of the Full Moon*, one of the major sources for our knowledge of the Nasrid Golden Age.

But the greatest of those poets, who turned the Alhambra into what has been called the most sumptuous book of verse ever produced, was Ibn al-Khatib's ruthless protégé **Ibn Zamrak** (1333-92). Born to a Granadan ironworker, and an early beneficiary of the city's newly founded *madrasa* (a collegiate institution with bursaries for the poor), Ibn Zamrak supplanted his mentor as vizier by spreading rumours that led to the man's flight to Morocco and eventual murder by strangling. As with all but one of the Alhambra poets, Ibn Zamrak himself met a violent death, being killed with all his family on the orders of Yusuf II. The sordid political manoeuvrings of his life and times were in ironic contrast to his lyrical, panegyric verse, which is full of references to nuptial diadems, paradisal gardens, full moons, and other 'enfolding wonders'.

### AFTER THE RECONQUISTA
The many legends about the last days of Nasrid Spain were avidly assimilated by the Christians, and gave rise in c1550 to one of the most popular 16th-century novels, the anonymous *Story of the Abencerrage and the Beautiful Jarifa*.

In the meantime, the spirit of Christian triumphalism that set in during the reigns of Carlos V and Felipe II was reflected in the rhetorical, Italianate verse of **Fernando de Herrera** (1534-97), known to his contemporaries as 'The Divine'. A Sevillian who spent all his life in his native city (which he called, in his poem 'Sevilla', 'not a city but a universe'), Herrera acquired much of his great learning through belonging to one of Spain's earliest known intellectual salons or *tertulias*.

It was also attended by Columbus's great grandson, Álvaro Colón, whose wife Leonor was the subject of many of Herrera's tedious outpourings of platonic love. A rather more down-to-earth regular at this *tertulia* was **Baltasar del Alcázar** (1530-1606), a poet whose racy, light verse – which was never intended for publication – captures the sense of humour for which the Sevillians are famous. 'Three things', begins one of his best-known works, 'keep my heart love's captive:/the fair Inés, smoked ham/and aubergines with cheese'.

Beyond the rarified environment of Álvaro Colón's *tertulia* was a pungent, vibrant and crime-ridden Sevilla that was the scene of lively theatrical activity. The rough-and-ready plays of the Sevilla-born actor, writer and manager **Lope de Rueda** (c1505-65) were a prelude to the popular drama of the Spanish Shakespeare, **Lope de Vega** (1562-1635), whose comedy *El Arenal de Sevilla* captures the vitality and cosmopolitanism of the city's port. But no other writer evoked Sevilla's Golden Age better than **Miguel de Cervantes** (1547-1616), who spent much of the 1580s and '90s in Andalucía, living an itinerant existence, and still hoping to make a name as a playwright. His knowledge of Andalucía, and in particular of the lowlife of Sevilla (a place he described as 'the asylum of the poor and refuge of the outlaw'), is apparent in the entertaining short stories that make up his *Exemplary Novels* (1616).

The only leading Golden Age writer actually native to Andalucía was the poet **Luis de Góngora** (1561-1627). Born to a wealthy and cultured Córdoban family, he would celebrate his city in a poem ('To Córdoba') whose lines are inscribed today on a plaque facing the Roman bridge: 'Oh mighty wall, oh towers crowned with honour, majesty and gallantry! Oh great river, great king of Andalucía, with your noble, if not golden sands!...' After a dissolute youth of whoring, gambling and theatregoing, first as a student at Salamanca University, and then as a prebendary at Córdoba Cathedral, Góngora moved to Madrid, and developed an increasing melancholy and austerity. As a poet he became the master of a learned style pejoratively referred to in its time as *culteranismo*. Extremely artificial, full of obscure references, and with a Latinate syntax and vocabulary, it was the antithesis of the fresh and simple effects that contemporary Lope de Vega aimed to achieve. Góngora's masterpiece is the long and incomplete pastoral work *Solitudes* (the 1961 English translation by EM Wilson is even less intelligible than the original), which probably drew greatly from memories of the Córdoban countryside.

Writing at the same time as Góngora were a great number of minor Andalucian poets; for instance, the Utrera-born and Sevilla-based **Rodrigo Caro** (1573-1647), an archaeologist and antiquary who is best remembered for a poem bemoaning the fast disappearance of the Roman settlement of Itálica ('These empty fields before you,/Fabio, this parched mound of earth,/Were once, alas, the famed Itálica').

## THE ROMANTIC 19TH CENTURY

It was not until the early 19th century that Andalucía saw again a major flowering of literary talent, and this time it was the Moorish rather than the Roman ruins of the region that drew the attention of writers.

Almost all the main figures associated with the Romantic discovery of Andalucía were British and French travellers, attracted to Spain by improved communications, and the enormous publicity the country received in the wake of the Peninsular War (not to mention the wealth of works of art to be had on the cheap). The great focus of attention was the Alhambra in Granada, then a collapsing monument overrun by gypsies and vagrants.

> 'Borrow was a delightfully perverse traveller who noticeably avoided both the Alhambra and other British tourists.'

**François Renée Chateaubriand**, who visited Granada in 1807, transformed *The Story of the Abencerrage and the Beautiful Jarifa* into his novel *The Last of the Abencerrages* (1827), an international bestseller that heralded a spectacular revival of interest in Nasrid Spain. Two years later a young American diplomat, **Washington Irving**, then researching a book on the conquest of Granada, took up quarters in the Alhambra, which inspired his enormously successful and largely fictional concoction later entitled *Tales of the Alhambra* (1832).

So great was the tourist appeal of Spain from the 1830s onwards that Lord Byron's publisher, John Murray (Byron was himself an enthusiast

of Andalucía, and in particular of the women of Cádiz), commissioned in 1839 a volume on the country for the popular series Murray's Handbooks. The writer who took on the commission was the aristocratic **Richard Ford**, who had been based in Sevilla and Granada from 1830 to 1833. The resulting *Handbook to Spain* (1845) strengthened the misleading view that Andalucía was the quintessential Spanish region, but nevertheless remains the most detailed and scholarly guide to Spain ever written. But it is much more than this. Ford was a brilliant descriptive writer whose lyricism was tempered by a sense of humour that makes you frequently laugh out loud.

The two other outstanding literary achievements by foreign travellers of this period are **George Borrow**'s *The Bible in Spain* (1842) and **Théophile Gautier**'s *Journey to Spain* (1841). Borrow was a delightfully perverse traveller who noticeably avoided both the Alhambra and other British tourists, and preferred instead the company of gypsies and lowlifes. Gautier, despite having the conventional Orientalist biases of his generation, had a vividly pictorial descriptive style that the Spanish essayist and novelist Azorín would later praise for helping Spaniards achieve 'a poetic understanding' of their country.

Initially, Spanish writers lagged behind their foreign contemporaries in exploiting Andalucian Orientalist subject matter. The Alhambra, for instance, would not properly be celebrated in Spanish verse until the publication in 1852 of the two-volume *Granada* by the Castillian poet and playwright **José Zorrilla** (1817-93), a man later to be crowned Spain's national poet in a ceremony that took place in the Court of the Lions. The Sevillian **Gustavo Adolfo Bécquer** (1836-70), by far the greatest of this region's native Romantic writers, made no reference to al-Andalus in his works, lived for much of his short and unhappy life outside Andalucía, and devoted himself to themes of thwarted love, misery and solitude. His sparse poems were not brought together until after his death, in a publication, *Rimas*, that became the most popular book of Spanish verse until Lorca's *Romancero Gitano*.

Among Bécquer's Andalucian contemporaries, those who wrote about their region mainly concentrated on those local manners and customs – from fiestas to flamenco – that most appealed to the burgeoning tourist market. One of these so-called *costumbristas* was the Málaga-born **Serafín Estébanez Calderón** (1799-1867), whose *Andalucian Scenes* (1847) featured the first lengthy description of a gypsy festival in Triana. Another was the adopted Sevillian **Fernán**

**Luis de Góngora**. *See p35.*

**Caballero** (the pseudonym of Swiss-born Cecilia Boehl von Faber; 1796-1877), a pioneering compiler of regional folk songs, and the author of the much-translated novel of Andalucían life, *The Seagull* (1856).

But only the French writer, **Prosper Mérimée**, in his novella *Carmen* (1845), was able to turn to such typical *costumbrista* subjects as bullfights, bandits and gypsies, and create out of these a work of fiction that truly seized the European imagination.

The 19th-century craze for Andalucía (which reached new heights with Bizet's 1875 musical version of Mérimée's tale) was finally accompanied, from the 1870s onwards, by a renascence of native literature. The Guadix novelist **Pedro Antonio de Alarcón** (1833-91) popularised the wild mountainous district of the Alpujarras with his humorous short story *The Three-Cornered Hat* (1874), while a psychologically more penetrating portrait of Andalucian village life was given in the novels of the Cabra-born **Juan Valera** (1824-1905). An unequalled prose poem to Granada, *Granada the Beautiful* (1896), was written by the locally born **Ángel Ganivet** (1865-98).

### THE 20TH CENTURY TO TODAY

Above all, it was poetry that flourished. The Sevilla-born **Antonio Machado** (1875-1939) – a leading member, like Ganivet, of the Generation of 1898 group – was the most important Spanish poet immediately prior to Lorca. After a flirtation in Paris with modernism and the bohemian life, he gave this all up to become a provincial schoolteacher. The death of his young wife and muse Leonor in the Castillian town of Soria prompted him to move back to Andalucía in 1913, where he lived as an exile. While working in the small town of Baeza

in Jaén province, he continued to dream about the stark and empty Castillian countryside, and brought out in 1917 a much expanded edition of his greatest collection of verse, the *Campos de Castilla*, which is filled with musings on that landscape, and on the passing of old glories. The folkloric Andalucian themes that he rigorously avoided were the speciality of his brother, **Manuel Machado** (1874-1947).

Often considered as a link between one literary generation and the next was the Nobel-prizewinning poet **Juan Ramón Jímenez** (1881-1958). His best-loved work was a book ostensibly for children, *Platero and I* (1914), a series of prose poems describing life in the author's native town of Moguer de la Frontera.

The group – essentially of poets – who called themselves the Generation of 1927 (after their admiration for the then much-neglected Góngora, who died in 1627) included several Andalucians, notably the Sevilla-born **Luis Cernuda** (1902-63) and **Federico García Lorca** (1898-1936; see *p260*). Whereas the former left Andalucia at a very early age, and rarely referred to the region in his works, Lorca's poems and plays were not only heavily influenced by local folk culture, but also did much to perpetuate the romantic clichés about Andalucia, including a sentimental veneration of its Islamic past.

No Andalucían writer since Lorca has gained much of a reputation outside Spain. However, important and successful writers from elsewhere have continued to be lured by the region and its history. A number of recent novelists have been as fascinated as their Romantic predecessors by the eclipse of Nasrid civilisation, including **Amin Maalouf** in his memorable *Leo the African* (1986), **Tariq Ali** in the lightweight *Shadows of the Pomegranate Tree* (1992) and **Salman Rushdie** in *The Moor's Last Sigh* (1996), which gave new life to the tired legends about Boabdil. The Islamic legacy in Spain has also obsessed the Catalan novelist **Juan Goytisolo** (born 1928), the author of one of the starkest post-war travel accounts about Andalucia, *Campo de Níjar* (1959).

**Laurie Lee**, in *A Rose for Winter* (1955) and *As I Walked Out One Midsummer's Morning* (1969), evoked Andalucia in rich poetic prose; but he lacked the in-depth knowledge of the region that is such a feature of the writings of the Hispanist and Bloomsbury associate **Gerald Brenan**. The latter's *South From Granada* (1957), an idiosyncratic account of his time spent living in the remote Alpujarran village of Yegen, was the first of a number of British books dedicated to Andalucían rural life, of which the most charming recent examples are **Chris Stewart**'s *Driving over Lemons* (1999) and *A Parrot in the Pepper Tree* (2002).

# Food & Drink

Leave your preconceptions at the airport.

Few people come to southern Spain for the food. Old stereotypes die hard, and, while Andalucia's reputation for sun and scenic beauty is unassailable, many first-time visitors assume the trade-off is a monotonous, oily diet of fried fish and *gazpacho*. As with most stereotypes, there's an element of truth to it – olive oil is ubiquitous, many menus across the region are strikingly similar and there are a fair few bad restaurants out there. Yet the curious gastronome is far more likely to return from their holiday with their preconceptions in tatters.

Spain's ongoing culinary revolution has been slow to reach the far south, but it is now starting to make a mark (particularly in the cities of Málaga and Córdoba). Fine dining restaurants may be relatively few as yet, but many of those that are here are very fine indeed (*see p39* **Top ten**). However, it's the pleasures of simple local cooking that are likely to provide your most satisfying culinary reminiscences – nibbling on a skewer of freshly grilled sardines at a beachside *chiringuito*, perhaps, or tucking into a platter of tender, locally-raised lamb chops, accompanied by vegetables plucked from the cook's own garden, on the terrace of a mountain village *venta*.

And then there are tapas. Andalucia regards itself as the home of this most civilised way of eating, and ordering two or three of these little dishes to accompany drinks often makes a sit-down meal superfluous. Andalucians may be conservative in their eating habits, but,

contrary to popular belief (not least in the rest of Spain), there's a rich culinary tradition in the region, which is often most in evidence in the best tapas bars, where the variety of dishes on offer will come as a very pleasant surprise. (*See p42* **Lifting the lid on tapas**.)

### ESSENTIAL FLAVOURS AND DISHES

Andalucia's best-known dish is *gazpacho*, and all its many regional variations. In its traditional form it comes as a tomato, olive oil and garlic-based soup, served cold, often with ice cubes, and a selection of chopped onions, peppers, cucumber, croutons and egg to sprinkle on top. Each region has its own interpretation: Málaga's *ajo blanco*, with almonds and grapes; Antequera's *pimentón*, made with red peppers; Córdoba's thick *salmorejo* (made without water); Huelva's *gazpacho verde*, using parsley rather than tomatoes; and Cádiz's *sopa de picadillo*, which is spicier.

The region is also famous for its olives (*aceitunas*), which come in a multitude of forms: green, black, marinated in garlic and olive oil or vinegar, or stuffed with anchovies and peppers. Their extract – olive oil – is an intrinsic part of Spanish cuisine and is used in or on almost every Andalucian dish. Although some visitors complain about Spanish food being too 'greasy', it is important to realise that the Spaniards view olive oil almost as a dish in its own right; mopping-up some leftover oil with a hunk of bread is often the tastiest part of the meal.

*Jamón* (cured ham) is another Andalucían speciality that can be found in every bar in Spain, usually hanging in shanks from the ceiling. It comes in a variety of forms and at wildly different prices. The standard *jamón serrano* is the cheapest and is what usually ends up in sandwiches (*bocadillos*), while that from Jabugo in Huelva province is generally regarded as the finest, and is the most expensive. This is the *pata negra*, or *jamón iberico*, and is made from free-range black pigs that are fed only on acorns; the finest cut is awarded '*cinco jotas*' or five 'j's and costs much the same as gold (*see p160* **Hang 'em high**). High in the Alpujarras in Granada, the village of Trevélez produces snow-cured *jamón*, which is half the price of Jabugo ham, though not in the same league.

Each region, each town, sometimes each village in Andalucía has a different speciality. The inland provinces of Córdoba, Jaén and Sevilla concentrate on hearty meat meals, often in the form of stews (*cocidos*) like *estofado* flavoured with cloves, or game dishes, such as venison, partridge, rabbit and wild boar. *Rabo de toro*, made with oxtail, onions and tomatoes, is a Córdoban favourite, while the province's Jewish and Moorish heritage is revealed in dishes such as *caldereta*, a lamb stew with almonds. Granada and Jaén's wonderfully refreshing *remojón* (a salad of salt cod, oranges and olives) is another legacy of the Moors. The list goes on…

## MEAT, FISH AND SEAFOOD

Meat, be it beef, lamb or pork, is served straight up and simple; presentation is not a strong point in Andalucía, and even the most elaborate-sounding meat dish on the menu will often be served with just a few vegetables and a handful of chips. The pig is big in the region, and pork is the number-one meat of the south (particularly in the sierras). Pork products will be found on just about every menu – from *lomo* (loin) to *jamón* via a dozen variations on sausage (such as *chorizo* – paprika-spiked sausage; and *morcilla* – blood pudding); Lamb is nearly always excellent, as too is *ternera* (strictly, veal), which is slaughtered later in Spain than elsewhere in Europe, and thus resembles steak more than pale, milk-fed veal.

It's always worth trying the local game, which is common in season in mountainous areas in particular – Córdoba province, for example, is known for its wild boar and Jaén province for partridge.

With the Atlantic on one side and the Mediterranean on the other, it's no surprise that fish and seafood can be found all over Andalucía, but it is predominantly in the coastal provinces of Huelva, Cádiz and Málaga that these dishes are at their best. The city of Cádiz, and nearby

**Top ten** Resta

### Amanhavis
*Benahavis, Málaga province. See p*
Exquisite attention to detail marks ou
daily-changing menu served at this hotel
restaurant within a 350-year-old building.

### Bodegas Campos
*Córdoba. See p213.*
The perfect Córdoba patio restaurant, where
the beauty of the setting is matched by the
delicacy and imaginativeness of the food.

### La Casa del Angel
*Málaga. See p56.*
Not just superb regional dishes with an
Arabic twist, but amazing decor and world-
class art to peruse after eating.

### El Faro
*Cádiz. See p108.*
An extraordinary variety of fish and
seafood, simply but exquisitely prepared.

### El Faro del Puerto
*El Puerto de Santa María, Cádiz province.
See p125.*
Faultless, innovative preparation of seafood
of the highest quality.

### Hacienda Benazuza
*Sanlúcar la Mayor, Sevilla province.
See p195*
First venture down south from Catalan
super-chef Ferrán Adria delivers audacious,
and memorable culinary results.

### Rey de Copas
*Ribera Alta, Jaén province. See p232.*
The wonderfully original cooking here
blends the best of traditional Andalucían
cuisine with contemporary ideas.

### La Sarga
*Cazorla, Jaén province. See p244.*
Inventive mountain cuisine of superlative
quality is served in José and Rosa's pretty
restaurant; the game is particularly good.

### Tragabuches
*Ronda, Málaga province. See p94.*
Funky, modern, an excellent wine list and
inspired reinventions of regional cuisine.

### Tragaluz
*Granada. See p264.*
Informal, friendly, intimate, and with the
best Sephardic food in Spain.

as in Cádiz and Huelva, and flavoured with herbs. Inland and outside the main cities, the best fish you're likely to find is fresh trout, which teems in the sierra rivers in Huelva and Jaén.

Common across all of Andalucía is *arroz marinera*. It is basically the Andalucían version of paella, but far more soup-like and with more emphasis on seafood than the Valencian dish. Another ubiquitous seafood favourite is *zarzuela*, which is similar to bouillabaisse.

# Food glossary

For a glossary of common tapas, *see p42*
**Lifting the lid on tapas**.

## ESSENTIALS
**desayuno** breakfast; **almuerzo** lunch; **cena** dinner.
**carta** menu; **menú del día** set menu; **primer plato (entrante)** starter; **segundo plato** main course; **postre** dessert; **plato combinado** one-course meal.
**pan** bread; **mantequilla** butter; **sal** salt; **pimienta** pepper; **mostaza** mustard; **ketchup/salsa de tomate** ketchup; **aceite** oil; **vinagre** vinegar; **aceitunas** olives.
**cubiertos** cutlery; **cuchilla** knife; **tenedor** fork; **cuchara** spoon; **plato** plate; **botella** bottle; **vaso** glass.
**la cuenta** the bill; **servicio incluído** service included; **propina** tip.

## COOKING STYLES AND TECHNIQUES
**en adobo** marinated; **al ajillo** with olive oil and garlic; **caliente** hot; **al chilindrón** a spicy tomato, pepper, ham, onion and garlic sauce; **crudo** raw; **escabechado/en escabeche** marinated in vinegar with bay and garlic; **estofado** braised; **frío** cold; **frito** fried; **guisado** stewed; **hervido** boiled; **al horno/asado** baked/roasted; **a la marinera** (fish or shellfish) cooked with garlic, onions and white wine; **a la parilla** charcoal grilled; **picante** spicy; **al pil-pil** flash-fried in sizzling oil and garlic; **a la plancha/brasa** grilled; **relleno** stuffed; **a la Romana** deep-fried in batter; **en salsa** in sauce or gravy; **al vapor** steamed; **muy hecho** well done; **medio hecho/regular** medium; **poco hecho** rare.

## EGGS (HUEVOS)
**huevos fritos** fried eggs; **revuelto** scrambled eggs; **tortilla francesa** plain omelette; **tortilla de patatas/española** Spanish potato omelette.

## FISH AND SHELLFISH (PESCADOS Y MARISCOS)
**almejas** clams; **almendritas** small cuttlefish; **anchoas** anchovies; **anchoba** a type of mackerel; **anguila** eel; **angulás** baby eels; **atún/bonito** tuna; **bacalao** salt cod; **berberechos** cockles; **besugo** sea bream; **bogavante** lobster; **bonito** light tuna; **boquerones** anchovies; **caballa** mackerel; **calamares (en su tinta)** squid (in their own ink); **camarones** shrimps; **cangrejo** crab; **chipirones** baby squid; **choco** cuttlefish; **cigalas** crayfish; **coquinas** small clams; **corbina** sea bass; **dorada** gilthead bream; **erizo** sea urchin; **gambas** prawns; **langosta** spiny lobster; **langostinos** langoustines; **lenguado** sole; **lubina** sea bass; **mejillones** mussels; **merluza** hake; **mero** Mediterranean sea bass/grouper; **navajas** razor clams; **neceros** small crabs; **ostras** oysters; **pargo** bream; **perca** perch; **percebes** barnacles; **pescaditos** whiting; **pez espada** swordfish; **pijota** whiting; **pulpo** octopus; **puntillitas** tiny squid; **quisquilla** small shrimp; **rape** monkfish; **róbalo** sea perch; **roballo** turbot; **salmón** salmon; **salmonete** red mullet; **sardinas** sardines; **sargo** bream; **sepia** cuttlefish; **tortuga** turtle; **trucha** trout; **vieiras** scallops; **zarzuela** fish stew.

## MEAT, POULTRY, GAME AND CHARCUTERIE (CARNE, AVES, CAZA Y EMBUTIDOS)
**albóndigas** meatballs; **bistec** steak; **buey/vacuno** (cuts **entrecot** entrecôte, **filete** fillet, **solomillo** tenderloin) beef; **cabrito** kid; **callos** tripe; **capón** capon; **cerdo** pork; **chivo** goat; **chorizo** spicy sausage; **chuletas** chops; **chuletón** large steak; **cochinillo** roast suckling pig; **cocido** stew; **codorniz** quail; **conejo** rabbit; **cordero** lamb; **costillas** ribs; **empanada** pasty; **estofado** stew; **faisán** pheasant; **fiambres** cold cuts; **gallina** chicken; **ganso** goose;

## VEGETABLES AND FRUIT

Although Almería supplies most of the rest of Europe with year-round veg and fruit, vegetables do not feature prominently in Andalucian cuisine and are often served as separate dishes rather than with the main meal. Of the cooked dishes, *espinacas con garbanzos* (spinach with chickpeas) is probably the best known across the region, with grilled mushrooms, often in garlic and olive oil, another popular dish. Specialities include asparagus from the Trigueros region of Huelva, served with onions, coriander and lemon.

As for fruit, Huelva province is famed for its strawberries, and Málaga province for its fat, juicy muscatel grapes. More unusual fruit to look out for includes (in autumn) the *chirimoya* (custard fruit) and the delicious sweet, tomato-look-alike *caquis*.

**higado** liver; **jabalí** wild boar; **jamón (serrano)** cured ham; **jamón york** cooked ham; **lengua** tongue; **liebre** hare; **lomo** loin (usually pork); **morcilla** blood sausage; **oca** goose; **pato** duck; **pavo** turkey; **pechuga** breast; **perdiz** partridge; **pichón** pigeon; **pinchito** small kebab; **pollo** chicken; **rabo de toro** oxtail; **riñones** kidneys; **salchicha** sausage; **salchichón** salami; **sesos** brains; **ternera** veal; **tocino** bacon; **vaca** beef; **venado** venison.

## VEGETABLES AND PULSES (VERDURES Y LEGUMBRES)

**ajo** garlic; **alcachofas** artichokes; **arroz** rice; **berenjena** aubergine/eggplant; **calabacines** courgettes/zucchini; **cebolla** onion; **champiñones** mushrooms; **col** cabbage; **endivias** chicory/endive; **ensalada mixta** mixed salad; **ensalada verde** green salad; **espárragos** asparagus; **espinacas** spinach; **frijoles/habichuelas** red kidney beans; **garbanzos** chickpeas; **guisantes** peas; **habas** broad beans; **judías blancas** haricot beans; **judías verdes** green (French) beans; **judiones** large haricot beans; **lechuga** lettuce; **lechuga** lettuce; **lentejas** lentils; **maíz** sweetcorn; **patatas** potatoes; **patatas fritas** chips/french fries; **pepinillos** gherkins; **pepino** cucumber; **pimientos** (red/green/yellow) peppers; **puerro** leek; **remolacha** beetroot; **repollo** cabbage; **setas** wild mushrooms; **zanahoria** carrot.

## FRUIT (FRUTA)

**aguacate** avocado; **albaricoque** apricot; **cerezas** cherries; **ciruelas** plums; **frambuesas** raspberries; **fresas** strawberries; **granada** pomegranate; **higos** figs; **macedonia** fruit salad; **manzana** apple; **melocotón** peach; **melón** melon; **naranja** orange; **nectarina** nectarine; **pera** pear; **piña** pineapple; **plátano** banana; **pomelo** grapefruit; **sandía** watermelon; **tomate** tomato; **uvas** grapes.

## DESSERTS (POSTRES)

**arroz con leche** rice pudding; **flan** crème caramel; **helado** ice-cream; **queso** cheese; **tarta** cake.

## DRINKS (BEBIDAS)

**agua (del grifo)** (tap) water; **agua mineral (con gas/sin gas)** mineral water (sparkling/still); **aguardiente** aniseed spirit; **amontillado** dry, amber-coloured sherry; **anís** aniseed; **café (con leche)** coffee (with milk); **café cortado** small, strong coffee with a little milk; **café manchado/americano** milky coffee; **café solo** espresso; **carajillo** Irish coffee; **cava** sparkling wine; **cerveza** beer; **fino** pale, very dry sherry; **con hielo** with ice; **infusión de manzanilla** camomile tea; **leche** milk; **manzanilla** pale, very dry sherry; **oloroso** dark, strong, sometimes sweet sherry; **té (con leche)** tea (with milk); **vino (de la casa)** (house) wine; **vino blanco** white wine; **vino rosado** rosé; **vino tinto** red wine; **zumo** juice.

Vegetarians should note that many ostensibly vegetable-only dishes, such as *huevos a la flamenca* (eggs and vegetables), may be sprinkled with *jamón*. Salads (*ensaladas*) are served all over the region and are usually much more substantial than those served in the UK. A house salad, for example, will often consist of tuna, egg, asparagus, artichoke, olives, onion and a lot of olive oil, as well as lettuce and tomato. It's not easy to find much variety in salads – they tend to be essentially the same throughout the region.

## DESSERTS

Dessert is not Spain's forte, and this certainly applies in Andalucia. More often than not your only sweet choices will be fresh fruit, or a pud from the freezer in the corner of the restaurant with the Menorquina logo emblazoned on it. This company seems to have cornered the entire dessert market, supplying *helado* (ice-cream), *flan* or *tocinos de cielo* (both types of crème caramel), and *natillas* (custard) to all the restaurants in the region.

# Lifting the lid on tapas

The original tapa was a small dish that the *camarero* (barman) would place over your drink – hence the name: lid. The reason for this practice is unclear: perhaps it was to keep the flies off; perhaps it was the combination of poverty and heat, which made eating a large meal impractical. Either way, the important thing was that the snack was free.

Nowadays, tapas have evolved from those humble beginnings to become practically an art form in Sevilla and Granada. In some cities (Granada and Jaén for example) you will often automatically be given a tapa whenever you order a drink; in most other places expect to pay a couple of euros for most tapas.

There are four basic sizes of tapa: a *pincho* (more or less a mouthful), a *tapa* (a saucerful or so – though, traditionally, the same size as a *pincho*), a *media-ración* (half a plateful) and a *ración* (a plateful). Not all of these will always be offered.

The tapas list will be displayed on a menu at the bar, on a board on the wall or, most likely, you just take your pick of what you fancy from trays under a glass counter. If you eat at the bar, you'll pay the price on the menu; if you eat at a table or outside on the *terraza*, you'll end up paying about 25 per cent more. Settle the bill once you have finished eating, rather than when you order.

## CLASSIC TAPAS

**aceitunas (rellenos)** olives (stuffed); **albóndigas** meatballs; **almendras saladas** salted almonds; **boquerones en vinagre** fresh anchovies in vinegar; **calamares rellenos** stuffed baby squid; **calamares a la romana** fried battered squid rings; **calamares en su tinta** squid cooked in its ink; **chanquetes** whitebait; **chorizo al vino** spicy sausage in red wine; **croquetas** potato croquettes (sometimes with tuna, ham,

chicken, etc); **empanadas** flat pies, usually with a tuna filling; **empanadillas** small fried pasties, usually with a tomato and tuna filling; **ensaladilla rusa** Russian salad (potatoes, onions, red peppers, usually tuna and other ingredients in mayonnaise); **flamenquines** ham and pork rolls in breadcrumbs; **fritura de pescado** flash-fried fish; **gambas al ajillo** prawns in garlic; **huevos rellenos** stuffed, cold hard-boiled eggs; **jamón serrano** cured ham; **mejillones al vapor** steamed mussels; **pan con tomate** bread rubbed with fresh tomato and olive oil; **patatas ali oli** potatoes in garlic mayonnaise; **patatas bravas** potatoes in a spicy tomato sauce, sometimes known as *papas bravas*; **pimientas de Padrón** fried, hot small green peppers; **pincho moruno** grilled meat brochette; **pisto manchego** ratatouille with meat (usually ham) and egg; **pollo al ajillo** chicken in garlic and olive oil; **revuelto** scrambled eggs; **riñones al jerez** kidneys in sherry; **sobrassada** soft Mallorcan paprika sausage; **tortilla española** Spanish omelette.

Having said that, there are also some Andalucían specialities to look out for, especially in Granada, where the Moorish influence has lingered the longest: try *alfajores* (a type of pastry made with honey and almonds) or *piononos* (almond-based cakes soaked in liqueur). In Cádiz province the *crema de jerez* (sherry pudding) is worth ordering, and in Málaga *peras al vino* (pears baked in wine) is a great way to finish a meal. Other desserts include *yemas* (candied egg yolks) and *tocino del cielo* (crème caramel).

Cheese is not served as a dessert, but as a tapa, and there are few well-known varieties. Most are produced on a village-by-village basis and are unlikely to be found outside the local area. The one exception is *pedroches* from Córdoba (a soft goat's cheese, kept in oil and flavoured with herbs).

## DRINK

Sherry is the quintessential Andalucían drink. Forget the outmoded British view of it as sweet, dark-coloured mouthwash mainly associated with vicars and aged aunts. Sherry in Andalucía comes in a variety of styles (from ultra dry to syrupy sweet), is the perfect foil for a seafood tapa and is often drunk ice-cold with a full meal, a habit unique to the region. Production is centred on the 'sherry triangle' in Cádiz province, the three points of which are the towns of Jerez, Sanlúcar de Barrameda and El Puerto de Santa María. Most Spanish brandies also come from this area – among the best-known are Soberano, Carlos I and III, and Gran Duque de Alba. For more on brandy and on sherry styles, production and *bodega* tours, *see p118* **Cliché**.

A similar drink to sherry is produced in Montilla in southern Córdoba province (from which the name *amontillado* – meaning 'in the style of Montilla' – derives). Montilla is created in a comparable way to sherry and in similar styles, but with the significant difference that no alcohol is added to aid the fermentation process, so it is not fortified. Also, the main grape variety used is Pedro Ximenez (which is only used to make sweet dessert styles in Jerez) rather than palamino. In terms of flavour, Montilla has even more toasted, nutty, savoury flavours than sherry; its richness works wonders with the local food.

The wines of Andalucía are relatively few and are generally not highly regarded. The little wine that is produced in the region's wine-growing regions – the Villaviciosa area of Córdoba; parts of Sevilla; east of Úbeda, in Jaén province; the Condado de Huelva area; southern Granada; and Sanlúcar – is rarely found outside the area in which it is grown, with most restaurants serving well-known bottles from

Clams with white wine and garlic.

Rioja, Valdepeñas and Jumilla (in neighbouring Murcia), instead. However, this situation might be (very slowly) changing. Under the label Príncipe Alfonso, the Cortijo de las Monjas estate near Ronda, owned by socialite Alfonso von Hohenlohe, has produced first-rate reds from tempranillo grapes combined with French varieties (and with expert French help). It is up to other enterprising individuals to follow his lead. (Note that many red wines are served cold, especially during the summer.)

Andalucía's very strong and sweet (and underrated) dessert wines, made from the moscatel and Pedro Ximenez grapes, are particularly good, and enjoyed huge popularity in England (particularly in Elizabethan times, when they were known as 'Malaga-sack'). The main growing regions are the Axarquía, east of Málaga, and between Estepona and the border with Cádiz province, and the results are wines that are dark golden in colour and smell raisin-rich, with distinct flavours of chocolate and toffee.

Other tipples include *sangría*, which can be found all over the region, particularly in tourist areas (its variant *tinto de verano*, on the other hand, is drunk by locals too – ask for it with *casera blanca*, a fizzy drink less sweet than lemonade), and *aguadiente* (anis), which comes in a variety of different forms, sweet or dry, but is always very strong and is often drunk at breakfast (by locals). The best-known brands are Zalamea from Huelva, Rute from Córdoba and Cazalla de la Sierra from Sevilla.

Spaniards love beer (*cerveza*), and Andalucía produces three fine brands – Cruzcampo from

Sevilla, Alhambra from Granada and Alcázar from Jaén. The former can be found all over the region, while the latter two are largely restricted to their respective provinces. Beer is always served very cold, usually from a *caña* (on tap), and comes in glasses of about a third of a pint. A *tubo* is roughly half a pint and a *pinta* is a pint, but this measurement is rarely seen outside the British bars along the Costa del Sol (though, if you want a larger glass, ask for a *litrona* or a *jarra*).

You can rely on drinking excellent fresh coffee in Spain, without a grain of powder or a freeze-dried granule in sight (and that applies to decaffeinated – *descafeinado* – too, which is widely available). *Café con leche* (coffee with milk) is the Spanish equivalent of a *café au lait*; a *cortado* is a medium-sized strong coffee with milk; while a *café solo* is the equivalent of an espresso and is often drunk with a shot of *coñac*. *Té* (tea) is not common in Andalucía and will be served weak and black unless you specify otherwise, in which case you will also be given warm milk. *Té infusión* is the name for herbal tea.

### EATING HABITS AND PLACES TO EAT

Eating out is one of the delights of visiting Andalucia and should be enjoyed at an unhurried pace. The locals spend a large part of their lives socialising in bars and cafés, and you should do the same. Children are welcome everywhere, and at any time of the day or night – it's not uncommon to see young families out dining at midnight.

> ## 'The *menú del día* always represents excellent value for money.'

Andalucíans do not generally go in for large breakfasts. A coffee, sometimes with a shot of *coñac*, a *magdalena* (a sweet pastry), perhaps a croissant with butter and *mermelada* (often jam rather than marmalade) and a fruit juice, is usually sufficient. *Chocolate* (hot chocolate) with *churros* (fried doughnut strips that are dipped into the drink) is a popular alternative all over the region. By far the most popular Andalucian breakfast dish, though, is *tostada* (toast), served in the west of the region with spiced lard (*manteca colorada*) and in the east with tomatoes and olive oil.

Visitors will probably have to alter their eating habits radically to correspond to local schedules: do not expect to have lunch before 2pm or dinner before 10pm or 11pm, unless you want to eat in a deserted restaurant (or unless you are in a heavily touristed area, where eating times will correspond more

closely to those elsewhere in Europe). You can, though, expect tapas to be available throughout the day and evening.

The range of places to eat can be confusing for the first-time visitor. *Cervecerías* and *tascas* are both types of bars where you can get a basic meal and/or tapas. Often there will be a *comedor* (dining room) attached, usually serving simple, cheap food. You can order from the *carta* (menu) or from the *menú del día* (set menu). The *menú* will usually consist of a choice of three courses plus a drink and bread, and always represents excellent value for money. A *plato combinado* is a cheaper, single-dish option, which will usually consist of meat, chips and perhaps an egg. Cheaper still are *bocadillos* (baguette sandwiches), usually filled with meat, cheese or tortilla. Beware: if you ask for a sandwich, you will get two anaemic slices of white bread with processed cheese and ham inside.

Many bars, particularly in rural areas, are spit-and-sawdust places, with a limited menu and an emphasis on drinking and watching football on TV rather than eating. Others might look that way superficially, but serve up excellent home cooking. You may find sleeker, smarter places in large towns and cities, but they're not common.

*Ventas* are cheap, family-run establishments that serve up local dishes at reasonable prices. They are great fun on a Sunday when whole families visit for a prolonged lunch. *Mesones*, *bodegas* and *tabernas* are more like inns or pubs and will be slightly pricier, though most will serve tapas and *raciones* as well as full meals.

*Restaurantes* are officially rated with forks (rather than stars), usually according to price rather than quality. They usually offer a set menu at lunchtime in addition to à la carte, although upmarket establishments may have a *menú de degustación* that offers a number of dishes from the à la carte menu. Restaurant prices are still reasonable in most places compared to the rest of Europe, with an average meal for two plus wine costing about €30-€40. In some of the main cities and upmarket tourist areas, however, prices can sky-rocket.

Seafood eateries come in two main guises – *marisquerías*, which are often pricey but are good quality; and *chiringuitos*, small beachside grills that you'll find dotted all along the coast.

In Spain, few people leave a tip (*propina*), though it's common to round the bill up. You may also find tax (IVA) at seven per cent added on to your bill in some of the posher places. One thing you can be sure of, however, is that wine will be relatively cheap. *Vino de la casa* is always drinkable (at worst), and you can get some really fine wines for a fraction of the price you'd pay in a UK or US restaurant.

Semana Santa in Sevilla.

# Festivals & Events

Eat, drink, worship the Virgin and be merry.

Andalucíans will jump on any excuse to let their hair down. Whatever time of year you visit you can be almost certain of stumbling across some sort of fiesta during your stay. Many of the region's festivals are notable for their blending of religious and secular elements to create an unforgettable, emotionally charged atmosphere. Their ubiquity and passion may have contributed to the seductive image of Andalucía abroad, but they are also intrinsic to the region's complex culture.

### INFORMATION

For listings of the major events in the region get a copy of *52 and a half weeks*, available from most major tourist offices. There is also a monthly listings guide to the region called *¿Que Hacer? What's On?*. For details of all the festivals mentioned below, contact the relevant local tourist office. Look, too, on the website www.andalucia.org. Below we list the main festivals by type.

### SEMANA SANTA

Semana Santa (Holy Week; 21-27 March 2005, 10-16 April 2006) is celebrated throughout Andalucia with great fervour. It is characterised by elaborate religious processions, organised by local brotherhoods, known as *cofradías*.

Effigies of Christ on the Cross and the Virgin Mary in mourning are carried through the streets from the local church, watched by emotional and passionate crowds. The image of the Virgin or Christ is placed on a float, known as a *paso*, and carried by *costaleros*, who either walk on each side of it (as in Málaga) or underneath it (as in Sevilla). The procession is led by *penitentes*, known as *nazarenos* in Sevilla, who are dressed in the same conical white hoods worn by the Inquisition and latterly by the Ku Klux Klan. The *paso* leaves the church in which it has been stored and makes its way through the streets, usually accompanied by a band, although in some cases the procession may be silent. Maundy Thursday and Good Friday are the high points of the week, after which celebrations wane over the Easter weekend.

Though the celebrations are ostensibly religious, for many participants it's the worship of the images themselves, rather than what they represent, that is most important. Certainly in Sevilla there is much rivalry between the various brotherhoods in terms of who is carrying the most beautiful/moving/well-dressed Virgin.

The (possibly apocryphal) origins of the festival can be traced back to 1521, when Don Fadrique, the first Marquis of Tarifa, came back from the Holy Land and introduced the *Via Crucis*, or Stations of the Cross, to Sevilla. The idea caught on, and each year more and more people participated. The exact form of today's processions dates back to the early 20th century.

Semana Santa is celebrated in every town and village across the region, but is at its most impressive in **Sevilla**, and the other major

cities of **Málaga**, **Granada** and **Córdoba**.
**Jerez** and **Úbeda** also have striking
processions, while **Baena** wins the prize for
the loudest celebrations thanks to its deafening
drum-rolling competition.

## CORPUS CHRISTI

Corpus Christi, celebrating the presence
of the body of Christ in the Communion host,
has been a religious holiday in Spain since
the 13th century. Celebrations kick off on
the Wednesday after Trinity Sunday when
balconies and buildings of towns and cities are
bedecked with flowers. On the following day,
Corpus Christi itself (26 May 2005, 15 June
2006), a solemn procession carries images of the
infant Jesus and various saints through streets
strewn with cypress branches and flowers.

Corpus Christi is celebrated everywhere
in Andalucía, most famously in Granada.
In Sevilla, the key events are the procession
of the enormous silver monstrance from
the cathedral in the early hours of Thursday
morning, and 'Los Seises', a dance that takes
place on the steps of the cathedral. The dance
dates from the 13th century and involves
a group of ten children dressed in page-boy
outfits accompanied by a band. Ronda, Vejer
de la Frontera and Zahara de la Sierra also
have significant Corpus Christi celebrations.

## ROMERÍAS

Hugely popular throughout Andalucía,
*romerías* are community pilgrimages to shrines
around which fiestas are held. Although most
regional *romerías* lead to a local shrine a few
miles from the town, the name remembers
those pilgrims, or *romeros*, who walked all
the way to Rome. May is the most popular
month for *romerías*.

> **'The biggest and most
> important pilgrimage of
> the year is the Romería
> del Rocío.'**

On the last Sunday of April, the people
of **Andújar** in Jaén process from the town to
the sanctuary of the **Virgen de la Cabeza**,
overlooking the wild hills of the Sierra Morena.
The pilgrimage has its origins in the 13th
century, and now involves around half a million
people. It is followed shortly afterwards by
another important Jaén pilgrimage, on the first
two days of May, to the shrine of **Nuestra
Señora de la Estrella**, north of **Úbeda**.
Pilgrims sing songs called *mayos* to the Virgin
during the night and bid for the privilege of
carrying her into the hermitage.

Cordoba's summer *feria. See p48.*

In **Huelva**, the **Romería de San Benito
Abad** takes place on 4-6 May and includes
songs, hymns and traditional dances such
as the *fandango*. It often coincides with the
**Romería de Santa Eulalia** in **Almonaster
La Real** in northern Huelva on the first
weekend in May, for which the townsfolk dress
up in traditional garb, while *cofradías* compete
to create the finest crosses.

The **Romería de San Isidro** on 17 May
involves more than 500 horse riders and
decorated carts travelling to the Sierra de
San Pablo in Sevilla for traditional dancing
and lots of drinking. San Isidro is the patron
saint of farmers, and his feast day on 15 May
is celebrated in many rural Andalucian villages
with a procession through the fields and
a fiesta. **Montefrío** in Granada province
is a good place to join in the festivities.

The biggest and most important pilgrimage
of the year, however, is the **Romería del Rocío**,
which takes place at Whitsun (14-16 May 2005;
4-6 June 2006), and culminates at the Huelvan
village of **El Rocío**. The three traditional routes
start at Sanlúcar, Huelva and Triana in Sevilla,
and involve up to a million people.

Later in the summer, on 5 August, the
atmospheric **Romería de la Virgen de las
Nieves** sets off from the village of **Trevélez**
in the Alpujarras and heads up to a small shrine
on the peak of Mulhacén, the highest mountain
on the Iberian Peninsula, to celebrate the Virgin
of the Snows. As the summer draws to a close,

the people of Baeza, complete with carriages and horsemen, take part in the **Romería del Cristo de la Yedra** to return the Virgen del Rosel to her shrine (last Sunday in August or the first in September). The **Romería de Nuestra Señora de los Ángeles** is on 8 September, when brotherhoods on horseback from neighbouring villages dress up in traditional costume and process to the sanctuary of the Virgin in **Aracena** in northern Huelva, while the last *romería* of the season is the **Romería de Cristo del Paño** on 5 October in **Moclín** in Granada province – the most important in eastern Andalucía after the Andújar *romería*.

### SAINTS DAYS AND OTHER FESTIVALS

Every village and town has one or two patron saints, whose feast days are a perfect excuse for a holiday and fiesta. Although these events have a religious origin, they usually incorporate secular celebrations.

The **Fiesta de los Reyes** on the evening of 5 January marks the visit of the three wise men to the infant Jesus and is celebrated throughout Spain. Three men dressed as kings ride through the town in a procession, scattering sweets to the children. In Málaga the event is known as the **Cabalgata de los Reyes Magos**.

The feast of San Juan on 24 June is an important festival in many regions of Spain. In Vejer de la Frontera effigies representing evil are burnt on a big fire in the main square. The fires are known as the **Candelas de San Juan** and conclude with a flaming effigy of a bull that is paraded around the town accompanied by fireworks. On the coast, San Juan celebrations take the form of bonfires and fireworks.

For the coastal towns, the **Virgen del Carmen**, patron of sailors, is one of the most important saints. On 16 July statues of the Virgin are borne across the water in decorated boats, accompanied by music and fireworks. The old fishermen's quarter of Los Boliches in Fuengirola and the town of Estepona have particularly atmospheric celebrations.

In August (13-15), the **Fiesta de Guadalquivir** in **Sanlúcar de Barrameda** celebrates the **Virgen de la Caridad** with bullfights and flamenco, while the people of **Mojácar** honour their patron **San Agustín** with a five-day fiesta at the end of the month.

Highlights of September include the **Virgen de la Luz** festival in **Tarifa** and the **Día del Señor** festival in **Órgiva**, a noisy event dominated by fireworks and processions. Finally, the **Fiestas de Otoño** in **Jerez de la Frontera** celebrate the city's co-patron saints, the Virgen de la Merced and San Dionisio, with a prestigious horse festival

in late October and early November. The highlights are the Parada Hipica, in which more than 1,000 riders in traditional costume parade, and the horse races in the Plaza del Arenal.

### CARNAVAL

Most towns in Andalucía celebrate Carnaval, a Catholic festival centred around Shrove Tuesday (8 Feb 2005; 28 Feb 2006). The carnival is a last free-for-all before the abstentions and prohibitions of Lent. The breakdown of social hierarchies is represented by the wearing of masks and fancy dress, and the satirical lampooning of local politicans and dignitaries. The implicit anarchy of the festival led Franco to abolish Carnaval in 1937, although it continued under a different name in Cádiz and some other towns.

Today, **Cádiz**'s **Carnaval** is one of the most dazzling and exciting events in the Spanish calendar, signalling the start of the festive season in Andalucía with ten days of mayhem and fun all over the city, including floats, parades, costumes, live music and lots of drinking (*see p112* **¡Carnaval!**). It is followed by the **Carnaval de la Concha Fina** in **La Línea**, a four-day event with bands and music, and a masked ball in which the whole town wears fancy dress. Smaller versions of the Cádiz extravaganza can be found in towns all over Andalucía; the festivities in **El Puerto de Santa María** are particularly lively.

### MAY FESTIVALS

Throughout May a series of festivals enlivens the streets of **Córdoba**. The first of these is the **Cruz de Mayo**, which is celebrated in a number of towns and villages across Andalucía, culminating in the **Fiesta de Santa Cruz** on the third of the month. Crosses decorated with flowers are set up in town squares as the centrepiece for drinking, dancing and singing, before eventually being set alight. The most notable celebrations are in Córdoba, Granada, Conil de la Frontera (Cádiz), Vilacarillo (Jaén) and Ubrique (Cádiz). Once every three years, the Cruz de Mayo celebrations coincide with Córdoba's **Concurso Nacional de Arte Flamenco**, a prestigious week-long flamenco competition. This is followed in the second week of May by Córdoba's **Festival de los Patios**, in which homeowners compete for the prize for the most beautifully decorated patio. The map provided by the tourist office will help you find competing courtyards, which are open to the public during the day. At the same time is the **Cata del Vino** wine-tasting festival. Córdoba's festive month concludes with a fiesta, processions and bullfights to celebrate **Nuestra Señora de la Salud** from 25 May to 2 June.

## SUMMER FERIAS

Every town and village in Andalucía has its own *feria*. *Ferias* originated in the Middle Ages as livestock and produce fairs, but nowadays their purpose is pleasure rather than business, and they share many characteristics with local fiestas, including dressing up, drinking, bullfights, equestrian events and dancing.

**Sevilla**'s **Feria de Abril** (*see p193*) is one of the first of the annual *ferias* and is a welcome antidote to the solemnity of Semana Santa. It takes place two weeks after the end of Easter and is one of the most colourful events in Spain, described by writer Michael Jacobs as 'the ultimate secular manifestation of the baroque spirit of Andalucía'.

Horses have replaced livestock at the *feria*, largely thanks to the influence of the **Feria del Caballo** in **Jerez de la Frontera**, an older but much smaller event in early to mid May, in which locals dress up in traditional costume and compete in various equestrian events.

The Feria de Abril also marks the peak of the main bullfighting season, which begins at Easter and lasts until the **Feria de San Lucas** in mid October. This fair in **Jaén** features fights on horseback, a carriage procession and lots of competitions and events.

Posh **Marbella** kicks off Málaga province's party season with the **Feria de San Bernabé** during the second week of June, when the townspeople let their hair down for a five-day party. This is followed by *ferias* in **Conil de la Frontera** in **Cádiz** on 30 June, and the **Feria de San Francisco Solano** in **Montilla** in south Córdoba in the second week of July.

## 'The Alpujarras is one of the best regions to see pageants recreating battles between Moors and Christians.'

By August, things are really hotting up, with town fairs in **Aroche** in Huelva, **Grazalema** in eastern Cádiz, and the spectacular **Feria de Málaga** all taking place in the third week. Málaga's nine-day bash rivals Cádiz's Carnaval as one of the wildest events in all Andalucía, with a night fair and bullfights. Also in the third week of August is the **Feria de Algeciras**, one of the biggest bashes in Cadiz province. At the end of the month, the Virgen del Mar, patroness of Almería, is celebrated in a ten-day *feria* with floats and flowers, sports events, a flamenco festival and bullfighting. August finishes with the **Feria de Agosto** in **Antequera**, involving more bullfights, horse-drawn carriage competitions and concerts.

In the first two weeks of September, attention turns to **Ronda** for the town *feria* and the **Fiestas de Pedro Romero**. Two weeks of festivities are heralded by a traditional bullfight in 18th-century costume, known as the '*goyesca*'.

Next up is the **Feria de San Miguel**, celebrated in various places across Sevilla province on the last weekend in September. In the city of Sevilla the fair dates back to 1875, when it began as a replacement for the cattle fair that had been lost to the Feria de Abril. It was suspended under Franco and not revived until 2001; now it's held on the same site as the April *feria*, and includes *casetas* (marquees), a portable bullring, rides and exhibitions. **Úbeda**'s **San Miguel** festival is much the same but on a smaller scale.

Coinciding with the end of the bullfighting season is the horse parade at the **Feria del Rosario** in **Fuengirola**. The *feria* season finishes with the **Feria de San Pedro de Alcántara** in mid October.

## MOORS AND CHRISTIANS

In the city of **Granada** the feast of **San Basilio** (1-2 January) celebrates the entry of Fernando and Isabel into the city in 1492, signifying the end of Moorish rule in Andalucía. To the south-east of the city, the Alpujarras became the last refuge of the Spanish Moors in the 15th century and is now one of the best regions to see pageants recreating battles between Moors and Christians. Re-enactments take place in **Pampaneira** on 3 May and in **Trevélez** on 13-14 June to celebrate San Antonio, although the most famous pageant is at **Válor** in September, which uses a 19th-century script to tell the story of local *morisco* rebel Aben Humaya.

You can also catch *moros y cristianos* events in **Mojácar** and **Vélez Blanco** in Almería province, as part of the **Santo Cristo de la Yedra** celebrations during the second week of August. The fiesta dates to the 16th century.

## FLAMENCO FESTIVALS

It should come as no surprise that flamenco features prominently in Andalucía's cultural calendar. The first flamenco festival was held in Córdoba in 1956 and the custom soon spread to other towns and cities. Festivals and competitions are now held in the summer months throughout each of the eight provinces.

**Almería**'s **Peña de Taranto** in the first week of May attracts some of the biggest names in flamenco. This is followed by the **Alhaurín de la Torre** festival in Málaga province (23-26 June), which incorporates processions and one of the best flamenco competitions (the **Torre del Cante**) in the region.

In the first two weeks of September, attention turns to **Ronda** for the town *feria* and the **Fiestas de Pedro Romero**. Two weeks of festivities are heralded by a traditional bullfight in 18th-century costume, known as the *'goyesca'*.

Next up is the **Feria de San Miguel**, celebrated in various places across Sevilla province on the last weekend in September. In the city of Sevilla the fair dates back to 1875, when it began as a replacement for the cattle fair that had been lost to the Feria de Abril. It was suspended under Franco and not revived until 2001; now it's held on the same site as the April *feria*, and includes *casetas* (marquees), a portable bullring, rides and exhibitions. **Úbeda**'s **San Miguel** festival is much the same but on a smaller scale.

Coinciding with the end of the bullfighting season is the horse parade at the **Feria del Rosario** in **Fuengirola**. The *feria* season finishes with the **Feria de San Pedro de Alcántara** in mid October.

### MOORS AND CHRISTIANS

In the city of **Granada** the feast of **San Basilio** (1-2 January) celebrates the entry of Fernando and Isabel into the city in 1492, signifying the end of Moorish rule in Andalucía. To the south-east of the city, the Alpujarras became the last refuge of the Spanish Moors in the 15th century and is now one of the best regions to see pageants recreating battles between Moors and Christians. Re-enactments take place in **Pampaneira** on 3 May and in **Trevélez** on 13-14 June to celebrate San Antonio, although the most famous pageant is at **Válor** in September, which uses a 19th-century script to tell the story of local *morisco* rebel Aben Humaya.

You can also catch *moros y cristianos* events in **Mojácar** and **Vélez Blanco** in Almería province, as part of the **Santo Cristo de la Yedra** celebrations during the second week of August. The fiesta dates to the 16th century.

### FLAMENCO FESTIVALS

It should come as no surprise that flamenco features prominently in Andalucía's cultural calendar. The first flamenco festival was held in Córdoba in 1956 and the custom soon spread to other towns and cities. Festivals and competitions are now held in the summer months throughout each of the eight provinces.

**Almería**'s **Peña de Taranto** in the first week of May attracts some of the biggest names in flamenco. This is followed by the **Alhaurín de la Torre** festival in Málaga province (23-26 June), which incorporates processions and one of the best flamenco competitions (the **Torre del Cante**) in the region.

Throughout July, the town of **Sanlúcar de Barrameda** in Cádiz comes alive to the sound of flamenco at the annual **Feria de Flamenco**. The **Caracolá de Lebrija**, one of the oldest and most famous of Andalucía's flamenco festivals, takes place in the second half of July in Lebrija, between Sevilla and Jerez.

In **Vejer de la Frontera** in Cádiz locals celebrate the Virgen de la Oliva with a flamenco festival that attracts leading singers and dancers (10-24 August). Throughout September, during the **Fiesta de Bulería**, flamenco fills the streets of **Jerez de la Frontera**.

### CULTURAL AND SPORTING EVENTS

Flamenco also makes an appearance at the **Festival de Danza** in **Jerez** in late February/ early March and at the multi-disciplinary **Festival Internacional de Musica y Danza** in **Granada** from late June to early July. This month-long event is one of the most important cultural festivals in Spain and showcases music and dance from around the world.

The **Festival Internacional de la Guitarra** attracts global stars like Paco de Lucía and BB King to **Córdoba** in early July. It is followed by **Sevilla**'s **Festival de Música, Danza y Teatro de Itálica**, which runs until the middle of August among the Roman ruins of Itálica near Sevilla, and **Málaga**'s **Festival de Teatro**, a drama festival in the city's Roman theatre. At the end of July, **Etnosur**, a festival of leading international folk musicians, takes place in **Alcalá La Real** in Jaén province.

The **Colombinas** festival in **Huelva** on 3 August celebrates the discovery of the New World with sports events, bullfighting, cultural performances and a dance festival.

Once every two years, **Sevilla** hosts the **Festival Internacional de Música y Danza** for two weeks in September (next 2006).

In contrast to these prestigious events is the informal **Festival de Verdiales**, which takes place on 28 December at the Puerta de la Torre on the C3310 road towards Almogía, north-west of Málaga city. Groups of elaborately-dressed local musicians, known as *'pandas'*, compete on stage and take part in spontaneous jamming sessions while bottles of potent Málaga wine and *aguadiente* are passed around.

In addition to the *corridas* that form an essential element of so many local festivals, the region's calendar also supports any number of equestrian events. Among the best known are **Las Carreras de Caballos en la Playa** on Sanlúcar de Barrameda's beach in late August; these famous horse races attract thousands of onlookers and punters (*see p123* **Sea horses**).

# Taking time off?
# Take Time Out.

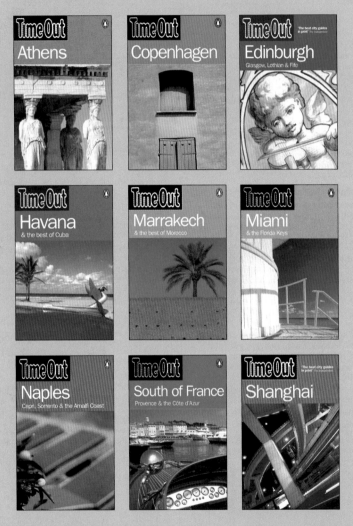

**Now with 48 titles in the series.**
Available from all good bookshops
and at www.timeout.com/shop

# Málaga Province

## Features

## Maps

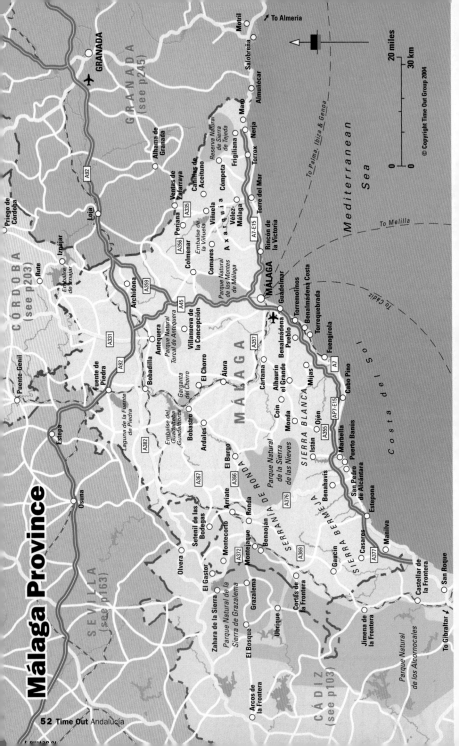

# Málaga Province

**To Almeria**

Motril
Salobreña
Almuñécar
Maro
Nerja
Torrox
Frigiliana
Torre del Mar
Vélez-Málaga
Rincón de la Victoria
Guadelmar
Torremolinos
Benalmádena Costa
Torrequebrada
Fuengirola
Calbo Pino

Mediterranean Sea

**To Palma, Ibiza & Genoa**

**To Melilla**

© Copyright Time Out Group 2004

20 miles
30 km

GRANADA (see p245)

GRANADA

Alhama de Granada
Cañhas de Aceituno
Ventas de Zafarraya
Perjana
Vélez
Viñuela
Cómpeta
Colmenar
Embalse de la Viñuela
Comares
Axarquia
Parque Natural de los Montes de Málaga
Reserva Natural de Sierra de Tejeda

MÁLAGA

Priego de Córdoba
Rute
Iznájar
Embalse de Iznájar
Archidona
Villanueva de la Concepción
Antequera
Parque Natural Torcal de Antequera
El Chorro
Bobadilla
Bobastro
Álora
Garganta del Chorro
Cártama
Benalmádena Pueblo
Alhaurín el Grande
Mijas
Coín
Monda
Ojén
Istán
Ardales
El Burgo
Parque Natural de la Sierra de las Nieves
Marbella
Puerto Banús
San Pedro de Alcántara
Estepona

CÓRDOBA (see p203)

CÓRDOBA

Fuente-Genil
Laguna de la Fuente de Piedra
Fuente de Piedra
Embalse del Guadalhorce
Arriate
Ronda
Setenil de las Bodegas
Montecorto
Benaoján
Benahavís
Casares
Manilva

SEVILLA (see p163)

SEVILLA

Osuna
Estepa
Olvera
El Gastor
Zahara de la Sierra
Parque Natural de la Sierra de Grazalema
Grazalema
El Bosque
Ubrique
Cortés de la Frontera
Montejaque
Gaucín
Jimena de la Frontera
Castellar de la Frontera
San Roque

CÁDIZ (see p103)

CÁDIZ

Arcos de la Frontera
Parque Natural de los Alcornocales

**To Gibraltar**

**To Cádiz**

Costa del Sol

SERRANÍA DE RONDA
SIERRA BLANCA
SIERRA BERMEJA

A92
A331
A359
A45
A357
A92
A382
A367
A366
A372
A376
A389
A377
A355
AP7-E15
A7
A7-E15
A335
A336
A356

# Málaga Province

Escape the overdeveloped coast and revel in the spectacular interior.

Nerja. *See p79.*

A third of all visitors to Andalucía don't get beyond Málaga province, and most of these don't go beyond the Costa del Sol. Yet the ravaged coastline is by far the least appealing area of this beautiful and varied region. Travel inland for 20 minutes and you'll feel like you're in a different country of wildly picturesque mountains and too-perfect whitewashed villages. Tourism is far from unknown in the interior, but it's much more in balance with its environment than on the coast.

### MÁLAGA CITY
Millions of package tourists may pass through its airport each year, but few of them trouble to visit the refreshingly Spanish provincial capital. There's history aplenty here, good shopping, a likeable, walkable centre, a new world-class Picasso museum and a varied and lively bar and restaurant scene that extends to the beaches east of the centre during summer.

### COSTA DEL SOL
Spain's most infamous *costa* is not a pretty sight. Much of it is an endless agglomeration of concrete high-rises and heaving beaches, backed by monotonous *urbanizaciones* stretching ever further inland. Yet, if you're in the mood, it's not without appeal. Mad-for-it Torremolinos can be great fun, Marbella's prettified old town is genuinely lovely, and villages such as Benalmádena Pueblo and Casares retain much of their charm. And if it's crazy nightlife you're after, it's here in spades.

### EAST OF MÁLAGA
Strictly speaking, the stretch of coastline east of Málaga is also part of the Costa del Sol, but it's generally less built-up. The resorts don't have much appeal until you reach Nerja – the most enjoyable town on the whole Costa. Stretching back from the coast is the relatively undiscovered and largely mountainous region known as the Axarquía, which contains any number of cute white-washed villages and offers fine walking.

### NORTH OF MÁLAGA
Despite its proximity to the Costa del Sol, the country north of Málaga feels a world away. The major town here, Antequera, is a fascinating place, and there are compelling natural attractions nearby: the weird rock formations of El Torcal and the dramatic gorge of El Chorro.

### WEST OF MÁLAGA
The wild yet accessible scenery of the Serranía de Ronda, scattered with countless white villages, is the great draw of western Málaga province. The spectacularly sited town of Ronda is the major tourist draw, and in and around it are a wealth of stylish places to stay and eat.

## The best…

### Architecture
Antequera (*p84*).

### Cool hotels, bars & restaurants
Ronda (*p90*).

### Natural wonders
El Chorro (*p87*); El Torcal (*p87*).

### Nightlife
Málaga City (*p56*); Marbella (*p68*); Nerja (*p81*); Torremolinos (*p61*).

### Prehistory
Antequera (*p84*); Cueva de la Pileta (*p99*).

### Towns
Antequera (*p84*); Marbella (*p66*); Nerja (*p79*); Ronda (*p90*).

### Villages
Too numerous to mention…

# Málaga City

So much more than a jumping-off spot for the Costa del Sol.

The **Teatro Romano**, backed by the **Alcazaba**. *See p55.*

A much underrated gem, Málaga is the most genuine of all the towns on the Costa del Sol. With its vibrant old town, spit-and-sawdust tapas bars, pint-sized *plazas*, labyrinthine Jewish quarter and sunny, beachside promenades, it has fiercely guarded its own special identity, refusing to become part of the resort frenzy further west. Add to that the enormous amount of money currently being thrown at it – pedestrianisation and beautification schemes, classy new hotels, the opening of the new Picasso Museum – and this is clearly one city that is on the move.

Founded by the Phoenicians as Malaka in the eighth century BC, Málaga later became a prosperous Roman port, exporting iron, copper and lead from mines in the hills near Ronda. In the eighth century AD it was taken by the Moors and prospered under their rule until 1487. The city began attracting tourists in the 19th century, and since the 1960s it has been a major hub for northern European sun-seekers.

Adored by the likes of Lorca (it was his favourite town) and Hans Christian Andersen (who dreamed of being buried here), Málaga has largely been ignored by contemporary travellers

as a destination in its own right. Used primarily as a stepping-stone to the Costa del Sol resorts, it remains at heart a truly Spanish town, and, because of this, it's a great place to sample a real slice of Iberian life. The concrete blocks of its sprawling suburbs aren't prepossessing, but the lively, compact historic centre has retained its charm, at the same time incorporating some great shopping. The beaches (particularly El Pedregalejo) are good for long, lazy lunches, and the leafy Paseo del Parque is the place to head to stroll in the evenings with the locals.

## Sightseeing

The most obvious place to begin is the **Catedral**, built on the site of the city's main mosque. Architecturally, it's a hotchpotch of styles: the heavy baroque façade was started in 1528, but not completed until the end of the 18th century, while the second bell tower was never built, earning the cathedral the nickname 'La Manquita' ('the cripple').

From here, Calle San Agustín leads past the site of the new **Museo Picasso Málaga** (*see p58* **Home is where the art is**) to Plaza de la Merced and the **Casa Natal de Picasso**, where the artist was born in 1881. Today, the square is lined with pavement cafés, all good places to sit and watch the world go by and a lively place for drinks at night. (Be warned, though: it's also notorious for pickpockets and bag-snatchers.)

Art enthusiasts may also be interested in checking out the **CAC Málaga**, Málaga's contemporary art museum, which opened in 2003 and hosts an impressive line-up of international and home-grown artists. It's located on the south-western edge of the city centre. (And there's more art at the museum-restaurant **La Casa del Angel**; *see p56*).

Just north-west of Plaza Merced is the **Teatro Cervantes**, the most important theatre on the Costa del Sol, which hosts big-name bands and international orchestras, as well as theatrical performances and the annual **Festival de Málaga Cine Español** (Málaga Spanish Film Festival) in April/May.

South of the *plaza* is the most impressive of Málaga's sights: the Moorish **Alcazaba**. It was started in the 700s, but most of the current structure dates from the second half of the 11th century (though what you see now is largely a later rebuilding), when the breakup of the Western Caliphate (*see p15*) allowed Málaga to declare its independence. Within the palace buildings is an archaeological museum. The grounds are an engaging series of rose gardens, interlaced with Moorish irrigation channels, stone fountains and brick archways. At the base of the Alcazaba, excavations of the impressive **Teatro Romano** (Roman Theatre) are just about complete after many years' work, though it is not yet open to the public. You can get a good view of the theatre from the entrance gates to the Alcazaba.

From here, a 20-minute climb up the hill brings you to the **Castillo de Gibralfaro**, commanding spectacular views over the city, and the **Jardines de Puerta Oscura**, where the Moors are believed to have entered Málaga. The castle was built in the eighth century and later rebuilt in the 14th and 15th centuries. This is also a prime spot for a bird's-eye view of the **Plaza de Toros**, the Costa's most active bullring. (The French Romantic traveller Théophile Gautier made a major detour during his 1840 Andalucían journey in order to watch a celebrated matador fight here: 'twenty-four bulls were killed, and ninety-six horses left dead on the arena.'). There's a shady café within the castle, a good spot to take in the views.

Five minutes' walk east of the bullring is the beautiful **Cementerio Inglés** (English Cemetery; open 9am-1pm, 3-5pm Mon-Fri, 9am-noon Sat, free, map off A3), founded in 1829 to save non-Catholics the . on the beach in the midd. the first of its kind in Spain and obsession of the British Mark, the lush cemetery, with views down to the sea, inspired Andersen to write that he 'could w how a splenetic Englishman might , own life in order to be buried in this place.

On the west side of the centre, by the Guadalmedina river and housed within a 17th-century inn, is the **Museo de Artes y Costumbres Populares**, an enjoyably diverse museum dedicated to everyday life and social history over the past few centuries.

A few kilometres to the north lies the **Jardín Botánico La Concepción**, founded in the mid 19th century by an Englishwoman, Amalia Livermore, and her Spanish husband, and now an impressive and important botanic garden.

A flea market takes place on Sunday mornings on Paseo de los Martiricos opposite La Rosaleda stadium, a couple of kilometres north of the centre.

And there's no better way to finish a day of sightseeing than with a long, luxurious Turkish bath and massage in the beautiful, marble-lined steam rooms of **El Hammam**.

### Alcazaba & the Castillo de Gibralfaro

*C/Alcazabilla (952 22 00 43).* **Open** *Apr-Sept* 9.30am-8pm daily. *Oct-Mar* 8.30am-7pm Tue-Sun. **Admission** €1.80; €3 for 2; 60¢ concessions; free after 2pm Sun. **No credit cards. Map** p57 D/E2.

### CAC Málaga

*C/Alemania s/n (952 12 00 55/www.cacmalaga.org).* **Open** 10am-8pm Tue-Sun; times may change, so phone to check. **Admission** free. **Map** p57 off A3.

### Casa Natal de Picasso

*Plaza de la Merced 15 (952 21 50 05/www.fundacion picasso.es).* **Open** 10am-8pm Mon-Sat; 10am-2pm Sun. **Admission** free. **Map** p57 D1.

### Catedral & Museo Diocesano

*C/Molina Lario s/n (952 21 59 17).* **Open** 10am-6.45pm Mon-Fri; 10am-5.45pm Sat. **Admission** €2; €1.50 concessions. **No credit cards. Map** p57 B/C2.

### El Hammam

*C/Tomás de Cózar 13 (952 21 23 27/ www.elhammam.com).* **Open** 10am-10pm daily. **Prices** *Bath* from €21. *Massage* from €29. *Bath & massage* from €50. Concessions 10% off. **Credit** AmEx, DC, MC, V. **Map** p57 C1/2.

### Jardín Botánico La Concepción

*A45 Autopista Antequera–Madrid (952 25 07 45).* **Open** *July, Aug* 10am-7.30pm daily. *Sept-June* 10am-6.30pm daily. Guided tour in English every hr on the hr, every half hr Sat, Sun. **Admission** €2.95; €1.50 concessions. **No credit cards.**

## ...o de Artes y ...stumbres Populares

*Pasillo de Santa Isabel 10 (952 21 71 37).*
**Open** 10am-1.30pm, 5-8pm Mon-Fri; 10am-1.30pm
Sat. **Admission** €2. **No credit cards. Map** p57 A1.

### Plaza de Toros

*Paseo de Reding s/n (952 22 17 27/museum 952 22
62 92/www.plazalamalagueta.com).* **Open** *Museum*
10am-1pm, 5-8pm Mon-Fri. **Admission** *Museum*
€1.80. *Fights* €12.50-€53. **Credit** *Fights only* DC, MC,
V. **Map** p57 E3.

### Teatro Cervantes

*C/Ramos Marín s/n (952 22 41 00/www.teatro
cervantes.com).* **Open** *Box office* 11am-2pm, 5.30-
8.30pm Mon-Sat. **Credit** DC, MC, V. **Map** p57 D1.

## Where to eat & drink

You can tell it's time to *tapeo* in Málaga when
the streets fill with the irresistible smells of
frying fish, grilled seafood and lemon juice. Do
as locals do and hop from one bar to another,
grazing as you go on local wines, cured meats,
cheeses, and the famed *fritura malagueño* (a
heap of golden fried fish). Particularly good
dishes to try are *rosado* (a white, meaty fish)
and *boquerones* (fresh anchovies). You should
also check out the local-packed *marisquerías*
(seafood joints) in the tiny alleyway of Calle
Comisario, off the Alameda Principal.

No culinary tour of Málaga is complete
without trying the local speciality, *sardinas
ensartadas* (a string of grilled sardines), from
any of the open-air cafés on El Pedregalejo
beach, such as **Las Acacias** (Paseo Marítimo
90, El Pedregalejo, 952 29 89 46, closed dinner
Mon-Thur, Sun, €€, map off D3).

For picnics, the wrought-iron **Mercado
Central de Atarazanas** (map A2) is fabulous
for perky fresh fruit and vegetables, *charcuterie*,
local cheeses and vats of olives.

### La Casa del Angel

*C/Madre de Dios 29 (952 60 87 50/www.lacasa
delangel.com).* **Open** 1-4pm, 8-11pm Tue-Sun.
**Average** €€€-€€€€. **Credit** AmEx, DC, MC, V.
**Map** p57 C/D1.
This remarkable restaurant-museum is owned by
the Spanish comedian Angel Caró. Its cuisine com-
bines Grandma's home cooking with the region's
Arabic heritage – with delicious results. The
museum showcases an extraordinary collection of
over 100 works from the 16th century to the present
day, including pieces by Pablo Picasso, Joan Miró
and Salvador Dalí. If you're not eating, it costs just
€3 including a drink for a look around.

### La Casa Guardia

*Alameda Principal 18 (952 21 46 80).* **Open** 9am-
10pm Mon-Sat. **Average** €. **No credit cards.**
**Map** p57 A2.

The original and still the best; this is the oldest
*taberna* in town (founded 1840). It serves Málaga
wines, *manzanillas* and other sherries straight from
the barrel, along with fresh grilled seafood tapas.

### El Chinitas

*C/Moreno Monroy 4-6 (952 21 09 72/952 22 64 40/
www.chinitas.arrakis.es).* **Open** 1-4pm, 8pm-midnight
daily. **Average** €€. **Credit** AmEx, DC, MC, V.
**Map** p57 B2.
Once upon a time El Chinitas was frequented by
bullfighters, artists and poets (including Lorca), and
paraphernalia from those glory days abounds. It still
offers an unarguably good feed, with dishes like rice
and lobster, and acorn-fed pork loin topping the bill.

### Pepa y Pepe

*C/Caldeiería 9 (952 60 82 99).* **Open** 1-11pm Tue-
Sun. **Average** €. **No credit cards. Map** p57 C1.
A tiny neighbourhood bar with upended barrels
providing outside seating. The Málaga wines here
start at a dangerously low 70¢ a glass, while the
super-fresh fried fish tapas will set you back a mere
€2.50 for a generous half *ración*. Bustling Bodega
Quitapeñas on C/Sanchez Pastor (no phone, €) offers
a similar deal, with a larger selection of seafood.

### La Posada de Antonio

*C/Granada 36 (952 60 21 23).* **Open** 1pm-midnight
daily. **Average** €€. **Credit** DC, MC, V. **Map** p57 C1.
Antonio Banderas' barbecued meat barn packs in
the punters for big juicy steaks, *chorizo*, chops, offal
and chicken in all its guises, served on sizzling
cast-iron platters.

### Rojo

*C/Granada 44 (952 22 74 86/www.restaurante
rojo.com).* **Open** 11am-2am Mon-Sat. **Average** €€.
**Credit** DC, MC, V. **Map** p57 C1.
Fresh, contemporary cuisine, interesting salads
and pasta dishes served in scarlet and snow-white
surrounds. It doubles as a lounge bar after hours.

### La Tetería

*C/San Agustín 9 (no phone).* **Open** varies.
**Average** €. **No credit cards. Map** p57 C2.
Situated right opposite the Museo Picasso, this
charming Moroccan tearoom is a quiet place to start
the day over a healthy breakfast of muesli and yogurt.

### El Tintero II

*Carretera Almería 99 (mobile 607 60 75 86).*
**Open** 12.30pm-1.30am daily. **Average** €€.
**No credit cards.**
On the seafront in El Palo, east of the centre, this
popular, lively fish restaurant is a real experience –
there's no menu, you just have to grab a waiter walking past with a plate of something you fancy.

## Nightlife

Málaga is a city of many bars and few discos –
most of the liveliest places can be found around
Calles Granada, San Agustín and Méndez

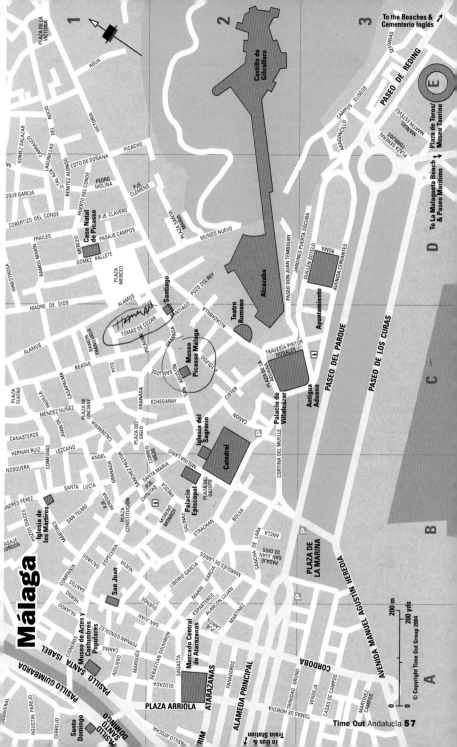

# Málaga

PLAZA DE LA VICTORIA

Casa Natal de Picasso

PLAZA MERCED

Santiago

Museo Picasso Málaga

Castillo de Gibralfaro

Alcazaba

Teatro Romano

Palacio de Villalcázar

Antigua Aduana

Ayuntamiento

PASEO DE REDING

PASEO DEL PARQUE

PASEO DE LOS CURAS

Iglesia del Sagrario

Catedral

Palacio Episcopal

Iglesia de los Mártires

San Juan

Museo de Artes y Costumbres Populares

Mercado Central de Atarazanas

PLAZA ARRIOLA

ALAMEDA PRINCIPAL

PLAZA DE LA MARINA

To the Beaches & Cementerio Inglés

Plaza de Toros / Museo Taurino

To La Malagueta Beach & Paseo Marítimo

to Bus & Train Station

200 m
200 yds

© Copyright Time Out Group 2004

Núñez, north of the cathedral. The **Bodegas El Pimpi** (C/Granada 62, 952 22 89 90, open 7pm-2am daily, map C1) is a classic drinking den, housed – not without some irony – in a 200-year-old convent; it's where Antonio Banderas and Melanie Griffith drink when in town. **Onda Pasadena** (C/Gomez Pallete 5, no phone, map D1) has live music every night of the week, covering jazz, blues and flamenco. For cocktails and DJ grooves every night, check out **Mondotike** (C/Mendes Núñez 3, no phone, open 4pm-4am daily, map C1). But for grown-up drinks, head for the roof terrace at the **Hotel Larios** (*see p59*) – you can't beat a balmy night here under the stars with views over the cathedral and up to the Castillo de Gibralfaro.

If Latin dancing is your thing, **Asúcar** (on the corner of Juan de Padilla and Lezcano, no phone, drop by for details, map C1) gets steamy well into the early hours, and has free dance classes from 10.30pm Tuesdays to Saturdays.

Though Málaga is not much of a flamenco city, there is a **Museo Flamenco** at Peña de Juan Breva (Callejón Picador 2, 952 21 08 76, open Tue, Fri, free, phone in advance, map C1), with shows from 11pm most Fridays. For live shows, **Tablao Flamenco Vista Andalucía** (Avenida de Los Guindos 29, Local 78, 952 23 11 75, www.vistaandalucia.com, open from 11pm Tue-Sat) has live music and dancing every Friday and Saturday.

Things really hot up during the *locos veranos* (or 'crazy summers') in the beach areas to the east of the centre, with endless bar-hopping and all-night music and dancing during July and August. **El Baneario** (Torre de San Telmo, 952 20 33 57, closed Sun) may seem tatty and run-down, but the kids love it.

## Where to stay

There's a handful of good hotels and *hostales* in the old centre, and another clutch in the streets just south of the Alameda Principal. An attractive alternative is to base yourself in the beachside neighbourhood of El Pedregalejo, which consists of low-rise, gingerbread houses set back from the beach, and cute, two-storey cottages along the shore. It was originally a fishing village (and has an unexpected underlying Caribbean flavour), yet is only a 30-minute walk from the centre.

# Home is where the art is

If Pablo Picasso (1881-1973) hadn't been born in Málaga, the city's ambitions might never have extended beyond the parochial. But the **Museo Picasso Málaga**, which opened in October 2003, has brought the city new money, a new role and, above all, hope for a sparkling future.

The gallery itself is a superb space. Converted from the sumptuous early-16th-century Palacio de los Condes de Buenavista, it is part 16th-century palace, complete with ornate carved wood ceilings and extravagant Renaissance and Mudéjar features; part straight-lined, creamy-white, futuristic architectural space.

Furthermore, excavations beneath the building, which uncovered Phoenician, Roman and Moorish remains, have been seamlessly incorporated into the museum's design, treating visitors to a vision of architecture spanning three millennia.

But it is the art itself that will draw the vast majority of people to the gallery. Thanks to the generosity of Picasso's heirs, specifically Christine Ruiz-Picasso, wife of the artist's eldest son Paulo, and her son Bernard, the museum's permanent collection boasts 204 original works, including oil paintings,

sculptures, drawings, sketchpads and ceramics, a large number of which are outright donations. The collection is estimated to be worth around €176 million.

Together, the works present a deeply personal retrospective of one of the most highly regarded artists of the 20th century. Laid out in chronological order, the collection traces the artist's development from his teenage years under the guidance of his father in *A Coruña* to his final piece *Man, Woman & Child*, which he painted seven months before his death. Many of the works have not been widely exhibited and some have never before been seen in public.

The hope is that with such a world-class art collection, Málaga will shake off its ill-fitting mantle of jump-off point for the Costa, and become a city destination in its own right.

### Museo Picasso Málaga

*Palacio de los Condes de Buenavista, C/San Agustín 8 (902 44 33 77/www.museopicasso malaga.org).* **Open** 10am-8pm Tue-Thur; 10am-9pm Fri, Sat; 10am-8pm Sun & hols. **Admission** *Collection* €6. *Exhibition* €4.50. *Combined* €8. Free children under 10. **No credit cards. Map** p57 C2.

## Cohíba Hotel

*Paseo Marítimo 64, El Pedregalejo (952 20 69 00/ www.cohibahotel.com).* **Rates** (incl breakfast) €57-€71 single; €86-€107 double; €114-141 suite. **Credit** AmEx, DC, MC, V.

The best little beach hotel in Málaga, this three-star Cuban-owned place has cheerful rooms and a communal kitchen. The best room is a penthouse suite that opens on to a pleasant rooftop terrace with jacuzzi. It's also a happening nightspot for tasty rum cocktails and salsa grooves.

## Hostal Blue Acacias

*Paseo de las Acacias 5 (952 20 62 20/www.blue acacias.com).* **Rates** €35-€45 single; €52-€61 double; €72-€100 suite with jacuzzi. **Credit** MC, V.

Minutes from the beach, this charming, duck-egg-blue *hostal* has a delightful, flower-filled garden with deckchairs and tables out back. The star room, a self-contained *casita*, is at the end of it.

## Hostal Derby

*4th floor, Pasaje San Juan de Dios 1 (952 22 13 01).* **Rates** €25-35 single; €36-€45 double. **No credit cards. Map** p57 B2.

A friendly *hostal* with cheap, cheerful rooms. The best is number 15, with corner windows giving fine views over the port. There's also a communal balcony.

## Hostal Juanita

*4th floor, C/Alarcon Lujan 8 (952 21 35 86).* **Rates** €25-€31 single; €35-€52 double; €48-€64 triple; €64-€86 quad. **No credit cards. Map** p57 A/B2.

A lift carries you to this fourth-floor *hostal* right in the centre of town. Rooms are simple but fresh, bright and airy.

## Hostal Larios

*3rd floor, C/Marqués de Larios 9 (952 22 54 90).* **Rates** €29-€32 single; €47-€60 double. **Credit** MC, V. **Map** p57 B2.

Newly opened in 2004, this *hostal* is simple and neat with bright rooms (the best have balconies), all with their own bathroom, TV and air-conditioning.

## Hostal Victoria

*C/Sancha de Lara 3 (952 22 42 23).* **Rates** €40-€48 single; €50-€80 double. **Credit** AmEx, DC, MC, V. **Map** p57 B2.

All rooms in this centrally located *hostal* have private bathroom and tub. Ask for one at the front of the building; the rooms at the rear are a little poky.

## Hotel Don Curro

*C/Sancha de Lara 9 (952 22 72 00/www.hoteldon curro.com).* **Rates** €69-€76 single; €98-€110 double; €126-€142 suite. **Credit** AmEx, DC, V. **Map** p57 B2.

This three-star hotel enjoys a central location and has modern, spacious rooms, a bar and a restaurant.

## Hotel Larios

*C/Marqués de Larios 2 (952 22 22 00/www.hotel-larios.com).* **Rates** €94-€123 single; €123-€164 double; €143-€199 suite. **Credit** AmEx, DC, MC, V. **Map** p57 B2.

The four-star 40-
choice when revisit
a fabulous roof terra
rooms. The hotel's Picas
€89 per person per night
entrance to the new museu
plimentary wine and cockta

## Málaga Palacio

*Avenida Cortina del Muelle 1 (952          /www.ac-hoteles.com).* **Rates** €106-€145. **Credit** AmEx, DC, MC, V. **Map** p57 B2.

Part of the chic AC chain, the 214-room Málaga Palacio is swish, ultra-modern and service oriented, with views over the leafy Paseo del Parque.

## Parador del Gibralfaro

*Camino de Gibralfaro s/n (952 22 19 02/www.parador. es).* **Rates** €106 single; €134 double; €176 superior double. **Credit** AmEx, DC, MC, V. **Map** p57 off E2.

With wonderful views over the city and the bay, this hilltop *parador* has luxurious, spacious rooms (all with terraces), a small rooftop pool and a restaurant.

# Resources

## Internet

*Ciber Teatro Romano, C/Alcazarilla s/n (952 60 45 22).* **Open** 10am-1am daily. **Map** p57 C2.
*Rent@net, C/Santiago 8 (952 22 02 41).* **Open** 10am-midnight daily. **Map** p57 C2.

## Police station

*Avenida de la Rosaleda s/n (952 12 65 00).* **Map** p57 off A1.

## Post office

*Avenida Andalucía 33 (952 32 35 28).*

## Tourist information

*Pasaje de Chinitas 4 (952 21 34 45/www.malaga turismo.com).* **Open** 8.30am-2.30pm, 4.30-7pm Mon-Fri; 8.30am-2.30pm Sat, Sun. **Map** p57 B2.
*Casa del Jardinero, Avenida Cervantes 1 (952 13 47 30).* **Open** 8.30am-2.30pm, 4.30-7pm Mon-Fri; 8.30am-2.30pm Sat, Sun. **Map** p57 C3.
*Plaza de la Marina (952 12 20 20).* **Open** 9am-7pm Mon-Fri; 10am-7pm Sat, Sun. **Map** p57 B3.

# Getting there

## By bus

The bus station is next to the rail station on Paseo de los Tilos (952 35 00 61). There are 10 daily buses to Granada (2hrs), 8 to Sevilla (2hrs 30mins) and Almería (3hrs 30mins), 5 to Córdoba (3hrs), 3 to Cádiz (4hrs) and Jaén (4hrs 30mins), plus 10 daily to Nerja (1hr 30mins) and one every 15mins along the Costa.

## By train

The rail station is at Explanada de la Estación (952 36 02 02), 15mins' walk from the centre. There are 5 daily direct trains to Sevilla (2hrs 30mins) and 9 daily to Córdoba (2hrs 20mins).

# osta del Sol

Package tourists, hedonists, millionaires and backpackers continue to jostle for space on Spain's most famous *costa*.

Escape the Torrie hordes in **La Carihuela**.

Though it's already overflowing with tourists and built up beyond any hope of redemption, Spain's most notorious *costa* still pulls in the crowds (though numbers are dropping; *see p24*). On first impressions it might seem like nothing more than one immense sprawl of monotonous development, but the coastal strip contains a surprising amount of diversity.

Rather like Vegas, Torremolinos (Torrie for short) is as wacky and kitsch as they come; so bad, you've just got to love it. Marbella, the pearl of the south, is a shopping mecca, the playground of royalty and celebs, and a yachties' and golfers' paradise, while Estepona offers a relatively quiet, family atmosphere and plenty of theme parks for the kids. It's all the result of Franco's ill-advised plan to turn Spain's Mediterranean coast into the 'Florida of Europe' – not just a holiday mecca, but home to huge numbers of British, German and Scandinavian expats, who have created their own micro-communities.

Just a few minutes' drive inland, however, life slows to a far more relaxed pace in some of the region's delightful white villages, such as Benahavis (otherwise known as the dining room of the South), Mijas and Casares. Meanwhile, in the nearby mountain reserves, rural tourism is quietly flourishing. Add to this impressively cheap air fares to Málaga and bargain-priced package deals, and the enduring appeal of the Costa del Sol isn't hard to fathom.

When driving along the Costa be warned that the A7 coastal road (the old N340) is often horribly jammed, and is notoriously dangerous; it is well worth paying a few euros to use the newer AP7 toll road (the former A7-E15) that runs parallel to it, particularly as the views from it are quite superb.

## Torremolinos

Located just a few kilometres south-west of Málaga airport, Torrie is so passionate about tourism that it even has a 'Tourist Day' (check with tourist office for date), in which thousands of servings of paella and fried fish get dished out along with cool beers, for free. Then, a few days later, they have 'Pescaíto Day' (3 June) in the neighbouring former fishing village of La Carihuela for anyone who missed out on the freebies the first time round.

How times have changed. Five hundred years ago, Torremolinos was a veritable spa town, revered for the quality of its underground springs, which filled the baths and spas of various nearby Roman settlements. In turn, this water supply fuelled the numerous watchtowers (*torres*) and mills (*molinos*) that dotted this coastline in the 15th century, and from whence the town takes its name.

The only real evidence of the town's past is the crumbling **Torre Vigia**, an Arab watchtower that pinpoints the heart of the old town. The steep streets that run down to the sea from here are more charming than you might expect given the resort's reputation. Though much of Torrie is still rather down at heel, the seafront has been smartened up considerably, and you can now walk along it all the way to Benalmádena Costa (*see p62*), passing the quieter village and beach of **La Carihuela** on the way. The latter is a good place to stay if the centre seems too much like hard work. For kids, the primary attraction (apart from the beach) is probably **Crocodile Park**, the star of which is Big Daddy – the largest croc in Europe at 600 kilos (94 stones) and 4.6 metres (15 feet).

The first tourist development on the Costa was the work of the philanthropist Englishman George Langworthy, who 'discovered' Torrie in the 1930s. Its first real pleasure hotel – the Pez Espada – was built in the 1950s (around the time that the town started becoming popular with American bohemians) and is still open, if a little faded round the edges. Since the '60s tourist boom, development has never really stopped; the town now has enough hotel rooms to accommodate around a quarter of a million visitors at any given time.

Full to bursting with bucket-and-spade shops, British pubs and greasy caffs serving egg and chips, Torrie nevertheless has legions of fans who return to enjoy its screeching, plastic madness year after year. It's a particularly fun gay destination, and if you're looking for a good time, Torremolinos has the beach, the bars and the nightlife to make it all happen.

### Crocodile Park

*C/Cuba 14, Torremolinos (952 05 17 82).* **Open** *Mar-June, Oct, Nov* 10am-6pm daily. *July-Sept* 10am-7pm daily. *Dec-Feb* 10am-5pm daily. **Admission** €8; €5.75 concessions. **Credit** MC, V.

## Where to eat & drink

You'll find no shortage of pub grub and fried breakfasts along the old town's frenzied central vein, Calle Miguel. Laying your hands on some solid Spanish fare, however, may prove more of a challenge. On the main drag, right opposite the Centro Comercial San Miguel, **La Chacha** (no phone) is little more than a hole-in-the-wall but serves an extraordinary array of fresh, grilled seafood by weight. In the old *barrio*, **Bodegas Quitapeñas** (C/Cuesta del Tajo 3, 952 38 62 44, €) is reliably excellent, offering fresh fish tapas with glasses of Málaga wine from the barrel. For traditional Spanish game dishes, try **La Mancha** (Avenida Los Manatiales, Plaza Goya, 952 38 01 46, closed Mon, €€-€€€).

Playa de la Carihuela is a top location for fish: the local favourite, **Casa Paco** (Paseo Maritimo La Carihuela s/n, 952 05 13 81, closed Mon and Dec & Jan, €€), does a huge skewer of freshly grilled sardines for around €5.

## Nightlife

Salsa fans head for **Atrevete** (Avenida Salvador Allende), a hot 'n' steamy joint near the beach in La Carihuela. Most of the super clubs and discos can be found on Avenida Carlota Alessandri and around Avenida Palma de Mallorca, west of the Plaza Costa del Sol. **Fun Beach** (Avenida Palma de Mallorca, 952 38 02 56) claims to be the biggest in Europe, with eight dancefloors, go-go dancers and stage performers. And the Ministry of Sound's flagship club, **Pacha** (for details, see www.pacha.com) has recently opened up on the Plaza Mayor. There's also quite a big, if obviously touristy, flamenco scene. **Pepe Lopez** (Plaza de la Gamba Alegre, 952 38 12 84, closed Sun all year and Mon-Thur Nov-Mar) also puts on a decent show.

Torrie's thriving gay scene centres mostly around the La Nogalera area, a hotbed of bars, discos and saunas for a mostly male clientele. The **Palladium** (Avenida Palma de Mallorca, 952 38 42 89, open Fri & Sat only) has a swimming pool, balloons, and smoke and fake snow billowing from every corner. An annual gay rave in August features big stars and international DJs.

## Where to stay

In the centre of town, the buttercup-yellow **Hotel Adriano** (Avenida de los Manantiales 1, 952 05 08 38, www.hoteladriano.info, double €75-€86) has a roof terrace with sea views, high above the chaos below, and fresh, clean rooms. Ask about special rates deals here, as the suites with private terraces and sun loungers often go for the same price as a double. The same family also own the cheery **Hostal Doña Lola** (C/Cruz 10, 952 38 20 84, double €35). In the so-called *'barri tipica'*, pretty **Hostal Micaela** (C/Bajondillo 4, 952 38 33 10, double €30-€45) is recognisable by its colourful Andalucian planters spilling over with geraniums; it's been around since 1972 and remains a hugely popular budget option. **Hotel El Pozo** (C/Casablanca 2, 952 38 06 02/22, double €40€62) has spacious, pleasant rooms, some with balconies.

In La Carihuela, the whimsical (and still resolutely Spanish) **Hotel Miami** (C/Cuesta del Tajo 8, 952 38 52 55, www.residencia-miami.com, double €34-€57) was built in the 1960s by Picasso's cousin and retains some of the house's original features, including a public area built in the style of the Sacramonte caves in Granada. The lush garden and swimming pool provide a blissful retreat. The three-star **Hotel Las Palomas** (Carmen Montes 1, 952 38 50 00, www.dorhoteles.com, double €44-€100) is popular with a young clubbing crowd. All rooms have balconies and there's a large swimming pool if the hangover's too bad for you to crawl to the beach.

## Resources

### Internet

*Cyber Café Caracas, C/La Nogalera, by C/San Miguel (952 38 72 37).* **Open** 10am-2pm, 4pm-midnight daily.

### Police station

*C/Rafael Quintana Rosado s/n (952 37 60 00).*

### Post office

*Avenida Palma de Mallorca 25 (952 38 45 18).*

### Tourist information

*Playa Bajondillo (952 37 19 09) & Plaza del Remo (952 37 29 56). Both* **Open** *July, Sept* 10am-2pm, 5-8pm Mon-Fri. *Aug* 10am-2pm, 5-8pm daily. *Sept-June* 9.30am-2.30pm Mon-Fri.
There are additional offices in the *Ayuntamiento* (Plaza Blas Infante, 952 37 95 12, open 8.30am-1.30pm Mon-Fri) and on Plaza de la Independencia (952 37 42 31, open 10am-1.30pm Mon-Fri).

## Benalmádena, Mijas & Fuengirola

Merging into Torremolinos, its brasher eastern neighbour, is **Benalmádena Costa**. The main attractions here are the **Puerto Deportivo**, the Costa's most happening nightspot, which is particularly popular among young Spaniards from Málaga, and a cable car (952 57 77 73, tickets €5.50, €4 concessions) that lifts you up into the hills, leaving you free to hike your way down on two well-marked paths. Benalmádena also has a couple of good theme parks: **SeaLife** is home to an impressive array of underwater installations, including a shark conservation tank and a seahorse breeding area, and turtle rescue schemes, while **Tivoli World** has the usual rides, amusements and shows.

Above the conurbation is **Benalmádena Pueblo**, an unexpectedly pretty village that gets two thumbs up for miraculously having escaped the overdevelopment all around. There's not much to do here, other than wander the streets, but it's a good place to stay if you want to be close to the coast.

High up in the **Sierra de Mijas**, around six kilometres (four miles) behind Benalmádena, is **Mijas**, which became a popular haven for new bohemians keen to escape the burgeoning coast during the 1960s. They were surprised to find in their midst the town's former mayor Manuel Cortes, who had gone into hiding in the village after the Civil War, and only emerged in 1968. Mijas was the subject of Ronald Fraser's anthropological classic *The Pueblo*.

Today, the village has grown to become the second-largest *pueblo* on the Costa del Sol; more than 40 per cent of residents are foreigners. In

season the town is overrun with day-trippers, though in the evening it becomes the locals' own once more. *Burro* (donkey) taxis are available for hire. Take one up the rocky path to the **Sanctuario del Calvario**, a 16th-century shrine of the barefooted Carmelite brothers. Also worth a look is the colourful grotto of the **Virgen de la Peña**, on the site where she appeared to two children in 1586. A small-scale running of the bulls takes place to celebrate the Virgen de la Peña festival in early September.

The **Carromato de Max** (closed for refurbishment at the time of writing) – a museum of the world's tiniest things, including a copy of the *Last Supper* painted on a grain of rice and some fully clothed fleas – is the town's most preposterous attraction. The pretty **Plaza de Toros** (952 48 52 48) is worth a visit, and if you feel so inclined there are *corridas* (bullfights) most Sundays. If that doesn't take your fancy, check out the town's thriving arts and crafts scene, which offers a better class of souvenir than can be found on the coast.

Whatever it is that **Fuengirola** has in mind for its regeneration – it is the coast's number one resort for Spanish tourists – it has been at it for several years now. Relentless drilling, cordoned-off roads and tarpaulin-wrapped buildings have long been the norm. It is a fairly cheap option, however, and public transport to the more attractive resorts of Mijas Costa and

**Hotel La Fonda**, Benalmádena. *See p63.*

Marbella is regular and good. Fuengirola's beach is heinously crowded, and rather than staggering your way through the sprawl of the old town you could kill an hour on the ramparts of the tenth-century **Castillo de Sohail**, at the south-western end of the beach. The town's best features are Andalucía's largest street market, held on Tuesdays on Avenida Jesús Santos Rein, and the night-time horse races held at the Hipódromo Costa del Sol on Saturdays throughout the summer.

### Carromato de Max

*Avenida del Compás s/n, Mijas (952 48 95 00).* **Open** *July-Sept* 10am-10pm daily. *Oct-June* 10am-7pm daily. **Admission** €3. **No credit cards.** Closed for refurbishment at time of going to press.

### Hipódromo Costa del Sol

*Urbanización El Chaparral s/n, Mijas Costa (952 59 27 00/www.hipodromomijas.com).* **Open** *July-Sept* 10pm-2am Sat. **Admission** free.

### SeaLife

*Puerto Deportivo de Benalmádena (952 56 01 50/www.sealife.es).* **Open** *June* 10am-8pm daily. *July, Aug* 10am-midnight daily. *Sept-May* 10am-6pm daily. **Admission** €9; €7 concessions. **Credit** AmEx, MC, V.

### Tivoli World

*Avenida de Tivoli s/n, Benalmádena (952 57 70 16/www.tivolicostadelsol.com).* **Open** *Easter-May, mid Sept-Oct* 4pm-1am daily. *June, early-mid Sept* 5pm-2am daily. *July, Aug* 6pm-3am daily. *Nov-Easter* 1-10pm Sat, Sun. **Admission** €4.50 **Credit** AmEx, DC, MC, V.

## Where to stay, eat & drink

In Benalmádena Pueblo, **Hotel La Fonda** (Santo Domingo 7, 952 56 83 24, double €72-€95) was designed by César Manrique. It's a beautiful colonial-style building constructed around a network of Moorish-style, cobblestoned patios, with a large pool and a balcony terrace with fine views. The catering school on site (952 56 86 25, open lunch only, closed Sat & Sun and July & Aug, €€) offers a good three-course tasting menu. **La Perla** (C/Ibiza 12, 952 56 81 66, closed Mon, €€€-€€€€) is an upmarket restaurant with a classy Mediterranean menu specialising in game, and is worth the trip up the hill. **El Bodegón del Muro** (C/Santo Domingo 23, 952 56 85 87, €€-€€€) has an intriguing menu featuring the likes of pickled frogs' legs and caviar vichyssoise.

On the Mijas Costa it seems nothing short of miraculous that a place like the **Beachhouse** (Urbanización El Chaparral, A7, km203, 95 249 45 40, www.beachhouse.nu, €125-€140) exists. Imagine waking up to the sound of waves crashing on the shore, and dazzling white archways surrounding a pretty tiled

**Málaga Province**

A quiet *plaza* in **Benalmádena Pueblo.** See p62.

# What Londoners take when they go out.

Millionaires' playground: the marina at **Puerto Banús**. *See p66.*

swimming pool with jawdropping views over the blue horizon – and you begin to get some idea of what it's like to stay here. Cool white walls and minimal Scandinavian furnishings ensure a blissful retreat from real life. There's no restaurant, but four minutes walk down the beach will bring you to **Sheriff** (A7, km202, Mijas Costa, 952 49 37 22, €€€), which serves decent steaks and fresh fish on tables on the beach.

In Mijas Pueblo, the family-run **Hostal La Posada** (C/Coín 47, 952 48 53 10, double €30-€45) has rooms and apartments and is deservedly popular with everyone from backpackers to middle-aged ramblers. The four-star **Hotel Mijas** (Urbanización Tamisa 2, 952 48 58 00, www.hotasa.es, double €106-€113) lets you kick back in style. For food you have many options, not all of them good. **El Mirlo Blanco** (Plaza de la Constitución, 952 48 57 00, closed 2wks Jan, €€-€€€), however, is truly superb, and, unusually in the male-dominated world of restaurants, is run by three generations of women from the Basque country. They specialise in the delicacies of home: *angulas* (mind-bogglingly expensive baby eels), *txangurro* (spider crab) and *kokotxas de bacalau* (cod cheeks). If you fancy something a little more down-to-earth, **Fiesta** (Avenida de Mexico, 952 48 57 67, closed Nov, €€) does a great barbecue, while **Bar La Gamba** (C/San Sebastián 11, 952 48 57 22, €€), hidden away on a quiet side street, offers

typical *casera* (home-style Spanish cooking) and – as you might guess from its name – prawns, on a pretty, vine-shaded roof terrace.

In Fuengirola, the three-star **Hotel Puerto** (Paseo Marítimo 32, 952 47 01 00, www.hotel-elpuerto.com, closed Nov, double €79-€122) gets points for being on the beach and for having a tenth-floor rooftop swimming pool. **Hostal Cuevas** (C/Capitán 7, 952 46 06 06, closed Jan & Dec, double €40-€55) is one of the better places in the town centre, safely tucked away from the noisy main drag. It offers no-frills accommodation, with clean, comfortable rooms with baths. Or there's the recently refurbished **Hostal Marbella** (C/Marbella 34, 952 66 45 03, www.hostalmarbella.info, double €42-€63), which has pleasant rooms and is handy for the beach. There are about 50 British pubs in Fuengirola; most are situated on and around Calle Capitán. Calle Moncayo is nose-to-tail with a variety of international restaurants. The Basque chain **Lizzaran** (Avenida Jesús Santos Rein 1, 952 47 38 29, €-€€) is probably your best bet for casual eats; it serves bite-sized *pintxos* (small pieces of bread with varied toppings) and *txacoli* (a fizzy Basque wine). Astonishingly, Fuengirola also has a Michelin one-starred restaurant, **Patrick Bausier** (Rotonda de la Luna 1, 952 58 51 20, €€€€), which serves reassuringly expensive, classical French cuisine.

In Benalmádena Costa, the Puerta Marina is a decent place to eat by day and is full of late-night *bares de copas* and a number of discos – the best are at the far end, looking towards Fuengirola; this is where people come to see and be seen from around 10pm.

## Resources

### Internet

**Benalmádena Costa** *Miramar, C/La Fragata, Darsena de Levante, Local A5 (952 57 75 75/ www.puerto-marina.com)*. **Open** 11am-11pm Mon-Fri; 2-6pm Sat, Sun.

### Tourist information

**Benalmádena Costa** *Avenida Antonio Machado 10, (952 44 12 95/24 94/turismo@benalmadena.com)*. **Open** 9am-3pm, 4-7pm Mon-Fri; 10am-1pm Sat.

**Fuengirola** *Avenida Jesús Santos Rein 6 (952 46 74 57)*. **Open** 9.30am-2pm, 5-7pm Mon-Fri; 10am-1pm Sat.

**Mijas** *Plaza Virgen de la Peña 2 (952 48 59 00)*. **Open** 9am-2pm, 4pm-7pm Mon-Fri; 10am-2pm Sat.

## Marbella

The most expensive resort in Spain, Marbella promotes a particular brand of luxury tourism conceived largely by the town's larger-than-life former mayor Jesús Gil y Gil. Gil finally stood down from office in 2002, and was given a three-year prison sentence for financial irregularities concerning his Atlético de Madrid football club. He died in May 2004. During his 11 years as mayor, Gil had his fingers in several notoriously sticky pies. In 1969 one of his apartment complexes collapsed, killing 58 people. He spent 18 months in jail, but was pardoned by Franco and released. Despite his dubious practices, Gil's property dealings have played no small part in Marbella's success. His replacement as mayor was his chosen successor and a close friend.

From the fine restaurants and glitzy hotels of the Golden Mile to the luxury yachts and exclusive nightclubs of nearby **Puerto Banús** (the Saudi king has a palace here), Marbella is a playground for royalty, celebrities and mafiosi. Yet despite a self-perpetuating reputation to the contrary, it is still easy to have fun in Marbella without being a millionaire.

Marbella's **Casco Antiguo** (old quarter) comes as a welcome relief after the high-rise horrors further east. It's a lovely tangle of narrow alleyways and twisted streets, free of lager louts and fish-and-chip shops, and filled with flowers; an annual prize is awarded to the town's prettiest street garden. Among the most attractive lanes is Calle Ortiz de Molinillos (just east of Plaza de los Naranjos), where creepers and vines choke wrought-iron balconies and a magnificent statue of the Virgin perches above it all in a turquoise-covered sentry box.

You can't miss the intimate central **Plaza de los Naranjos**, site of the old marketplace and orange orchard, and now jammed with café tables. The scent of blossom in the evenings can be quite intoxicating. Also worth seeing is the **Museo del Grabado Español Contemporáneo**, an engraving museum housing works by Dalí, Miró and Picasso. It occupies a striking Renaissance building, formerly a poor hospital and children's home.

Nearby, the church of **Nuestra Señora de la Encarnación** (open hours of services) was built in the 16th century, but like many Andalucían churches, was later remodelled in baroque style. One of the more curious of Marbella's sights is the **Museo de Bonsai**, the showcase of an obsessive collector.

During the summer, the Paseo Marítimo springs to life as cafés and bars open their doors to face the sea. At the easternmost end you'll find the **Puerto Deportivo**. Once better known as a place to score drugs and women, it has begun to clean up its act, with some of the more salubrious business owners doing their best to promote it as a hip alternative to Puerto Banús.

**Cabo Pino** (between Marbella and Fuengirola) is a delightful little port with a number of decent eateries, and the area's main nudist beach, while a string of beaches west of town are the scenes of all-night beach parties ruled by Europe's top DJs in high season.

Just outside Marbella are a couple of interesting archaeological sites, including a well-preserved Roman mosaic of Medusa. Free guided tours in English depart from Arco de San Pedro Alcantara (952 78 13 60) at noon on Mondays, Wednesdays and Fridays. Book at least a day in advance. You'll need to provide your own transport to the site.

### Museo de Bonsai

*Parque Arroyo de la Represa, Avenida Doctor Mais Viñal (952 86 29 26)*. **Open** *July, Aug* 10.30am-1.30pm, 4-7pm daily. *Sept-June* 10am-1.30pm, 4-7pm daily. **Admission** €3; €1.50 concessions. **No credit cards**. Map p67 C1.

### Museo del Grabado Español Contemporáneo

*C/Hospital Bazán s/n (952 82 50 35/www.museo delgrabado.com)*. **Open** *June-Sept* 10am-2pm, 6-9pm Tue-Sat. *Oct-May* 10am-2pm, 5.30-8.30pm Tue-Sat. **Admission** €2.50. **No credit cards**. Map p67 C2.

## Where to eat & drink

With more than 600 restaurants to choose from, Marbella offers just about anything from anywhere in every price bracket. The Paseo Marítimo is good for funky bars and beachfront dining; head for the Golden Mile and Puerto Banús for posh dinners and world-class cuisine; but for sheer atmosphere, you can't beat the Casco Antiguo.

**Bar Altamirano** (Plaza Altamirano 4, 952 82 49 32, closed Wed and mid Jan-mid Feb, €, map C2) remains one of the old town's best kept secrets, serving some of the freshest fish and seafood tapas on the coast. It's always lively with locals, and doubles as a shrine to Spanish football. Opposite the lighthouse on the Paseo Marítimo is **La Pesquera del Faro** (Avenida José Melia 2, 952 76 41 74, www.lapesquera. com, €€€), part of a chain that serves reliably good grub; this branch has tables on the sand.

In the Casco Antiguo it's worth hunting out Calle San Lázaro (map A2) – an alleyway off Plaza Victoria – which has a range of eateries from expensive but seductively romantic to dirt cheap and basic. The tapas bar **El Estrecho** (C/Lazazro s/n, 952 77 00 04, closed Sun and mid May-mid June, €€) is much loved by locals.

Wander along Calle Ortiz de Molinillo (map B1) for local eats. **El Balcón de la Virgen** (C/Remedios 2, 952 77 60 92, closed Sun and mid Dec-mid Jan, €€, map B1) seems stuck in another time and place, with hearty, country fare to match. Try **La Querencía** (C/Tetuán 9, no phone, €, map B2) for cheap and tasty North African dishes. Heading a little more upmarket, **La Cuisine** (Plaza Puente de Ronda, 952 82 33 32, closed Sun, €€-€€€, map A/B1) proffers its own particular brand of tasty French-Swedish cuisine in a lovingly restored old townhouse with a laid-back atmosphere. **ZoZoi** (Plaza Altamirano 1, 952 85 88 68, closed Sun, €€€-€€€€, map C2) is the new darling of Marbella's hip young things for its adventurous Med cooking and romantic terrace and dining rooms.

A pint-sized place offering food fit for kings, visitors are spoiled for choice when it comes to eating out in the village of **Benahavis**, just ten minutes' drive inland from Marbella. Standards

**Málaga Province**

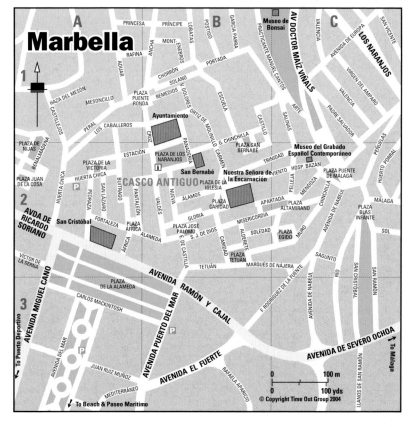

are high, with prices to match, but it is *the* place to go on the Costa for foodies, offering a good range of cooking styles and regional dishes. Reserving is nearly always advisable, and be sure to check on opening hours; many places are open for dinner only. **Los Abanicos** (C/Málaga 15, 952 85 50 22, €€€-€€€€) is one of the old hands and remains a favourite among locals and expats for well-executed Mediterranean and international fare. For giant portions of tender, juicy chargrilled meat try **Rufinos** (C/Montemayor 5, 952 85 52 62, €€-€€€). For a truly special evening of fine food and wine, a fabulously detailed menu and splendid surrounds, the hotel **Amanhavis** (*see p70*) is well worth fitting into your itinerary.

**Marbella** beach.

## Nightlife

Things don't get going until after midnight in Marbella, so eat late, before heading out to enjoy the flashiest club scene on the Costa. In the Puerto Deportivo (about ten minutes' walk from the Casco Antiguo), the **House of Silk** (Local 9)

makes a good start to the evening before going on to one of the bigger clubs elsewhere; there's free beer and a barbecue on Sundays, served to the beat of chilled-out reggae. Nearby are **Loco's** for live music and **El Colonial** for lively flamenco. The superclubs are clustered at the Puerto Banús end of the Golden Mile. **Dreamers** (A7, km175, 952 81 20 80, www.dreamers-disco.com) is a great-looking

# The Costa del Crime

The Costa del Sol may be losing its touch as Spain's best-loved coastline among tourists, but it's still a favourite hiding place for shadier visitors. From drug barons to fugitive train robbers, con-artists to wannabe gangsters, the Costa del Sol is a criminals' playground, where the crimes themselves range from the brutal to the bizarre.

Curiously, crime on the eastern Costa (east of Málaga) has risen by about 20 per cent in recent years, while that on the western strip has remained much as it was. Experts say this is due to population explosions in towns like Vélez-Málaga and Torrox in the east, creating a fertile breeding ground for organised crime, such as drug trafficking, fraud and sexual exploitation. These nouveau criminals have no fear of established gangs – as is the case west of Málaga – and so are free to engage in their own forms of modern-day banditry.

The best-known Costa crooks have become minor celebrities, like Charlie Wilson, one of the Great Train Robbers, who escaped his high-security cell in Winson Green prison in Birmingham in 1964. It was four years before the authorities caught up with him and put him back behind bars. When he was finally released from jail, he moved to the Costa del Sol and turned his hand to drug trafficking until he was gunned down by a hit man in 1990.

More recently, the case of Tony King, accused of a double murder on the Costa del Sol, made the headlines both in Spain and abroad. Dolores Vázquez had already served 17 months in prison for one of the murders, that of 19-year-old Rocío Wanninkhof, when King became the chief suspect in the murder of 17-year-old Sonia Carabantes. He confessed to both murders initially, before changing his story and blaming his erstwhile friend Robert Graham and Vázquez. However, in August 2004 a court ruled that King would stand trial alone for the murder of Wanninkhof.

Local thieves may not make international headlines, but they cause one hell of a stir on their own stomping grounds. In June 2004 a bank in the quiet and decidedly unexciting village of Maro – home to the Nerja caves – was the victim of an armed robbery in which the thieves made off with €50,000. It is the third time the same bank has been targeted in the last few years. Locals say there just isn't enough of a police presence in the area, though one could be forgiven for thinking it wasn't necessary in a village with a population of just 800.

Two months earlier, national police busted Europe's biggest and best-quality coin counterfeiting operation, which was being run by two Italians out of a house in venue and plays a good variety of music, including sounds from the Berlin underground, while the **Lounge Suite** at the Hotel Puente Romano, A7, km177, 952 82 09 00, closed Sun-Wed) is good for R&B, soul and Latin house. Things get steadily more glam at **La Notte** (Camino de la Cruz, 952 86 69 96), but for sheer class you can't beat **Olivia Valere** (Carretera de Istán, km0.8, Marbella, 952 82 88 61/45, www.oliviavalere.com). The playground of royalty and celebrities, and housed in a hybrid replica of the Alhambra and the Mezquita, this is one of the most beautiful nightclubs in the world.

For cocktails, **Astral** (Playa Levante, Puerto Banús, mobile 610 01 58 15) has a beautiful terrace on the beach; it's a top spot to start an evening in this ritzy part of town. For lounging with the jet set, check out **Liquid Lounge** (Marina Banús, 952 90 88 31).

Famed veteran flamenco artist Ana María's **Tablao Ana María** offers evenings of foot-stamping action (Plaza Santo Cristo 4/5, 952 77 56 46, 952 86 07 04, closed Mon and Nov & Dec, admission €22 incl drink, map off B1).

## Where to stay

Budget accommodation is mostly in the Casco Antiguo and ranges from fun, friendly backpackers' hostels to simple hotels in restored townhouses. **Hostal del Pilar** (C/Mesoncillo 4, off C/Peral, 952 82 99 36, www.hostel-marbella. com, double €27-€37, map A1) was built in 1635 to accommodate monks travelling from Madrid. The current co-owner Michael Wright has tried to continue the building's legacy by creating a home for 'travelling pilgrims'. You'll find like-minded folk from all over the world swapping travel stories while basking on the roof terrace with a beer. Nearby, **Hostal Paco** (C/Peral 16, 952 77 12 00, hostalpacomarbella@hotmail.com, double €42-€52, map A1) is a fresh, clean, no-frills *hostal* with friendly staff. Alternatively, **Puerto de Aduares** (C/Aduar 18, 952 82 13 12, mobile 646 20 92 65, double €56-€76, map A1) is a good deal for its country-style self-catering apartments smack in the centre of town, all with kitchen, en suite bathrooms and terrace.

---

Benalmádena. The duo – both previously jewellers – had been merrily stamping out as many as 2,000 freshly faked two-euro coins a day for the past four years before police tracked them down. Reportedly a shopkeeper in Estepona became suspicious when someone tried to pay for an item using 200 of them.

Fraudulent real estate, meanwhile, is providing rich pickings for dodgy Britons, as in the case of Lemon Falls, a fictitious mobile-home park near Málaga. Lots were sold to unsuspecting buyers over the internet at €17,000 a time, before the bogus company behind the scam, Citylist, suddenly disappeared with all the cash.

But it's not just bogus businesses on the take; the region is notorious for scoundrels ready to take you for all you've got. Such was the case with lottery winner Tom Papworth, who won £6 million on the UK lotto only to be swindled out of it by con-man Joe Wilkins (aka John Fay) on the Costa del Crime. Fay persuaded Papworth to invest in a luxury apartment and place the rest of his winnings in a Marbella bank account. Shortly afterwards Papworth was arrested when cocaine was discovered in his brand-new Mercedes. While he served 30 months in jail, Fay did a bunk with the deeds to

his apartment and the contents of his bank account. Fay died suddenly in Estepona, just as his scam came to light.

One of the more disturbing recent cases was that of a Muslim cleric from Fuengirola, who was sentenced to a 15-month jail sentence and the rather more peculiar fine of €8 a day for eight days, after writing a book entitled *Women in Islam*. In it he advised men on how to beat their wives without marking them, provoking international outrage. Andalucía is the worst province in Spain for death by domestic violence, accounting for 15 fatalities in 2003.

Finally, watch out for shady goings-on in clandestine kitchens – the latest scandal to come under scrutiny on the Costa – where some restaurants are serving illegal, undersize fish to preferred customers who phone up and order them in advance. So far, 450 kilos of illegal fish have been seized from restaurants in Málaga, Torre del Mar and Benalmádena. Aside from the ecological and environmental damage caused by illegal fishing, undersize fish are sometimes preserved in substances like boric acid or formaldehyde, posing serious health risks to consumers.

Don't have nightmares – but you have been warned.

There are two noteworthy newcomers to the boutique hotel scene, both less expensive than you might imagine. **La Morada Mas Hermosa Hotel** (C/Montenebros 16A, 952 92 44 67, www.lamoradamashermosa.com, double €59-€86, map B1) is tucked down a leafy mews and has just five simply but elegantly decorated rooms. The best room (twin beds) has a spiral staircase leading up to a private terrace. **The Townhouse** (C/Alderete 7, Plaza Tetuán, www.townhouse.nu, 952 90 17 91, double €95-€120, map B2), owned by the same people as the Beachhouse (*see p63*), is elegance personified, with carved wood ceilings, sumptuous fabrics, chandeliers, glittering tiles and lots of marble. All rooms are individually decorated (a four-poster bed in number 6, a private terrace for number 9) and there's a rooftop terrace with views over the city's skyline, and tables and chairs in the *plaza*.

Sandwiched between the sea and the town centre, the big four-star **El Fuerte** (Avenida El Fuerte, 952 92 00 00, www.fuertehoteles.com, double €98-€187, map B3) does a splendid job at offering a personal service despite its size, and has all the facilities you'd expect, plus spa treatments at its sister hotel just down the road.

Located in the hills about 20 minutes drive north-west of Marbella, the **Amanhavis Hotel and Restaurant** (C/del Pilar 3, Benahavis, 952 85 60 26, www.amanhavis.com, closed 7 Jan-3 Feb, double €127-€181) is a wonderful, intriguing place to stay. Surrounding an intimate garden and plunge pool, nine unique rooms each tell a different story: the Astronomer's Observatory provides star-gazers with a skylight and brass telescope, while Sultan Boabdil's chamber is a sumptuous silken retreat, ideal for honeymooners. The dining room is housed in part of the original 350-year-old building, and the excellent food shows amazing attention to detail.

## Resources

### Police station
*C/Juan de la Cierva s/n (952 89 99 00).*

### Post office
*C/Jacinto Benavente 14 (952 77 28 98).*

### Tourist information
*Plaza de los Naranjos 1 (952 82 35 50/www.turismo marbella.com).* **Open** 9am-9pm Mon-Fri; 10am-2pm Sat. **Map** p67 B2.
There are other offices at Glorietas de la Fontanilla s/n (952 77 14 42) and at Arco de Marbella (952 82 28 18), tucked beneath the pearly concrete arch as you drive into town on the A7.

## Sierra Blanca

Towering behind Marbella are the hills of the **Sierra Blanca**, offering a much-needed escape route when all that partying gets too much. Eight kilometres (five miles) north of Marbella on the A355, the small sugar-cube village of **Ojén** clings to a valley wall at the base of the Sierra, sprouting a good many orange orchards. It makes an ideal base for exploring the area. The village's main attraction is the **Museo del Vino Málaga**, which does wine tastings and sells a large selection of Málaga province's most revered bottles, including the 'Viejo Abuelo 10-años', which won a gold medal at the World Wine Fair in 2002. The museum is housed in an 18th-century building, which was founded as Andalucía's first *aguardiente* distillery in 1830. It became so famous that for a long time in Spain it was common to ask simply for a 'copa de Ojén'. In the 1930s the abandoned distillery became the headquarters of the CNT – the syndicate of Spanish anarchists.

From here, a 15-minute drive will take you up to the **Refugio de Juanar**, at 760 metres (2,500 feet). The hotel (*see p71*) provides a good map of the area, with hiking routes and photographs of the flora and fauna you may encounter.

Should you happen to be in the town of **Monda** (11 kilometres/7 miles on from Ojén) on a particular Sunday in March, you can join in celebrations for the 'world's biggest soup' – a dubious-looking gloop of bread, peppers, tomatoes, garlic, oil and eggs, served to anyone who wants it from a gigantic wooden bowl. If that doesn't take your fancy, you can always have lunch at the **Hotel El Castillo** (*see p71*).

A number of local companies offer tours and specialist activities in the Sierra Blanca: among them are **Guías Daidín** in Marbella (C/Nuestra Señora de Gracia 4, 952 77 55 44, www.daidin.com) for trekking and archaeological digs; **Monte Aventura** (Plaza de Andalucía 1, Ojén, 952 88 15 19 Mon-Fri, mobile 656 96 04 78 Sat, Sun) for guided tours; and the **Safari Shop** in Puerto Banús (Centro Comercial Cristamar B61, Avenida Naciónes Unidas, 952 90 50 82 Mon-Fri, mobile 609 51 75 17 Sat, Sun, www.Spain4Fun.com) for canoeing, spelunking and rock-climbing expeditions.

### Museo del Vino Málaga
*C/Carrera 39, Ojén (952 88 14 53).* **Open** *July, Aug* 11am-3pm, 5.30-9.30pm daily. *Sept-June* 11am-3pm, 4-8pm daily. **Admission** free.

## Where to stay, eat & drink

In Ojén, **La Posada del Ángel** (C/Mesones 21, 952 88 18 08, www.laposadadelangel.com, double €70-€93) is a beautifully restored village house built around a wood-columned courtyard and furnished with country antiques. Some rooms have balconies; all have cable TV and internet access. A cheaper, more basic option with great views is the **Hostal El Solar** (C/Córdoba 2, 952 88 11 49, double €24-€40). Eat at **El Patio** (no phone, €) on the main *plaza*, which offers local dishes including *migas* (fried breadcrumbs, used much like couscous).

High in the mountains, the **Refugio de Juanar** (Sierra Blanca s/n, 952 88 10 00, www.juanar.com, double €86-€98) is where Charles de Gaulle chose to finish his memoirs in 1970. The best rooms have open fireplaces and jacuzzis, while the restaurant, housed in a converted hunting lodge, specialises in locally caught game.

For an unusual treat, stay at **Hotel El Castillo de Monda** (Avenida de Castillo s/n, 952 45 71 42, www.costadelsol.spa.es/hotel/monda, double €113-€224) on its perch above the town of the same name. It's the epitome of Moorish splendour, and has preserved some macabre artefacts, including a few human

**Amanhavis Hotel and Restaurant.** *See p70.*

skulls, which glint from darkened corners. The **Santa Fe Hotel Restaurante** (Carretera de Monda, km3, 952 45 29 16, www.santafe-hotel.com, closed 2wks Nov & 2wks Jan-Feb, double €66, restaurant €€) is another gem, with just five rustic bedrooms above a great little pub. Facilities include a swimming pool, conservatory and a roaring fire in winter.

## Estepona & around

West of Marbella is the not particularly distinguished resort of **San Pedro de Alcántara**. There are plenty of exclusive mansions scattered around the area, and countless golf courses (this part of the coast is commonly known as the Costa del Golf). The next big town along, heading south, is **Estepona**. Roman in origin, this is a pretty, if somewhat jaded, place, and the most genuinely Spanish town between here and Málaga. Development has been kept on a fairly strict leash, though the front has recently been dug up to make way for a vast underground car park, which should have been completed by the time this guide goes to press. Estepona's beaches boast the cleanest water on the coast and are flanked not by high-rises but by a handful of palm-thatched *chiringuitos*. Though it doesn't possess the good looks of Marbella's Casco Antiguo, its old town, particularly the attractive squares of **Plaza Las Flores** and **Plaza Arce**, is well worth exploring. Pick up the excellent information pack from the tourist office.

Around 16 kilometres (ten miles) west of Estepona, up in the **Sierra Bermeja**, the road to Casares resembles Tolkien's hobbits' Shire, with lush green hillsides and wild flowers blooming everywhere in spring. Locally known as the 'hanging village', due to the steepness of its streets and its strategic location perched on top of a rocky outcrop, **Casares** is one of the most spectacular of the *pueblos blancos*. Presided over by an 18th-century church and a Moorish castle, the upper reaches appear dangerously fragile when viewed from the road spiralling out of town towards Manilva. The surrounding countryside is virtually untouched and great for rambling. Eddie Taylor (mobile 609 50 07 80, www.adventureboundspain.com) offers guided hiking trips into the surrounding natural parks.

Casares takes its name from Julius Caesar, who was fighting Gaius Pompey for control of Spain in these parts around 45 BC. The battle took place near where present-day Monda stands, but, according to local legend, Caesar stopped en route to bathe in **Manilva**'s sulphurous springs, known as **La Hedionda**

**Málaga Province**

(the foul-smelling woman), where he reputedly rid himself of a nasty skin infection. If you want to share his bathwater, follow signs from the main road to the **Roman Oasis Restaurant** (Camino Sabanias Alcazares s/n, 952 89 23 80, www.insanctum.com, closed Oct-May, €€-€€€), then take a dirt road upstream until you spy a small white dome on the riverbank. Beneath these arches, the eerie blue sulphurous water lapping against the ancient stone produces a magical effect. Six kilometres (four miles) out of the town, on the private estate of Alechipe, are the remains of the Roman town of **Lacipo**, itself built over an Iberian settlement. Ask at the tourist office for more information about visiting this extraordinary site.

## Where to stay, eat & drink

In Estepona, if you're on a budget, **Hostal El Pilar** (Plaza de Las Flores 10, 952 80 00 18, www.anit.es/juanvit/hostal.htm, double €30-€47) is charming and has been in the same family since 1870; the best rooms have balconies opening on to the *plaza*. Opposite, **Hostal La Malagueña** (C/Castillo 1, 952 80 00 11, www.hlmestepona.com, double €30-€50) has light, airy top-floor rooms with sunny terraces. In the last few years nearly all of the hotels on the seafront have been refurbished. Many of the rooms at the freshly painted **Hotel Mediterráneo** (Avenida de España 68, 952 79 38 93, double €45-€60) have sea views.

Eating options in Estepona are numerous, from beachfront *chiringuitos* and classic Spanish tapas in town to world-class restaurants at the countless five-star hotels in the area. **Los Rosales** (C/Damas 12, 952 79 29 45, www.infhos.com/losrosales, closed Sun and 3wks Oct, 3wks Feb, restaurant €€), does excellent seafood at its simplest and freshest, but if you're looking for the ultimate fisherman's lunch, **La Escollera** (Puerto Pesquero de Estepona, 952 80 63 54, closed Mon, €€) will not disappoint. Portions are huge and the *navajas* (razor clams) are peerless. (To reach it, walk past the marina towards the docks and you'll find it by the beach entrance.) **La Casa de Mi Abuela** (C/Caridad 54, 952 79 19 67, closed Tue and May, €€) serves prime, Argentinian steaks, while at the Marbella end of the street, the ceilings at **Sabor Andaluz** (C/Caridad 44, 952 79 52 93, €€) are dripping with acorn-fed *jamones*, *salchichones* and other piggy delicacies. Nearby, **La Posá Dos** (C/Caridad 95, 952 80 00 29, closed lunch July-Sept, €€-€€€) is the perfect setting for a romantic meal out, with its blush hues, dripping candle wax and an

alcove made for two, plus a roof terrace. Most of the town's night-time action is centred around Calles Real and Caridad.

Hikers will find Casares a good base, but bear in mind that many of its streets are too steep and narrow to be reached by car. The **Hotel Rural Casares** (C/Copera 52, 952 89 52 11, www.hotelcasares.com, double €60) has pleasant rooms featuring brick archways and exposed beams. There are a couple of cheaper *pensiones* around Plaza de España, where the **Bar Nuevo Antiguo** (Plaza de España 17, 952 89 44 31, closed Tue and Nov, €) offers good meals and tapas. The roof terrace at **La Bodeguita de Medio** (Plaza de España 15, 952 89 40 36, closed Mon, €) is lovely for drinks. Or head up to one of the restaurants tucked under the crumbling ramparts of the castle for panoramic vistas.

The best place in the area for food, **The Forge** (Finca el Forjador, Carretera de Casares, km10, 952 89 51 20, www.forgerestaurant. netfirms.com, closed Mon & Tue and Feb, €€-€€€) is largely hidden by thick cork and oak woods, olive trees and wild blooms. The two- and three-course menus combine Middle Eastern-, African- and Greek-inspired dishes. Book several weeks in advance for lunch on Sundays.

## Resources

### Police station
**Estepona** *Avenida Los Frutales 1 (952 80 02 43).*

### Post office
**Estepona** *C/Martínez Campos 1 (952 80 05 37).*

### Tourist information
**Casares** *C/Villa 29 (952 89 41 26).* **Open** 11am-2.30pm, 4-6.30pm Mon-Fri; 11am-4pm Sat.
**Estepona** *Avenida San Lorenzo 1 (952 80 20 02/09 13/www.estepona.com).* **Open** 9am-8pm Mon-Fri; 10am-1.30pm Sat.

### By bus
Buses run from Málaga to Marbella (Avenida Trapiche, 952 76 44 00) via Torremolinos (C/Hoyos, 952 38 24 19) and Fuengirola (Avenida Matias Saez de Tejada, 952 47 50 66) every 15mins daily. From Marbella, hourly buses serve the main towns along the rest of the coast, and there are also less frequent buses on to Algeciras and Cádiz. Buses also run inland from Marbella to Ronda.

### By train
From Málaga (via the airport) trains run every 30mins to Torremolinos (15mins from airport), Benalmádena Costa and Fuengirola (30mins from airport).

# East of Málaga

The pace is still slow on the eastern portion of the Costa del Sol.

Typical white village in the **Axarquía**.

In marked contrast to the Costa del Sol west of Málaga, the eastern Costa is less developed (largely because its beaches are less appealing) and, as a result, the towns here have retained much of their Spanish flavour, though none are wildly interesting. The exception (on both counts) is the relaxed, Brit-dominated resort of Nerja, which has a charming old town, pretty sculpted coves and plenty to keep visitors amused in terms of bars and restaurants. Inland, the Axarquía (literally, 'land to the east') is a wonderland for walkers and great country for exploring *pueblos blancos* where, despite the expat resident count continually rising, life goes on pretty much as it did decades ago. It is especially tranquil out of season.

## The Montes de Málaga

Local people often talk of Málaga's two lungs: one is the Mediterranean, the other is the deep green, pine-forested **Parque Natural de los Montes de Málaga**, reaching up to 1,031 metres (3,383 feet) above the city to the north-east. Rarely visited by tourists, the park covers 4,956 hectares (19 square miles) of deep gorges, sun-dappled forests of pine trees, holm oaks and

olives, and lush valleys. Just 30 or so minutes' drive from the city centre, it's a quick and convenient retreat from the bustle of the town and is exhilarating hiking and mountain-biking territory. The tourist offices in Málaga can supply information about the Montes.

## Where to stay & eat

Many *ventas* (country inns) line the mountain road through the Montes de Málaga, and their menus have changed little since the days when bandits sheltered here. There are also two exceptional places to stay. If total solitude is what you're seeking, the **Hotel Humaina** (Carretera Colmenar s/n, 952 64 10 25, www. hotelhumaina.es, double €74-€80, restaurant €€) is a family-run retreat in the heart of the park, nestling halfway down a valley, surrounded on all sides by walls of verdant green. It feels more like going to stay with friends in the country than being in a hotel. The restaurant specialises in hearty mountain fare, as well as home-made breads and jams.

Alternatively, **Hotel Cortijo La Reina** (Carretera Málaga–Comenar, km549.5, 951 01 40 00, www.hotelcortijolareina.com, double

€128-€160, restaurant €€-€€€) offers luxury accommodation in a converted mansion. Most of the original details have been preserved; you eat breakfast in what would have been the family kitchen, a gleaming tiled affair. There's an in-house *bodega* for tasting the local wines, and individually decorated bedrooms, all with either a fireplace or a pot-bellied stove.

## The coast to Torre del Mar

Travelling east from Málaga to Torre del Mar takes you along one of the most banal stretches of coastline in Spain. A 30-kilometre (19-mile) wall of nondescript concrete high-rises, it has neither the madness of Torrie nor the glamour of Marbella's golden mile. What it does offer, however, are some of the few genuinely Spanish coastal towns remaining on the Costa del Sol.

The first sizeable resort you come to is unappealing **Rincón de la Victoria**, which only warrants a stop to explore the nearby grottoes of the **Cueva del Tesoro**. According to legend, this is where the Moorish emirs hid their treasure, though the loot has never been found. After a trip to the caves, head for local favourite **Bar Marisqueria La Alegría** (Paseo Maritimo El Carmen 87, mobile 678 41 99 15, closed dinner Mon, all Sun and Oct-Apr, €) for char-grilled sardines on a stick.

The next major settlement along the coast is **Torre del Mar**, the most Spanish of the resorts on this stretch of coast. It's less gloomy than it might first appear, especially since major improvement works in 2002. Should you end up here, there are some decent places to eat, and a large American-style mall, El Ingenio, with a 12-screen cinema – a useful fallback in bad weather. The Paseo de Larios has become the new heart of the city and is leafy and graceful, with numerous pavement cafés, tapas bars and fish restaurants (the pick is unglamorous-looking **La Cueva** at Paseo de Larios 12, 952 54 02 23, closed Mon, €). The seafront is likewise busy and bustling with bars, disco-pubs and seafood joints. Unfortunately, the beach itself, though long and wide, remains a fairly miserable-looking stretch of sand.

If you want pretty beaches but a lively resort, Nerja (*see p79*), a further 21 kilometres (13 miles) east, has no competition along this stretch of coast.

## The Axarquía

Far more appealing than the built-up coast is the rolling interior, known as the **Axarquía**, which stretches back from the sea towards the hills that mark the border with Granada province. This white village-specked region

is easily accessible from Málaga, and is slowly being discovered by tourists in search of an alternative holiday. It's a good winter destination, when cooler temperatures are kinder to walkers, and the hotels, restaurants and bars that stay open are real travellers' rests, warmed by wood-burning fires and serving hearty, home cooking.

Despite attempts to preserve the area for rural tourism, development, mainly in the form of faux-white village *urbanizaciones*, is slowly creeping its way into the hills, and there is a real danger that more intensive exploitation of the Axarquía might be on the way (*see p77* **Going, going, gone?**)

The capital of the Axarquía is the busy town of **Vélez-Málaga**, just four kilometres (2.5 miles) inland from Torre del Mar. In 1487 this was one of the last Moorish strongholds to fall to Christian forces. The (restored) tower of the Moorish castle still looks over the largely modern town, which is a pleasant place for a wander, containing a handful of interesting *palacios* and churches. The best day to visit is Wednesday, when a lively street market takes place; plans for a regular 'medieval' market on the Paseo Nuevo, at least one weekend a month, look set to go ahead – check with the tourist office for details.

It's worth exploring the more out-of-the-way villages, such as **Comares**, one of the highest settlements in Andalucía; **El Borge**, tucked into a hollow in a valley; **Sedella**, a Moorish village rarely visited by tourists, though that is likely to change when the region's new walking centre opens here sometime in 2005; and **Periana**, which presides over the **Embalse de la Viñuela**, where you can rent pedalos to mess about on the glassy reservoir. An enjoyable drive follows the main A335 up through the impressive Zafarraya pass, into western Granada province and on to Alhama de Granada (*see p270*).

Marking the eastern boundary of the Axarquía and Málaga province is a *jamón*-shaped hunk of mountainous national reserve known as the **Sierra de Tejeda**. Less than an hour's drive from Málaga, and very handy from Nerja, it offers a convenient foray into the wilds, and superb hiking trails, horse-riding and wildlife-spotting opportunities.

For a long time this area was a notorious haunt of *bandoleros* (bandits), who preyed upon traders carrying produce from Granada to the coast. Later, guerrillas used the craggy outpost as a camp during the Civil War. Interested visitors can hike the Ruta del Acebuchal Puerto Blanquillo, following a marked trail from the roadside (the first left heading north from Frigiliana). It takes about two hours each way.

*Málaga Province*

Just seven kilometres (four miles) north of Nerja, the whitewashed houses of **Frigiliana** cling to the flank of the Sierra de Tejeda like limpets to a rock. This is the most visited of the villages of the Axarquía, and it is incredibly pretty; so much so that it has become something of a theme park. If you have your own transport it is far more pleasant to visit in the early evening when most of the daytrippers have returned to the coast. Frigiliana is developing at a shocking rate, with multi-storied apartment blocks springing up all around the pretty centre. The old town, however, is picture-perfect, with ornately patterned cobblestoned streets, and flowers and ferns tumbling out of every available windowsill, wheelbarrow and watering can in town. It's also not a bad place for stocking up on local ceramics, olive-wood bowls and the local sweet wines, the once-revered 'Málaga-sack'. There's a market in the village on Wednesdays. For good historical tours contact 952 53 42 40, www.frigiliana.com (€5).

The conical hill, **El Fuerte**, that rises up behind Frigiliana makes a decent early evening hike. Just climb the steep streets out of the old town and follow your nose until the cobblestones turn to dusty goat tracks and the whitewashed homes are replaced by fig trees and views of the Mediterranean. It was here that the 1569 rebellion of the Moriscos was finally defeated.

Heading north of the town, the valleys and ridges become less populated, save for the odd itinerant goat grazing on the steps and terraces where farmers grow their citrus and avocado crops. As the road to the village of **Cómpeta** reaches higher ground, these are replaced with olive groves and vines. Originally a Moorish settlement, there's not a great deal to see or do here except enjoy the tranquillity of the place, and sample Cómpeta's most prized product: Jaral. All the bars here serve it. If you happen to be in the village on 15 August, the annual festival – Noche del Vino – celebrates the grape and its harvest by doling out as much free wine as the revellers can handle.

### Cueva del Tesoro

*A7-E15, Rincón de la Victoria (952 40 61 62/ www.sopde.es/naturaleza).* **Guided tours** *Mid June-mid Sept* 10.45am, 11.30am, 12.15pm, 1pm, 4.45pm, 5.30pm, 6.15pm, 7pm daily. *Mid Sept-mid June* 10.45am, 11.30am, 12.15pm, 1pm, 3.45pm, 4.30pm, 5.15pm daily. **Admission** (incl guided tour in English) €4.10; €2.40 concessions. **No credit cards.**

## Where to stay & eat

The Axarquía is full of small, out-of-the-way places to stay and eat, and nearly all of them are blessed with spectacular settings and superb views. Just 30 minutes' drive from the coast in El Borge, the stone cottage of **Posada del Bandolero** (C/Cristo 1, El Borge, 952 51 94 50, double €35-€40, restaurant closed Wed) is a treat. Andalucía's answer to Dick Turpin, Luis Muñoz García, was born here, and the inn, with its crooked beams and cobbled floors, oozes old-fashioned warmth and character; it also has a good regional restaurant.

In the northern Axarquía, where the olive terraces finally give way to bald-headed peaks of navy granite, the **Venta de Alfarnate** (Antigua Carretera de Málaga–Granada, km513, 952 75 93 88, closed June-Sept, €€-€€€) stands on the outskirts of Alfarnate. Believed to be the oldest functioning inn in Andalucía, dating back to the early 1800s, it was once notorious for harbouring the bandits and highwaymen who terrorised travellers on the old road from Málaga to Granada, while at the same time providing shelter for such dignitaries as King Alfonso XIII. Dig in to meaty dishes in a jumble of different dining rooms, most with crackling fires. Should you wish to stay and explore the area on foot, **Cortijo Pulgarín Bajo** (Alfarnatejo, 952 46 23 02, mobile 620 05 97 87, €120 for a 2-bed house for a weekend, €300 for a week) gives a taste of *finca* living. Old-fashioned and basic, the *cortijo*'s big draws are feeling like you've travelled back in time, and the bracing mountain scenery. A more modern touch is the good-sized pool.

On the edge of the Sierra de Tejeda in Sedella, **La Casa Pinta** (952 50 89 55, www.lacasapinta.com, double €48) is the only place to stay in town, and commands a spectacular position on a ridge above it. The recently decorated rooms are cool and spacious, and have tea- and coffee-making facilities. In the restaurant you can expect English and Spanish dishes (all made with local produce) and an internet terminal.

Across the valley in the small lakeside village of Puente Don Manuel, near Alcaucín, the British-run **Hotel Romero** (A335, 952 51 08 04, double €55), has ten rooms, a cosy living area and lively bar and restaurant.

For a retreat-style holiday, **Montaña Palmera** (El Cañuelo, Periana, 952 53 65 06, www.montanapalmera.com, closed Nov, double €53) offers week-long yoga courses, trips to local hot springs and massage. A great hideout for people travelling alone and peace-loving couples (no kids allowed), it also has a pretty swimming pool overlooking the rolling hills.

Above Frigiliana, the mountaintop **Hotel Los Caracoles** (Carretera Frigiliana–Torrox, km4.6, 952 03 06 09, www.hotelloscaracoles.com, double €59-€83, caracol room €78-€110), inspired by Gaudí's creations in Barcelona, is the most unusual hotel in the area. The spiral-shaped

# Going, going, gone?

Some people just don't know when they're on to a good thing. Such is the case in the Axarquía, for many years one of the Costa del Sol's best-kept secrets: an area of pristine walking country and sea views, snow-white *pueblos blancos* barely changed in centuries and superb flora and fauna.

Now, as boom coastal towns like Nerja are beginning to run out of space to expand and developers are belatedly waking up to the potential of the eastern Costa del Sol, encroaching building works are sneaking their way up the valleys. As the economics of small-scale farming get more and more dicey, many farmers are happy to take the easy money and sell their land for construction.

A decade ago the eastern part of Málaga province had just 20 hotels, most of them in Nerja. Today, with a massive push in the direction of rural tourism and vast numbers of expats moving into the area, there are more than 400 *casas rurales* (country home-style accommodation) spread across 27 villages.

But is yet more development really the answer? Recent reports from the Costa del Sol's tourism board points to stagnation in the tourist industry. Visits, particularly on the western Costa, are down on previous years and the length of time that people are staying is also decreasing. Resorts like Torremolinos are struggling to fill their hotel rooms.

The south's largest tour operator, Servitour, has gone so far as to put forward a motion to decrease the number of budget airlines flying into Málaga because they attract the wrong kind of tourist – the skint kind, that is. Even the tourism board president, Juan Fraile, recognises that the area is no longer Europe's number-one spot for sun-seekers. The points most criticised by tourists are beach cleanliness, over-development, traffic, public transport and infrastructure.

On the positive side, the Axarquía is making concerted efforts to prevent itself going the way of the Costa del Sol by actively promoting the area for rural tourism and adventure sports. New land laws introduced in 2003 have succeeded in cracking down on illegal construction works in rural areas of the Axarquía by fining developers heavily, with the result that illegal building has fallen between 50 and 90 per cent.

All good news until you hear about the battle between the golfing conglomerates –

the scourge of water-starved southern Spain – and the ecologists. Golf means big fat euro signs to developers, but the cost to the environment is astronomical. Nerja has been fighting for its own 18-hole golf course for more than 16 years. If it gets the go-ahead, it would eat into huge chunks of the Sierra Tejeda Natural Park. The regional government opposed the proposal. However, by the end of 2003 a bid of 15.1 million euros by Med Group Development had been accepted. The project is currently stalled over boundary issues, and, some suspect, for political reasons – a new 18-hole golf course in the east would threaten golfing interests on the western Costa.

Still more worrying are Vélez-Málaga Town Council's proposals for huge new residential zones throughout the area, and as many as eight new golf courses.

'It's a contradiction between concepts of development,' said Rafael Yus, the president of GENA – Ecologists in Action, which has been active in the area for 20 years. 'For some, development should imitate the western Costa del Sol: building in the country, more golf courses, more marina leisure complexes. For others, development could be of a higher aesthetic quality and be environmentally friendly. Quantity or quality, that's the question.'

So, let the golfers go west, and save what redeeming features the eastern Costa del Sol still has left. There is still time, but is the will there?

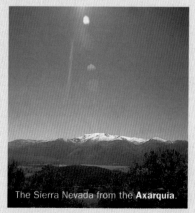

The Sierra Nevada from the **Axarquía**.

The **Balcón de Europa**, **Nerja**. *See p80*.

**Vélez-Málaga**'s Moorish tower. *See p75.*

cottages (*caracol* means 'snail') have living areas and private terraces, ideal for a romantic getaway. There's a good Moorish-influenced restaurant too (€-€€, closed Mon and Jan & Feb). Another good bet is the 12-room **Hotel Rural La Posada Morisca** (Loma de la Cruz, Carretera Montaña Frigiliana–Torrox, 952 53 41 51, www.laposadamorisca.com, double €85, restaurant €€, closed lunch and all Sun) built along a ridge just above Frigiliana. All rooms have terraces and wood-burning stoves, making it an especially snug choice out of season, and the views are magnificent. The restaurant offers interesting salads, such as watercress and eel, and unfussy mains.

In Frigiliana, the recently opened **Hotel Villa Frigiliana** (C/San Sebastián, 952 53 33 93, www.villafrigiliana.com, double €73-€103) is closer to a four-star than its three-star badge might convey. Rooms are spacious and pleasant – the best are on the fourth floor and have their own terraces. There's a swimming pool too.

Frigiliana has numerous places to eat, but the best is the atmospheric **La Bodeguilla** (C/Chorruelo 7, 952 53 41 16, €), consisting of a series of heavily planted, interconnecting *plazitas* off a tiny street. Rosario started the restaurant from her living room 20 years ago, and now, with the help of her four daughters, she knocks out exemplary regional cooking. Alternatively, the **Garden Restaurant** (follow signs from the town centre, 952 53 31 85, closed Tue, €€-€€€) is set in an elegant, lush garden, tucked into the side of the mountain, with wonderful views and a varied menu of barbecue ribs, Thai curries and Greek salads.

In Cómpeta, very pleasant self-catering accommodation is available at **Casa La Piedra** (Plazoleta 17, 952 51 63 29, casa@2sandra.com, double €70). **Las Tres Abejas** (C/Panaderos 43/45, 952 55 33 73, mobile 628 06 97 03, www.lastresabejas.com, double €48) is a cosy, pint-sized B&B, with friendly British owners and plenty of cute features, such as a plunge pool on the upper roof terrace. The village's wonderful wood-stove bakery is opposite. Alternatively, the three-star **El Balcón de Cómpeta** (C/San Antonio 75, 952 55 35 35, €64-€79) has the usual mod cons, plus tennis courts and a good swimming pool – ask for a room with a balcony.

The **Museo del Vino** (Avenida Constitución 6, 952 55 33 14, closed Mon, €) is a fun, atmospheric place for wine and tapas, while the tiny *finca* **Bodegas Almijara**, a couple of kilometres out of town (Carretera de Canillas de Albaida, 952 55 32 85) does free tastings for potential customers. For eats, the long-established **El Pilón** (C/Laberinto, 952 55 35 12, €-€€) is a firm favourite for grills, and also does an excellent pot-roasted rabbit dish. For top-quality Spanish nosh, head uptown to **Cortijo Paco** (Avenida Canillas 6, 952 55 36 47, mobile 657 32 44 91, www.cortijopaco.com, closed Mon and June-Aug, €-€€).

## Resources

### Internet
**Vélez-Málaga** *Ciber-Café Intern@te, C/Doctor Laureano Casquero, Bajo 5 (952 50 44 54).* **Open** 10am-midnight Mon-Sat; 4pm-midnight Sun.

### Police station
**Frigiliana** *Plaza del Ingenio (658 79 27 51).* **Vélez-Málaga** *Plaza de San Roque s/n (952 54 92 38).*

### Post office
**Frigiliana** *C/Den Inmán 1 (no phone).* **Vélez-Málaga** *Plaza San Roque 12 (952 50 01 43).*

### Tourist information
**Cómpeta** *Plaza Almijara s/n (952 55 33 01).* **Open** *July-Aug* 10am-2pm Tue-Sat; *Sept-June* 10am-2pm Wed-Sun. **Frigiliana** *Plaza del Ingenio s/n (952 53 31 26).* **Open** 10am-2pm Mon, Wed-Sat. **Torre del Mar/Vélez-Málaga** *Paseo de Larios s/n (952 54 11 04).* **Open** 8am-3pm Mon-Fri.

## Nerja

Around 50 kilometres (30 miles) east of Málaga, **Nerja** is one of the very few towns on the Costa del Sol that has not had its charms submerged under a sea of concrete. Since the 1960s boom in tourism, this once tiny fishing village has grown to a population of around 16,000, of whom a fifth are foreign residents (75 per cent of these are British) – you are more likely to hear English spoken than any other language. Wedged between the Mediterranean and the umber, ice-cream-cone peaks of the Sierra de Tejeda, it's difficult to beat the town as a base for exploring the Axarquía.

Nerja's focal point is the **Balcón de Europa**, justly famed as one of the most beautiful promenades on the coast. Built on the site of a Moorish castle, it juts out towards the sea, flanked by towering palms and lined with ice-cream vendors, cafés, dried fruit and nut stands, and the odd touristy horse and carriage.

But if you really want to get a taste of how things were before the boom, follow the town wall west of the Balcón to **El Salón** beach. Its scrubby cliffs made development impossible and the only buildings you'll see are two or three small fishing cottages. Sadly, cliff erosion is occurring at such an alarming rate that the old cliff path that connected all the town's beaches is unlikely to open again. The horseshoe shaped *playas* **Carabeo** and **Calahonda**, however, are still easily accessed via steps from the old town.

Nerja really comes alive in the summer, particularly during the festival of San Isidro, which takes place in the caves in May, and on the Eve of San Juan in July, which features the best beach party of the year. Young and old gather on the strands at midnight and stagger backwards into the sea, before dancing till dawn.

By far the biggest attraction in the area is the **Cueva de Nerja**, which dates back five million years. This spectacular series of caves resembles something from Tolkien. The grand central column in Cataclysm Hall, at 32 metres (105 feet) high, is the tallest in the world and took 1,000 billion drops of water to form. It is possible to take spelunking tours of the caves by prior arrangement, and if you happen to be in town at the end of July,

do check out the **International Festival of Music and Dance**, which takes place here.

Another draw is Nerja's enjoyable Tuesday morning market (9.30am-2pm), based around Calle Chanquete in the east part of town.

If you want to escape the crowds (other than on summer weekends and throughout August), head for the beautiful – naturist-friendly – beach of **Cantariján**, ten kilometres (six miles) east of Nerja, which has a couple of excellent *chiringuitos* that can rustle up a mean paella.

There's no shortage of adventure sports and activities available in the area. **Scuba Nerja** (Playa Burriana, 952 52 72 51, www.scubanerja. com) runs one- and two-tank dives, and offers day trips aboard its catamaran along the coast, stopping at one of the area's best beaches for a paella lunch. **Cortijo Hidalgo** (Castillo Alto, Casa 73E, 952 52 10 23) organises horseback tours of the nearby Sierra Tejeda.

### Cueva de Nerja

*Carretera Maro (952 52 95 20).* **Open** *July, Aug* 10am-2pm, 4-8pm daily. *Sept-June* 10am-2pm, 4-6.30pm daily. **Admission** €5; €2.50 concessions. **No credit cards**.

## Where to eat

There are about 300 bars and restaurants in Nerja, some of them excellent, others way south of mediocre. However, the scene is varied and offers a good many international options for a town its size. Among the stars is **Scarletta's** (C/Cristo 38, 952 52 00 11, closed Sun and mid Nov-mid Feb, €€-€€€), a trendy eaterie with bags of style and a firm focus on top-quality ingredients. The menu offers a range of classics from around the world, from Thai curries and barbecue ribs to fat, juicy *gambas pil-pil* (prawns fried in garlic). It has two outside terraces.

Following a close second, **Mama Rosa's** (C/Chaparil, 952 52 12 62, closed Sun and July, Aug, €) serves up delicious Spanish home cooking. And for mammoth portions of home-

Picture-perfect **Frigiliana**. *See p76.*

made pasta and 28 different sauces, try **El Gato Negro** (C/Carabeo 19, 952 52 56 11, €€), an intimate little Italian bistro decorated with baroque drapes, stone statues and a painted ceiling. It doubles as a shrine to Pavarotti, whose hits will serenade you through dinner.

For traditional tapas, Nerja has a handful of options. Among the best are **Los Mariscos** (C/Cristo 17, 952 52 27 14, closed Mon and mid-Nov-Jan, €), which specialises in fried fish and seafood *raciones*, served in two simple interior patios, and **Esquina Paulina** (C/Almirante Ferrandiz 45, 952 52 21 81, closed Sun and Nov & Dec, €), where you can munch on platters of cured meats, cheeses, anchovies and olives.

On the international circuit, the **Taste of India** (C/Carabeo 51, 952 50 00 43, €€-€€€) has an extensive menu. Or, for something a little more wacky (and for great food and friendly service), check out the cave-like interior and colourful decor of Mexican restaurant **El Cielito Lindo** (C/El Barrio 26, 952 52 36 21, €€-€€€). Specials include a gargantuan spear of chargrilled meats.

A once quiet fishing beach, Playa Burriana is now chock-full of eateries, bars and *chiringuitos* barbecuing fish out of old Nerja fishing boats. Favourites remain **Merendero Ayo** (Playa Burriana s/n, 952 52 22 89, €) for paella cooked in a giant pan over open flames, and the Belgian-owned **Nerja de Nerja** (Playa Burriana, 952 52 09 28, closed Wed, €-€€) for mussels and seriously stiff drinks.

For panoramic views over the Med, **El Ancladero** (Playa El Capistrano, 952 52 19 55, closed Tue Oct-May and 2wks Dec-Jan, €-€€) commands an enviable position on the clifftop above the beach, and has a pleasant swimming pool and patio. The menu offers seafood, steaks and a selection of English favourites, and there are flamenco shows on Saturdays.

For posh nosh, head for the restaurant in the apart-hotel **Pepe Rico** (Almirante Ferrandiz 28, 952 52 02 47, closed Sun, €€€); the setting is a little formal, but the food is superb – strong on fish and with a choice of vegetarian meals too.

## Where to drink/nightlife

One of Nerja's prettiest bars, the **Mirador del Bendito Café** (no phone), is hacked into the cliff just beneath Plaza Cueva del Bendito, offering shade beneath lovely palm-thatched umbrellas in a luxuriant sub-tropical garden.

Most of the dancing and late-night drinking places (open until 4 or 5am) are found around Calle Antonio Millón and Plaza Tutti-Frutti (both north-west of the Balcón). **La Iguana** (C/Antonio Millón C/1, Edificio Jábega II, no phone) and **Casbah** are two of the most

Nerja's Balcón de Europa. *See p80.*

popular hang-out joints. **Cayma** (C/Cristo 56, no phone) is good for '60s, '70s and '80s disco music. Try **Jimmy's** (C/Antonio Millón C/6, Edificio Venus, 952 52 19 15, closed mid Sept-May) for a boogie or **Castillo** (C/Diputación 12, no phone), one of the best discos in town.

There are innumerable places offering flamenco *espectáculos* (shows) at varying prices and with varying degrees of talent. **El Colono** (C/Granada 6, 952 52 18 26, mobile 670 86 78 01, dinner shows 9pm, 10pm, 11pm Wed, Fri) claims to stage *flamenco puro*. Reservations are recommended for this twice-weekly dinner-dance extravaganza; tickets cost from €25. **El Burro Blanco** (C/Gloria 3, no phone) is more casual and has raucous singing and dancing every night from 10pm.

## Where to stay

There is no shortage of options, and the quality is generally high. Calle Pintada is home to several budget *hostales*, all similar in price and quality. One of the best cheap places is the centrally located **Hostal Miguel** (C/Almirante Ferrandiz 33, 952 52 15 23, www.hostalmiguel.com, double €27-€45), which was taken over by a young, enthusiastic English couple in 2004. This popular eight-room *hostal* is set to become something altogether more funky, with updated decor, a cool new lounge area and a revamped roof terrace.

Málaga Province

# Walk Cómpeta circuit

**Distance** 9km (5 miles)
**Time required** 4-4.5 hours

This easy circuit is a good introduction to the hills, valleys and irrigated terraces around Cómpeta. It passes through two of the region's prettiest villages, and there's a lovely section of path along the river Cájula.

The walk begins in Cómpeta in the Plaza de la Almijara, next to the church of Nuestra Señora de la Asunción. Leave the *plaza* at its top, left-hand corner and go along Calle de San Antonio. You pass the Museo del Jamón and the *consultorio*, the hotel Balcón de Cómpeta and then the Chapel of San Antón. Just after the chapel you come to a three-way split in the road. The street that you have been following bears right, another goes left, but you should take the middle way, a concrete section of road that drops steeply down and after just 20 metres (65 feet) becomes a path. It leads you down through groves of citrus, crosses a stream and then comes to fork in the path. Take the left fork that leads you towards a modern house with a row of cypress trees to its right.

The path passes just to the right of the house and then meets with the Cómpeta/Canillas road. Turn left here and continue until you are opposite a house with a white bench, Casa Paraíso. Here turn right off the road by the Jaral vineyard (tastings possible) onto a track. The first section is paved. Continue past Casa Mimosa, sticking to the main track. Ignore a track that leads off to the right. Soon you begin to descend through the almond groves and come to a point where a fence with green netting runs just left of the track. Turn right here onto another track that drops steeply down through the terraces of olives, almonds and vines. The village of Árchez soon comes into view. Pass beneath some pylons and you will then see a line of concrete posts to your left.

Leave the track at this point and pick up a narrow path that drops down, indistinctly at first, following the line of pylons. It soon improves and leads you down past stands of agave, cacti and prickly pears. You pass a house to your left. Here the path becomes paved for a short section. You come to a tarmac road.

Turn right here and soon you'll reach the outskirts of Árchez. Go past Bar Avenida, the *consultorio* and *Ayuntamiento* and you arrive at the Plazuela Mudéjar with its beautiful 13th-century *alminar* (minaret). Leave the square via the narrow street just to the right of the *alminar*. It passes a ceramic painting depicting the village's history.

Turn right at the end of this street onto a track that hugs the right bank of the River Cájula and passes an old mill, La Fábrica. You cross the river on stepping stones, pass by a second mill and then cross back to the right bank of the river.

Shortly you'll reach a red marker post, next to a grove of avocado trees, with an ugly concrete-posted fence. Careful! Don't go right here but swing left, cross the river again (you may see a cairn on the other side) and climb up the left bank on a steep track.

On the seafront, the **Hostal Marazul** (Avenida del Mediterráneo, 952 52 41 91, double €30-€47) is another good deal; all rooms are sea-facing and the best have private sun terraces. On the other side of the Balcón, **Hostal Tres Soles** (C/Carabeo 40, 952 52 51 57, double €29-€43) is clean and simple, with all mod cons, including satellite TV, and is very kid-friendly.

If you want to stay on the Balcón, the four-star **Hotel Balcón de Europa** (Paseo Balcón de Europa 1, 952 52 08 00, double €89-€157) is the best-known option, but for a fraction of the cost, the **Hostal Marissal** (Paseo Balcón de Europa 3, 952 52 01 99, www.marissal.net, double €40-€60, restaurant €€-€€€) next door is highly recommended. Located above a good bar-restaurant, its immaculate rooms are superb value for money. Nearby, the three-star **Hotel Cavana** (Plaza Cavana 10, 952 52 40 00, double €80-€110) is modern, if a little clinical. Its main selling points are indoor and rooftop pools, a sauna and a jacuzzi.

The most luxurious place to stay in town is the **Parador de Nerja** (C/Almuñécar 8, 952 52 00 50, www.parador.es, double €104-€112), despite an exterior that resembles a multi-storey car park. It has spacious, elegant bedrooms (most are sea-facing), manicured lawns, two swimming pools, tennis courts, a restaurant and piano bar. It's worth enquiring about the multitude of different packages on offer.

If you're after boutique-style accommodation, two places stand out. The **Hotel Paraíso del Mar** (C/Prolongación de Carabeo 22, 952 25 16 21, www.hotelparaisodelmar.com, double €64-€150) has wonderful terraced gardens carved

Just 150 metres (525 feet) after crossing the river, at a point where the track narrows, you come to an old carob tree. Here branch left onto a narrow mule track that zigzags steeply uphill, crosses a water channel, passes more carob trees and then merges with a dirt track. The track leads up to a small farm where it bends right and along a ridge from where there are good views of Canillas.

The road forks. Go right and climb towards a house with a round tower. Don't branch up to the house but rather keep to the main track. You'll soon pass a farm with buttressed walls and high palm trees. The track meets with a paved road where you turn right down the hill.

After just 150 metres (500 feet), branch off on a narrow track that descends to the river. As you descend you can see the track on the other side of the valley that you soon must follow, twisting its way up to Canillas.

You cross the River Cájula via a pretty old bridge, wind up to the road, turn right and, after just 25 metres (82 feet), turn left onto the narrow path you could see earlier. The path leads you up towards Canillas.

When you come to a paved road, bear left, wind up to a green railing, and continue climbing. You enter the village along Calle La Plazoleta. Bearing right at the end, you reach the main square. Either Bar Romero or Restaurante La Plaza would make a good stop for refreshments. Remember that you now have a short, steep section of the walk to negotiate.

At the end of the square, climb Calle Hornos to house no.13, where you swing left, then sharp right, and continue climbing. At the next fork bear right. Then at the next junction, go left and carry on up Calle Canovas del Castillo. You come to another fork. Here take the right option and climb steeply towards an ugly breeze-block wall and soon you reach the Ermita de Santa Ana.

Climb up to the *ermita* for great panoramic views. When you leave the chapel, take the track that leads away from the main porch, back down to the tarmac road. Here you'll see two dirt tracks. Don't go left (signposted Zona Recreativa La Fábrica) but rather bear right and climb up towards an olive grove, passing by a large water deposit to the left of the track.

Continue on up the track for ten metres (32 feet), and after a second water deposit you reach a fork in the track. Here, bear right, pass just to the left of a pylon, descend and then bear sharply left on a track that passes above a house with a swimming pool. It narrows to become a path that runs beside an irrigation channel. Stick to the main path, which eventually meets with a new tarmac road. Turn right here and after 270 metres (880 feet), at a cairn in front of an oleander bush, bear left and pick up the path, which runs towards Cómpeta through a beautiful swathe of irrigated terraces.

Eventually the path becomes a track and then meets with the road. Go right here, and then left, and retrace your footsteps along the Calle de San Antonio to the main square. *From* Walking in Andalucía *by Guy Hunter-Watts (Santana)*

out of the cliff leading down to Burriana beach. Alternatively, in the neighbouring village of Maro (about three kilometres/two miles east of Nerja), **Hotel Romantico Casa Maro** (952 52 95 52, www.hotel-casa-maro.com, double €40-€89, restaurant €€-€€€) offers cliff-top views, cute bedrooms and an intimate covered terrace. It's also a good place for fish and seafood.

## Resources

### Internet
*Europaweb, C/Málaga s/n (952 52 61 47).*
**Open** *June-Aug* 10am-midnight daily. *Sept-May* 10am-10pm daily.

### Police station
*C/Virgen de Pilar 1 (952 52 15 45).*

### Post office
*C/Almirante Ferrandiz 6 (952 52 17 49).*

### Tourist information
*Puerta del Mar 2 (952 52 15 31/www.nerja.org).*
**Open** 10am-2pm, 5-8pm Mon-Fri; 10am-1pm Sat.

## Getting there

There's no public transport in the Montes de Málaga, and very little in the Axarquía, so renting a car is advisable.

### By bus
Alsina Graells (952 52 15 04) runs hourly buses from Málaga to Nerja (via main towns on the coast), and 3 a day from Nerja to Cómpeta. An hourly bus runs daily from Nerja to Frigiliana. Frequent buses run from Torre del Mar to Vélez-Málaga.

# North of Málaga

A treasure trove of history, both man-made and natural.

Antequera.

## Antequera

Málaga and the Costa del Sol may be less than half-an-hour's drive away to the south, but the unique town of **Antequera** feels a world away from the excesses of the kiss-me-quick coast, and provides one of the region's historical and architectural showpieces. Nestled among steep, rugged mountain peaks, it is a thriving settlement of around 40,000 inhabitants, with a perfectly preserved ancient centre and some world-class prehistoric sights. Boasting everything from Neolithic dolmens to a ninth-century Moorish castle and some of Andalucía's finest baroque interiors, the town encapsulates the history of the entire region, which, in the last 2,000 years, has passed through Roman, Arab and Christian hands. The result is a fascinating synthesis of all three periods.

Known even to the Romans as 'Antiquaria' or the 'Ancient City', Antequera was probably a significant settlement as far back as 2,500 BC. The size and sophistication of the town's three dolmens, which would have required hundreds of men to build them, suggest the presence of a large, well-organised prehistoric community of nobles and workers with powerful leaders and strong religious beliefs. With the arrival of the Romans in the first century AD came great wealth and magnificent villas. One such mansion is currently being excavated near the station, an effort that has already revealed an outstanding set of mosaics and priceless artefacts (now on show at the town's Museo Municipal, *see p85*). Recognising Antequera's strategic importance (and therefore vulnerability), the Moors, who took control of the area in the ninth century, endowed it with an imposing Alcazaba (hilltop castle). It was, however, one of the first Granadan border fortresses to fall during the *reconquista*, in 1410. Under Spanish Christian rule, the town expanded both literally (down into the plains) and culturally, emerging as a prestigious centre of literature and learning during the 16th century. Elsewhere, fine palaces and churches continued to be built right up until the late 19th century to create the Antequera you see today.

### Sightseeing

Get hold of a street map at the tourist office on the central Plaza San Sebastián and start your tour at the **Arco de los Gigantes**. Located in the oldest part of town on Calle Colegio, this imposing triumphal arch was erected in 1585 by Felipe II, who decorated it with Roman sculptures, tableaux and fragments. Known as Spain's oldest (and smallest) open-air museum, the arch can be climbed via a stone stairway.

The same stairway leads to the medieval **Alcazaba**, which occupies the highest point in the town. Once a great defensive fortress, it is now reduced to a collection of expertly restored exterior walls that have been incorporated into a simple but lovely formal garden, largely comprising cypresses and yews. The most complete structures within the Alcazaba are two keeps, one of which, the **Torre del Homenaje**, can normally be visited (10am-2pm Tue-Sun, free). Before leaving the castle, take a moment to admire the distant view of **La Peña de los Enamorados** (Lovers' Rock), known colloquially as 'Franco's Nose'. Shaped like the head of a sleeping giant, this huge natural formation is located halfway between Antequera and neighbouring Archidona. Its official name comes from a touching local legend about a Moorish girl and a Christian boy who fell in love shortly before the conquest of Granada in 1492. Realising they could never be together, the young couple hurled themselves from the top of the rock, choosing togetherness in death over life apart.

Just beyond the triumphal arch and castle stands the **Real Colegiata de Santa María la Mayor**. Constructed between 1514 and 1550, the church is the principal feature of the beautifully proportioned Plaza de los Escribanos. The exterior, set against dramatic mountain scenery, is notable for its elegant early Renaissance façade. A plaque describing the prestigious Professorship of Grammar that was established in the church college during the 16th century indicates Antequera's religious and intellectual importance at that time. The college became an important focal point for humanists and poets, producing revered bards such as Pedro Espinosa, whose statue stands in front of the church.

Beyond the imposing, Arab-style door is an elegant interior, with a fine Mudéjar *artesanado* ceiling. Notice the small side chapel (on the left as you enter), which contains Roman remains. Just before you reach the altar there is another, larger side chapel with a lovely Moorish-style wooden ceiling and some delicate stucco work around the paintings. Before leaving the square, take a moment to admire the excavated Roman baths to one side of Santa María.

If Santa María is arresting thanks to its austerity, the nearby church of **El Carmen** is precisely the opposite. Located just below Plaza de los Escribanos on Plaza El Carmen, it boasts

a stunningly elaborate late-baroque interior hidden away behind a deceptively simple façade. Its *retablo* is one of the most intricate in all Andalucía, and an excellent example of the churrigueresque style. Carved in unpainted red pine, it is littered with delicately sculpted biblical figures, saints, bishops and angels. Away from the altar, every inch of the church is decorated with frescoes and ornate stucco-work.

From Plaza El Carmen, descend Cuesta de los Rojas to reach the **Museo Conventual de las Descalzas**, the first of the town's two small but interesting museums. Housed in a 17th-century convent built for the Barefoot (*descalzas*) Carmelites, it contains a substantial collection of religious art, including a painting by Lucas Giordano of St Teresa of Avila, the 16th-century founder of the religious order. Note that at the time of writing, the museum was closed for renovation.

Around the corner, on Plaza del Coso Viejo, Antequera's excellent **Museo Municipal** occupies a beautiful 18th-century palace with a fine Mudéjar-baroque bell tower. Once the private residence of the aristocratic Nájera family, the *palacio* has an interior courtyard now used to display Roman artefacts, and several exhibition rooms containing – among other things – a collection of 17th-century paintings by the Mexican artist Juan Correa, a rare 18th-century statue of the pregnant Virgin Mary and a surprisingly lifelike portrait of St Francis by Pedro de Mena. The museum's prize exhibit, however, is a complete Roman bronze of a nude boy known as 'Ephebus of Antequera'. The statue, which stands 1.4 metres (4.6 feet) high, is one of only six such figures in the world and is probably the finest piece of Roman sculpture in Spain. Unearthed on a local farm in the 1950s (note the hole in his back where the tractor hit the metal), the graceful young man, who dates from the first century AD, is a typical Roman toy boy and a superb example of the sensual nature of Imperial art at that time; it was found at a Roman villa located near the station. The villa is still being excavated, but when it eventually opens to the public, it will be a world-class archaeological site thanks to its spectacular mosaics, a large proportion of which remain intact.

Antequera's historical wealth means that it possesses a disproportionately large number of architecturally significant churches. One of the most striking is **San Sebastián** (open hours of services), a 16th-century building on Plaza San Sebastián, which succeeded Santa María as the town's principal centre of learning in the late 17th century. Located next to a fin-de-siècle palace, the church's exterior has two outstanding and somewhat contradictory features: a

Renaissance-style façade adorned with statues of saints Paul, Peter and Sebastian, plus Emperor Carlos V's coat of arms; and a graceful baroque-Mudéjar tower, constructed in the early 18th century with intricate brickwork and a glazed ceramic spire crowned by a weathercock.

From Plaza San Sebastián, take Calle Cuesta de la Paz and follow it all the way to Plaza El Portichuelo, an enchanting square containing the pretty church of **Jesús** (open 10am-12.30pm daily). It was constructed in the 18th century in baroque-Mudéjar style using pink and white bricks, and incorporates the **Capilla Tribuna del Portichuelo**, which houses the Virgen del Socorro, a key focus in the town's Semana Santa celebrations. Further north, the simple 18th-century church of **Santiago** (open hours of services) stands practically side-by-side at the junction of Cuesta de Archidona and Calle de Belén with the ornate 17th-century baroque **Convento de Belén** (open 8am-5.30pm daily).

What most distinctively marks out Antequera from other southern Spanish towns, however, are its three Neolithic dolmens (burial chambers), located on the north-eastern outskirts of town, which rate as some of the most important prehistoric remains in the country. The largest and oldest, **Dólmen de Viera** and **Dólmen de Menga**, are only a short distance from the city centre on the Archidona–Granada road (if you're on foot, turn right down Calle Belén by the church of Santiago, following the 'Dólmenes' sign for ten minutes). The Menga dolmen (roughly 4,500 years old and probably the tomb of an important nobleman) consists of a huge underground gallery lined with 32 vertical stone slabs, the largest of which weighs 180 tonnes. Don't miss the engraved symbols and human figures at the entrance. Thought to be slightly more recent, the Viera dolmen has a long, narrow tunnel leading to a small burial chamber. (Out of normal opening hours you might well be approached by an old man who'll show you how to sneak in through a hole in the fence – in return for a couple of euros.) To reach **El Romeral** dolmen, continue on the same road past Menga and Viera for three kilometres (two miles). Turn left after the industrial estate following signs for Córdoba and Sevilla. After 500 metres (quarter of a mile), turn left at a roundabout and follow the signs for 'Dólmen El Romeral' (the tourist office has a map showing how to reach the dolmen if you have trouble locating it). Located under a mound in the grounds of a sugar factory, this is the most recent (a mere 3,800 years old) and most sophisticated of the three sites, with two domed brick chambers, the smallest of which would have been used for making offerings to the dead.

## El Carmen

*Plaza del Carmen (952 84 29 22).* **Open** *June-Sept* 10am-2pm, 5-8pm Mon-Sat; 10am-2pm Sun. *Oct-May* 10am-2pm, 4-7pm Mon-Sat; 10am-2pm Sun. **Admission** €1.50; €0.60 concessions. **No credit cards.**

## Dólmen el Romeral

*Cerro Romeral s/n (no phone).* **Open** 9am-3.30pm Tue; 9am-6pm Wed-Sat; 9.30am-2.30pm Sun. **Admission** free.

## Dólmenes de Viera & Menga

*Carretera Antequera–Archidona (no phone).* **Open** 9am-3.30pm Tue; 9am-6pm Wed-Sat; 9.30am-2.30pm Sun. **Admission** free.

## Museo Conventual de las Descalzas

*Plaza de las Descalzas 3 (952 84 19 59).* **Open** *July-Sept* 10am-1.30pm, 5-7pm Tue-Fri; 10am-noon Sat, Sun. *Oct-June* 10.30am-1.30pm, 5-6.30pm Tue-Fri; 10am-noon Sat, Sun. **Admission** €2.40. Obligatory guided tours every 30mins. **No credit cards.**

## Museo Municipal

*Palacio de Nájera, Plaza de Coso Viejo s/n (952 70 40 51).* **Open** *June* 9am-3pm Tue-Sun. *July-Sept* 10am-1.30pm, 8.30-10.30pm Tue-Fri; 10am-1.30pm Sat, Sun. *Oct-May* 10am-1.30pm, 4.30-6.30pm Tue-Fri; 10am-1.30pm Sat, Sun. **Admission** free under-18s. Obligatory guided tours every 30mins. **No credit cards.** Opening hours are subject to change, so call ahead.

## Real Colegiata de Santa María la Mayor

*Plaza de los Escribanos (952 84 61 43).* **Open** *June* 9am-3pm Tue-Fri; 10.30am-2pm Sat; 11.30am-2pm Sun. *July-mid Sept* 10.30am-2pm, 8.30-10.30pm Tue-Fri; 10.30am-2pm Sat; 11.30am-2pm Sun. *Mid Sept-May* 10.30am-2pm, 4.30-6.30pm Tue-Fri; 10.30am-2pm Sat; 11.30am-2pm Sun. **Admission** free.

---

# Where to eat & drink

Most of Antequera's (very limited) nightlife is to be found in the bars and tapas joints along Calle Alameda, near the bullring, to the west of the old town.

## El Angelote

*Plaza Coso Viejo (952 70 34 65).* **Open** noon-5pm, 7-11pm Tue-Sun. Closed 2wks Aug. **Average** €€. **Credit** AmEx, MC, V.

Next to the Museo Municipal, this is one of Antequera's best-known eateries. Local specialities such as *porra antequerana* (a dip like gazpacho before water is added) are served in a pleasant, rustic-style dining room.

## Bar-Restaurante Plaza San Sebastián

*Plaza San Sebastián 4 (952 84 42 39).* **Open** 7am-2.30am daily. **Average** €. **Credit** AmEx, MC, V.

Antequera's **Arco de los Gigantes**. *See p84.*

This central bar-restaurant-hotel (€39 double) draws tourists to its terrace and locals into its cavernous exterior for good simple tapas and *raciones*.

### Caserío de San Benito
*Carretera Córdoba–Málaga, km108 (952 11 11 03/ www.caseriodesanbenito.com).* **Open** *Mid July-mid Sept* noon-5pm, 8pm-midnight Tue-Sun. *Mid Sept-June* 8pm-midnight Fri-Sun. Closed 2wks early July. **Average** €€€. **Credit** AmEx, MC, V.
One of the region's best restaurants and well worth the 20-kilometre (12-mile) drive from Antequera. The dining room occupies the ground floor of a renovated farmhouse. Try the likes of *arroz con conejo* (rice with rabbit), and leave room for pudding.

### El Escribano
*Plaza de los Escribanos 11 (952 70 65 33).* **Open** *July-Sept* 11am-11.30pm Tue-Sun. *Oct-June* 11am-11.30pm Tue-Sat; 11am-4pm Sun. Closed 2wks Sept & Oct. **Average** €€. **Credit** MC, V.
A simple restaurant with tables spilling out on to the *plaza*, serving good, traditional dishes in a glorious location facing the church of Santa María la Mayor.

### Restaurante La Espuela
*C/San Agustín 1 (952 70 34 24).* **Open** 1-4.15pm, 7-11.30pm daily. **Average** €€. **Credit** MC, V.
Reputedly the first Spanish restaurant located inside a bullring, this attractive, white-walled place serves excellent grilled meats and local specialities.

## Where to stay

In addition to the places below, the following are all decent central options: **Hotel Colón** (C/Infante Don Fernando 29, 952 84 00 10, www.castelcolon.com, double €35-€40),

**Pensión Reyes** (C/La Tercia 4, 952 84 10 28, double €20-€30), the three-star **Hotel Papabellotas** (C/Encarnación 5, 952 70 50 45, double €49-€71) and the **Bar-Restaurante Plaza San Sebastián** (*see p86*).

### Hotel Antequera Golf
*Urbanización Santa Catalina (952 70 45 31/ www.hotelantequera.com).* **Rates** €75-€81 single; €81-€101 double; €161 suite. **Credit** AmEx, MC, V.
The town's parador is a comfortable, modern building, located just outside the centre. The rooms are spacious, and it has every modern convenience, including a bar, pool and its own golf course.

### Hotel Castilla
*C/Infante Don Fernando 40 (952 84 30 90/ www.castillahotel.com).* **Rates** €25-€33 single; €39-€42 double; €51-€55 triple. **Credit** MC, V.
A new building in the heart of the old town, the two-star Castilla has comfortable, if rather bland, rooms equipped with satellite television and air-con.

### Pensión Madrona
*C/Calzada 31 (952 28 40 14).* **Rates** €21 single; €29 double; €42 triple. **Credit** MC, V.
Clean, basic accommodation located a five-minute walk north-east of Plaza San Sebastián. Don't miss out on the delicious *churros* and breakfasts.

## Around Antequera

Located just to the south of the town is the **Paraje Natural Torcal de Antequera**, better known as **El Torcal**, a nature reserve containing some spectacularly weird rock formations. The park covers 2,000 hectares (eight square miles) and is dominated by a 1,369-metre (4,491-foot) mountain that has been splintered, gnarled, serrated and fractured over approximately 150 million years into bizarrely shaped calceous rocks. The 1.4-kilometre (one-mile) Ruta Verde walk starts and ends near the visitors' centre and is marked by green posts. You will need a car to get to the park, which is signed from the C3310 between Antequera and Villanueva de la Concepción.

West of El Torcal lies the area's other great natural wonder, the deep, rugged canyon of the Río Guadalhorce, known as the **Garganta del Chorro** (El Chorro Gorge). Here, breathtakingly steep limestone walls create some of the most dramatic scenery in Spain. To reach it, follow the signs for Camping El Chorro and, when you reach the entrance to the campsite, continue past it for a few minutes on a rough track until you reach a small car park, with a metal gate blocking the way just beyond it. Leave your car here and take the wide track heading upwards for around 15 minutes. You'll soon see the gorge and a green-painted railway bridge ahead of you. Although officially prohibited, many

**Málaga Province**

Crazy rock formations in **El Torcal**. *See p87.*

visitors then cross over the rail bridge and walk through the rail tunnel for more stunning views.

El Chorro's most famous (and frightening) sight is the crumbling concrete walkway, known as the **Caminito del Rey** (King's Pathway), that snakes along the walls of the gorge. Constructed in 1901-05 to move workers and materials between El Chorro Falls and the Gaitanejo Falls on the other side of the gorge, it earned its name when it was walked by Alfonso XIII in 1921 on the occasion of his opening of the Conde del Guadalhorce dam. It has been closed now for some years following its partial collapse and the deaths of a number of people who attempted to walk it. In 2004 the regional government finally gave the go-ahead for a seven-million-euro restoration to be undertaken, though this is likely to take some years yet.

While you're in the area, seek out the ninth-century Christian church and fortress remains of **Bobastro**, just west of El Chorro. Hidden away behind a rocky hill (which you'll have to climb), the church is unusual for several reasons: it was built as a Christian place of worship when Andalucía was ruled by Muslims; it is entirely cut out of bare rock; and it is supposed to contain the tomb of Ibn Hafsun, a Christian emir who founded a short-lived independent state in the region in 880.

Heading north-west towards Sevilla from Antequera for about 20 kilometres (12 miles) brings you to one of the area's most unexpected natural features, the **Laguna de Fuente de Piedra** (*see p89* **Top five**), the largest natural lake in Andalucía and one of Europe's principal breeding grounds for the Greater Flamingo. Surrounded by unusual flora and fauna thanks to the high salt content of the water, vast numbers of flamingoes fly over from Senegal in January and February, hatch their chicks in April and May and then depart for Africa in August when the water dries up. Tip: be sure to take a pair of binoculars.

Eighteen kilometres (11 miles) north-east of Antequera, the town of **Archidona** is chiefly

of note for its unique and largely unaltered octagonal main square, built in 1780-86 with stone from El Torcal.

## Where to stay & eat

The outstanding place to stay near **El Torcal** is **La Posada del Torcal** (Villanueva de la Concepción, 952 03 11 77, www.eltorcal.com/ PosadaTorcal, closed Dec or Jan, double €134-€279, restaurant €€€), a hilltop *cortijo* with ten luxurious rooms, a pool and a good restaurant. A much cheaper option in the same village is the small, friendly **Casa de Elrond** (Barrio Seco s/n, Villanueva de la Concepción, 952 75 40 91, closed Dec & Jan, double €55). If you want to stay near El Chorro, **La Garganta** (Barriada del Chorro, 952 49 51 19, apartments to sleep 2-6 people €40-€85) offers excellent apartments with views, a pool and a restaurant.

## Resources

### Police station
Antequera *Avenida de la Legión (952 70 81 04).*

### Post office
Antequera *C/Nájera 26 (952 84 20 83).*

### Tourist information
Antequera *Plaza de San Sebastián 7 (952 70 25 05/ www.antequera.es).* **Open** *Mid June-mid Sept* 11am-2pm, 5-8pm Mon-Sat; 10am-2pm Sun. *Mid Sept-mid June* 10.30am-1.30pm, 4-7pm Mon-Sat; 10.30am-1.30pm Sun.
**Paraje Natural Torcal de Antequera** *Centro de Visitantes 'Torcal Alto', C3310, Torcal de Antequera (952 03 13 89).* **Open** 10am-5pm daily.
**Reserva Natural Laguna de Fuente de Piedra** *Centro de Información José Antonio Valerde, Cerro del Palo s/n, Fuente de Piedra (952 11 17 15).* **Open** *Apr-Sept* 10am-1pm, 6-8pm Tue; 10am-2pm, 6-8pm Wed-Sun. *Oct-Mar* 10am-1pm, 4-6pm Tue; 10am-2pm, 4-6pm Wed-Sun.

## Getting there

### By bus
From Antequera, Alsina Graells (952 84 13 65) runs 7 or so buses daily to Málaga (1hr 15mins), 6 to Sevilla (2hrs 40mins), 5 to Granada (1hr 45mins) and 2 to Córdoba (2hrs 15mins). Antequera's bus station is near the bullring, a 5-10min walk from the centre.

### By train
Antequera's rail station is on Avenida de la Estación (952 84 32 26/952 87 16 73), 1.5km north of the centre. There are 5 trains a day to/from Granada (1hr 30mins), 4 to Sevilla (1hr 30mins) and 3 to Algeciras (2hrs 50mins) via Ronda (1hr 10mins). For Málaga and Córdoba, change at Bobadilla. A couple of trains a day from Málaga stop at El Chorro (40mins).

**Málaga Province**

## Top five Birding spots

Andalucía is twitcher heaven. Thanks to its unique geographical position, almost within touching distance of Africa and on major migration routes, and its huge ecological and climatic diversity, southern Spain supports a huge range of breeding and migrant species. Many – such as the red-knobbed coot and white-rumped swift – are found nowhere else on the continent, and even the uninitiated will get a kick from witnessing the exoticism of many of the passerines and wetland species and the majesty of the soaring raptors. Below we list five of the region's best birdwatching locations.

For more details, get hold of Ernest Garcia and Andrew Patterson's authoritative *Where to Watch Birds in Southern and Western Spain* and check the website of the Spanish Ornithological Society (Sociedad Española de Ornitología, www.seo.org).

### DONANA

This immense National Park and its surrounding protected areas occupy more than 1,300 square kilometres (500 square miles) of the western Guadalquivir estuary at the boundary of Huelva and Sevilla provinces. The Doñana is one of the most important wetland sites in Europe, supporting huge concentrations of wildfowl in winter, as well as breeding populations of cattle and little egrets, grey, night, purple and squacco herons, and glossy ibises. There are raptors aplenty, including around 15 pairs of the ultra-rare Spanish imperial eagle. The interior of the park is accessible only by guided tour but there are a variety of good sites on the periphery, including El Rocío, where you may be able to spot up to 70 species. The park's information centre, El Acebuche (*see p152* **The last wilderness**), is one and a half kilometres (one mile) west of the Matalascañas–Almonte road at km29.

### GIBRALTAR, TARIFA AND AROUND

The southern tip of the continent is the place to head for the best views of migrating raptors and seabirds. Thanks to its elevation, Gibraltar allows up-close views of the former (it's possible to see more than a dozen species on a good day in spring or autumn). The area around Tarifa has the edge for watching stork and crane migrations, while Tarifa's beach (Playa de los Lances) is thronged in winter with waders and gulls

(including Audouin's gulls). Punta Secreta, on the CA223 south from Algeciras, is another great spot for migration-watching. The steppe-like plain of La Janda (viewable from the minor road from Facinas to Benalup) offers the chance to see species such as little bustards and stone curlews. Up the Costa de la Luz at Sierra de la Plata (near Bolonia) is the first known breeding site in Europe of the white-rumped swift.

### LAGUNA DE FUENTE DE PIEDRA

The chief draw of this large, shallow saline lake in Málaga province is the only regular breeding colony of greater flamingoes in Spain (*see picture*). The lagoon attracts as many as 16,000 pairs annually. It lies close to the village of Fuente de Piedra, just off the A92 motorway between Sevilla and Granada. *See also p88.*

### PUNTE ENTINAS TO ROQUETAS DE MAR

The west of Andalucía has the edge in birdwatching terms over the east of the region, but the coastal strip between Almerimar and Roquetas de Mar in Almería province is well worth a visit. Its mix of dunes, scrub and salt pans shelters the likes of white-headed ducks, yellow wagtails, lesser short-toed larks and, incongruously, a colony of mute swans. There are large numbers of gulls, terns and waders too.

### RIO GUADALQUIVIR, CÓRDOBA

Right in the heart of the city, in reed beds by the Puente Romano in front of the Mezquita, is a remarkable and highly visible egret colony. As well as cattle and little egrets, there's a wide variety of other species to be seen, including night and squacco herons, white storks, little bitterns and purple gallinules. On the Mezquita itself is a lesser kestrel colony. *See p211.*

# West of Málaga

One of Andalucía's most likeable and spectacularly located towns, jaw-dropping mountain scenery and *pueblos blancos* galore.

## Ronda

Spread out along a high cliff that has been cleft in two by the mighty Guadalevín gorge, and surrounded on all sides by rumpled mountains, it is easy to see why **Ronda** has long captured the imagination of travellers and has become the most visited town in western Andalucía. With the Costa del Sol little more than half an hour away by car (albeit via a heart-stopping road that cuts a series of dizzy loops up and up from San Pedro), the town sometimes struggles to cope with the huge influx of tourists who are disgorged by the coachload from mid-morning onwards. In order to avoid being swamped by the bumbag brigade, try to leave exploring the town until later in the day. Once the coaches are heading back down the hill Ronda once again becomes a magical place, the *ciudad soñada* (town of dreams) of artists and poets.

Ronda's reputation is no recent phenomenon. When the 19th-century Romantic movement espoused Spain, the region became an obligatory stop on the Grand Tour. The likes of Victor Hugo, Théophile Gautier, David Roberts, George Borrow and Richard Ford all waxed lyrical about the town's extraordinary beauty, and later it was to beguile Rainer Maria Rilke, Ernest Hemingway and Orson Welles, among others. For Hemingway and Welles the town's central role in the history of bullfighting was a major draw; both coincided with the apogee of Ronda's most famous *torero*, Antonio Ordóñez. Hemingway quipped that this was the perfect place to spend a honeymoon 'because there's nothing to do' and Welles was so taken by the place that he asked for his ashes be scattered in the patio of Ordóñez's farm, just north of the town.

The classic postcard view of Ronda is looking up at the cliff-top buildings ranged on either side of the dramatic gorge of the Guadalevín, known by all locals simply as 'El Tajo'. The gorge is spanned by the late 18th-century **Puente Nuevo** (New Bridge), which was eventually completed, after works spanning more than four decades, in 1793, and which has become the town's neural centre as well as its adopted symbol. It links the old Moorish citadel in the south to the newer town, which could only develop once the gorge had been spanned. Most shops, bars and restaurants

Ronda's El Tajo gorge.

are in the newer town (the **Mercadillo** quarter), while the majority of the interesting buildings and boutique hotels are in the old town (known as **La Ciudad**). Beyond La Ciudad, the *barrio* of San Francisco is far less touristy and contains some of Ronda's best tapas bars.

In most guidebooks you'll come across the tragicomic legend of the Puente Nuevo's architect, Martín de Aldehuela, who supposedly fell to his death during his final inspection of the bridge when he lunged to grab his hat, which had been blown off by the wind. (The truth is disappointingly prosaic: he died in a hospital bed in Málaga.) During the Civil War both Nationalist and Republican prisoners were forced to jump to their deaths in the gorge, events that were to act as a touchstone for Hemingway's *For Whom the Bell Tolls*. Above the bridge's central arch was a tiny prison cell that later became a bar and now houses a small museum.

Crossing the bridge into the old town, take the first left to reach the fancifully named **Casa del Rey Moro** (House of the Moorish King). It actually dates from 1709, although beneath the house is a lengthy rock-cut stairway, **La Mina**, which dates back to Moorish times. If you're feeling fit you can descend the 365 steps to the bottom of the gorge, where you emerge beside the Guadalevín via a keyhole-arched doorway. There are wonderful views from the gardens, which were laid out by the French landscape gardener de Forestier.

Further down the hill is the 18th-century **Palacio del Marqués de Salvatierra**. The unusual figurines carved on its façade were inspired by Native American art. If you continue downhill – passing beneath the **Arco de Felipe V**, then crossing over the **Puente de San Miguel**, Ronda's oldest bridge – you reach the **Baños Arabes** (Arab Baths). Although much of the marble and mosaic that once adorned the baths is gone, most of the main 13th-century structure remains intact, making this probably Andalucía's best-preserved *hammam*.

Back up in the old town, past the 14th-century **Minarete de San Sebastián** (a Nasrid-style minaret) and the **Museo del Bandolero**, devoted to the bandits who once dominated the surrounding country (*see p98* **Cliché**), is the lovely orange-tree-lined **Plaza Duquesa de Parcent**. Prior to the completion of the bullring, *corridas* were frequently held here.

To one side is the town hall and across the way stands the church of **Santa María la Mayor**. It has had many incarnations: first it was a Roman Temple dedicated to Julius Caesar, then a mosque and finally the town's main church. The construction of the present building began in the early 16th century after Ronda fell to the Christians following a protracted siege. You can see the remains of the ornate *mihrab* (the prayer niche where the Koran was kept) in the entrance hall as well as the minaret, which, embellished with a lantern, became the Christian belfry. The church's most beautiful paintings and *retablos* (altarpieces) were destroyed during the Civil War and were replaced by an extraordinary series of paintings depicting strangely hermaphrodite saints and apostles.

Just west of the church is the most emblematic of Ronda's many fine buildings, the **Palacio de Mondragón**. Home to a succession of Moorish governors until the *Reconquista* (King Fernando slept here after the siege of Ronda in 1485), it was converted into a Mudéjar-Renaissance mansion named after the knight Melchor de Mondragón, whose coat of arms is above the palace's main entrance. It now houses a museum of local archaeology and an offshoot of Málaga University, which organises intensive Spanish courses. But by far its most charming feature is its formal garden, which runs right to the edge of the cliff and provides a backdrop for photographs of newly-weds and children taking first communion. In the 1960s the palace became the home of the writer Alastair Boyd (Lord Kilmarnock), who opened a school for studying Spanish here. A number of well-heeled Brits passed through as well as a succession of writers, including Patrick Leigh Fermor and Martin Amis. Boyd's two books about the area, *In the Sierras of the South* and *The Road from Ronda* (both recently republished by Santana Books), are essential reading for anyone with more than a passing interest in the area.

From the nearby Plaza del Campillo, a path winds down the gorge below the Puente Nuevo to a rocky outcrop, from where you can take the classic gorge snap. Persevere to the bottom and, in spring, you'll find yourself wandering through a multi-hued ocean of wild flowers. From here you can loop back up to the Barrio de San Francisco. There's also a wonderful walk (much enjoyed by Rilke) from Ronda to the **Ermita de la Virgen de la Cabeza** (ask at the tourist office for details), passing the house where the painter David Bomberg lived during the last years of his life. Considered to be one of the greatest artists of the Spanish landscape, Bomberg died in 1957, largely ignored by the British art world, and an unknown figure in Spain. Not until 2004, when a plaque to him was placed in the centre of Ronda, did he finally receive some form of acknowledgement in the country that had so inspired him.

Back across the Puente Nuevo in the new part of town is the **Plaza de España** and a stunningly sited *parador* (*see p97*) with views across the gorge to the old town.

Just beyond it is the **Plaza de Toros**, built in 1785 by the Puente Nuevo's architect Martin de Aldehuela. It is one of the oldest, most beautiful rings in Spain. It was here that local *torero* Pedro Romero (1754-1839) established the blueprint for modern bullfighting techniques and style. In his long career (he retired aged 72), Romero killed 6,000 bulls and was never seriously injured.

The history of Ronda's bullring is the history of bullfighting itself and dates back to 1572, when Felipe II set up the Real Maestranza de Caballería, an exclusive academy in Ronda that aimed to teach young noblemen the art of horsemanship in battle at a time when the *morisco* rebellions threatened the established order. A century or so later, Pedro Romero's grandfather came to the rescue of a nobleman who had been unseated while testing his horsemanship against wild bulls by sweeping his wide-brimmed Andalucían hat in front of the bull to distract it. Thus was born the *corrida de toros*. In time the academy became a training school for young bullfighters. The pricey museum is a taxidermist's paradise, full of massive bulls' heads. There are also blood-stained matador costumes and photos of the *corrida* spanning several decades.

Since 1957 Ronda has celebrated the **Fiestas de Pedro Romero** (on the Saturday of the September *feria*) with traditional Goya-esque bullfights (Goya was a friend of Romero), where fighters don the traditional costumes that were worn at the end of the 18th century. It remains one of the most important events on the bullfighting calendar and tickets change hands on the black market for huge sums.

Behind the bullring a walkway, the **Paseo de los Ingleses**, runs along the cliff edge, giving wonderful views towards the old town and out over open countryside. It takes its name from the many Brits who stayed in Ronda when it became a hill station for the Gibraltar garrison.

If you've an interest in art, it's well worth visiting **Ronda-Art** (C/Pozo 11, 952 19 04 90, www.ronda-art.com, closed Mon), just to the north of the Plaza de Merced church. This small gallery, run by friendly Brit Andy Cairns, exhibits work by the best of the local artists.

### Baños Arabes

*Barrio de Padre Jesús (mobile 656 95 09 37).* **Open** *Mar-Oct* 10am-7pm daily. *Nov-Feb* 10am-6pm Mon-Fri; 10am-3pm Sat, Sun. **Admission** €2; €1 concessions; free under-14s. **No credit cards.** **Map** p93 A2.

### Casa del Rey Moro

*C/Santo Domingo 17 (952 18 72 00).* **Open** *Mar-Oct* 10am-8pm daily. *Nov-Feb* 10am-7pm daily. **Admission** €4; €2 concessions. **Credit** AmEx, DC, MC, V. **Map** p93 A2.

### Museo del Bandolero

*C/Armiñán 65 (952 87 77 85/www.museo bandolero.com).* **Open** *Mar-Oct* 10.30am-8.30pm daily. *Nov-Feb* 10.30am-6.30pm daily. **Admission** €2.70; €2.40 concessions. **No credit cards.** **Map** p93 A1.

### Palacio de Mondragón

*Plaza de Mondragón s/n (952 87 84 50/08 18).* **Open** *Mar-Oct* 10am-7pm Mon-Fri. *Nov-Feb* 10am-6pm Sat; 10am-3pm Sun. **Admission** €2; €1 concessions. **No credit cards.** **Map** p93 B1.

### Plaza de Toros/Museo Taurino

*C/Virgen de la Paz 15 (952 87 15 39).* **Open** *Corridas* phone for details. *Museum* Apr-Sept 10am-8pm daily. Mar, Oct 10am-7pm daily. Nov-Feb 10am-6pm daily. **Admission** €5; €3.50 concessions. **No credit cards.** **Map** p93 B3.

### Santa María la Mayor

*Plaza Duquesa de Parcent s/n (952 87 86 53/ www.colegiata.com).* **Open** *Apr-Oct* 10am-8pm daily. *Nov-Mar* 10am-6pm daily. **Admission** €2; €1.50 concessions. **No credit cards.** **Map** p93 A1.

---

## Where to eat & drink

There's a huge selection of places to eat in Ronda, from the Michelin-starred to simple spit-and-sawdust tapas bars. You're best off avoiding the plentiful tourist traps around the Plaza de España, where world-weary waiters try to entice you in for the *menú del día*. Instead, head for the untouristy Barrio de San Francisco at the end of the old town, or to places further into the new town. Note that a number of Ronda's hotels (*see p95*) have excellent restaurants.

### Bar La Farola

*C/Plaza de Carmen Abela 9 (952 87 74 20).* **Open** 9am-6pm Mon-Sat. **Average** €. **No credit cards.** **Map** p93 A3.
One of the longest-established and best-loved tapas joints in town. La Farola's specialities include *chorizo* (paprika-spiced sausages), *berenjenas* (fried aubergine) and *chipirones* (baby squid).

### Bar Restaurante Almocábar

*C/Ruedo Alameda 5 (952 87 59 77).* **Open** 1-5pm, 7-11.30pm Mon, Wed-Sun. Closed mid Aug-mid Sept. **Average** €€-€€€. **Credit** AmEx, DC, MC, V. **Map** p93 off A1.
One of Ronda's best places for tapas or a full-blown meal. The front bar is popular with a young, local crowd and there's an attractive restaurant attached, with interesting Arab-Andalus dishes, volcanic stone-grilled meat and exceptional roast lamb.

### Bar Restaurante Moreno
*Avenida Ricardo Naverrete 4 (952 87 58 88).*
**Open** 12.30-4.30pm, 8pm-midnight Mon, Thur-Sun;
12.30-4.30pm Tue. **Average** €€. **Credit** DC, MC, V.
**Map** p93 off A3.
Tucked behind the railway station, Moreno's is one
of the most popular eateries in town and is well away
from the tourist trail. The place is always buzzing
and the food is excellent. Choose from the fresh fish
and seafood piled up on ice or order a charcoal-grilled
steak, and be sure to try the house speciality as an
accompaniment: *cogollos con anchoas* (baby gem
lettuces draped in anchovies drizzled with hot olive
oil and garlic). It has a great wine list too.

### Casa María
*C/Ruedo Alameda 27 (952 87 62 12/mobile 670
79 24 38).* **Open** 1-5pm, 7.30pm-12.30am Tue-Sun.
Closed mid Dec-mid Jan. **Average** €€. **Credit** MC,
V. **Map** p93 off A1.
Casa María has a good range of fresh seafood, great
steaks and some interesting salads; try the Basque
cod or marinated goose liver. Its tables spill out on
to the square, and it's nearly always packed, so be
sure to book, especially in winter when dining space
inside is limited. The wine list is one of the best in
Ronda. Popular with the local expat crowd.

### Los Cazadores
*C/Rosal 1 (952 19 03 16).*
**Open** 1-4.30pm, 8pm-midnight
Mon, Tue, Thur-Sun. Closed Sept.
**Average** €-€€. **Credit** MC, V.
**Map** p93 off A3.
Good, simple tapas and *raciones*,
including a decent selection of fish
dishes and fantastic *berenjenas*
(fried aubergine slices). Very
popular with locals, especially at
lunchtime, so it's best to book.

### Faustino
*C/Santa Cecilia 4 (952 19 03 07).*
**Open** 11.30am-1am Tue-Sun.
Closed 2wks Sept. **Average** €.
**No credit cards**. **Map** p93 A2/3.
Faustino is among the most popular tapas bars in town and draws
in locals and visitors with its
friendly, lively atmosphere and
very reliable food. Try a *serranito*
– a small sandwich of *jamón
serrano*, green pepper and pork.

### La Giralda
*C/Nueva 19 (952 87 28 02).*
**Open** noon-5pm, 8pm-midnight
Mon, Tue, Thur-Sun. Closed 2wks
Nov. **Average** €. **Credit** MC, V.
**Map** p93 B2/3.
Named after Sevilla's famous tower,
La Giralda's most delicious culi-
nary treat is its *pinchito de gambas*
(prawn kebab), spiked with the

owner's secret seasoning. Be sure to order at least
three or four per person. Other fresh seafood dishes
include *mejillones* (mussels), or try the delicious
grilled *setas* (wild mushrooms).

### La Gota de Vino
*C/Sevilla 13 (952 87 57 16).* **Open** 1-4pm, 8pm-
midnight Tue-Sat. **Average** €€. **Credit** AmEx, MC,
V. **Map** p93 A/B3.
Friendly owner Luigi Pignatelli refers to his bar as
a *vinoteca* and offers a superb selection of his
favourite wines, ranging from €7 to €40 per bottle.
An excellent young chef magics up creative cuisine
using Italian and Spanish ingredients as well as
whatever is best in the local market. La Gota de Vino
is fast becoming one of *the* Ronda eateries for the
local expat crowd.

### Relax
*C/Los Remedios 27 (952 87 72 07/www.relax
cafebar.com).* **Open** May-Sept 10am-4pm, 8pm-
midnight daily. *Oct-Apr* 1-4pm, 8pm-midnight daily.
**Average** €. **No credit cards**. **Map** p93 A2/3.
The only vegetarian eatery in Ronda. Relax's owner
Damaris is an adventurous English girl with heaps
of enthusiasm and culinary talent. Quiches, Mexican
dishes, exotic salads, dips and baked beans are all
on offer, accompanied by smoothies or herbal teas.
And there are now interesting curries on Sundays.

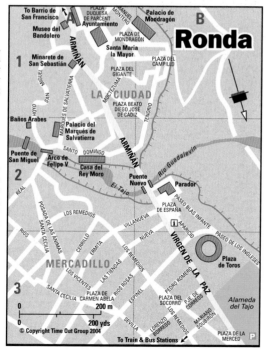

*Málaga Province*

### La Taberna de Rafael Espejo
*Pasaje de Correos 1 (mobile 630 46 24 20).*
**Open** 2-5pm, 9pm-midnight Mon-Sat. **Average** €.
**No credit cards**. Map p93 B3.
A family-run no-frills tapas bar, popular with locals and plastered with photos of flamenco artists (the owner Rafael included). If you are lucky you may hear an impromptu flamenco performance. Regional cheeses, cured ham and superb grilled liver kebabs are among the dishes on offer, and there's a decent selection of casked sherries too. A great place for an aperitif.

### Tetería Al-Zahra
*C/Las Tiendas 19 (mobile 607 74 51 73).*
**Open** 4pm-midnight Mon, Wed-Sun. **Average** €.
**No credit cards**. Map p93 A3.
This atmospheric, traditional cushion-floored Moroccan tearoom is very popular with a young Ronda crowd. Join them and owner Daniel for mint tea, Moroccan pancakes and cakes. Part of a new vogue for all things Moroccan that has recently taken root in Andalucía.

### Tragabuches
*C/José Aparicio 1 (952 19 02 91/www.tragabuches.com).* **Open** 1.30-4pm, 8-10.30pm Tue-Sat; 1.30-4pm Sun. **Average** €€€€. **Credit** AmEx, DC, MC, V. Map p93 B2.
Named after an infamous local *torero*, flamenco singer and bandit, this celebrated restaurant has been a haven of light, modern southern Spanish cuisine for many years now. Traditional dishes are cleverly and skilfully reinterpreted (cherry

# Walk Mr Henderson's railway

**Distance** 9 kilometres (5.5 miles)
**Time required** 3 hours

This short and easy walk follows a delightful riverside path that links the sleepy village of Estación de Benaoján with the sleepier-still hamlet of Estación de Jimera de Líbar.
It begins at El Molino del Santo, a hotel and restaurant just up from the railway line (*see p101*). What makes it such a lovely half-day walk is that you can set off after a late breakfast, dawdle along the way, have a long lazy lunch in the excellent Quercus restaurant in Estación de Jimera de Líbar, then return by train later in the afternoon to the Molino or to your car (departure from Jimera is 4.48pm, arriving at Estación de Benaoján at 4.56pm; be sure to check times). If this idea appeals, begin this walk at about 11am. You could turn it into a longer walk by simply retracing your footsteps back along the Guadalete valley from Jimera.
From El Molino del Santo in Estación de Benaoján, turn left out of its main entrance and walk down the hill until you reach a stop sign at a level crossing. Turn left along the railway line, cross over a fast-flowing river and, at a second level crossing, turn right and cross over the railway track.
The road drops down, crosses the River Guadiaro and leads up to a sign marking the beginning of the official walk that recommends you allow (a very generous) four hours. Turn right off the road at the sign and follow a track that soon passes by an abandoned farm with three magnificent palm trees. The railway and the river are now to your right.

A British engineer, Mr Henderson, was responsible for the construction of the Ronda–Algeciras line. The train that plied this route came to be known as the Smugglers' Express. It went so slowly that contraband butter, cocoa and tobacco from Gibraltar could be sold from the train windows.
The track narrows to a path, which shortly crosses a small wooden bridge and then bears round to the right and passes a ruined farm.
Shortly after this farm the path divides. You should take the left fork, which leads you slightly away from the river. Your path takes you through a gate and, shortly afterwards, you'll see that the railway is now on your side of the river. Carry on along this same path. You eventually drop down, cross a (dry) stream and, a little further on, a concrete water channel runs to the left of your path.
Continue along the path and soon you'll see a sign for Via Pecuaria. You are on the old drovers' path that leads from Cortes to Ronda. You reach a small olive grove. Here the path, which previously continued straight ahead, bears sharply right, crosses the railway line and then swings left towards Jimera de Líbar. As you approach the village you come to the Quercus restaurant in a converted railway shed. The railway station is just a hundred metres (330 feet) further on.
After lunch, you have two choices. You could return by the same route that you followed earlier in the day or take the train back to Benaoján. It's a less than ten-minute ride back along Mr Henderson's railway line.

*From Walking in Andalucía by Guy Hunter-Watts (Santana)*

gazpacho or thyme ice-cream, for instance), but the inventiveness never descends into mere gimmickry. Splash out and go for the *menú degustación*.

## Nightlife

Ronda's previously rather conservative nightlife scene has picked up somewhat in the last couple of years. Bars and clubs tend to spring up and disappear from year to year, but look out for hip new places such as **Kopas** (C/Rios Rosas 9, map A3) and **Limbo** (Plaza Carmen de Abela, map A3), which often feature DJs. In summer a huge *discoteca de verano* (summer disco) opens at the far end of Avenida de Málaga, just beyond the roundabout on the Campillos road, where the young and not-so-young rock on all the way through until dawn on Friday and Saturday nights.

## Shopping

Ronda has some of the cheapest high-quality leather-goods stores in Spain, much of their merchandise produced in nearby Ubrique, leather capital of the South. And there are also masses of shops selling local ceramics, as well as lots of imported stuff from Morocco (which you may well be told is 'local'). Much of it is surprisingly cheap. Ronda is also famous for its rustic pine furniture (*mueble rondeño*), which more often than not is made from new pine planks that have been scraped and battered to give the patina of time. If you want fresh produce your best bet is the Sunday morning market (10.30am-2pm), just off the Ronda bypass near the Cobrero supermarket. There's also a daily market at the top end of the Calle Espinel behind the Mercadona supermarket. Shops are open 10am to 2pm and 5pm to 9pm Monday to Friday, and from 10am to 2pm on Saturday. Large supermarkets like Hipersol remain open until 9pm six days a week.

## Where to stay

In and around Ronda there is a huge range of characterful and often dashingly chic accommodation options. But be sure to book as far in advance as possible.

### Alavera de los Baños

*Hoyo San Miguel s/n (952 87 91 43/www.andalucia. com/alavera).* Closed early Dec-early Jan. **Rates** (incl breakfast) €50-€60 single; €75-€90. **Average** €€. **Credit** MC, V. **Map** p93 A1.
Next door to one of Spain's best-preserved *hammams* (Arab baths; *see p91*), this intimate hotel has great views across open country to the new Real Maestranza riding school. The decor is a colourful mix of things rustic and North African. Bedrooms

have wrought-iron beds and oak furniture but are generally small: it is well worth shelling out extra for a room with a terrace. The restaurant offers organic Spanish, Mediterranean and North African dishes with some interesting vegetarian options and excellent salads. Breakfast is superb and there is a pretty garden with masses of greenery and a small plunge pool.

### Cortijo Puerto Llano

*MA449, km8 (952 11 42 27/www.andalucia.com/ accommodation/puertollano).* **Rates** (incl breakfast) €60 single; €96 double. **No credit cards.**
This tastefully converted farmhouse, close to the Roman site of Acinipo/Ronda La Vieja (*see p99*), is impeccably run by artist Aart van Kruiselbergen. Aart will prepare you a delicious breakfast or you can self-cater in the guest kitchen, which is just to one side of a beautiful, secluded swimming pool. Only 15 minutes' drive from Ronda but with a wonderfully isolated feel.

### EnFrenteArte

*C/Real 40-42 (952 87 90 88/47 33/www.enfrente arte.com).* **Rates** €45 single; €78-€100 double. **Credit** MC, V. **Map** p93 A2.
Owned and run by Belgian entrepreneur Filip Eyckmans, EnFrenteArte is not your average hostelry. Wine, beer, coffee and freshly-squeezed orange juices, a buffet breakfast and lunch are all laid on for no extra charge. Resident chef Encarni González prepares dishes like tortilla and grilled king prawn salad. The decor is stylish and most rooms are large, with four-poster beds and en suite bathrooms, the best with their own terrace. Use of the internet, swimming pool, sauna, jacuzzi, games and music room is also included in the room price.

### Hotel La Española

*C/José Aparicio 5 (952 87 10 51/www.ronda.net/ usuar/laespanola).* **Rates** €36-€44 single; €74-€88 double. **Credit** AmEx, MC, V. **Map** p93 B2.
A good option if you're travelling on a tight budget, La Española is tucked away in the narrow pedestrian street leading from the bullring to the *parador*. Four of its sixteen rooms have extraordinary views out across the cliff, so try to book room 205, 206, 207 or 208. The staff are friendly, and right next door are the famous Tragabuches restaurant (*see p94*) and the diminutive *tasquita* (sherry bar) Échate'-pa'llá, where you can start your evening with a *fino* and a *montadito* (a small toasted sandwich).

### Hotel La Fuente de la Higuera

*Partido de los Frontones s/n (952 11 43 55/ www.hotellafuente.com).* **Rates** (incl breakfast) €144 double; €178-€210 suite. **Average** €€€€. **Credit** MC, V.
This is the best expensive option in the Ronda area for those wishing to relax in a country setting in style and tranquillity. The hotel, run by Pom and Tina Piek, exudes the kind of cool chic that has glossy magazine editors drooling, with sleek wooden interiors imported from the Far East and

Alavera de los Baños.
See p95.

The **Serranía de Ronda**, from the castle at **Gaucín**. *See p97 and p99.*

contemporary art on the walls. From the hotel's terrace restaurant undulating farmland rolls up towards Ronda. Life centres around the poolside terrace in summer or the dining room in winter, where there is a huge CD collection including everything from flamenco to jazz to blues to chill. It is located a few kilometres north of Ronda.

### Hotel San Gabriel

*C/Marqués de Moctezuma 19 (952 19 03 92/ www.hotelsangabriel.com).* Closed mid Dec-early Jan. **Rates** €75-€98 double; €98-€109 suite. **Credit** AmEx, DC, MC, V. **Map** p93 A1.
Run by an exceptionally friendly local family, this gem of a hotel in the old town has cool, beautifully restored wooden interiors (rescued from the old town hall) in the billiard room, a small poetry library (to which guests are encouraged to contribute) and a ten-seat mini-DVD cinema (salvaged from the town theatre). Bullfighting memorabilia and signed photos of celebrity guests such as Bob Hoskins and Isabella Rosellini adorn the walls.

### El Juncal

*A366, km1 (952 16 11 70/www.eljuncal.com).* **Rates** €118-€162 double; €198-€257 suite. **Credit** AmEx, DC, MC, V.
Located just outside Ronda, in a converted 17th-century house, El Juncal is a boutique hotel owned by the same people as the Tragabuches restaurant (*see p94*). It has eight spacious rooms, each with a private terrace, plus two villa suites. Decor and ambience are Zen-meets-Alessi, and highlights include a swimming pool, jacuzzi, sauna and an adjacent *bodega*, where you can sample the hotel's wine,

Pasos Largos (named, like Tragabuches, after a local bandit; *see p98* **Cliche**). Some visitors think the hotel lacks atmosphere.

### Parador de Ronda

*Plaza de España s/n (952 87 75 00/www.parador.es).* **Rates** €102 single; €128 double; €197 duplex. **Average** €€-€€€. **Credit** AmEx, DC, MC, V. **Map** p93 B2.
The position of Ronda's *parador* can't be bettered, perched right at the edge of the gorge with views across to the old town and to the mountain ridge beyond. The decor is a surprisingly innovative postmodern pot-pourri: most of it works well. Bedrooms are sleek and plush (many have stupendous views) and bathrooms are up to the usual high *parador* standards. There's an outdoor pool, which enjoys views across the gorge, and the restaurant is one of the best places to eat in town, thanks to the culinary skills of Jaén-born chef José Gomez. But you need to book well ahead – the place has a near hundred per cent occupancy rate, one of the highest of any hotel in Spain.

## Resources

### Internet

*El Choque Ideal, C/Espíritu Santo 9 (952 16 19 18).* **Map** p93 off A1.

### Police station

*Ayuntamiento, Plaza Duquesa de Parcent 3 (952 87 32 40).* **Map** p93 A1.

### Post office

*C/Virgen de la Paz 20 (952 87 25 57).* **Map** p93 B3.

## Tourist information

*Paseo Blas Infante s/n (952 18 71 19/www.turismo deronda.es).* **Open** 9.30am 7.30pm Mon-Fri; 10am-2pm, 3.30-7pm Sat, Sun. **Map** p93 B2.
By far the most helpful of Ronda's tourist offices.

*Plaza de España 9 (952 87 12 72).* **Open** 9am-8pm Mon-Fri; 10am-2pm Sat, Sun. **Map** p93 B2.

## The Serranía de Ronda & the Pueblos Blancos

The mountainous country around Ronda, the **Serranía de Ronda**, is some of the wildest and most beautiful in Andalucía, and you'll soon see why it has long captured the imagination of the Romantics and landscape artists. Depending on the season, it can appear mercilessly parched and raw or lushly green with a spectacular profusion of wild flowers. As long as you avoid the hottest part of the day in summer, the walking in this area is truly exceptional. Tourist offices can supply details of local routes. (*See also p94 and p100.*)

The area is famed for its *pueblos blancos* (white villages). Although you'll come across picture-postcard whitewashed hamlets throughout Andalucía, some of the very prettiest are to be found in the Serranía, and you could easily spend a fortnight's holiday driving (or

# Cliché Bandits

Despite the creeping cancer of the tourist *urbanizaciones* moving ever further inland and the spider's web of ever faster roads appearing across the region, much of Andalucía remains resolutely remote and reassuringly wild. Today's adventurous visitors head to the hills for incomparable climbing, hiking, mountain biking, paragliding and other adrenaline sports. 160 years ago intrepid travellers got their kicks in the same mountains, not from pitting themselves against nature, but rather from hoping for the thrill of a close encounter with *bandoleros* – bandits.

By the early 19th century Andalucía had become notorious across Europe as prime bandit country. Mountainous, remote, sparsely populated areas through which trade and travellers' routes ran offered prime pickings for bandits, and an easy escape into the wilderness. So it was that the Sierra Morena, the Serranía de Ronda and the Alpujarras, in particular, became infamous for their brigands (the Guardia Civil was set up in 1844 specifically to deal with the problem).

In the popular imagination the Andalucían *bandoleros* were often conceived of as Robin Hood-like figures, driven to a life of crime by the injustices of the social and economic system. One such was the bullfighter **José Ulloa** 'El Tragabuches' (born 1781; after whom Ronda's most famous restaurant is named), who took to banditry to escape the consequences of a crime of passion.

The most celebrated of all the region's outlaws was **José María Hinojosa Cabacho** 'El Tempranillo' (1805-33), who once pronounced that 'the King rules in Spain, but I rule in the sierra'. Having killed a man when he was 13, he fled to join a bandit gang and later ran a lucrative protection racket in the Sierra Morena, assuring travellers of safe passage on payment of a consideration. His concern for the poor and civilised treatment of his victims earned him a royal pardon just before his death.

Generally, however, chivalry wasn't foremost among the *bandolero*'s character traits. Ruthlessness and violence were far more common, as the white crosses planted beside the main routes chillingly (and thrillingly) reminded travellers. When Théophile Gautier passed through the region in the 1840s he delighted in reporting that:

'Danger surrounds you, follows and precedes you; you hear nothing on all sides but whispered tales of terror and mystery… No doubt there is much exaggeration in all this; but, however incredulous one may be, one is forced to believe something when one sees at every turn of the road wooden crosses bearing such inscriptions as "Here they killed a man", "Here died by violence…"'

Yet even by Gautier's time banditry was disappointingly elusive: 'The Spanish brigand was for us a purely fictitious being, an abstraction, a mere poem.'

By the 1870s the crackdown on banditry was producing results. The last of the famed *bandoleros* was **Juan Mingolla Gallardo** 'Pasos Largos' ('Long Steps') (1874-1934), whose demise in a shoot-out with the Guardia Civil was a suitably dramatic coda to the history of banditry in the region.

If you want to learn more, the **Museo del Bandolero** in Ronda (*see p92*) tells the story of many of the region's most famous bandits and the background to banditry in Andalucía.

walking) from one to the next. Tourism in this area has not reached anything like the scale of the Costa, but for a decade or two the Serranía has figured large on the tourist map and increasing numbers of expats are setting up home in the region. There are those who feel that, like in the Alpujarras (*see p274-82*), this influx of foreigners is changing the character of the region and putting otherwise affordable village houses out of the range of young Andalucíans. But as a visitor you'll benefit from the fact that there is an ever-increasing number of excellent places to stay and eat, and you can hardly blame anyone for wanting to live in this uniquely beautiful part of Spain.

One of the most popular and interesting excursions from Ronda is to the prehistoric **Cueva de la Pileta**. Discovered in 1905 by local farmer José Bullón (or by a British officer collecting chough's eggs, as another version of the story has it), the cave remains in the Bullón family's possession, in spite of periodic attempts by the local government to expropriate it. The tours, by the light of spluttering Davey lamps, are without doubt the most atmospheric and exciting in Andalucía. As well as the usual stalactites and stalagmites, there are naturalistic cave paintings of animals and fish dating from the late palaeolithic period (around 25,000 BC). These are almost certainly the oldest cave paintings in Andalucía. To reach the cave, take the MA505 (which becomes the MA561) towards Montejaque and Benaoján (both villages are worth a visit) from the A376 Ronda–Sevilla main road and look for the signs. You can't pre-book a visit but need to wait outside the cave entrance for the previous group to emerge or, if you are there first thing, for a member of the Bullón family to arrive from their farm in the valley below. The maximum number allowed to visit at one time (it tends to vary, but was 24 at the last count) is written on a sign outside the cave. So, if you arrive and there are more than this number already waiting, it's advisable to come back at some other time. Take warm clothes with you in the cooler months: the area outside the cave catches the winds that are funnelled along the Guadiaro valley.

A few kilometres north-west of Ronda are the hilltop Roman ruins of **Ronda La Vieja**. This was the site of the Roman town of **Acinipo**, whose heyday was during the first century AD. Much remains to be excavated, but the massive theatre, hewn out of the limestone hillside, gives some clue to the town's former importance. You can also see the remains of the forum and the public baths. To the north-west, a ten-minute drive brings you to the village of **Setenil de las Bodegas**, many of whose houses are carved into the side of an overhanging gorge. A number of them have become bars and restaurants. It is worth visiting the castle and church at the top end of the village.

Another popular excursion from Ronda is west into the **Parque Natural de la Sierra de Grazalema**, just over the border in Cádiz province (*see p128*). Far less visited is the **Parque Natural de la Sierra de las Nieves** to the south-east, but you have about a half-hour drive from Ronda before you reach good walking country. The Ronda tourist office sells a guide, in Spanish, listing walks.

The A369, heading south-west from Ronda, is a spectacular mountain road that passes several pristine *pueblos blancos* before arriving in **Gaucín**, one of the best-known villages in the area. The first foreigners to come here were British officers serving in Gibraltar during the 19th century, who would ride through en route to Ronda. Since then Gaucin has become hugely popular amongst wealthy expats, its property prices have rocketed and hotels, restaurants and bars seem to open by the day. Yet its winding streets, thankfully unsuitable for coach parties, retain much charm and the locals remain friendly. Gaucin is perched more than 600 metres (1,970 feet) up in the Serranía; on a clear day you can see the mountains of Morocco and, at night, the twinkling lights of Tangier. It has long been a strategic stronghold, as is easy to imagine as you clamber around the romantically ruined Moorish castle that overlooks the town. An old man usually hangs around by its entrance and will open up the gate and show you inside the chapel in return for a little loose change.

If you want to rent a villa or house in the area, contact the ever-helpful Conchi at **Cestur Hogar Turismo Rural** (C/Lorenzo Garcia 26, Gaucin, 952 15 16 00, mobile 607 94 93 53).

Based just outside Gaucin, in the hamlet of **Estación de Cortes**, two young Brits, Melanie and Tristram Templar of **Unseen Andalucía** (952 15 33 30, mobile 650 41 51 34, melytigre@eresmas.com), have been organising walks for several years. They can take you on a full- or half-day hike with a picnic provided or can put together a longer, bespoke itinerary.

Continuing along the A369 you cross into Cádiz province and come to **Jimena de la Frontera**, a large hill village beneath an extensive ruined Moorish castle. As in Gaucin, there's a strong expat (particularly British) influence here. Try to find time to hike along the spectacular Hozgarganta river valley beneath the village where, weather permitting, there are some wonderful places to swim. Jimena now hosts an annual international music festival at the beginning of summer.

# Walk Jimena circuit

**Distance** 14 kilometres (9 miles)
**Time required** 4 hours

This is an easy half-day walk out from Jimena de la Frontera that is best taken at a leisurely pace: the exceptionally pretty section of path leading down the Arroyo del Cañuelo should not be rushed. There are rock pools for bathing, and the old mill itself (about halfway into the walk) is a great spot for a picnic. On the higher sections of the walk there are wonderful views back to Jimena and across the beautiful Hozgarganta valley. And, apart from an initial steep section, there is not too much climbing involved. Note: this route should not be attempted when the Arroyo del Cañuelo stream is in spate.

The walk begins in Jimena de la Frontera's Plaza de la Constitución, which is just to the left of the road as you arrive at the bottom of the village. Leave the square at the top left-hand corner near Disco-Bar Calem and head up Calle San Sebastian, following signs for Hostal El Anon. Turn left into Calle Barrera, and at its end cross a small square into Calle La Vaca. Drop steeply down this street, then bear left into Chorro de la Calle. Pass a spring and at the end of the road bear sharp

left, then right, and drop down the hill past some ugly houses. Continue on past a sign marking the beginning of the Sendero del Río Hozgarganta. Your road merges with another, then crosses a bridge over the Hozgarganta river.

After a few hundred metres you reach a fork where you bear right up the hill. (Note: don't go left on the GR7.) Pass between two wooden posts with faint red-and-white markings and the road levels. There are lovely views back to Jimena. Careful! 30 metres past an entrance to a farm to the left of the road, at a point where there are eucalyptus trees, you should turn right off the road at a faint red dot on a low wall.

The path climbs, passes between a stand of eucalyptus and arrives at a ruined farmhouse. Swing left in front of the farm and, just past a stone-walled pen, bear sharp right and pick up a rough track that loops steeply up above the farm. There are occasional red dots.

Soon the track ends. Go right at a red dot and follow a narrow path steeply upwards. Soon it crosses a track and leads up to the top of a rather more open, eroded swathe

Jimena de la Frontera's castle. *See p99.*

South of Jimena, off to one side of the road leading to Algeciras, is the uniquely beautiful but claustrophobic village of **Castellar de la Frontera**. The original inhabitants were obliged to leave the village in the late 1960s when it seemed that the rising waters from a new reservoir would cut off access. It never happened and a band of hippies, most of them German, moved in to squat the village. An uneasy standoff between the newcomers and the locals ensued and continues to this day – even if most of the hippies have given up drug-dealing, bought their squatted houses, and embarked on new careers

managing tea and souvenir shops. There are plans to convert the castle into a hotel.

Both villages are on the borders of the huge **Parque Natural de los Alcornocales**, which takes up most of south-eastern Cádiz province (*see p128*).

### Cueva de la Pileta
*MA561 (952 16 73 43).* **Tours** hourly 10am-1pm, 4-6pm daily, on the hour. **Admission** €6. **No credit cards**.

### Ronda La Vieja
*MA449 (mobile 630 42 99 49).* **Open** 10am-3pm Tue-Sun. **Admission** free.

of hillside. At the top it bears right and you again pick up a track that leads on and up through the oaks. This track soon peters out. Go left and climb up through the cork oaks to the top of the ridge, ignoring a large red square painted on a rock.

At the crest of the ridge, there are great views up the Hozganganta valley. Pick up a track that runs to the left, along the top of the ridge. It soon runs parallel to a wall and a fence, over to your right. The vegetation becomes sparser – again there are amazing views – and the track bears slightly left, away from the wall, then drops down to a fence with a wire-and-post gate.

On the other side of the gate you'll see a tarmac road immediately ahead of you. Continue parallel to the road, just to its right, and you reach an indistinct track cutting directly in from the road. Bear sharp right onto this track (you should see a red arrow painted on a rock), drop over the top of the ridge and then bear left. There may be a chain across the track at this point. Follow this track all the way down through the cork oaks to the bottom of the valley. The track loops lazily downhill and you can occasionally cut off a corner. There are good views of the *lajas* (jagged ridges) on the other side of the valley.

The path becomes stonier and looser underfoot. Towards the bottom of the valley wild olives begin to take the place of the cork oaks. Cross a (dry) stream and, just before reaching the valley floor, the track loops hard to the left. Here look right for a cairn where you swing right away from the track and then drop down through the wild olives. The oleander-filled stream bed is to your left. (If you reach a concrete bridge across the Cañuelo, you have

come slightly too far and should retrace your footsteps to the sharp bend described earlier.)

The path is overgrown in parts but is easy enough to follow. Soon it crosses the stream, then follows the left bank of the Cañuelo. Cross the stream once again, this time via stepping stones. The sandy path improves as it winds through the rocks.

You cross a third time at a place where the stream has been shored up and pick up a beautiful cobbled footpath. It climbs away from the river before bearing right, following a water channel. Soon you arrive at a derelict mill (a wonderful picnic spot), and just beneath you there is a great place to swim.

Just 75 metres past the mill the path descends and crosses the riverbed. Look for a cairn. The castle of Jimena is visible up ahead. You pass another good bathing spot and the path climbs slightly away from the river into the cork oaks and passes between two huge rocks. At the next fork bear left, drop down and pass just to the right of a cork oak. The Hozganganta river soon comes into sight. The path again becomes cobbled and leads you through a wire-and-post gate.

On the other side of the gate the path turns right and, shortly afterwards, follows a fence on a course roughly parallel to the Hozganganta river, now on your left. Where the fence cuts uphill your path bears left and eventually brings you back to the tarmac road. Turn left onto the road, cross the river and you have a final steep climb back up into Jimena to the Plaza de la Constitución, retracing the route that you followed earlier in the walk.

*From* Walking in Andalucía *by Guy Hunter-Watts (Santana)*

## Where to stay & eat

The best of Setenil's bars is **Bar Frasquito** (C/Cuevas del Sol 75, 956 13 44 71, closed lunch and all day Mon, €), an atmospheric *bodega* bar with tables made from old sherry casks and a range of largely pork-based tapas.

In the sleepy village of Montecorto, a few kilometres south of the Roman theatre of Acinipo, is a great, friendly, laid-back B&B, **El Tejar** (952 18 40 53, double €65-€70, closed June-Aug). The house is the highest in the village and all the bedrooms have wonderful views out to the peaks of the Grazalema park.

There's a spring-fed pool surrounded by tall bamboo and a great collection of music and books, as well as a well-stocked honesty bar. The owner has written walking guides and has masses of route descriptions and maps.

Close to the rail station in Benaoján, west of Ronda, is **El Molino del Santo** (Estación de Benaoján, 952 16 71 51, www.andalucia.com/molino, closed mid Nov-mid Feb, double €80-€178, restaurant €-€€). This converted watermill, set in the beautiful Guadiaro valley, attracts large numbers of mainly British guests of all ages; it's an ideal place for families with young children. The staff are friendly and efficient without being obsequious and the restaurant has a more-interesting-than-most menu that mixes international and local dishes with some veggie alternatives.

If you prefer the idea of cheap local tapas, walk down the road to the entrance of the village opposite the railway station to **Bar Stop** (Barriada, Estación de Benaoján, 952 16 71 42, closed Sat, €), run by Doña Anita and Señor Pepe. The restaurant is packed at lunchtime on weekdays when local workers turn up for the excellent *menú del día*.

In Gaucín the best food in town can be found at the **Hotel Restaurante La Fructuosa** (C/Convento 67, 952 15 10 72, www.lafructuosa. com, double €92, restaurant open dinner Wed-Sat May-Oct, €€), run by Luis and Jesús, who prepare Moroccan-style dishes; there are also five beautifully decorated rooms.

The luxurious and deservedly popular **Hotel Casablanca** (C/Teodoro de Molina 12, 952 15 10 19, www.casablanca-gaucin.com, closed late Oct-early Mar, double €80-€105, restaurant €€), recently under new management, has had a complete facelift and promises to be as good as ever. This surprisingly grand village house has bags of relaxed character, a small pool and a crow's-nest of a raised terrace from which you can see Africa on a clear day.

A great spot to stay between Ronda and Gaucín is **Hotel El Gecko** (C/Cañada del Real Tesoro 39, Estación de Cortes de la Frontera, 952 15 33 15, www.hotelelgecko.com, hotel closed Jan, Feb, double €78, restaurant €€-€€€, closed Mon). The five bedrooms are decorated in impeccable less-is-more taste (four look out over the river) and there's a lovely restaurant terrace, where first-rate globally inspired bistro favourites are served alongside more sophisticated dishes to an almost exclusively expat clientele. There's a heated pool too. To reach El Gecko, take the MA508 off the A369 Ronda–Gaucín road.

There are two top-notch places to stay in Jimena. **Hostal Anon** (C/Consuelo 36, 956 64 01 13, www.andalucia.com/jimena/hostal anon/info.htm, hotel closed 2wks end of June & 2wks end of Nov, double €55, apartments €65, restaurant €€, closed Wed) is run by Suzie Odell, who came to Jimena in the '70s. The *hostal* has become the main port of call for walkers and backpackers in Jimena, while its reputation for good food brings day-trippers up from the coast. Rooms vary considerably – some are enormous and with views, others are smaller with dim lighting. There is a small rooftop plunge pool, a little bar that is decked out like an English pub and a beamed restaurant offering international food. In Jimena you will also find the relaxed, friendly **Posada**

**La Casa Grande** (C/Fuentenueva 42, 956 64 05 78, http://personal.iddeo.es/casagrande, double €35-€45, apartments €60, restaurant €-€€, closed Tue) run by another expat, Tom Andresen, from Norway. Rooms are spacious, bright and there are self-catering apartments as well. The recently opened restaurant offers a simple tapas menu.

There are plenty of other eating options in Jimena. **Restaurante-Bar España** (C/Sevilla 82, no phone, closed Sun, €-€€) knocks out a decent range of regional dishes at rock-bottom prices. A slightly more expensive choice is the **Restaurante-Bar Cuenca** (Avenida los Deportes 21, 956 64 01 52, closed Tue, €€), one of the oldest restaurants in town, serving tapas as well as fresh shellfish. **Meson Campoy** (Mesila de los Angeles 36, 956 64 10 60, closed Wed and late July-early Aug, €€) has international dishes, including home-made pizzas and barbecued meats. There are a good range of tapas bars in Jimena; the main meeting point for the local expat crowd is boisterous **Bar El Ventorrillero** (Plaza de la Constitución 2, 956 64 09 97, closed last 2wks Sept, €). Another option is **Café Lorca** (C/Sevilla 18, 956 64 05 88, closed Tue, €), a decent place for a quiet drink in a comfy setting with English-speaking bar staff.

## Resources

### Tourist information

**Parque Natural de la Sierra de las Nieves**
*Casa del Guarda, C/Alameda de Tajo s/n, Ronda (952 87 77 78).* **Open** 8am-1.30pm Mon-Fri.

## Getting there

### By bus

Ronda's bus station (952 87 22 60, mobile 657 91 44 48) is on Plaza Redondo, close to the rail station and around 15mins on foot from the Puente Nuevo. For a timetable of buses to and from Ronda get hold of a copy of the local newspaper, *Ronda Semanal*. There's 1 daily bus to Benaoján and Montejaque, and 1 to Gaucín and Jimena, 6 daily to Málaga, 4 daily to Arcos, 3 daily to Cádiz, 5 to Marbella, 5 to Sevilla, and 2 to Grazalema and Zahara de la Sierra.

### By train

Ronda's rail station (902 24 02 02) is in the new town on Avenida de Andalucía, about a 20min walk from the Puente Nuevo. Tickets can also be bought over the phone on 952 87 16 62. Ronda is on the rail line between Granada and Algeciras. There are 3 trains a day from Granada to Ronda (2hrs 30mins) and 6 daily from Ronda to Algeciras (1hr 40mins), 3 of which call at the stations in the Guadiaro valley and Jimena. For trains to and from Málaga, Córdoba, Sevilla and Cádiz, change at Bobadilla. Estación de Gaucín is 13km (8 miles) from Gaucín.

# Cádiz Province & Gibraltar

# Cádiz Province

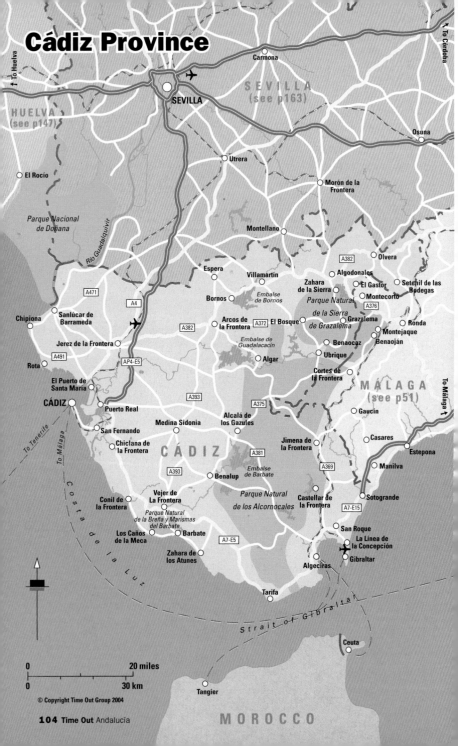

To Córdoba

To Huelva

**Carmona**

**SEVILLA**

**S E V I L L A**
(see p163)

**HUELVA**
(see p147)

**Osuna**

**El Rocío**

**Utrera**

**Morón de la
Frontera**

*Parque Nacional
de Doñana*

**Montellano**

*Río Guadalquivir*

A382

**Olvera**

**Espera**

**Villamartín**

**Algodonales**

**Zahara
de la Sierra**

**El Gastor**

**Setenil de las
Bodegas**

A471

A4

**Bornos**

*Embalse
de Bornos*

**Montecorto**

A376

*Parque Natural
de la Sierra*

**Chipiona**

**Sanlúcar de
Barrameda**

**Arcos de
la Frontera**

A372  **El Bosque**

*de Grazalema*

**Grazalema**

**Ronda**

A382

**Montejaque**

**Benaoján**

**Jerez de la Frontera**

*Embalse de
Guadalacacín*

**Benaocaz**

A491

AP4-E5

**Algar**

**Ubrique**

**Rota**

**Cortes de
la Frontera**

**El Puerto de
Santa María**

A393

A375

**M Á L A G A**
(see p51)

To Málaga

**CÁDIZ**

**Puerto Real**

**Gaucín**

**Alcalá de
los Gazules**

To Tenerife

To Málaga

**San Fernando**

**Medina Sidonia**

**Casares**

**Chiclana de
la Frontera**

**Jimena de
la Frontera**

A381

**Estepona**

**C Á D I Z**

*Costa de la Luz*

A393

A369

**Manilva**

**Benalup**

*Embalse
de Barbate*

**Castellar de
la Frontera**

**Sotogrande**

**Vejer de
La Frontera**

*Parque Natural
de los Alcornocales*

A7-E15

**Conil de
la Frontera**

*Parque Natural
de la Breña y Marismas
del Barbate*

**San Roque**

**Los Caños
de la Meca**

**Barbate**

A7-E5

**La Línea de
la Concepción**

**Zahara de
los Atunes**

**Algeciras**

**Gibraltar**

**Tarifa**

*Strait of Gibraltar*

**Ceuta**

0      20 miles

0      30 km

© Copyright Time Out Group 2004

**Tangier**

**M O R O C C O**

# Cádiz Province & Gibraltar

Wild country, pristine beaches, classic Spanish towns and a defiantly British Rock.

If you were to pick one province that represented the distillation of all things Andalucian, then it would have to be Cádiz. A distinctive and enjoyable provincial capital, a largely virgin coastline facing the untamed Atlantic, a dramatically hilly interior specked with white villages, vibrant towns, wonderful seafood, sherry, horses, flamenco and a political hot potato (or, rather, Rock) on its doorstep…

## CÁDIZ CITY

The provincial capital, dramatically isolated on a spit of land, and surrounded by the sea, is a singular place. Its old town, with long straight streets and projecting glazed balconies, is heavy with atmosphere and feels quite unlike any other Andalucian city. There are fine museums and churches plus, unsurprisingly, some of the best seafood in the region – and probably the top carnival in all Spain.

## NORTH OF CÁDIZ

Just to the north of Cádiz lies the famous sherry triangle, made up of the towns of Jerez, El Puerto and Sanlúcar, all appealing places to visit in their own right. Apart from their *bodegas*, all three are famed for the excellence of their tapas. Jerez is also known for flamenco and horses, while Sanlúcar is a gateway to the wilderness of the Doñana National Park.

## EAST OF CÁDIZ

The inland portion of Cádiz province is chiefly known for its collection of *pueblos blancos* (white villages), scattered like patches of pristine snow among the spectacular hills that merge into Málaga province. Arcos de la Frontera, one of the most impressively sited, makes an excellent base from which to explore some of the wild, lesser populated areas around.

## COSTA DE LA LUZ

Running from Cádiz to Tarifa is the longest stretch of unspoilt coastline in Andalucía. Though development is proceeding at an alarming rate, there are still endless swathes of virgin golden sand to enjoy. The coast is at its most dramatic around the laid-back hippyish little resort of Los Caños de Meca,

while Vejer de la Frontera, back from the coast, is the most perfect *pueblo blanco* in the area. The enjoyable town of Tarifa has a cool surf-dude vibe, and the constant winds around here draw in windsurfers from all over Europe.

## GIBRALTAR

Geographically awe-inspiring, historically fascinating, aesthetically horrifying, Britain's controversial Mediterranean outpost raises strong emotions whether you're Gibraltarian, Spanish or just a visitor. Coming from Spain, its retro UK seaside town vibe is a shock, and beyond the apes and the siege tunnels, it's appeal is largely limited to homesick Brits in search of cheap booze and fags.

## The best...

**Architecture & history**
Cádiz City (*p106-11*).

**Beaches**
All along the **Costa de la Luz** (*p131-41*).

**Flamenco**
Jerez (*p113*).

**Low-key resorts**
**Los Caños de la Meca** (*p132*);
**Zahara de los Atunes** (*p132*).

**Natural beauty**
**Doñana** (*p122*); **Los Alcornocales** (*p128*);
**Sierra de Grazalema** (*p128*).

**Seafood & sherry**
**Jerez** (*p113*); **El Puerto de Santa María** (*p124*); **Sanlúcar de Barrameda** (*p121*).

**White villages**
**Arcos de la Frontera** (*p126*); **Vejer de la Frontera** (*p133*); **Zahara de la Sierra** (*p129*).

**Windsurfing**
**Tarifa** (*p138*).

# Cádiz City

Bask in the faded glory of this historic, atmospheric port.

Isolated at the end of a narrow strip of land, hammered by the sea on three sides and seemingly unchanged in more than 200 years, Cádiz – at least the old part of town – encapsulates every romantic notion of a port. To walk along the seafront as sunset turns to dusk, to lose yourself in the maze of narrow streets and marvel at the ungainly gold-topped cathedral – the first thing a returning sailor would see from his ship – is like taking a walk through history.

Cádiz today is made up of two distinct parts – the old city, crammed onto the fist-shaped headland, and the unappealing new town, stretching back from here to the mainland on either side of the Avenida de Andalucía.

The city claims to be the oldest in western Europe and dates its history back to 1100 BC, when the Phoenicians knew it as Gadir – hence the name of its citizens, *gaditanos*. It was used as a base by the Carthaginians for military campaigns in the peninsula and prospered under Roman rule after Julius Caesar granted Gades, as it became known, the privileges of a Roman town.

After the Romans left Cádiz declined, and it was only of minor importance under the Moors. Trade with the Americas helped revive its fortunes in the 16th century (though an English raid in 1596 destroyed a third of the city). The city's period of greatest prosperity began in 1717, when the silting up of the Guadalquivir led the Chamber of Commerce of the Americas to move here from Sevilla.

A century later, the town achieved its historical zenith when, in 1812, the short-lived Cortes (Spanish parliament) met here to declare the first Spanish constitution.

Today, Cádiz is a youthful, vibrant city of around 150,000, though the old town is haunted by an appealingly melancholic air. It remains undiscovered by mass foreign tourism and hosts what is indisputably the best carnival on mainland Spain (*see p112* **¡Carnaval!**).

## Sightseeing

The old part of Cádiz is compact and can be seen on foot in a day. The city retains an air of faded grandeur; many of the buildings are in dire need of repair and, although a certain amount of restoration is taking place, the city authorities are not keen to prettify the place too much. The architecture of the old town dates mainly from the late 18th and early 19th centuries, and reflects a strong influence from France, with elegant neo-classical detailing and buildings arranged in long, straight rows. Another striking feature is the number of projecting glazed balconies.

A (now faded) red line through the town leads visitors from the Plaza San Juan de Dios, one of the town's prettiest squares, through the oldest part of town, the medieval **Barrio del Pópulo**, via a number of other lovely streets and squares.

**Plaza San Juan de Dios** is a fine palm-fringed square fronted by the huge *Ayuntamiento* and lined with numerous bars and cafés. Head west from here along Calle Pelota and you will reach Plaza de la Catedral.

Begun in 1722 when money from the Americas was pouring into Cádiz, the immense **Catedral Nueva** was designed by Vicente Acero and should have been one of the most architecturally memorable churches in Spain. However, money ran short and the project took

Plaza San Juan de Dios.

far longer than expected, so that when it was finally completed (in 1853) it consisted of a mishmash of jarring styles. It is also fighting a losing battle against the elements and is visibly crumbling. Inside, there is a small museum with a collection of silver, the centrepiece of which is the so-called *Millón*, an over-the-top *custodia* encrusted with one million gems and precious stones. The tomb of locally born composer Manuel de Falla is in the crypt.

Just east of the current cathedral, in the Barrio del Pópulo, is Cádiz's former cathedral, now the church of **Santa Cruz** (open times of services). It was built in 1260 over a mosque, and was all but destroyed by the English in 1596; most of what you see today dates from the 17th century. The church is notable for its *retablos*.

Just beyond Santa Cruz lies the (currently closed) **Teatro Romano** (Roman theatre), dating from the first century BC. Ongoing excavations on the site have revealed much of the interior seating and galleries, as well as the remains of a Moorish fortress.

From Plaza de la Catedral, Calle Compañía leads north-west to Plaza de las Flores, another attractive square that is home to the town's **Mercado Central** (Central Market), set mainly in a dilapidated 19th-century building, surrounded by bustling bars and cafés.

West of the square, just off Calle Sacramento is the **Torre Tavira**, part of an 18th-century mansion and the tallest tower in the old city. It contains a camera obscura, giving stunning views over the city, and an exhibition on Cádiz's seafaring past.

A right turn on to Calle Sagasta and first left on to Calle Santa Inés bring you to two of Cádiz's most important and interesting buildings, the town's history museum, **Museo de las Cortes de Cádiz**, and the **Oratorio de San Felipe Neri**. Historically one of the most significant buildings in Spain, the Oratorio is where a group of liberals assembled on 29 March 1812, in defiance of Napoleon, to draft the Cortes, a radical document, way ahead of its time, that posited a Spanish constitution and declared Spain an independent republic with full religious and political freedom.

The revolution was short-lived and it took another 163 years before Spain emerged as a fully fledged democracy, but the ideas of the Cádiz Cortes played a major part in shaping modern European politics. The church itself has a very pretty interior, with two sets of balconies framing the central space and large windows in the dome to illuminate the predominantly blue decor. The altar is decorated with an Immaculate Conception by Murillo. Next door, the centrepiece of the museum is an enormous scale model of the city as it was in 1777, which shows how little

the old part of the city has changed in more than 200 years. The museum also contains numerous artefacts related to events in 1812.

A short walk west from here lies Cádiz's main theatre, the neo-Moorish **Gran Teatro Falla**, named after one of the town's most famous sons, composer Manuel de Falla.

Another couple of minutes' walk west lies the delightful **Parque Genovés**, laid out along the seafront and home to a centuries-old dragon tree, imported from the Canary Islands. Follow the gardens round to the north-east to reach the **Baluarte de Candelaria**, a promontory that adjoins the Alameda de Marqués de Comillas, where you'll find more seafront gardens with some ancient trees.

Inland from here, de Falla's birthplace is marked by a plaque in the garden-filled Plaza de Mina, also the site of the **Museo de Cádiz**. The museum is divided between three floors. On the ground floor is a display of archaeological finds from the province covering the Roman, Phoenician and Greek periods, including glassware, amphorae, marbles and pottery – the two Phoenician tombs here are the equal of any in Spain. The fine-art museum on the second floor contains some impressive paintings by Murillo, Zurbarán (an important series of panels from the charterhouse in Jerez) and Alonso Cano, and a Rubens, while the third floor concentrates on local ceramics and textiles as well as an antique puppet collection.

Just east of the Plaza de Mina is the church of **San Francisco** (open hours of services) in the square of the same name and the nearby **Oratorio de Santa Cueva**, which contains the only Goya frescoes in Andalucía. They depict three key moments in Christ's life, including the Last Supper at which Christ and the disciples are shown eating on the floor. Steps head down to a gloomy chapel.

The streets leading east from here – Calle San Francisco, Calle Rosario and, a few blocks south, Calle Ancha, are some of the most attractive in the city, full of bars, restaurants and little shops. Calle Ancha also contains a well-preserved 19th-century mansion, **Casa Museo Palacio de Mora**, which provides a glimpse of life during that era. Rooms are full of artefacts and arranged round a pretty patio.

North-east of Plaza de San Francisco is the huge but rather soulless Plaza de España, with a monument to the Cortes at its centre. The *plaza* gives on to the bus station and the port area, from where boats depart for the Canary Islands.

At the opposite end of the old town, in the far south-western corner, is the old fishermen's quarter known as the **Barrio de la Viña**. The streets here are full of bars and restaurants as well as a number of *peñas de flamenco*.

Just beyond it, fronting the old town's beach, Playa de la Caleta, are enormous, ancient dragon trees, which are particularly beautiful when floodlit at night. **Playa de la Caleta** is small, a bit dirty and gets incredibly crowded in high season; **Playa de Santa María**, just outside the old town, suffers from a similar fate. If you're after some sun and sea, your best bet is to head to the enormous expanse of the **Playa de la Victoria**, further into the new town, which is huge, clean and hosts all the night-time action during the summer.

### Casa Museo Palacio de Mora

*C/Ancha 26 (956 21 14 09).* **Open** phone for details. **Admission** free. **Map** p109 B2.

### Catedral Nueva

*Plaza de la Catedral; entrance to museum on Plaza Fray Félix s/n (956 25 98 12).* **Open** 10am-1.30pm, 4.30-7pm Tue-Fri; 10am-1pm Sat. **Admission** €2.50. No credit cards. **Map** p109 C2.

### Gran Teatro Falla

*Plaza de Falla s/n (956 22 08 34).* **Open** Box office noon-2pm, 6-9pm Tue-Fri; also prior to performances. **Tickets** from €3.50. No credit cards. **Map** p109 A2.

### Museo de Cádiz

*Plaza Mina s/n (956 21 22 81).* **Open** 2.30-8pm Tue; 9am-8.30pm Wed-Sat; 9am-2.30pm Sun. **Admission** €1.50; free with EU passport. No credit cards. **Map** p109 B1.

### Museo de las Cortes de Cádiz

*C/Santa Inés 9 (956 22 17 88).* **Open** 9am-1pm, 5-7pm Tue-Fri; 9am-1pm Sat, Sun. **Admission** free. **Map** p109 B2.

### Oratorio de San Felipe Neri

*Plaza San Felipe Neri (956 21 16 12).* **Open** 10am-1.30pm Mon-Sat. **Admission** €1.20. No credit cards. **Map** p109 B2.

### Oratorio de Santa Cueva

*C/Rosario 10 (956 22 22 62).* **Open** 9am-1pm, 5-8pm Tue-Fri; 9am-1pm Sat, Sun. **Admission** €2. No credit cards. **Map** p109 B1.

### Torre Tavira

*C/Marqués del Real Tesoro 10 (956 21 29 10/ www.torretavira.com).* **Open** Mid June-mid Sept 10am-7.30pm daily. Mid Sept-mid June 10am-5.30pm daily. **Admission** €3.50; €2.80 concessions. No credit cards. **Map** p109 B2.

## Where to eat & drink

### Old town

In addition to the places below, if you yearn for a taste of the real Cádiz (and aren't too fussy about decor) try the tapas bars **La Rambla** and **Noya** in Calle Sopranis (which leads off Plaza San Juan de Dios, map C1).

### Achuri

*C/Plocia 15 (956 25 36 13).* **Open** 1-4.30pm Mon-Wed, Sun; 1-4.30pm, 8.30pm-midnight Thur-Sat. Closed 24 Dec-6 Jan. **Average** €€. **Credit** AmEx, V. **Map** p109 C1.
This place is popular with *gaditanos* and specialises in Basque and Andalucian dishes, including *morros de cerdo* (meat from the face of a pig, in spicy sauce).

### El Aljibe

*C/Plocia 25 (956 26 66 56).* **Open** 12.30-4.30pm, 8pm-midnight daily. **Average** €€€. **Credit** DC, MC, V. **Map** p109 C1.
Located in a restored historic house (and named after the old well in the basement), El Aljibe has an excellent menu and superb tapas.

### Balandro

*Paseo Alameda de Apodaca 22 (956 22 09 92).* **Open** noon-4.30pm, 8pm-1.30am Tue-Sat. **Average** €€€. **Credit** AmEx, DC, MC, V. **Map** p109 A1.
Enjoying fine sea views, this stylish restaurant offers first-rate seafood and meat dishes as well as tapas. The house special is *rollitos de dorado* (rolls of dorado fish).

### Bar Terraza Pelayo

*Plaza de la Catedral 3 (956 28 26 05).* **Open** Mid June-mid Sept 10am-midnight Mon-Sat. Mid Sept-mid June 10am-midnight Tue-Sun. **Average** €€€.
**Credit** AmEx, DC, MC, V. **Map** p109 C2.
In a superb spot by the cathedral, this 50-year-old institution serves high-quality regional dishes, but you do pay a premium for the location.

### La Caleta

*Plaza San Juan de Dios 1 (956 27 27 81).* **Open** 10am-midnight daily. **Average** €€. **Credit** AmEx, DC, MC, V. **Map** p109 C1.
Now the only restaurant left in this beautiful square, La Caleta turns out relatively standard fare (specialising in prawn and clam dishes) plus numerous tapas and *raciones*. The location is one of the best in town.

### Cervecería-Marisquería Joselito

*C/San Francisco 38 (956 26 65 48).* **Open** 11am-4pm, 8pm-midnight Mon-Sat. **Average** €€. **Credit** AmEx, DC, MC, V. **Map** p109 B1.
Owned by three friendly brothers, this much-loved twin-fronted institution occupies both a traditional spot on C/San Francisco and a trendy terrace overlooking the port. The house speciality *almejas joselito* (clams) and fried fish are excellent.

### El Faro

*C/San Félix 15 (956 21 10 68).* **Open** 1-4.30pm, 8.30pm-midnight daily. **Average** €€€. **Credit** AmEx, DC, MC, V. **Map** p109 B3.
Widely considered to be the number-one restaurant in town (and one of the best in the province), El Faro specialises in, of course, seafood. The menu has an extraordinary range and the quality of execution is sublime. House specialities include *lubina* (bass) and *cigalas* (crayfish). If you can't afford the restaurant, there is a first-class tapas bar too.

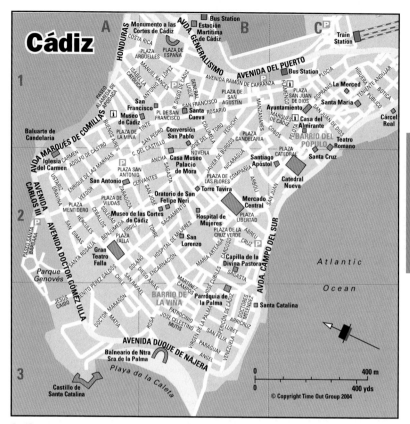

Cádiz

## Gotinga

*Plaza Mentidero 15 (956 07 05 80).* **Open** 1pm-1am Mon-Sat. **Average** €€. **Credit** AmEx, DC, MC, V. **Map** p109 A2.

The only foreign-owned bar in town, this German-run place makes a refreshing change from traditional Spanish eateries, and offers a wide range of international tapas, good salads, bottled beers and 12 types of tea.

## Merodio

*C/Libertad 4, Mercado Central, Plaza de Abastos (956 21 43 10).* **Open** 9am-midnight daily. **Average** €. **No credit cards**. **Map** p109 B2.

This Cádiz institution fronts the Mercado Central and is consequently always busy, especially at Carnaval time when it traditionally becomes a focal point for drunken revellers.

## Pablito

*Avenida de Ramón de Carranza 30 (956 28 31 55).* **Open** 9am-1am daily. **Average** €. **Credit** AmEx, DC, MC, V. **Map** p109 B/C1.

A well-established spot offering simple but tasty fare, including *cazón de abodo* (fried fish) and a good-value *menú del dia*.

## Taberna el Albero

*C/San Félix 2 (956 22 08 38).* **Open** noon-4pm, 8pm-1am daily. **Average** €. **Credit** AmEx, DC, MC, V. **Map** p109 B3.

Run by a one-time *toreador*, this little bar, full of bullfighting memorabilia, is popular with local characters. Try the delicious *tortillitas de camarones* (prawn fritters).

# New town

## Arte Serrano

*Paseo Marítimo 2 (956 27 72 58).* **Open** 1-5pm, 8pm-midnight daily. **Average** €€. **Credit** AmEx, DC, V.

If you're tired of fish, then try this excellent meat restaurant, dedicated to porky products. All the *jamones* (hams), *lomos* (pork loins) and *chorizos*

**Parque Genovés.** *See p107.*

(paprika-spiced sausages) are produced locally. It's not expensive and there is also an excellent selection of meaty tapas.

### El Baro

*Below Residencia Tiempo Libre, Paseo Marítimo s/n (956 25 79 57).* **Open** *May-Oct* 1pm-midnight daily. *Nov-Apr* noon-5pm, 7pm-midnight daily. **Average** €€. **Credit** DC, MC, V.

Serving fine fresh fish and shellfish, El Baro is a cheaper alternative to La Marea just up the road (*see below*).

### La Leyenda

*Paseo Marítimo 20 (956 26 21 85).* **Open** 1-5pm, 9pm-midnight Tue-Sat; 1-5pm Sun. **Average** €€. **Credit** AmEx, DC, MC, V.

For a first-class three-course meal try this smart new town restaurant, which shares the same owner as Balandro (*see p108*). The food is excellent – try the chicken in Pedro Ximénez sauce.

### La Marea

*Paseo Marítimo 1 (956 28 03 47).* **Open** 1-5pm, 8pm-1am daily. **Average** €€. **Credit** AmEx, DC, MC, V.

Regarded as the best seafood restaurant in this part of town, La Marea is not particularly classy, but prices are very reasonable and the menu is enormous: everything from the bay is here, including *lubina* (bass) and *langostinos* (langoustines). There's a bar attached if you'd rather sample a few tapas than have a full meal.

## Nightlife

Apart from during the joyful chaos of Carnaval, and despite a large student population, Cádiz does not have a hugely exciting nightlife during the winter months. The most popular area for after-dark revelry is the **Punta de San Felipe** at the tip of the harbour, which is crammed with bars and discos, most of which get going after midnight. One of the best of these is **El Malecon** (Paseo Almirante Pascual Perry Junquera s/n, 956 22 45 19, closed Mon-Wed all year and Thur mid Sept-mid June), which is a Latin dance venue popular with all ages.

Try also the streets around Plaza de Candelaria, Plaza de San Antonio and Plaza de Mina, which are popular with students. Plaza San Francisco gets packed on Friday and Saturday nights with students who buy spirits and mixers from nearby shops.

The **Barrio de la Viña** is a good area to find flamenco, although popular spots from the past like **El Quini** on C/San Felix and **Juan Vilar** at C/Puerta la Caleta only rarely put on shows these days. This area is also the heart of Carnaval preparations; the modern-day interpretation of Carnaval began in the late 19th century in the Plaza del Tio de la Tiza (named after the man who revived the festivities), and many costumes and effigies are still made in this district.

Venues in the old town that put on regular flamenco shows include **La Cava** (C/Antonio Lopez, 956 21 18 66, www.flamencolacava.com, closed Mon-Wed, Fri & Sun in winter, shows 9pm, €22 with drink, map B1) and **Pena la Perla** (C/Carlos Ollero, 956 27 98 02, open 10pm-late Thur, Fri), next to the Cárcel Vieja.

**Woodstock** (C/Manuel Rances 13, no phone, 8pm-3am Mon-Fri, 8pm-4am Sat, Sun, map B1) is an international bar that serves a decent pint and plays rock music. There are two other branches in Cádiz, on the Paseo Marítimo and on Calle Canovas del Castillo. For varied live shows, try **Pay Pay** (no phone, closed Mon & Sun, free, map C1/2) on the corner of Calles Meson and Silencio, just behind the Teatro Romano. You can see anything here – flamenco, rock, tango and acoustic performances.

As soon as it starts to get warm *gaditanos* decamp to the new town and the hundreds of bars and discos around the **Playa de la Victoria**. Most discos play a standard diet of dodgy Spanish techno called *bacalao*.

## Shopping

The main shopping area in the old town is concentrated along and around four main streets: Calles Ancha, Columela (which has branches of Spanish clothing favourites Zara and Mango), San Francisco and Compañia. In the new town, shops flank both sides of the Avenida de Andalucía from the Plaza de la Constitución until the turn-off for the bridge. **Mediterráneo** (C/San Pedro 12, 956 22 70 89, closed Sun, map B1) is the best place in town for tasteful pottery, candles, rugs and small presents, while **Mareta** (C/San Pedro 8-10, 956 21 18 17, closed Sun, map B1) stocks stylish household goods including glass and cushions, many of which are recycled or made from natural products. The two branches of **Máspapeles** at Calle San José 6 (956 22 07 91, map B2) and Avenida de Andalucía 84 (956 28 16 99) have a good range of stationery plus hand-painted gifts including bags and purses (closed Sun all year and Sat June-Sept).

If you're after something original from the province, try **Hecho en Cádiz** (Plaza Candelaria s/n, 956 28 31 97, closed Sun, map B1), which has typical local art and sculpture, or **Los Duros Antiguos** (C/Beato Diego 7, 956 21 11 68, closed Sun, map B1), which is designed like an old boat and has Carnaval memorabilia and piratical knick-knacks. **Aguamanil** (C/Plocia 21, 956 28 81 85, closed Sun, map C1) sells high-quality local art, much of it reflecting the history of Cádiz.

## Where to stay

The old town is the place to stay, though accommodation is more luxurious in the new town, which may be a good option if you want to be where the action is in the summer. Other than at Carnaval time, you will always be able to find a room: the old town, particularly off Plaza San Juan de Dios, is full of *hostales* and *pensiones*.

## Old town

### Hospederia Las Cortes De Cadiz
*C/San Francisco 9 (956 21 26 68/www.hotel lascortes.com).* **Rates** (incl breakfast) €72-€98 single; €102-€128 double. **Credit** AmEx, DC, MC, V. **Map** p109 B1.
This stylish three-star hotel opened in early 2004 and is a welcome addition to the accommodation options in the old town. Rates include an all-you-can-eat breakfast served in the hotel's classy café. Rooms overlooking the central courtyard can get noisy.

### Hostal Centro Sol
*C/Manzanares 7 (956 28 31 03/www.hostalcentrosol cadiz.com).* **Rates** €32-€40 single; €40-€49 double. **Credit** AmEx, DC, MC, V. **Map** p109 B1.
This decent, clean guesthouse enjoys a convenient central location.

### Hostal Marqués
*C/Marqués de Cádiz 1 (956 28 58 54).* **Rates** €18 single; €25-€35 double. **No credit cards.** **Map** p109 C1.
This typical Cádiz house in the city centre is 100m (330ft) from a car park. Rooms are a little spartan.

### Hotel Atlántico
*Avenida Duque de Nájera 9 (956 22 69 05/ www.parador.es).* **Rates** (incl breakfast) €79-€93 single; €106-€123 double; €176-€239 suite. **Credit** AmEx, DC, MC, V. **Map** p109 A/B1.
This four-star *parador* is a modern building in an excellent position right on the seafront, near the town centre. It has a large swimming pool and a tiny

spot of beach. Rooms are modern and comfortable; go for the suites with sea views. There's a good restaurant and plenty of parking.

### Hotel Francia y Paris
*Plaza San Francisco 6 (956 22 23 48/ www.hotelfrancia.com).* **Rates** €56-€62 single; €70-€77 double. **Credit** AmEx, DC, MC, V. **Map** p109 B1.
A charming three-star hotel right in the heart of the city on a very pretty square, this is an excellent option if you want to soak up the old town atmosphere. Rooms are comfortable, but the square gets very noisy on weekend nights.

### Pensión Colón
*C/Marqués de Cádiz 6 (956 28 53 51).* **Rates** €32-€55 double. **No credit cards.** **Map** p109 C1.
Run by a friendly elderly couple, this *pensión* has good-value, clean rooms, some en suite.

### Pensión Fantoni
*C/Flamenco 5 (956 28 27 04/www.hostal fantoni.com).* **Rates** €15-€20 single; €25-€55 double; €35-€75 triple; €60-€80 family room. **No credit cards.** **Map** p109 C1.
Budget accommodation in an 18th-century house decorated with tiles and marble, and with a pleasant terrace. Undergoing renovation at the time of writing, it's due to re-open in January 2005.

## New town

### Hotel Playa Victoria
*C/Ingeniero la Cierva 4 (956 20 51 00/ www.palafoxhoteles.com).* **Rates** €124-€166 double; €300-€333 suite. **Credit** AmEx, DC, MC, V.
This four-star is by far the most luxurious option in the city, situated in a fantastic spot right on the beach and beside a strip of the best new town restaurants. Rooms are big, modern and comfortable, with balconies and sea views. The hotel pool is virtually on the beach, and there's a good restaurant and bar.

### Hotel Tryp La Caleta
*Avenida Amilcar Barca 47 (956 25 93 22/ www.solmelia.com).* **Rates** phone for details. **Credit** AmEx, DC, MC, V.
Despite the ugly exterior and characterless atmosphere this new four-star is located right on the Playa de Victoria and has excellent facilities.

## Resources

### Internet
*Cibercafé, C/Abreu 9, bajo, near Plaza Cruz Verde (956 22 58 88/www.cibercafe.com).* **Open** 11am-3pm, 6pm-midnight daily.
*Enred@2, C/Isabel la Catolica, off Plaza de San Francisco (956 21 44 30).* **Open** 11am-11pm daily. **Map** p109 B1. There is another branch on the corner of C/Cervantes and C/San José (956 21 39 96; same opening hours).

# ¡Carnaval!

It's impossible to overestimate the importance of this ten-day orgy of excess to the average *gaditano*. Many locals spend all year designing costumes or rehearsing for a band. Starting in the second week of February, it's the biggest and best carnival on mainland Spain (the one in Tenerife is its only rival), and signifies the start of the *feria* season in Andalucía. People come from all over the country and beyond to join in the festivities, so accommodation is at a premium.

Carnaval is about more than just drinking and dancing in the streets though. Like Las Fallas in Valencia it has an overtly political message, with many people in satirical costumes lampooning local figures.

It took its current form in the late 19th century thanks to a man called Antonio Rodríguez Martínez (El Tío de la Tiza), who is remembered by a plaque in the square of the same name. He organised bands of musicians to roam the streets of the old town. These (usually male) groups, in various stages of drunkenness, are still a major feature of Carnaval. Some are professional musicians or serious amateur singers, others are simply clueless and legless.

Throughout the ten days, floats, parades, competitions and concerts entertain revellers in many of the squares. If you stay for the whole time, you will find the festivities get progressively more chaotic; crowds of

people throng the streets getting increasingly drunk and staggering around in outlandish costumes. There is also an almost continuous stream of revellers arriving on special Carnaval buses and trains from Jerez and Sevilla, and from the towns nearby, in particular from the US naval base at Rota.

### Post office
*Plaza Tapete s/n (956 21 05 11).*

### Police station
*Plaza San Juan de Puerto Rico (956 24 11 00).*

### Tourist information
*Avenida Ramón de Carranza s/n (956 25 86 46/ otcadiz@andalucia.org).* **Open** 9am-7pm Mon-Fri; 10am-1.30pm Sat, Sun. **Map** p109 B1. Info on the whole province.
*Plaza San Juan de Dios 11 (956 24 10 01).* **Open** 9am-2pm, 5-8pm daily. **Map** p109 C1. City-specific information.

## Getting there

### By bus
The Amarillos line, which runs from the bus station at Avenida Ramón de Carranza 31 (956 29 08 00, map C1), has frequent services to the nearby resorts of El Puerto, Sanlúcar and Chipiona. Estación de Comes (Plaza de la Hispanidad, next to Plaza de España, 956

80 70 59) is used for long-distance services to Sevilla, points along the coast to Algeciras and beyond, and inland to Granada and Córdoba. There's also an El Puerto/Rota service from here. Secorbus runs 6 buses daily between Avenida José Leon de Carranza 20 (902 22 92 92, www.socibus.es, map B1) and Madrid.

### By boat
Boat services run to Tenerife, Las Palmas de Gran Canaria and La Palma every Tuesday. Tickets and information are available from Transmediterránea (Avenida Ramón de Carranza 26-8, 902 45 46 45, www.transmediterranea.es, map B/C1). El Vapor, the ferry across the bay to El Puerto, also departs from the port (629 46 80 14, www.vapordeelpuerto.com).

### By train
The train station (Plaza de Sevilla, 902 24 02 02, map C1) is a few minutes' walk from the main square, Plaza San Juan de Dios. There are around 14 daily trains to Sevilla (2hrs), all of which call at El Puerto de Santa María (25mins from Cádiz) and Jerez (45mins from Cádiz). Four direct trains a day run to Córdoba (4hrs), and one a day to Jaén (5hrs).

# North of Cádiz

This tiny sliver of Andalucía has it all – characterful towns, beaches, superlative seafood, authentic flamenco and, of course… sherry.

Jacarandas in bloom in **Jerez**.

The north-west corner of Cádiz province is small in area but rich in attractions. This is sherry country, and the lively, likeable town of Jerez is its heart. The two other points of the 'sherry triangle' – Sanlúcar de Barrameda and El Puerto de Santa María – are also enjoyable places to visit. Both are famed for their seafood, and the former is one of the access points to the wild Parque Nacional de Doñana (*see also p152* **The last wilderness**). The stretch of coast here, including the resorts of Chipiona and Rota, is a favoured holiday spot for *sevillanos* and *gaditanos*, and in July and August you will be hard-pressed to find a room.

## Jerez de la Frontera

The economy of the largest city in Cádiz province (36 kilometres/22 miles north-east of the provincial capital) is almost entirely dependent on the production and export – mainly to Britain – of sherry and brandy, but in recent years the famous brands have seen a fall in demand and

profits, resulting in **Jerez de la Frontera** having one of the highest unemployment rates in Andalucia. Not that this is apparent as you wander around the well-maintained streets of the town, and it remains a relaxed and pleasant place to while away a day or two. As well as sherry and brandy in abundance, the town boasts superb tapas bars, some authentic flamenco venues and many outstanding buildings.

The name Jerez is an anglicised version of the Phoenician 'Xeres' – the town formed part of the ancient empire of Tartessus. The Moors, who called the town 'Sherrish', ruled until 1264, and it is from around this time that the 'de la Frontera' was added – like so many Andalucían towns it was on the front line of the constant skirmishes between Christians and Moors.

Aside from sherry, Jerez has two other main preoccupations: horses and flamenco. The Real Escuela Andaluz del Arte Ecuestre – the Royal Riding School – is based here, and, in the first half of May, the whole town dresses up for the **Fería del Caballo** (Horse Fair). In 2002 the town hosted the World Equestrian Games, the most important event in the equestrian calendar. Jerez also claims to be the home of flamenco; the flamenco archive, the Centro Andaluz de Flamenco, is based here, and the city has one of the largest remaining gypsy populations in Andalucia.

### Sightseeing

The heart of the city is Calle Larga, which is also the main shopping drag. Its northern reaches are overlooked by the **Iglesia-Convento de Santo Domingo** (956 34 10 37, open 7.30-10am, 7.30-8.30pm Mon-Fri, Sun, 9-10am, 7.30-8.30pm Sat), which has a masterful baroque altar – and the **Palacio Domecq**. This imposing late-baroque 18th-century pile is typical of the type of homes the sherry barons built. Inside, the rooms are ranged around a beautiful marble-floored patio, which you can usually sneak a peek at from outside. Halfway down Calle Larga is the **Gallo Azul**, a distinctive circular building from the late 19th century where *jerezanos* meet for a coffee or a *fino*. Calle Larga leads south to Plaza del Arenal, scene of occasional horse races and the best area for tapas bars – not the square itself, but the streets leading off it.

Jerez's **Catedral de San Salvador** and the **Bodegas González-Byass**.

North lies Plaza de la Asunción and the 16th-century Renaissance/plateresque **Cabildo Municipal** (old Town Hall). Opposite is the church of **San Dionisio** (closed for restoration; due to reopen 2006), a Mudéjar building dedicated to Jerez's patron saint.

West along Calle José Luis Diez stands the **Catedral de San Salvador**, also known as La Colegiata. Built on the site of an old mosque, with a free-standing bell tower (probably its minaret), it is a mix of Gothic, Renaissance and baroque styles. Begun in the 17th century but not finished until the late 18th, it is largely the work of Vicente Acero. Inside is a good painting by Zurbarán, *La Virgen de Niña*, and sculptures by Juan de Mesa. The first grapes of the wine harvest are pressed on the cathedral steps in early September.

Just south-west of the cathedral is the **Puerta del Arroyo**, a city gate dating from 1500. On either side of the gate are two of the town's largest *bodegas*: **González-Byass** and **Domecq** (*see p118* **Cliché**).

South of the cathedral is the 12th-century **Alcázar de Jerez**. The entrance has three sharp turnings to disorientate intruders, a characteristic it shares with just one other structure: the Puerta de Justicia in the Alhambra. Inside is a former mosque, later converted into the chapel of **Santa María la Real** (with a beautiful eight-sided cupola and *mihrab*), a bath house and a camera obscura, offering great views over the city.

North-west of the cathedral lies the gypsy district, the **Barrio de Santiago**. Consisting of a maze of winding streets lined by crumbling houses and churches, this is one of the most intact gypsy quarters in Andalucía and remains largely untouched by tourism. Within the *barrio*, located in two conjoined 16th-century palaces on Plaza del Mercado, is the **Museo Arqueológico**. The museum displays archaeological finds from the city and around, including the nearby town of Hasta Regia. The star exhibit is an almost intact Greek helmet dating from 700 BC, which is believed to be the oldest Greek artefact found on the peninsula. There's also a fine Roman coin collection, Moorish ceramics, some cute idols with big starry eyes and a number of sculpted candles.

North-west of here, along Calle Cordobeses, is a chunk of the old 12th-century Moorish walls (*murallas*) that once surrounded the town (other remnants are scattered around Jerez). Calle Muro leads to Plaza de Santiago and the largely Gothic church of **Santiago** (956 18 08 39, open 7am-8pm Mon-Fri), the spiritual heart of the gypsy quarter.

South along Calle Oliva is Plaza San Juan and the **Centro Andaluz de Flamenco** (*see p116* **Flamenco *puro***). This is Spain's central library and research centre for flamenco, and it puts on daily screenings of flamenco shows in a small cinema, and offers dance and guitar classes and study rooms.

A few minutes' walk north-west of Plaza de Santiago along the weirdly named Calle Taxdirt is the **Parque Zoológico**, which is primarily a centre for the rehabilitation of injured or endangered animals endemic to the Peninsula. It is home to red panda, ibis and Iberian lynx, as well as two white tigers, a mother and daughter – not albinos, just missing their fur pigmentation. The zoo is set in botanical gardens, where 33 pairs of storks nest.

Heading north-east from Plaza de Santiago brings you to the **Centro Temático La Atalaya** (closed at the time of writing; due to re-open at the end of 2004). This area, once home to a worthy but dull clock museum and a few disused *bodegas*, was developed as a result of Jerez's high-profile hosting of the 2002 World Equestrian Games; the results are impressive. Within extensive grounds are two exhibitions, the **Palacio del Tiempo** (Palace of Time) and the **Misterio de Jerez** (Mystery of Sherry). Billed as a 'journey through time', the former consists of an enjoyable guided tour (introduced by a life-sized hologram of a person in 18th-century garb) through exquisitely designed

rooms housing a collection of 302 antique working clocks. The latter is a multimedia show, using four enormous screens and a floor projection, which traces the origins, history, production and importance of sherry to the town.

North-east of La Atalaya is the **Real Escuela Andaluz del Arte Ecuestre** (Royal Riding School), the training and breeding centre of thoroughbred, or *pura raza*, Andalucian horses, whose lineage can be traced back to the 15th-century horses of La Cartuja (*see p116*). The school is open for visits to the stables, saddlery and museum and also for the world-famous 'Dancing Horses' show. This is split into six or eight parts and lasts about an hour-and-a-half with a break. For some this is sublime: the horses conduct a series of steps, skips and jumps to classical music; for others it seems entirely unnatural. Apparently, horses have poor memories and it takes them four years to learn all the moves.

**Cádiz Province**

Just outside Jerez is the monastery of **La Cartuja** (A381, km4, 956 15 64 65), founded in the 15th century, and one of the most architecturally and artistically important buildings in the province. Its centrepiece is a stunning baroque façade added two centuries later, with sculptures by Alonso Cano among others. The interior of the monastery can only be visited by men (and by appointment), but it's worth a look at from the outside.

Just off the A382 heading towards Arcos is a rather different type of attraction: the **Circuito de Jerez** (A382, km10, 956 15 11 00, www. circuitodejerez.com). The circuit plays host to some major biking events, as well as occasional

Formula One meets. There are ambitious plans to turn the track into a year-round attraction based around the theme of speed and racing, but, as yet, these have not got off the ground.

### Alcázar de Jerez

*C/Alameda Vieja s/n (956 31 97 98).* **Open** *May- mid June* 10am-8pm daily. *Mid June-mid Sept* 10am-6pm Mon-Sat; 10am-3pm Sun. *Mid Sept-Apr* 10am-6pm daily. **Admission** *Alcázar* €1.35; 65¢ concessions. *Alcázar & camera obscura* €3.35; €2.65 concessions. **No credit cards**. **Map** p115 B3.

### Catedral de San Salvador

*Plaza de la Encarnación 5 (956 34 84 82).* **Open** 11am-1pm, 6-8pm Mon-Sat; 11am-2pm Sun. **Admission** free. **Map** p115 B3.

# Flamenco *puro*

Flamenco in Jerez is far less commercialised than elsewhere in Andalucía, and there are no big tourist flamenco shows, such as you'll find in Sevilla and Córdoba. The best place to find flamenco is in the gypsy quarter, the Barrio de Santiago, which is full of *peñas* (semi-private flamenco clubs), some of which are for *socios* (members) and some of which you can walk into off the street. The central section of the old quarter near Plaza Belén has been earmarked for development into a 'barrio de flamenco', a move that will transform the town when completed.

The nature of the art is such that there are no set times or programmes: if someone is feeling particularly melancholic (or drunk), he (it is always he) may break into song. If someone else feels like dancing, he or she may get up and do a few turns. True flamenco is not about castanets and bright dresses, it's about smoky bars, a single guitar and tales of woe.

A full list of *peñas* and a map are available from the tourist office; some of the better known ones are listed below. Authentic *peñas* don't have regular opening hours and don't usually charge admission. Shows often rotate between the different *peñas* of the district on a monthly basis. Your best chance of catching a performance is at around 10pm on a Friday or Saturday night, but it is recommend to ring beforehand to check what's on. Another way to catch some quality flamenco is to visit during the month-long flamenco festival in September.

For more on flamenco, *see p184* **Cliché**.

### La Buena Gente

*Plaza de San Lucas 9 (956 33 84 04).* **Map** p115 A2.

### Don Antonio Chacón

*C/Salas 12 (956 34 74 72).* **Open** *Shows* Oct-June 10pm-late Sat. **Map** p115 A2. This is more of a cultural centre, which has weekly renditions on a Saturday.

### El Garbanzo

*C/Santa Clara 9 (956 33 76 67).* **Map** p115 off C3.

### El Lagá de Tío Parrilla

*Plaza del Mercado s/n (956 33 83 34).* **Open** 8pm-late Mon-Sat. **Shows** 10.30pm Mon-Sat. **Admission** (incl first drink) €12. **Credit** DC, MC, V. **Map** p115 A2. Tourist venue next to the archaeological museum, with daily shows and a restaurant.

### La Taberna Flamenca

*C/Angostillo de Santiago 3 (956 32 36 93/ mobile 649 38 39 78/www.lataberna flamenca.com).* **Open** 1.30-4pm, 8pm-midnight Tue-Sat. **Shows** 2.30pm, 10.30pm Tue-Sat. **Admission** (incl 2 drinks) €15; (incl meal & drink) €30. **No credit cards**. **Map** p115 A1. Right beside the church, and perhaps the most touristy of the venues, with daily shows and a restaurant attached. (At the time of writing the Taberna was planning to start opening on Sunday and Monday evenings too; call for details.)

### Tío José de Paula

*C/Merced 11 (956 32 01 96).* **Map** p115 A1/2.

### Centro Andaluz de Flamenco
*Plaza San Juan 1 (956 34 92 65/http://caf.cica.es).*
**Open** 9am-2pm Mon-Fri. **Admission** free.
**Map** p115 B2.

### Centro Temático La Atalaya
*C/Cervantes 3 (956 18 21 00/www.elmisteriodejerez.*
*org).* **Open** *Mid June-mid Sept* 10am-2pm, 6-8pm Tue-
Sat; 10am-2pm Sun. *Mid Sept-mid June* 10am-2pm, 5-
7pm Tue-Sat; 10am-2pm Sun. **Admission** *Palacio del*
*Tiempo only* €5.10; €2.70 concessions. *Combined ticket*
€9; €4.50 concessions. **No credit cards. Map** p115 B1.

### Museo Arqueológico
*Plaza del Mercado s/n (956 33 33 16).*
**Open** *Mid June-Aug* 10am-2.30pm Tue-Sun.
*Sept-mid June* 10am-2pm, 4-7pm Tue-Fri; 10am-
2.30pm Sat, Sun. **Admission** €1.70; 70¢ concessions.
**No credit cards. Map** p115 A2.

### Parque Zoológico
*C/Taxdirt s/n (956 18 23 97).* **Open** *June-Sept*
10am-8pm daily. *Oct-May* 10am-6pm Tue-Sun.
**Admission** €4.20; €2.60 concessions. **No credit
cards. Map** p115 off A1.

### Real Escuela Andaluz del Arte Ecuestre
*Avenida Duque de Abrantes s/n (956 31 96 35/*
*www.realescuela.org).* **Open** Guided tours *Mar-Oct*
10am-1pm Mon, Wed, Fri. *Nov-Feb* 10am-1pm
Mon-Wed, Fri. Shows *Mar-July, Sept, Oct* noon Tue,
Thur. *Aug* noon Tue, Thur, Fri. *Nov-Feb* noon Thur.
**Admission** *Tour* €6; €3 concessions. *Show* €13-
€21; €5.20-€8.40 concessions. **Credit** AmEx, MC, V.
**Map** p115 off B1.

## Where to eat & drink

The streets off Plaza del Arenal are home to some
great tapas bars, particularly Calle Pescadería
Vieja (a covered passageway, leading off to
the north-west). For bars, try the streets around
Avenida Domecq, particularly Calles Divina
Pastora, Cádiz and Paul, and the area around the
bullring. A hidden gem is **Bereber**, just off Plaza
del Mercado in the Barrio de Santiago, a classy
bar with a beautiful courtyard setting, ideal for
hot summer nights (C/Cabezas 10, 956 34 42 46).

### Bar Juanito
*C/Pescadería Vieja 8 & 10 (956 33 48 38).*
**Open** 1-5pm, 8.30-11.30pm Tue-Sun. **Average** €€.
**Credit** AmEx, DC, MC, V. **Map** p115 B3.
Winner of numerous awards and regarded as the
best tapas bar in town, Bar Juanito has an enormous
selection of tapas and *raciones*, including *alcachofas*
*en salsa* (artichokes in sauce) and *costillas* (ribs).

### Cafeteria Arenal 15
*Plaza Arenal 15 (956 34 79 79/www.arenal15.com).*
**Open** 8am-midnight Mon-Fri; 8am-5pm Sat. **Average**
€€. **Credit** AmEx, DC, MC, V. **Map** p115 B3.
A popular terrace restaurant offering award-
winning tapas, including good seafood.

### La Carboná
*C/San Francisco de Paula 2 (956 34 74 75).*
**Open** 12.30-4.30pm, 8pm-12.30am Mon, Wed-Sun.
Closed 2wks July. **Average** €€. **Credit** AmEx, DC,
MC, V. **Map** p115 off C3.
A huge barn of a place set inside an old *bodega* and
specialising in generous portions of barbecued fish
and meat. Often lays on entertainment, such as live
music or flamenco Thursdays to Saturdays.

### Gaitán
*C/Gaitán 3 (956 34 58 59/www.restaurante*
*gaitan.com).* **Open** 1-4.30pm, 8-11.30pm Mon-Sat;
1-4.30pm Sun. **Average** €€. **Credit** AmEx, DC, MC,
V. **Map** p115 B1.
Popular with locals who want good Andalucian and
Basque specialities (with an emphasis on meat) at a
decent price. It's slightly chaotic but homely, and the
waiters all seem to be over 100 years old.

### El Marqués
*Corner of C/Pizarro & Pozo del Olivar (956 03 15*
*00).* **Open** 1-4.30pm, 8-11.30pm daily. **Average**
€€€. **Credit** AmEx, DC, MC, V. **Map** p115 B1.
Close to the riding school, and part of the Hotel
Prestige-Palmera Plaza (*see p120*), this suberb
restaurant is housed in a grand restored *bodega*.

### La Mesa Redonda
*C/Manuel de Quintana 3 (956 34 00 69/www.*
*restaurantedmesaredonda.com).* **Open** 1.30-4pm, 9-
11.30pm Mon-Sat. Closed mid Jul-mid Aug. **Average**
€€€. **Credit** AmEx, DC, MC, V. **Map** p115 off C1.
Contender for best place in town. The interior is full
of old furniture and paintings; you imagine youself
in a private *palacio*. The constantly changing menu
includes innovative dishes such as shark, oxtail, and
stewed veal tongue. Press the buzzer to be let into
the residential complex in which it's located.

### Taberna Marinera
*Plaza Rivero 2 (956 33 44 27).* **Open** *Sept-mid July*
noon-4pm, 8pm-midnight daily. *Mid July-Aug*
7.30pm-1.30am daily. **Average** €€. **No credit
cards. Map** p115 B/C2.
A tiny place selling various *embutidos* and good red
wines in a pleasant square with a number of other
decent bars. Try the *bacalao ahumado con salmorejo*
(smoked cod in *salmorejo – gazpacho* without water).

## Shopping

The main shopping area is pedestrianised Calle
Larga and the streets around it, including Calle
Honda and Calle San Francisco, which fronts the
main market. Calle Porvera and the streets off
it are better for smaller shops selling the likes
of flamenco dresses and horse-related items.

The best place to buy sherry, *catavinos*
(sherry glasses) and *venencias* (the long-handled
things the pros use to pour), are the shops in
the *bodegas*. There is a *rastro* (street market)
in Plaza del Mercado on Sunday mornings.

# Cliché Sherry (& brandy)

The towns of Jerez, Sanlúcar de Barrameda and El Puerto de Santa María have a unique aroma. Wandering through their streets you may well pick up the scent of something savoury, tangy, sometimes even nutty, with a sweet richness. That will be the sherry. Vast quantities of the stuff sit maturing in wooden casks behind the ancient whitewashed walls of the *bodegas*.

Few drinks are as closely identified with their place of origin as sherry. The grapes are not native to this part of the world – it is thought that the Phoenicians introduced them around 1,000 BC, but it was not until Roman times that sherry really caught on, and was exported right across the Empire. The drink is mentioned in *The Canterbury Tales* and was a favourite tipple of Falstaff, referred to by Shakespeare as 'sack'. The Moors, despite their religion, were also known to have been fond of 'Sherrish'.

Sherry's modern history can be traced back to 1730, when Pedro Domecq founded the first *bodega* in Jerez (which can still be visited). Others soon followed, virtually all of them started by British families: González-Byass, Sandeman, Harveys, Williams and Humbert. Most are no longer in private hands, the one main exception being González-Byass, makers of the ubiquitous Tío Pepe, which is in the fifth generation of the family.

The grapes can be seen growing in tidy, disciplined rows in the land surrounding the sherry towns. The best are grown on a type of soil called *albarizo*, recognisable by its dazzling white sheen. This chalky soil helps the grapes retain water in the blistering heat by forming a hard crust on its surface. Palomino is the variety most widely used for making sherry, although other varieties, such as Pedro Xímenez and Moscatel, are used to make sweet styles. The sherry harvest requires an enormous amount of itinerant labour, as the grapes are picked by hand.

The sherry-making process is an ancient one, and has changed little since the mid 17th century. In fact, many of the barrels – all American oak – date back to that period. The barrels (called 'butts') are not filled to the brim, and on many, a layer of yeast, known as flor, forms on top of the grape must. It is the flor that gives *fino* and *manzanilla* (*fino* made in Sanlúcar) its trademark savoury edge and appley freshness, and it thrives in Andalucía.

Although most sherry starts as *fino* or *manzanilla*, how it develops varies greatly. Mystery has always surrounded winemaking, of course, but making sherry is even more mysterious. No one, for example, knows why some barrels of wine grow flor but others don't. The final style and flavour of the wine depend on a number of factors, such as whether or not the flor grows, the length of time the sherry spends in a *solera* (the complex system of ageing sherry in several 'scales', or rows, of barrels of varying ages), and whether any sweetening wine is added at the end. The longer the time spent ageing in a *solera*, the greater the intensity and the alcoholic strength of the wine.

Fresh **fino** and **manzanilla** have a taste unlike any other wine. They're bracingly dry, with hints of bready yeast and a light nuttiness. Some say that *manzanilla* has a 'salty' tang, owing to Sanlúcar's proximity to the sea, but that may be a bit fanciful. After fortification they have an alcoholic strength of 15-18 degrees.

**Amontillado** is sherry that starts its life as a *fino* (or as *manzanilla* in Sanlúcar), under a blanket of flor. After several years, the flor dies off (the reason why is another mystery), exposing the wine to oxygen. The wine slowly oxidises, taking on hazel-nutty, savoury flavours in the process. The older it gets, the more concentrated and robust the flavours become, while the colour changes from pale amber to deep auburn. It has an alcoholic strength of 16-22 degrees.

Unlike *amontillado*, **oloroso** sherries have never developed a protective blanket of flor. Despite popular misconceptions, in their natural state they are bone dry. Dark amber to walnut brown in colour, they have a flavour reminiscent of walnuts and an evolved, savoury, sometimes iodine-like intensity. Alcoholic strength is 17-22 degrees.

So, if *amontillado* and *oloroso* are naturally dry, why do so many sherries taste sweet? That's because some are blended with sweet grape must, usually made from Moscatel or Pedro Xímenez grapes. The level of sweetness depends on how much must is added. At the sweet end of the spectrum, thick, treacle-dark 100 per cent **Pedro Xímenez** sherries are some of the most wonderful dessert wines around.

Throughout Andalucía, with every meal, snack or tapa, *fino* or *manzanilla* is enjoyed with gusto. There is perhaps no other drink that can complement regional foods – such as gutsy *salmorejo*, thinly sliced *pata negra* ham, savoury marinated anchovies or ultra-fresh fish and seafood – with the aplomb that sherry can.

## BRANDY DE JEREZ

After a long lunch or dinner, a large glass of brandy is a favourite way to round off a meal (among the older generation anyway). Brandy de Jerez is different from French brandies such as Cognac and Armagnac. It tends to be darker, richer, sweeter, and it gains complexity by being aged in a *solera* system, the same as sherry.

In fact, most *bodegas* age their brandies in casks that were used to age *oloroso* sherry, which imparts a rich, nutty flavour to the finished brandy; some *bodegas* favour old Pedro Ximenez casks, which give a rounder, sweeter, more raisiny flavour.

Do avoid the cheaper brandies, however, as their flavour can be harsh and raw, little more than alcohol dandied up with sugar and caramel.

## BODEGA TOURS

Below are details of the major Jerez sherry tours; many smaller *bodegas* also offer tours, as do those in El Puerto and Sanlúcar – ask at the relevant tourist office for details. At all times of year it is a good idea to ring ahead to reserve your place on a tour.

### Bodegas González-Byass

*C/Manuel María González 12
(956 35 70 16/www.gonzalezbyass.es).*
**Open** (tours in English) *July, Aug* Standard tour 11.30am, 12.30pm, 1.30pm, 4.30pm, 5.30pm, 6.30pm daily; tour with tapas 2pm daily. *Sept-June* Standard tour 11.30am, 12.30pm, 1.30pm, 3.30pm, 4.30pm, 5.30pm daily; tour with tapas 2pm daily. **Admission** *Standard tour* €8. *Tour with tapas* €12. **Credit** AmEx, DC, MC, V. **Map** p115 A/B3.
By far the most commercialized of the sherry tours in town, with a cheesy video, children's train ride and the chance to have your photo taken with the 'Tío Pepe Girl' (for a fee of €3.70). Overall, something of a disheartening experience.

### Bodegas Domecq

*C/San Idefonso 3 (956 15 15 00/
www.domecq.es).* **Tours** *Apr-Sept* 10am, 11am, noon, 1pm Mon-Fri; noon Sat. *Oct-Mar* 10am, 11am, noon, 1pm Mon-Fri. **Admission** Mon-Fri €5; Sat €7; free under-12s. **Credit** MC, V. **Map** p115 A3.
A much more personable and interesting experience than that offered by González-Byass, with a generous sampling of sherries and a decent video.

### Bodegas Sandeman

*C/Pizarro 10 (956 15 17 00/reservations 956 31 29 95/www.sandeman.com).*
**Open** *Mid Mar-Oct* 10am-5.30pm Mon-Fri. *Nov-mid Mar* 10am-3pm. **Tours** *Mid Mar-Oct* 10.30am, noon, 1pm, 2pm, 3.30pm Mon-Fri; selected weekends (call to check). *Nov-mid Mar* 10.30am, noon, 1pm, 2pm Mon-Fri. **Admission** *Standard tour* €5; free under-12s. *Special tours* €4.50-€15. **Credit** AmEx, DC, MC, V. **Map** p115 B1.
An efficient and down-to-earth tour showing bottling and cooling facilities rather than just the sexy stuff. Call ahead to find out the times of the English-speaking tours.

## Where to stay

Jerez is well-served with hotels for all budgets, although rooms are scarce during the Horse Fair in May and the motorcycle championship. Many of the top hotels are located north-east of the town centre, around Avenida Alvaro Domecq. They include the five-star **Hotel Prestige-Palmera Plaza** (C/Pizarro 1, 956 03 15 00, www.palmeraplaza.com, double €187-253, map off B1), which has comfortable, understated rooms, most with balconies, in a serene setting. Facilities include a pool, gym and sauna.

The number of three-star hotels is increasing, and includes the ultra-modern **Hotel La Albarizuela** (C/Honsario 6, 956 34 68 62, www.hotelalbarizuela.com, double €60-€150, map off C3) and **Tierras de Jerez** (C/Corredera 58, 956 34 64 00, www.intergrouphotels.com, double €86-€133, map C3), in an excellent spot just off Plaza Arenal.

For the cheapest *hostales*, try Calles Morenos, Arcos and Higueras. Good bets include **San Andrés** (C/Morenos 12-14, 956 34 09 83, double €35-€38, map C2/3), a pleasant place with a lovely patio, **San Martín** (C/Caballeros 28, 956 33 70 40, double €36-€42, map C3) and **Trujillo** (C/Medina 36, 956 34 24 38, www.hoteltrujillo.com, double €52-€81, map C3).

### El Ancla
*Plaza Mamelón 13 (956 32 12 97/www.helancla.com).* **Rates** €32-€64 single; €48-€107 double. **Credit** MC, V. **Map** p115 C1.
A good spot and good prices; simple rooms with a pleasant café below.

### Doña Blanca
*C/Bodegas 11 (956 34 87 61/www.hoteldona blanca.com).* **Rates** €59-€119 single; €76-€151 double. **Credit** AmEx, DC, MC, V. **Map** p115 C3.
The best hotel in the town centre: smart clean rooms, friendly service, a garage and satellite TV.

### Guadalete
*Avenida del Duque de Abrantes 50 (956 18 22 88/ www.hotelguadalete.com).* **Rates** €68-€140 single; €82-€168 double; €237-€355 suite. **Credit** AmEx, DC, MC, V. **Map** p115 off B1.
The Guadalete's rooms are comfortable and of a decent size, and there's an outdoor pool and a decent restaurant. Good value for the quality, but a bit of a trek from the centre.

### Hotel Villa Jerez
*Avenida de la Cruz Roja 7 (956 15 31 00/www.villa jerez.com).* **Rates** €204-€235 single; €254-€283 double; €317-€395 junior suite; €570-€678 suite. **Credit** AmEx, DC, MC, V. **Map** p115 off B1.
Even more luxurious than its five-star sister hotel further out of town, this is a beautiful spot to stay, with lush gardens, pool and gym.

Relaxing by the **Alcázar** in Jerez. *See p114.*

### Monte Castillo
*A382, km9.6 (956 15 12 00/www.montecastillo.com).* **Rates** (incl breakfast) €202-€285 single; €218-€316 double; €566-€1,076 suite. **Credit** AmEx, DC, MC, V.
The best hotel in the area is where Manchester United choose to stay when they come to Jerez to train. If you are after unabashed luxury in an idyllic setting and you are a golf fan with very deep pockets, then this five-star joint is definitely the place for you.

### Royal Sherry Park
*Avenida Alvaro Domecq 11 (956 31 76 14/ www.hiphotels.com).* **Rates** €110-€269 single; €138-€269 double; €270-€352 suite. **Credit** AmEx, DC, MC, V. **Map** p115 C1.
Modern and comfortable, this stylishly decorated oasis of luxury has an indoor and an outdoor pool, and a good restaurant.

### Serit
*C/Higueras 7 (956 34 07 00/www.hotelserit.com).* **Rates** €43-€97 single; €59-€82 double. **Credit** AmEx, DC, MC, V. **Map** p115 C3.
The Serit enjoys an excellent town-centre location, and offers quiet, comfortable and very reasonably priced rooms; those on the upper floors are lighter and roomier.

## Resources

### Internet
*Rueca de Fabulas, C/Corredera 42 (956 32 20 68).* **Open** *Mid June-Sept* 10am-2pm, 6-10pm Mon-Sat; 6-10pm Sun. *Oct-mid June* 10am-1pm, 6-9pm Mon-Sat; 6-9pm Sun. **Map** p115 C3.

### Police station
*Avenida de la Comedia s/n (956 35 99 00).*

### Post office
*C/Cerrón 2 (956 32 67 29).* **Map** p115 C3.

## Tourist information

*Edificio los Claustros, Alameda Cristina s/n (956 33 11 50/www.turismojerez.com).* **Open** *Mid June-mid Sept* 10am-3pm, 5-7pm Mon-Fri; 9.30am-2.30pm Sat, Sun. *Mid Sept-mid June* 9.30am-2.30pm, 4.30-6.30pm Mon-Fri; 9.30am-2.30pm Sat, Sun. **Map** p115 B3.

## Sanlúcar de Barrameda

In his book, *Inside Andalusia*, David Baird describes **Sanlúcar de Barrameda** as having the 'seedy demeanour of a colony in the tropics left behind by the *Conquistadores'* – and that's its appeal. This sizeable seaside town, 22 kilometres (14 miles) north-west of Jerez, is famed for its *manzanilla* (*see p118* **Cliché**), the lightest and driest of all sherries, which supposedly has a salty tang imparted by the sea breezes – it's a perfect accompaniment to the seafood for which Sanlúcar is also known. It's an agreeably sleepy place outside high season, with a distinctive atmosphere and a crumbling charm, largely untouched by foreign tourism.

Sanlúcar has an illustrious history as one of the most important ports in the region, situated as it is on the mouth of the Guadalquivir. Magellan set sail from, and returned to, Sanlúcar on his round-the-world voyage; Columbus launched his second Indies voyage and third Americas trip from here in 1498; Francisco Pacheco, Velázquez's mentor and teacher, was born in Sanlúcar, and the town was the main base of the powerful Dukes of Medina Sidonia (the current Duchess still lives here).

Today, Sanlúcar is split into two main districts: the **Barrio Alto**, the old town on the hill, and the **Barrio Bajo** below it, leading down to the port area of the **Bajo de Guía**, a 15-minute walk from the Barrio Alto. All the sights are within the old town, the focus of which is the tapas bar-strewn Plaza Cabildo. Calle Ancha, which crosses the top of the square and leads west into Calle San Juan, is the town's main shopping street. At the end of the eastern end of Calle Ancha are three churches: 16th-century **Santo Domingo**, **San Francisco**, built in the 17th century by the Dukes of Medina Sidonia, and **San Nicolás**.

South of here, up the hill, a flight of steps (Carril de Los Angeles) leads to the crumbling 15th-century **Castillo de Santiago** (closed for restoration). Opposite the castle is the town's largest sherry maker, **Barbadillo** (founded in 1821). The company accounts for three-quarters of all *manzanilla* production, and also makes Castillo de San Diego white wine from the same grape. You can visit the *bodega* (and several of the smaller producers,

too – ask at the tourist office for a list), though reservations should be made in advance. Barbadillo also recently opened a museum (open 11am-3pm Mon-Sat).

From the *bodega*, Calle Sevilla leads into Calle Luis Eguilaz and Sanlúcar's oldest church, **Nuestra Señora de la O** (open hours of services). Dating from the 14th century, it has an impressive Gothic façade and a 16th-century Mudéjar doorway. Beside it is the **Palacio de los Duques de Medina Sidonia**, a 16th-century pile that is still inhabited by the current bearer of the title, a duchess known locally as the Red Duchess for her campaigning on behalf of the very people her ancestors used to oppress. The building contains extensive archives (including a huge amount of documentation relating to the Spanish Armada) and is home to a number of valuable works of art, including some paintings by Goya.

Opposite the church is a very pretty square, Plaza de la Paz. Just west of here, on the corner of Calle Caballeros and Cuesta de Belén, the *Ayuntamiento* (Town Hall) is in another palace, the **Palacio de Orleáns y Borbón**. This 19th-century neo-Moorish building with a curious Swiss-style chalet in the courtyard was the ducal home of the Montpensier family; you are free to wander around the public areas, which include a small park and patio (ask at the tourist office for details of more extensive tours).

The town market, off the Plaza del Roque, is one of the finest in the whole of Andalucía, with an enormous variety of local seafood and fresh vegetables on sale.

Sanlúcar is one of the main gateways into the wild and remote **Parque Nacional de Doñana**, just across the estuary. Four-hour tours can be arranged via the park visitors' centre (*see below*); they include a stop at an old village within the park, at a hide where you can spot birds (and if you're lucky, deer and wild boar), and at the salt flats where flamingoes congregate. For more information on the park, and for points of entry in Huelva province, *see p152* **The last wilderness**.

### Barbadillo

*C/Luis Eguilaz 11 (956 38 55 00/ www.barbadillo.com).* **Open** 9am-3pm Mon-Sat. *Tours* (in English) 11am. **Admission** €3. **Credit** AmEx, DC, MC, V.

### Palacio de los Duques de Medina Sidonia

*Plaza Condes de Niebla 1 (956 36 01 61).* **Open** (guided tours only) 11am, noon Sun. **Admission** €3. **No credit cards.**

### Palacio de Orleáns y Borbón

*Cuesta de Belén s/n (956 38 80 00).* **Open** 8am-2pm Mon-Fri. **Admission** free.

**Cádiz Province**

## Where to eat & drink

The smartest places to eat and drink are the restaurants of Bajo de Guía, the old fishing district by the beach, which are widely regarded as some of the best in Andalucía, while the tapas bars on the central Plaza Cabildo and, indeed, throughout the town, are almost all first-rate. In the old fishing quarter, one of the most celebrated is **Casa Bigote** (Bajo de Guía s/n, 956 36 26 96, closed Sun and all Nov, €€), a shrine to squeakily fresh seafood, which is delivered daily from the nearby port of Bonanza. The same management runs a cheaper tapas bar next door. The other big name in the area is **Mirador de Doñana** (Bajo de Guía s/n, 956 36 42 05, closed mid Jan-mid Feb, €€), where the speciality is known as *mi barca mirador*, a white fish in tomato sauce; wonderful *cigalas* (crayfish), *chocos* (cuttlefish) and *angulas* (eels) are also served, and there's a good tapas bar attached. Both places have fine views over the water to the Doñana.

Other restaurants well worth trying here are **Marisquería Poma** (Bajo de Guía s/n, 956 36 51 53, closed Jan, €€ ) and **Joselito Huerta** (Bajo de Guía 30, 956 36 26 94, closed Mon & all Nov, €-€€), a simple place, favoured by locals, with fine views from the upstairs dining room.

Around Plaza Cabildo, the star tapas bar is undoubtedly **Casa Balbino** (Plaza del Cabildo 14, 956 36 26 47, closed Jan, €€), which has a dauntingly long menu. House specials include *ortiguillas* (sea anemones) and *langostinos* (langoustines). There are plenty of other good places for sampling tapas in the immediate area – just follow your nose.

## Where to stay

Sanlúcar has few hotels, and none over three stars. In the summer it's almost impossible to find anywhere to stay so book ahead. The nicest hotel in town is the three-star **Los Helechos** (Plaza Madre de Dios 9, 956 36 13 49, www.hotelhelechos.com, double €45-€63), with large, airy rooms and a delightful plant-filled patio. Also good is the atmospheric two-star **Posada del Palacio** (C/Caballero 11, 956 36 48 40, phone for prices), opposite the town hall. The modern, comfortable **Hotel Doñana** (C/Orfeón Santa Cecilia s/n, 956 36 50 00, www.partner-hotels.com, double €60-€104) is well placed for the beach and restaurants by the old port. You can't miss the **Hotel Guadalquivir** (Calzada del Ejército 20, 956 36 07 42, double €53-€97), towering over the main square. The location's great but it's rather characterless inside. Of the cheaper places, **Pensión La Bohemia** (C/Don Claudio 5, 956 36 95 99, double €33-38) is in a quiet street in the old town; it's not well signed so you'll have to hunt it out. Even more basic, **Pensión Blanca Paloma** (Plaza de San Roque 15, 956 36 36 44, double €27) is in a good location, off lively Plaza Cabildo.

## Resources

### Internet

*Cyber Guadalquivir, C/Infanta Beatriz 11 (956 36 74 03).* **Open** 10am-12.30am Mon-Sat; noon-12.30am Sun. **Credit** MC, V.

### Tourist information

*Calzada del Ejército s/n (956 36 61 10/ www.aytosanlucar.org).* **Open** *Mar-May, Oct, Nov* 10am-2pm, 5-7pm daily. *June-Sept* 10am-2pm, 6-8pm daily. *Dec-Feb* 10am-2pm, 4-6pm daily.
*Centro de Visitantes de Doñana Fabrica de Hielo, Avenida Bajo de Guía s/n (956 38 16 35/ www.visitdonana.com).* **Open** *Apr-Oct* 9am-8pm daily. *Nov-Mar* 9am-7pm daily. **Tickets** (for boat) €15.04; €7.52-€10.49 concessions. **Credit** MC, V.

# Chipiona & Rota

Nine kilometres (six miles) west of Sanlúcar is the pleasant seaside town of **Chipiona**, which makes a nice stop if you're after a few days lazing on the beach. Its 69-metre (226-foot) lighthouse (*faro*) is the tallest in Spain and the third highest in the world; on clear nights its beam can be seen from the coast of Portugal. If you're feeling fit you can climb the 344 steps (enquire at the tourist office about guided tours in English and for opening times).

There is little else to detain you in the way of sights, but the town does have a lovely old quarter of winding streets and shaded *plazas*. One such is Plaza de Juan Carlos, which is home to one of the prettiest buildings in town, the 16th-century **Parroquia de Nuestra Señora de la O** (Plaza San Carlos I s/n, 956 37 01 02, open hours of services). The 14th-century former monastery of **Nuestra Señora de Regla** (Paseo Costa de la Luz s/n, 956 37 01 89, open open 7.30am-noon, 5-7.30pm Mon-Fri, 8am-12.30pm, 5-9pm Sat, Sun) is at the far end of the main beach, Playa de Regla. Chipiona's castle is undergoing long-term restoration work and is closed indefinitely.

Chipiona's real draw is its beaches – 12 kilometres (7.5 miles) of clean golden sand. The best is **Playa de Regla**, which gets very crowded in summer. For more peace, try Playas **Cruz del Mar** or **Las Canteras**. The once pristine stretch of coast between Chipiona and Rota has been dubbed the Costa Ballena (Whale Coast, despite there being none) and is currently disappearing under a sea of concrete and characterless five-star hotels and golf courses.

Rota's main claim to fame is as the site of one of the US's largest military bases in Spain. Franco, desperate for US aid in the 1950s, and keen to improve Spain's standing in the eyes of the rest of the world, gave a large chunk of land along this coast in return for financial help. The town (17 kilometres/11 miles south of Sanlúcar and Chipiona) has some lovely beaches, including an EU blue-flagged one, the **Playa de la Costilla**, and a large marina, but little charm. The main sight is the oft-restored Moorish **Castillo de Luna**, which houses the tourist office. The castle dates from the 12th century; its centrepiece is a very pretty patio with a fountain and a covered balcony. The 16th-century **Nuestra Señora de la O** (Plaza Bartolomé Pérez s/n, 956 81 00 84, open 8am-1pm, 6.30-9pm daily) is a mix of architectural styles – Gothic, plateresque and baroque.

### Castillo de Luna

C/Cuna 2, Rota (no phone). **Open** (guided tours only) *Mid June-mid Sept* noon, 6pm Sat, Sun. *Mid Sept-mid June* 11am Wed. **Admission** free.

### Where to stay, eat & drink

Chipiona is bursting with *pensiones* and *hostales*. The only time you may find it difficult to find somewhere to stay is in summer. If you want four-star luxury, rooms with balconies and sea views, and a pool, try the **Hotel Cruz del Mar** (Avenida de Sanlúcar de Barrameda 1, 956 37 11 00, www.hotelcruzdelmar.com, closed Nov-Mar, double €65-€119). The best mid-

priced option is the spotless, spacious **La Española** (C/Isaac Peral 4-6, 956 37 37 71, www.hotellaespanola.com, double €47-€57) – many of its rooms have sea views. The modest **Hostal Gran Capitán** (C/Fray Baldomero González, 956 37 09 29, closed Nov-Feb, double €33-€50) dates from the 1500s and was once the family home of El Gran Capitán, the Catholic monarchs' famed military commander.

Chipiona is not known for its restaurants. Perhaps the best is **Paco** (Puerto Deportivo, 956 37 46 64, closed Tue Oct-May and all Nov, €-€€), which draws customers – despite being badly signed and out of the way in the sailing marina – with seafood so fresh that a menu isn't deemed necessary or practical. **La Pañueleta** (C/Isaac Peral 4-6, 956 37 37 71, €) is another reasonable choice, offering a good selection of local fish in pleasant surroundings. **Peña Bética** (C/Larga 46, 956 37 43 44, €) is popular with local families and supporters of Real Betis, on which the decor is based. The food is simple, tasty and excellent value.

There are also numerous beach bars. Chipiona's nightlife takes place along Paseo Costa de la Luz and Calle Tolosa Latour.

By far the best place to stay in Rota, in a prime location just off the beach, is the stylish four-star **Hotel Duque de Najera** (C/Gravina 2, 956 84 60 20, www.hotelduquedenajera.com, double €123-€177), which has a pool. At the other end of the scale is the one-star **Hotel Nuestra Señora del Rosario** (C/Higuereta 23, 956 81 06 00, double €42-€69), which also

# Sea horses

Once a year Sanlúcar erupts in a frenzy of gambling and partying, and the salty air is filled by the thunder of hooves on damp sand and the roar of the crowd. This maritime town is famed throughout Spain for its spectacular horse races, **Las Carreras de Caballos en la Playa**, which take place on its long golden beach in late August.

Around 40,000 spectators come each year to Sanlúcar to watch some of the top jockeys from all over Europe in action at one of the most prestigious (and downright snobby) festivals of the Spanish summer; the action is presided over by the King himself. There are two cycles of races, running roughly from the 8th to the 10th and the 22nd to the 24th of August, depending on the retreating tide, which leaves an unlikely hippodrome on Sanlúcar's main beach, Playa Calzadaon;

the fine sand and wide strand makes it ideal for afternoon racing at low tide. Riders wear brightly coloured jerseys and caps; race distances covered are 1,500 and 1,800 metres, similar to the Derby in England.

The Sanlúcar races were the first regulated horse races in Spain, and some of the oldest in Europe – the first took place in 1845. Their origin is said to be in informal contests organised by the owners of the horses that transported seafood on the beach. In 160 years they've been transformed into an international fixture on the racing calendar and one of Andalucía's premier social events. But, this being Spain, don't expect the refinement of Ascot or Cheltenham – the parties held in the bars and restaurants along the riverfront during the races are as fun and raucous as any you'll come across in a village *fería*.

enjoys a fine location, overlooking the Playa de la Costilla, but isn't in the best of conditions inside. Relatively new on the scene is the charming *hostal-restaurante* **Sixto** (Plaza Barroso 6, 956 84 63 10, double €65-€86, restaurant €), on a quiet square.

For food and drink in Rota, the best places are the restaurants on Calle Mina. **Bodega la Mina** (C/Mina 27, no phone, €) is a friendly venue offering typical local dishes and occasionally hosting flamenco and jazz shows; try the *arrenque roteno* (a dry version of *gazpacho*). In high season, late-night drinking and dancing can be found along the Mirador de las Almenas, which flanks the Playa del Rompidillo.

## Resources

### Tourist information

**Chipiona** *C/Larga 74 (956 37 71 50/www.chipiona. net).* **Open** *June-Sept* 8am-2pm, 6-8pm Mon-Fri; 11am-1.30pm Sat, Sun. *Oct-May* 8am-3pm, 5-7pm Mon-Fri; 11am-1.30pm Sat.

**Rota** *Castillo de la Luna, C/Cuna 2 (956 84 63 45/ www.turismorota.com).* **Open** *July-Sept* 9am-2pm, 6-9pm Mon-Fri; 10am-2pm, 6-9pm Sat, Sun. *Oct-June* 9am-1.30pm, 5-7.30pm Mon-Fri; 10am-2pm, 5-8pm Sat, Sun.

Midway between Cádiz and Jerez lies the third town in the 'sherry triangle'. **El Puerto de Santa María**, famed for its seafood, is something of a hidden gem, where foreign (though not Spanish) tourists are a rare sight. The town is set on the bay at the mouth of the Río Guadalete and surrounded by pretty beaches, and, though it has been marred by a lot of ugly modern development, its old quarter is an enchanting grid of streets running back from the waterfront, packed with restaurants, tapas bars and *bodegas*.

If you arrive by the *vapor* boat from Cádiz, you'll disembark by a riverside street, the Ribera del Marisco, directly opposite **El Fuente de las Galeras**, an 18th-century fountain with six spouts, which used to supply ships bound for the Americas with water. The old town stretches back from here. Calle Luna leads west past the tourist office up to Plaza de España and the **Iglesia Mayor Prioral** (open 8.30am-12.30pm, 6.30-8.30pm Mon-Fri, 8.30am-noon, 6.30-8.30pm Sat, 8.30am-1.45pm, 6.30-8.30pm Sun). The church dates from the 15th century and was rebuilt in the 17th. Inside, it houses the effigy of the patron saint of the town, the Virgen de los Milagros.

On the other side of the square is the **Museo Municipal**, which contains a few archaeological remains, mainly dating from the Palaeolithic era. Calle Santa Lucía runs from Plaza de España to El Puerto's **Plaza de Toros**, the third-largest bullring in Spain after those of Madrid and Sevilla, and one revered by fans. From Calle Santa Lucía, Calle Federico Rubio leads towards the river, past the heavily restored 13th-century **Castillo de San Marcos**. Built on the site of a mosque and watchtower by Alfonso X (the Wise), the castle is well worth a look – particularly the pretty Mudéjar church inside.

The streets behind the castle contain a number of *palacios* left over from when the great sherry barons virtually ruled the town. Some are in a dreadful state of disrepair and are closed, others are being turned into hotels or smart apartments and some can be visited – the main ones being **Terry**, **501** and the biggest producer of Spanish brandy **Osborne** (reservations essential; the huge cut-out black bulls you see dotted along the highways of Spain represent Osborne). For more on brandy, *see p118* **Cliché**.

### Bodega Terry

*C/Toneleros s/n (956 85 77 00).* **Open** *Guided tour only* Apr-Sept 10am, noon Mon-Fri; noon Sat. Oct-Mar 10am, noon Mon-Fri. *Guided tour with tasting & show* (July-Sept only) 11am Wed, Fri, Sat. **Admission** *Guided tour* €4.50; free under-12s. *Tour with tasting & show* Wed, Fri €10; €6 under-12s; Sat €12; €8 under-12s. **Credit** AmEx, DC, MC, V.

### Bodega El Tiro

*A4, km651 (956 85 42 28/www.osborne.es).* **Open** 10.30am-1.30pm Mon-Fri. *Guided tours* (in English) 11.30am Mon-Fri. **Admission** €5; €1.50 concessions; free under-10s. **No credit cards**.

### Bodegas 501 del Puerto

*C/Valdés 9 (956 85 55 11/www.bodegas501.com).* **Open** 9am-2pm Mon-Fri. **Admission** €4; free under-15s. **Credit** AmEx, MC, V.

### Bodegas Osborne

*Sherry Bodega de Mora, C/Los Moros s/n (956 86 91 00/www.osborne.es).* **Open** 10.30am-1.30pm Mon-Fri. *Guided tours* (in English) 10.30am Mon-Fri. **Admission** €5; concessions varies. **No credit cards**.

### Castillo de San Marcos

*C/Alfonso X el Sabio s/n (956 85 17 51).* **Open** *July-Sept* 10am-2pm Tue-Sun. *Oct-June* 11am-1.30pm Tue, Thur, Sat. **Admission** €5; €2 concessions. **No credit cards**.

### Museo Municipal

*C/Pagador 1 (956 54 27 05).* **Open** 10am-2pm Tue-Fri; 10.30am-2pm Sat, Sun. **Admission** free.

### Plaza de Toros

*956 54 15 78.* **Open** 11am-1.30pm, 6-7.30pm Tue-Sun, except the day before & after a *corrida*. **Admission** *Corrida* phone for details; other times free.

The *fería* at **El Puerto de Santa María**.

## Where to eat & drink

There are an enormous number of restaurants and tapas bars in El Puerto, most of them specialising in seafood fresh from the bay, and most superb. Many can be found along the riverside Ribera del Marisco and the lanes running off it. The king of them all, and possibly the finest seafood restaurant in Andalucía, is **El Faro del Puerto** (Carretera de Fuentebravía, km0.5, 956 87 09 52, www.elfarodelpuerto.com, closed dinner Sun, €€€) – presentation is exquisite, preparation is innovative and the ingredients are of the highest quality. **Casa Flores** (C/Ribera del Rio 9, 956 54 35 12, www.casaflores.com, €€€) is another exemplary restaurant, and one of the best in the province, with a beautiful tiled interior and the freshest seafood. The other contender for El Puerto's culinary crown is **Los Portales** (C/Ribera del Rio 13, 956 54 21 16, www.losportales.com, €€€), which also offers great seafood and two *menús gastronomicos*. Far simpler, but equally famous, **El Romerijo** (C/Jose Antonio Romero Zarazaga, 956 54 12 54, www.romerijo.com, €€), serves fine, simple seafood at keen prices. Many locals buy their *gambas* (prawns) at the restaurant's takeaway counter and then eat at one of the many tables.

For drinking, Calle Micaela Aramburu is packed with pubs and bars, while for later-night action, head towards the bars and discos along the **Playa Santa Catalina** in the Vistahermosa district, west of the centre (take a cab), popular with a young, trendy Spanish crowd, and without a tourist in sight.

## Where to stay

The beautiful five-star **Hotel Duques de Medinaceli** (Plaza de los Jazmines 2, 956 86 07 77, www.jale.com/dmedinaceli, double €169-€236) is a stunning 17th-century mansion, once home of the Irish Terry family of sherry and brandy fame. It contains a botanical garden, swimming pool and first-class restaurant.

Also recommended is the sumptuous four-star **Monasterio San Miguel** (C/Virgen de los Milagros 27, 956 54 04 40, www.jale.com/monasterio, double €144-€180), set in a 16th-century monastery, with a good restaurant and pool. Another fine place is the three-star **Los Cántaros** (C/Curva 6, 956 54 02 40, www.hotel loscantaros.com, double €75-€117), off pretty Ribera del Marisco, with a bar and parking.

## Resources

### Internet

*Rush@Net, C/Larga 137 (no phone).* **Open** 10am-2pm, 5.30-10.30pm Mon-Sat; 5-10pm Sun.

### Tourist information

*C/Luna 22 (956 54 24 13/www.elpuertosm.es).* **Open** *May-Sept* 10am-2pm, 6-8pm daily. *Oct-Mar* 10am-2pm, 5.30-7.30pm daily.

## Getting there

### By air

Jerez airport (info 956 15 00 00) is located 7km (4 miles) north-east of the town, off the A4 and AP4 (*see p308*).

### By boat

El Vapor runs across from Cádiz to El Puerto several times daily. The journey takes around 45mins.

### By bus

There are numerous daily services between Cádiz, El Puerto, Rota, Chipiona, Sanlúcar, Jerez, and on to Arcos and Sevilla. The main operating companies are Comes (956 80 70 59, 902 19 92 08), Linesur (also known as La Valenciana, 956 34 10 63, www.linesur.com) and Los Amarillos (956 38 50 60). The bus station in Jerez (956 34 52 07) is on C/Cartuja, east of the centre. In Sanlúcar, Linesur buses (to and from Jerez) leave from C/Herman Fermín, near the tourist office; Los Amarillos services go from Plaza de la Salle (serving Chipiona, Cádiz and Sevilla). In El Puerto buses stop at the bullring.

### By train

Jerez and El Puerto are 10mins apart by train; services between Cádiz and Sevilla (around 15 per day) stop at both towns. It's about 30mins from El Puerto to Cádiz, and around 1hr 20mins from Jerez to Sevilla. Jerez's train station (956 33 48 13) is on the east side of the city on Plaza de la Estación, at the end of C/Cartuja. El Puerto's station (956 54 25 85) is on the north side of town, a 10-min walk from the old town.

# East of Cádiz

Take a walk (or a drive) on the wild side… via sublime white villages.

## Arcos de la Frontera

Arrayed along a long, narrow strip of sheer cliff (*la peña*) overlooking the fertile Guadalete valley, 30 kilometres (19 miles) east of Jerez, Arcos de la Frontera is one of the most spectacular of the *pueblos blancos*.

There was an early Celtic settlement here, and during the Roman period a garrison post known as Arcos Briga was established on the easily defended plateau. During the Moorish period the town grew considerably and briefly even became an independent kingdom; all that remains from this time is the 11th-century castle. Arcos held out against the Christians until 1250, after which it took its 'de la Frontera' appellation.

The historic part of the town, the *barrio antiguo*, stretches from the Cuesta de Belén to the Puerta de Matrera; it was declared a national monument in 1962. At its heart is the pretty **Plaza del Cabildo**, the cobbled main square that unpicturesquely doubles as a car park. To one side of the square stands the castle, rebuilt by the Christians in the 15th century (it is now privately owned and not open to the public). On its southern side is a *mirador* from where there are the best views along the cliff face. Look down and you'll see evidence of a recent rockfall that left the restaurant of the next-door *parador* hanging in space. The *parador*

terrace (now safely underpinned) is a wonderful place for a sundowner and for watching the wheeling kestrels and choughs.

On the square's north-west side, the church of **Santa María** (956 70 00 06, open same hours as tourist office, *see p128*, closed Jan & Feb) is a real hotchpotch of architectural styles. Its main body dates from the late 18th century, although work began immediately following the Christian capture of Arcos in the 13th century, when a smaller church was built on the site of the old mosque. Most remarkable is its 15th-century plateresque façade and the incomplete baroque bell tower that was built to replace the one destroyed by shocks from the Lisbon earthquake of 1755. Santa María was described in 1764 by the Holy Tribune in Rome as 'the oldest, most distinguished parish in Arcos', a declaration that put an end to its long-running rivalry with the 16th-century church of **San Pedro** (C/San Pedro 4, open 10.30am-2pm Mon-Sat), a few minutes' walk to the east, which perches precariously on the cliff's edge. From its tower there are wonderful views out across the town and eastwards to the Grazalema massif.

If you're interested in local crafts, it's worth seeking out the **Galería de Arte Arx-Arcis** (C/Marqués de Torresoto 11, 956 70 39 51), a labyrinthine building displaying handicrafts from the area, including blankets, paintings and ceramics. Or if you'd prefer local products of an edible nature, head for the **Convento de**

**Grazalema**. *See p129.*

Mercedarias Descalzas (C/de los Escribanos s/n, 8.30am-2.30pm, 5-7pm daily), which is home to a closed order of nuns who raise funds by selling cakes and excellent biscuits. You'll see the convent entrance on the right-hand side in the narrow passageway leading from the *parador* to the Hotel Los Conventos. You ring a bell, make your order through a small grille and then have your goodies delivered on a revolving lantern, all without any face-to-face contact.

Other than the above, there isn't a vast amount of sightseeing to be done in Arcos. The best way to get a feel for the place is simply to wander through the backstreets of the old town and then to head for the new part of town to people-watch from one of its many terrace cafés. The town comes to life during its *feria* (at the end of September) and the 'Toro de Alelulya' on Easter Sunday, when bulls are run through the old town.

## Where to eat & drink

The best tapas bars in the old town can be found on and around the Callejón de las Monjas, a continuation of Cuesta de Belén, which at its eastern end becomes Calle Botica. Check out the recently opened **Don Fernando** (C/Botica s/n, no phone, €) for *raciones* of excellent ham and cheeses or, next door, the quieter **Mesón de Lola** (C/Botica s/n, no phone, €). One of the most atmospheric of the old town bars is **Alcaraván** (C/Nueva 1, no phone, closed Mon, €), in a vaulted cellar just beneath the castle. There are great tapas as well as grilled meats.

But there is far more action back down the Cuesta de Belén, beyond the Plaza de España, in the new part of town. There are several terrace bars (try **El Faro** or **La Tasquita**), tapas galore and a lighter mood than in the *barrio antiguo*, where some of the bar owners seem a mite world-weary. On the lively *plaza* there are free outdoor concerts on Fridays throughout July and August.

For a full meal, try **El Convento** (C/Marqués de Torresoto 7, 956 70 32 22, closed 1st week July and 2wks Jan, €€-€€€), which is housed in a 17th-century palace and specialises in game. It is often closed one day a week, so call ahead. Or head for **Mesón El Patio** (Callejon de las Monjas 4, 956 70 23 02, mobile 605 86 64 82, www.mesonelpatio.com, closed Wed, €). Sawdust covers the floor of this down-to-earth tapas joint, serving up local dishes such as wild asparagus omelette and steamed snails. Antonio, the gregarious owner, also runs the barber's next door and the adjoining pensión (*see p128*). It's usually standing room only at 'Joselito's', as the **Taberna José de la Viuda** (Plaza Rafael Perez del Alamo 13, 956 70 12 09,

€) is informally known. Goat's and sheep's cheeses and cured hams hang from the ceiling, and there's an impressive selection of 89 tapas and *raciones*. Resident DJ Joselito has a massive collection of flamenco tracks.

The town's flamenco club, **Peña Flamenca de Arcos** (Plaza de la Caridad, 956 70 12 51) organises shows most Saturday nights during the summer and occasionally in winter. You may also find live flamenco at **Los Jovenes Flamencos** (C/Julio Mariscal 5, no phone, erratic opening times); just turn up any day after about 10pm and take pot luck.

If you are looking for some action late into the night, head for the area close to the bus station: you'll be in lively company through to the early hours. Check out **El Burladero** (where you may get a bit of impromptu flamenco), **Quo Vadis** or **Murga**. And if you fancy dancing until dawn in the summer months take a cab out to the lakeside disco-bar **Porto Alegre**, which doesn't really get going until past midnight.

## Where to stay

### La Casa Grande

*C/Maldonado 10 (956 70 39 30/www.lacasa grande.net).* Closed last 2 wks Jan. **Rates** €65-€75 double; €88-€95 suite. **Credit** AmEx, DC, MC, V.
Without doubt the number one accommodation choice in Arcos. This 18th-century mansion was built at the very edge of the cliff and was the home of dancer Antonio Ruiz Soler before being bought by its present Catalan owners. They have converted the building into an elegant and intimate hotel. There are just four doubles and two suites, all tucked away at the top of the house and eclectically decorated, fusing Moroccan details with traditional local design. The Casa's most attractive feature is its rooftop terrace, which looks out across the rolling Cádiz plains.

### Hotel El Convento

*C/Maldonado 2 (956 70 23 33/www.webdearcos.com/ elconvento).* **Rates** €35-€55 single; €50-€80 double. Closed 2wks Jan. **Credit** AmEx, DC, MC, V.
The next-best option to La Casa Grande is just along the street. This former convent has 11 rooms, most with amazing views looking down on to the Gaudalete river valley and the castle. The best rooms are in an annex next door to the hotel. There's a rooftop terrace and the staff are really on the ball.

### Hotel Los Olivos

*Paseo de Boliches 30 (956 70 08 11).* **Rates** €40-€45 single; €60-€70 double. **Credit** AmEx, DC, MC, V.
Back down the hill towards the new town, Los Olivos is cheaper and less intimate than its sister hotel El Convento (*see above*) and the views are not nearly as spectacular. Still, it's bright, modern and cool and has a large roof terrace and a sunny, plant-filled courtyard where a buffet breakfast is served. Popular with tour groups.

## Hotel Real de Veas

*C/Corredera 12 (956 71 73 70).* **Rates** (incl breakfast) €73-€88 double; €102-€107 suite. **Credit** AmEx, DC, MC, V.

This airy 19th-century townhouse has recently been converted to a small hotel by its friendly Spanish owners. Bedrooms are spotless and come with air-conditioning, TV, hydro-massage baths and mini-bars, yet still have a reasonable price tag.

## Parador Arcos de la Frontera

*Plaza del Cabildo s/n (956 70 05 00/www.parador.es).* **Rates** €97 single; €122 double; €143 double with terrace. **Credit** AmEx, DC, MC, V.

This elegant building in the centre of old Arcos is one of Andalucía's very best *paradores*. It was formerly 'La Casa del Corregidor' (a *corregidor* was the 16th-century equivalent of a mayor). The decor is a classy take on traditional Andalucían style: attractive tiles, oak furniture and earthy colours. The hotel's restaurant serves excellent food (set menu €26) and has stunning views. Both the central patio and poolside terrace bar are great places for a drink.

## Pensión Callejón de las Monjas

*C/Dean Espinosa 4 (956 70 23 02/mobile 605 86 64 82/mobile.mesonelpatio.com).* **Rates** €20-€22 single; €33-€39 double. **Credit** AmEx, MC, V.

This family-run *pensión* (the Mesón el Patio is owned by the same family, *see p127*) is very handy for the old part of town and all the best tapas bars. The rooms are clean and bright but don't expect much of a view, and beware the noise coming from the bar next door.

## Resources

### Tourist information

*Plaza del Cabildo s/n (956 70 22 64/ www.ayuntamientoarcos.org).* **Open** *Mid Mar-mid Oct* 10am-2pm, 4-8pm Mon-Sat; 10.30am-1.30pm Sun. *Mid Oct-mid Mar* 10am-2pm, 3.30-7.30pm Mon-Sat; 10.30am-1.30pm Sun.

*Paseo de Andalucia (no phone).* **Open** *Mid Feb-mid Nov* 10.30am-1.30pm, 5-6.30pm Mon-Fri; 10am-2pm Sat. Usually closed mid Nov-mid Feb.

The tourist offices offer daily guided tours in English of the old town; call for details.

## South & east of Arcos

The rolling countryside south of Arcos, heading towards the Costa de la Luz, is sparsely populated. The major settlement, **Medina Sidonia** (37 kilometres/23 miles south of Arcos) is perched on a hill, with views out over undulating wheat fields. It's a peaceful, pretty little town, well off the main *pueblos blancos* trail, with a number of fine buildings and a ruined Moorish castle. The ducal title of Medina Sidonia (awarded to the decendants of Gúzman 'El Bueno', who took the town from the Moors) has long been one of the most distinguished in

Spain and, thanks to royal favours granted at the time of the *reconquista*, the family came to be one of the wealthiest in Andalucía, owning several vast estates. Famous family members have included the commander of the Spanish Armada, while the present 'red' Duchess lives in Sanlúcar (*see p121*) and is, puzzlingly, one of Andalucía's most outspoken socialists.

East from here is the vast, rugged **Parque Natural de los Alcornocales** (168,600 hectares/650 square miles), which extends along almost all of Cádiz province's eastern boundary. There are few roads and fewer people within the park, making for fine walking. In a forest glade on its northern edge are the ruins of the village of **La Sauceda**, which was destroyed by Franco for harbouring Republicans and criminals on the run; the surviving houses are now used as refuges for hikers. Technically, you need permission to visit the park from the park office in **Alcalá de los Gazules**, a village with commanding views over the surrounding country located on the edge of the park (23 kilometres/14 miles east of Medina Sidonia).

While south-central Cádiz province is relatively neglected by visitors, the countryside east of Arcos is well-trodden tourist territory. The *Ruta de los Pueblos Blancos* links up a series of picture-postcard white villages, which are dotted among some of the most spectacular and varied mountain scenery in Spain.

The first place you reach heading east along the A372 is **El Bosque** (32 kilometres/20 miles from Arcos), which makes a good base for exploring the **Parque Natural de la Sierra de Grazalema** (53,500 hectares/207 square miles). A UNESCO Biosphere Reserve since 1984, and one of the first Natural Parks established in Andalucía, the park contains some 1,300 plant species, as well as herds of red and roe deer, wild boar and ibex. Birds of prey, such as ospreys, Egyptian and griffon vultures, booted, short-toed and golden eagles are commonly seen. The park's botanical jewel is the hardy Abies pinsapo fir tree, which survived the last ice age and now only grows in three small areas in southern Spain and northern Morocco. Due to the rarity of these unique trees, and the risk of forest fires, you need to pick up a permit from the park's main visitor centre in El Bosque if you wish to walk through the pinsapo forest. You also require a permit to hike through the spectacular gorge of **Garganta Verde** (which lies close to the Zahara–Grazalema road; path at km3 – you'll need ropes and a high degree of fitness; the less athletic can just hike down to the canyon floor to the huge cave known as the **Ermita de la Garganta**) or if you wish to climb the park's highest peak, **El Torrejón** (1,640 metres/5,380 feet). A far easier

**Arcos de la Frontera.**
*See p126.*

path to follow, with no permit required, follows the river between El Bosque and Benamahoma. It begins just behind Hotel Las Trucha and the walk takes little more than an hour.

The road east of El Bosque (A372) is one of the most scenic byways in Spain (and has featured in more than one car advert) and after 18 kilometres (11 miles) brings you to the village of **Grazalema**. This was a centre of the wool industry and became famous for its textiles during the 18th and 19th centuries. A number of grander-than-most village houses bear witness to an age when the village was so prosperous that it was known as 'Cádiz el Chico' (Little Cádiz). The **Artesanía Téxtil de Grazalema**, more commonly known as the museum of the 'Fábrica de mantas' (A372, 956 13 20 08, open Sept-June 8am-2pm, 3-6.30pm Mon-Thur, 8am-2pm Fri, July 7am-3pm Mon-Fri, closed Aug, free), is devoted to traditional methods of cloth-making and blanket-weaving. Fine blankets, as well as shawls and scarves, are still produced on industrial looms next door. The village was the subject of Pitt-Rivers' classic sociological study *People of the Sierra*.

Although Grazalema is undeniably pretty, it seems a little ill at ease with the huge seasonal influx of tourists, most of them day-trippers from Cádiz and Sevilla. At the weekend facilities are often over-stretched and it is not unusual to have to queue for a table at one of the restaurants.

The best way to escape the hordes is to take to the hills: superb scenery, wildlife and amazing geology make the Park a mecca for mountain-sports enthusiasts. Walking, rock climbing, camping expeditions and orienteering are organised by **Ocio Natural** (C/Empedrada 25, mobile 678 38 91 92, www.ocionatural.net). If you want to get your adrenaline really pumping, try bungie-jumping, potholing or abseiling with **Horizon** (Corrales Terceros 29, 956 13 23 63, www.horizonaventura.com). For guided walks around Grazalema contact

Jo Carter (956 13 23 97, mobile 627 70 51 25, www.grazalema.ws/eww1.html), who has lived in the village for several years, or, for longer, more remote rambles with great picnic lunches and 4x4 excursions call Guy Hunter-Watts (952 18 40 53, mobile 616 05 71 84).

Though it still gets its fair share of visitors, delightful little **Zahara de la Sierra** (17 kilometres/11 miles north of Grazalema by way of another stunning road that loops over the Paloma pass), seems to cope far better. Its hillside location, overlooking a reservoir, is wonderful. An 18th-century baroque church stands in the pretty main square, where there are a number of bars. Be sure to climb up to the restored Moorish castle for the most spectacular view of the village and lake. You'll often be treated to close encounters with soaring Griffon Vultures, which are part of the huge colony that nests in the nearby **Garganta Verde**.

Following the road south along the southern side of the reservoir for five kilometres (three miles) you reach **Arroyomolinos**, where a river has been dammed to create a wonderful swimming area (but steer clear of it on busy summer weekends). Outside of the village, on the road to Grazalema, is the oldest olive oil mill in the Sierra, **El Vínculo** (956 12 30 02, mobile 696 40 43 68, www.zaharadelasierra.info/elvinculo, open 10am-7.30pm daily, visits by appointment only, €3-€6 per person); it makes for an interesting visit, especially when its gracious owner Juan Urruti is there to explain how his pure virgin olive oil is produced.

Half an hour's drive south-west of Grazalema, in the heart of the Parque Natural, is **Ubrique**. Famous for its leather (you'll see scores of handbag and shoe shops lining the streets), it's larger, more industrious and less picturesque than Grazalema and Zahara. It is also the home of bullfighter-megastar Jesulin de Ubrique, who owns a ritzy ranch just outside of town.

The main attraction in the area is the Roman city of **Ocuri**, which stands on the Benalfi crags, a kilometre from Ubrique. To reach it, take the mountain path leading to Benaocaz and La Manga de Villaluenga (ask at the tourist office). This path is, in fact, one of Spain's best preserved Roman roads, and the walk to loftily situated Benaocaz (where there are several bars with panoramic views). Only discovered during the last century, the Ocuri site contains incredibly well preserved terraced walls (*oppidum*) and round houses comparable to those of Pompeii. Archaeological excavations began in the 1970s and unearthed a first-century crematorium, public baths, a necropolis and irrigation aquifers. Guided walks around the site can be arranged by the tourist office in Ubrique every Saturday and Sunday.

## Where to stay & eat

There has always been a dearth of decent accommodation in Medina Sidonia but the gap has now been filled by **Casa La Loba** (C/Padre Felix 21, 956 41 20 51, mobile 617 00 11 76, www.casalaloba.com, double €95-€105). This grand old townhouse has just three guest rooms (one a suite with its own lounge) and has been sympathetically decorated and restored by its Scottish owner, James Barr. There's a Moorish style patio and a small walled garden.

Just outside El Bosque is the attractive **Las Truchas** (Avenida de la Diputación s/n, 956 71 60 61, www.tugasa.com, double €57-€65, restaurant €€), which has a pool and an enormous, high-ceilinged restaurant specialising (as you might guess from the name) in trout from the fish farm just down the road. Many of the rooms have large balconies. On the outskirts of Grazalema, looking back across to the village, is the **Villa Turística Grazalema** (Carretera Olivar s/n, 956 13 21 36, www.tugasa.com, double €57-€65, apartment for 2 €68-€81). In the village itself is the four-star **Hotel Puerta de la Villa** (Plaza Pequeña 8, 956 13 23 76, www.grazhotel.com, double €103-€129), a plush, slightly Forté-style place with a small pool, jacuzzi, gym and sauna. For budget travellers, **Casa de las Piedras** (C/Las Piedras 32, 956 13 20 14, www.casadelas piedras.net, double €43, restaurant €€) is by far the best bet. It's deservedly popular with walking groups, and the young owners operate the town's only taxi service. Some rooms have en suite bathrooms – the best are on the top floor of the new wing – and there's a lively patio restaurant offering hearty local dishes.

There are a number of good places to stay in Zahara. On the main drag, **Hotel Marqués de Zahara** (C/San Juan 3, 956 12 30 61, www.marquesdezahara.com, double €41-€46) offers simply furnished rooms around a cool, central patio. A cheaper option is family-run **Pensión Los Tadeos** (Paseo de la Fuente s/n, 956 12 30 86, double €40), which has excellent views and is next to the public swimming pool. There are stunning views and good food at the two-star 17-room **Arco de la Villa** (Paseo Nazarí s/n, 956 12 32 30, www.tugasa.com, double €57-€65). The **Mesón los Estribos** (C/Fuerte 3, 956 12 31 45, €€), opposite the main church, offers the best food in Zahara. Enjoy specialities such as (enormous) steaks, lamb stew and *perdiz encebollada* (roast partridge in an onion sauce) while enjoying wonderful views across the reservoir. Another good food option, back along the main street, is **Bar Los Naranjos** (C/San Juan 12, 956 12 33 14, €€). This is the best place in town

for *alfresco* dining, with tables set out under the orange trees; the roast lamb is excellent, and there's a great selection of tapas.

## Resources

### Tourist information

**Grazalema** *Plaza de España 11 (956 13 22 25)*. **Open** *Apr-Sept* 10am-2pm, 5-8pm Tue-Sun. *Oct-Mar* 10am-2pm, 4-6pm Tue-Sun.

**Medina Sidonia** *Plaza Iglesia Mayor s/n (956 41 24 04/www.medinasidonia.com)*. **Open** *Mar-June, Sept, Oct* 10am-2pm, 4-8pm daily. *July, Aug* 9.30am-2pm, 4-9.30pm daily. *Nov-Feb* 10.30am-2pm, 4-6.30pm daily.

**Parque Natural de la Sierra de Grazalema** *Avenida de la Diputación, El Bosque (956 72 70 29)*. **Open** *Apr-Sept* 10am-2pm, 6-8pm Mon-Sat; 10am-2pm Sun. *Oct-Mar* 10am-2pm, 4-6pm Mon-Sat; 10am-2pm Sun.

**Ubrique** *C/Moreno de Mora 19A (956 46 49 00/ www.ayuntamientoubrique.es)*. **Open** 10am-2pm, 5-7.30pm Tue-Sun.

**Zahara de la Sierra** *Plaza del Rey 3 (956 12 31 14/www.zaharadelasierra.info)*. **Open** 9am-2pm, 4-7pm Mon-Sat; 9am-2pm Sun.

## Getting there

### By bus

From Arcos (C/Corregidores, in the new town) Los Amarillos (956 70 49 77/956 32 93 47) runs up to 20 buses a day to Jerez (40mins), around 6 to El Bosque and a handful to other towns and villages in the region (it takes 2.5hrs to Ronda, 2hrs to Sevilla, 1.5hrs to Cádiz). Comes (902 19 92 08/956 34 21 74) also runs a number of services in the area.

**Zahara de la Sierra.** *See p129.*

# Costa de la Luz

Spain's untamed Atlantic coastline feels a million miles away from the Costa del Sol.

Sun, sea, sand and sunflowers, outside **Conil de la Frontera**.

With its unspoilt coastal villages, miles of golden beaches, towering cliffs, and rolling hillsides that wouldn't look out of place in the Scottish Highlands, the Costa de la Luz ('Coast of Light') is dramatically beautiful. Add to this the crashing Atlantic and persistent winds that provide for world-class windsurfing, a vibrant party scene in towns like Los Caños de la Meca and Tarifa, superb food and affordable boutique hotels, and it's not surprising that this coastline is turning into the hip new Spanish holiday destination.

Of course, with discovery comes development, and plans to extend the AP7 motorway from Algeciras to Cádiz look set to go ahead and will undoubtedly impact the number of visitors to the area. However, the Costa de la Luz attracts a different breed of foreigner than the Costa del Sol: New Age travellers, surfers and rat-race refugees, most of whom want to see this spectacular, wind-lashed chunk of the world stay as it is. Much of the area is being granted protection, and building along the magnificent stretch of open ocean and flat alluvial plains from Conil to Caños de la Meca is strictly prohibited, while beautiful Parques Naturales already protect much of the area around Barbate and Tarifa.

## Conil to Vejer

The immediate environs of Cádiz are not beguiling; heading south, the first resort with any appeal is **Conil de la Frontera**, 40 kilometres (25 miles) south of the provincial capital. Though it is not quite the 'Land of Delights' described by Arab colonisers, the quiet little town of Conil has a pretty, if tiny, historic quarter (it gets quite lively at the weekend) and huge expanses of beach. The town has several churches, all housing impressive religious artworks. Of particular note is the the 16th-century convent **La Parróquia de Santa Catalina** (open hours of services) on Plaza Constitución, with its kitschy gilded altar and piped music; while the town's icon, the dilapidated 15th-century watchtower, built by the famous soldier

Guzmán el Bueno, is a good landmark for the 'tapas triangle' (*see p135*) should the straggly streets confuse you. Storks like to nest here in spring, filling the streets with the sound of clattering beaks.

The best beaches are west of the central **Playa de los Bateles**; here you'll find the reddish coloured, cliff-hugging coves of **Calas de Roche**, **Fontanilla** and **Fuente del Gallo**. To reach them by car, follow signs to Puerto Pesquero and then hoof it over the rocks. If you fancy scuba diving in the area, contact **Marbella Diving Conil Adventure** (mobile 630 23 44 26, www.divetarifa.com), which is based at the Hotel Fuerte Conil (*see p135*). Prices range from €25 without equipment to €45 all inclusive.

From here, it's a 10-minute drive to **El Palmar**, an extensive stretch of windswept ocean and magnificent beach backed by low dunes, which is the coast's top spot for surfers.

Around 16 kilometres (ten miles) further south is **Los Caños de la Meca**, once the coast's best-kept secret until, like many of the hippy colonies around the world, it got 'discovered'. With most of the true hippies gone, the summer campsites rival the infamous beach parties of Goa and Thailand in high season, though its chilled-out, alternative lifestyle vibes endure.

Situated at the base of the **Parque Natural de la Breña y Marismas del Barbate**, Los Caños' beaches are backed by 30-metre (100-foot) cliffs, while the little town itself is overlooked by a giant pine-hooded sand dune, known locally as the 'magic mountain'; it's a calf-numbing hike to the top, but an exhilarating speed thrill coming down via the fire break. There are several great walks from here through the park (which has picnic and barbecue areas off the road) to Barbate along the cliffs and to the fresh waterfall of Las Cortinas in the same direction. West of the village, a narrow lane leads to the **Faro de Trafalgar**, which continues to light the bay where Admiral Nelson met an untimely death during the Battle of Trafalgar in 1805. Below the lighthouse, in the direction of Conil, extends the beach of **Zahora** (not to be confused with Zahara de los Atunes; *see below*), with mile upon mile of white powder sand. It tends to be a little more sheltered from the persistent wind than most places along this coastline.

A further 12 kilometres (seven-and-a-half miles) along the coast, **Barbate** (sometimes referred to as Barbate de Franco; the dictator liked to summer here) has something of an insalubrious reputation for drugs and crime. The car parks for the Parque Natural, for example, are notorious for break-ins. That

said, if you're willing to brave the dodgy night-time characters, it is something of a hub for authentic flamenco, with a very active centre hosting regular performances (Peña Flamenca, Plaza Generalísimo Franco 14, 956 43 03 60). The unprepossessing town itself is dominated by the fishing industry and it has an excellent fish market that is worth a look (Mercado Abastos-OMIC, Avenida de Andalucía, 956 43 46 27). Tuna is still caught using traditional trapnets or *almadrabas* during the season from February to May, as tuna reach the end of their long journey from the cold waters of Norway. The method dates back 3,000 years and involves vertical walls of netting, which funnel the fish into a central area from where they can easily be lifted on to boats. Considered to be the best tuna in the world for sushi, the port often hosts two or three Japanese fishing trawlers, who take around 85 per cent of all the tuna caught here.

A must-see for fans of modern art, the **Fundación NMAC (Montenmedio Arte Contemporáneo)** is a unique project in Spain that marries contemporary art and nature. Boasting an extraordinary collection of outdoor sculpture, installations, photography and paintings by contemporary artists from all over the world, and sitting pretty in the heart of Mediterranean forest and bush off the main A7, this site is one of the most daring and original contemporary art projects in Europe.

Ten kilometres (six miles) on from Barbate, the once thriving tuna fishing port of **Zahara de los Atunes** ('of the tuna') is now a popular and agreeably low-key summer resort (mainly for Spaniards) with a fine golden strand. The town now has two claims to fame. The first, according to locals, is that Cervantes was imprisoned here on charges of espionage, and mentions the town in his book *La Fregona Ilustre* ('The Illustrious Mop'). In it he says that no one deserves the name *pícaro* (lowlife) unless they've spent a couple of months tuna fishing out of Zahara. The second, is that the wedding scene in Spanish director Pablo Carbonell's film, *Atún y Chocolate*, which tells the tale of three Barbate fishermen whose lives are turned upside-down when one of their sons decides to get married, was shot in Zahara's spectacular church, **Nuestra Señorita Carmen** (C/Gobernador Sanchez González). Sadly, the town's only other landmark building, the 15th-century **Castillo de las Almadrabas**, built by the Dukes of Medina Sidonia to protect the town against pirates and later used by fishermen to store their tuna fishing equipment, is in ruins.

This stretch of the coast has long been colonised by Germans since the time of Franco, who offered sizeable plots of land belonging to the Spanish military to neo-Nazis.

Ten kilometres (six miles) inland from Barbate, **Vejer de la Frontera** is a delightful brilliant-white village that a few years ago was barely known to the outside world. Since then it's been 'discovered' and, intriguingly, attracts a curious array of rock dinosaurs and minor celebrities. Hopefully it won't change its authentic character and flavour too much. Perched high on a hill, it was originally built to protect the fishing grounds and factories along the coast from marauders attacking from the north. Later it became an important Moorish agricultural centre and it retains a strongly Moorish atmosphere – the four gates of the original Moorish settlement survive.

Due north of the tourist office on Calle Marqués de Tamarón, the 14th-century church of **Divino Salvador** is built on the site of a mosque in an intriguing mix of Mudéjar and Gothic styles. From here, follow Calle Ramón y Cajal west to the **Convento de las Monjas Concepcionistas**, a restored 16th-century Renaissance building currently used as a venue for cultural events. This gives way to the **Arco de las Monjas**, a row of narrow arches framing a huddle of Vejer rooftops that lead into the Jewish quarter. Continue west along Calle Judería to the **Arco de Puerta Cerrada** – the closed door. Also known as the Berber Gate, it was kept shut between the tenth and 12th centuries by Jewish residents fearful of attack by Barbary Coast pirates. The lovely little **Plazuela**, centred around an exuberant polychrome fountain, on the edge of the old Moorish village, has a number of good bars and restaurants.

Perhaps one of the most striking features of the Moors' presence here (until 1250) was *el cobijado*, a black, all-encompassing garment somewhere between a burka and a nun's habit, which was worn by the women of the town until 1931. Today, the only place you're likely to see it is on a postcard or during the Fiesta Patronales in August. Other fun times to visit include the running of the bulls during **El Toro Embolao** on Easter Sunday and the **Eve of San Juan** (23 June), when effigies representing evil are burned in a big fire in the main square. This is followed by a flaming effigy of a bull, which is paraded around the town, to the accompaniment of fireworks.

From Vejer, the main road runs south-east for 50 kilometres (31 miles) towards Tarifa. After 35 kilometres (22 miles), a right turn on to the CA9004 leads to the old Roman settlement of **Baelo Claudia**. For their completeness, the romantically sited ruins are considered to be one of the most important Roman archaeological sites on the Iberian peninsula. A two-kilometre (one-and-a-quarter miles) walk around the site reveals the temples of Egyptian goddess Isis, and the Roman gods Juno, Jupiter and Minerva. From the remains of the basilica, marketplace, amphitheatre, hot

**Vejer de la Frontera.**

baths, forum and fish-salting factories, visitors get a very real impression of what life here in Roman times would have been like.

The nearby tiny village of **Bolonia** is somewhat overshadowed by its famous historical neighbour, but it's also worth a visit for its breathtaking position beneath craggy peaks and pasture that runs down to meet the sea. It has a beauty of a beach, and a visit here can easily combine a little local history with some relaxing sun-worshipping.

### Baelo Claudia

*Bolonia (956 68 85 30)*. **Open** *June-Sept* 10am-8pm Tue-Sat; 10am-2pm Sun. *Oct-May* 10am-6pm Mon-Sat; 10am-2pm Sun. **Admission** €1.50; free with EU passport. **No credit cards**.

### Fundación NMAC (Montenmedio Arte Contemporáneo)

*A7-E5, km42.5 (956 45 51 34/www.fundacion nmac.com)*. **Open** *July, Aug* 10am-2.30pm, 4.30-8.30pm Tue-Sun. *Sept-June* 10am-2.30pm, 4-7pm Tue-Sun. **Admission** €3; free under-12s. **No credit cards**.

## Where to stay & eat

In Conil de la Frontera, the **Hostal Los Hermanos** (C/Virgen 2, 956 44 01 96, double €25-€45) was the birthplace of Conil's most famous poet and musician, Antonio Rodríguez Martínez. The building is 200 years old and, stepping through the hefty wooden doors into a flower-filled courtyard, you can easily believe it. The rooms, though extremely old-fashioned and low-ceilinged, are clean and comfortable. **Hostal-Restaurante La Posada** (C/Quevedo s/n, 956 44 41 71, double €35-€65, restaurant €) offers more modern comforts, with the best of its eight rooms opening on to a roof terrace. Recently refurbished, it also has a handsome conservatory-style restaurant and a flower-filled garden for outdoor dining. The **Hotel Almadraba** (C/Señores Curas 4, 956 45 60 37, www.hotelalmadrabaconil.com, double €59-€107) is a smart newcomer to the historic centre and is situated in a restored Andalucian house built around a patio. Best of all is its fabulous

# Crossing continents

Should your holiday take you anywhere near the Costa del Sol or the Costa de la Luz, it seems almost foolhardy not to make a quick trip across to the next continent. Boats to Tangier run from Algeciras, Gibraltar and Tarifa several times a day, and at their speediest take just 35 minutes to drop you at the gateway to Africa.

Once considered the pearl of the Mediterranean, **Tangier** was one of the most fashionable resorts frequented by Europeans in the first half of the 20th century, and by the 1950s half of her 120,000 strong population were expats. Among them was Barbara Hutton, the Woolworth's heiress who was renowned for her decadent parties and extravagance. She once had the steep, whip-thin streets widened to accommodate her Rolls-Royce. And you can still occasionally hear the hawkers screeching 'Woolworth's price' in the souks and bazaars.

The town also became the adopted home of many of the 20th century's greatest writers and artists, who were mesmerised by its exoticism, its crystalline light, its Moorish architecture and its seemingly endless supply of vice. Tangier's period as an 'International Zone' exempted it from many laws and created a playground for hedonists. Immortalised by Paul Bowles in his novels

*The Sheltering Sky* and *Let It Come Down*, both set in Fez and Tangier, the town became a magnet for the beat generation: William Burroughs wrote *The Naked Lunch* from his room at the Hotel El Muniria on the rue Magellan, while Jack Kerouac followed later to help edit it. Ian Fleming gleaned much of his inspiration for the 007 series at the Café de Paris on the Place du Faro, where spies traded secrets during World War II. Oscar Wilde, Francis Bacon and Joe Orton were all fans, drawn by its reputation as a city of sin.

Moroccan independence in 1956, however, soon put a stop to the partying – alcohol was banned in the *medina* (old town), brothels were cleared out and there was a general cleaning up. Today, it is difficult to imagine the town attracting anyone, much less the in-crowd. Dirty, run-down and impoverished, many visitors turn on their heels the moment they arrive, and unsurprisingly so: Tangier is easier to loathe than to love.

Yet those who can see past the festering chaos they behold on arrival will discover a place unlike any other Mediterranean destination. Founded in the fourth century BC as Tingis, it has been fought over by Carthaginians and Romans, Phoenicians, Vandals, Arabs and Spaniards, resulting in a unique mongrel town reflecting its position

roof terrace. Rooms are tastefully decorated and fully kitted out with four-star facilities. A little removed from the centre, **Hostal Lojo** (C/Canarias 2, 956 44 15 31, www.hostal-lojo.com, double €25-€60) is quiet and has a very pretty interior patio filled with ferns and geraniums. It also has a small dive school and snack bar.

A frightening number of four-star hotels are mushrooming up along the cliffs, north of the centre. The best is the ecologically run **Hotel Fuerte Conil** (Playa de la Fontanilla s/n, 956 44 33 44, www.fuerte hoteles.com, closed mid Nov-mid Feb, double €92-€178). It has indoor and outdoor pools, a spa centre and a good international restaurant. For food, head for the so-called 'tapas triangle' between Plazas de España, Andalucía and Santa Catalina. On Santa Catalina, **El Resbalón** (No.7, 956 44 04 97, closed Oct-Feb, €) has a hefty tapas menu and very weird decor: cuttlefish bones and other cadavers of the deep swing ominously from the ceiling. For picnic fodder, **Casa Manuela** (C/José Valarde) stocks excellent *charcuterie* and cheeses. The best seafood and fish are from either of the *chiringuitos* on the beach below Hotel Fuerte Conil. **Restaurante La Fontanilla** (Playa de la Fontanilla, 956 44 11 30, closed Wed Nov-July, €€) has a couple of branches around town and serves excellent grilled fish and tender, juicy steaks from locally reared cattle; it also has a decent wine list.

El Palmar has several *hostales*, all pretty basic but they do the job. **Hostal La Ilusión** (956 23 23 98, closed Nov-Jan, double €42-€60) has comfortable rooms, some with sea views, and a pleasant garden. At the southern end of the beach you'll find **La Chanca** (Carretera de la Playa, mobile 659 97 74 20, closed Feb and Tue Mar & Apr), situated in restored stone farm buildings. The restaurant has a pretty lawn overlooking the shore. Fish is a better bet than meat here, and they do a superb version of the local dish, prawns and spinach. At the other end of the beach, **So.Co** (mobile 670 08 12 23, €) does breakfast from 10am, and cheap,

as a crossroads where the Atlantic meets the Mediterranean, Spain meets Africa, and Christianity and Islam live side by side.

There is only one way to deal with Tangier, and that is with an open mind and senses ready and willing to soak up every strange sight, smell and sound that it has to throw at you. Abandon yourself to it, and it's just possible that the side of Tangier that so inspired writers and artists less than a century ago will begin to reveal itself.

It is not a city of many traditional sights, but there's more than enough to fill a day. The **Kasbah** is housed in a former 17th-century Sultan's palace – Dar el Makhzen – and has impressive carved wood ceilings and stunning views that take in both continents. You can literally watch the sun rise in the east and set in the west by facing in different directions.

Below, the **Grand Socco** (the Spanish word for souk) no longer has a market, but has become the town's hub, a meeting spot for tradesmen and a good place to breathe in the life of the town and watch Rif women in colourful garb drift by, before hurling yourself into the *medina* after them. Here the streets and passageways are filled with bright mountains of spices and colourful handicrafts – brightly embroidered shirts, *djellabas* and leather goods. If you speak a little French, all the better for bargain hunting.

The **Petit Socco** is at heart of the *medina* and is the town's most attractive spot. No visit to Tangier is complete without passing time sipping hot, sugary mint tea in the *plaza* and watching the world go by. It's also the best place in town to feast on hearty tagines and couscous, before heading back to fortress Europe.

As Paul Bowles wrote in his 1958 essay 'The Worlds of Tangier': 'For the nine sight-seers who are mildly amused by the chaos and absurdity of the place, frankly repelled by its ugliness and squalour, or simply indifferent to whatever it may have to offer, there is a tenth one who straight away falls in love with it.'

### GETTING THERE
**FRS** (956 68 18 30/43 25, www.frs.es) high-speed catamarans leave the Spanish coast daily from Tarifa (€24 one way, 35 minutes), Algeciras (€26.50 one way, 70 minutes) and Gibraltar (€19 one way, 80 minutes). The same company also offers day trips with an English-speaking guide, lunch and transfer for €49.50, overnight trips staying in Tangier for €86, or, two nights in the laid-back seaside resort of Asilah for €79. Travellers must carry a passport.

tasty Mexican fare thereafter, though the popularity of its table-football with local teenagers does little to help the ambience.

In Los Caños de la Meca, few places give a taste of the good life quite so successfully as **Casas Karen** (C/Fuente del Madroño 6, 956 43 70 67, mobile 649 78 08 34, www.casas karen.com, double in small straw cottage €48-€85 per night, €260-€390 per week); a rare piece of Eden if your idea of a proper holiday is to read, relax and take long walks on the beach. The creation of sparky English expat Karen Abrahams, it's a unique *campo* of straw houses (*chozas*), Andalucian cottages and a restored farmhouse, all surrounded by unruly gardens. Life coaching and a range of holistic and massage treatments are also available. It's quite easy to miss so keep your eyes peeled for a sign reading '*apartamentos* and bungalows', about half a kilometre (a third of a mile) after the turning for Faro de Trafalgar as you head into Los Caños. Casas Karen is at the end of sandy, pot-holed lane. The **Hostal Madreselva** (956 43 72 55, www.madreselvahotel.com/ canos, double €66-€79) owned by the same people as the Hurricane (*see p140*), is a low-rise villa built around a ficus-filled courtyard presided over by a giant fig tree, with a pool off to the side. Rooms are comfortable, with wrought-iron trimmings, and each has a walled terrace. For being close to the sea, though, **Hostal Mar de Frente** (Avenida Trafalgar 3, 956 43 70 25, double €50-€60) is a spruce newcomer built on the edge of the cliff above Caños beach.

Due to Los Caños de la Meca's transient summer community, new bars and restaurants are constantly opening and closing. Most can be found along Los Caños's main street, Avenida de Trafalgar, so you can't miss them; more often than not they're filled with disconsolate surfers waiting for their wave to come in. **La Pequeña Lulu** (Avenida de Trafalgar 2, 956 43 73 55, €) is a hippy-chic hangout, with glowing stars on the ceilings and a twinkle-light terrace. It does a good-value three-course vegetarian menu. **El Pirata** (Avenida de Trafalgar s/n, 956 43 73 96, €) is a long-standing favourite for sunsets and cocktails.

About five kilometres (three miles) east of Los Caños, a tangle of sandy lanes leading to Playa de Zahora contains several isolated guesthouses and restaurants. Open year-round, the **Saboy Bar** (C/Mangeta 357, 956 43 73 46, €) is a cosy stone-and-thatch tavern with live music at the weekend. It also rents out some two-up, two-down cottages. Try **Venta Curro** (Playa de Zahora, 956 43 70 64, closed Tue in

**Casas Karen** in Los Caños de Meca.

winter, €-€€) for hearty, home cooking. The ranch-like atmosphere of **Sajorami** (Playa de Zahora, 956 43 74 24, mobile 650 76 68 89, www.sajoramibeach.com, double €50-€80, restaurant €) was inspired by the owner's love of Cuba and is a good base for outdoorsy holidays. Horse riding, mountain biking and kayaking are all available in the area. Accommodation ranges from cool, stone high-ceilinged rooms to wooden, beachfront houses. The beachfront restaurant specialises in a Creole-style barbecue and is worth making the trip for, even if you aren't staying here.

Another decent alternative-style guesthouse, **Casa Montecote** (La Muela 200, CA125, 956 44 84 89, www.casamontecote.com, apartment for 2 €40-€58 per night, €260-€390 per week) is tucked away in the hills, with large, unkempt gardens, a gym, sauna and swimming pool, plus opportunities for rambling, mountain biking, horse riding and hiking.

In Zahara, the nicest place to stay is the colonial-style **Hotel Gran Sol** (Avenida de la Playa 20, 956 43 93 09, www.gransolhotel.com, double €72-€127), whose walled gardens and swimming pool front the beach; ask for a room with a sea view and balcony over the pool. Next to the main *plaza*, the marble-lined **Hotel Doña Lola** (Plaza Thomson 1, 956 43 90 09, d.lola@teleline.es, closed Dec-Feb, double €58-€120) offers ultra-modern rooms with TV, music system and telephone. The figure-of-eight-shaped pool is sheltered and there are two decent restaurants for more upmarket dining. More standard four-star comfort is available a little away from the main village at **Antonio II** (C/Atlanterra 1, 956 43 91 41, www.antoniohoteles.com, closed Nov-Jan, double €82-€132). The two-star **Antonio** next door is run by the same people (same number, closed Nov-Jan, double €62-€94). If you're on a budget, **Hotel Nicolas** (C/Maria Luisa 13, 956 43 92 74, closed Nov, double €42-€55 or half board July & Aug €86) has small but comfortable rooms, all with bath, telephone and TV; some with small balconies that give on to the street. The hotel also serves a good, hearty breakfast.

Food-wise, you'll find a handful of beach bars in season. In town, the nautically themed **Casa Juanito** (C/Sagasta 7, 956 43 92 11, www.casajuanito.com, closed Nov-Jan, €), established in 1948, is the oldest bar in town and the top spot for sampling locally caught tuna tapas and Spanish wines. **El Vapor** (no phone, €) is a cute fishing cottage that serves beautifully fresh fish and seafood tapas, one block from the beach at Calle Zapal and Calle Yerbabuena. There's also a thumping, open-air pizzeria and grill on Calle General Franco. Most of the night-time watering holes are on Calle Maria Luisa.

Vejer boasts some of the most exceptional small hotels in the region. **Casa Cinco** (C/Sancho IV El Bravo 5, 956 45 50 29, www.hotelcasacinco.com, closed Jan, double €86-€112) has just four individually decorated rooms, a cosy reading room stacked high with books and glossy magazines and a Moroccan-inspired roof terrace strewn with rugs and cushions and lit with candles. Owners Colette and Glen's gourmet cooking can be enjoyed two nights a week (often accompanied by local flamenco artists) and is well worth sampling. **Escondrijo** (Callejon Oscuro 3, 956 44 74 38, www.escondrijo.com, double €74-€121) is another recently opened and highly classy place, constructed from the remains of an old chapel. It also has four stylish, characterful rooms, two with private terraces and all with stereos. There's a main sun terrace, guest bar, movie lounge and internet access too. The **Casablanca** (C/Canalejas 8, just behind Plaza de España, 956 44 75 69, www.andaluciacasablanca.com, closed late Dec-late Jan, double €50) offers several individually decorated studio apartments, combining the comforts of a modern home with a colourful Moorish ambience. Its prize-winning interior patio, a large roof terrace and basement caves that provide a private bar for guests are added bonuses. The labyrinthine **Hotel La Casa**

**del Califa** (Plaza de España 16, 956 44 77 30, www.vejer.com/califa, double €59-€77, restaurant €€) does a splendid job of blending the old with the new, offering a mix of rooms from standard doubles to suites furnished with antiques. Among numerous communal areas is a cushion-filled Arab-style lounge and a well-stocked library. Descending into the catacombs you'll discover a gorgeous secret garden and restaurant. Its location outdoes the cuisine, but the Moroccan- and Middle Eastern-style cooking is perfectly adequate. The **Convento de San Francisco** (La Plazuela s/n, 956 45 10 01, www.tujasa.com, double €67-€78, restaurant €) dates back to the 17th century. With its long, silent corridors and monastic features, there is something ethereal about this place.

Vejer is also gaining a well-deserved reputation as the dining room of the Costa de la Luz. For market-fresh tapas, **El Palenque** (C/Francisco 1, 956 45 17 04, closed Jan, €) occupies a fine sun-trap in a patio behind the market. The Scandinavia-meets-Morocco decor of **Restaurante Trafalgar** (Plaza de España 31, 956 44 76 38, closed Jan-mid Feb, €€-€€€) and the numerous designer cookbooks on display give it a trendy edge over other places in town. Modern regional food is a speciality. For cutting-edge French cuisine in a restored 16th-century chapel, **La Vera Cruz** (C/Eduardo Shelly 1, 956 45 16 83, closed Wed Oct-mid July and all Jan, €€€-€€€€) is rapidly blazing a trail as one of the region's best restaurants; choose from an interesting menu and short but decent and not overpriced wine list. The homemade foie gras, local red mullet with compote of leeks, and duck breast with citrus glaze are all superb.

Vejer is not a town with much nightlife, but **La Bodeguita** (C/Marqués de Tamarón, 956 45 25 82) is a fun place to start or end the night – chances are, one will blur into the other. Also check out the **Peña Flamenca** (C/Rosario, no phone), located in a former church. Thanks to the sudden influx of mainly foreign residents, flamenco performances are becoming a more regular occurrence, led by locals from Barbate and Cádiz. You can also find out what's on while stocking up on CDs at specialist flamenco shop **Zoco Flamenco** (C/Juan Relinque 28).

Bolonia is the place to be if you just want some quality seaside R&R. More places to stay are gradually springing up, but the best remains **Hostal Lola** (C/El Lentiscal 26, 956 68 85 36, www.hostallola.com, double €37-€56), with a lush garden overlooking the hills, and fresh, cheerful rooms. Alternatively, **Hostal Rios** (956 68 85 44, closed Nov, double

€50-€77, apartment €50-€67) has basic, clean rooms and apartments overlooking the beach. For eats, the *chiringuitos* in front of Baelo Claudia are decent lunch stops (evening meals in high season only). Or, at the opposite end of town, where the coast road finally peters out, **La Cabaña** is a lovely, thatched bar serving killer cocktails as the sun sets.

## Resources

### Internet

**Barbate** *CB Systems, C/Lope de Vega 3 (956 43 43 64).* **Open** 10.30am-2pm, 5.30-9pm Mon-Sat; 5.30-9pm Sun.

**Conil de la Frontera** *Café de la Habana, Plaza de Santa Catalina s/n (956 44 34 84).* **Open** 10am-midnight Mon-Thur, Sun; 11am-2am Fri, Sat.

**Vejer de la Frontera** *Por Ir Ya Estoy, Plaza San Francisco s/n (no phone).* **Open** varies.

### Tourist information

**Barbate** *C/Vázquez Mella 2 (956 43 39 62/ www.dipucadiz.com).* **Open** 8am-2pm Mon-Fri. *Paseo Marítimo s/n, Playa de Carmen (no phone).* **Open** 9am-2pm, 5-8pm daily.

**Conil de la Frontera** *C/Carretera 1 (956 44 05 01/www.conil.org).* **Open** *June-Sept* 9.30am-2pm, 6-9pm daily. *Oct-Apr* 9.30am-2pm daily.

**Vejer de la Frontera** *C/Los Remedios 2 (956 45 17 36/www.turismovejer.com).* **Open** *July-Sept* 9am-3pm, 4-8pm Mon-Sat; 11am-2pm Sun. *Oct-June* 9am-3pm Mon-Fri.

**Zahara de los Atunes** *C/Doctor Sanchez Rodriguez s/n (956 44 95 25/turismo@aytobarbate.com).* **Open** noon-6pm Mon-Fri; noon-5pm Sat.

## Tarifa

Welcome to the capital of the 'Costa del Windsurf' and the most happening town on the Costa de la Luz. With its lively, party atmosphere, brightly painted bars, sunny *plazas*, and warren-like, cobblestoned streets, **Tarifa** has a unique vibe that belongs more to the Caribbean, California and even nearby Africa than it does to Spain. It is one of the foremost windsurfing and kitesurfing destinations in the world, and the constant wind has led to hundreds of power-generating windmills being erected in the area. It's also the most southerly point of Europe – just 11 kilometres (seven miles) across the straits from Africa and a mere 35 minutes by boat (*see p134* **Crossing continents**).

Tarifa's name derives from that of Tarif ibn Malik, the Moorish leader who took the town in 710 – the first Moorish possession in Spain – and made it the springboard for the Arab conquest. Castilian troops captured Tarifa almost 600 years later (in 1292), and two-thirds

of the city walls that they built, plus the main gate, the **Puerta de Jerez**, are still standing. The 15th-century church of **San Mateo** (open hours of services) hides a beautiful late-Gothic interior behind a baroque exterior (added in the 18th century). It's also worth stopping in at the neo-Mudéjar market on Calle Colón. The most impressive sight of all, however, is across the straits – the smoky-blue outline of Africa's Rif Mountains, best seen from atop the ramparts of the tenth-century Castillo de Guzmán el Bueno.

A tour of the **Castillo de Guzmán el Bueno** begins with the grisly account of how, during the Moorish siege of 1292, the enemies of Christian commander Alonso Pérez de Guzmán captured his nine-year-old son and demanded the keys to the castle in exchange for the boy's life. Refusing to give up his cause, Guzmán threw down his own knife from the ramparts in defiance, and was forced to watch as the Moors slit the boy's throat before him. He did, however, save Tarifa from the Moors, who returned to Africa empty-handed.

The majority of visitors, though, come to Tarifa for the sand, surf and summer beach parties along **Playa de los Lances**, due west of the town centre. However, conditions that make it a hot spot for windsurfers can make it sandblasting hell for anyone who just wants to lie in the sun. Tiny, scallop-shaped **Playa Chicitita** is better for more sheltered bathing. Several miles west, a turn-off to Punta Paloma leads to a giant sand dune called **Playa de Valdevaqueros**, which is parked up with innumerable surfers' camper-vans in high season. But from here you can walk along the coast looking for more secluded coves and easily escape any crowds.

If you fancy taking advantage of the wealth of activities available in the area, try **Club Mistral** (Hurricane Hotel, A7, km78, 956 68 90 98, *see p140*) for kitesurfing and windsurfing; **Aventura Marina** (€45 incl all equipment, with a second dive for just €26) at Club de Buceo Bahia (Avenida Andalucía 1, www.aventuramarina.org, 956 05 46 26, mobile 609 59 40 20) for scuba diving; **FIRMM España** (C/Pedro Cortés 4, 956 62 70 08, tickets €27 for 2hr trip) or **Whale Watch España** (Avenida de la Constitución 6, 956 62 70 13, www.whalewatchtarifa.com, tickets €27) for whale- and dolphin-watching; and **Hurricane Hipica** (A7, km78, 956 68 90 92, www.tarifahip.com) for horse riding.

### Castillo de Guzmán el Bueno

**Open** *June-mid Sept* 11am-2pm, 6-8pm Tue-Sat; 11am-2pm Sun. *Mid Sept-May* 11am-2pm, 5-7pm Tue-Sat; 11am-2pm Sun. **Admission** €1.80. **No credit cards.**

Windsurfing capital of Europe, **Tarifa**.

For more upmarket dining, the restaurant at the **Hotel Hurricane** (*see p140*, €€) creates imaginative dishes using local produce. The A7 from Tarifa to Barbate also has an abundance of roadside eateries, ranging from *ventas* (country inn-style taverns) to theme bars.

If not on the beach, most of the nightlife kicks off around Calle San Francisco. You'll find **Tanaka's** nightclub on Plaza de San Hiscio. For hole-in-the-wall-type street bars and beer gardens wander down Calle Carniceria. The **Soul Café** attracts a more sophisticated crowd. The **Peña Flamenca Tarifena**, on Plaza Santa Maria, often has live performances on weekend nights during the summer.

On a street with no name, the **Mariposa Nocturna Teteria** (first right under the Puerta Jerez, 626 53 84 23, closed Wed & Sun, €) is a colourful Moroccan-style tea room, complete with drums, heavily embroidered rugs and ornate hanging lanterns.

## Where to stay

To get an idea of the kind of crowds to expect in high season (July and August), note that the campsites that line the shore provide space for around 4,000 tents. It's fiendishly difficult to get a room at this time, so, if you're coming for the party, booking is essential.

Out of season, take your pick from cheap and cheerful backpackers' *hostales* to chic boutique hotels. In the historic quarter just along from the church, the **Pensión Correo** (C/Coronel Moscardó 8, 956 68 02 06, www.pension correo.com, closed 2wks late Dec, double €30-€50) is a delightful, family-run *hostal* with just eight brightly decorated rooms. The best is a penthouse double with private roof terrace. **Misiana** (C/Sancho IV el Bravo, 956 62 70 83, www.misiana.com, double €61-€112) has gone a bit mad with the paint box: the funky bar looks as if someone upset a bowl of tutti-frutti all over it, but it does serve good, imaginative tapas (daytime only, €), morphing into the town's hippest music venue at night. The rooms upstairs offer more candy colours and, if being cocooned in shocking lilac, hot pink and intense turquoise is your thing, you'll be very happy here. The penthouse is a treat, with lots of dark wood and leather. It also boasts the highest roof terrace in Tarifa, with stunning views over the town. Across the street, **La Sacristía** (C/San Donato 8, 956 68 17 59, www.lasacristia.net, double €115-€135) is more subtle, if a little busy, with its restaurant, coffee bar and clothing shop all crammed into the pint-sized patio. Rooms are cool and romantic, with four-poster beds and mosaic-tiled bathrooms.

## Where to eat & drink

Tarifa has one of the most varied international restaurant scenes on the coast, ranging from pizza and pasta to Mexican, Greek and North African. Just the other side of the main road from the old town, the blue-and-white Greek taverna **Iris Manau** (C/San Sebastian, 956 62 74 08, closed Mon, €€) does a good range of tasty vegetarian dishes as well as more classical Greek dishes like tangy chicken with lemon. It's well worth calling ahead to pre-order the superb leg of lamb roasted in wine, garlic and herbs.

**Hostal Restaurante La Casa del Comandante** (C/Alcalde Juan Nuñez 8, 956 68 19 25, www.tarifadiving.com, closed Tue Sept-June, €€-€€€) overlooks the shipyard, and specialises in more unusual fish dishes, such as spider crab and octopus 'Tarifa style', as well as the catch of the day. It also has pleasant rooms to rent and a dive school.

Calle Sancho IV el Bravo is a good daytime grazing ground, with **Café Central** the prime spot for people-watching and soaking up the sun; next door, **Ali Baba** (€) does a mean falafel.

You'll find most of the good dinner places around Calle San Francisco, none of which open much before 9pm. **Bistro Point** (€) boasts more than 100 types of crêpes, while **Mosquito** is the place to go for potent cocktails. Another good bet for lively restaurants and funky hangouts is on the main drag, Calle Batalla del Salado.

**Casa Amarilla** (C/Sancho IV el Bravo 9, 956 68 19 93, www.lacasaamarilla.net, apartment for 2 €42-€64) is great for longer stays, offering 11 colourful Moorish-style apartments. **Hostal Africa** (C/María Antonia Toledo 12, 956 68 02 20, mobile 606 91 42 94, www.hostalafrica.com, double €30-€45) is a snappily restored townhouse, popular with backpackers, with airy rooms, a roof terrace and storage space for bikes and boards. Just on the other side of the Puerta Jerez, **Hostal Asturiano** (C/Amador de los Rios 8, 956 68 06 19, double €40-€60) is a good bet if you can't find a room right in the centre. All rooms are fresh and new, tastefully furnished and with their own bathrooms. It also does a good value lunch *menú*.

Resort-type hotels face the beach a few kilometres out of town to the north. **Dos Mares** (A7, 956 68 40 35, www.dosmares.com, double €60-€130) offers basic rooms, bungalows and *cabañas*; most have sea views. It is hugely popular with families and has its own stables, kitesurfing school and windsurfing. Next door, the **ArteVida** (A7, km79.5, 956 68 52 46, www.hotelartevida.com, double €85-€130) is overrun with bronzed and beautiful wind- and kitesurfers. It has funky rooms with lots of flowing white linen, hammocks and, of course, those amazing views. Another good place, primarily popular with the surfing fraternity is the wackily named **100% Fun** (A7, km76, 956 68 03 30, www.tarifa.net/100fun, closed Nov-Feb, double €53-€92, restaurant €). It's on the main road but close to the beach, and has a swimming pool, a jungle-like garden, a Caribbean-feel beach-hut design and a good Tex-Mex restaurant. With its dramatic two-storey arches, Eastern-inspired bedrooms, subtropical gardens and palm-fringed views of the sea, the **Hotel Hurricane** (A7, km78, 956 68 49 19, www.hurricanehotel.com, double €80-€140) looks like the kind of super-cool designer hotel you'd expect to pay a fortune for after reading about it in *Wallpaper\**. In fact it's far more down-to-earth, very friendly and worth every penny to feel like one of the 'beautiful people' for a couple of days. Don't forget your kaftan. The eclectic restaurant (*see p139*) also tends toward the hip rather than stuffy, with lounge music to match.

## Resources

For windsurf/kitesurf emergencies, call 900 21 22 02.

### Internet
*Papeleria Pandor@, C/Sancho IV el Bravo, opposite Café Central (956 68 16 45).* **Open** varies.

### Police station
*Plaza Santa María 3 (956 68 41 86).*

### Post office
*C/Coronel Moscardó 9 (956 68 42 37).*

### Tourist information
*Paseo de la Alameda s/n (956 68 09 93/www.ayto tarifa.com).* **Open** *July-mid Sept* 9am-9pm daily. *Mid Sept-June* 9am-3pm daily.

## Algeciras

As you cross the mountain range that separates Tarifa from **Algeciras** (stopping en route at the Mirador El Estrecho to take in the views), there is a sudden transformation in the scenery from the green, rolling hills, craggy mountaintops and blustery skies of the Costa de la Luz to the parched desert-like landscapes of the Costa del Sol.

The greatest temptation on approaching Algeciras is to keep going. It's a polluted, industrial port, riddled with dodgy characters selling any illicit substance they can get their hands on. As the ghetto of southern Spain, it is somewhat ironic that the name Algeciras derives from the Arabic 'Al-Jazira-al-Khadra', meaning 'Green Island'. Most visitors today are here for one reason only: to catch the next ferry to Ceuta or Tangier on the North African coast.

That said, because Algeciras' lack of appeal is so well documented, it does mean it's a town still waiting to be discovered. The San Isidro neighbourhood, around the leafy **Parque María Christina**, is one of the oldest parts of the city, and its narrow, cobblestoned streets and crooked houses are unexpectedly charming. Recent excavations of the Merinid town of **al-Binya**, discovered north of the Miel River and dating back to 1279, can now be clearly seen behind the fencing, and could finally put the town on the cultural map, at least for archaeology buffs.

The vibrant Andalucian flavour of the old town contrasts sharply with the heavy Arab influence elsewhere, particularly in July and August when the port bustles with Moroccan migrants returning home from their jobs in other parts of Spain and Europe. Around the port, the small bazaars and Moroccan tea shops serving sweet mint tea are OK if you don't have time to head across the straits for the real thing (*see p134* **Crossing continents**). Be warned, this area is notorious for bag-snatchers and pickpockets. Finally, for rail-travel enthusiasts, the train journey from here to Ronda is one of the most beautiful in Andalucia, passing through Gaucin and some of the most appealing *pueblos blancos* in southern Spain.

## Where to stay & eat

You'll find numerous cheap *hostales* in the streets behind Avenida de la Marina and the port, and they vary considerably in quality. The **Hotel Marina Victoria** (Avenida de la Marina 7, 956 65 01 11, double €45-€52) is a good bet if you're crossing the straits to Morocco early in the morning. The best rooms look directly over the port and across to Gibraltar. A few blocks behind this, the **Hostal Fez** (C/Rio 7, 956 66 97 62, double €24-€30) is unexpectedly pleasant and a bargain. A townhouse built in typical colonial style, with arches giving on to a tiled courtyard, its rooms are clean and modern, all with private bathrooms, and it has the added bonus of a small cafeteria for snacks. The most upmarket place (and the first hotel to be built on the Andalucian coast) is the four-star **Reina Cristina** (Paseo de la Conferencia s/n, 956 60 26 22, www.reinacristina.com, double €64-€98), a beautiful colonial building set in verdant gardens that has welcomed the likes of Churchill, Roosevelt, Conan Doyle, Lorca, Orson Welles, Rock Hudson and Cole Porter. It was built by the British at the same time as they constructed the railway to Ronda.

More of a home than a hotel, the **Monte de la Torre** (Apartado de Correos 66, 956 66 00 00, www.andalucia.com/montedelatorre, closed mid Dec-mid Jan, double €120), five or so kilometres north of Algeciras in los Barrios, is a good base for exploring the nearby Parque Natural de los Alcornocales (*see p128*). It's a fine 100-year-old house with period decor and vast gardens, surrounded by cork oak forests. Another good out-of-town option is the converted 15th-century convent of **La Almoraima** (A369, km22, 956 69 30 02, www.la-almoraima.com, double €90) with its original tower still intact. The convent has been sensitively remodelled, with tastefully furnished rooms arranged around a quiet courtyard, surrounded by gardens.

In the town centre you'll find a number of decent restaurants around Plazas Alta and Palma serving good fish and seafood. **Restaurante Montes** (C/Juan Morrison 27, 956 65 42 07, €-€€€) is one of the more established places, offering a reasonable set menu. It specialises in *urta* (a succulent white fish, a member of the bream family). **Casa Castro** (Avenida Blas Infante 5, no phone) is a classic, characterful drinking den, while the **Café Opera** (C/Alfonso XI 8, 956 66 48 50) attracts a well-heeled clientele; the pavement terrace is a choice locale for supping on a good cup of java and watching the world go by. The bazaars around the port offer Moroccan-style snacks. Otherwise, pack a picnic lunch from the market on Plaza Palma, and head for the leafy Parque de María Cristina.

The most famous restaurant in the area is the Michelin-starred **Los Remos** (Finca Villa Victoria, C351, km2.8, 956 69 84 12, closed dinner Sun, €€-€€€€), which serves superb fish in an old house surrounded by gardens, but alas overlooked by oil refineries.

## Resources

### Internet
*Boo Meranj, C/Senaco s/n (no phone).* **Open** varies.

### Tourist information
*C/Juan de la Cierva s/n (956 57 26 36/www.ayto-algeciras.es).* **Open** 9am-2pm Mon-Fri.

## Getting there

### By boat
There are 2 daily sailings between Tarifa and Tangier by Ferries Rapidos de Sur (956 68 18 30; journey time 35mins). From Algeciras there are almost hourly ferry crossings every day to Ceuta and Tangier, taking around 1hr and 2hrs respectively. The fast ferry (*rapido*) to Ceuta takes 40mins, but is more expensive. Be sure to buy a ticket in advance during the summer months. Several companies operate out of Algeciras port. Euro Ferries (956 65 11 78) and Transmediterránea (956 65 17 55) operate frequent daily passenger and car ferries to both destinations.

### By bus
Tarifa bus station is at C/Batalla del Salado (956 68 40 38). There are 1 or 2 daily buses to Madrid and most major cities in Andalucía, and around 10 a day between Tarifa and Algeciras. Algeciras has two bus stations. The Comes station (C/San Bernardo, 956 65 34 56) runs daily buses locally to towns like La Linea, Tarifa and Cádiz, and to Madrid. For other main Andalucian cities, Portillo runs services from Avenida Virgen del Carmen 15 (956 65 10 55). The Bacoma service (956 66 50 67) runs from the airport or from Puerto Maritimo, while Estación Maritima Local B11 runs to Barcelona, Valencia, Alicante and other European destinations. There are buses connecting the towns and villages along the Costa de la Luz, although their schedules tend to be erratic. In Conil, buses stop on C/Carretera de Punto, in front of Hotel Don Pelayo (956 44 29 16); in Barbate the main bus stop is at Avenida Generalísimo 1 (956 43 05 94), and in Vejer it's at La Plazuela (956 44 71 46).

### By train
There are no rail services on the Costa de la Luz. Algeciras rail station (902 24 02 02) is at Carretera de Cádiz s/n, with 2 daily services to Madrid (fastest is 6hrs), 3 to Granada (4hrs 20mins) and 4 trains to Ronda (1hr 50mins) that call at the stations along the Guadiaro valley. For Sevilla, Córdoba, Málaga and Cádiz, change at Bobadilla.

# We reign in Spain

# Gibraltar

Little Britain-on-sea.

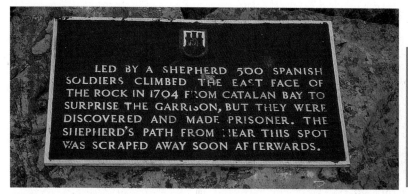

LED BY A SHEPHERD 500 SPANISH SOLDIERS CLIMBED THE EAST FACE OF THE ROCK IN 1704 FROM CATALAN BAY TO SURPRISE THE GARRISON, BUT THEY WERE DISCOVERED AND MADE PRISONER. THE SHEPHERD'S PATH FROM NEAR THIS SPOT WAS SCRAPED AWAY SOON AFTERWARDS.

Something of a curio, Gibraltar sticks out of the bottom of Spain like a gigantic Roman nose. Viewed from afar, it is an undeniably impressive sight, rising from the sea to a height of 426 metres (1,398 feet). Up close, the town is nothing if not eccentric and, though you probably won't want to spend a huge amount of time here, it is certainly worth experiencing the place where John Lennon and Yoko Ono got married in 1969, and which, in 2004, celebrated its 300th birthday as British territory.

## HISTORY

The gatekeeper of two continents, Europe and Africa, it is often said that Gibraltar has more history than it knows what to do with. To the ancients, Gibraltar was known as Monscalpe – one of the mythical pillars of Hercules, said to be a religious shrine and an entrance to Hades (the other is Jbel Musa, on the African side). More recently it has been a key military outpost, long fought over by the European powers.

The name Gibraltar comes from a corruption of the Arabic Jebel Tariq (literally 'Tariq's Mountain'). The Tariq in question was Tariq ibn Ziyad, the Governor of Tangier, who landed here in 711 and used it as a staging post for the Islamic conquest of Spain. Gibraltar remained under Moorish occupation for the next six centuries until it was reconquered by Spanish armies in 1462. In 1704 it fell to the British, and, by the 1713 Treaty of Utrecht, was ceded to Britain in perpetuity. Hankering after its lost appendage, Spain laid siege to the rock twice, in 1727 and 1779, but ultimately failed to regain it.

During the 18th and 19th centuries Britain developed Gibraltar as an important naval base. Miles of tunnels and chambers were dug out of the limestone, and a self-supporting underground city was constructed.

The Rock played a pivotal role in World War II, while the post-war years were marked by expansion, turning Gibraltar into a residential and commercial centre. In 1963 the question of Gibraltar's status came before the United Nations, and Spain seized the opportunity to revive her claim to the Rock. This coincided with increasing restrictions at the border between Gibraltar and Spain, which culminated in the complete closure of the border by Franco in 1969. It remained closed for the next 15 years, causing huge resentment among the locals that is still very much alive today. Though Spain still continues to vie for the reintegration of Gibraltar into her territory, Gibraltarians continue to insist on their right to self-determination.

Interestingly, despite the trappings of Britishness – from the electric points and telephone jacks to the bobbies on the beat and the Gibraltar pound (you'll pay more using euro), the population is a complete stew. Gibraltarians – 75 per cent of the population – are a mix of Genoese, Jewish, Maltese, Spanish and British ancestry. About 14 per cent are really British, and about seven per cent are Moroccan. Yet, to many Gibraltarians, Spain seems as remote, hostile and alien as Mars.

With most of the garrison now gone, Gibraltar relies on tourism, banking and gambling to fuel its economy. It's also a tax haven for cheap booze, cigarettes, perfume and petrol. The town centre is an even grimmer version of run-down British seaside towns everywhere: chip shops, sweet rock and the smell of stale beer wafting out of grubby pubs.

This 'familiarity' is part of its appeal; the Rock currently gets some six million day visitors a year. Since 2000, the local government has sponsored the refurbishment of hotels in an attempt to attract business from cruise ship passengers. And the Gibraltar cruise terminal welcomes 180 liners a year – an increase of nearly 50 per cent from 2001. Tourism officials dream of Gibraltar becoming the 'new Monaco'.

## Sightseeing

There's certainly no excuse for getting bored in Gibraltar. Despite covering a mere six square kilometres (two-and-a-half square miles), the Rock has no shortage of things to do, especially if military history is your thing. A cable car runs from Grand Parade at the far end of Main Street to the top of the Rock, with a stop at the **Apes' Den**, about halfway up. (Many people continue to the top and then see the Den on the way down.) The famous Barbary apes (brought over from Morocco by the Moors) are Gibraltar's most popular attraction, but don't forget that they aren't pets and have been known to bite, to steal and, more humorously, to urinate on tourists while sitting on their heads. Don't feed them (they are given a properly balanced diet) and keep your belongings clutched tightly to you. The apes live in two dens. Traditionally it's been said that if the apes ever disappear from Gibraltar, so too will the British.

Gibraltar is riddled with caves. More than 140 have been discovered so far (most of which cannot be visited). The most famous is **St Michael's Cave**, to the south of the summit, which was long believed to be bottomless and a possible subterranean link to Africa. Summer concerts and recitals are often held inside its vast 'auditorium', some of which are free for visitors. James Joyce fans take note: this was the site of Molly Bloom's deflowering in *Ulysses*.

Excavated by the British army in the late 18th century, the **Great Siege Tunnels** form part of what is arguably the most impressive defence system in the world. What you see today, including the office of General Eisenhower, is only a small part of what was once a 51-kilometre (32-mile) network that housed up to 18,000 Allied soldiers during World War II.

Further down the rock, the **Moorish Castle** has a small museum showing two or three examples of intricately patterned Berber carpets from the High Atlas Mountains. In Moorish times, woven shapes within

the fabric were used as code between the rulers of the day. The detailed intricacy of some carpets meant that the eyesight of the women making them deteriorated to such an extent that they could only make three in a lifetime.

In town, the **Gibraltar Museum** offers an interesting journey into Gibraltar's 200-million-year history, from the time when it was still geographically part of Africa. Highlights include the skull of a Neanderthal woman, discovered on the Rock in 1848, eight years before a similar skull was found in the Neander Valley, near Düsseldorf. Neanderthal Man should have more accurately been called Gibraltar (Wo)Man.

Close by is the **Nefusot Yehuda Synagogue**. Dating from 1724, it is one of the oldest synagogues on the Iberian Peninsula. Tours, including a short history of the local Jewish community, are available with Holy Land Travel (75965) for a minimum donation of £2.

The **Shrine of Our Lady of Europe** (71230, open 10.30am-1pm, 2-6pm Mon-Fri, 11am-1pm, 2-6pm Sat, Sun), originally a mosque, was converted into a chapel by the Spanish in 1462. This was the original Gibraltar lighthouse, which was sacked by the fearsome pirate Barbarossa. Miraculously, according to devotees, he missed the 15th-century statue of the Virgin and Child, which is still in place. Nearby, the **Ibrahim-Al-Ibrahim Mosque** (47693) was a gift from King Fahd of Saudi Arabia to the thousands of Moroccans who came to work on the Rock when the border was closed. For a tour contact Shuli a day in advance on 41104, mobile 588 93000.

The beaches, though not a patch on anything over the border, are fine for catching a few rays. The best is on the east side, at **Catalan Bay**. It's also worth taking a stroll around **Marina Bay** on the west side to look at the boats.

A number of charter businesses cater to dolphin lovers. The best one is **The Original Dolphin Safari** (Marina Bay Complex, Marina Bay, 71914, mobile 607 290 400, www.dolphin safari.gi, tours at 11am, 12.30pm, 2pm, 4pm in the summer, call in advance in winter, £27, £22 concessions).

Gibraltar is probably the best spot in Andalucia for scuba diving, due to the nature of the Rock and the underwater life that dwells there. It's also among the cheapest. Try **Rock Marine Dive Gibraltar** (The Square, Marina Bay, 73147, www.divegibraltar.com). It's BSAC accredited and offers a one-tank dive for £25, night dives for £25 and discovery dives for £30.

### Cable Car

*Lower station 77826/Upper station 78759.* **Open** *Departs from lower station 9.30am-5.15pm daily. Returns to lower station 9.30am-5.45pm daily.* **Tickets** return £5.90; £3.95 concessions. **No credit cards.**

## Gibraltar Museum

*18-20 Bomb House Lane (74289/www.gib.gi/ museum).* **Open** 10am-6pm Mon-Fri; 10am-2pm Sat. **Admission** £2; £1 concessions. **No credit cards.**

## Upper Rock Nature Reserve

*Upper Rock.* **Open** 9.30am-7pm daily. **Admission** *Nature reserve only £2. Nature reserve & attractions* £7; £4 concessions; £1.50 vehicles. **No credit cards.** The Apes' Den, the Moorish Castle, the Great Siege Tunnels and St Michael's Cave are all part of the Nature Reserve.

## Where to eat & drink

If you've arrived from Spain, you'll need to revert to British eating hours and prices. You won't find any shortage of pub grub, fried breakfasts and fish-and-chip shops. However, with the recent smartening up of Gibraltar's image, the Rock's culinary efforts seem to be on the up too, and there's plenty of variety. For all-day English fry-ups, the **Star Bar** (12 Parliament Lane, 75924, £) is apparently one of the best, and is Gibraltar's oldest bar. **The Clipper** (78B Irish Town, 79791, £) offers hearty, home-cooked meals in a trad pub atmosphere. Something of a Gibraltar institution, **Bunters** (1 College Lane, 70482, closed Sat, £) continues to be good for more upscale British cooking, with dishes like stilton and Guinness pâté. However, it could soon be outclassed by **Simon's** (44 Cornwall's Lane, 47515, closed Sun, ££), a small, intimate bistro offering dishes like king prawn and spinach tart, and grilled swordfish with crayfish tail sauce.

**Sacarello Coffee House** (57 Irish Town, 70625, closed Sun, £) is a good bet for vegetarian snacks and home-made cakes, and **The Breadbin** (49 Main Street, 44558, closed Sun) makes a good range of tasty sandwiches, ideal for the beach or picnics. One thing the Rock does really well is curry, and **The Viceroy of India**, just off Main Street (9/4 Horse Barrack Court, 70381, closed Sun, £), won't disappoint with its whopping menu of old favourites; booking is advised.

**Al Andalus** (3 College Lane, 49184, closed Sun, £) is good for Moroccan dishes, or try **Café Solo** (Unit 3, Casemates Square, 44449, £) for unfussy, well prepared Italian dishes. **El Burlaero** (5 Governors Parade, 79008, closed Sun, £) is one of very few genuinely Spanish bars in town. Another one is **Mesón Jabugo** (The Tower, Marina Bay, 71771, £); it's located on Marina Bay, which has many waterfront restaurants overlooking the yachts. **The Little Mermaid** (4/5 Admiral's Walk, Marina Bay, 77660, closed Sun, £-££) does Danish fare, such as marinated herring, and smoked eel and scrambled eggs. **Bianca's** (6/7 Admiral's

Walk, Marina Bay, 73379, £) has a decent and reasonably priced bar menu and is hugely popular for after-work drinks, while **Da Paolo** (Marina Bay, 76799, closed Sun, £-££) is a great spot for fresh fish and has a fine wine list.

**La Mamela** (Catalan Bay, 72373, £-££), meaning 'woman's breast', is named after the rock jutting out of the wash at the southern end of the beach. It's far and away the best fish restaurant in town, with specialities such as *caldereta del pescado y marisco* (a hearty seafood stew). The owners also have a decent tapas bar, **El Patio** (11 Casemates Square, 70822, closed lunch Sat & all Sun, £).

For truly world-class cooking there are two options: **Nuno's** Italian restaurant at the Caleta Hotel (*see p146*) is a highly sophisticated eaterie (£££) serving excellent pasta and breads made on the premises, and fine Italian wines, in a dramatic promontory location. On the other side of the Rock, **The Rib Room** at The Rock hotel (*see p146, £££*) also has fine sea views and an interesting menu including the likes of quail and pigeon breast and baked fish on braised fennel, capers and pickled lemons.

## Nightlife

Although there are supposedly over 360 pubs here, Gib's nightlife is modest to say the least, and follows British licensing hours. The few more upmarket bars around Casemates Square attract a young, trendy crowd. **Cool Blues Café** (310 Main Street, 43111) is popular with young, image-conscious townies, while **Corks Wine Bar** (79 Irish Town, 75566, closed Sun) gets busy mainly at weekends and has a touch

The Rock.

more class than the local boozers, plus occasional live music. After hours, head to **The Market Tavern** (next door to the market, 50800) which stays open until 4am; its karaoke nights every Wednesday and Saturday are legendary and by its own admission can get 'messy'. For dancing there is the **UnderGround** (8 West Place of Arms, 40651), with two dancefloors; however, more discerning clubbers hop across to Spain, where **Gabba** in La Linea is about the hottest thing around. Your only other option is to hit the tables of the **Casino** (7 Europa Road, 76666) next to The Rock hotel.

## Where to stay

In the last couple of years, many of the hotels on the Rock have also been given a face-lift, or at least a makeover, although accommodation remains considerably more expensive than back on across the border. If you book a room in any of Gibraltar's more pricey hotels out of season, be sure to ask if any cut-price deals are available; rates are frequently negotiable if the hotel isn't full. If you're on a strict budget, you're much better off staying in La Linea.

On the east side, the four-star **Caleta Hotel** (Sir Herbert Miles Road, 76501, www.caleta hotel.com, double £69-£140), gets full marks as the Rock's most characterful hotel, and it presides over Gibraltar's nicest beach. Its garden is a pleasant place for afternoon tea, while an Argentinian grill is a summer feature. The cliff terraces and swimming pool are spectacular.

On the west side, **The Rock** (3 Europa Road, 73000, www.rockhotelgibraltar.com, double £120-£165) was built by the Marquis of Bute in 1932 and is a Gibraltan institution. Recently refurbished, it seems to have lost some of its character with modernisation, but it's good for comfort and offers a range of facilities including several bars, lounges and terraces.

Another four-star is the **Eliott Hotel** (Governors Parade, 70500, www.gibraltar.gi/ eliotthotel, double £165, restaurant ££), which is popular with business travellers but is the most central of the upmarket hotels, and has a rooftop pool and an international restaurant.

**Queens Hotel** (1 Boyd Street, 74000, www.queenshotel.gi, £50-£70) is a friendly, family-run mid-range option just outside the old city walls. Rooms are air-conditioned and most have either a sun terrace or balcony.

For a B&B in the centre of town, try the **Continental Hotel** (1 Engineer Lane, 76900, double £55, where the bedrooms (each with TV and phone) surround a central, oval-shaped atrium that has seen better days. Nearby, **The Cannon** (9 Cannon Lane, 51711, double £36.50-£45) is a no-frills hotel situated in a building

dating back to the 18th century with modernised, pleasant rooms (lots of pine), and a small bar and a lunchtime restaurant (closed Sat, Sun, £).

## Resources

To phone Gibraltar from outside Spain, dial the international access number, then 350 and the local five-digit number. From within Spain, call 9567, and then the local number, unless you're within Cádiz province, where you dial 7 then the local number.

**Rock Tours by Taxi** (from any taxi stand, 70052) will take you anywhere on Gibraltar. Guides are knowledgeable and offer colourful anecdotes. Tours last about 1hr 30mins and cost £7 per person (minimum 4 people).

### Internet
*Café Cyberworld, Units 14-16, Ocean Heights Gallery (51416).* **Open** noon-midnight daily.

### Police station
*New Mole House, Rosia Road (72500).*

### Post office
*104 Main Street (75714).*

### Tourist information
*Gibraltar Tourist Board, Duke of Kent House, Cathedral Square (74950/www.gibraltar.gi).* **Open** 9am-5.30pm Mon-Fri. *Casemates Square office (74982).* **Open** 10am-3pm Sat; 10am-1pm Sun.

## Getting there

### By air
There are direct flights from the UK to Gibraltar. For details on the airport, *see p308.*

### By boat
There are daily ferries from Tarifa and Algeciras, (£35 day return) and one catamaran a week from Tangier (1hr15mins, £19 single, £32 return). Info for both: Turner Travel, 65-67 Irish Town (78305, www.frs.es).

### By bus & car
Regular buses run from most of the major towns on the Costa to Gibraltar (most tourist offices can provide details of day excursions to Gib from €15 to €20) and/or La Linea, on the Spanish side (the bus station is a 5min walk from the border). If you're only visiting Gibraltar on a day trip, the easiest and quickest approach is to park your car at La Linea and walk or catch a bus (numbers 3 and 9) to the border. With the border now open 24 hours a day, the interminable queues of cars that once plagued the frontier are now reduced; average waiting time is around 20mins. You'll need a passport – an official ID card for EU nationals is not enough – and, if you're travelling by car, insurance and rental documents, a certificate of registration, a nationality plate and a valid driving licence.

# Huelva Province

# Huelva Province

PORTUGAL

EXTREMADURA

Parque Natural
de la Sierra de Aracena y
Picos de Aroche

Rosal de
la Frontera
N433
Aroche

Cortegana

Jabugo
Galarya
Los Marines
Fuenteheridos
Aracena

El Real
de la Jara

A493
Almonaster
la Real
Alájar
Linares de
la Sierra

Santa Olalla
del Cala

Zufre
N630-E803

Santa Bárbara
de Casa
H120
A479

N435
A461

A499
Cabezas
Rubias

Minas de
Riotinto
Nerva

H124
Calañas
Zalamea
la Real

Puebla de
Guzmán
A495

Valverde del
Camino

Villanueva de
los Castillejos

H U E L V A

N435
A493

San Bartolomé
de la Torre

Beas
A499
A495
Gibraleón
Trigueros
Villarrasa
La Palma
del Condado

E1-A49
N431
Lepe
Niebla
A472
A49-E1

HUELVA
Moguer
Bollullos
del Condado

Ayamonte
Palos de la Frontera
La Rábida
Almonte
SEVILLA
(see p163)

Isla Cristina
Punta Umbría
A483

Isla Canela
Mazagón

El Rocío

A494

To Sevilla

ATLANTIC OCEAN

Matalascañas

Parque Nacional
de Doñana

Sanlúcar de
Barrameda

0                    20 miles
0                    30 km

Chipiona
CÁDIZ
(see p103)

© Copyright Time Out Group 2004

Jerez de la Frontera

Rota

**148** Time Out Andalucía

El Puerto de
Santa María
CÁDIZ

# Huelva Province

Virgin beaches and mountains are the chief lures of this under-appreciated corner of the region.

Andalucía's westernmost province features on relatively few foreign tourists' itineraries. Part of this is understandable, part is just ignorance. With Portugal on its western flank, Extremadura to the north, Sevilla to the east and the Atlantic to the south, Huelva has long been thought of as little more than a region to pass through in order to get somewhere else. Apart from the many wonderful beaches, much of the southern part of the province is scenically dreary, yet the hilly north is hugely beguiling, and, if major blockbuster attractions are few, there is plenty of interest for the visitor who cares to look.

## HUELVA CITY AND THE COAST

Visually, Huelva is the least appealing of Andalucía's provincial capitals, with its small but attractive historic centre surrounded by modern apartment blocks and an ugly industrial

El Rocío. See p154.

## The best...

**Beaches**
Mazagón (p154); Punta Umbría (p152).

**Birds**
Parque Nacional de Doñana (p152).

**Castles**
Aracena (p158); Aroche (p156); Cortegana (p156).

**Caves**
Gruta de las Maravillas (p158).

**Cowboys**
El Rocío (p154).

**Ham**
Jabugo (p157 & p160).

**Mariners**
The Columbus Trail (p151).

**Mines**
Minas de Riotinto (p158).

**Villages**
Alájar (p157); Almonaster La Real (p156); Aracena (p158); Zufre (p158).

fringe. However, the area immediately south of the city is rich in maritime heritage, particularly in relation to the pioneering voyages of Christopher Columbus. And much of the coastline is blessed with superb (though often windswept) white sand beaches, and resorts that boast some of Spain's best seafood restaurants. Although somewhat dull out of season, the resorts burst into life from Easter onwards, with mainly Spanish visitors. The most significant attraction on the coast is the immense expanse of the Parque Nacional de Doñana, a rigorously protected haven for bird- and wildlife and one of Europe's most important wetlands. The curious Wild West-style town of El Rocío, on the park's western edge, is the most interesting settlement in the area.

## NORTH OF HUELVA

Without doubt, the most alluring region of Huelva province is the mountainous Sierra de Aracena in the north. Part of the huge Sierra Morena range that defines the northern boundary of Andalucía, the Sierra de Aracena is a rewarding and relatively compact area of modest peaks and wooded valleys, of friendly, pretty villages and memorable walking. This is the home, too, of the internationally salivated-over Jabugo ham. Tourism in these parts is low-key, though attractions such as Aracena's Gruta de las Maravillas (Cave of Marvels) are the equal of any in southern Spain.

# Huelva City & the Coast

Go west... to Andalucía's final frontier.

Columbus woz 'ere: **La Rábida**. *See p151.*

Extending from the Portuguese coast in the west to the Doñana National Park in the east, the Huelvan coast is essentially one endless stretch of exposed virgin beach, punctuated by mostly modern resorts (though at least there's not a full English breakfast in sight). Apart from tourism, the area relies on fishing and strawberry growing, and there's also evidence of declining mining and thriving petrochemical industries to blight some of the best views.

## Huelva City

The city of Huelva offers little to attract tourists, though, if you're using public transport, it makes a handy base from which to explore the area. You may find it easier and cheaper to get accommodation here than in the resorts.

Huelva was a historically important city: its port supplied the Roman Empire with silver and copper, and Christopher Columbus set off on his historic voyages from the coast nearby

(*see p151*). Remains of its former glory can be seen in the curious **Barrio Reina Victoria**, an estate of mock-Tudor villas built in the early 1900s by the British Rio Tinto Mining Company to house its British workers. The town's **Museo Provincial** has remains from the Phoenician, Greek and Roman eras.

In the centre there are some pleasant pedestrianised shopping streets, or you can knock elbows with the locals at the no-nonsense market, **Mercado del Carmen** (C/Carmen), where marble slabs display an array of glistening fish. You can also buy *mojama* (cured tuna), a Costa de la Luz delicacy. For a view, climb up to **Parque Moret** and the **Santuario de Nuestra Señora de la Cinta** (a couple of kilometres north of the centre), where Columbus prayed before one of his voyages.

Another Columbus-related sight is the **Monumento a Colón** (Columbus Monument), sculpted by Gertrude V Whitney and donated by the US in 1929, standing huge, square and forlorn at the **Punta del Sebo**, the point where the rivers Odiel and Tinto meet. Back towards the city, curving gracefully out from the harbourside, is the massive **Muelle Río Tinto** (Río Tinto Pier), an impressive 19th-century iron structure from which the British used to ship out minerals from the Río Tinto Mines in the north of the province (*see p158*).

Huelva is on the edge of the **Paraje Natural Marismas del Odiel**, 7,100 hectares (27 square miles) of marshland that's home to herons, spoonbills and flamingoes. The Centro Visitantes de Calatilla (*see p151*) has exhibitions, information on footpaths, and a café. **Erebea** (mobile 660 41 49 20) organises excursions into the park on foot, by boat or with a 4x4.

### Museo Provincial
*Alameda Sundheim 13 (959 25 93 00).* **Open** 2.30-8.30pm Tue; 9am-8.30pm Wed-Sat; 9am-2.30pm Sun. **Admission** free.

## Where to eat & drink

Next to the Barrio Reina Victoria is the Galician restaurant **Las Meigas** (Avenida de Guatemala 44, 959 27 19 58, closed Sun, €€), a mecca for fish aficionados. The old-school, flamenco atmosphere of **El Rinconcito** near the market is more local (C/Marina 4, no phone, €); try the Huelvan speciality *adobo de mero* (fried marinated fish). On a pedestrianised street off Avenida Martín Alsonso Pinzón is **Café-Rehilites** (Paseo Santa Fe s/n, 959 28 20 88, breakfast €), good for a coffee or breakfast.

The best-known restaurant in the area is located eight kilometres (five miles) west of the city in Aljaraque – **Las Candelas** on the Punta Umbría road (959 31 83 01, closed Sun, €€); it serves up superb seafood at keen prices.

## Where to stay

Most people stay at the **Hotel Luz Huelva** (Alameda Sundheim 26, 959 25 00 11, www.nh-hoteles.com, double €107), a large, smart but bland member of the NH chain. For something more unusual, the two-star **Hotel Costa de la Luz** (C/José María Amo 8-10, 959 25 64 22, double €47.58-€51.57), near the market, is a weird and wonderful timewarp of '70s kitsch.

## Resources

### Police station
*Avenida Tomás Dominguez 2, off Avenida de Italia (959 21 02 21).*

### Post office
*Avenida Tomás Dominguez s/n (959 54 03 61).*

### Tourist information
*Avenida de Alemania 12 (959 00 44 33).* **Open** 9am-7pm Mon-Fri; 10am-2pm Sat, Sun. *Centro Visitantes de Calatilla, Carretera de Enrique Kima Carlos 1, km2.8 (959 50 90 11).* **Open** *Apr-Sept* 9am-2pm, 6-8pm Wed-Sun. *Oct-Mar* 10am-2pm, 6-8pm Wed-Sun.

## The Columbus Trail

Apart from its world-beating Jabugo ham (*see p160* **Hang 'em high**), the province of Huelva is chiefly famed as the starting point of Christopher Columbus's first historic voyage to the New World. **La Rábida** (seven kilometres/four miles south of Huelva) is the main site for Columbus-related sightseeing. Take a monk-led tour through the simple, whitewashed **Monasterio de Santa María de la Rábida**, where Columbus (known in Spanish as Cristóbal Colón) spent time waiting for the go-ahead for his epic voyage. The monastery's church holds the tomb of local hero Captain Martín Alonso Pinzón (who accompanied Columbus across the Atlantic), as well as the only image of the Virgin Mary in Spain to have been blessed by the Pope. The flag room contains the flags of Latin American countries and coffers of sand from each land.

At the waterfront you'll find the **Muelle de las Carabelas** (Pier of the Caravels), where full-scale replicas of Columbus's ships – the *Niña*, the *Pinta* and the *Santa María* – are moored. Though technically impressive, the ships are kitted out with laughable wooden parrots, plastic turtles and models of naked natives. More interesting is the mock 15th-century European village, with real chickens scratching around and displays of period crafts. There's also a bar with a terrace.

Those keen to complete the Columbus tour can visit neighbouring **Palos de la Frontera**, which supplied Columbus with much of his crew, including the captains of the *Niña* and *Pinta*: Vincente Yañez Pinzón and Martín Alonso Pinzón. Columbus performed a vigil in the **Convento de Santa Clara** in **Moguer**, eight kilometres (five miles) north of Palos.

### Convento de Santa Clara
*Plaza de las Monjas s/n, Moguer (959 37 01 07).* **Open** *Guided tours only (in Spanish, every hr on the hr)* 11am-1pm, 5-7pm Tue-Fri. **Admission** €1.80; €1.20 concessions. **No credit cards.**

### Monasterio de Santa María de la Rábida
*La Rábida (959 35 04 11).* **Open** 10am-1pm, 4-7pm Tue-Sat. *Guided tours (in Spanish only)* every 45mins. **Admission** *Guided tour* €2.50. *Audio guide* €3; €1.50 concessions. **No credit cards.**

### Muelle de las Carabelas
*Paraje de La Rábida (959 53 05 97).* **Open** *Apr-Sept* 10am-2pm, 5-9pm Tue-Fri; 11am-8pm Sat, Sun. *Oct-Mar* 10am-7pm Tue-Sun. Phone for details of guided tours. **Admission** €3; €1.25 concessions. **No credit cards.**

## Resources

### Tourist information
**Moguer** *C/Castillo s/n (959 37 18 98/www.ayto moguer.es).* **Open** 10am-1.30pm, 5-7pm Mon-Fri. **La Rábida** *Paraje de la Rábida s/n (959 53 05 35/65).* **Open** *Apr-Sept* 10am-2pm, 5-9pm Tue-Fri; 11am-8pm Sat, Sun. *Oct-Mar* 10am-7pm Tue-Sun.

## West of Huelva

Between the mouth of the Río de Huelva and the Portuguese border lies a string of beach resorts, ports and marshes. The roads here skirt around estuaries and streams, making driving a round-the-houses affair. In recent years large stretches of the coast west of Huelva (particularly around El Rompido and Ayamonte) have been given over to intensive farming of oysters, clams and prawns; seafood production now forms a major pillar of the Huelvan economy.

**Ayamonte** has few sights, but its pedestrianised shopping streets and agreeable squares are pleasant enough for a stroll. Situated

# The last wilderness

Nowhere in Europe is quite like the Doñana. Protected since the 1960s as the **Parque Nacional de Doñana** and declared a UNESCO Biospheric Reserve, the vast floodplains of the Guadalquivir river, east of Huelva, incorporate some of the most important natural ecosystems in Europe.

The park consists of 50,720 hectares (196 square miles – surrounded by a further 26,540 hectares/102 square miles of protected buffer zone) of virgin beach, pine-covered sand dunes, marshland, riverbank, thickets of heather and gorse, and forests of cork and pine. This diversity of habitats attracts huge numbers of birds – over six million stop here on their annual migration – and shelters some highly endangered species. Among them is one of the only remaining populations (about 40 animals) of the world's most endangered feline, the Iberian lynx, and 15 pairs of the extremely rare Spanish Imperial Eagle.

If you want to get beyond the limited number of marked footpaths on the park's periphery, you will have to join a guided tour in an all-terrain vehicle. There are two main points of entry to the park from the Huelva side – El Rocío (generally better for birdlife) and Matalascañas (better for a variety of landscapes and of animal species).

At the beach you can see hordes of seabirds: sanderlings, cormorants and the rare Audouin's gull, as well as peregrine falcons nesting in the ruins of the coastal defensive towers. In the forest of juniper, olive, pine and eucalyptus you'll spot deer and wild boar. The dunes in the park are immense (parts of *Lawrence of Arabia* were filmed here) and move three to six metres (10-20 feet) a year, swallowing up swathes of pine trees on their way. The juniper bushes 'ride' the dunes, their roots allowing them to move up and down on top of the sand. A major part of the park is marshland, whose unsuitability for agricultural exploitation has been the saving grace for nature in this area. The marsh is best in spring, when thousands of breeding birds can be seen. (For more on the birds that can be found in the park, *see p89* **Top five**).

A tour of the Doñana is a rare opportunity to experience one of the few really wild places left in Europe, and also to support the important conservation work that goes on here. The park continues to be under threat, however, by hotel developments (most notably at Matalascañas) that are nibbling at its edges, and agricultural activities, which cause pollution and put pressure on the park's water supply.

For access to the park from Cádiz province, *see p121*.

## Centro de Visitantes 'El Acebuche'

A483, km26 (959 44 87 11/tours 959 43 04 32/www.donanavisitas.com). **Open** June-Sept 8am-9pm daily. Oct-May 8.30am-3pm, 4-7pm Tue-Sun. **Rates** €20 for 4hr tour. **No credit cards.**

on the Guadiana river, facing Portugal, this is Andalucía's westernmost town. The border is crossed by an elegant suspension bridge that can be seen straddling the skyline from some distance. The construction of the bridge (which opened in 1991) led to a huge slump in the local economy, as car drivers sped straight through the town now they no longer needed to take the ferry from Ayamonte to Portugal. You can, though, still take a ferry across the river with **Transporte Fluvial del Guadiana** (959 47 06 17, €1.10). Ferries leave from the Muelle de Portugal every half hour daily from July to September, and every 40 minutes on weekdays from October to June; there are hourly services on Sundays. **Grupa Guiamundo** (959 47 16 30) offers pleasure trips up the Guadiana (€42 incl lunch, €19 children aged 9-11, free under-11s), also leaving from the Muelle de Portugal.

**Isla Canela** is the closest beach to Ayamonte (seven kilometres/four miles to the south-east), a soulless, purpose-built resort with a long, wide, rather exposed strand. Across the marshy inlet of the Marismas de Isla Cristina is **Isla Cristina**, which has a spacious beach backed by pines. The fishing boats in the harbour create a lovely scene at sunset, and you can buy some of their catch, canned or salted, from the harbourside factories. On the way into town, pop into the **Terra Exotica** crocodile park on the N431 to feed the crocs.

Heading along the coast east from here, you cross a peninsula of pines and dunes to reach **Punta Umbría**. This fishing port and holiday resort (the province's liveliest) was first developed in 1880 by the British managers of the Rio Tinto Mining Company (*see p158*). The town still has a certain British salt-and-vinegary

Black-winged stilt.

in advance. The centre also has a bar/café, a giftshop where you can hire binoculars and an exhibition (in Spanish). A 1.5-km (one mile) footpath, 'Laguna del Acebuche', starts from the centre, winding through scrub to eight observation points around the lake.

### Club Hipico El Pasodoble

*Parque Dunar, Matalascañas (horse treks 959 44 82 41/4x4 tours 629 06 05 45/ www.marismadedonana.com).* **Rates** *Horse treks €22. 4x4 tours €21.* **No credit cards**.
El Pasodoble offers trips on horseback or in a 4x4 for all levels and ages through the park, mostly over the beach and dunes. Two-hour horse treks start at 9am, 6pm and 8pm daily in summer, and 10am and 5pm in winter daily (depending on demand). Four-hour 4x4 tours are at 8am and 5pm daily in summer, and 8am and 3pm daily in winter. Reserve both in advance.

### Discovering Doñana

*C/Aguila Imperial 150, El Rocío (959 44 24 66/620 96 43 69/www.discoveringdonana. com).* **Rates** *Group of 2-3 €110 half day, €140 whole day. Group of 4-6 €140 half day, €210 whole day.* **No credit cards**.
Discovering Doñana organises enjoyable half-day or full-day excursions in all-terrain vehicles for groups of up to six people, and supplies binoculars and an ornithologist guide. It can also organise airport transfers and accommodation. Excursions leave daily at 8am and 5pm.

The 80-kilometre (50-mile), four-hour tour sets off at 8.30am and 3pm in winter (Tue-Sun) and at 8.30am and 5pm in summer (Tue-Sun in May and Mon-Sat June-Sept). The all-terrain vehicles hold about 20 people, and in peak season you should book a week

feel to it – tatty, but with a down-to-earth charm. The 13-kilometre (eight-mile) long blue flag-standard beach has soft sand and a scattering of beach bars, as well as a string of high-rise hotels.

### Terra Exotica

*Isla Cristina (959 38 24 39).* **Open** *July, Aug* 10.30am-2pm, 4-8pm daily. *Sept-June* 10.30am-2pm, 4-7pm daily. **Admission** *Guided tour only (some in English)* €6; €4 concessions. **No credit cards**.

## Where to eat & drink

At weekends the Ayamonte locals head for the bars and cafés lining the main square, Plaza de Laguna, and the long promenade of the Plaza de Ribera, opposite the marina. The friendly **La Puerta Ancha** (Plaza de la Laguna 14, 959 32 19 96, closed Mon, €) claims to be the oldest

bar in Ayamonte and offers cheap tapas, with tables in the square. Also on the *plaza* is the **Passage Café** (No.11, 959 47 09 78, closed 2wks late Sept, €), a good spot for coffee and cake. Try the famous Huelvan *charcuterie* at **Mesones Juan Macías** (Paseo de la Ribera 2, 959 47 16 95, closed Mon and 2wks late Oct, €€), or, for fish straight from the boat, visit the cheerful **El Cocedero de Ayamonte** (Plaza de la Coronación 15, no phone, €). Choose your seafood from the chalkboard menus outside or from the trays on display on the bar inside.

Opposite the beach in Isla Canela, the **Espuma del Mar** bar-restaurant (Paseo de los Gavilanes s/n, 959 47 72 85, €€) specialises in fresh local fish and shellfish and has outdoor tables. There are also *chiringuitos*, or beach-bar barbecues, serving food on the sand during the summer. Isla Cristina is famous for its *raya con* *tomate* (skate with tomato) and *mechado con atún* (tuna minced with bacon, garlic and parsley and cooked in the oven with an onion and wine sauce). Try them in any of the bars in town, or go for something flashier at the prizewinning **Casa Rufino** (Avenida de la Playa Central s/n, 959 33 08 10, closed Jan, €€€), which is possibly the best restaurant on the coast. You can sample seafood fresh off the boats in Punta Umbría at the bars opposite the port or along the nearby pedestrianised Calle Ancha. Try the locally caught *chirlas* (clams) at **El Marinero** (C/Ancha 61, no phone, €). Calle Ancha is the lively hub of Punta Umbría, with cafés, ice-cream shops and late-night bars.

## Where to stay

Ayamonte, Isla Cristina and Punta Umbría are very busy in summer (particularly in July and August), when accommodation is hard to find without a reservation. Ayamonte's accommodation options include the good-value **Parador de Ayamonte** (C/El Castillito s/n, 959 32 07 00, www.parador.es, double €99-€123, restaurant €€€); its restaurant offers classily presented local dishes. Isla Canela has the neo-Moorish splendour of the **Hotel Riu Canela** (Paseo de los Gavilanes s/n, 959 47 71 24, www.riu.com, closed Nov-Jan, double €100-€194 per person incl breakfast & dinner), which features the usual four-star facilities among lovely tiled patios and terraced pools. In Isla Cristina try the friendly, characterful **Hotel Los Geranios** (Avenida de la Playa s/n, 959 33 18 00, www.bd-andalucia.es, double €61-€146), which has a swimming pool. In Punta Umbría, an attractive option is the traditional Andalucian-style **Barceló Punta Umbría** (Avenida del Océano s/n, 959 49 54 00, www.barcelo.com, double €96-€209). Near Calle Ancha, the friendly **Hostal Casa Manuela** (C/Carmen 8, 959 31 07 60, closed Oct-Mar, double €30-€60) has rooms with bath and TV.

## Resources

### Tourist information

**Ayamonte** *Avenida Ramón y Cajal s/n (959 32 18 71).* **Open** *June-Oct* 10am-1pm, 6-9pm Mon-Sat. *Nov-May* 10am-1pm, 5-8.30pm Mon-Fri; 10.30am-1pm, 6-8.30pm Sat; 6-8.30pm Sun.

**Isla Cristina** *Avenida de Madrid s/n (959 33 26 94).* **Open** *Mar-Oct* 10am-2pm, 5.30-7.30pm daily. *Nov-Feb* 10am-2pm daily.

**Punta Umbría** *Avenida Ciudad de Huelva, at Avenida de Andalucía s/n (959 49 51 60).* **Open** *June-Sept* 10am-2pm, 6-9pm Mon-Fri; 10am-1pm Sat, Sun. *Oct-May* 10am-2pm, 5-8pm Mon-Fri; 10am-1pm Sat.

## East of Huelva

The beach resorts of Mazagón and Matalascañas mark either end of a long stretch of sandy coastline between Huelva city and the **Parque Nacional de Doñana** (*see p152* **The last wilderness**). Neither offers much beyond sand, sea, dunes, pines and wind, and the usual seaside resort facilities. There's a nudist beach – the Cuesta de Maneli – at the 38 kilometre point on the C442 beach road.

**Mazagón** is a reasonable, low-rise resort. The best beach in the area, sheltered by steep cliffs, is six kilometres (four miles) east of town near the Parador de Mazagón (*see p155*). Further east, and right on the edge of the National Park, **Matalascañas** shocks with its unrelenting maze of tourist hotels and villas, arranged in 'sectors' and '*parcelas*'. Nature fights back in the **Parque Dunar** (959 44 80 86), a new development with walking and cycling routes through the dunes, picnic areas and a museum of marine life. The town beach itself is expansive and has fine sand, but, despite its EU blue flag, it gets rather littered, so you're better off wandering east towards the Doñana park. Matalascañas claims to have Spain's first ecological golf course, the **Golf Dunas de Doñana** (959 44 18 10, www.golf dunasdedonana.com, €45-€55 per 18-hole round), which is irrigated with recycled water and fed with organic fertilisers.

Heading inland through watery flatlands for 16 kilometres (ten miles) from Matalascañas brings you to one of the strangest little places in Andalucía: **El Rocío**. Looking for all the world like a Remember-the-Alamo-style Wild West town, its wide sand-strewn streets are lined by hitching posts for horses and Spanish colonial houses and churches. In fact, the resemblance is neither artifice nor coincidence. Many of the Spanish pioneers in North America originated from this corner of Andalucía, and took their style of domestic architecture with them. Horses remain the preferred mode of transport here – if you want to hire one, try **Doñana Ecuestre** (Avenida Canariega s/n, 959 44 24 74, €15 for first hour, €6 per hour thereafter, available afternoons Mon-Fri and all day Sat, Sun).

El Rocío is famous throughout Spain for the **Romería del Rocío**, a raucous pilgrimage held at Pentecost. The pilgrims are grouped into brotherhoods (*hermandades*), each with its own base in town. The subject of all this attention, the statue of the Virgen del Rocío, can be seen in the **Ermita** (open summer 8am-10pm daily, winter 8.30am-8pm daily).

Flamingoes, herons, red kites and countless other species of birds flock to the **Marisma del Rocío** (the marshy lake fronting the town).

## Where to stay, eat & drink

**The Parador de Mazagón** (A494, km30, 959 53 63 00, www.parador.es, double €114-€132), six kilometres (four miles) south-east of Mazagón, built in the '60s, offers typical *parador* service and style, and a large garden (with pool) running down to clifftop views over the ocean. A good, basic, cheap option nearby is the **Albergue-Campamento Juvenil Mazagón** (C/Cuesta de la Barca s/n, 959 53 62 62, www.inturjoven.com, open Easter, July & Aug only), which has four-person cabins with private bathroom (€13-€17 per person) and a campsite (open summer only). Alternatively, the attractive three-star **Hotel Albaida** (Carretera Huelva–Matalascañas, km18.3, Urbanización El Faro, 959 37 60 29, www.hotelalbaida.com, double €59-€86) sits in pine groves near the beach. For good-value seafood, take your pick from the *marisquerías* and *freidurías* lining the central Avenida Fuentepiña.

Don't even try to find accommodation in El Rocío during the Romería. At other times of year, the main hotel is the **Hotel Toruño** (Plaza de Acebuchal 22, 959 44 23 23, www.toruno.com, double €80-€375). Most rooms have balconies overlooking the *marisma* and a minibar and TV. For a treat, stay just outside town at **El Cortijo de los Mimbrales** (A483, km30, 959 44 22 37, www.cortijomimbrales.com, double €134-€161, cottage for 4 €375 per night). Beautiful cottages and rooms in a converted *finca* sit around gorgeous patios and gardens. If you can't afford to stay, you can eat at the superb restaurant (959 44 22 11, €€€). El Rocío's other classy joint, the **Aires de Doñana** restaurant (Avenida de la Canariega 1, 959 44 27 19, closed Mon and first 3wks July, €€), has picture windows and a terrace overlooking the *marisma*, and serves up imaginative dishes

such as carpaccio of *bacalao* with grapes and rosemary oil. **Bar El Pocito** (C/Ermita 9, 959 44 25 55, closed Wed, €) is a cheaper option for tapas, conveniently located next to the Ermita with a view of the *marisma* from its terrace.

## Resources

### Tourist information

**Matalascañas** *Avenida de las Adelfas s/n (959 43 00 86).* **Open** 9.30am-2pm Mon-Fri; 10am-2pm Sat.

**Mazagón** *Avenida de los Conquistadores s/n (959 37 60 44/63 00).* **Open** 10am-2pm Mon-Fri.

**El Rocío** *Avenida Canariega s/n (959 44 38 08).* **Open** 10am-2pm, 5-7pm Mon-Sat; 9am-2pm Sun.

## Getting there

### By bus

Most services are run by Damas (959 25 69 00, www.damas-sa.es). Huelva bus station (C/Doctor Rubio) has frequent buses to Sevilla and west and east along the coast (with connections at Almonte for El Rocío). There are also a few buses a day to the Sierra de Aracena and Portugal, and a daily service to Cádiz and Málaga. Ayamonte bus station is at Avenida de Andalucía (959 32 11 71). From here there are 2 buses to Faro in Portugal (except Sunday), plus services to Isla Canela and Isla Cristina. Isla Cristina bus station is at C/Manuel Siurot s/n (959 33 16 52); the bus station in Punta Umbría is at Avenida Ciudad de Huelva s/n (no telephone). El Rocío is served by regular buses to and from Huelva (via Almonte) and Sevilla.

### By train

Huelva station is at Avenida Italia, opposite C/Alfonso (902 24 02 02). There are 3 trains daily to and from Sevilla (1hr 30mins), 1 to Córdoba (2hrs 30mins) and Madrid (4hrs 50mins), and 2 services north to Almonaster-Cortegana (1hr 20mins-2hrs 40mins).

**Huelva Province**

El Rocío.

# North of Huelva

Spain's finest *jamón*, the world's oldest mines and vast tracts of wilderness are attracting more and more visitors to Andalucía's north-west corner.

The northern part of Huelva province was popular up until the 1980s almost exclusively with weekend and summer visitors from Sevilla. Greatly improved access has now made the area almost as anglicised as Granada's Alpujarras. Its charm is certainly easy to understand. Most of it falls within the boundaries of the densely forested 187,000-hectare (722 square-mile) **Parque Natural de la Sierra de Aracena y Picos de Aroche**, where small whitewashed villages cling to steep cliffs or nestle half-hidden in wooded valleys. The economy is rural, producing world-renowned ham, as well as cheese and honey. It's gently pretty in parts, spectacularly beautiful in others, and its locals are as yet unjaded by too many tourists. There's a distinctive culture to be discovered here, and the best way to do this may be as part of an organised tour, on foot, horse or bike. If you prefer to go it alone, your own transport is a must; unless, of course, you choose to explore some of the many hiking paths that have been marked out throughout the area.

## West Sierra de Aracena

Due to its proximity to the Portuguese border (28 kilometres/17 miles away), **Aroche** has been the subject of territorial disputes since the 13th century. Today, it is one of the best preserved and least touristy villages in the area. The **Castillo de Aroche**, at the top of its steep cobbled streets, bears witness to its contentious position. It was originally built in the 11th and 12th centuries but has been renovated almost continually ever since; it's now used as offices and a bullring.

On the road into Aroche is the weird **Museo del Santo Rosario**, which displays rosary beads fingered by such saintly figures as Franco and Nixon. More religious relics can be seen in the 15th- to 17th-century church of Nuestra Señora de la Asunción (open times of services), another much-renovated Aroche monument. It's an intriguing church, with Giralda-like tiers on its outer walls, a jumble of ancient doors and an incredibly ornate altar. In the fascinating **Museo Arqueológico** are artefacts that have been found around Aroche, including some Roman remains.

The well restored 13th-century castle in **Cortegana**, 14 kilometres (nine miles) east of Aroche on the N433, also bears witness to border disputes with Portugal. Today, you can enjoy one of the finest 360-degree views of the Sierra from its battlements. Be transported back to the Middle Ages during the four-day **Jornadas Medievales** *feria*, usually held over the first weekend of August, when the locals display their archery and falconry skills, as well as indulging in medieval music, theatre, drinking and dancing. Cortegana's decayed casino is a wonderful (and, in Andalucía, rare) art nouveau building.

Seven kilometres (four-and-a-half miles) south-east of Cortegana is the lovely village of **Almonaster La Real**, built around a stunning tenth-century mosque and citadel (usually open; if not, ask at the *Ayuntamiento* for the key), which overlooks the village. The mosque shares the site with some Roman and Visigothic remains and a 19th-century bullring. Inside the crumbling, atmospheric walls you'll find archways, columns with Arabic inscriptions, a Muslim fountain for washing, a prayer niche, and faded murals. Climb the tower (carefully) for views across Almonaster and into the bullring. A good time to visit is during the colourful **Las Cruces de Mayo** festival on the first Sunday in May.

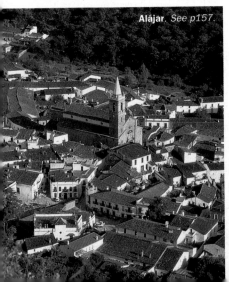

**Alájar.** *See p157.*

Ten kilometres (six miles) east of Cortegana is the village of **Jabugo**, home of Huelva's world-famous export– *jamón Ibérico*, ham made from pampered black Iberian pigs that are fed exclusively on acorns (*see p160* **Hang 'em high**). A couple of kilometres further east, **Galaroza** is a crafts centre, with a number of workshops producing ceramics and rush-backed furniture. It's worth a visit on 6 September for the **Fiesta de los Jarritos**, when everyone runs around throwing water at each other. Galaroza is also the starting point for a number of superb waymarked walks to neighbouring villages, including Jabugo, Fuenteheridos, Castaño del Robledo and Valdelarco. The latter is worth a visit for its superb restaurant, **La Maja** (*see below*).

### Castillo de Aroche

*Aroche (no phone).* Contact Manuel Amigo (*see below*).

### Castillo de Cortegana

*Cortegana (mobile 649 26 51 26).* **Open** *Apr-Sept* 11am-2pm, 5-8pm Tue-Sun. *Oct-Mar* 11am-2pm, 4-6.30pm. **Admission** €1.25; free under-8s.

### Museo Arqueológico

*Cilla de los Jerónimos, Aroche (no phone).* Contact Manuel Amigo (*see below*).

### Museo del Santo Rosario

*Paseo Ordóñez Valdés s/n, Aroche (no phone).* Contact Manuel Amigo (*see below*).

## Where to stay, eat & drink

In Aroche's Plaza Juan Carlos, check out **Cafetería Las Peñas** (959 14 04 15, €), which serves great tapas and, at weekends, seafood caught off Isla Cristina. Climb the steps next to it to reach **Bar Lalo** (no phone) through the first door on the right. It's a small, smartish bar with cute balconies overlooking the *plaza*. Opposite Las Peñas, **La Caja** (no phone) is a male-oriented bar with a good selection of local firewater made from acorns (*bellotas*) or anis. If you have one too many, rest your head at **Hostal Picos de Aroche** (Carretera de Lavita 12, 959 14 04 75, double €30).

Two kilometres (about one mile) from Cortegana towards Almonaster, you pass the delightful **Casas Rurales Los Gallos** (Finca Los Gallos, Estación de Almonaster, 959 50 11 67, mobile 687 36 57 54, www.alojamientolos gallos.com, cottage for 2 €59-€65, for 4 €97-€107, for 6 €138-€157, with reductions on weekly rates). Several whitewashed self-catering cottages are scattered around beautiful leafy gardens with patios, arches, wells and a swimming pool. If you don't want to cook, visit the friendly restaurant **El Fogón** (Antigua Estación Siglo XIX, Carretera Almonaster–Cortegana, mobile 617 90 06 65, closed Mon, €) nearby, with its great terrace by the railway line.

Just outside Almonaster, **El Rincón de Curro** (Carretera Almonaster–Cortegana, km1, 959 14 31 49, €€) dishes up tasty traditional local cuisine. Curro himself will talk you through his specialities, including a delicious *sopa de olores* (soup of smells). A good place to stay in Almonaster is the smart and popular **Hotel-Restaurante Casa García** (Avenida San Martin 2, 959 14 31 09, double €51), which has lovely views. The restaurant (€€) offers local specialities using seasonal ingredients.

The village of Valdelarco is home to the wonderful restaurant **La Maja** (C/Doctor Rodiño 27, 959 12 48 43, closed Mon-Fri except public holidays, €€), which serves up some original dishes, like *pimientos rellenos de jabalí* (peppers stuffed with wild boar), and has a terrace with lovely views of the surrounding countryside.

## Resources

### Tourist information

**Aroche** *Centro de Visitantes, Antiguo Convento de la Cilla (no phone).* **Open** 11am-2pm, 4-6pm Fri-Sun & hols.

The local authorised guide is Manuel Amigo (959 14 02 61), who holds the keys for the castle, Museo del Santo Rosario and the Museo Arqueológico, and will give you a tour of these (in Spanish only) for a voluntary contribution. He can be found at his house: C/Cilla 2, signposted from the main square, or ring in advance to arrange a time.

## East Sierra de Aracena

One of the Sierra's most picturesque villages, and an excellent base for exploring the area, **Alájar** (15 kilometres/nine miles east of Almonaster) is a tight knot of mossy, uneven cobbled streets and rickety old stone buildings, dotted with better-preserved examples of baroque churches and fine houses. The cobbles are often arranged in patterns, a common custom in the Sierra villages. Alájar shelters under the **Peña de Arias Montano**, a steep, leafy cliff, with caves at its foot and religious sites at its summit. This has been a spiritual area for centuries: ancient Iberian shamans are said to have had mushroom-induced visions here. This tradition was continued by Benito Arias Montano, Felipe II's confessor, who came here to meditate – on one occasion with his monarch. On the summit is a 16th-century church, Nuestra Señora de los Angeles (usually open), filled with pilgrims' offerings. The hallowed atmosphere is spoilt somewhat by the hordes that arrive on weekends and the tacky stalls outside selling local produce. Visit during

**Huelva Province**

the week and stroll in the woods for solitude and peace. To find out more about Arias Montano, visit the Centro de Visitantes (open 9am-2pm Mon-Fri). The exuberent **Romería de Nuestra Señora de los Angeles**, the Sierra's patron saint, takes place on 7-8 September, when processions from the surrounding villages congregate at the Peña for a day of eating, drinking and singing.

A few kilometres north of Alájar is the pretty village of **Fuenteheridos**. The lovely central square here has a 12-spring fountain surrounded by dark, ham-hung bars that are great for rubbing shoulders with gossiping locals. There's also the best *artesanía* shop in the Sierra, selling fine locally made handicrafts.

Heading west from Alájar for four kilometres (two-and-a-half miles) brings you to **Linares de la Sierra**, where houses have their own personalised cobblestone thresholds. Narrow streets converge on an open sandy square that doubles as a bullring. It's worth stopping off at the **Restaurante Arrieros** (*see p161*).

A further six kilometres (four miles) east is the Sierra's main town, **Aracena**. There's an air of cool confidence about its well-preserved streets, pleasant squares and whitewashed houses with casement windows. At the top of the picturesque, cobbled Calle Pozo de la Nieve, with its water features, souvenir shops, bars and restaurants, is the entrance to Aracena's main draw – the truly wonderful **Gruta de las Maravillas** (Cave of Marvels), where much of *Journey to the Centre of the Earth* and *Tarzan* were filmed. Visits to the caves are by guided tour only and numbers are limited. The tour takes an hour and leads you past spectacular rock formations and underground lakes that are reminiscent of *The Lord of the Rings*. There's a sign at the entrance warning visitors about the 95 to 98 per cent humidity and potential claustrophobia, though perhaps it would be better to prepare them for the eye-wateringly massive phallic shapes formed by some of the stalactites. The tour is in clear Spanish and the pleasant guides will usually help out any foreign tourists. Unlike many of Spain's caves, the Gruta de las Maravillas has been left almost untouched, which means you can really appreciate this incredible feat of nature.

The tourist office is opposite the cave entrance, with maps of Aracena and the Sierra, and walking guides. The Centro de Visitantes, housed in the Cabildo Viejo on Plaza Alta, has maps and information about the town, but is mainly the central information point for the Parque Natural de la Sierra de Aracena y Picos de Aroche. It has some interesting displays on the Sierra's history, geology, flora and fauna. Climb further up the hill to reach

the ruins of the Templar castle, with a 13th-century Gothic-Mudéjar church within its walls. There are fine views of the town from here.

Towards the eastern reaches of the province, about 23 kilometres (14 miles) south-east of Aracena, the curious, vertiginous village of **Zufre** perches on the edge of a cliff, with terraced *huertas* (allotments) below. Look down across the plain to the Embalse de Zufre reservoir from the *mirador* of the elegant Paseo de los Alcaldes (C/Nuestra Señora del Puerto). The tranquility of this small park of rose trees, lime trees and hedges is disturbed only by old gents engaged in fierce debates, swifts diving to and fro, and nesting storks clacking their beaks. On the first Saturday of every month there is a small but bustling *artesanía* market, where you can buy locally produced organic fruit, vegetables and cheeses, as well as leather and ceramic handicrafts.

As you walk Zufre's cobbled streets, you'll pass fountains and water features that have been used to irrigate the *huertas* for about half a century. On Plaza de la Iglesia are Zufre's monuments: the *Ayuntamiento*, with old stone, throne-like seats that were used by the Inquisition, and the 16th-century church of La Purísima de Concepción (open times of services), attributed to Hernán Ruiz, who was also responsible for Sevilla's Giralda.

## Gruta de las Maravillas

*C/Pozo de la Nieve s/n (959 12 83 55).* **Open** 10am-1.30pm, 3-6pm daily. **Admission** €7.70; €5.50 concessions. **No credit cards.**

## The Río Tinto Mines

Just south of the Sierra de Aracena, you come to mining country. This area has been exploited for its mineral wealth for over 5,000 years; the **Minas de Riotinto** (Río Tinto Mines) are the world's oldest, and allegedly the original King Solomon's mines. The Phoenicians extracted copper, followed by the Romans, who mined silver extensively using slaves. The mines were then forgotten until the 18th century, when the Spanish government sold them to the British Rio Tinto Mining Company for a bargain price. The Brits ran the mines in typical efficient colonial style, building an English-style estate of Victorian villas to house British management and engineers, complete with a village green, and church. They also built the first golf course and football pitch in Spain.

The mines returned to Spanish control in 1954, and today the area is more tourist attraction than industrial site. The landscape is a sight in itself, with the Río Tinto tracing a rust-red line through the multicoloured earth. Despite its

# Walk Alájar circuit

**Distance** 13km (8 miles)
**Time required** 4.5/5hrs

This is one of the loveliest walks in the Sierra. It links two exceptionally pretty villages, is easy to follow and has only one steep climb. It is best combined with a leisurely picnic beneath one of the old oaks or olives that you pass before reaching Linares de la Sierra. Or you could eat at the excellent Restaurante Arrieros in Linares (*see p161*).

The walk begins in the main *plaza* in Alájar. At the bottom of the square, head up Calle San Bartolomé, passing the Caja de San Fernando to your left. When you reach a church, turn left into Calle San Marcos.

The road soon bears right, passes the small Plaza de Miguel Moya, then drops down Calle Pintor Antonio Miña past the restaurant Casa El Padrino. At the end of the street you climb slightly and will see a sign for Sendero Aldea de los Madroñeros. At this, turn left and climb up a steep track that is at first concreted. In a little while you are descending between old stone walls over cobbled sections of path. There are wonderful views to the south. Soon you see the small hamlet of Los Madroñeros up ahead.

You come to a sign. It tells that in the mid 19th century the hamlet had a population of 150 but that it is now *deshabitado* (uninhabited), apart from on the last Sunday of August, when a pilgrimage takes place in honour of Nuestra Señora de la Salud Venderada. The path drops steeply down to the hamlet. Once you reach the first houses bear left, away from the church, to reach a large cobbled central square.

Go directly across this open area, pass between two houses, and you'll pick up a path that leads between beautiful old walls, taking you away from the hamlet.

You should pick up waymarking. Cross a (dry) stream and follow the winding path onwards between evergreens and cork oaks. The path reaches a gate. Go through the gate and climb gently upwards. Pass by Cortijo Mailozana and soon your path descends and crosses the poplar-lined course of the Barranco de los Madroñeros. Then continue along a pretty cobbled path. Somewhere around here would make a nice picnic spot. The path, sandier now, passes an old ivy-covered palm tree, bears left and goes behind a farm.

You wind past old olive groves and grubbing pigs and shortly Linares comes into sight, down below you to your left. Go through a wire-and-post gate and the path narrows once again. Continue down on a final steep cobbled section of path, cross a stream via a footbridge and then loop to the outskirts of the village, which you enter beside a newish small hotel.

Make sure to climb up and visit the village – one of the prettiest in the Sierra. Then retrace your footsteps back to the hotel and here bear sharply to the right, then immediately left, and follow a narrow path that runs between high walls and has citrus groves on either side. You reach a wooden gate. Bear right here and you come to a fork by a dead tree. Take the right fork and at the end of the path you reach a cobbled track where you turn left. You should see a sign here reading 'Alájar 8.9km'.

You pass the village cemetery and soon will have the oleander-filled stream to your left. Continue along this track, pass a picnic site and prepare yourself for a long, steep climb. The countryside opens out and you occasionally see the road up above you to the right. The track narrows, becomes a path and continues to climb upwards, cobbled at times.

Eventually, you meet the Alájar–Linares road. Here you turn left and, after just 20 metres, turn left again and descend sharply on a track that is paved for the first few metres. After about 100 metres, at a fork in front of a blue metal gate, go left. There is a signpost that points the way to Alájar.

Drop down a path that at first hugs the left bank of the stream before crossing over to its right bank. Soon the path reverts to track and continues descending until it reaches the first houses of Alájar, where it meets with the road. Bear left here and wind down Calle Rafael Montesinos. At the end of the street, bear left again by a public telephone, continue along Calle Virgen de la Salud, then bear right in front of the Casa de Padrino.

Follow the wall of the church of San Marco and then turn to the right and drop down past the Caja de San Fernando back to Alájar's main square.

*From* Walking in Andalucía *by Guy Hunter-Watts (Santana)*

Spring flowers in the **Sierra de Aracena**.
*See p156.*

lunar appearance, Río Tinto may prove to have more in common with Mars than the moon, according to NASA, which believes that the area has a mineral and bacterial composition similar to the Red Planet. In 2003 it began drilling in the area to simulate a future mission to Mars.

The **Museo Minero** displays mining artefacts, a reconstruction of a Roman mine and Queen Victoria's sumptuous train carriage. From the museum you can go on a tour (in Spanish only) to one of the largest opencast mines in the world, the jaw-droppingly vast **Corta Atalaya**. Probably the best attraction is the 22-kilometre (15-mile) **Ferrocarril Turístico Minero**, with its restored steam train from the 1900s, which runs along the Río Tinto and through a spectacular mining landscape.

### Museo Minero

*Plaza Ernest Lluch s/n, Minas de Riotinto (959 59 00 25).* **Open** 10.30am-3pm, 4-7pm daily. Steam train runs daily June-Sept, weekend afternoons only Oct-May. **Admission** *Museum* €3. *Museum & Corte Atalaya* €7. *Museum, Corte Atalaya & Ferrocarril Turístico Minero* €15. **Credit** DC, MC, V.

### Where to stay, eat & drink

Alájar has a great choice of places to eat. One of the best is **Mesón El Corcho** (Plaza España s/n, 959 12 57 79, closed Tue & Thur and last 2wks June, €€), a bar-restaurant with a decor based on the eponymous cork; treat yourself to its *gambones a la plancha* (grilled king-sized prawns). The nearby **Hotel La Posada**

# Hang 'em high

Throughout the Sierra de Aracena, black Iberian pigs (*cerdos Ibéricos*) snuffling in the ground for acorns *(bellotas)* are a common sight. The animal's meat is a ubiquitous feature on tapas menus in the Sierra, so much so that vegetarian visitors will suffer in this predominantly pig-rearing area. Traditionally, most families kept a pig or two, which provided a year-round supply of pork products. The whole family and their friends helped at the *matanza* (pig slaughter), with the men doing the butchering while the women made the sausages. Not for the squeamish, a *matanza* is a celebratory occasion where a pig is killed for all to see. Every part of the beast is used, from its distinctive black trotter – or *pata negra*, another name for *jamón Ibérico* – to its tail and its snout. Today, the custom of the *matanza* is in decline, mainly because of stringent EU regulations.

However, with the increasing popularity of *jamón Ibérico* from Jabugo, the pork industry still contributes significantly to the local economy, employing many locals during the winter, the *matanza* season. *Jamón de Jabugo* is regarded as the best in Spain, partly because the Sierra's air is ideal for drying hams. Other factors that contribute to the ham's quality are the breed of pig and its diet, consisting primarily of acorns. The free-ranging Iberian pig has a better distribution of fat than its more inactive counterparts, and deposits distinctive finely-marbled fat in its muscles. It is significantly high in oleaic acid, like olive oil, and so

helps to reduce cholesterol, as well as being lower in calories than other types of ham.

There are three types of *jamón Ibérico*: *jamón de bellota* is the most expensive and comes from pigs that feed almost exclusively on acorns; *jamón de recebo* is from pigs that feed on acorns and cereals, mainly maize; *jamón de pienso* is the cheapest and is from pigs fed only cereals and *pienso* (processed animal feed). To prepare the hams, they are first buried in sea salt for up to a month and then hung up to be dried in fresh air. The third stage of curing lasts 18 to 24 months, when hams are hung in a *bodega* (cellar).

The top producer is Sánchez Romero Carvajal, which has created grades of *cinco jotas* ('five Js', the 'J' standing for 'Jabugo') to classify *jamón* quality. You can visit **Mesón Sánchez Romero Carvajal** (C/San Juan del Puerto, 959 12 10 71, €€) in Jabugo; the prices can be a little steep, but it's certainly worth a splurge. You can also buy its ham in local supermarkets; a *jamón* is the back leg, and a *paleta* is the front. Expect to pay around €27/kg for *jamón de bellota* and €15/kg for *jamón de recebo*.

You can see *jamón* being sliced at bars throughout the Sierra, which parade an endless variety of pig-derived dishes. Apart from another cured delicacy, *caña de lomo* (cured pork loin sausage), there are various cuts of pork – *lomo, solomillo, presa, pluma, secreto*; and parts of the pig – *lengua* (tongue), *hígado* (liver), *orejas* (ears), *riñones* (kidneys), *carrillera* (cheek), *costillas* (ribs) and *castañuelas* (saliva glands).

View from **Aracena**'s castle. *See p158.*

(C/Médico Emilio González 2, 959 12 57 12, laposadadealajar@telefonica.net, closed last 3wks June, double €55) boasts green credentials like solar-powered hot water and organic locally produced food. A short walk away is the Dutch-run **Molino Río Alájar** (Finca Cabeza del Molino s/n, 959 50 12 82, www.molinorioalajar.com, cottage for 2 €225 per weekend, €492 per week, cottage for 4-6 €385 per weekend, €824 per week, 7-night minimum stay in July, Aug & Christmas). Beautifully furnished self-catering stone cottages are set in a leafy valley, and there's a swimming pool.

In Linares de la Sierra, reserve a table in advance at **Restaurante Arrieros** (C/Arrieros 2, 959 46 37 17, closed Wed and all July, €€). This smart but cosy restaurant has an open fire and a terrace, and serves delicious local specialities.

Near the little village of Los Marines, between Fuenteheridos and Aracena, you can hire a self-catering cottage in the British-run **Finca Buen Vino** (N433, km95, 959 12 40 34, www.fincabuenvino.com, double €128-€171, cottage for 4 with pool €433-€939 per week). Surrounded by chestnut woods, orchards and grazing sheep, the cottages have private swimming pools and barbecue areas, or you can stay and eat handsomely in the main house. This gorgeously peaceful and relaxing oasis is perhaps the best accommodation in the area. The owners also run cookery courses.

In Fuenteheridos, visit **Restaurante Biarritz** (C/Virgen de la Fuente 25, 959 12 50 88, closed dinner Mon-Thur and closed last wk June-1st wk July, €), a popular restaurant/tapas bar serving melt-in-the-mouth *caña de lomo* (cured pork sausage) and *solomillo con crema de jamón* (pork fillet with ham and cream sauce).

Despite being more on the tourist drag than its neighbours, rooms are limited in Aracena. The main hotel, **Los Castaños** (Avenida Huelva 5, 959 12 63 00, double €50), is a spruce two-star, with rooms decorated in rather depressing pinks and beiges. A cheaper, simpler option is **Casa Manolo** (C/Barberos 6, 959 12 80 14, double €22) for basic doubles without a bath. Situated in a beautiful wooded valley a kilometre out of Aracena is the lovely **Finca Valbono** (Carretera Aracena–Carboneras, km1, 959 12 77 11, www.finca valbono.com, double €68-€89, cottage for 3 €76-€92, cottage for 5 €135-€149). Hotel rooms and cottages are furnished in rustic style and there is a swimming pool and tennis court, as well as horse riding and walks. On Aracena's main square, Plaza del Marqués de Aracena, is **Café-Bar Manzano** (959 12 63 37, closed Tue and last wk Sept, €), with one of the best and most extensive tapas menus in the Sierra. For dessert, try some devilish cakes from the nearby **Confitería Casa Rufino** (C/Constitución 3, 959 12 81 21), an ornately tiled, 100-year-old cake and pastry shop – the best known in this part of Andalucía. Near the Gruta is the swish **Restaurante Montecruz** (C/San Pedro s/n, 959 12 60 13, closed Wed & 2wks July, €€), serving some tasty game and typical Sierra fare like wild mushrooms and the ubiquitous pork. If you've pigged out, then head to the nearby **La Tetería Andalusí** (Avenida Reina Isabel de los Angeles, 959 12 78 97, closed Mon, €) where you can sink into comfy floor cushions, sip a mint tea and enjoy sumptuous Moroccan-style surroundings. Besides home-made teas, there are fine tagines and couscous dishes.

## Resources

### Tourist information

**Parque Natural de la Sierra de Aracena y Picos de Aroche** *Centro de Visitantes, Cabildo Viejo, Plaza Alta s/n, Aracena (959 12 88 25).* **Open** *Apr-Sept* 10am-2pm, 6-8pm Tue-Sun. *Oct-Mar* 10am-2pm, 4-6pm Tue-Sun. **Aracena** *C/Pozo de la Nieve (959 12 82 06.* **Open** 10am-2pm, 4-7.30pm daily.

## Getting there

### By bus

Damas runs a limited service from Huelva (959 25 69 00) and Casal from Sevilla (954 90 69 77) to Aracena. There's a twice-daily service between Aracena and the other towns and larger villages.

### By train

One railway line runs north–south through Huelva province. The most convenient station for exploring the Sierra de Aracena is Estación de Almonaster-Cortegana, about 3km (1.5 miles) north of Almonaster on the way to Cortegana. It is served by a couple of trains a day to and from Huelva (2hrs).

# Sevilla Province

## Features

## Maps

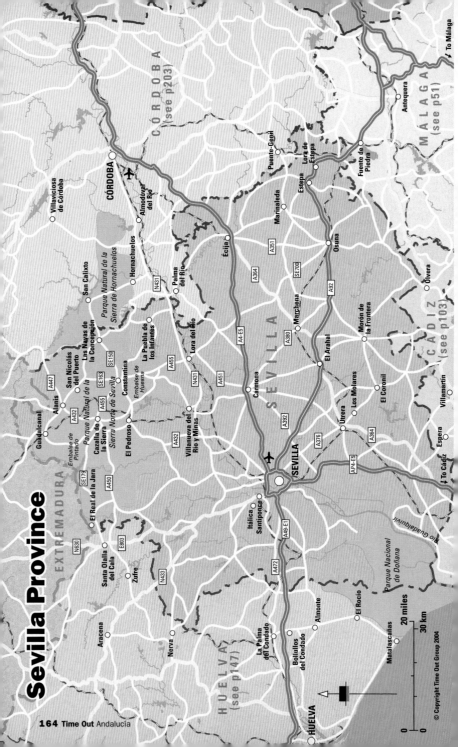

# Sevilla Province

© Copyright Time Out Group 2004

# Sevilla Province

The big city's the big draw, but don't overlook the rest of the province.

The city of Sevilla is one place in Andalucía that needs little introduction, featuring on most visitors' itineraries, yet the rest of the province is all but ignored by tourists. That's their loss, for the vast undulating plains to the east towards Córdoba contain some of the best-preserved historic towns in southern Spain, while the wilds to the north offer endless possibilities for nature boys and girls.

## SEVILLA CITY

With a population of more than 700,000, Sevilla is easily the largest city in Andalucía (and the fourth biggest in Spain); it's also one of the most romanticised – an exotic, steamy cauldron, scented with oranges and populated by passionate Carmens and flamenco-obsessed gypsies. While much of this reputation is pure fancy, and it certainly suffers from big city problems (unemployment, crime), Sevilla is, nevertheless, an intoxicating, immensely appealing city, packed with enough to see and do to easily fill a week or more. The gargantuan cathedral, the Alcázar and the winding alleyways of the *barrio* of Santa Cruz are where most visitors flock, but it's easy to avoid the crowds and discover tranquil, little-visited corners. And after you've had your fill of sightseeing, feast on superlative tapas and enjoy the youthful nightlife.

## EAST OF SEVILLA

The area east of Sevilla, bounded by the Guadalquivir river to the north and the hills of the Sierra del Sur to the south, is known as La Campiña. This gently rolling countryside is an important agricultural area, patchworked with olive groves and cereals rippling in the breeze. At their best, La Campiña's towns – Carmona, Écija and Osuna are the pick – are beautifully preserved architectural history lessons, where you'll find Iberian sculptures, Roman walls, Visigothic churches, Moorish fortresses and palatial baroque townhouses.

## NORTH OF SEVILLA

The northern reaches of Sevilla province are dominated by the most dramatic portion of the vast Sierra Morena range – the Sierra Norte. Hair-raising mountain roads offer stunning views of verdant valleys below and swirling vultures above. This is one of the lesser-known areas of Andalucía, with few large towns, and wonderful hiking opportunities.

## The best...

**Architecture, history, tapas, nightlife, bulls, oranges... the lot**
Sevilla City (*p166-95*).

**Church towers**
Écija (*p197*).

**Necropolis**
Carmona (*p196*).

**Towns**
Carmona (*p196*); Osuna (*p198*).

**Wilderness**
Sierra Norte de Sevilla (*p200*).

The **Palacio del Marqués de la Gomera** in **Osuna**. *See p199.*

# Sevilla City

*Toreros* and tapas, flamenco and *ferias* – Andalucía's essence is concentrated in the regional capital.

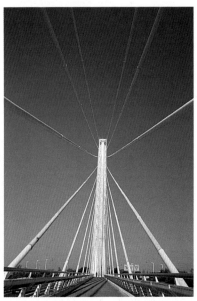

The **Puente del Alamillo**. *See p179.*

Madrid might exude more grandeur, and Barcelona more style, but it is to Sevilla we go to fulfil our deepest, most indulgent fantasies about Spain. Here is the pungent aroma of orange trees and jasmine, the *machismo* and violence of the bullfight, the vivacity of the Feria de Abril, the pious intensity of Semana Santa, the twisting cobbled streets of the Barrio de Santa Cruz specked with venerable tapas bars, the plaintive cry of the *canto jonde* singer… All clichés, to be sure, but all grounded in reality. Indeed, it's a wonder the city hasn't become a museum, a fossilised theme park of Andalucían archetypes. But Sevilla is also a workaday hub of industry and commerce, with a serious traffic problem, unlovely sprawling suburbs and a whole basket full of social and economic issues on its plate.

Yet none of this dampens the fun-loving spirit of *sevillanos* – and their energy, and wonderful capacity to share their social spaces with countless tourists, means the city's social scene is constantly renewed by young blood and contemporary cultural events. At the same time, locals of all generations are rightly proud of their southern 'capital' and even teenagers eagerly embrace the oldest traditions – go to a packed flamenco *peña* and you can bet it's *sevillanos* doing the tricky clapping in time.

The best time to visit is spring, when the weather is comfortably warm and every tree and plant is in blossom – the purple haze of jacarandas along the banks of the Guadalquivir and in the parks is strikingly beautiful. If you can afford to stay during either of the big festivals that take place at this time, Semana Santa and the Feria de Abril, you are guaranteed an unforgettable experience.

## HISTORY

Sevilla was first settled in about 600-700 BC by native Iberians, who were drawn to the Rio Guadalquivir and its fertile plains. The Iberians traded ceramics and minerals with the Phoenicians who had settled along the coast, until around 500 BC, when the Phoenicians conquered the Iberian settlement and renamed it Hispalis. Research suggests Hispalis may have been one of the towns that made up the fabled kingdom of Tartessus, a theory that is supported by archaeological remains found in the area.

The Phoenicians were defeated by the Carthaginians, who in turn succumbed to Roman invaders, who founded the neighbouring city of Itálica (*see p179*) in AD 205. Hispalis and Itálica grew in size and significance under Roman rule, becoming two of the most important population centres in Baetica, the Spanish part of the Roman Empire. In the early part of the fifth century Hispalis was conquered by the Vandals, but flourished again under Archbishop San Isidro, a native of the city.

In 712 'Isbiliya' was named the capital of Moorish al-Andalus, but lost its status to Córdoba just two years later. Nevertheless, the city flourished under Moorish rule, becoming an independent kingdom in the middle of the 11th century. By the end of the 12th century, the Almohads had made it their capital and built the Giralda as a mark of its significance.

When the city was conquered by Christian forces in 1248 a significant decline followed. Half the population fled as a wave of religious persecution was unleashed by Fernando III. It remained a favoured city for subsequent rulers, however, including Pedro I, who enlarged the royal residence, the Alcázar (employing a huge force of Moorish craftsmen).

It was the discovery of the Americas that signalled the city's entrance on to the world stage. Sevilla's monopoly on American trade for the best part of two centuries saw it grow to become the largest city in Spain, with a population of 150,000. The city suffered severe plagues in the early 17th century, and by the end of the century its fortunes had changed yet again. The silting up of the Guadalquivir forced the focus of trade to move to Cádiz, and for Sevilla there followed a slow slide into relative obscurity. The following decades were marked by more plagues, the widespread devastation of the 1755 Lisbon earthquake and the Napoleonic invasion of 1810-12.

Its lack of prominence did not prevent increasing numbers of European writers visiting the city throughout this period and waxing lyrical about its beauty and character in books and verse. Their outpourings attracted in turn a steady stream of 'romantic' tourists.

Sevilla attempted to re-establish itself on the world stage with the huge Ibero-American Exhibition of 1929. It had a signficant impact on the appearance of the city – the Parque de María Luisa and the Plaza de España were one result – but left the city bankrupt (and it had not fully recovered by the time of the 1992 Expo).

Sevilla fell quickly in the Civil War, becoming the first major prize for Franco in 1936. The years that followed saw a gradual revival of the city's status, although it remained the capital of one of the poorest, most backward regions of Spain. Sevilla's current fortunes are largely down to one man – Felipe González, a native *sevillano*, whose ruling Socialist party encouraged the enormous spending spree that presaged Expo '92, and led to the city becoming bankrupt once again.

Today, Sevilla is a modern city with modern city problems – increasing crime, horrendous congestion and the highest unemployment rate in Andalucía. It welcomes huge numbers of tourists every year, all hoping to find the version of Sevilla that each has created in his or her mind's eye. The city plays by its own rules, though, and it doesn't take long to adapt to its ways – long lunches, lazy afternoons and late dinners enjoyed in buzzing bars and cafés in shady squares.

## Sightseeing

Sevilla is a big city and requires at least a week to explore thoroughly. It would be impossible to see all the sights in a day or even two, especially in mid summer when temperatures

soar, so take your time, and make the most of Sevilla's charms. If you want a quick glance at everything, or find walking in the heat too much, check out **Sevilla Tour** (902 10 10 81, www.sevillatour.com) and **Tour por Sevilla** (954 56 06 93, http://sevirama.cjb.net), hop-on, hop-off bus services that pass all the major monuments and provide a guide to the Expo '29 and Expo '92 areas. The Torre de Oro is the most central pick-up stop. Even lazier – but rather cheesy – are the **Cruceros Torre del Oro** riverboat cruises (954 56 16 92, www.crucerostorredeloro.com, €13), which depart from the same spot for 90-minute cruises of the Guadalquivir.

## The Catedral & around

It's the sheer size of Sevilla's **Catedral** that first takes your breath away. Not just the height of its most emblematic structure, the Giralda, but the mass of the building. Allow a few minutes to walk around outside to marvel at the size of the Roman pillars, connected by huge metal chains, and at the enormous double flying buttresses.

Until the early 1400s the Christians of Sevilla worshipped in the 12th-century Almohad mosque, which had been adapted as a church by Fernando III in 1248. By 1401 the building was beginning to show signs of wear and tear so the church authorities resolved to pull it down and replace it with a magnificent new structure that would be an unsurpassed monument to the Christian faith, 'a church which those who see it finished will think we were mad for attempting'.

Nothing like it had been constructed before. Although it was Gothic in design, the shape of the cathedral had no clear precedents, and the architects – all 17 of them – were constrained by the floorplans of the original mosque. Construction began in 1434 and was completed, incredibly, by 1517. Today, the cathedral is considered the largest church in the world – bigger in volume than St Peter's in Rome.

The building's Moorish past is most clearly evident at the original entrance to the old mosque, the Almohad-style **Puerta del Perdón**, whose 12th-century bronze doors have inscriptions from the Koran. This gateway leads into the **Patio de los Naranjos**, where orange trees follow the outline of the original courtyard in which the faithful performed their ablutions before entering the mosque; the fountain in the centre and a number of the walls date from the Moorish period. The east wall contains the **Biblioteca Colombina**, a library of manuscripts from Christopher Columbus's journeys, founded by his son.

# Sevilla

© Copyright Time Out Group 2004

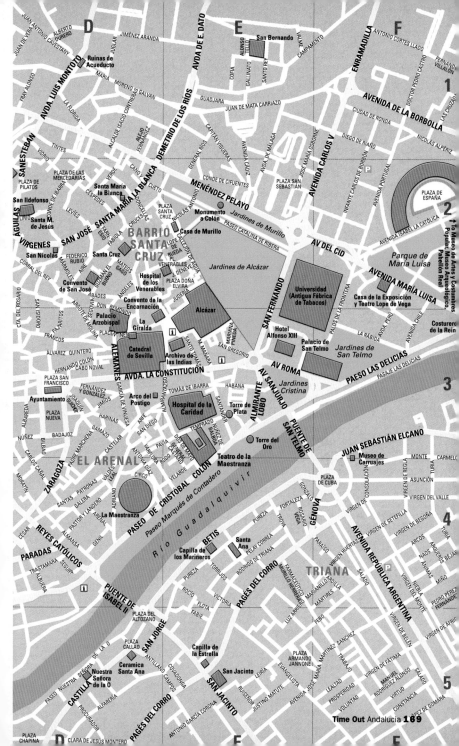

Once inside the cathedral, as your eyes grow accustomed to the darkness, you'll notice the tops of columns soaring towards the ceiling and enormous arches sweeping across the tops of the naves. The sheer scale of the structure is undeniably impressive and would no doubt have cowed the original worshippers. At its highest point, the central nave rises to almost 43 metres (140 feet), supported by columns that are 3.6 metres (12 feet) thick. The *retablo* of the main altar is the largest in the world at almost 37 metres (120 feet) high.

The chapels along the sides of the building contain works such as Murillo's *Vision of St Anthony* and *Baptism of Christ*; Zurbarán's *retablo* of the life of St Paul; and Goya's *Saints Justa and Refina*, which takes pride of place in the **Sacristía de los Cálices**.

The centrepiece of the cathedral is the main altar in the **Capilla Mayor**, an extraordinary work begun in 1482 and completed a century later. It contains more than 1,000 sculptures in wood and gold depicting 45 scenes from the Bible. Opposite the altar, the massed ranks of the choir stalls line up in front of the vast organ.

Behind the Capilla Mayor, against the eastern wall, is the **Capilla Real**, housing the ornate tomb of Fernando III, his wife Beatrice and his son Alfonso the Wise. On the south side of the cathedral is another impressive tomb held aloft by four pallbearers representing the kingdoms of Castilla, León, Navarra and Aragón. This may or may not be the final resting place of Christopher Columbus. The explorer's body was moved so many times after his death in 1506 that no one is entirely sure if he is buried here or in the Dominican Republic.

To the left of the tomb lies the **Sacristía Mayor**, a huge space topped by a dome designed in 1528 by Diego de Riaño. It's full of art, including more works by Murillo and Zurbarán, and an impressive *Deposition* by 16th-century Flemish-born Pedro de Campaña, which greatly influenced Velázquez and the other artists of the Golden Age. The centrepiece, though, is an incredible three-metre-high (ten-foot) 16th-century monstrance made entirely of silver by Juan de Arfe. East of the main sacristy is the stunning **Sala Capitular** (Chapter House). Conceived by Hernán Ruiz II in 1558, it represents the first oval design by a Renaissance architect, although it was modified upon his death and finally completed in 1591. The domed ceiling, with an *Immaculate Conception* by Murillo, and the beautiful marble floor make this an architectural gem.

At the north-east corner of the cathedral lies the entrance to the **Giralda**, the symbol of Sevilla and a landmark from almost anywhere in the city. The minaret of the original mosque was built between 1172 and 1195 during Almohad rule and was topped by four shiny globes, designed to catch the light and be visible from far beyond the city. These fell during an earthquake in the 13th century and were replaced after the *reconquista* by a spire and a weathervane representing faith, called El Giraldillo, from which the tower takes its name. The exquisite decoration of the minaret is completely unlike anything to be found on any other Almohad monument, and is often said to be an example of the ascetic Almohads succumbing to the sensuality of al-Andalus. Despite being more than 91 metres (300 feet) high, it's surprisingly easy to climb the Giralda due to the gently inclining ramps inside. They were designed to allow the *muezzin* (whose job it was to call the faithful to prayer five times a day) to ride his horse to the top. It need hardly be said that the views from here are magnificent.

Across the Plaza del Triunfo from the cathedral is the entrance to the **Alcázar** palace and grounds. The fortress palace of Pedro I ('the Cruel') contains the finest examples of 14th-century Moorish architecture outside the Alhambra. Its origins go back to the eighth century, but most of the design you see today dates from the 1360s, when Pedro installed himself and his mistress María de Padilla here.

You enter the complex through the **Puerta de León**, which contains traces of the original Almohad wall and opens on to a courtyard where Pedro received visitors and passed judgement on offenders. On the left is the **Sala de Justicia**, built by Alfonso XI of Castilla in around 1330, with a beautiful coffered ceiling and exquisite plasterwork. The **Patio del Yeso** (Plaster Courtyard) has more of the same and is the only surviving part of the original 12th-century palace.

From the **Patio de la Montería** (Hunting Courtyard), you can contemplate the wonderful Mudéjar façade of the palace, built by Pedro in 1364. It is a perfect synthesis of the different cultural and architectural styles that were present in Andalucía at that time. Muslim artists from Granada worked alongside Mudéjar carpenters from Toledo; Christian and Kufic inscriptions were carved side by side; and graceful Mudéjar columns bear heraldic lions and castles signifying Pedro's kingdom.

To the right of the palace lies the rather dreary **Casa de la Contratacción**, where Fernando and Isabel planned much of the conquest of the Americas – there's a stunning painting here by Alejo Fernández of the Virgin protecting the navigators. Pass through here to the interior of the palace, where the breath-taking designs rival those of the Alhambra.

Symbol of the city: the **Giralda**. *See p170.*

complex by Carlos V. The classical-style rooms are full of Flemish tapestries and unlikely to hold your attention for long. Instead, continue to the gardens, which are among the loveliest in all Spain. Huge palms tower over the paths, flowers and fish ponds, and birdsong fills the air in all seasons. The gardens are a combination of Moorish design and later Italian influence, resulting in trickling streams and little fountains interspersed with gaudy grottoes and wildly-staring sculptures. There is also a small maze at the far end. Near here is the **Pabellón de Carlos V**, a gem of Spanish Renaissance architecture, with a marvellous combination of classical and Moorish elements.

Tucked in between the cathedral and the Alcázar is the city's old merchant exchange, **La Lonja** (Avenida de la Constitución 3, 954 21 12 34, closed for renovation at the time of writing). Built in response to a complaint in 1572 by Archbishop Cristóbal de Rojas de Sandoval concerning the number of business transactions taking place on the steps of the cathedral, La Lonja soon became the commercial centre of Sevilla. Although numerous architects worked on the building, Juan de Herrera (Felipe II's favourite architect) oversaw construction, and his hand is everywhere, from the stern lines and simple design to the trademark pyramids topped with balls on the roof. The central courtyard is a study in restraint, with double-decked Doric columns surrounding a black and white marble square.

By the 1780s Sevilla had been usurped by Cádiz as the centre of trade with the Americas, so Carlos III converted La Lonja into a huge storehouse to hold the records for the Spanish Empire. The **Archivo de las Indias** consists of almost 40,000 documents kept on hundreds of 18th-century mahogany shelves.

Diagonally across from La Lonja, on Plaza Virgen de los Reyes, is the **Palacio Arzobispal**, with its beautiful baroque façade, twin patios and a 17th-century staircase. Next door is the **Convento de la Encarnación**, founded in 1591 and containing a collection of sculptures.

In keeping with Moorish custom the palace is divided into public and private domains. Among the public areas is the palace's largest courtyard, the **Patio de las Doncellas**, named after Christian maidens who were presented to the Moors as an annual peace offering. (The patio is currently being excavated – the remains of two previous Moorish palaces have been found here.) The arches are supported by matching marble columns, and the 14th-century tiling is perhaps the prettiest in the Alcázar. A gallery was added by Carlos V on the occasion of his marriage in 1525. This leads to the **Salón de Embajadores** (Hall of Ambassadors), which is overwhelming in its beauty and craftsmanship. Take time to gaze at the wooden dome, gilded and painted with spots of bright red, green, blue and gold, and decorated with stalactite designs. (The balconies were added by Felipe II.)

Pass through the bedroom next door to reach the intimate **Patio de las Muñecas**, once the living room of the palace and named after two tiny dolls' faces carved into the honeycombed arches. The columns were taken from the ruins of the Moorish palace outside Córdoba, Medina Azahara (*see p207* **The lost city**). Numerous other bedrooms and *salas*, as well as an entire palace, were tacked on to the east side of the

### Alcázar
*Patio de Banderas s/n (954 50 23 23/www. patronato-alcazarsevilla.es).* **Open** *Apr-Sept* 9.30am-7pm Tue-Sat; 9.30am-5pm Sun. *Oct-Mar* 9.30am-5pm Tue-Sat; 9.30am-1.30pm Sun. **Admission** €5; free concessions. **Credit** AmEx, DC, MC, V. **Map** p169 E2/3.

### Catedral & La Giralda
*Avenida de la Constitución s/n (954 21 49 71/ www.catedralsevilla.org).* **Open** *July, Aug* 9.30am-3.30pm Mon-Sat; 2.30-6pm Sun. *Sept-June* 11am-5pm Mon-Sat; 2.30-6pm Sun. **Admission** €7; €1.50 concessions; free under-12s; free to all Sun. **No credit cards**. **Map** p169 D3.

## Barrio de Santa Cruz

The maze of streets leading away east from the Catedral and Alcázar make up the old Jewish quarter and should be the most atmospheric part of the city. Here you'll find tiny squares studded with orange trees and jasmine, narrow, whitewashed streets filled with needle-sharp sunlight and shadows, plant-covered patios behind iron railings and shady bars serving *finos*, cured ham and cold beers. This whole area was drastically restored in the 1920s by the founder of the *parador* hotel group, the Marquis of Vega-Inclán, Spain's first minister of tourism. Unfortunately, Santa Cruz today can feel like a theme park in high season, when the whole area is jammed with tour groups. If you're here in summer, try to visit early in the morning, before 9am, when you'll find the streets practically deserted. The prettiest lanes are those backing on to the north-east wall of the Alcázar. Follow Calles Judería and Vida as they twist and turn along to Plaza de Doña Elvira, a beautiful square fringed by orange trees and with a pretty fountain in the middle; it's home to the **Corral de Comedias**, where playwright Lope de Rueda began his career.

On one side of the plaza is the **Hospital de los Venerables**, the best-known building in the *barrio*. It was built as a home for old and sick priests on the initiative of a local canon in 1676. Juan Domínguez began the work but Leonardo de Figueroa took over and created what may well be the prettiest patio in all Andalucia. Four tiled staircases lead down to a sunken terracotta courtyard with a tiny fountain at its centre and orange trees in each corner. The patio is surrounded by slender arched columns and first-floor balconies. Inside there's an art gallery with various works, including a large oil painting (part of the *retablo*) of the Last Supper by Lucas Valdés.

Running alongside the walls of the palace gardens is the Callejón de Agua, a lovely tree-shaded street whose name derives from the watercourse that ran along the top of the wall. Leading off it are Calle Pimienta (Pepper Street) – supposedly named after an incident involving a Jewish spice merchant who found a pepper tree growing outside his front door – and Calle Susona, where, according to legend, a beautiful Jewish girl and her entire family were killed by her Christian lover (in fact, she betrayed her family to the Christians, and then killed herself). An *azulejo* (glazed tile) in the street records the incident. The *callejón* leads to Plaza Alfaro, inspiration for the balcony scene between the young lovers in the *Barber of Seville*; continue along to the **Jardines de Murillo**, a slender landscaped park of ancient peepul trees, lady of the night and jasmine trees, with shaded corners and water features.

Plaza Alfaro almost adjoins one of the prettiest squares in the *barrio*, Plaza Santa Cruz. In the centre, flowers and orange trees surround a wrought-iron cross, known as La Cerrajería, indicating where the original church once stood; it was pulled down by the French in 1810. In one corner of the square is **La Albahaca**, the former home of the architect Talavera and now a fine restaurant (*see p180*), while at No.8 is the last home of the Sevillian artist Murillo. The house now contains a

The **Alcázar**.
*See 170.*

small museum, the **Museo Casa de Murillo** (C/Santa Teresa 8, only open for special exhibitions, call tourist office for details).

The church of **Santa Cruz** (C/Mateos Gago s/n, 954 22 73 38), with a façade by Juan Talavera, is a minute's walk away along Calle Santa Teresa, and nearby is the **Convento de San José** (C/Gúzman el Bueno 10), a 16th-century church that contains beautiful Mudéjar decoration. A further minute to the east, through Plaza de las Cruces, is the church of **Santa María la Blanca** (C/Santa María la Blanca 5), a Visigothic temple that was used as a synagogue in the 13th century before being converted into a church in 1391. Further alterations took place in 1659 – the heavy baroque plasterwork is striking. Inside are some wonderful *azulejos* and a *Last Supper* by Murillo.

Calle Santa María la Blanca opens up into a small square with a number of good bars and restaurants; it marks the northern edge of the *barrio*. The streets and houses beyond retain little of Santa Cruz's unique atmosphere, but it's worth pressing on to the north-east to see Sevilla's prettiest mansion, the **Casa de Pilatos** on Calle Esteban. The house's name (according to one theory) comes from the mistaken belief that it was built to the same dimensions as Pontius Pilate's house in Jerusalem, after one of the original owners went there on a pilgrimage. Work was started in 1481 by Don Pedro Enríquez, a former governor of Andalucía, but it was his son, Don Fadrique, who redesigned it in a mixture of Mudéjar, Renaissance and Gothic styles. You enter via a triumphal arch to the *apaedero*, where carriages waited, and into the central courtyard with its harmonious mixture of Moorish and European architectural styles. Around the courtyard are rooms with busts of emperors and kings, many sculpted in Italy. The Praetorium Room has a beautiful coffered ceiling and 16th-century *muqarna* cones (stalactite designs) by Andrés de Juarra. The stairs leading to the upper floors are magnificent – a dazzling array of tiles in light blues, greens and reds, covered by a coffered ceiling with more stalactite designs; these floors are occupied and can only be visited on a guided tour. They contain paintings and frescoes, including the *Apotheosis of Hercules* ceiling by Francisco Pacheco, the mentor of Velázquez, and three oil paintings by *sevillano* artist Sebastián de Llanos Valdés. The gardens are stunning too.

### Casa de Pilatos

*Plaza de Pilatos 1 (954 22 52 98).* **Open** *Mar-Sept* 9am-7pm daily. *Oct-Feb* 9am-6pm daily. **Admission** *Ground floor & gardens* €5. *Both floors & gardens* €8. **No credit cards. Map** p168 C2.

### Hospital de los Venerables

*Plaza de los Venerables 8 (954 56 26 96/ www.focus.abengoa.es).* **Open** 10am-2pm, 4-8pm daily. **Admission** €4.75; €2.40 concessions. **No credit cards. Map** p169 D/E2.

## El Arenal

The old port area, directly west of the cathedral across the Avenida de la Constitución, was once a stinking marshland and red-light district. It's not as pretty as Santa Cruz, but it seems a lot more authentic, mainly due to the lack of tourists. It's a good area in which to lose yourself for a few hours, dipping into the many excellent bars and restaurants.

Its main sight is **La Maestranza**, Sevilla's bullring on the Paseo de Colón, an enormous complex containing offices, apartments and a museum and ticket office at the western end. The so-called Cathedral of Bullfighting holds 13,500 people; it's not as big as Las Ventas in Madrid but is regarded by aficionados as the most beautiful and important in the world. It was begun in 1761 under the orders of its current owners, the Real Maestranza de Caballería, and was constructed over the next 119 years. Delays contributed to its oval shape, as architects and builders attempted to work around new buildings. Despite the size of La Maestranza, its incredible acoustics allow you to hear everything that takes place, wherever you are sitting. It was a key backdrop to the action in Bizet's *Carmen*, as testified by the statue across the road. The **Museo de la Maestranza** contains the heads of slain animals, posters, matadors' jackets and other *toro*-related memorabilia. The bullfighting season begins on Easter Monday and continues daily throughout the Feria de Abril and then every Sunday in May and June. There are also *corridas* in July and August, but they are not as highly regarded. (For more information on bullfighting, *see p174* Cliché.) All around this area are atmospheric old spit-and-sawdust bars that pack out before and after *corridas*. Also on the riverside *paseo* is the **Teatro de la Maestranza** (*see p190*), constructed for the 1929 Expo.

Behind the theatre is the **Hospital de la Caridad**, built on land where criminals were once hanged. This was a small fraternity languishing in the backwaters of the city until the admission of Miguel de Mañara, the rakish son of a wealthy landowner. Mañara (who may have been the inspiration for the mythical Don Juan) resolved to change his ways, becoming prior and spending his entire inheritance on the building we see today (built 1673-82). The hospital now houses one of the best collections of paintings and sculptures in Sevilla. Highlights

*Sevilla Province*

# Cliché Bullfighting

Forget football stars, say traditionalists – Spain's real macho heroes are the handsome chaps who take on the big black bulls. And it's in steaming Sevilla that the definitive bullfight, in the definitive bullring, can be seen. Although the pitting of *hombre* against *toro* is far from exclusive to Andalucía, it was here (in Ronda; *see p92*) that the form and substance of the *corrida* were developed, and here that its spiritual heart remains. If you can overcome any squeamishness and moral objections you might have, and want to experience first-hand what it's all about, here's what to expect...

In the *venta de taquillas* (ticket office) you'll find little maps of the bullring hanging on the wall. There are two things to decide: how near you want to be to the action and whether you want to be in the *sol* (sun) or *sombra* (shade). *Sol* is always cheaper than *sombra*, but that's largely due to the fact that most of the action takes place in shadow.

To smell the bulls and look directly down at the matadors, choose a seat in the first three rows, known as *filas*. These seats, actually little more than concrete benches, are uncomfortable and allow a close-up view of the action that is definitely not for the squeamish. The next few rows are known as *tendidos*. They offer a little more comfort (they have backs) but you'll have to put up with a lot of people, including the beer vendors, walking past. Beyond here is the *balcón*, where the seats are cheaper the further back you sit.

## THE CORRIDA

A typical *corrida* lasts for at least a couple of hours, during which time six bulls are killed. The show begins with a procession, accompanied by a band, in which you see the entire cast of characters: the three matadors, their *cuadrillas* (helpers) – two mounted *picadores* and three *banderilleros* – followed by the mule teams who will carry off the dead animals. At the front of the procession are two *alguacilillos* whose job it is to open the enclosure and let in the bull.

Once the ring is cleared the fight begins. First the bull storms in, snorting and magnificent. He is goaded by *banderilleros* with capes, partly to tire him, and partly to ascertain how angry he is.

Next come the *picadores* on horseback. For many observers, this is the most objectionable part of the *corrida*. Although the horses are covered in heavy padding and blindfolded, they are well aware of what's going on, and it's a shocking sight when one is tossed and gored on the bull's horns (though at least they don't die in their dozens, as used to be the case before padding was introduced). The horses' silence has nothing to do with their stoicism: their vocal cords are cut before they come into the ring. The idea of this part of the fight is to allow the *picador* to stab the bull's neck, thus weakening its muscles and forcing it to lower its head, making the kill easier for the matador.

A horn sounds, the ring is cleared and on march the *banderilleros*, whose job it is to stick three sets of *banderillas* (poles festooned in bright ribbons with barbed ends) into the bull's shoulders. This can be nerve-wracking to watch, and involves an enormous amount of skill and courage – though, again, animal rights groups contest that the odds are unfairly stacked against the bull, who is soon bleeding heavily and dizzy through lack of oxygen.

include a series of paintings by Murillo (a good friend of Mañara), who decorated the *azulejo* tiles on the façade of the chapel. Valdés Leal also contributed to the collection, with a series of paintings so realistic in their depictions of death that Murillo commented, 'one has to hold one's nose to look at them'.

On Calle Santander is the **Torre de Plata** (Tower of Silver), a Moorish watchtower, while the better-known **Torre del Oro** (Tower of Gold) stands on the riverbank close by. The latter was constructed by the Almohads in 1220 to mark the edge of the city's defences.

If the city came under attack, a chain would be stretched across the river from the tower to a small keep in Triana. The chain was broken during the conquest of Sevilla by the invading Christian fleet in 1248. In Moorish times the tower was covered by golden-coloured tiles that reflected the sunlight. Later, it became the warehouse for gold from the Americas.

## Hospital de la Caridad

*C/Temprado 3 (954 22 32 32).* **Open** 9am-1.30pm, 3.30-7.30pm Mon-Sat; 9am-1pm Sun. **Admission** €4. **No credit cards. Map** p169 E3.

closer to him as it charges the cape. Often the matador will contemptuously turn his back on the animal and walk away. When the matador judges it's time to despatch the bull, he grabs his sword and holds it under the cape, readying himself. He needs the animal right in front of him, head bowed to allow him to thrust the sword between its shoulders and through to its heart for a quick kill.

If the matador is accurate and swift, there is little blood; the animal pauses and there is total silence in the ring; it sways slightly, staggers, its front legs give way and it collapses. However, if the kill is not clean, things can get very messy indeed: the bull will start staggering around, glassy-eyed, throwing up gallons of blood all over the pristine yellow sand while the matador either tries to finish the job himself with a second sword or instructs one of his men to stab the bull in the brain with a tiny dagger. Either way, it's horribly distressing to watch.

Finally, the bull is dragged away, the sand is cleaned and the crowd make clear their feelings – either by shouting abuse or waving white handkerchiefs. The president will then decide whether the matador should be awarded one ear, both ears, or both ears and a tail, if the matador's performance has been especially impressive.

The fourth and final act involves the matador who strides on in brilliantly coloured garb carrying the traditional cape (pink on one side, gold on the other). At this point all chatter ceases and you can actually hear the swoosh of the cape and the matador's words as he whispers to the bull, '*vamos toro... vamos toro...* '. The skill of a professional matador can be mesmerising: he may choose to 'flirt' with the bull, placing his arm across its back and circling with it in a weird dance, or he may get the animal to come closer and

The whole event is repeated a further five times until, like at the end of a play, the entire cast (minus the bulls) comes on for a few laps round the ring. If they've done well, the audience will shower them with red roses. After a particularly fine show, the matador may be carried out on the shoulders of his *cuadrilla* and led through the main door of the bull ring – this rarely happens in Sevilla, where the aficionados are considered the most discerning (and fussy) in Spain.

### La Maestranza & Museo de la Maestranza

*Paseo de Colón 18. Corrida ticket sales: C/Adriano 37 (corrida tickets 954 50 13 82/museum 954 22 45 77/ www.realmaestranza.com).* **Open** *Museum* 9.30am-7pm daily (9.30am-3pm on fight days). **Admission** *Corridas* €3-€110. *Museum* €4. **No credit cards**. **Map** p169 D4.

### Teatro de la Maestranza

*Paseo de Colón 22 (information 954 22 33 44/tickets 954 22 65 73/www.teatromaestranza.com).* **Open** *Ticket office* 10am-2pm, 6-9pm Mon-Sun. **Tickets** €18-€48. **Credit** AmEx, DC, MC, V. **Map** p169 D4.

### Torre del Oro

*Paseo de Colón s/n (954 22 24 19).* **Open** 10am-2pm Tue-Fri; 11am-2pm Sat, Sun. Closed Aug. **Admission** €1; free to all Tue. **No credit cards**. **Map** p169 E3.

## Centro

The Plaza San Francisco is the logical place to start a tour of central Sevilla. This smart but soulless square was rebuilt at the same time as the **Ayuntamiento**, whose entrance lies to the west in modern Plaza Nueva. Work on the town hall began in 1526 under Diego de Riaño and was completed in 1571 after his death. Beneath the layers of grime is a plateresque façade incorporating hundreds of ornate designs. Inside is an impressive art collection, with works by Velázquez and Zurbarán.

North of here lie the main shopping streets of the city – Calles Sierpes, Tetuán and Velázquez – which also contain a number of good bars and restaurants. Between Sierpes and Tetuán is the exquisite, tiny **Capillita de San José** (C/Jovellanos 10), one of the best examples of baroque architecture in the city, while a couple of minutes' walk to the west is the church of **La Magdalena** (C/San Pablo s/n). The church was rebuilt by Leonardo de Figueroa at the end of the 17th and beginning of the 18th centuries, and contains a *Life of Dominic* by Zurbarán.

A little to the north-west is the **Museo de Bellas Artes**, which has a collection of mainly Spanish art that is regarded as the finest outside Madrid. The museum was founded in 1835 and is housed in the beautiful **Convento de la Merced**, rebuilt by Juan de Oviedo in 1612 and renovated by Leonardo de Figueroa in 1724. The galleries are arranged around three pretty courtyards. Room one concentrates on Gothic painting and sculpture from the 14th and 15th centuries, and includes two works by local sculptor Pedro Millán. Room two has Renaissance pieces, both European and Sevillian, including El Greco's portrait of his son; the wooden *St Jerome* by Pietro Torregiano is another highlight. Room three looks at *retablo* history in the second half of the 16th century and features artists such as Pacheco and Montañes. Room four has a fantastic *Last Supper* by Alonso Vázquez and a gruesome picture of the severed head of John the Baptist by Núñez Delgado. Through a courtyard and past the impressive main staircase, you reach room five, probably the most outstanding in terms of design, with murals by Domingo Martínez all over the domed ceiling. The centrepiece is Zurbarán's *Apotheosis of St Thomas* (1631), and there are plenty of good works by Murillo too. The upper floor is dedicated to the baroque, with works by Ribera and Zurbarán (room six), Murillo (room seven), Valdés Leal (room eight) and Zurbarán again (room nine), including his *Miracle of St Hugo*.

Head back east from the museum along Calle Alfonso XII to see the rest of Centro. The **Palacio de Lebrija** on Calle Cuna has three ornate patios and a collection of Roman artefacts from the nearby settlement of Itálica. Close by is the church of **La Anunciación** (C/Laraña), which flanks the Plaza de la Encarnación, and further east, the Gothic **San Pedro** (Plaza de San Pedro) and **Santa Catalina** (Plaza de Santa Catalina s/n), whose tower is a copy of the Giralda. Just behind here, on Calle Gerona, is Sevilla's oldest tapas bar, **El Rinconcillo** (*see p183*).

From San Pedro, Calle Sales Ferrer takes you to the perpetually lively Plaza Alfalfa, full of bars, cafés and small alternative shops, while heading west from here along Calle Alcaicería will take you towards Plaza del Salvador, dominated by its church. Originally a ninth-century mosque, the church of **El Salvador** (954 21 16 79, www.colegialsalvador.org, currently closed for restoration) was converted into a church in 1672. The inside is dominated by a baroque *retablo* and various wooden carvings, including *Cristo del Amor* by Juan de Mesa and *Señor de la Pasión* and *San Cristóbal*, both by Juan Martínez Montañes. The minaret (now the bell tower) and a central patio are from the original mosque.

### Ayuntamiento

*Plaza Nueva 1 (954 59 01 01).* **Open** (by pre-booked guided tour only) 5.30pm, 6pm Tue-Thur; noon Sat. Closed mid July-mid Sept. **Admission** free with passport/ID. **Map** p169 D3.

### Museo de Bellas Artes

*Plaza del Museo 9 (954 22 07 90/www.ccul.junta-andalucia.es/museos).* **Open** 2.30-8.30pm Tue; 9am-8pm Wed-Sat; 9am-2.30pm Sun. **Admission** €1.50; free with EU passport. **No credit cards.** **Map** p168 C4.

### Palacio de Lebrija

*C/Cuna 8 (954 22 78 02/www.palaciodelebrija.com).* **Open** *June-Aug* 10.30am-1.30pm, 5-8pm Mon-Fri; 10am-2pm Sat. *Sept-May* 10.30am-1.30pm, 4.30-7.30pm Mon-Fri; 10am-2pm Sat. **Admission** *Ground floor* €4. *Both floors (including tour)* €7. **No credit cards.** **Map** p168 C3.

## La Alameda & La Macarena

The northern part of the city centre is somewhat run down and slightly seedy, but retains a strong character and a number of monuments worth searching out. It has long been a solidly working-class area, and was long home to the city's now dwindling gypsy population, though many gypsies have moved out to the suburbs as the middle classes gradually move in.

La Alameda, in the north-west, was for a long time the red-light district, but has recently enjoyed a new lease of life and is now an up-and-coming area, full of alternative shops, bars, discos and a fledgling gay scene, centred around the long, rectangular Alameda de Hercules. Once polluted marshland, this was developed in 1574 into a smart tree-lined promenade. The two columns at the southern end support statues of Hercules and Caesar, while at the other end are statues of two flamenco greats. The Alameda really comes alive at night, and on Thursdays and Sundays, when it is the site of a flea market.

From the southern end, heading west down Calle Conde de Barajas brings you to the 17th-century church of **San Lorenzo** and the more modern **Jesús del Gran Poder** (both on Plaza San Lorenzo). A short walk north and you arrive at the **Convento de Santa Clara** and the **Torre de Don Fadrique** (C/Santa Clara 40, 954 37 99 05, currently closed for renovation), a 13th-century tower probably built by Fernando III's son to protect his palace. Calle Santa Clara leads to the **Monasterio de San Clemente** (C/Reposo 9, 954 37 80 40, currently closed for renovation), the city's oldest monastery, which was built over a Moorish palace. Inside is one of the finest baroque *retablos* in the city, made of gilded wood by Felipe de Rivas.

From here you can see the graceful **Puente de la Barqueta** (built for the 1992 Expo) crossing the Guadalquivir. South-west along the river is the restored area of **Torneo**, once a backwater but now the city's summer nightlife area, packed with bars and discos.

From the monastery, the main road Calle Resolana runs east along the line of the old city walls past the **Hospital de Cinco Llagas**, a Renaissance hospital that is now home to the Andalucian parliament. Opposite are part of the old walls and the **Puerta de Córdoba**, the gateway into the La Macarena *barrio*. It was built by the Almoravids in the 12th century and strengthened by later rulers. Beside it is the **Basílica de la Macarena**, which contains the Virgen de la Macarena, the most revered of all the Semana Santa effigies. The Virgin was designed by Luisa Roldán in the last part of the 17th century, and is the image that attracts the most weeping and wailing during the Easter processions. She is transported on a solid silver *paso*, accompanied by an image of Christ, carved by Felipe de Morales Nieto in 1654. The church museum contains some fairly garish jewels and outfits worn by the Virgin on her days out. The church itself, built in 1949, is nothing special.

There are a number of other churches in the immediate vicinity: **San Gil** (C/San Gil s/n), with its Mudéjar tower and ceiling; **San Luis** (C/San Luis 37), a superb example of Sevillian baroque, designed by Figueroa; the 13th-century Gothic-Mudéjar **Santa Marina** (C/San Luis 31), restored by Pedro I after an earthquake and featuring fine plasterworks and stalactite designs; the 14th-century **San Julián** (C/San Hermenegildo); and **San Marcos** (Plaza San Marcos), with a Mudéjar tower.

Also in the area is the **Convento de Santa Paula**, the only closed convent in Sevilla that can be officially visited. Built in the late 15th century, it is worth seeing for its beautiful 17th-century coffered ceiling, and for the entrance portal, decorated by Millán in 1504, and covered in glazed tiles by Pisano. Seek out the gilded *retablo* depicting St John the Evangelist by Alonso Cano (1635), which incorporates a wonderful sculpture of the saint by Montañes. The museum has paintings by artists including Zurbarán and Alonso Vázquez. You can buy the nuns' delicious home-made *dulces* and jams.

### Basílica de la Macarena

C/Bécquer 1 (954 90 18 00/www.hermandaddela macarena.org). **Open** *Church* 9am-2pm, 5-9pm daily. *Museum* 9.30am-2pm, 5-8pm daily. **Admission** *Museum* €3; €1.50 concessions. **No credit cards**. **Map** p168 A2.

### Convento de Santa Paula

C/Santa Paula 11 (954 53 63 30). **Open** *Museum* 10am-1pm Tue-Sun. Convent not open to public. **Admission** *Museum* €2. **No credit cards**. **Map** p168 B1.

# The Parque de María Luisa & the Plaza de España

Beyond the gardens of the Alcázar to the south is the **Parque de María Luisa**, a truly delightful expanse of palms, cypresses, water features, formal rose gardens and Andalucian tiled patios. There are plenty of places to sit in the shade and listen to the ferocious cooing of the park's multitudinous doves, and gardening fans can follow the 'botanic itinerary' of 127 species, exotic and indigenous, mapped out on signs for a self-guided walk.

Constructed for the 1929 Expo, the whole concept is much better integrated with the city than the Isla de Cartuja (site of the '92 Expo), chiefly because its grand, opulent buildings were built to last. Today, the majority are embassies, but there are still a number that are open to the public. Probably the most pleasant way to visit the park is by horse-drawn carriage. Pick one up from Plaza del Triunfo for a 45-minute tour (€24).

On the north-east side of the park is the **Plaza de España**, a huge, semi-circular complex of buildings decorated in bright tiles representing each of the 40 regions of Spain. It's a stunning sight, and a good spot to read in the shade for a while. Little boats can be hired to potter around on the arc of canal echoing the shape of the structure.

To the south of the park two of the fair's most impressive mansions have been converted into museums. The city's **Museo Arqueológico** has a comprehensive collection of artefacts, from prehistory to the *reconquista*, including Roman mosaics, gold jewellery (possibly from the mythical kingdom of Tartessus), Mudéjar ceramics and numerous finds from Itálica. Opposite is the beautiful **Museo de Costumbres Populares** (Popular Arts Museum), which houses a random collection of everything from Semana Santa costumes to old photos and kitchen implements.

Closer to the centre of town are numerous other buildings of note, including the **Casa de la Exposición**, the **Teatro Lope de Vega** (Avenida de María Luisa s/n, *see p190*), and the ultra-posh **Hotel Alfonso XIII** (C/San Fernando; *see p191*). Beside it is the **Antigua Fábrica de Tabacos** (Old Tobacco Factory), now owned by the university. The hulking 18th-century factory employed up to 10,000 women at its zenith in the 19th century, and is famed as the workplace of Carmen, the character immortalised in Prosper Merimée's novella and Bizet's opera.

Nearby, next to the river, the **Palacio de San Telmo** is a baroque extravaganza, built in the early 18th-century as a training academy for the Indies fleet. It was later bought by the Dukes of Montpensier, whose relation – the Dowager Duchess María Luisa de la Borbón – donated part of the grounds (and her name) to the park.

## Museo Arqueológico

*Plaza de América s/n (954 23 24 01/www.juntade andalucia.es/cultura).* **Open** 3-8.30pm Tue; 9am-8.30pm Wed-Sat; 9am-2.30pm Sun. **Admission** €1.50; free with EU passport & for students with ID. **No credit cards. Map** p169 off F2.

## Museo de Costumbres Populares

*Plaza de América 3 (954 23 25 76).* **Open** 2.30-8.30pm Tue; 9am-8.30pm Wed-Sat; 9am-2.30pm Sun. **Admission** €1.50; free with EU passport & for students with ID. **No credit cards. Map** p169 off F2.

## Triana

Located across the water, on the west bank of the Río Guadalquivir, the *barrio* of Triana takes its name from the Emperor Trajan, who was born in nearby Itálica (*see p179*). It is the old gypsy quarter and is considered the spiritual heart of the flamenco tradition. You won't find many gypsies here now, though. The district's been smartened up considerably over the past few years and its eastern section, flanking the river between two bridges, is nearly as full of tourists as Santa Cruz. It still retains some traditions, however. This is one of the many starting points for the **Romería del Rocío**, the most important pilgrimage in the Andalucían calendar (*see p46*), and is where the Virgen de la Esperanza begins her procession during Semana Santa.

From 1171 Triana was connected to the city by a pontoon bridge, which was replaced by the Puente de Isabel II in 1854. Cross the bridge – known to *sevillanos* as the **Puente de Triana** – to reach the charming Plaza Altozano, lined with bars and restaurants, and on to nearby Plaza Callao, where you'll find the beautiful tiled façade of the **Ceramica Santa Ana**. Triana was long the centre of *azulejo* production in the city, and this is the oldest of the remaining factories.

North-west along Calle Castilla lies the 17th-century church of **Nuestra Señora de la O** (C/Castilla). The chapel has a stunning crucified Christ by Francisco Antonio Gijón, known popularly as *El Cacharro*. It was supposedly inspired by the dead body of a gypsy singer killed outside. Five hundred years ago, the most infamous building in Sevilla was located just south of here, on the site of the current food market. The **Castilla de Triana** was the residence of the Inquisition until it was formally abolished in 1820. You could continue north from Calle Castillo to **Isla de Cartuja** (*see below*), or double back towards the church of **San Jacinto** (C/Pagés del Corro s/n).

Running south-east along the riverbank from the Puente de Triana is Calle Betis, lined with good bars and restaurants. Halfway along is the church of **Santa Ana**. The oldest church in Triana, it was built by Alfonso X in 1276 and houses a masterful 16th-century *retablo* by Pedro de Campaña, a double row of choir stalls carved in 1620 by Miguel Cano and a silver monstrance made by Andrés Ossorio in 1726. The gypsy quarter used to spread out through the streets and squares behind the church. Wander around and you'll spot some of the original gypsy homes, known as *corrales*. To get back to the centre, cross the **Puente de San Telmo**, off Plaza de Cuba.

## Isla de Cartuja

Until the early 1990s the Isla de Cartuja, north of Triana on the west bank of the river, was filled with slum dwellings. The city resolved to clear it up for the '92 Expo, displacing a lot of the residents in the process, many of whom now live in the shanty towns that ring the city. An enormous public works programme was begun, which involved not only building the Expo, but also creating the necessary infrastructure to welcome the world and beautify the entire city.

The fair itself was meant to be a joint effort with the US, but in the event Sevilla was left to finance the extravaganza itself. Over the course of half a year the Expo attracted a whopping 42.5 million visitors, but even these hordes were not enough to cover costs, and the city was left with debts of some 60 billion pesetas (€360 million). Politicians may argue that the Expo was a success, but many *sevillanos* believe it was a dreadful waste of money.

However, even the most staunch critics cannot deny the Expo's lasting legacy: not the island itself, but the infrastructure that came with it. Four new bridges were constructed to link the site to the city, including the **Puente de Alamillo**, designed by Santiago Calatrava. Its lyre-like shape has since become a symbol of Sevilla. The Santa Justa train station formed a terminus for a new high-speed train link to Madrid, and an international airport, San Pablo, was built to bring foreign visitors to the city.

The Isla de Cartuja today consists mainly of offices and a faculty of the university. However, the 14th-century Carthusian monastery, with its modern art gallery, is worth a visit, and the Isla Mágica amusement park is popular with kids.

Built in 1400 by the Archbishop of Sevilla, Gonzalo de Mena, the tranquil monastery **La Cartuja de Santa María** was a self-sufficient village, entirely cut off from the rest of the city. It was here that Columbus stayed before his visits to the Americas. The monastery suffered numerous indignities in the succeeding centuries: it was occupied by French troops in 1810-12, became a ceramics factory for

much of the 19th and 20th centuries, and was not restored until the Expo. From the stables and servants' quarters, a courtyard leads to the main cloister, which includes the **Capilla de Santa Ana** and a tomb, where Columbus's bones rested for 27 years. The church has the remains of a Mudéjar gallery and a beautiful stained-glass window, surrounded by tiles in blue and honey tones. Several rooms lead off the Mudéjar cloister, including the refectory with its extraordinary *artesando* ceiling, used as a shooting gallery by French troops during the occupation. Also worth a look is the **Capítulo de Monjes** (chapter house), in which the patrons of the monastery are buried. Outside are the chimneys of the restored kiln works and pretty gardens full of orange trees. A separate building in the monastery complex now houses the **Centro Andaluz de Arte Contemporáneo**. This is Andalucía's only contemporary art museum and holds a small permanent collection, plus temporary shows highlighting modern Andalucian artists.

The only other attraction of note on the island is the **Isla Mágica**, a theme park created from the remains of the Expo site. The park has plenty of rides, plus a lake, a giant-screen cinema and the Torre Panoramica, which offers great views of the city.

### La Cartuja de Santa María

*Isla de Cartuja (955 03 70 83/www.caac.es).* **Open** *Apr-Sept* 10am-9pm Tue-Fri; 11am-8pm Sat; 10am-3pm Sun. *Oct-Mar* 10am-8pm Tue-Fri; 11am-8pm Sat; 10am-3pm Sun. **Admission** €3; free Tue. **No credit cards**. **Map** p168 B5.

### Centro Andaluz de Arte Contemporáneo

*Avenida Américo Vespucio 2, Isla de Cartuja (955 03 70 70/www.caac.es).* **Open** *as for La Cartuja above.* **Admission** *Collection & exhibition* €3. *Exhibition only* €1.80; free Tue. **No credit cards**. **Map** p168 B5.

### Isla Mágica

*Pabellón España, Isla de Cartuja; entrance opposite Puente de la Barqueta (902 16 17 16/www.isla magica.es).* **Open** *Apr-mid July* 11am-7pm Tue-Fri; 11am-10pm Sat, Sun. *Mid-end July* 11am-10pm Tue-Fri; 11am-midnight Sat, Sun. *Aug* 11am-midnight daily. *Early-mid Sept* 11am-10pm daily. *Mid Sept-Oct* 11am-9pm Sat, Sun. Closed Nov-Mar. **Admission** *Daytime* €19-€21; €13-€14.50 concessions. *Evening* €13-€14.50; €10-€11 concessions. **Credit** AmEx, MC, V. **Map** p168 off A4.

---

## Outside the city

Nine kilometres (five miles) north of Sevilla, near the village of Santiponce, are the ruins of what was once the third largest city in the Roman Empire. Founded in 206 BC, **Itálica**

*Antigua Fábrica de Tabacos. See p178.*

**Sevilla Province**

rose to prominence during the reign of Hadrian in the second century AD and boasted a population of almost half a million. Hadrian was one of three Roman Emperors born in the city, the others being Trajan and Theodosius. The Visigothic invasion signaled the end for Itálica, and subsequent centuries saw it despoiled and looted for much of its stone.

Today, it's a rather forlorn and barren spot, although the amphitheatre, with seating for 40,000, is undeniably impressive. Various streets, with the ruins of villas, temples and bath houses, are also clearly visible, and there are some beautiful mosaics in the Casa Neptune and the Casa de los Pájaros. The fascinating monastic complex of San Isidro del Campo (at the Sevilla entrance to Itálica) has recently been opened to the public, and holds an exceptional collection of art, from Medieval frescoes to a superb late Renaissance high altar by Pablo de Rojas.

### Itálica

*Avenida de Extremadura 2, Santiponce (955 99 65 83).* **Open** *Apr-Sept* 8.30am-8.30pm Tue-Sat; 9am-3pm Sun. *Oct-Mar* 9am-5.30pm Tue-Sat; 10am-4pm Sun. **Admission** €1.50; free with EU passport. **No credit cards**.

## Where to eat & drink

The best food in Sevilla is generally to be had in tapas bars – which is no surprise in the city that invented the tapa. You'll find all kinds of places, from humble backstreet bars offering a few olives or slices of cheese to quality restaurant-bars preparing elaborate, extravagant dishes. Watch out for overpriced tourist traps, which abound in the city centre. Instead, venture a few streets beyond the major monuments and you'll discover some hidden gems, where your bill is chalked up on the bar, *jamones* hang from the ceiling, and old men yack about politics in a haze of Ducados smoke.

## The Barrio de Santa Cruz & around the Catedral

Bars and restaurants here tend to be overpriced and full of tourists – but there are a number of outstanding exceptions.

### La Albahaca

*Plaza Santa Cruz 12 (954 22 07 14/www.andalunet. com/la-albahaca).* **Open** *July, Aug* 8pm-midnight Mon; 1-4pm, 8pm-midnight Tue-Sat. *Sept-June* 1-4pm, 8pm-midnight Mon-Sat. **Average** €€. **Credit** AmEx, DC, MC, V. **Map** p169 E2.
This dreamy place is located in a fine converted palace (by Juan Talavera) on one of Sevilla's most romantic squares. Inside it's decorated with *azulejos*, antique furniture and chandeliers; a

perfect setting for inventive dishes like fillet of sea bass with apple and almond sauce, and venison with mushrooms and almonds.

### Altamira

*C/Santa María la Blanca 4 (954 42 50 30).* **Open** 9am-2am daily. **Average** €-€€. **Credit** DC, MC, V. **Map** p169 D2.
This lovely bar in a pretty square serves ice-cold *fino*, huge salads and a wide range of tapas and *raciones*, including *berenjenas rellenas* (stuffed aubergines) and *gambas al ajillo* (prawns with garlic).

### Bar España

*C/San Fernando 41 (954 22 72 54).* **Open** 9am-1am Mon-Sat. Closed Aug. **Average** €. **Credit** AmEx, DC, MC, V. **Map** p169 E2.
A short walk from the cathedral, on the edge of the Jardines de Murillo, this tapas bar adjoins the Egaña Oriza restaurant (*see p181*). It's very smart but reasonably priced, considering the quality of its huge range of exquisite tapas. Try the ham croquettes or the house special: stuffed mussels with béchamel sauce.

### Bar Modesto

*C/Cano y Cueto 5 (954 41 68 11/www.grupo modesto.com).* **Open** 8am-2am daily. **Average** €€. **Credit** AmEx, DC, MC, V. **Map** p169 D2.
This place began life as a tapas bar, but it's now more of a restaurant. It's still hugely popular among *sevillanos*, though, who flock here for the enormous range of excellent, reasonably priced tapas.

### La Bodeguita

*C/Hernando Colón 1-3 (954 22 25 61).* **Open** 9am-11.30pm daily. **Average** €. **Credit** AmEx, DC, MC, V. **Map** p169 D3.
It may be tiny, but La Bodeguita has an enormous range of tasty and inventive tapas including *berenjenas rellenas de jamón y gambas* (aubergines stuffed with ham and prawns).

### Casa Morales

*C/García de Vinuesa 11 (954 22 12 42).* **Open** *July, Aug* noon-4pm, 8pm-midnight Mon-Fri. *Sept-June* noon-4pm, 8pm-midnight Mon-Sat. **Average** €. **Credit** AmEx, DC, MC, V. **Map** p169 D3.
Founded in 1850 and largely unchanged since, this is allegedly the second-oldest bar in town and it's a great place to do a *degustación* (wine tasting). The atmosphere is traditional and the tapas are simple: *queso* and *jamón* on slices of bread.

### Casa Placido

*C/Mesón del Moro 5 & C/Ximénez Enciso 11 (954 56 39 71).* **Open** noon-4pm, 8pm-midnight daily. **Average** €. **Credit** DC, MC, V. **Map** p169 D2.
This traditional *fino* bar makes no concessions to tourists, despite being at the heart of tourist Sevilla. It looks as though it hasn't changed in centuries, with *jamones* hanging from the ceiling, sherries served from the barrel and ancient posters adorning the walls.

## Casa Robles

*C/Álvarez Quintero 58 (954 21 31 50/
www.roblesrestaurantes.com).* **Open** 1-6pm, 9pm-
1am daily. **Average** €€. **Credit** AmEx, DC, MC, V.
**Map** p169 D3.
This is supposedly one of the best restaurants in
town, but it's now resting on its laurels. The meat
and fish can be fine, but they can also be overcooked,
and badly presented with a handful of limp vegetables. There are two saving graces: an extensive wine
list and superb desserts; the *tocino de cielo* (a rich
custard) is particularly tasty.
**Other locations: Robles Placentines**
C/Placentines 2 (954 21 31 62); **Robles Aljarafe**
Carretera Bormujos 2-3 (954 16 92 60).

## Casa Román

*Plaza de los Venerables 1 (954 22 84 83).*
**Open** 9.30am-4pm, 7.30pm-midnight Mon-Fri;
11am-4pm, 7.30pm-midnight Sat, Sun. **Average** €.
**Credit** MC, DC, V. **Map** p169 E2.
Despite being in a prime spot in one of the *barrio*'s
most popular squares, this excellent old bar manages
to retain a traditional feel. The menu is in Spanish
only, there are fag ends and napkins all over the floor,
and the *jamón* is among the finest in the city.

## Cervecería Giralda

*C/Mateos Gago 1 (954 22 74 35).* **Open** 9am-
midnight Mon-Sat; 10am-midnight Sun. **Average** €.
**Credit** AmEx, DC, MC, V. **Map** p169 D2.
With the Giralda as a backdrop, this place gets
understandably mobbed. Neither the service nor
the tapas seem to suffer though. Excellent house
specials include *patatas importancia* (baked potatoes with ham and cheese).

## Corral del Agua

*Callejón del Agua 6 (954 22 48 41/www.andalunet.
com/corral-agua).* **Open** noon-4pm, 8pm-midnight
Mon-Sat. Closed Jan, Feb. **Average** €€. **Credit**
AmEx, DC, MC, V. **Map** p169 E2.
Under the same management as the excellent
La Albahaca (*see p180*), Corral del Agua serves
simpler dishes, such as sea bass in sherry, and
*salmorejo*. The restaurant is in a converted 18th-
century palace with a plant-filled patio, a pretty
fountain and a garden.

## Daz El Mehdi

*C/Federico Rubio 8 (mobile 636 41 53 47).*
**Open** 6pm-1am daily. **Average** €. **No credit
cards. Map** p169 D2.
When you tire of coffee and sherry, this friendly
Maghrebi-style *tetería* is great for mint tea,
Argentinian *mate* and North African pastries.
Downstairs it's all carpets and sofas straight out of
your best kif-fuelled Kasbah dreams.

## Egaña Oriza

*C/San Fernando 41 (954 22 72 11/
www.restauranteoriza.com).* **Open** 1.30-3.30pm,
9-11.30pm Mon-Fri; 9-11.30pm Sat. Closed Aug.
**Average** €€€€. **Credit** AmEx, DC, MC, V.
**Map** p169 E2.

The smartest and perhaps most upmarket restaurant
in town is also one of the most expensive. This is
where *sevillano* businessmen entertain their clients by
day and well-heeled couples sup in the evening. The
Basque food is imaginative and delicate, though somewhat overrated, while the atmosphere and the setting,
right beside the Jardines de Murillo, is perfect. It has
an adjacent tapas bar, Bar España (*see p180*).

## Horno de San Buenaventura

*Avenida de la Constitución 16 (954 22 18 19).*
**Open** 8am-8.30pm daily. **Average** €.
**Credit** AmEx, DC, MC, V. **Map** p169 D/E3.
Claiming to have existed since 1385, this is actually
a very modern, comfortable, air-conditioned space
for trying generous portions of classic tapas – the
*tortilla especial* lives up to its name – and quite amazing, calorific creamy pastries. Upstairs is quieter.

## Hostería del Laurel

*Plaza de los Venerables 5 (954 22 02 95/
www.hosteriadellaurel.com).* **Open** noon-4pm, 8pm-
midnight daily. **Average** €. **Credit** AmEx, DC, MC,
V. **Map** p169 D/E2.
Beautiful tiles from Triana and a ceiling full of
*jamones* add atmosphere to this place, which has
retained its ambience against the odds. House
specials are *espinacas* (spinach) and squid in garlic.
Trivia point: the Hostería del Laurel is mentioned
in the first act of *Don Juan*. The attached hotel has
double rooms from €75.

## La Judería

*C/Cano y Cueto 13 (954 41 20 52/www.grupo
modesto.com).* **Open** 1-5pm, 7.30pm-12.30am daily.
Closed last 2wks Aug. **Average** €-€€. **Credit**
AmEx, DC, MC, V. **Map** p169 D2.
A few doors down from Bar Modesto (*see p180*) and
part of the same chain, La Judería is another good
tapas place, with a large informal *comedor* at the back.
Specials include *cola de toro* and spinach with cheese.

## La Sacristía

*C/Mateos Gago 18 (954 21 92 07).* **Open** 12.30pm-
midnight daily. **Average** €. **Credit** AmEx, MC, V.
**Map** p169 D3.
Stylish (even down to the toilets) but friendly, La
Sacristía has a wide range of good-sized tapas, such
as *flamenquín caseros* (croquettes with bacon and
mushrooms) and hearty *tortillas* laced with whisky
or roquefort, and a decent wine list.

## Salvador Rojo

*C/San Fernando 23 (954 22 97 25).* **Open** noon-
4.30pm, 8.30pm-1am Mon-Sat. Closed last 2wks Aug.
**Average** €€-€€€. **Credit** AmEx, DC, MC, V.
**Map** p169 E2.
The design is warm and simple, the service is
superb, and the dishes, though generously proportioned, are delicate and refined. Try the *salteado de
langostinos* with Thai rice or the *colitas de cigalas* as
a starter; for mains, the fish and lighter meat dishes are recommended, particularly *carne de cordero*
(slices of lamb with potato purée).

Las Piletas.

### El Toisón

*C/Fernández y González 36-38, corner of*
*C/García Vinuesa (954 21 21 11).* **Open** noon-
4.30pm, 8pm-midnight Mon-Fri; noon-4.30pm Sat.
Closed Aug. **Average** €. **Credit** AmEx, DC, MC, V.
**Map** p169 D3.
This modern place makes a pleasant change if
you've had enough of cobwebby old local bars.
El Toisón offers some elaborate tapas, including
flaked cod with raisins and pine nuts, and salmon
in cream of asparagus.

## El Arenal

### Adriano

*C/Arfe 11 (954 21 68 45).* **Open** noon-late daily.
**Average** €. **No credit cards. Map** p169 D3.
This *taberna* and occasional flamenco venue close
to the bullring is handily placed for a post-*corrida*
beer and snack.

### Antonio Romero

*C/Antonia Díaz 19 (954 22 39 39).* **Open** noon-
1am Tue-Sun. Closed Aug. **Average** €-€€.
**Credit** AmEx, DC, MC, V. **Map** p169 D4.
The perfect stop after a *corrida*, Antonio Romero is
always crowded, always lively and typical of the
spit-and-sawdust establishments in this area. Both
branches serve excellent tapas, particularly the
*salmorejo* topped with salt cod.
**Other locations**: C/Gamazo 16 (954 21 05 85).

### Bodega San José

*C/Adriano 10 (954 22 41 05).* **Open** 8am-11.30pm
Mon-Sat; 8am-3pm Sun. **Average** €. **No credit
cards. Map** p169 D4.
Drinks are chalked up on the bar and sherry is
served from the barrels behind. The walls are
covered in Semana Santa posters and the floor is
covered in napkins and olive stones. Noisy, friendly: a real taste of old Sevilla.

### Cinco Jotas

*C/Castelar 1, corner of C/Arfe (902 38 88 38/954 21
58 62).* **Open** *July, Aug* 11am-midnight Mon-Thur,
Sun; 11am-1am Fri, Sat. *Sept-June* 9am-midnight
Mon-Thur, Sun; 10am-1am Fri, Sat. **Average** €-€€.
**Credit** AmEx, DC, MC, V. **Map** p169 D3.
The first of an excellent chain of smart tapas bars
serving the finest *jamón*, matured cheeses and Rioja.

### La Leyenda

*C/Reyes Católicos 4 (954 22 89 00).* **Open** 8am-
11pm daily. **Average** €. **Credit** AmEx, DC, MC, V.
**Map** p169 D4.
Attached to the Hotel Bécquer, this smart bar-restaurant with a half-dozen tables on the pavement is
more popular with office workers on their way home
than tourists. Those in the know come to feast on
creative tapas of turkey paté with blueberry jam,
venison ragout, duck in sherry reduction, and even
slightly orientalised bites – all sizeable and all cheap.

### Las Piletas

*C/Marqués de Paradas 28 (954 22 04 04/
www.andalunet.com/piletas).* **Open** 7am-1am daily.
**Average** €€. **Credit** AmEx, DC, MC, V. **Map** p168
C4/p169 D4.
Bulls' heads and matador posters hang everywhere
in this high-ceilinged temple to taurine culture,
where excellent barbecued lamb, steaks and *rabo de
toro* (bull's tail) is served accompanied by heavy red
wines. Solo men come to watch the football at the
bar, while a partitioned section offers seclusion.

### Porta Rossa

*C/Pastor y Landero 20 (954 21 61 39).* **Open** *July*
9am-noon Mon; 2-4pm, 9pm-midnight Tue-Sat. *Sept-
June* 9am-noon, 2-4pm Tue-Sat; 2-4pm Sun. Closed
Aug. **Average** €€-€€€. **Credit** AmEx, DC, MC, V.
**Map** p169 D4.
If you need a change from Spanish cuisine, and
fancy a refined atmosphere and superlative Italian
cooking (with a Sevillian touch), then this is the place

for you. The decor is upmarket, stylish and modern, and the menu offers delicate pastas and subtle sauces. Recommended.

### El Rincón Gallego
*C/Harinas 21 (954 22 43 11).* **Open** noon-4.30pm, 8.30-11pm Mon-Sat. **Average** €. **Credit** AmEx, MC, V. **Map** p169 D3.
A tiny spot that specialises in food from Galicia, in particular seafood from the Rías Baxas.

### Taberna del Alabardero
*C/Zaragoza 20 (954 50 27 21/www.tabernadel alabardero.com).* **Open** 1-4pm, 8pm-1am daily. Closed Aug. **Average** €€-€€€. **Credit** AmEx, DC, MC, V. **Map** p169 D4.
This (one) Michelin-starred restaurant is one of Sevilla's best eateries. The setting is exemplary: all dark woods, soft lights, starched tablecloths and chandeliers. The emphasis is on meat dishes, including cheeks of Iberian pork and venison stew, but there's also seafood (spiny lobsters are actually reared on site) and an extensive wine list. The restaurateur, Juan Marcos García, also runs a training school for chefs here and a fine hotel (*see p191*).

# Centro

Plaza Alfalfa and the streets and squares off it are packed full of little bars and cafés.

### La Alicantina
*Plaza del Salvador 2-3 (954 22 61 22).* **Open** *July, Aug* 11am-1am Mon-Sat. *Sept-June* 11am-1am Mon-Sat; 11am-5pm Sun. **Average** €. **Credit** AmEx, DC, MC, V. **Map** p168 C3.
Very popular place with a great *terraza* in the middle of a bustling square. Specialises in seafood, particularly shellfish, at reasonable prices.

### Bar Europa
*C/Siete Revueltas 35 (954 22 13 54).* **Open** 8am-1am daily. **Average** €. **Credit** MC, V. **Map** p168 C3.
One of the best bars in the area – for breakfast, lunch or late-night drinks. The food is outstanding and varied: house specials include a delicious *crema de calabacín al aroma de curry,* a kind of creamy soup made from courgette, with a curry flavouring.

### Bar Manolo
*Plaza Alfalfa 3 (954 21 41 76).* **Open** 7am-midnight daily. **Average** €-€€. **No credit cards.** **Map** p168 C2.
Bar Manolo is a good spot for a morning coffee or a lunchtime snack. Specialises in *pescado frito.*

### Barbacoa Cólóniales
*Plaza del Cristo de Burgos 19 (954 50 11 36/37).* **Open** *June-Aug* noon-4pm, 8pm-midnight daily. *Sept-May* noon-midnight daily. Closed first 3wks Aug. **Average** €. **Credit** AmEx, DC, MC, V. **Map** p168 C2.
An old-style bar with lots of simple tapas and grilled fish and meats, on a pleasant square (south of Plaza San Pedro).

### Bodega Amarillo Albero
*Plaza de la Gavidia 5 (954 21 90 85).* **Open** noon-5pm, 7pm-midnight daily. **Average** €. **Credit** AmEx, DC, MC, V. **Map** p168 B3.
The walls of this bodega are lined with sherry bottles and old photos, wine barrels stand in for tables, and there is a good selection of tapas.

### Bodega Dos de Mayo
*Plaza de la Gavidia 6 (954 90 40 63).* **Open** *July, Aug* 12.30-4pm, 7pm-midnight Mon-Sat. *Sept-June* 12.30-4pm, 7pm-midnight daily. **Average** €. **No credit cards.** **Map** p168 B3.
A big, buzzing place with pretty *azulejos* on the walls and *jamones* hanging from the ceiling. There's a good choice of sherries from the cask to wash down the variety of inexpensive tapas.

### Confitería La Campaña
*C/Sierpes 1 & 3 (954223570/www.confiteriala campana.com).* **Open** 9am-10pm daily. **Average** €. **Credit** AmEx, MC, DC, V. **Map** p168 C3.
This dusty, gorgeous old-style city caff was founded in 1885 and specialises in home-made chocolate, nougats, *yemas* and all things unhealthy and sweet, and is good for coffee and cakes too.

### La Habanita
*C/Golfo 3, off C/Pérez Galdos (954 21 95 16/ www.andalunet.com/habanita).* **Open** 12.30-4.30pm, 8pm-12.30am Mon-Sat; 8pm-12.30am Sun. **Average** €. **Credit** MC, V. **Map** p168 C2.
A fab restaurant in a tiny square close to Plaza Alfalfa specialising in tasty Cuban dishes like *arepes* (cornmeal rolls), fried bananas and black beans, and chicken breast in coconut sauce. It's also one of the few places in the city offering vegetarian and vegan dishes.

### Patio San Eloy
*C/San Eloy 9 (954 22 11 48).* **Open** 11.30am-5pm, 7-11.30pm daily. **Average** €. **Credit** MC, V. **Map** p168 C3/4.
Big, noisy, chaotic and hugely atmospheric. Locals drop by for a quick post-shopping snack, waiters shout out orders and there are mountains of simple sandwiches to munch on.

### El Rinconcillo
*C/Gerona 40 (954 22 31 83).* **Open** 1pm-1am daily. **Average** €. **Credit** AmEx, DC, MC, V. **Map** p168 C2.
The city's oldest bar dates from 1670 and is an essential stop for a real slice of *sevillano* atmosphere. The scene is set with *azulejos,* ancient wood fittings, bills chalked up on the bar, and a haze of smoke and noise from *fino-* and *vino-*fuelled conversations. The tapas, particularly *espinacas con garbanzos* (spinach with chickpeas) and *jamón y queso,* are excellent.

### San Marco
*C/Cuna 6 (954 22 46 09).* **Open** 1.15-4.30pm, 9.15pm-12.30am Mon-Fri, Sun; 1.15-5pm, 8.15pm-1am Sat. **Average** €€. **Credit** AmEx, DC, MC, V. **Map** p168 C3.

# Cliché Flamenco

It's not *all* flamenco in southern Spain (salsa, for instance, is hugely popular), but no musical form is as closely identified with the region. It is in flamenco that *andaluces* find their soul and character evoked, explored and exaggerated. The essential elements of the genre – the heartfelt song, the guitar and the dance – have a long history in Andalucía, but there was no smooth development over the centuries to produce the flamenco we know today, despite the attempts of the likes of Federico García Lorca and the composer Manuel de Falla to claim as much. (Lorca was a huge enthusiast for flamenco, believing it to be 'one of the most gigantic creations of the Spanish people', and did much to bring it mainstream respectability.) In fact, flamenco in a recognisable form probably doesn't date from earlier than the end of the 18th century.

Another common cliché is that only *gitanos* (gypsies) can perform real flamenco, although one of the greatest contemporary flamenco performers, Paco de Lucía, is a *payo* (non-gypsy). However, flamenco did originate in the tightly knit, myth-shrouded communities of Spain's gypsies, somewhere within the 'flamenco triangle' of Sevilla, Jerez and Cádiz – and it's also true that the vast majority of flamenco greats are gypsies.

Feeling is at the heart of flamenco. Much is spontaneous and improvised, though there are strict conventions (most of the lyrics, for instance, have been set for well over a century). Flamenco songs fall into two general categories – the light, lyrical *cante flamenco* or *cante chico* ('small song'), of which *malagueñas* and *bulerías* are examples; and the emotion-wrenching *cante jondo* ('deep song'), with often tragic lyrics, which demands an extraordinary passionate intensity to be performed at its best.

The latter is considered by aficionados to be the heart of true flamenco, and achieves its apotheosis when the performer imbues the song with a semi-mystical quality known as *duende* – an emotional transcendence, a sort of sublime communication between performer and audience (though the word is seldom used today, other than by romantically minded foreign writers). The unromantic truth is that (the perception of) this elusive *duende* is often influenced by the large quantity of alcohol and (often) class-A drugs consumed at traditional gypsy *juergas*

(spontaneous gatherings). It's no coincidence that some of the greatest names in flamenco have met with an untimely demise due to the excesses of their lifestyles.

The spontaneity and unpredictability of the best flamenco means that *duende* and commercial flamenco aren't compatible. By its nature, great flamenco is volatile and elusive. You have to take your chance, hoping to stumble into a backstreet *peña* late at night at the moment when the right mood takes the right performer at the right time, though if you only have a couple of nights in Sevilla, try La Carbonería (*p189*), where the trios are informal but intense and committed.

Flamenco is far from being an ossified musical form and contemporary musicians continue to explore its possibilities. Migrants from North Africa keep alive Moorish strains – as do Javier Ruibal and Radio Tarifa, successfully fusing these elements with modern European rhythms. Flamenco jazz is another popular offshoot (with saxophonist Jorge Pardo one of its most prominent exponents), and there is also an important local Sefardi tradition of Jewish music. Classic national traditions – the *fandango*, the *seguidilla* and a variety of *boleros* – are also preserved in Andalucía.

Flamenco virgins will probably find sufficient pain and passion on compilations like EMI's *100 Años de Flamenco*, the *Rough Guide to Flamenco* (World Music Network) or the 'new flamenco' collection *Con Duende* (RTVE). But for those who've been seduced by the sound, here are six stars worth getting to know better.

### MANOLO CARACOL (1909-73)

Singing since the age of 13, this much-loved *sevillano cantaor* has never been surpassed for depth of feeling and raw energy – his voice is memorable for its rough, gritty sonorities. An academician as well as a star, Caracol's collections are veritable bibles for students of flamenco song and culture. For all that, he was a populist, and performed in countless shows and film soundtracks – his statue stands on the Alameda de Hércules. Check out the disc *Early Cante Flamenco (1934-39)*, released in 1990.

### EL CAMARÓN DE LA ISLA (1950-92)

The 'Mick Jagger of Cádiz' was born in San Fernando, near Cádiz, and began to sing in public at the age of eight. While his streetwise, stridently modern style (and his use of Moogs, Fender piano, zither and other un-flamenco instruments) has its detractors, there was something gutsy and marginal about Camarón's songs and an earthiness in his rough-edged vocal style. *La leyenda del tiempo* (1980) is a key album in his musical evolution. Look out also for his collaborations with Tomatito and Paco de Lucía.

### PACO DE LUCÍA (1947-)
The most widely known contemporary flamenco guitarist, this son of the port of Algeciras was born into a family of flamenco strummers. At 12 he won awards at an international festival in Jerez and then toured with the José Greco Company in 1963. In New York he worked with Sabicas and Mario Escudero, and then moved to Madrid, going on to perform with jazz fusionists such as Al Di Meola, John McLaughlin and Chick Corea. His work was enriched by these contacts, but his first solo record, *La fabulosa guitarra de Paco de Lucía* (1984), is still astounding for its pure flamenco sound. Check out *Siroco* (1987), *Ziryab* (1990) and *Live in America* (1994) for more recent crossover experiments.

### CARMEN LINARES (1951-)
With a stunning command of all the *cante* styles, the intense, lushly voiced Carmen Linares (*pictured*) emerged in the 1990s as a formidable female talent in a notoriously male-dominated scene. Born in the little village of Linares, near Jaén, she moved to Madrid with her family and played alongside scores of major flamenco singers and leading dance troupes during the '70s. Later she would tour and perform memorably at the Lincoln Center with the New York Philharmonic and has picked up countless awards in Europe and the US. Rather than opt for crass vogueishly 'modern' takes on flamenco, Linares revolutionises from inside the genre – her album *La Luna en el Río* (1991) is a good choice to get a feel for Linares' vocal range and raw emotion.

### JERÓNIMO (1977-)
The *Diario de Sevilla*'s respected flamenco critic Juan Vergillos dubbed Jerónimo Maya's 2004 debut 'one of the records of the year'. Performing since he was a child, Jerónimo handles all the sub-genres, such as tango, *zapateao*, *solea*, *bulería* and *seguiriyas*, with

a muscular youthfulness. He is arguably the most promising new talent in Andalucía and his album, simply called *Jerónimo*, is a gem.

### KETAMA
One of the leading groups of the *flamenco nuevo* scene, Ketama represents a new wave of more improvisational and international flamenco, fusing it with salsa, reggae, funk and jazz. Ketama has collaborated with major names like Paco de Lucía, Enrique Morente, Celia Cruz, Paquito D'Rivera and Arturo Sandoval and, more recently, Toumani Diabate from Mali. Two albums recorded in 1988 and 1994 with Diabate, *Songhai I* and *Songhai II*, brought together African percussion and vocals with flamenco rhythm and dance.

Carmen Linares.

Jacarandas in bloom on **Plaza de la Concordia**.

Stylish San Marco offers French and Italian dishes at reasonable prices. The main restaurant is in an 18th-century palace with Moorish features, while the other branch serves great pizza and pasta in an old Arabic bath house near the Hospital de los Venerables. **Other locations**: Pizzeria San Marco, C/Mesón del Moro 6 (954 21 43 90).

## La Alameda

### Bar San Lorenzo
*Plaza de San Lorenzo 7 (954 38 15 58).*
**Open** 8am-midnight Mon-Fri; 8am-2pm Sat.
**Average** €. **No credit cards**. **Map** p168 B3.
This ancient place has hardly changed since it was established in 1893. It's the winner of various awards in the Feria de Tapa for house specials such as *bacalao con tomate* (salt cod with tomato).

### Eslava
*C/Eslava 3-5 (954 90 65 68).* **Open** *Bar* noon-12.30am Tue-Sat; noon-4pm Sun. *Restaurant* 1.30-4pm, 9-11pm Tue-Sat; 1.30-4pm Sun. Closed 1st 3wks Aug. **Average** €-€€. **Credit** AmEx, DC, MC, V. **Map** p168 B3.
One of Sevilla's finest tapas bars, Eslava is permanently crowded. Specials include courgette quiche, steak in blue cheese, spinach strudel and a deliciously creamy *salmorejo*. The dining room at the back has one of the best and cheapest set lunches in town.

### La Ilustre Victima
*C/Correduria 35 (954 38 94 90).*
**Open** noon-midnight daily. Closed Aug. **Average** €. **Credit** AmEx, DC, MC, V. **Map** p168 B3.
A writers' café/bar/restaurant with a laid-back feel, warm, dark wood furniture and bright murals on the walls. A decent selection of tapas is served, as well as couscous, kebabs and fajitas.

## Triana

Lovely to wander round after dusk, Triana is packed with restaurants and bars on the river bank (Calle Betis) and parallel Calle Pelay Correa.

### Bar Bistec
*C/Pelay Correa 34 (954 27 47 59).* **Open** noon-4pm, 7.30pm-1am daily. **Average** €. **Credit** AmEx, DC, MC, V. **Map** p169 E4.
One of the best-known bars in the area. Traditional and atmospheric, and serving a fine selection of tapas, including delicious quail stews.

### Bar Santa Ana
*C/Pureza 82 (954 27 21 02).* **Open** 7.30am-1am Mon-Sat; 7.30am-4pm Sun. **Average** €. **Credit** AmEx, DC, MC, V. **Map** p169 E4.
Simple but well-sourced tapas are dealt out swiftly at this delightful corner shrine to bullfighting, Virgins and the Crucifixion. The bar hums with local banter, or you can eat bites like the sizeable pork steak and snails at tables by the church.

### Los Chorritos
*C/Betis s/n (954 33 14 99).* **Open** 11am-4pm Tue, Thur-Sun; 8pm-1am Tue-Sun. **Average** €.
**Credit** AmEx, DC, MC, V. **Map** p169 E4.
Popular with Triana locals, this riverside shack serves up a tender pork flank (*secreto Ibérico*) and good roasted peppers. Great views of El Arenal, especially at sunset.

### Ezcaray
*C/Salado 5-7 (954 28 38 89/www.restaurante ezcaray.com).* **Open** 1pm-midnight Mon-Fri. Closed Aug. **Average** €€-€€€. **Credit** AmEx, DC, MC, V. **Map** p169 F4.
On a street full of restaurants, Ezcaray really stands out as a special eatery. It's a Basque place and specialises in delicious home-style cooking. There's a good wine cellar here too.

### La María
*C/Betis 12 (954 33 84 61).* **Open** *July-mid Sept* 1-4.30pm, 8pm-1am daily. *Mid Sept-June* noon-1am daily. **Average** €-€€. **Credit** MC, V. **Map** p169 E4.
La María bills itself as a *parilla Argentina* and serves some fine cuts of meats. It also offers a good selection of fish and seafood, including *dorada* (sea bream) and enormous *langostinos* from Sanlúcar.

### Restaurante Casa Manolo
*C/San Jorge 16 (954 33 32 08).* **Open** 9am-6pm, 8pm-1am Tue-Sun. **Average** €. **Credit** MC, V. **Map** p169 D5.
A real locals' place with a traditional atmosphere. Casa Manolo attracts a diverse crowd, who are drawn by the good selection of cheap tapas.

### Restaurante María Angeles
*Puente de Isabel II s/n (954 33 74 98).* **Open** *Restaurant* 11am-4.30pm, 7.30pm-12.30am Mon-Fri. *Bar* 10am-1am Mon-Fri. **Average** €-€€. **Credit** DC, MC, V. **Map** p169 D4.
A great spot by the bridge means that wherever you sit – in the restaurant, tapas bar or on the *terraza* – you will get a fantastic view of the river and the city. Despite the setting, the food is simple – mostly fresh fish and meats – and very reasonably priced.

### Río Grande
*C/Betis s/n (954 27 39 56/www.riogrande-sevilla. com).* **Open** 1-4pm, 8pm-midnight daily. **Average** €€. **Credit** AmEx, DC, MC, V. **Map** p169 E4.
The best-known restaurant on this side of the river, due to its views of the Torre del Oro and the Giralda. They provide a perfect backdrop for some tasty dishes such as *langostinos* from Isla Cristina and *almejas de Faro en salsa verde* (clams in green sauce).

### El Tejar
*C/San Jacinto 68 (954 33 41 52).* **Open** 8am-3am daily. **Average** €. **Credit** AmEx, DC, MC, V. **Map** p169 E5.
This pretty little café covered in tiles does a selection of tapas and *montaditos* (bite-size sandwiches) from €1.50. There are flamenco shows here on Wednesday and Thursday nights from 10pm and regular exhibitions of work by *sevillano* artists.

**Sevilla Province**

## Nervión

This suburb (east of the centre, not far from the train station) has recently become known for its tapas bars, concentrated around two areas: a grid of streets bordered by Calle Los Pirineos and Avenida de la Buhaira, and further east around the Gran Plaza.

### Al-Mutamid

*C/Alfonso XI 1, corner of Gran Plaza (954 92 55 04/ www.grupomodesto.com).* **Open** noon-5pm, 8pm-midnight daily. Closed 2wks late Aug. **Average** €-€€. **Credit** AmEx, DC, MC, V.

Part of the excellent Modesto chain and a cut above the other branches, Al-Mutamid offers excellent service, upmarket surroundings and fine cuisine, with an emphasis on seafood.

### El Fogón de Leña

*Avenida Luis de Morales s/n, near Nervión Plaza (954 53 90 36).* **Open** 1-4.30pm, 8pm-midnight daily. **Average** €€. **Credit** AmEx, DC, MC, V.

This excellent restaurant mini-chain (there's another in Cádiz and a couple more in Sevilla) serves up huge cuts of meat on an open grill. It's simple, hearty Andalucian cooking at its best, served in a farm-house-style atmosphere.

### La Taberna de Azafrán

*Avenida Luis Montoto 148 (954 57 66 97).* **Open** 12.30-4.30pm, 8.30pm-12.30am Mon-Sat. Closed Aug. **Average** €. **Credit** AmEx, DC, MC, V.

Probably the most popular bar in the area, it's big and smart, and attracts a friendly crowd. The extensive list of tapas includes baked fish.

### La Monumental

*Edificio Corona 6-8, C/Diego Angulo Íñiguez (954 42 33 85).* **Open** *July* 8am-1am Mon-Sat. *Sept-June* 8am-1am Tue-Sun. Closed Aug. **Average** €. **Credit** AmEx, DC, MC, V.

An up-and-coming venue whose profile was boosted after it won first prize at the Feria de Tapas for its smoked salmon and shellfish *gratinado*.

### Nervión

*La Dorada, Edificio Viapol, Avenida Ramón y Cajal s/n (954 92 10 66).* **Open** *July, Aug* noon-4pm, 8.30pm-midnight Mon-Sat. *Sept-June* 8am-4.30pm, 8.30pm-midnight daily. **Average** €€. **Credit** AmEx, DC, MC, V.

Nervión attracts a fairly smart clientele, who come to dine on seafood in rooms decorated with marine memorabilia. The branch at Paseo de Colón 3 (954 22 78 28) has a lovely *terraza* overlooking the river.

## Nightlife

The best nightspots vary by season. When the university term ends in late May/early June and the weather starts to heat up, the action shifts to the so-called Costa de Guadalquivir on Calle Torneo (map A/B4), where the riverbank is packed with bars and discos that are open into the early hours. Opposite, on the Isla de Cartuja, the crowd is young and the emphasis is more on rave-style *discotecas*. Upriver in Triana, Calle Betis (map E4) is where all the bars and pubs spill out into the street in the summer. In the cooler months, the nightlife is spread across town among the venues detailed below.

There are more bars and cafés in the area around Plaza Alfalfa than anywhere else in town. At weekends the sheer number of people in the streets gridlocks the traffic; the *marcha* goes on until sunrise. Elsewhere in Centro, look out for the following: **Bestiario** (C/Zaragoza, map D4), an early morning club for up-for-it party people; **El Garlochi** café (C/Boteros 4, map C2) – camper than a row of tents and full of kitsch Semana Santa memorabilia; the friendly Irish theme bar **Flaherty's** (C/Alemanes 7, 954 21 04 51, www.pflahertys.com, map D3), with live music on Thursdays from September to May; and **Histeria** (off Plaza Nueva, map D3), an after-hours *discoteca* pumping out house and trance until daybreak and beyond; **Los Soportales** and **La Antigua Bodeguita**, both on Plaza del Salvador (map C3), are where thirtysomething *sevillano* society spills out onto the streets on Friday evenings.

Towards Puente de Isabel II, a stylish spot for cocktails and, on Thursdays from 10.30pm, live Cuban bands and occasional flamenco is **Nu Yor Café** (C/Marqués de Paradas 30, 954 21 28 89, closed Mon & all Aug, map C4). There are a couple of laid-back gay bars at the corner where Reyes Católicos meets the river – check out **Café El Paseo** and its neighbour **Café Bar Ysbillya** (Paseo de Cristóbal Colon 2, map D4).

Once run-down and rather seedy, La Alameda has now become a sought-after 'alternative' destination. Check out: **Barón Rampante** (C/Arias Montano 3, map B3), a key bar in the emerging gay scene; the cool **Café del Mar** (C/Jesús del Gran Poder 83, map B3), one of the best bars in this area, attracting a young, trendy crowd, and with an emphasis on Ibizan-style house, with a bit of jungle or R&B some nights; **Fun Club** (Alameda de Hercules 86, map B3), a live rock and pop venue; **Habanilla Café** (Alameda de Hercules 63, 954 90 27 18, map B3), an excellent boho café at the northern end of the square, facing **Café Central**, another hip, young hangout; **La Imperdible** (Plaza San Antonio de Padua 9, map B3), a café-bar that puts on alternative theatre, jazz and flamenco.

In Triana, try cyber-café-cum-restaurant-cum-bar **Mex Rock/Tequila Connection** (C/Betis 41A/B, 954 28 40 12, www.tequila connection.net, map E4), with its fine line in tequila-based cocktails and shots, loud music and good atmosphere.

## Arts & entertainment

For full listings of what's on where and when in Sevilla, get hold of a copy of the excellent *El Giraldillo* or the monthly listings magazines – *Guia de Ocio de Andalucía* and *¿Que Hacer?/What's On?*

### Film

There's not a major art house scene in Sevilla, but you can see mainstream Spanish releases and undubbed Hollywood standards at the **Avenida V.O** cinema (C/Marqués de Paradas 15, 954 29 30 25, www.cineciudad.com, €4.80, map C4).

# Extreme unction

If, after one *fino* too many in one bar too many, you catch a sudden flash of purple and the glint of a gold cross, and then on second glance you swear you see a posse of beer-swigging prelates propping up the counter, your eyes may not be deceiving you. For Sevilla's drinking dens are a favourite haunt of the cardinals of Clemente Domínguez, otherwise known – by himself and his followers at least – as **Pope Gregorio XVII**, Sevilla's own anti-Pope.

Having supposedly witnessed visions of the Virgin at El Palmar de Troya, near Utrera, south of Sevilla, in 1968, the 22-year-old Domínguez went on to found the ultra-reactionary Carmelites of the Holy Face in 1975, who raged against the supposed 'progressivism' of the Roman Church, and sanctified General Franco and José Antonio Primo de Rivera (founder of the Spanish fascist Falange party) to make their point. A year later the order's rotund leader went blind (as a result of his battles with Satan, according to his supporters, but more directly as the consequence of a car accident), and in 1978 he had his cardinals proclaim him Pope in a ceremony in Sevilla.

It would be easy to dismiss Domínguez as an eccentric were his followers not so committed and so wealthy. They built their leader a huge and hideous basilica at El Palmar de Troya (which can be visited by those soberly enough dressed), and believe that he will be the last ever Pontiff, destined to be crucified in Jerusalem.

### Flamenco

Although Sevilla may claim to be the home of flamenco, most of what you'll see here is the pre-packaged stuff – a fine spectacle, but hardly authentic. If you are after real, spontaneous flamenco, you'll need to search hard; disappear off the beaten track into La Macarena and you may stumble across a *peña*. Look out for the free bi-monthly magazine *alma100*, the '*revista de flamenco*', in any of the venues; it contains tips on new records and gig information. For more information on flamenco, *see p184* **Cliché**.

In addition to the places listed below, try **Bar El Mundo** (C/Siete Revueltas 5, 954 21 79 08, map C3) or **La Anselma** (C/Pagés del Corro 49, map E5).

#### El Arenal

*C/Rodo 7 (954 21 64 92/www.tablaoelarenal.com).* **Shows** 9pm, 11pm nightly. **Admission** €31.50 incl drink; €61 incl dinner. **Credit** MC, V. **Map** p169 E3/4.
Between the bullring and the theatre, this is one of the better tourist shows in the city.

#### La Carbonería

*C/Levíes 18 (954 21 44 60).* **Open** 8pm-3.30am daily. **Admission** free. **Map** p169 D2.
A great place with a relaxed atmosphere and an eclectic mix of people. It's not solely dedicated to flamenco, but there are often spontaneous performances (usually on a Thursday) if the right people come in. It was a favourite haunt of Camarón, a flamenco great who died of a heroin overdose.

#### Casa de la Memoría de al-Andalus

*C/Ximénez Enciso 28 (954 56 06 70).* **Open** 9am-2pm, 6-8pm daily. **Shows** 9pm daily. **Admission** *Cultural centre* €1. *Flamenco shows* €11; €9 concessions. **Credit** MC, V. **Map** p169 D2.
This is the closest you'll get to anything authentic without walking the backstreets all night. Traditional flamenco dominates, but there are also concerts of medieval music and Sefardi Judeo-Spanish music shows – all performed in an exquisite patio.

#### Los Gallos

*Plaza Santa Cruz 11 (954 21 69 81/www.tablao losgallos.com).* **Shows** 9pm, 11.30pm daily. Closed Jan. **Admission** €27 incl drink. **Credit** AmEx, DC, MC, V. **Map** p169 E2.
A two-hour show is held in a small room on two levels. It can get quite intense on a good night; get there early for a seat on the lower floor.

#### El Palacio Andaluz

*C/María Auxiliadora 18B (954 53 47 20/www.el palacioandaluz.com).* **Open** *Dinner* 9.30pm daily. *Shows* 10pm daily. **Admission** €28.25 incl drink; €49.50 incl dinner. **Credit** AmEx, MC, V. **Map** p168 B1.
In the north of the city, opposite the Jardines del Valle, this is a huge show with a large cast. A great spectacle, if miles away from true flamenco.

**Sevilla Province**

### Sol Café Cantante

*C/Sol 5, just off Plaza de los Terceros (954 22 51 65).*
**Open** (shows only) *July, Aug* 9-10.30pm Thur-Sat. *Sept-June* 9-10.30pm Wed-Sat. **Admission** €18 incl drink; €11 concessions. **No credit cards. Map** p168 C2.
As a showcase for young performers and new flamenco styles, this dark cabaret-type café-bar maintains a busy schedule of gigs. Though touting its services to tourists, the constantly changing artists means there's no tired show element, and some of the emerging talents are impressive.

### El Tamboril

*Plaza Santa Cruz s/n (954 56 15 90).* **Open** *July, Aug* Bar 6.30pm-3am Mon-Sat. Shows midnight Mon-Thur. *Sept-June* Bar 6.30pm-3am daily. Shows midnight daily. **Admission** free. **Map** p169 E2.
Much less formal than Los Gallos (*see p189*), El Tamboril promises spontaneous singing, guitar-playing and hand-clapping, if the mood is right.

## Sport

For information on bullfighting at the famed **La Maestranza**, *see p173*, and for *corrida* basics, *see p174* **Cliché**.
More popular locally is football. The city's two first division teams are **Sevilla** (Estadio Sánchez Pizjuán, Avenida Eduardo Dato s/n, 954 53 53 53, www.sevillafc.es) and **Real Betis** (Estadio Ruiz de Lopera, Avenida de Heliópolis s/n, 954 61 03 40, www.realbetisbalompie.es).

## Theatre & music

Opera, operetta, flamenco and classical music are performed regularly at the **Teatro Maestranza** (*see p173*), the city's most important performing arts venue, and home to the **Real Orquesta Sinfónica de Sevilla**. **Teatro Lope de Vega** (Avenida de María Luisa s/n, 954 59 08 46, 954 59 08 53, closed July, Aug, map F2), housed in the Pabellón de Sevilla, puts on both modern and classical musical and dramatic performances throughout the year, while **Teatro Alameda** (C/Credito 13, 954 38 83 12, closed July, Aug, map A3) is the place for contemporary Andalucían theatre.
For pop concerts, flamenco, theatre and classical music, try the **Teatro Central** on the Isla de Cartuja (C/José de Gálvez s/n, 955 03 72 00, www.teatrocentral.com, closed July, Aug). Also here is **El Palenque** concert venue (C/Blas Pascal s/n, 954 46 71 70, www.palenque.org, map A5). In early June, the **Territorios Sevilla** series of gigs (954 59 08 67, www.territorios sevilla.com, tickets €12-€45) attracts Spanish stars such as Bebe, international artists like Nitin Sawnhey and Cuba's Bebo Valdés Cuarteto; tickets are available from Palenque, Sevilla Rock (*see p190*) and the Teatro Lope de Vega.

## Shopping

Sevilla's enormous shopping area stretches from the bullring to Plaza Alfalfa, extending to Plaza del Duque in the north and the cathedral in the south. Slick boutiques and chain stores share the pedestrianised thoroughfares and backstreets with more traditional shops. Unless stated otherwise, all shops close on Sundays.
At its heart is Calle Sierpes and the streets running parallel with it: Calles Velázquez, Tetuán, Francos and Cuna. This is where you'll find shops selling outfits for the Feria de Abril, shoes, fabrics and clothes. Among them are branches of **El Corte Inglés** (Plaza del Duque s/n, 954 57 14 40, map C3), Spain's perennially popular department store, and fashion favourites **Mango** (C/Velazquez 7-9, 954 22 33 89, www.mango.es, map C3) and **Zara** (Plaza Duque 1, 954 56 00 96, www.zara.com, map C3). For youthful, trendy garb, check out **Pimkie** (C/Velázquez 6, 954 56 43 53, map C3) and **Sexto Sentido** (C/Alcaicería de la Loza 9, 954 21 35 35, map C3), which sells shoes, jackets and jeans from Miss Sixty and Replay.
Further along the same street, **Porta Gayola** (C/Alcaicería de la Loza 26, 954 21 49 39, map C3) is a small shop selling trendy shoes, clothes and watches, and you can accessorise at the same address, with handmade bags and jewellery from **Alfalfa** (C/Alcaicería de la Loza 26, 954 22 55 11, map C3). **Angeles Méndez** at No.24 (954 22 48 59, map C3) has all the *sevillana* gear you could wish for, while **Sasa** (Plaza Adolfo Rodriguez Jurado 2, Avenida de la Constitución, 954 22 43 97, map E3) stocks Gucci and Prada leather goods.
For rock, world, folk and flamenco CDs, visit **Sevilla Rock** (C/Alfonso XII 1, at the corner of Plaza Duque, 954 22 97 38, map C3), though if you want some guidance on flamenco, *zarzuela* and ethnic Andalucian sounds, the calmer, classier **Allegro** (C/Dos de Mayo 38, 954 21 61 93, map E3) is a rare store. An outstanding shop for Spanish guitars is **Guitarras de Artesanía** (Zaragoza 4, 954 22 45 57, www.juanluiscayuela.com, map D4), where Señor Cayuela's immaculate handiwork is sold from €108 to €2,700.
For unique, arty homewares check out **Sargadelos** (C/Albareda 17, 954 21 67 08, www.sargadelos.com, closed Sat in July & Aug, map D3). Art collectors who like old posters should take a look at **Felix** (Avenida de la Constitución 26, 954 21 80 26, map D3), opposite the west wall of the cathedral, where Spanish artists and themes dominate; for antiques, the pretty little circular patio behind this store is home to three small stores. If you want to take back sherry, pickles, hams, cheeses and

local wines, visit one of Sevilla's six **Baco** *delisupermercado* outlets (Zaragoza 7, 954 21 11 99, other outlets listed at www.baco.es, map D4).

The two main shopping centres in town are the small, upmarket **Tiendas Peyra** (C/Francos 42 & C/Álvarez Quintero 27, map D3), which sells designer clothes, sunglasses and books, and the old train station on Plaza de Armas (map C4/5), which has been converted into a very pleasant shopping and entertainment complex.

**Plaza Duque de la Victoria** (map C3) has an open-air market on Fridays and Saturdays selling beads, cheap jewellery and ethnic gear, and there's an antiques market on Thursdays on **Calle Feria** (map B2).

## Where to stay

Accommodation is geared towards the upper end of the market; you will notice a marked hike in hotel prices compared to the rest of the province. Sevilla has pioneered *casa particular* and *palacio* conversions, exquisite former private homes turned into boutique-style hotels. It struggles to provide good quality rooms in the lower categories, with *pensiones* and *hostales* often significantly overpriced.

In terms of room rates, Sevilla has four seasons: low season includes July and August when prices drop but temperatures go through the roof; mid season is from March to June (excluding the *fiestas*) and from September to mid November; high season is Semana Santa; and very high, or 'extra', is the Feria de Abril. As well as being prohibitively expensive to stay in the city during high or extra periods, it is almost impossible to find any accommodation at all unless you book months in advance.

**Note**: the hotels are listed below in descending order of price for a double room within each area.

## Barrio de Santa Cruz, El Arenal & around the Catedral

### Hotel Alfonso XIII

*C/San Fernando 2 (954 91 70 00/www.westin.com).* **Rates** €371-€570 single; €487-€640 double; €1,006 junior suite; €1,493 executive suite; €1,926 royal suite. **Credit** AmEx, DC, MC, V. **Map** p169 E3. It's a shame that this five-star hotel – once the finest in all Spain – has been taken over by a chain, whose bland and incongruous Americanisms have the effect of diluting its unique character. But it's still a beautiful place, built by King Alfonso for the 1929 Expo as accommodation for the royal family, visiting heads of state, leading *matadores* and the like. Breakfast includes champagne and caviar, and its two top-class restaurants – one Japanese, the other 'international' – are popular with wealthy *sevillanos*.

### Casa Numero 7

*C/Virgenes 7 (954 22 15 81/21 45 27/www.casa numero7.com).* **Rates** (incl breakfast) €190-€294 single/double. **Credit** MC, V. **Map** p169 D2. Staying here is more like being a visitor to someone's private mansion than a guest in a hotel. The *casa* is owned by a director of González-Byass, who restored the house as a labour of love (it took three years). The six guestrooms (ask for the yellow room) are each individually designed, and furnished with original paintings and antiques. The roof terrace has views of the Giralda, and in the dining room a white-gloved butler serves the best scrambled eggs in Sevilla.

### Hotel Taberna del Alabardero

*C/Zaragoza 20 (954 56 06 37/www.tabernadel alabardero.com).* Closed Aug. **Rates** (incl breakfast) €124-€209 single; €155-€251 double; €190-€292 junior suite. **Credit** AmEx, DC, MC, V. **Map** p169 D4. This four-star has been converted from the 19th-century home of poet Juan Antonio Cavestany and is one of the most tastefully designed and supremely elegant small hotels in Sevilla. The seven rooms, all with jacuzzi, are ranged round a patio draped in hanging vines and flooded with light. The restaurant is one of the best in town (*see p183*).

As you stroll around Sevilla, you won't miss a strange emblem on lamp-posts, manhole covers, municipal buildings, and even on the base of Columbus's tomb. It looks like 'NO-8-DO', with the figure eight representing a looped skein of wool or *madeja*. The pun reads 'NO-madeja-DO' or 'no me ha dejado' – literally 'she never abandoned me' – and was famously uttered by Alfonso the Wise after the city remained loyal to him in a battle with his son Sancho during the 13th century. The phrase still conjures up pride in the people of Sevilla, and the *madeja* has become an enduring symbol of the city.

Sevilla Province

## Hotel Rey Alfonso X

*C/Ximénez Enciso 35 (954 21 00 70/www.rey
alfonsox.com).* **Rates** €120-€173 single; €156-€193
double; €187-€225 suite. **Credit** AmEx, DC, MC, V.
**Map** p169 D2.

Very modern and extremely stylish, this well-locat-
ed four-star boasts a rooftop pool with views over
the cathedral. The 18th-century tiles in the reception
are balanced by cutting-edge designer bathrooms
and understated decor. The 35 rooms either look in
to a quiet patio or out to the noisy square, but they
are all soundproofed and have little balconies.

## Los Seises

*C/Segovia 6 (954 22 94 95/www.hotellosseises.com).*
**Rates** €109-€150 single; €144-€209 double.
**Credit** AmEx, DC, MC, V. **Map** p169 D2/3.

This 16th-century former archbishop's palace is like
a miniature museum, stuffed full of Roman and
Arabic artefacts. The four-star en suite rooms are
comfortable and tastefully designed, and there's an
excellent restaurant attached, not to mention a
rooftop swimming pool with views of the Giralda.
The in-house restaurant, La Cocina de los Seises, is
set in a pretty courtyard.

## Hotel Bécquer

*C/Reyes Católicos 4 (954 22 89 00/www.hotel
becquer.com).* **Rates** €86-€118 single; €133-€180
double. **Credit** AmEx, DC, MC, V. **Map** p169 D1.

An elegant, old-fashioned hotel that draws an interesting mixture of independent travellers and business people. Rooms are comfortable but smallish,
with smart modern furnishings. The brand new spa
– offering mud, clay, salt, water and aroma therapies – is one of the best in town, and the hotel has
its own excellent tapas bar, La Leyenda (*see p182*).

## Hotel Vincci La Rábida

*C/Castelar 24 (954 50 12 80/www.vinccihoteles.com).*
**Rates** €118-€173 single; €118-€207 double.
**Credit** AmEx, DC, MC, V. **Map** p169 D3.

This 80-room, two-star hotel in an 18th-century
palace is tucked into the streets of El Arenal, halfway between the bullring and the cathedral. The
rooms are set around two patios.

## Las Casas de los Mercaderes

*C/Álvarez Quintero 9-13 (954 22 58 58/
www.casasypalacios.com).* **Rates** €77-€94 single;
€112-€137 double. **Credit** AmEx, DC, MC, V.
**Map** p169 D3.

This very pretty 18th-century building has been converted into a stylish three-star. Rooms are arranged
around a stunning patio, complete with columns,
balcony, mosaic tiling and an elaborate roof.

## Doña María

*C/Don Remondo 19 (954 22 49 98/www.hdmaria.
com).* **Rates** €64-€107 single; €107-€235 double.
**Credit** AmEx, DC, MC, V. **Map** p169 D2/3.

What sells this four-star – besides its antique fittings
and four-poster beds – is the swimming pool on
the roof. Paddling about with the Giralda as your

backdrop is a pretty unique experience. It's extremely comfortable, and pretty reasonably priced considering the perfect location.

## Hotel Amadeus

*C/Farnesio 6 (954 50 14 43/www.hotelamadeus
sevilla.com).* **Rates** €67 single; €81-€96 double; €134
junior suite. **Credit** DC, MC, V. **Map** p169 D2.

This is an excellent-value option, a few minutes'
walk from the heart of the *barrio*. An 18th-century
home has been converted into a tasteful hotel with
a musical theme. You are serenaded in the light-filled
entrance, and pianos, sheet music and paintings of
famous composers are dotted around. Each of the 14
rooms is prettily designed, and there is a roof terrace
with views of the Giralda.

## Hotel Simón

*C/García de Vinuesa 19 (954 22 66 60/
www.hotelsimonsevilla.com).* **Rates** €50-€57 single;
€75-€92 double; €107-€121 suite. **Credit** DC, MC, V.
**Map** p169 D3.

This 18th-century conversion has a patio, columns,
foliage and a large amount of antique furniture and
fittings: gilded mirrors, chandeliers, carpets and cab-
inets full of silver. The one-star bedrooms are nothing special, though, and the location, across the road
from the cathedral, means it can get a bit noisy.

## Hotel Alcántara

*C/Ximénez Enciso 28 (954 50 05 95/www.hotel
alcantara.net).* **Rates** €60-€112 single; €60-€140
double; €82-€165 triple. **Credit** AmEx, DC, MC, V.
**Map** p169 D2.

In terms of value, style and location, this two-star is
hard to beat. It's a new building (built March 2002)
rather than a conversion, with rooms decorated in
cool greys and whites, and bathrooms in steel and
marble, like a much more expensive designer hotel.
Rooms look out on to a charming modern patio.

**Los Seises.**

# Sacred and profane celebrations

## Semana Santa

Holy Week celebrations are not unique to Sevilla but they are unquestionably at their finest and most moving here. The build-up lasts for weeks and if you're in the city before Easter you'll see *cofradías* (brotherhoods) practising for the processions by carrying *pasos* (the platforms that hold the effigies of Christ and the Virgin), and bands warming up all over town.

Events officially begin on Palm Sunday, when the streets of the city fill with people and the bars stay open all night – a good spot to watch the goings-on is in the Parque de María Luisa. Processions begin at noon at their respective churches, head to the cathedral, through it and back again. This continues until Thursday evening, when the men dress up in dark suits, the women don their black *mantilla* shawls, and expectations rise for the three most important processions of the week: **El Gran Poder**, **La Esperanza de Triana** and **La Macarena**, which head off from their churches at midnight. The streets are heaving with people throughout the night, and the atmosphere around the churches is electric. The processions fizzle out on Good Friday, with just four taking place on Easter Saturday, and on Sunday they make way for the first bullfight of the season.

As an outsider it's difficult to know what's going on, where to look and why people may be cheering or crying. Your best bet is to pick up the excellent pocket guide published by the tourist office, which provides information on the terminology, routes and timing, so you know where to be and when. *See also p45.*

## Feria de Abril

The sometimes sombre religious atmosphere of Semana Santa is blown away in the second half of the month by the Feria de Abril, a week-long round of parades, dancing, dressing-up, bullfighting and drinking. The fairground takes up a large area on the west bank of the Río Guadalquivir in Barrio Los Remedios, although space restrictions may force it to move to the Charco de la Pava near the Isla de Cartuja in years to come.

The *feria* is still dominated by *casetas* (marquees), once the setting for business transactions (when the *feria* was a cattle fair), but now used for socialising. Some *casetas* are public, but most are owned by companies, families or societies, and you'll need an invitation to get inside. They contain little more than ample supplies of sherry or *manzanilla* (the main tipples throughout the festival) and crowds of people. During the day the fairground and much of the rest of the city is a riot of colour: women wear stunning flamenco creations in bright colours, while the men, dressed in traditional leather trousers and waistcoats, ride groomed horses around town. As the day wears on, the *sevillanas* dancing starts and continues until dawn. *See also p48.*

## Hostal Goya

*C/Mateos Gago 31 (954 21 11 70/www.hostal goyasevilla.com).* **Rates** €43 single; €70 double. **Credit** MC, V. **Map** p169 D2.
Located on one of Sevilla's many labyrinthine backstreets, this 20-room townhouse is a good low-budget option. The gold façade looks grand but inside it's a cosy, simple affair.

## YH Giralda

*C/Abades 30 (954 22 83 24/www.yh-hoteles.com).* **Rates** €59-€139 single/double; €80-€187 triple; €86-€193 suite. **Credit** AmEx, DC, MC, V. **Map** p169 D2.
One of very few mansion conversions – in this case an 18th-century abbot's home – that won't break the *banco*, with ultra-stylish decor and fittings. Rooms are simple but elegant, and quiet by Santa Cruz standards.

## Hostal Picasso & Hostal Van Gogh

*C/San Gregorio 1 & C/Miguel de Mañara 4 (954 21 08 64/www.grupo-piramide.com).* **Rates** €61-€86 double. **Credit** AmEx, DC, MC, V. **Map** p169 E3.

These two *hostales* are under the same management. Both offer decent value and locations convenient for the cathedral and the Alcázar. They are designed in bold, bright colours and festooned with pot plants. The en suite rooms are clean and comfortable, and most have air-conditioning.

## Hotel San Francisco

*C/Álvarez Quintero 38 (954 50 15 41/www.san franciscoh.com).* **Rates** €43-€59 single; €53-€73 double; €66-€86 triple. **Credit** AmEx, DC, MC, V. **Map** p169 D3.
Located just round the corner from the cathedral, this adequate one-star has diminutive but clean en suite rooms. The busy pedestrian street can be noisy at night.

## Hotel Murillo

*C/Lope de Rueda 9 (954 21 60 95/www.sol.com/ hotel/murillo).* **Rates** €36-€83 single; €50-€104 double; €63-€128 triple. **Credit** AmEx, DC, MC, V. **Map** p169 D/E2.

Themed after the Sevillian artist, this two-star has fairly standard rooms and smallish bathrooms, but there's a pleasant, old-fashioned feel to it and the common areas are impressive. If it's full, try the Apartamentos Murillo nearby (C/Reinosa 6, 954 21 09 59, www.sol.com/apartamentos/murillo).

### Hostal Arias

*C/Mariana Pineda 9 (954 21 83 89/www.hostal arias.com).* **Rates** €34-€43 single; €45-€59 double; €62-€81 triple. **Credit** DC, MC, V. **Map** p169 E3.
A good-value, functional, comfortable place in an excellent location, literally round the corner from the Alcázar. Rooms and bathrooms are of a decent size, uninspiring, but clean.

### Pensión Virgen de la Luz

*C/Virgen de la Luz 18 (954 53 79 63).* **Rates** €43-€48 double. **No credit cards**. **Map** p169 D1.
Tucked down a quiet side street off C/San Esteban, this is a very basic but good budget option, with small rooms (some en suite) around a tiny patio. Clean and friendly.

# Centro, La Alameda & La Macarena

### Hotel Casa Imperial

*C/Imperial 29 (954 50 03 00/www.casaimperial.com).* **Rates** €182-€364 junior suite; €257-€439 suite; €326-€546 triple. **Credit** AmEx, DC, MC, V. **Map** p168 C2.
A 16th-century *palacio*, originally owned by the Villafranco family (you can see their coat of arms carved into the stone entrance), has been turned into an exquisite, rambling five-star hotel made up of a series of beautiful interconnecting patios. Each luxury guest room is individually designed, with tiled floors, big beds and chunky antique furniture. Many bathrooms have sunken baths and twin washbasins. Rates include the use of a nearby gym and pool.

### Las Casas del Rey de Baeza

*Plaza Jesús de la Redención 2, off C/Santiago (954 56 14 96/www.hospes.es).* **Rates** €133-€280 single; €152-€308 double. **Credit** AmEx, DC, MC, V. **Map** p168 C2.
Possibly the most stylish conversion in town, this place oozes cool and luxury: the bedrooms are fitted with sleek hi-fis and huge comfy beds; the public spaces have slate floors and fresh flowers, and the starkly designed dining room is a great setting in which to enjoy an inventive menu. The pool and two guest reading rooms are similarly swanky.

### La Casa del Maestro

*C/Almudena 5 (954 50 00 07/www.lacasadel maestro.com).* Closed last wk July & all Aug. **Rates** €93-€118 single; €107-€146 double. **Credit** AmEx, DC, MC, V. **Map** p168 C2.
La Casa del Maestro is a hidden gem with bags of character, located in a quiet street. The house once belonged to renowned guitarist Niño Ricardo and the sympathetic conversion is full of pictures of El

Maestro and other flamenco greats. The guest rooms are lovely, with big beds, fluffy pillows and designer furniture, while the bathrooms are decorated in blue and white porcelain with deep baths. At the centre of the building is a pretty patio where guests can enjoy breakfast.

### Hotel Cervantes

*C/Cervantes 10 (954 90 02 80/www.hotel-cervantes.com).* **Rates** €69-€169 single; €89-€204 double. **Credit** AmEx, DC, MC, V. **Map** p168 B3.
A recently built three-star with a plant-festooned, light-filled patio topped with a glass ceiling. It's off the tourist trail, near the newly trendy Alameda, but is still only ten minutes' walk from the cathedral. The rooms are all of a decent size, and pleasantly if uninspiringly decorated; all have a minibar and air-conditioning.

### Hotel NH Plaza de Armas

*C/Marqués de Parada s/n (954 90 19 92/www.nh-hotels.com).* **Rates** €86-€237 single/double; €135-€285 suite. **Credit** AmEx, DC, MC, V. **Map** p168 C4.
Built for the 1992 Expo, this riverside tower displays all the marks of a boutique-style corporate NH hotel. The impressive curve of the building, the minimalist lobby and artworks, and the gentle brown and beige furnishings are verging on iconoclasm in what is, in design and hotelling terms, a conservative city. Function rooms make it one of the centre's few good business hotels, and there's a pool, satellite TV and babysitting for tourists. The surrounding Plaza de Armas is evolving as a lively leisure spot, with good non-Spanish restaurants.

### Hotel Don Pedro

*C/Gerona 22 (954 29 33 33/www.hoteldonpedro.net).* **Rates** €54-€72 single; €83-€128 double. **Credit** AmEx, DC, MC, V. **Map** p168 C2.
A good-value two-star in a converted 18th-century palace, on a quiet street just a few doors down from the famed El Rinconcillo tapas bar (*see p183*). Breakfast is served on the pretty patio.

### Aparthotel Patios de Sevilla

*C/Lumbreras 8-10 (954 90 29 00/www.patiosde sevilla.com); Alameda de Hercules 56 (954 90 49 99).* **Rates** €62-€69 single; €79-€97 double. **Credit** AmEx, DC, MC, V. **Map** p168 A3.
Two lovely terracotta-daubed *sevillano* houses share between them 56 brightly decorated apartments, each with a balcony or patio, double bed, sofabed and essential mod-cons, and just a minute's walk from the coolest part of town.

### Hotel Corregidor

*C/Morgado 17, corner of C/Amor de Dios (954 38 51 11/www.hotelcorregidorsevilla.net).* **Rates** €53-€77 single; €75-€148 double; €115-€123 triple. **Credit** AmEx, DC, MC, V. **Map** p168 B3.
Set in its own grounds not far from the Alameda de Hercules, this beautiful place is surprisingly tranquil. The three-star rooms are big and bright, and set round an exquisite patio.

### Hostal Sierpes

*C/Corral del Rey 22 (954 22 49 48/www.hsierpes. com)*. **Rates** €37-€78 single; €51-€103 double; €66-€134 triple. **Credit** AmEx, MC, V. **Map** p169 D2.
Good value *pensión* in the heart of the action. The rooms are surprisingly big and light, and ranged around a small patio. There's even a garage and a decent restaurant attached.

### Hostal Atenas

*C/Caballerizas 1 (954 21 80 47/atenas@jed.es)*. **Rates** €29-€40 single; €45-€95 double; €70-€120 triple. **Credit** AmEx, DC, MC, V. **Map** p168 C2.
This is a good budget option, with plenty of plants and tiles, and clean, comfortable rooms.

### Hostal La Muralla

*C/Fray Diego de Cádiz 39 (954 37 10 49)*. **Rates** €43-€86 single/double; €64-€107 triple. **Credit** MC, V. **Map** p168 A2.
If you want to be in the heart of La Macarena, this is a good place, hard by the old city walls.

## Outside the city

### El Bulli Hotel Hacienda Benazuza

*Sanlúcar La Mayor (955 70 33 44/www.hbenazuza. com)*. **Rates** €310-€1,130 double. **Credit** AmEx, DC, MC, V.
Located 12 kilometres (7.5 miles) west of the city is superstar chef Ferran Adrià's first foray into the world of hotels. The famed force behind Catalonia's El Bulli restaurant has created the ultimate fairytale fantasy lodgings – 'You don't come here to stay,' gushes the publicity, 'you come here to be.' And nowhere is just 'being' more fabulous. From the sumptuous suites, where once the Catholic monarchs rested their heads, and secluded cottages with bubbling alfresco hot tubs, to the day beds that shelter like teak-wood cattle beneath the trees, the Hacienda Benazuza is a serious contender for the sexiest hotel on earth. And, of course, the food is a key part of the experience – chef Rafa Morales flirts and seduces with a 33-course tasting menu that easily rivals that of the mother restaurant up north, while the El Bulli Breakfast – a seven-course extravaganza – gives guests the wake-up-call of their lives. Inevitably, all this indulgence comes with a hefty price tag.

## Resources

### Internet

*Amazonas Cyber, Conde de Barajas 6, off Alameda de Hercules (954 37 24 91/www.amazonascyber. com)*. **Open** 10.30am-2.30pm, 5-10.30pm Mon-Fri; 11am-2.30pm, 5-10.30pm Sat; 5.30-10.30pm Sun. **Map** p168 B3.
*Email Place, C/Sierpes 54 2A, off Pasaje de las Delicias (954 21 85 92/www.sevillaonline.com)*. **Open** 11am-10pm Mon-Fri; noon-9pm Sat, Sun. **Map** p168 C3.
*Seville Internet Centre, C/Almirantazgo 2, 1E (954 50 02 75/www.sevilleinternetcenter.com)*. **Open** 9am-10pm Mon-Fri; 10am-10pm Sat, Sun. **Map** p168 D/E3.

### Police station

*Pabellón de Brasil, Isla de la Cartuja (092)*.

### Post office

*Avenida de la Constitución 32 (954 21 11 81/ www.correos.es)*. **Open** 10am-11pm Mon-Fri; 11am-midnight Sat; noon-11pm Sun. **Map** p169 D/E3.

### Tourist information

*Turismo de Sevilla, Avenida de la Constitución 21 (954 22 14 04)*. **Open** 9am-7pm Mon-Fri; 10am-2pm, 3-7pm Sat; 10am-2pm Sun. **Map** p169 E3.
*Provincial Tourist Office, Plaza del Triunfo 1-3 (954 50 10 01/www.turismosevilla.org)*. **Open** 10.30am-2.30pm, 3.30-8pm Mon-Fri. **Map** p169 E3.
*Turismo, C/Arjona 28 (954 22 17 14)*. **Open** *July, Aug* 8am-2pm Mon-Fri. *Sept-June* 8.15am-8.45pm Mon-Fri; 9am-2pm Sat, Sun. **Map** p169 D4.
There are also tourist information offices at the airport (954 44 91 28) and the train station (954 53 76 26).

## Getting around

Sevilla has a chronic traffic problem. The first line of a four-line metro system is due to open by 2006. In the meantime, walking remains the best way of getting around the centre.

### By bus

The city bus service (900 71 01 71) doesn't pass through the centre. Routes C3 and C4 loop the old city on the Ronda; C1 and C2 take in Triana, Isla de Cartuja and Santa Justa; nightbuses are prefixed with 'A'. A 'bono bus' ticket allows unlimited travel; it's available from the main station in Plaza de Armas (map C4/5). There is also a hop-on, hop-off tour bus (954 56 06 93) that you can catch every 20mins (10am-11pm daily) anywhere along the east bank of the river between the Puente Triana and Torre del Oro.

## Getting there

### By air

The Aeropuerto de San Pablo is located 12kms (7.5 miles) east of the city, just off the A4-E5. *See p308.*

### By bus

Buses leave from Plaza de Armas (C/Cristo de la Expiración s/n, map C4/5) to Huelva and Lisbon (Damas, 954 90 77 37) and hourly to Madrid 8am-1am (Socibus, 902 22 92 92, www.socibus.es). Buses to Cádiz, Córdoba, Málaga, Granada and Almeria leave from El Prado de San Sebastián (Plaza de San Sebastián s/n, 954 41 71 11, map E2).

### By train

Estación Santa Justa is on Avenida Kansas City (a 20min walk east of the centre). The super-fast AVE gets you from Sevilla via Córdoba to Madrid in 2hrs 30mins – or your money back. Alternatively, the Talgo train takes a more sedate 3hrs 30mins. Every day there are 15 trains to Cádiz (1hr 45mins), 15 to Jerez (1hr), 30 to Córdoba (40mins-1hr 10mins), 6 to Málaga (2hrs 25mins), 4 to Granada (3hrs), 4 to Almeria (5hrs 20mins) and 1 to Jaén (3hrs).

# East of Sevilla

A vast plain and some of the region's finest towns.

The **Parador Alcázar del Rey Don Pedro** in **Carmona**. *See p197*.

## Carmona

The beautifully preserved town of **Carmona** (38 kilometres/24 miles east of Sevilla) is one of the oldest settlements in Spain, the site of human habitation for over half a million years. Its attraction for settlers is obvious: perched on a terraced escarpment, it enjoys a defensively perfect outlook across the *vega*. Today it's a prosperous, refined place, replete with classy boutiques, chic hotels and first-rate restaurants.

The efficient, friendly tourist office is a good place to start a tour of Carmona. It's located on the ground floor of the **Alcázar de la Puerta de Sevilla**. The Carthaginians set the template for this fortress, which was subsequently altered and developed by Roman and medieval rulers; climb the tower for a view of the town and surrounding plain. Carmona's other surviving gate, the **Puerta de Córdoba** (an elegant composite of Roman, Moorish and Renaissance elements), is at the opposite end of town on Calle Dolores Quintanilla. Approaching it from the direction of Córdoba, you get a view of the remains of the city walls, the **Alcázar del Rey Don Pedro** (originally an Almohad fortress, now a *parador; see p197*) and the Roman bridge.

From the tourist office, Calle Prim leads east to the town's main square, Plaza San Fernando, around which are a number of good places to eat and drink. Off the south-eastern side

of the *plaza* is Carmona's **Ayuntamiento** (C/El Salvador 2, 954 14 00 11), housed in a converted monastery; check out the Roman mosaic discovered in its courtyard in the 1920s.

Just to the north-east, on Calle San Ildefonso, is the cathedral-like **Prioral de Santa María**, which has a beautiful orange tree patio (the only surviving part of the original mosque) with a unique Visigothic liturgical calendar from the sixth century inscribed on one of its pillars. The church itself is a soaring treasure trove of gold-plated altarpieces. You can't miss the statue of the Virgin of Grace (from c1300) – it's as ornate as a Fabergé egg. Among the crucifixes and chasubles you'll also find a sword owned by the founder of the Jesuits, Ignatius Loyola.

Next door, the town museum, the **Museo de la Ciudad**, is housed in the Casa Palacio Marqués de las Torres, one of Carmona's many ornately fronted baroque townhouses. This old-fashioned museum is gradually being modernised with more audio-visual exhibits. Highlights include vivid descriptions of Moorish kitchens and markets (with a shelf of spices to sniff), as well as recordings of typical folk songs.

The highlight of Roman Carmona is the **Necropolis** (around a kilometre south-west of the centre), which was used from the second century BC to the fourth century AD. The Tomb of Servilia and the Tomb of the Elephant can only be visited on a guided tour; call in advance to book. Both tombs contain the remains of chambers, courtyards and sarcophagi. You can also climb down into a typical family burial vault containing the original cremation urns stored in niches in the curved chamber wall. The site also has an informative and well-presented museum.

### Alcázar de la Puerta de Sevilla

*Arco de la Puerta de Sevilla s/n (tourist office 954 19 09 55).* **Open** 10am-6pm Mon-Sat; 10am-3pm Sun. **Admission** €2; €1 concessions. **No credit cards.**

### Museo de la Ciudad

*Casa Palacio Marqués de las Torres, C/San Ildefonso 1 (954 28 01 14/www.museociudad.carmona.org).* **Open** *Mid June-Aug* 10am-2pm, 6.30-8.30pm Mon, Wed-Sat; 10am-2pm Tue, Sun. *Sept-mid June* 11am-7pm Mon, Wed-Sun; 11am-2pm Tue. **Admission** €2; €1 concessions. **Credit** AmEx, DC, MC,V.

### Necropolis

*Avenida Jorge Bonsor 9 (954 14 08 11/www.junta andalucia.es/cultura).* **Open** (always phone ahead as visits must be accompanied) *Mid June-mid Sept* 8.30am-2pm Tue-Fri; 10am-2pm Sat. *Mid Sept-mid June* 9am-5pm Tue-Fri; 10am-2pm Sat, Sun. **Admission** €2; free with EU passport. **No credit cards.**

### Prioral de Santa María

*Plaza Marqués de las Torres s/n (954 14 13 30).* **Open** *Apr-Sept* 9am-2pm, 5.30-7.30pm Mon-Fri. *Oct-Mar* 9am-2pm, 5-7pm Mon-Fri. Closed last 2wks Aug. **Admission** €3; €1.50 concessions. **No credit cards.**

## Where to eat & drink

For high-class international cuisine try Carmona's top hotels, especially the **Alcázar de la Reina**'s **La Ferrara** restaurant (*see below*, €€), which has a vegetarian menu, and the **Casa de Carmona**'s sumptuous restaurant (*see below*, €€€), which has exquisite food (including Andalucían specialities) and service. A non-hotel alternative is the genteel, slightly snooty **San Fernando** (C/Sacramento 3, 954 14 35 56, closed dinner Sun, all Mon and all Aug, €€-€€€).

The tapas bar-restaurant in the town museum, **Mesón Sierra Mayor** (C/San Ildefonso 1, 954 14 44 04, €€), is a converted stable with the horses' nameplates still on the wall above their stalls. **Bar Plaza** (Plaza San Fernando 2, 954 19 00 67, closed dinner Mon, €-€€), on the main square, has terrace tables and does a good value *menú* for €9. A stone's throw from the *parador* is **Meson Molino de la Romera** (C/Pedro I s/n, 954 14 20 00, closed lunch Sat, lunch Sun and 1st 2wks July, €€), specialising in regional dishes and roast meats. Set within a restored 15th-century olive oil mill it also serves superbly fresh vegetarian dishes, including *espincas estilo carmona* (spinach with chick peas). The best tapas in Carmona are to be found in the simple outdoor

bar **An Cá Carmela** (€-€€) (954 14 21 06, €) on the arcaded Plaza de los Abastos, where the local market is held.

## Where to stay

Carmona has three first-rate hotels. The **Parador Alcázar del Rey Don Pedro** (C/Alcázar s/n, 954 14 10 10, www.parador.es, double €128) is built on the ruins of a 14th-century fortified palace and has a beautiful pool with a view. Feel free to wander around inside and along the walls or have a drink in the bar. In a similar vein, but with a more homely, cosy feel, is the **Alcázar de la Reina** (Plaza de Lasso 2, 954 19 62 00, www.alcazar-reina.es, double €100-€200), which has fantastic views over the plain; the facilities, restaurant and staff are wonderful. At the luxurious five-star **Hotel Casa de Carmona** (Plaza de Lasso 1, 954 19 10 00, www.casadecarmona.com, double €120-€240) you feel as if you're staying in a private, if palatial, home. Books and musical instruments are strewn around the sumptuous rooms, and you can help yourself from the drinks trolley in the library. Budget choice is very limited. The best is **Hostal Comercio** (C/Torre del Oro 56, 954 14 00 18, double €45-€60, restaurant closed Sun, €), part of which dates from the 15th century. It has 14 spacious, tasteful, well-kept rooms and a lovely central patio.

## Resources

### Tourist information

*Alcázar de la Puerta de Sevilla s/n (954 19 09 55/ www.turismo.carmona.org).* **Open** 10am-6pm Mon-Sat; 10am-3pm Sun.

## Écija

Écija, 53 kilometres/33 miles east of Carmona, is sometimes known as the City of Towers, referring to the 11 distinctive tiled towers that adorn the town's churches and convents. From afar they provide an enchanting, twinkling welcome to the town. However, the sun that illuminates these towers has also been known to raise temperatures in the town to a vicious 52°C (126°F) in summer. At such times, the best thing to do is to slink from shade to shade, discovering Écija's crumbling, evocative Gothic-Mudéjar churches and grand baroque *palacios*.

Note: the recent tourism surge has inspired a fever of long-overdue restoration work in an attempt to reverse the decay of many of Écija's monuments (enquire at the tourist office to find out which are open). The town's main square, Plaza de España, should be a glorious open promenade surrounded by grand palaces and churches, but has been boarded up for years while the authorities build an underground car park and restore the square's buildings.

On the west side of the plaza is the tall **Ayuntamiento**, on the top floor of which is a camera obscura, with great views over the town (open 9.30am-2.30/3pm Mon-Fri, €1.80, €1.50 concessions). Next door is the church of **Santa María** (Plaza de Santa María s/n, 954 83 04 30, open 10am-1pm, 5.30-9pm Mon-Sat, 10am-noon Sun), of interest chiefly for the archaeological artefacts within its patio.

Calle Canovas del Castillo leads south-west from the *plaza* to the superb 18th-century **Palacio de Benamejí**, the fancy floral marble portals of which belie its former status as an army barracks. The building contains the tourist office, a good restaurant and the **Museo Histórico Municipal** (currently partially closed for renovations; due to re-open 2006).

From here, Calle Emilio Castellar runs east to another grand *palacio*, with a gracious patio and an ornate plasterwork stairwell, the **Palacio de Peñaflor** (open 10am-1pm Mon-Fri, 11am-1pm Sat, Sun, free). A little north of here, on Plaza San Juan, stands the church of **San Juan Bautista** (open noon-2pm daily), with perhaps the most outstanding and ornate baroque tower in town.

A few minutes' walk north of the Plaza de España is one of the most attractive of Écija's churches, the **Iglesia Mayor de Santa Cruz** (Plaza Nuestra Señora del Valle, open 9am-9pm Mon-Sat, 10am-1pm, 6-8pm Sun). Its grounds contain the remains of a Muslim archway, a grand Renaissance arch and beautiful leafy gardens. The church's tower echoes details of Sevilla's Giralda. The patron saint of the city, Nuestra Señora del Valle, is housed here apart from on her feast day (9 September), when she's carried around the streets.

### Museo Histórico Municipal

*C/Canovas del Castillo 4 (954 83 04 31/ http://museo.ecija.org).* **Open** *June-Sept* 9am-2pm Tue-Sun. *Oct-May* 9.30am-1.30pm, 4.30-6.30pm Mon-Fri; 9am-2pm Sat, Sun. **Admission** free.

### Where to stay & eat

If you want to overnight, you can do no better than the **Palacio de los Granados** (C/Emilio Castelar 42, 955 90 53 44/www.palaciogranados. com, doubles €128-€160), a superbly restored and stylish 18th-century *palacio* hotel, which opened in summer 2003. The only budget option in town is **Pensión Santa Cruz** (C/Practicante Romero Gordillo 8, 954 83 02 22, double €26-€30), an old-fashioned *casa familiar*, and very central, although the decor is a little shabby. **Hotel Platería** (C/Platería 4, 955 90 27 54, www.hotelplateria.com, double €60-€75,

restaurant €-€€) has less character but is a bit more comfortable. The restaurant offers good traditional food, including *gachas*, a hot pudding made with milk, flour, toast and aniseed.

**Restaurant Las Ninfas** in the Palacio de Benamejí (C/Elvira 1, 955 90 45 92, closed Mon, €-€€) serves local dishes in cool, stylish and historical surroundings. The cosy **Bar La Reja** (C/Garcilópez 1, 954 83 30 12, closed Sun) is a favourite with locals for a leisurely drink, gossip and delicious snacks. For a taste of one of Spain's top cuisines, visit the popular Galician restaurant **Bodegón de Gallego** (C/Arcipreste Aparicio 3, 954 83 26 18, closed Aug, €-€€): be brave and order *percebes* (barnacles).

## Resources

### Tourist information

*Ayuntamiento, Plaza de España 1 (955 90 29 33/ www.ecija.org).* **Open** 9.30am-3pm Mon-Fri; 10.30am-1.30pm Sat-Sun.

## Osuna

Residents of **Osuna** (34 kilometres/21 miles south of Écija) will proudly tell you that it lies at the geographical heart of Andalucía. Certainly, Osuna's location explains its importance since Iberian times (it thrived particularly, as Urso, under the Romans), and today it is one of the most beautifully preserved little towns in the whole of Andalucía.

Evidence of Osuna's ancient inhabitants can be seen in the tiny **Museo Arqueológico**, a 12th-century tower (and one-time prison). A few of the most important finds, including bronze inscriptions of the laws of the Roman settlement, are now housed in the national museum in Madrid, although copies are displayed here.

Up the hill from here, overlooking the town, is the 16th-century **Colegiata de Santa María de la Asunción**. It's an impressive, sturdy piece of Spanish Renaissance architecture, containing a hoard of sacred art including key works by José Ribera and important pieces by Juan de Mesa. The eccentric woman who has been showing visitors around the building for nearly a quarter of a century will happily play a Renaissance portable organ kept in one of the chapels for you; she will also lead you into an exquisite classical plateresque courtyard that recently re-opened after renovation. The guided tour continues down to the funerary chapel of the Dukes of Osuna, a Renaissance jewel encrusted with magnificent carvings, and taking the form of a miniature church, complete with central choir. The Dukes of Osuna are buried in the wood and stone sarcophagi that lie beyond this.

The local ducal families were responsible for the town's ornate *casas señoriales* and convents, built to show off the family's wealth. Stroll down beautiful Calle Sevilla, with its intricate façades, to get a good overview of Osuna's architecture. One of its highlights is the **Palacio del Marqués de la Gomera** (now a wonderful hotel, *see below*), which has one of the finest examples of a grand Osuna portico (one of the most original baroque porticoes in Spain). The front of the **Palacio del Cabildo Colegial** at No.16 displays a copy of Sevilla's Giralda, flanked by the Sevillian martyrs Santa Justa and Santa Rufina.

While in the area, it's worth visiting the town of **Estepa** (24 kilometres/15 miles east of Osuna), which also contains some lovely baroque *palacios* and churches, and is famed within Spain for its lard-based almond biscuits known as *polvorones*.

### Colegiata de Santa María de la Asunción

*Plaza de la Encarnación s/n (954 81 04 44).* **Open** *May, June, Sept* 10am-1.30pm, 4-7pm daily. *July, Aug* 10am-1.30pm, 4-7pm Mon-Sat; 10am-1.30pm Sun. *Oct-Apr* 10am-1.30pm, 3.30-6.30pm daily. **Admission** €2. **No credit cards.**

### Museo Arqueológico

*Plaza de la Duquesa s/n (954 81 12 07).* **Open** *June* 10am-1.30pm, 4-7pm daily. *July, Aug* 10am-1.30pm, 4-7pm Mon-Sat; 10am-1.30pm Sun. *Sept-May* 10am-1.30pm, 3.30-6.30pm daily. **Admission** €1.60. **No credit cards.**

## Where to stay & eat

The four-star **Hotel Palacio del Marqués de la Gomera** (C/San Pedro 20, 954 81 22 23, www.hotelpalaciodelmarques.com, double €90-€166, restaurant €€) is a reason to visit Osuna all on its own. A stunning *casa palacio* with its own baroque chapel, it has been tastefully and imaginatively restored, with 20 characterful, individually decorated rooms (the tower room, with its 180-degree views, is impossibly romantic). A rooftop pool and bar were added in 2004. The hotel restaurant serves imaginative interpretations of traditional dishes in a refined atmosphere. **Hostal-Restaurante El Caballo Blanco** (C/Granada 1, 954 81 01 84, www.ursoweb.com, double €45) is a well-maintained, smart-looking *pensión*, but its en suite, air-conditioned rooms are rather poky. There's parking and a restaurant serving traditional dishes (closed Sun, €-€€).

For solidly traditional, fresh and lovingly prepared food, try **Restaurante Doña Guadalupe** (Plaza Guadalupe 6-8, 954 81 05 58, closed Tue and first 2wks Aug, €-€€), situated in a courtyard between Calles Guadalupe and

Écija. See p197.

Quijada. It specialises in egg dishes and soups such as *ardoria* (a heavier, spicier version of *gazpacho*), as well as local game and homemade desserts. The town's outstanding tapas bar is tiny **Casa Curro** (Plaza Salitre 5, 955 82 07 58, closed Mon, €), south-west of the Plaza Mayor. Also recommended is the very pleasant, good-value bar-restaurant **El Mesón del Duque** (Plaza de la Duquesa 2, 954 81 28 45, closed Wed, €-€€). Recommended for a relaxed drink and snack at any time of the day is **Casino de Osuna** (Plaza Mayor s/n, 954 81 05 19, €), which has 1920s Mudéjar-style decor and views across the square.

## Resources

### Tourist information

*Ayuntamiento, Plaza Mayor (954 81 58 51/ www.ayto-osuna.es).* **Open** 9am-2pm, 4-6pm Mon-Fri.

## Getting there

### By bus

Buses stop on Paseo del Estatuto in Carmona, with frequent services to Sevilla by Alsina (954 41 88 11), Casal (954 90 69 77) and Sevibús (954 90 11 60); there are also 2 buses daily to Écija. Écija is served by Linesur (954 98 82 22) to Sevilla, and Graells (957 25 81 00) to Córdoba. There are 11 buses daily between Sevilla and Osuna. Osuna's bus station (954 81 01 46) is on Avenida de la Constitución.

### By train

Osuna rail station (954 81 03 08) is on Avenida de la Estación – it's a 20min uphill walk into the centre of town. There are 5 daily trains to Málaga (1hr 30mins), 8 to Sevilla (1hr), 3 to Granada (2hrs 20mins) and 3 to Almería (4hrs 50mins).

# North of Sevilla

Embrace the Great Outdoors.

A feathered resident of the 15th-century charterhouse **La Cartuja de Cazalla**.

The attractions of the wild **Sierra Norte** mountains of northern Sevilla province may be well known to *sevillanos*, but few foreign tourists venture into this sparsely populated corner of Andalucía. A chunk of the vast Sierra Morena range forms the border with Extremadura, and largely falls within the protected 167,400-hectare (646-square-mile) **Parque Natural de la Sierra Norte de Sevilla**.

None of the villages stand out in terms of sights. Indeed, they can seem bewilderingly similar, with their castle on a hill, bar-lined *paseo* and Mudéjar church. Here, untamed nature is the draw. This is a resolutely rural area, and the best way to get to know it is by staying in a remote converted *finca* and taking part in outdoor pursuits, such as fishing, riding, climbing and hiking; contact the tourist offices for details.

One of the two main settlements in northern Sevilla province, **Cazalla de la Sierra** (around 90 kilometres/56 miles north of Sevilla city), is a small town of typically steep cobbled streets lined with whitewashed houses. It's a bustling (in other words often traffic-jammed)

town, with a *paseo* – Paseo del Carmen – for summer drinking al fresco, and plenty of shops, banks and bars. The main sight is the large church of **Nuestra Señora de la Consolación** (open hours of services) on Plaza Mayor. Started in the 14th century, it's an architectural hotchpotch of Gothic-Mudéjar, Renaissance and baroque styles. There's a ruined castle on top of the hill behind the village.

Four kilometres (two-and-a-half miles) from Cazalla along the A455 towards Constantina is **La Cartuja de Cazalla**, a 15th-century charterhouse that has been slowly restored over many years and is now part hotel (*see p201*), part arts centre and gallery (954 88 45 16, www.skill.es/cartuja, open 8am-2pm, 5-9pm daily, €3).

North of Cazalla, the A432 becomes the A447 and winds through stunning, lonely scenery towards the remote north of Córdoba province (*see pp218-20*) – it's a marvellous drive, during which you're unlikely to pass more than a couple of other cars.

For true wilderness, head west from Cazalla on the SE179 towards El Real de la Jara on the outer reaches of the Sierra. The 46-kilometre

(29-mile) journey takes you through green, densely wooded valleys, over high passes and along the side of the **Embalse del Pintado** reservoir, a wild and beautiful spot. Non-motorised watersports are allowed on the lake, and there's a picnic area and jetty at the water's edge.

**El Real de la Jara** is a small, squat collection of whitewashed buildings, nestled beneath a recently renovated castle. Its now intact ramparts offer views north to the edge of Extremadura. In the town, the **Museo de Ciencas Naturales** (Torre de Reloj, C/Cervantes 44 s/n, contact the tourist office on 954 73 34 54, www.sierranortedesevilla.com for details) has two rooms full of stuffed animals – birds of prey, a lynx, a frog riding a tortoise and a selection of mammals having a grimacing competition. This weird collection is complemented by strange, oversized animal sculptures scattered about the village's streets. From here, the road continues onwards to Santa Olalla del Cala and northern Huelva province (*see pp156-61*).

Taking the A455 east from Cazalla towards Constantina, you drive alongside a pretty burbling stream. At the eight-kilometre mark is a turning for **San Nicolás del Puerto**. This village sits by the River Hueznar and has made the most of its watery position by trying to create an artificial beach on the banks of the river. However, the sloping concrete banks leading to a rather slimy trickle of algae-filled water aren't exactly appealing. More attractive is the pretty **Isla Margarita** picnic area, just off the A455, where footpaths flank a rushing stream with small cascades. Picnic tables and barbecues are scattered under firs and willows. Nearby, you'll find the train station serving both Cazalla and Constantina.

**Constantina** (20 kilometres/12.5 miles south-west of Cazalla) is the most populated town in the Sierra Norte. Its genteel air is intensified by a number of *casas señoriales* with wrought-iron covered windows, tiled walls and old wooden doors. Among the town's sights is the 16th-century church of **Santa María de la Encarnación** (open hours of services). The church's ornately carved portal (Puerta de Perdón) is attributed to Hernán Ruíz (the architect of Córdoba cathedral and the belfry of Sevilla's Giralda). You can climb the Mudéjar tower as long as there are no storks nesting on the top. Looking down on the church from a hilltop position are the ruins of the **Castillo de la Armada**. Climb steep, stepped streets to reach the terraces of flowers, shrubs and cherry trees that gather at the castle's foot. The castle was the scene of countless squabbles between local nobles, as well as acting as a fortress against the French in 1810.

The SE150 winds east from Constantina for 22 kilometres (14 miles) to **Las Navas de la Concepción**. This small town marks the eastern end of the Sierra, and its tourist office enthusiastically promotes Sierra activities. Many are organised by the **Hostal Los Monteros** (*see p202*), including cheesemaking, honey-collecting, mushroom-picking, and *matanza* – the traditional slaughtering and butchering of the valuable *cerdo ibérico* pig, with the chance to make your own *embutidos* (sausages). The tourist office also has a leaflet detailing local walks.

## Where to stay, eat & drink

Cazalla has the biggest concentration of accommodation in the Sierra (the area is very popular with weekenders from Sevilla). The **Posada del Moro** (Paseo del Moro 46, 954 88 48 58, www.laposadadelmoro.com, double €60, restaurant €) is a well-furnished, relaxed hotel-restaurant run by two sisters and various relations. There's a terrace and pool, and all rooms have a TV and faux-rustic frills. The restaurant serves simple but ample, well-prepared local dishes.

Grander lodgings can be found at the ten-room **Palacio de San Benito** (C/San Benito s/n, 954 88 33 36, www.palaciodesanbenito.com, double €128-€225), which was restored to its 17th-century glory by the present owners in 1997. The decor is ornate and the rooms luxurious, and there's the added draw of a lovely swimming pool in the garden.

Just outside town, the **Villa Turística de Cazalla** (A455, km3, 954 88 33 10) is a modern development of 3 bedrooms (double €64-€77) and 26 self-catering apartments (€74-€89 for 2 people, €110-€133 for 4) with wonderful views over a wooded valley. There's a pool, tennis court and a restaurant (try the superb wild boar with thyme), and activities such as 4x4 excursions, horse-riding and mushroom gathering can be arranged.

Some of the most interesting lodgings can be found next door at the **Hospedería La Cartuja de Cazalla** (A455, km2.5, 954 88 45 16, www.skill.es/cartuja, double €96). This former Carthusian monastery (1476), which sits on a plateau near a natural spring, has been restored by the indomitable Carmen Ladrón de Guevara y Bracho. As well as creating a hotel with cosy suites and rooms (a little pricey for the standard) in the monastery cloister, and a self-catering house in the grounds, Señora Carmen has turned part of the complex into

**Sevilla Province**

a centre for contemporary art and culture. The restaurant uses home-grown organic produce for its no-choice *menú* (expensive at €20); there's a charming pool, and horse-riding excursions can be arranged.

**Las Navezuelas** (A432, km43.5, 954 88 47 64, www.lasnavezuelas.com, closed early Jan-late Feb), on the road south towards El Pedroso, is a converted 16th-century olive mill and *finca*, surrounded by huge grounds. The garden has leafy archways, old whitewashed patios and a pool. There are singles (€43-€48), doubles (€67-€71) and suites (€79-€86) in the main building and self-catering apartments for two (€91-€96), four (€104-€111) or six (€139, weekly rentals only Apr-Sept, €856) in the grounds. The lovely owner Luca Cicerella prepares one menu a day (lunch in winter, dinner in summer) from his own produce.

For food in Cazalla, try the great tapas at **Bar Los Mellis** (C/La Plazuela s/n, 954 88 42 95, €), next to the Casino, or **Bar Bencomo** (C/Cervantes 55, no phone, €), a stylish little place specialising in *arroces* (rice dishes), with friendly staff and classical music on the stereo.

King Juan Carlos is an occasional visitor to tapas bar/restaurant **Cambio de Tercio** in Constantina (C/Virgen del Robledo 51 bajo, 955 88 10 80, closed Tue and last wk Sept, €€). The front tapas bar is small and overcrowded at lunch, while the more formal restaurant at the back specialises in local game, such as wild boar and partridge. The town's other local specialities are aniseed hooch and olive oil.

**Casa María Pepe** in Constantina (C/José de la Bastida 25, 955 88 02 82, double €42-€50) has nicely decorated rooms (with or without bath) in a lovingly converted mansion. From the town centre, a steep climb leads you to the three-star **Hotel San Blas** (C/Miraflores s/n, 955 88 00 77, double €46-€62), a welcoming place with light, cool, well-equipped rooms and a pool. The hotel can help with excursions and activities. **El Martinete** (SE168, km12, 955 88 65 33, closed Mon, €) is a dinky bar-restaurant attached to a campsite, just outside San Nicolás. From the restaurant, a path leads alongside a stream to an open barbecue area and on to waterfalls, woods and the campsite reception.

In Las Navas de la Concepción, the **Hostal Los Monteros** (SE150, km0.2, 955 88 50 62, double €38) offers en suite rooms with air-conditioning and TV.

## Resources

### Tourist information

**Cazalla de la Sierra** *Plaza Mayor s/n (954 88 35 62/www.ayto-cazalladelasierra.org).* **Open** 10am-2pm Tue, Wed; 10am-2pm, 5-7pm Thur-Sat; 11am-1pm Sun.

Cazalla de la Sierra. *See p200.*

Abandoned mine, **Sierra Norte**. *See p200.*

**Constantina** *C/Eduardo Dato 7 (955 88 07 00/ www.constantina.org).* **Open** 8am-3pm Mon-Fri.

**Las Navas de la Concepción** *Plaza España 5 (955 88 51 12/sfd@lasnavasdelaconcepcion.com).* **Open** *July, Aug* 9am-2pm, 6-8pm Mon-Fri, Sun; 9am-2pm Sat. *Sept-June* 9am-2pm, 6-8pm Mon-Fri, Sun.

**Parque Natural de la Sierra Norte de Sevilla** *Centro de Visitantes 'El Robledo', A452, km1 (955 88 15 97).* **Open** *May, June* 10am-2pm Tue-Thur; 10am-2pm, 6-8pm Fri, Sat. *July-Sept* 6-8pm Fri; 10am-2pm, 6-8pm Sat, Sun. *Oct-Apr* 10am-2pm Tue-Thur; 10am-2pm, 4-6pm Sat, Sun.

**San Nicolás del Puerto** *C/Real 4 (955 88 65 00/ www.dipusevilla.es).* **Open** 8am-3pm Mon-Thur; 8am-2pm Fri.

## Getting there

### By bus

Linesur/Betica (954 98 82 20, www.linesur.com) runs buses between Sevilla and most towns in the Sierra Norte. However, the services between towns are erratic, and there are no buses to either Huelva or Córdoba provinces. For further information, ask at Bar Gregorio in Constantina (C/Alférez Cabrera 11) or call 954 98 82 22.

### By train

There are 2 trains daily from Sevilla to El Pedroso (1hr 30mins), Cazalla-Constantina (1hr 45mins) and Guadalcanal (2hrs 20mins). Another 2 trains travel in the opposite direction from Mérida. Be aware that Cazalla-Constantina station is several kilometres from both places.

# Córdoba Province

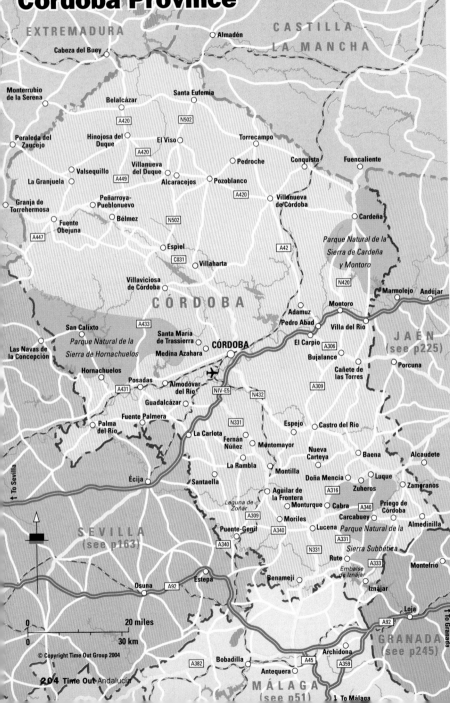

# Córdoba Province

EXTREMADURA

CASTILLA - LA MANCHA

Almadén

Cabeza del Buey

Monterrubio de la Serena

Belalcázar

Santa Eufemia

Peraleda del Zaucejo

Hinojosa del Duque

El Viso

Torrecampo

A420

N502

A420

Villanueva del Duque

Pedroche

Conquista

Fuencaliente

Valsequillo

Alcaracejos

Pozoblanco

La Granjuela

A449

Peñarroya-Pueblonuevo

Villanueva de Córdoba

Cardeña

Granja de Torrehermosa

Bélmez

N502

Villaharta

Parque Natural de la Sierra de Cardeña y Montoro

Fuente Obejuna

A447

Espiel

C031

N420

Villaviciosa de Córdoba

Marmolejo

Andújar

CÓRDOBA

Montoro

San Calíxto

A433

Adamuz

Pedro Abad

Villa del Río

Santa María de Trassierra

CÓRDOBA

El Carpio

JAÉN

(see p225)

Parque Natural de la Sierra de Hornachuelos

Medina Azahara

A306

Bujalance

Porcuna

Las Navas de la Concepción

Hornachuelos

Posadas

Almodóvar del Río

Cañete de las Torres

A431

A309

Guadalcázar

NIV-E5

N432

Palma del Río

Fuente Palmera

N331

Espejo

Castro del Río

La Carlota

Fernán Núñez

Montemayor

Alcaudete

To Sevilla

Baena

Écija

Santaella

La Rambla

Montilla

Nueva Carteya

Doña Mencía

Luque

Zamoranos

Laguna de Zoñar

Aguilar de la Frontera

A316

Zuheros

Priego de Córdoba

A309

Monturque

Cabra

A340

Almedinilla

Moriles

Carcabuey

SEVILLA

(see p163)

Puente-Genil

A340

Lucena

Parque Natural de la

A331

Sierra Subbética

Montefrío

Rute

A333

Osuna

A92

Estepa

Benamejí

Embalse de Iznájar

Iznájar

Loja

20 miles

A92

To Granada

30 km

GRANADA

(see p245)

© Copyright Time Out Group 2004

Archidona

Bobadilla

A382

Antequera

A45

A359

MÁLAGA

(see p51)

To Málaga

# Córdoba Province

Echoes of Moorish glories, wide open spaces and olive- and vine-clad hills.

The city of Córdoba and, more specifically, its far-famed mosque, finds a place on most visitors' hit lists, but the huge and hugely varied province at the heart of which it sits is far less known to tourists. The Guadalquivir river valley has long nurtured agriculture and ancient towns; to the north, huge skies and vast empty plains predominate; to the south, wine and olive oil production fuels a series of likeable industrious towns.

## CÓRDOBA CITY

The regional capital is a compact, attractive city that is perfect for exploring on foot. Its premier draw is the magnificent Mezquita, the most ambitious mosque ever built and a potent symbol of the city's pre-eminence in the glory days of al-Andalus. Around the Mezquita, the city's Jewish quarter is a network of whitewashed alleys and patios, while to the north are a sprinkling of lovely Renaissance churches. Córdoba is also famed within Andalucía for its fine restaurants – probably

the best in the region. Close to the city are the remains of Medina Azahara, a huge fairytale palace built by successive Caliphs.

## THE GUADALQUIVIR VALLEY AND NORTH OF CÓRDOBA

The Guadalquivir valley, running east and west from Córdoba, is a gentle, fertile place with some attractive towns. Almodóvar del Río, to the west, stands out for miles for the cinematic splendour of its hilltop castle, while Montoro clings to steep cliffs that rise up from the river. There are two Natural Parks in this area, both with unmissable scenery, flora and fauna. North from the Guadalquivir valley, a wilder, harsher landscape emerges and towns take on a road-movie edge. Among the heights of the Sierra Morena, and far off the tourist trail, neglected castles and old mining towns wait to be explored.

## SOUTH OF CÓRDOBA

The landscape and economy south of Córdoba are dominated by the twin liquid resources of wine and olive oil. Montilla is home to the sherry-like drink of the same name, while Baena produces some of the best olive oil in Europe. The olive tree is ubiquitous in this region, covering both the gentle swathes of fertile land known as the Campiña and the more dramatic heights of the Parque Natural de la Sierra Subbética. Roman and Moorish remains have been found in many of the towns in this area, and there are some spectacular baroque churches to discover, particularly in Priego de Córdoba.

## The best...

**Baroque architecture**
Priego de Córdoba (p223).

**Festivals**
Cabra (p221); Córdoba City (p206).

**Ham**
Los Pedroches (p220).

**Mosque**
Córdoba City (p206).

**Olive oil**
Baena (p223).

**Restaurants**
Córdoba City (p206).

**Wildernesses**
Sierra de Cardeña y Montoro (p219);
Sierra de Hornachuelos (p218);
Sierra Subbética (p223).

**Wines**
Montilla (p221).

Córdoba Province

# Córdoba City

With its Moorish heritage, blooming patios and local flamenco and bullfighting stars, Córdoba is stereotypical Andalucía writ large.

The city of Córdoba wears many masks: living museum, sleepy Andalucian backwater and bustling modern city, all crammed into a relatively small area. At its heart is the resplendent **Mezquita** – one of the greatest of all Moorish monuments. This heart's arteries, the tiny whitewashed streets of the Judería, are clogged with tacky and twee establishments serving tourists' needs. Yet, away from the Mezquita, the whitewashed streets can sometimes feel like those of a somnolent country village, even though only a couple of minutes' walk away broad avenues roar with traffic and the peripheral parks are alive with the chatter of families.

Apart from the Mezquita and the nearby ruins of **Medina Azahara** (*see p207* **The lost city**), Córdoba has only a few sights: museums, galleries and pleasant botanical gardens. Gastronomy is, perhaps, a greater draw, for there's arguably better eating to be had in Córdoba than anywhere else in the region. The favourite time to visit is during the unique **Concurso de Patios** in May (the second or third weekend), when hundreds of flower-filled private patios are opened to the public.

## HISTORY

Córdoba first came to prominence as a Roman port on the highest navigable stretch of the Guadalquivir river. It was then famed for its olive oil and its poetry – Roman wordsmiths Seneca and Lucan were both born here. With the decline of the Roman Empire, Córdoba fell to the Vandals and then the Visigoths, before being taken by the Moors in 755.

The next three centuries were Córdoba's Golden Age. The Umayyad prince Abd al-Rahman I established the independent state of al-Andalus with Córdoba as its capital, and started the building of the Mezquita. But it was Abd al-Rahman III (912-61) who really put Córdoba on the map, ushering in a period of major civic and cultural prosperity and building the large, dreamlike royal city of Medina Azahara. Though certainly exaggerated, the statistics quoted by the 17th-century Arab historian al-Maqqari give an idea of the splendour of the city at its peak. According to him, Córdoba boasted 3,000 mosques, 80,000 shops, 400,000 books in the library, 27 schools, 50 hospitals, 900 public baths, and public lighting in the streets.

Abd al-Rahman III's son, al-Hakam II (961-76), was a scholarly, peace-loving leader who built one of the great libraries of the age. In contrast was the warlike al-Mansur (977-1002), who used his position as regent to overthrow the child successor Hisham II, and famously stole the huge cathedral bells from Santiago de Compostela and had them melted down to make lamps for the Mezquita. (Two and a half

The **Mezquita**. *See p208.*

# The lost city

In 929, when the Emir of Córdoba, Abd al-Rahman III, became Caliph, he set about building a new palace and *medina* to firmly establish his authority and the magnificence of the fledgling Caliphate. The complex was named after his favourite wife Az-Zahra (the Radiant) and has been described by the historian Felipe Fernández-Armesto as 'worldly and ostentatious… both a pleasure-dome and a power-house'.

Work on Medina Azahara began in 936 on a huge site west of Córdoba. In addition to palace buildings the complex contained a zoo, aviary, four huge fish ponds, 300 baths, 400 houses, weapons factories and barracks for the royal guard, as well as numerous markets, workshops and mosques. The *medina* reputedly accommodated 4,000 slaves and a harem of over 6,000 women.

At the heart of the complex was the Alcázar, or palace. Chroniclers tell of its extraordinary beauty, in particular the splendour of the Throne Hall and the Golden Salon, both decorated with arches of ebony and ivory, and ornaments of marble, gold and precious stones. Another hall was built around a huge shallow bowl of mercury that would be rocked by a slave to send sunbeams skittering about the room.

After some stable years under al-Hakam II, who continued to endow the new royal city, greater opulence was to come under tough-guy al-Mansur. As a calculated snub to the dynasty he nominally served, the soldier-ruler built yet another palace, larger than Abd al-Rahman III's, and finished in just two years. Al-Mansur died in 1002 and his younger son failed to rise to the challenge of his father's legacy. In 1009 Medina Azahara was looted and sacked by Berber mutineers who ravaged the entire complex.

For the following centuries Medina Azahara existed only in history as 'old Córdoba', until excavations brought its stories back to life in 1910. The site is around ten kilometres (six miles) west of the provincial capital, on gentle fertile slopes, dotted with cypresses, below the Sierra Morena. Excavations are ongoing

and only a tenth of the original walled city has been exposed, corresponding to the central section of the Alcázar. The directed route through the complex ends on the lower terraces at the Chamber of Abd al-Rahman III. This hall would have been used for majestic receptions, although a vivid imagination is needed to conjure up the gleaming white marble floors and jewelled walls. Although the ruins only hint at past grandeur, they offer a tantalising glimpse into this short-lived but fantastic city.

### Medina Azahara

*A431, km6 (957 32 91 30).* **Open** *May-mid Sept* 10am-8.30pm Tue-Sat; 10am-2pm Sun. *Mid Sept-Apr* 10am-6pm Tue-Sat; 10am-2pm Sun. **Admission** €1.50; free with EU passport. **No credit cards**.

centuries later, when Fernando III conquered Córdoba, his first action was to have the lamps carried back to Santiago and remade into bells.)

Al-Mansur was the last of the great Córdoban leaders. Eventually, his Berber army revolted against its master, and the puppet Caliphs that

followed never regained the brilliance of their predecessors. However, Córdoba's reputation as a centre for culture and scholarship remained until the Christian conquest in 1236. Many of the period's greatest philosophers and scientists were born, lived or died here, such as the great astronomer and mathematician Maslama al-Mayriti, the 'father of surgery' al-Zahrawi (Abulcasis) and the multi-talented Jewish doctor, rabbi and scholar Maimonides.

Today, Córdoba flourishes modestly but happily, with an economy based on agriculture, tourism and light industry. The university was re-established in 1971, turning the city once again into a centre of learning, with a faculty devoted to the study of Muslim history and culture.

## Sightseeing

### The Mezquita

The Mezquita, the most ambitious mosque ever built by the Moors, was started by Abd al-Rahman I in 786 on the site of a former Visigoth cathedral, which had itself been built on top of a Roman temple dedicated to Janus. Subsequent Caliphs and Emirs all left their mark on the mosque, but the most surprising addition is the incongruous Renaissance cathedral constructed at its very heart.

The mosque is the origin of the Caliphal architectural style, combining Roman, Visigothic, Byzantine, Syrian and Persian elements, and became the reference point for all Arabian-Hispanic architecture until the *reconquista*. It conforms to the Muslim tradition of creating buildings that have humble, plain exteriors with dog-legged entrances that serve as a tease before the opulence and splendour of their interiors. In contrast to narrow Christian churches, the Mezquita is broad, to allow as many worshippers as possible to the front of the mosque, where they are closest to Mecca.

Considering the alterations and additions to which it has been subjected, the Mezquita could easily have become a mess of conflicting styles and extensions. However, the building hangs together supremely well, helped by its predominantly uniform rectangular design.

Its imposing outer walls retain their original highly decorated entrances, although only one – the **Puerta del Perdón** (Gate of Forgiveness) – now opens. It leads into the **Patio de los Naranjos**, an immense courtyard of orange trees, palms and fountains, originally used for ablutions by Muslims before prayer. At the corner of the patio, Abd al-Rahman III's beautiful minaret has been replaced by a 16th-century bell tower (closed to the public).

From here, 19 doors originally opened into the mosque itself, flooding the interior with sunlight. Now only one (the Puerta de las Palmas, or Gate of Palms) opens into the original section of the mosque, built by Abd al-Rahman I. In the subdued half-light you can

just pick out the astounding number of columns and the striking terracotta- and white-striped double arches. The impressive design is due to architectural improvisation. The Mezquita's architect was given a hotchpotch of old columns from Córdoba's Visigothic cathedral, the city's Roman buildings and others shipped in from Constantinople – making it difficult to achieve a uniform ceiling height. The solution was to use the tall columns as a base, on which were placed the smaller columns to create the ceiling arches. These evoke the shape of the date palm, much favoured in Moorish architecture, and may have been inspired by the designs of Roman aqueducts, which also used arcading.

The unity of the interior is broken by Abd al-Hakam II's tenth-century extension, which doubled the size of the mosque and created a magnificent *mihrab* (prayer-niche), meant to indicate the direction of Mecca and amplify the words of the Imam. (However, this mosque is, unusually, oriented towards Damascus rather than Mecca, perhaps due to Abd Al-Rahman I's nostalgia for his hometown.) The *mihrab* was constructed by Byzantine craftsmen. Its inner chamber has a shell-shaped ceiling carved from one piece of marble. To the side, chambers decorated with elaborate mosaics of gold, red, turquoise and green form the *maksura*, where the Caliph and his attendants would have prayed.

Opposite the *mihrab* is the **Capilla de Villaviciosa**, built in 1377 with convoluted Mudéjar arches, and the **Capilla Real**, constructed as a small funeral chapel for Fernando IV and Alfonso XI of Castilla. These relatively small-scale, sensitive Christian additions are in stark contrast to the Renaissance cathedral, built in 1523 with the support of Carlos V, which crouches in the centre of the Mezquita. Construction involved blocking up the mosque's open arches. It may be a blot on the Mezquita's original landscape, but the cathedral has some worthy architectural details, particularly its churrigueresque choir stalls. Carlos V failed to see its virtues, however, lamenting after it had been built that he had 'destroyed something that was unique in the world'. Yet, overall, the Christian elements of the Mezquita are eclipsed by the overwhelming Islamic architecture bearing down on all sides. Even today, when locals come to worship here, they say they are 'going to mass at the mosque'.

### The Mezquita

*C/Torrijos s/n (957 47 05 12).* **Open** *Mar, July-Oct* 10am-6.30pm Mon-Sat; 9am-10.15am, 2-6.30pm Sun. *Feb, Nov* 10am-5.30pm Mon-Sat; 9am-10.15am, 2-5.30pm Sun. *Jan, Dec* 10am-5pm Mon-Sat; 9am-10.15am, 2-5pm Sun. *Apr-June* 10am-7pm Mon-Sat; 9am-10.15am, 2-7pm Sun. **Admission** €6.50. **Credit** AmEx, DC, MC, V. **Map** p209 B3.

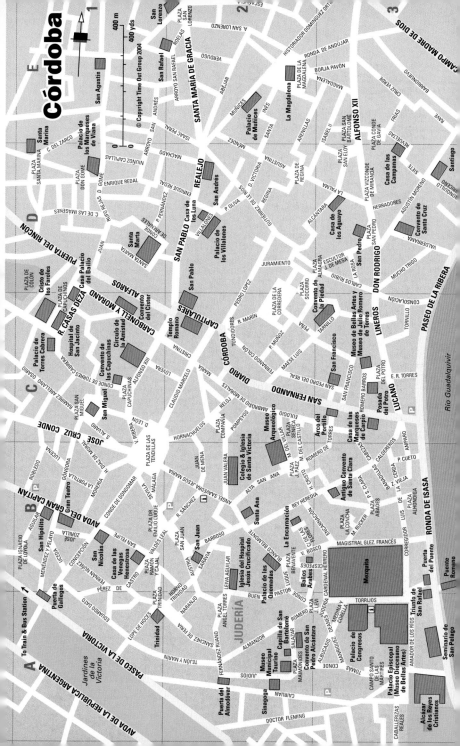

# Cliché Julio Romero Torres

You won't be in Córdoba long before you see the bare-breasted woman nestling oranges suggestively beneath her bosom. No, it's not a desperate greengrocer; she's the subject of one of the most famous paintings (*Naranjas y Limones; see below*) by locally celebrated 19th-20th century Córdoban artist Julio Romero Torres.

Romero Torres was born in 1874 in the Córdoban provincial art museum, where his father, also a painter, was curator, and which is now a museum dedicated to Romero himself. As a young artist he was subject to varying influences, and his own style became a curious mixture of Romanticism, Naturalism, Realism and Modernism.

Perhaps the most important aspect of his work, though, is its folkloric nature, representing what he saw as the spirit of Andalucían and *gitano* (gypsy) culture. His works are filled with long-legged, silken-skinned, dusky-eyed maidens, displaying flesh with a casual sensuality; with murderously jealous bullfighters and defiantly dignified prostitutes; and with scenes of passion and despair. They are variously seen as insightful and sensitive representations of the Andalucían soul with hints of social satire – a two-dimensional representation of the melancholic flamenco song style, the *copla*;

as sentimental popularist art without any lasting value; or as chocolate-box soft-porn.

Romero certainly had a deep authentic connection with the flamenco world, both personal and professional. Some of his favourite models/muses were Andalucían flamenco performers, such as the dancer Elisa Muñiz 'Amarantina' and the singer Dolores Castro Ruiz 'Dora La Cordobesita' – the model for Romero's famous *La Cordobesa* anís bottle labels. It's said he had affairs with these and the other Andalucían lovelies he painted, keeping locks of their hair stuffed in a cushion as mementoes. Such goings-on created scandal in certain circles, but also bolstered his persona as both embodiment and interpreter of 'fundamental Andalucían values'.

His flamenco credentials were recently endorsed by a fellow Córdoban, the flamenco guitarist Paco Peña. Peña has created a show based on Romero's life and works, and named it after perhaps his most famous work – *La Musa Gitana*, which one critic described as 'one of the most important contributions of Spanish painting to universal art'.

Whatever is thought of him now, Romero was certainly celebrated in his own lifetime, exalted in Madrid's artistic circles and exhibited with great success in London, Paris and South America. In 1930 he started his last work at his home-studio in the Plaza del Potro. He died in May of that year leaving *La Chiquita Piconera* unfinished – a fate that has elevated this work's significance and, in doing so, perhaps denigrated Romero's overall legacy, his whole oeuvre being coloured by judgement of this last painting. It's a portrait of an overly long-limbed, coal-eyed girl, with half-off blouse and stockings, poking at dying embers and staring defiantly at the viewer. It inspires the typical dichotomy of reactions to Romero's work, being seen as either a moving portrayal of dignity in poverty, or an example of his overwrought, sentimental voyeurism.

But whatever the rest of the world thinks, Córdoba loved this dapper, black-caped, well-coiffured would-be gypsy – every shop, bar and office closed for his funeral – and it loves him still, as witnessed by the hundreds of posters of that dusky maiden with her eyes (and breasts) following unsuspecting tourists round every street corner.

# The Judería & around

A good place to start a tour of the old Jewish quarter, which radiates out from the Mezquita, is the tourist office at Calle Torrijos where you can pick up a map and the all-important, ever-changing monument and museum opening times. Next door is the **Museo Diocesano de Bellas Artes** in the former Palacio Episcopal, which can be visited with the Mezquita ticket. The palace was constructed on the site of the original Moorish Alcázar and has a beautiful, airy patio. Medieval wood sculpture, religious tapestries and a collection of psalm books, as well as works by local artists, are among the exhibits. Next to this is another *palacio*, the **Palacio de Congresos y Exposiciones**. If it's not closed for a function, visit the lovely patio where you can sit and have a drink and tapas, or browse the ceramics shop in its cloisters.

South of here stands the **Alcázar de los Reyes Cristianos**, a fortified palace beside the river built in 1328 by Alfonso XI. The building was used by the Inquisition from the 1500s until 1820, and later became a prison until the 1950s, resulting in the loss of much of its original grandeur. However, it still incorporates remarkable Arabian baths, Roman mosaics, a marble sarcophagus from the third century and three of its original towers. The small museum is worth a visit, and the gorgeous Moorish-style gardens are a delight.

The tiny **Calleja de las Flores**, just west of the Mezquita, draws in a constant stream of camera-toting tourists for its neatly framed view of the mosque's bell tower. It's also home to some of the last remaining workshops where Córdoba's famous worked-leather goods are made and sold (*see p214*).

The nearby **Museo Arqueológico** is set inside the beautiful Renaissance **Casa Páez**. During its conversion, a Roman patio was discovered, which is now exhibited along with other Roman, Iberian and Moorish remains.

South-west of the Mezquita, heading towards the Puerta de Almodóvar, Córdoba's last standing old town gate, you'll find the **Museo Municipal Taurino** and the 14th-century **Sinagoga** (synagogue). The bullfighting museum is housed in the beautiful **Casa de las Bulas**, which has another splendid patio. The synagogue in Calle Maimonides was built in 1315 and is one of only three surviving original synagogues from this period in Spain.

The **Puerta de Almodóvar** is the city's only surviving 14th-century gate. From here, a pleasant walk leads east along the old city walls towards the Guadalquivir river. Alternatively, head west to reach the **Jardines de la Victoria**, the city's main promenade park.

## Alcázar de los Reyes Cristianos

*Campo Santo de los Mártires s/n (957 42 01 51).*
**Open** *Mid June-Sept* 8.30am-2pm Tue-Sat; 9.30am-2pm Sun. *Oct-mid June* 10am-2pm, 5.30-6.30pm Tue-Sat; 9.30am-2pm Sun. **Admission** €3; €1.50 concessions; free to all Fri. **No credit cards.** **Map** p209 A3.

## Museo Arqueológico

*Plaza Jerónimo Páez 7 (957 47 40 11).*
**Open** 2.30-8.30pm Tue; 9am-8.30pm Wed-Sat; 9am-2.30pm Sun. **Admission** €1.50; free with EU passport. **No credit cards.** **Map** p209 B/C2.

## Museo Diocesano de Bellas Artes

*Palacio Episcopal, C/Torrijos 12 (957 49 60 85).*
**Open** 9.30am-1.30pm, 4-6pm Mon-Fri; 9.30am-1.30pm Sat. **Admission** €1.50; free with Mezquita ticket. **No credit cards. Map** p209 A3.

## Museo Municipal Taurino

*Casa de las Bulas, Plaza Judíos s/n (957 20 10 56).*
**Open** 10am-1.30pm, 5.30-6.30pm Tue-Sat; 9.30am-2.30pm Sun. **Admission** €3; free to all Fri. **No credit cards. Map** p209 A2.

## Palacio de Congresos y Exposiciones de Córdoba

*C/Torrijos 10 (957 48 31 12).* **Open** 9.30am-2.30pm, 5-8pm Mon-Fri; occasionally weekends. **Admission** free. **Map** p209 A3.

## Sinagoga

*C/Maimonides s/n (957 20 29 28).* **Open** 9.30am-2pm, 3.30-5.30pm Tue-Sat; 9.30am-1.30pm Sun. **Admission** 30¢; free with EU passport. **No credit cards. Map** p209 A2.

# Along the Guadalquivir

Head towards the river from the Mezquita and you'll see the **Puente Romano**, the much altered Roman bridge. At its western end stands the **Triunfo de San Rafael** (Triumph of San Rafael monument) and the **Puerta del Puente** (Bridge Gate), built by Felipe II in 1572, replacing an original Roman structure. On the bridge's far side rises the **Torre de la Calahorra**. Built in 1369 as a lookout, it now contains a small museum of Córdoba's history, focusing on the 'three cultures' – Muslim, Jewish and Christian – in the 12th and 13th centuries. On the river are the remains of the **Molino de la Albolafia**, one of several Moorish mills along the Guadalquivir. The reedbeds around the Puente Romano are home to a remarkable collection of birdlife (*see p89* **Top five**).

Follow the river south along its western bank to Córdoba's **Jardín Botánico** (Botanical Garden), which offers a fragrant, leafy respite from the heat and noise. You can also visit the garden's paeleontology and ethnobotany museums, a café and a small gift shop.

### Jardín Botánico

*Avenida de Linneo s/n (957 20 00 18).*
**Open** *Gardens* Mid June-Sept 10am-2.30pm Tue-
Sun (occasionally open evenings 9pm-midnight;
call to check). Oct-mid June 10am-9pm Tue-Sat;
10am-2.30pm Sun. *Museo de Etnobotanica & Museo
de Paleobotanico* Mid June-Sept 10am-2.30pm Tue-
Sun. Oct-mid June 10am-2.30pm, 5-8pm Tue-Sat;
10am-2.30pm Sun. **Admission** €2; €1.30 concessions.
**No credit cards. Map** p209 off A3.

### Torre de la Calahorra

*Puente Romano (957 29 39 29/www.torrecalahorra.
com).* **Open** *Museum* May-Sept 10am-2pm, 4.30-
8.30pm daily. Oct-Apr 10am-6pm daily. *'Multivision'
tours* May-Sept 10.30am, 11.30am, 12.30pm, 6pm, 7pm.
Oct-Apr 11am, noon, 1pm, 3pm, 4pm. **Admission**
*Museum* €4; €2.50 concessions. *'Multivision'* €1.20.
**No credit cards. Map** p209 off B3.

## Plaza del Potro & Plaza de la Corredera

On the river side of the Mezquita, Calle
Corregidor Luis de la Cerda leads northwards
to the **Medina Califal**, a Moorish-style modern
bathhouse with hot and cold baths, massage and
other treatments. Reservations are obligatory.

Continuing in the same direction, you pass
through a rabbit warren of alleys and streets
to arrive at **Plaza del Potro**. The inn on
its south side, the **Posada del Potro**, is
mentioned in *Don Quijote* and almost certainly
accommodated Cervantes on his visits to the
city. It now hosts contemporary art exhibitions.

Opposite, the **Museo de Bellas Artes**,
housed in the former 16th-century Hospital de
la Caridad, has a collection of works by local
artists. Across the hospital's pretty courtyard
is the former home of the Córdoban artist **Julio
Romero de Torres** (1885-1930), now a small
museum (*see p210* **Cliché**).

West of here is the splendour of the **Plaza
de la Corredera**. A huge arcaded square,
it hosted horse races, bullfights and public
executions in the Middle Ages; today it still
holds cultural and sporting events, but its main
draw is the indoor market on one side, and the
bars and bric-a-brac stalls that line its cloisters.

A few minutes walk north along Calle Pedro
Lopez brings you to Plaza Luis Venegas, where
the stark modern lines of the **Museo Regina**
jewellery museum rise from ancient stone
foundations. Visits are by guided tour only
(English available) and pre-booking is advisable.

### Medina Califal

*C/Corregidor Luis de la Cerda 51 (957 48 47 46/
www.hammamspain.com).* **Open** 10am-midnight
daily. **Rates** *Bath, massage & aromatherapy* €22;
€18.50 concessions, 10am-4pm only. *Bath only* €15.
**Credit** MC, V. **Map** p209 B3.

### Museo de Bellas Artes

*Plaza del Potro 1 (957 47 13 14).* **Open** 2.30-8.30pm
Tue; 9am-8.30pm Wed-Sat. **Admission** €1.50; free
with EU passport. **No credit cards. Map** p209 A3.

### Museo de Julio Romero de Torres

*Plaza del Potro 1 (957 49 19 09).* **Open** *Mid June-
mid Sept* 8.30am-2.30pm Tue-Sat; 9.30am-2.30pm
Sun. *Mid Sept-mid June* 10am-2pm, 4.30-6.30pm Tue-
Sat; 9.30am-2.30pm Sun. **Admission** €3; free to all
Fri. **No credit cards. Map** p209 C3.

### Museo Regina

*Plaza Luis Venegas 1, off Calle Pedro Lopez (957 49
68 89/www.museoregina.com).* **Open** *June-mid Sept*
9am-2pm, 5.30-9pm daily. *Mid Sept-May* 10am-3pm,
5-8pm daily. **Admission** €3; €1.50 concessions.
**Credit** AmEx, DC, MC, V. **Map** p209 D2.

### Posada del Potro

*Plaza del Potro s/n (957 47 20 00).* **Open** 9am-2pm,
6-9pm daily. **Admission** free. **Map** p209 C3.

## Plaza de las Tendillas & beyond

West of Plaza de la Corredera, the modern city
starts to assert itself. Its focal point is **Plaza
de las Tendillas**, from which Córdoba's
main shopping streets radiate. The square is
dominated by an old fountain and an equestian
statue of El Gran Capitán, a Córdoban general
whose Italian campaigns in the late 15th
century brought him international fame.

Calle Claudio Marcelo leads from the *plaza*
to the **Templo Romano** (reconstructed pillars
from a first-century Roman temple) and the
church of **San Pablo** (open hours of services).
The architecture of the latter displays the
transition between the Romanesque and
the Gothic, with Mudéjar features. Further
north-east is a trio of *reconquista* churches:
**San Andrés** on Calle Realejo, the neoclassical
**San Rafael** on Calle Roelas and the stunning
Gothic-Mudéjar **San Lorenzo** on Calle Maria
Auxiliadora (all open hours of services). The
latter has a converted minaret tower and a
beautiful rose window.

The twisting streets and small squares west
of here shelter several more beautiful Gothic
churches built soon after the *reconquista*.
**Santa Marina** (open hours of services) has
a particularly attractive setting in a small *plaza*
(Plaza Santa Marina) with a monument to the
legendary local-born bullfighter Manolete.

Just south-east of here is the splendid
**Palacio de Viana**. The compulsory guided
tour takes you through the interior, which still
contains the furnishings of the Viana family,
but the highlight is the palace's 14 beautiful
patios and gardens, constructed between
the 14th and 18th centuries. The gardens and
patios can be visited without a guided tour.

for instance, has become famed for its light variations on traditional dishes and for its El Bulli-inspired innovations, while **Bodegas Campos** is another haven of lightness of touch and culinary imagination.

### Al Khyma

*C/Céspedes 11 (mobile 679 59 04 83).* **Open** 1pm-midnight Mon-Fri; noon-2am Sat, Sun. **Average** €. **No credit cards. Map** p209 B2/3.
Popular with a young local crowd, this Moorish-style tea room serves teas, infusions and fresh juices. The decor is *A Thousand and One Nights*, with horseshoe arches, ornate tiles and embroidered cushions.

### Amapola

*Paseo de la Ribera 9 (957 47 37 40).* **Open** noon-3am daily. **Average** €. **No credit cards. Map** p209 C3.
Aquamarine tiles, black graphic squiggles and green leather banquettes signal this recently opened bar's cool credentials. The crowd is mixed, though, with an emphasis on the young and good-looking, and the music ranges from lounge to retro rock.

### Bodegas Campos

*C/Lineros 32 (957 49 75 00/www.bodegas campos.com).* **Open** 1-5pm, 8.30pm-midnight Mon-Sat; 1-5pm Sun. **Average** €€€€. **Credit** DC, MC, V. **Map** p209 C3.
This elegant and sensationally beautiful restaurant (with its numerous patios) may not be cheap, but each dish is produced using top ingredients and great skill. Highlights include a superb *remojón* (salt cod and orange salad), suckling lamb and four-chocolate tart with cinnamon ice-cream. The staff are usually very friendly, and the head waitress, Manoli, is a motherly Córdoban institution.

### Cafeteria El Rincón de Carmen

*C/Romero 4 (957 29 10 55).* **Open** noon-4pm, 8-11pm Mon-Sat; noon-4pm Sun. **Average** €. **Credit** AmEx, MC, V. **Map** p209 A2.
Settle into large wicker chairs to breakfast cheaply on *tostadas* and freshly squeezed orange juice at this airy café. There's a small patio restaurant next door.

### Casa Pepe de la Judería

*C/Romero 1 (957 20 07 44).* **Open** 1-4pm, 8.30-11.30pm daily. **Average** *tapas* €-€€; *restaurant* €€-€€€. **Credit** AmEx, DC, MC, V. **Map** p209 A2.
This innovative restaurant has a tangle of dining rooms and a gorgeous roof terrace with views of the Mezquita. The menu is diverse, with delicacies such as the Morisco dish *mazamorra* (egg, garlic and oil soup). It proudly claims of its desserts: 'We make and we think sensual delight are the sweetest... Sugar pleased!!!' Tapas are served in the busy side bar.

### Casa El Pisto

*Plaza San Miguel 1 (957 47 01 66).* **Open** noon-4pm, 8.30pm-midnight Mon-Sat; noon-4pm Sun. Closed Aug. **Average** €. **Credit** AmEx, DC, MC, V. **Map** p209 C1.

The **Jardines de la Victoria**. *See p211.*

A little south of Santa Marina is the **Plaza de Capuchinos**, a raised, enclosed *plaza* dominated by the famous 18th-century statue of *El Cristo de los Faroles* (Christ of the Lanterns), which seems especially mystical when lit up at night.

Just west of here are the ornate gardens of the **Plaza de Colón**, flanked on the western side by the very grand baroque **Palacio de la Diputación**. North-west of the *plaza* is the **Torre de la Malmuerta** ('bad death'), a 15th-century battlement tower, supposedly built in contrition by a nobleman who had murdered his adulterous wife – another story is that he bricked up his unfaithful wife in the walls.

There are several churches worth a visit on the route from here back towards the Judería, including **San Miguel** (open hours of services). It is located in a pretty *plaza* of the same name (which has some good café-bars) and houses a wonderful 18th-century *retablo* in red marble.

### Palacio de Viana

*Plaza Don Gome 2 (957 49 67 41).* **Open** 10am-1pm, 4-6pm Mon-Fri; 10am-1pm Sat. **Admission** *Patios only* €3. *Palace (guided tour only) & patios* €6. **No credit cards. Map** p209 D1.

## Where to eat & drink

Córdoba is Andalucía's culinary capital. Spain's ongoing culinary revolution (inventive cuisine; light, fresh flavours) is taking a while to filter into the regional restaurant scene – but Córdoba is in its vanguard down south. **Casa Pepe,**

**Córdoba Province**

'The Barrel' is a legendary Córdoban bar in a delightful old house, with great *montilla* and a busy, buzzy atmosphere. Be warned that none of the tables in the neighbouring square belong to this bar.

### La Cávea

*Plaza de Jerónimo Páez s/n (957 47 29 32).* **Open** 9.30am-midnight Tue-Sun. Closed mid June-mid July. **Average** €. **Credit** DC, MC, V. **Map** p209 B2.
This recently opened tapas bar near the archaeological museum has outdoor tables on a leafy terrace. The selection of mixed tapas is good value: the *salmorejo* is gloriously garlicky and the *pinchos morunos* (little skewers of grilled meat) are both Moorish and moreish.

### El Churrasco

*C/Romero 16 (957 29 08 19/www.elchurrasco.com).* **Open** 1-4pm, 8.30pm-midnight daily. Closed Aug. **Average** €€-€€€€. **Credit** AmEx, DC, MC, V. **Map** p209 A2.
Loved by locals and tourists (and Tony Blair), this is a safe bet for traditional Andalucian fare and old-style waiter service. Try El Churrasco's signature dish: *churrasco Cordobés con salsas Árabes* (pork loin with 'Arabic' sweet-and-sour sauce). There are two patios and some beautiful private salons.

### El Faro

*C/Blanco Belmonte 6 (957 48 62 14).* **Open** 1-4pm, 8.30pm-12.30am Tue-Sun. **Average** €€. **Credit** AmEx, DC, MC, V. **Map** p209 B2.
A modest side entrance makes this quiet, unpretentious restaurant easy to miss (just west of the Mezquita). Splash out on a mixed seafood platter or try the simple but tasty fried red mullet. The restaurant also has an excellent sister seafood bar – look out for its cute lighthouse-themed exterior.
**Other location:** El Faro, C/Sevilla 3 (957 47 83 51).

### Los Marqueses

*C/Tomás Conde 8 (957 20 20 94).* **Open** 2.30-4pm, 8.30-11.30pm Sun. 2.30-4pm Sun. **Average** €€€-€€€€. **Credit** AmEx, MC, V. **Map** p209 A2.
The *marqueses* after whom this extremely smart restaurant is named gaze down imperiously from oil paintings that dominate the small, elegant dining room. The highlights of the menu are the lobster salad and shoulder of suckling lamb, but all the dishes are expertly executed with creative touches.

### El Sotano

*Plaza de la Corredera 1 (957 48 45 70).* **Open** *Mid June-Oct* 9am-5pm, 8pm-2am daily. *Nov-mid June* 9am-2am daily. **Average** €. **Credit** AmEx, DC, MC, V. **Map** p209 C2.
This funky little bar, run by two friendly young guys, is decorated in warm yellows and oranges. With a couple of terrace tables, it's a chilled spot for a drink or reasonably priced snacks.

### Soul

*C/Alfonso XIII 3 (957 49 15 80).* **Open** 9am-3am Mon-Fri; 5pm-3am Sat, Sun. **Average** €. **No credit cards. Map** p209 C1.

Soul puts its namesake into its breakfasts, with bread baked in a wood-burning oven (Omega3, raisin-and-walnut, and multicereal varieties), topped with honey or speciality jams. Later in the day and into the evening a young crowd lounges among the funky decor. There's live music or DJs on Wednesday to Saturday nights.

### Taberna Casa Bravo

*C/Puerta de Almodóvar s/n (957 29 29 79).* **Open** noon-4pm, 8pm-midnight Tue-Sun. **Average** €-€€. **Credit** AmEx, DC, MC, V. **Map** p209 A2.
This extremely friendly (especially the English-speaking Anglophile proprietor) tapas bar-restaurant is well patronised by locals, most of whom choose to linger in the small atmospheric bar area, laden with bullfighting photos and posters, rather than the larger dining room. Everything is excellent quality, from a simple dish of plump cracked green olives to the ominous-sounding, but delicious 'meat in sauce' (*carne en salsa*).

### Taberna Salinas

*C/Tundidores 3 (957 48 01 35).* **Open** noon-4pm, 8pm-midnight Mon-Sat. Closed Aug. **Average** €. **Credit** DC, MC, V. **Map** p209 C2.
This bustling bar and great patio restaurant with barrels of *montilla* and antique olive-wood furniture has been around since 1879. Try the excellent tapas, including fried squid, pigs' trotters and ewe's cheese. Located between Plaza de la Corredera and Calle Fernando Colón.

### Taberna Sociedad de Plateros

*C/San Francisco 6 (957 47 00 42).* **Open** noon-4pm, 8pm-midnight Tue-Sat. **Average** €€. **Credit** AmEx, DC, MC, V. **Map** p209 C3.
Many of Córdoba's old *bodegas* are run by the silversmiths' guild (Sociedad de Plateros). This airy, popular place is a great favourite of the guitarist Paco Peña, who lives around the corner. Service ranges from charming to indifferent, depending on the waiter, and you may have to be quite pushy to get a table. Low prices may tempt you to over-order the exceedingly generous *raciones*. Food is basic but good, with heavy-duty highlights such as an enormous entrecôte.

## Shopping

For general and high-street shops, head for the streets off Plaza de las Tendillas. Note: many of the smaller shops close on Saturday afternoon as well as all day Sunday.

Córdoba has a strong tradition in jewellery-making (especially in silver) and leather-working, and the handcrafted results of these traditions make great gifts. **Plata Natura** (C/Cardenal González 53, 957 49 87 18) showcases stylish jewellery from contemporary designers in a small gallery-like showroom/shop near the river. Perhaps the only place where you can still buy genuine handcrafted leather goods in Córdoba is **Meryan** (Calleja de las Flores 2, 957 48 71 65, www.meryancor.com, map B2), opened by Angel and Mercedes López-Obrero in the 1950s, and now run by their sons. Prices range from a few euros for a comb case to around a thousand for an embossed chair or trunk.

Córdoba is the gastronomic hub of Andalucía, and there are plenty of good delis. Try **Andalusí** (C/Rodriguez Marín 22, 957 48 89 61, map C2) or the family-run **Bodegas Mezquita** (C/Corregidor Luis de la Cerda 73, 957 49 81 17, www.bodegasmezquita.com, map B3). The produce market on Plaza de la Corredera (9am-1.30pm Mon-Sat) is also a good bet for picnic goodies. For something to drink, head for **La Bodega** (Calleja Herradores s/n, off C/Alfonso XII, no phone, map D/E3), a tiny, well-hidden *bodega*. The friendly owner sits sewing in the window until locals come to fill their empty bottles with wines from the barrel.

For clothes, accessories and homewares with a touch of Moorish style, head for **Bessara** (C/Rodriguez Marín 16, 957 47 44 94, map C2), off the Plaza de la Corredera; best buys include handmade ceramics and Arabic-style slippers.

## Arts & entertainment

### Film

The **Filmoteca de Andalucía** (C/Medina y Corella 5, 957 48 18 35, www.filmotecade andalucia.com, map A3) is the centre for film in Andalucía. Housed in a wonderful patioed art-house cinema, it is worth seeking out to see classic, original-language, subtitled (in Spanish, of course) films. Note: there are no screenings during July and August.

## Music, drama and dance

The **Gran Teatro** (Avenida Gran Capitán 3, 957 48 06 44, www.teatrocordoba.com, map B1) is the city's grandest performing-arts venue and hosts performances of drama, dance and music, including concerts by the Orquesta de Córdoba.

The **Festival de Córdoba-Guitarra**, held every July, attracts national and international stars to play in some of the city's most iconic sites. Concerts by flamenco, jazz and classical guitarists (such as Paco Peña, Carlos Santana and BB King) are complemented by workshops, exhibitions and films.

## Flamenco

Córdoba is the home of the modern flamenco star Paco Peña, and puts on good, reasonably authentic flamenco all year round. Look out for performances by internationally acclaimed stars at the **Gran Teatro** (*see above*), which also hosts (although only every three years, next due in 2007) the **Concurso Nacional de Arte Flamenco** competition. Next door to the tourist office, opposite the Mezquita, is **Tablao Flamenco Cardenal** (C/Torrijos 10, 957 48 31 12, shows 10.30pm Mon-Sat, tickets €18 incl

Looking north towards **Plaza del Potro**. See p212.

drink, map A3), where performances by an array of established artists are held in a high-ceilinged hall or on the patio. Book to reserve a table close to the stage.

## Sport

If you're interested in seeing a *corrida* while you're in Córdoba, details and tickets are available from the **Plaza de Toros** on Avenida Gran Via Parque (957 23 35 07, tickets from €25) to the north-west of the city. Guided tours of the bullring are also available. The city's capable football team, Córdoba, can be checked out at **El Nuevo Arcángel** stadium, east of the river (Avenida del Arcángel s/n, 957 75 19 34, www.cordobacf.com, tickets €15.50-€52).

## Where to stay

Most beds in Córdoba are found in the Judería around the Mezquita. One of the pleasures of staying here is that even the meanest *hostal* is likely to have a cute flower-filled patio. Check if your hotel has parking – a reserved space is more important than a reserved bed. It's best not to drive in Córdoba at all, or else dump your car as soon as possible. Hotel rates can soar during Semana Santa and the May fiestas. Although unfinished at the time of writing, the boutique hotel **Hospedería de Churrasco** (www.elchurrasco.com, due to open in late 2004) on Calle Romero looks like it will be an attractive and unusual addition to Córdoba's accommodation offerings.

**Note**: the hotels below are listed with the most expensive first and the cheapest last.

### NH Amistad

*Plaza de Maimonides 3 (957 42 03 35/ www.nh-hoteles.com).* **Rates** €150-€164 double. **Credit** AmEx, DC, MC, V. **Map** p209 A2.
Built on the southern edge of the Judería into the old city walls, this is a quiet, cool and stylish hotel. The large patio is a calm, airy place in which to relax over a coffee, and, when it's too hot for sightseeing, there's a plunge pool and sun terrace on the third floor of the neighbouring building to enjoy. Bedrooms are a touch corporate but luxurious, and breakfast is a buffet feast, with a chef on hand to cook to order.

### Hotel Casa de los Azulejos

*C/Fernando Colón 5 (957 47 00 00/www.casa delosazulejos.com).* **Rates** (incl breakfast) €54-€96 single; €89-€128 double; €112-€166 suite. **Credit** AmEx, MC, V. **Map** p209 C2.
One of only two boutique hotels in Córdoba, Casa de los Azulejos is a stunningly converted *palacio* with eight individually decorated rooms overlooking leafy patios. Original features, including a majestic staircase, carved woodwork and Sevillian wall tiles, have been complemented with playful modern

touches, such as colourful bathrooms. The hotel also has a South American-Andalucían fusion restaurant and a Mexican *cantina*.

### Hotel Posada de Vallina

*C/Corregidor Luis de la Cerda 83 (957 49 87 50/ www.hotelvallina.com).* **Rates** (incl breakfast) €70-€86 single; €86-€107 double. **Credit** AmEx, DC, MC, V.
This historic inn on the east side of the Mezquita once housed the labourers who built part of the old mosque, and Columbus is rumoured to have stayed in room 104. Compared to its colourful history and the atmospheric breakfast patio, the rooms can seem a bit bland. However, they're good-sized and well-equipped.

### Hotel Lola

*C/Romero 3 (957 20 03 05/www.hotelconencanto lola.com).* **Rates** (incl breakfast) €80-€115 double. **Credit** AmEx, DC, MC, V. **Map** p209 A2.
Located in the heart of the Judería, with a roof terrace that overlooks the Mezquita's bell tower, this traditional Córdoban house is a charming and unusual small hotel with friendly staff. The eight individual guest rooms feel like old movie-sets, with clusters of antiques and baroque touches.

### Hostal Lineros

*C/Lineros 38 (957 48 25 17/www.hostallineros38. com).* **Rates** €32-€51 single; €51-€58 double; €64-€83 triple; €83-€96 quad; €77-€96 suite. **Credit** MC, V. **Map** p209 C3.
This good-value *hostal* features lovely Moorish detailing. The two internal patios contain a *Salon de Té*, decorated with leather pouffes, deep-cushioned

**Hotel Casa de los Azulejos.**

seating and a stained-glass ceiling. Splash out and stay in Room 8, an atmospheric suite with a wooden four-poster bed, two further beds and a jacuzzi.

### Hotel Mezquita

*Plaza Santa Catalina 1 (957 47 55 85/hotelmezquita @wanadoo.es).* **Rates** €27-€51 single; €44-€100 double. **Credit** AmEx, MC, V. **Map** p209 B3.

A superbly located two-star hotel in a restored 16th-century mansion right by the Mezquita (at the end of Calle M Rucker). Room 4 is a nice, light corner room overlooking the Mezquita walls.

### Hotel González

*C/Manriquez 3 (957 47 98 19/hotelgonzalez@ wanadoo.es).* **Rates** €27-€48 single; €42-€97 double. **Credit** AmEx, MC, V. **Map** p209 A3.

This popular hotel near the Mezquita is housed in a restored 16th-century *palacio*, once home to relations of Córdoban painter Julio Romero de Torres (*see p210*). The rooms are decorated with reproduction antique furniture and heavy curtains. Breakfast is served in a traditional, plant-filled patio.

### Hostal Séneca

*C/Conde y Luque 7 (957 47 32 34/hostalseneca@ erasmas.com).* **Rates** (incl breakfast) €22-€34 single; €39-€47 double. **Credit** V. **Map** p209 A/B2.

This friendly, old-fashioned *hostal* is a very popular and cheap place to stay, with gorgeous stained-glass windows on the first floor and a delightful patio at ground level. The cheaper rooms don't have en suite bathrooms. You may need to book well ahead.

### Hotel, Hostal y Apartamentos Maestre

*C/Romero Barros 4 & 6 (957 47 24 10/www.hotel maestre.com).* **Rates** *Hostal* €35 double. *Hotel* €47 double. *Apartments* €50 (2 people); €54 (3 people); €58 (4 people). **Credit** AmEx, DC, MC, V. **Map** p209 C3.

The Maestre is a bit of muddle – stark, modern marble-and-chrome reception rooms clash with pleasant leafy patios. There's a hotel with well-equipped but rather dully decorated rooms, a *hostal* with a touch more character and (your best bet) some smart apartments fantastically situated on Plaza del Potro.

### Hostal El Reposo de Bagdad

*C/Fernández Ruano 11 (957 20 28 54/www.hostal bagdad.en.eresmas.com).* **Rates** €20 single; €33-€36 double. **Credit** MC, V. **Map** p209 B3.

This new *hostal* near the Puerta de Almodóvar, offers characterful, comfortable en suite rooms at a bargain price. The upper rooms are calm and comfy, with white walls and bed linen. Two rooms can be used together as an 'apartment' by up to five people. The ground floor has beautiful (though dark) Moorish-style tiled bedrooms, a leafy patio and a tea room.

### Hostal El Portillo

*C/Cabezas 2 (957 47 20 91/angelquintero@ tiscali.es).* **Rates** €18 single; €30-€35 double; €45-€49 triple. **No credit cards**. **Map** p209 B3.

A plain but homely *hostal*, with touches of character (such as roof-tile lampshades) and a friendly atmosphere, tucked away in the warren of streets north of the Mezquita. Room 2 is a double with a small balcony overlooking the quaint and quiet street. Other rooms face the small, flower-filled internal patio. The cheaper rooms have no air-conditioning or en suite bathrooms.

## Resources

### Internet

*Odisea, Plaza Mármol de Bañuelos 1, off C/Diego de León (957 47 38 10).* **Open** 10am-11pm Mon-Sat; 4-11pm Sun. **Map** p209 C1.

### Police station

*Avenida Doctor Fleming 2 (957 59 45 00).* **Map** p209 A2.

### Post office

*Correos Jefatura Provincial, C/José Cruz Conde 15 (957 49 63 42).* **Open** 8.30am-8.30pm Mon-Fri; 9.30am-2pm Sat. **Map** p209 B/C1.

### Tourist information

*Palacio de Exposiciones y Congresos, C/Torrijos 10 (957 47 12 35/otcordoba@andalucia.org).* **Open** 9.30am-7pm daily. **Map** p209 A3.

*C/Angel de Saavedra 4 (957 49 16 78/ www.turiscordoba.es).* **Open** *June-Oct* 9.30am-1.30pm, 6-9pm Mon-Sat; 10am-2pm hols. *Nov-May* 9.30am-1.30pm, 5-8pm Mon-Sat; 10am-2pm hols. **Map** p209 B2.

## Getting there

### By bus

The main bus station is at Plaza de las Tres Culturas (957 40 40 40), next to the AVE train station (map off A1). Times change frequently, so check with the relevant bus companies. Alsina Graells (957 27 81 00, www.alsinagraells.es) runs buses between Córdoba and Granada (3hrs), Málaga (3hrs) and Sevilla (2hrs), with less frequent connections and extensions to other destinations, including Cádiz, Algeciras and the Costa del Sol. Bacoma (957 27 98 60) runs one bus a day between Córdoba and Alicante and three a day to Barcelona and Valencia. Secorbús (902 22 92 92) runs about five buses a day between Madrid and Córdoba.

### By train

Córdoba's station is at Avenida de América (map off A1), 30 minutes' walk west of the Mezquita; there's also a ticket office in town at Ronda de los Tejares 10 near Plaza de Colón (map C/D1). The AVE high-speed train links Córdoba with Sevilla (45min) and Madrid (2hrs). There are about 20 trains a day in both directions. The Talgo train links Córdoba and Málaga (6 times daily, 2hrs). There are four trains a day to Barcelona, including two sleepers. There are also standard daily services to Cádiz (4 trains, 3hrs), Málaga (10 trains, 2hrs 15mins) and other Andalucían cities. For train information, contact RENFE (902 24 02 02, www.renfe.es).

**Córdoba Province**

# The Guadalquivir Valley & North of Córdoba

The historically key river valley and a remote, untamed wilderness.

The 'Cathedral of the Sierra',
**Hinojosa del Duque**. *See p220.*

Córdoba Province

## The Guadalquivir valley

Twenty-five kilometres (16 miles) west of Córdoba city along the A431 lies **Almodóvar del Río**, dominated by its castle. Originally built in the eighth century, but much altered and restored since (most of it is now an ugly neo-Gothic pastiche), it was one of the most formidable fortresses in the region. There is a great view across the Guadalquivir valley from the precipitous battlements.

A further 30 kilometres (19 miles) west, **Palma del Río**, originally a strategic Roman settlement, lies on the border with Sevilla province. Some of the town's 12th-century walls survive, but the real attraction is the 15th-century monastery that has been converted into the **Hospedería de San Francisco**, a luxurious hotel (*see p219*). Pop in for a drink. Palma is the birthplace of the famously reckless matador Manuel Benítez, better known as El Cordobés.

Heading north from Palma del Río, the CO140 passes through a beautiful slice of countryside, where prairie-like fields are interrupted by old wooden bridges and water towers. After 17 kilometres (11 miles), you reach **Hornachuelos**, a small, whitewashed village balanced on steep cliffs around the ruins of its old Moorish castle.

From here, the CO142 enters the **Parque Natural de la Sierra de Hornachuelos**, with a bumpy track leading to the gorgeous **Monasterio de Santa María de los Angeles**; it's privately owned but worth a look from the outside. Much of the park is made up of gentle slopes covered in holm and gall oaks, pine and cork, and broken only by modest mountains (the highest is just 673 metres/2,208 feet). It is home to Andalucía's second largest colony of black vultures, but more common spottings are of Imperial and Royal eagles. Continue on the CO142 to eventually reach **San Calixto**, a community of around 20 Carmelite nuns, who sell home-made cakes and biscuits through a quirky, revolving window.

Another scenic drive can be enjoyed by taking the rural A433, nine kilometres (six miles) west of Almodóvar del Río at Posadas, which curves north for 63 kilometres (39 miles) to join the main N432 from Córdoba. The stunning journey takes you from the fertile lowlands to heights where cork gives way to fir.

The attractive town of **Montoro**, 42 kilometres (26 miles) east of Córdoba city on the A4-E5 motorway, sits atop a hill overlooking the **Puente de la Doñadas**. It is said that the bridge, which took 50 years to build (it was finished in 1480), was only completed because the local women sold their jewellery to raise the necessary funds (hence its name, 'bridge of the lay sisters'). The prominent tower belongs to the 15th-century church of **San Bartolomé** (open hours of services) on the central Plaza de España. In the same square, the old ducal palace (now the town hall) houses the tourist office and the **Museo Arqueológico Municipal**.

For a taste of big-time kitsch, seek out **Casa de las Conchas** (C/Grajas 17), a house decorated entirely in shells that have been collected by the owner Francisco del Río.

He will proudly show off his home for a small fee. Montoro is also the site of one of the oldest churches in the province (on C/B Comacho, just north of the square), the 13th-century **Santa María de la Mota** (open hours of services).

From Montoro there is a delightful route through the Sierra Morena on the CO414 west to **Adamuz**, a good-sized village with a laid-back atmosphere. Alternatively, the N420 north goes through the western edge of the beautiful **Parque Natural de la Sierra de Cardeña y Montoro**, with views to the peaks of the Sierra de Andújar. The **Presa de Martín Gonzalo**, 17 kilometres (11 miles) north-east of Montoro, is a good picnic spot by a lake. If you want to overnight in the area, stop off in **Cardeña** (33 kilometres/20 miles north of Montoro), which has a fair selection of hotels and bars.

A few kilometres south-west of Montoro in **Pedro Abad** you'll find the first mosque founded in Spain since the time of Moors. The foundation stone of the Ahmadiyya sect's Basharat Mosque was laid in 1980 (though Marbella's mosque was completed first).

### Castillo de Almodóvar del Río

*Almodóvar del Río (957 63 51 16/www.castillo dealmodovar.com).* **Open** 11am-2.30pm, 4-8pm daily. **Admission** €4.50; €2.50 concessions. **No credit cards**.

### Museo Arqueológico Municipal

*Plaza Santa Maria de la Mota s/n, Montoro (957 16 00 89).* **Open** 11am-1pm Sat, Sun. **Admission** free.

## Where to stay, eat & drink

In Almodóvar del Rio, the unfussy **La Taverna** (C/Antonio Machado 24, 957 71 36 84, closed Sun in July, Mon Sept-June & all Aug, €€-€€€) has a deserved reputation for posh home cooking.

In Palma del Rio stay at the stylish, stark but luxurious **Hospedería de San Francisco** (Avenida Pio XII 35, 957 71 01 83, www.casas ypalacios.com, double €84-€111). The hotel is a converted 15th-century monastery with an exquisite swimming pool and a good restaurant (closed Sun and all Aug, €€-€€€).

Budget travellers could try the good-value **El Alamo** (Carretera Comarcal 141, 957 64 04 76, www.hornaocio.com, double €39-€59), eight kilometres (five miles) outside Hornachuelos.

If you stop in Montoro, **Bar Yepez** (Plaza del Charco 4, 957 16 01 23) is a good watering hole and tapas joint, and the attractive neo-Moorish **Casino** (off Plaza M Benitez) is a good place to try no-nonsense tapas like pigs' brains.

If you crave tranquillity and a remote rural setting, head for **Hacienda La Colora** (C0414, km16, 957 33 60 77, www.lacolora.com, 2-person *casita* €65-€75), an 18th-century

former olive oil-producing farm, now converted into a hotel, offering studios and apartments. There are lovely walks around the estate, plus a pool and restaurant.

## Resources

### Tourist information

**Montoro** *Plaza de España 8 (957 16 00 89).* **Open** 9am-3pm Mon-Fri; 10am-1pm Sat. **Palma del Río** *C/Cardenal Potocarrerro s/n (957 64 43 70).* **Open** *Mid June-mid Sept* 10am-2pm Tue-Sat; 11am-2pm Sun. *Mid Sept-mid June* 5-8pm Tue-Sat; 11am-2pm Sun.

## North of Córdoba

The wild landscapes north of Córdoba – mountainous in the west and east, broad and gently rolling in the north – stand out from the rest of Andalucía. It's poor, brutally beautiful and sparsely populated, with echoes of the endless, untamed spaces of the American West.

The main N432 runs north-west from Córdoba into the high Sierra Morena and on to Extremadura. After 50 kilometres (31 miles), it's worth taking the N502 north on a lengthy detour towards the far north. There's not a lot to do up here, but the driving is magnificent.

At Alcaracejos, a right turn takes you after 11 kilometres (seven miles) to the large, busy town of **Pozoblanco** – a good place to catch bullfights. The increasingly flat landscape around here can seem repetitive, but there's a worthwhile excursion on the A437 north-east for ten kilometres (six miles) to the small town of **Pedroche**, which has a Roman bridge and a fine 16th-century Gothic church.

Springtime in northern Córdoba.

Carrying straight on along the N502 at Alcaracejos brings you after 25 kilometres (16 miles) to the pretty village of **Santa Eufemia**, surrounded by fine walking country and topped by a ruined Moorish castle. The 15th-century church of **La Encarnación** (open hours of services) on the Plaza Mayor is also worth a look.

A left turn at Alcaracejos onto the A420 leads you through a wide-open landscape of olive groves, oaks and farmland, and, after 20 kilometres (12.5 miles), you arrive in **Hinojosa del Duque**, with views to the distant mountains. Hinojosa is a fly-blown workaday town, but its so-called 'Cathedral of the Sierra', **San Juan Bautista** (open hours of services) is well worth a look. Largely Gothic-Renaissance in style, it has a portal by Hernán Ruiz (who designed the cathedral within the Mezquita in Córdoba), a fine Mudéjar stuccoed ceiling, a baroque altar and some *trompe l'oeil* carving on the window to the left of the main door. There are a couple of tapas places in the same square.

East of here is an area known as **Los Pedroches**. The Moors referred to it as the 'land of acorns' and it's still densely covered with holm oaks. The acorns are essential food for the small brown-black pigs that produce the province's famed (and expensive) *jamón ibérico* (sometimes known as *pata negra*, from the pigs' black trotters). It's very dark in colour, compared to the lighter pink of *jamón serrano*, and very tender, with a rich, sweet, oaky taste. There are a number of other quality pork products made in the region. Red and black blood sausages known as *chine canas* are made in Fuente Obejuna; fine *salchichón* (salami) and *chorizo* (paprika sausage) are produced in Pozoblanco, and a blood sausage mixed with onion and *chorizo* is the speciality of Pedroche.

Ten minutes' drive north of Hinojosa on the A420 is the little town of **Belalcázar**, with its wonderfully ravaged castle on the outskirts. **El Castillo de Sotomayor**, dominated by an eccentric 50-metre (164-foot) keep, was built in the mid 15th century on Moorish foundations. Alas, it isn't open to the public, but is still worth seeing from the outside. Afterwards, stop for a drink at one of the *tabernas* on the main square.

South of Hinojosa, back on the N432, is the small and uninviting town of **Bélmez**, distinguished by its dramatically sited Moorish castle high up on a rocky outcrop. Eight kilometres (five miles) to the north-west is by far the largest settlement in northern Córdoba, **Peñarroya-Pueblonuevo**; it's a busy, unremarkable industrial town.

Fifteen kilometres (nine miles) west of here is a more interesting spot, historically at least. **Fuente Obejuna**'s moment came in 1476 when the villagers dragged their

tyrannical lord from his palace and hacked him to pieces in the town square. The event was immortalised in a play by the 17th-century playwright Lope de Vega (Lorca directed a production in the village in 1933). Sadly, more than 500 years later, little has changed, with the majority of the local population split between a handful of landowners and a mass of poor day labourers. There's a neglected art deco mansion in the town, **Casa Cardena**, which seems utterly out of keeping with its surroundings.

From Fuente Obejuna, the wild, lonely and stunning A447 winds through the mountains into northern Sevilla province (*see p200*).

## Where to stay, eat & drink

Accommodation in this area tends to be cheap and simple. In Bélmez, **Hostal Javi** (C/Córdoba 31, 957 57 30 99, double €43) is good value, with clean rooms around a pretty patio. In Belalcázar, **Hostal La Bolera** (C/Padre Torrero 17, 957 14 63 00, raulbolera@hotmail.com, double €34-€38) is a no-nonsense *hostal* with uninspiring rooms, but an appealing restaurant serving good food. A more charming option is the **Hostal La Paloma** in Santa Eufemia (N502, km2, 957 15 82 42, double €26), where some rooms have balconies with mountain views. Delicious home-cooked food and cheap tapas are served in the bar area. Just down the road is the **Bar Las Catalanas** (N502, 957 15 82 69, €) for snacks. Outside Pozoblanco is the delightful **Cortijo Palomar de la Morra** (Avenida Argentina 8, C0421, km3, 957 77 15 85, mobile 678 42 89 23, www.palomar delamorra.com, from €239 for 4-6 people). Simple, traditional bedrooms share use of a homely communal lounge and a swimming pool – a luxury for these parts.

## Resources

### Tourist information

**Fuente Obejuna** *C/Luis Rodríguez 27 (957 58 49 00)*. **Open** 10am-2pm Mon-Fri.
**Santa Eufemia** *Ayuntamiento, Plaza Mayor 1 (957 15 82 29)*. **Open** 9am-2.30pm Mon-Fri.

### By bus

Buses run from Córdoba to the main towns in the region, but few head in to the north. For information, call 957 40 40 40.

### By train

Six trains a day run from Córdoba to Sevilla via Palma del Río. There are no rail services in the north of Córdoba province.

# South of Córdoba

Indulge yourself in wine and olive country.

## Montilla & around

South of Córdoba, the N331 branches off the A4-E5 motorway to Sevilla on what has been dubbed the *Ruta del Vino* (Wine Route) by the tourist board. It passes through wide, rolling sweeps of wheat fields before reaching picturesque castle-topped **Montemayor**, perched on the highest hill in the area, with stunning views from the town's *mirador*. In Plaza de la Constitución is a miniature copy of the Alhambra's Fountain of the Lions, and a fascinating stash of local archaeological finds in the **Museo Arqueológico Ulía**. A five-minute drive south-west from here brings you to **La Rambla**, famed for its pottery. Plenty of shops sell the spouted drinking vessels known as *botijos*. Around here, olive trees and vines start to dominate the undulating landscape.

Twelve kilometres (7.5 miles) east of La Rambla is **Montilla**, site of the crucial Battle of Munda in 45 BC, where Julius Caesar beat the supporters of Pompey, bringing to an end the Roman civil war and giving Caesar authority, albeit briefly, over the entire Roman Empire. Apart from the obvious temptation of its superb wines, the town is not hugely appealing, though it does have a fascinating small museum, the **Casa Museo del Inca Garcilaso**, dedicated to the Hispano-Inca son of a *conquistador*, who chronicled Inca civilisation in the 16th century. Also in Montilla, the church of **Santa Clara** (open hours of services) has a fine late-Gothic façade and paintings by Alonso Cano.

If you want to visit a *bodega*, try **Bodegas Alvear**, one of the major producers. Montilla wine has long lived in the shadow of its more famous cousin, sherry. Unlike its coastal relation, Montilla (lacking an outlet to the sea and, thus, easy shipping abroad) is little-known internationally, yet many of its wines are superb and deserve to be better appreciated (*see p43*).

Ten kilometres (six miles) south of Montilla is **Aguilar de la Frontera**, an attractive town where the striking and unusual octagonal Plaza de San José (designed by the Salamanca architect Vincente Gutierrez in 1806, and inspired by a similar square in Archidona) has managed to retain its dignity, despite being used as a car park. Check out the impressive tower, **Torre Civil del Reloj**, nearby, or, for the best views, head for the **Peñon de Moro**, the site of the old castle. Close by is the church of **Santa María del Soterraño** (open hours of services), which dates originally from the Middle Ages, but was replaced in 1530 by a Gothic-Mudéjar building.

South-west of Aguilar, off the A309, is the tranquil **Laguna de Zóñar**, a protected area that's home to many migratory birds, including flamingoes, while another ten minutes' drive further on is the town of **Puente-Genil**, where you can sample the fine local quince jam.

Turning east off the N331 at Monturque on to the A342 takes you, after a fine 12-kilometre (7.5-mile) drive through olive groves, to **Cabra**. The pleasant town (birthplace of realist novelist Juan Valera) was an important Roman colony, a Visigothic bishopric and a provincial capital under the Moors, as related in its **Museo Arqueológico Municipal**. The spectacular church of **La Asunción** (open hours of services) near the castle is converted from a mosque, and retains 44 red marble columns, reminiscent of the Mezquita. Today, Cabra is big on candle-making and festivals. It has a spectacular Easter Sunday extravaganza, followed by its own patio festival at the beginning of May. On 4 September the Virgen de la Sierra is brought into town for a week-long celebration, including cultural events, *corridas* and a flower fight. For the rest of the

Priego de Córdoba's Barrio de la Villa. See p223.

year, she rests in her sanctuary, off the A340 towards Priego de Córdoba. Off the same road is **La Fuente del Rio**, a natural spring with a series of swimming pools and a picnic area.

South from Cabra, on the main N331, is the sizeable town of **Lucena**, a furniture centre with American-style warehouse showrooms on its outskirts and a real baroque treat at its heart. Until the 12th century, Lucena was an independent Jewish republic within the Córdoban Caliphate, and, in 1483, the site of a battle that resulted in the capture of Boadil, the last Moorish ruler of Granada. Today it is one of the wealthiest towns (per capita) in Spain. The church of **San Mateo** (open hours of services) on Plaza Nueva has an 18th-century octagonal *sagrario* chapel, whose central shrine is crammed with flying cherubs and exquisite plasterwork – it's one of the masterpieces of the Andalucían baroque. Climb uphill to the **Sanctuario de la Virgen de Araceli**, where there is a bar selling excellent home-produced *charcuterie*, and wonderful views.

The A331 runs from Lucena south-east for 20 kilometres (12.5 miles) towards **Rute**. The appeal of the village's Moorish castle and baroque church is eclipsed by the attraction of the potent *anís* spirit that is distilled here. Many *bodegas* offer a taste, while the **Museo Anís** explains the manufacture and history of the spirit, followed by a chance to sample and buy the stuff at the end.

The Spanish are not known for their tender-hearted attitude to animals, but just beyond the museum is the **Sanctuario de Burros** (Donkey Sanctuary), the first one of its kind in Spain, which was set up by a local draper in 1989, and can be visited.

For energetic visitors there's a scenic 18-kilometre (11-mile) walk from Rute around the **Embalse de Iznájar** (the largest reservoir in Andalucia), and on to the lovely little town of Iznájar. **Iznájar** sits high above the reservoir, near the Granada province border, and has an attractive ruined **Alcazaba** dating from the eighth century, and the church of **Santiago** (open hours of services), built inside its walls in the 16th century; call at the *Ayuntamiento* to collect the key for both. Canoes and dinghies can be hired from the sailing club. A sleepy place today, Iznájar was the setting for an 1861 peasants' revolt against the landowners; inevitably, it was swiftly and brutally crushed.

### Bodegas Alvear

*Avenida de María Auxiliadora 1, Montilla (957 66 40 14/www.alvear.es).* **Open** *July, Aug* 10am-2pm Mon-Fri; 11am-2pm Sat. *Sept-June* 10am-2pm, 5-7pm Mon-Fri; 11am-2pm Sat. **Admission** €2.95 Mon-Fri, €3.95 Sat; €1 Mon-Fri, €2 Sat concessions. **No credit cards.** Recommended to call in advance.

### Casa Museo del Inca Garcilaso

*C/Capitán Alonso de Varga 3, Montilla (957 65 24 62).* **Open** *July, Aug* 10am-2pm Mon-Fri; 11am-2pm Sat, Sun. *Sept-June* 10am-2pm, 5-7pm Mon-Fri; 11am-2pm Sat, Sun. **Admission** free.

### Museo Anís

*Paseo del Fresno s/n, Rute (957 53 81 43/54/ www.museodelanis.com).* **Open** *June-Aug* 8am-3pm Mon-Fri; 11am-2pm Sat, Sun (call in advance at weekends). *Sept-May* 9am-2pm, 4-7pm Mon-Fri; 11am-2pm Sat, Sun. Ring bell if closed. **Admission** free.

### Museo Arqueológico Municipal

*C/Martín Belda 23, Cabra (957 52 01 10/ cultura@cabra.com).* **Open** 10am-2pm, 6-9pm Mon-Fri; 11.30am-2pm Sat. **Admission** free.

### Museo Arqueológico Ulía

*Plaza de la Constitución s/n, Montemayor (957 38 42 53).* **Open** 9.30-11am, 7-8.30pm Mon, Tue, Thur-Sun. **Admission** free.

### Sanctuario de Burros

*follow road from Museo Anís towards campsite (957 53 20 32/mobile 610 84 17 20).* **Open** by appointment; call in advance. **Admission** free.

## Where to stay & eat

In Aguilar de la Frontera, the basic but cheap **Hostal Queen III** (C/Pescaderias 6, off Plaza de San José, 957 66 02 22, double €42-€53, restaurant €) has a bar and a simple choice of food. For slightly more fancy Andalucían fare, try **Restaurante Guillermo** (C/Moralejo 47, 957 66 00 48, €). The popular **Gran Bar** (C/Andalucía 23, no phone, €) also serves tapas.

In Puente-Genil, **Café Bar El Poncho** (Plaza España 9, 957 60 12 35, closed Mon, €) serves generous portions of basic, hearty fare.

There are some cheap *hostales* in Montilla, but just outside town is the lovely eight-room **Finca Buytrón** (C/Gran Capitán 24, 957 65 01 52, www.fincabuytron.com, double €60), a homely, rural farmhouse dating back to 1567, which has an outdoor pool. The finca is often rented out completely, so call in advance if you only want a room. For food, try the award-winning **Las Camachas** (Avenida de Europa 3, 957 65 00 04, €€-€€€), which serves fine local specialities and has a bargain-priced *menú*.

In Lucena, the 28-room **Husa Santo Domingo** is housed in the converted convent of Santo Domingo (C/Juan Jiménez Cuenca 13, 957 51 11 00, www.husa.es, double €96-€114). Much of the building's original character has been lost, but it's luxurious, in a predictable way.

The **María Luisa** (A331, km22, 957 53 80 96, www.zercahoteles.com, double €64-€80) is a good-value modern roadside hotel just south of Rute, with 30 rooms, a small indoor pool, jacuzzi and sauna.

Córdoba Province

## Resources

### Tourist information

**Cabra** *C/Santa Rosalía 2 (957 52 01 10/ www.cabra.net).* **Open** *June-Sept* 9am-2pm Tue-Sun. *Oct-May* 10.30am-1.30pm, 6.30-8.30pm Tue-Sun.

**Laguna de Zóñar** *9km south-west of Aguilar on the A309 road to Puente-Genil (957 33 52 52).* **Open** *Apr-June* 9am-2pm Tue-Fri, Sun; 9am-2pm, 6-8pm Sat. *July-Sept* 9am-2pm, 6-8pm Sat, Sun & hols. *Oct-Mar* 9am-2pm, 4-6pm Tue-Sun.

**Lucena** *Castillo del Moral, Pasaje Cristo del Amor 1 (957 51 32 82/www.turlucena.com).* **Open** *Mid June-Sept* 9am-2pm, 6-10pm Tue-Fri; 11am-2pm, 7-9pm Sat, Sun. *Oct-mid June* 9am-2pm, 5-9pm Tue-Fri; 11am-2pm, 6-8pm Sat, Sun.

**Montilla** *C/Capitán Alonso de Vergas 3 (957 65 24 62/www.turismomontilla.com).* **Open** *July, Aug* 10am-2pm Mon-Fri; 11am-2pm Sat, Sun. *Sept-June* 10am-2pm, 5-7pm Mon-Fri; 11am-2pm Sat, Sun.

**Puente-Genil** *Casa del Ciudadano, Paseo Antonio Fernandez Diaz s/n (957 60 91 61).* **Open** *Mid June-mid Sept* 9am-3pm Mon-Fri. *Mid Sept-mid June* 10am-2pm, 5-8pm Mon-Fri.

## Priego de Córdoba & around

From Córdoba, the N432 leads south-east, along what has been dubbed the *Ruta del Aceite* (Oil Route), towards the heights of the Sierra Subbética. After ten or so minutes' driving, the stunning fortress of **Torres Cabrera** lurches into view above the wheat plains and olive groves, setting the tone for further Moorish castle-topped towns like beautiful **Espejo** and **Castro del Río**. The latter is well known for its traditional olive-wood furniture, and the old part of town, La Villa, is very attractive.

Twenty kilometres (12.5 miles) south-east of Castro is **Baena**, famed for the quality of its olive oil. The town's premier producer is **Nuñez de Prado**, a family-owned concern that has been in the business since 1795; call in advance to visit its palatial factory. For those interested in ancient oil production, the **Museo Arqueológico** is worth a visit. The same building also houses the **Museo de Semana Santa**, which explains Baena's unusual Easter ritual in which hundreds of brightly dressed drummers in plumed helmets, divided into rival teams known as the *Coliblancos* and the *Colinegros*, try to outdo each other in volume and stamina. Elsewhere, check out the 18th-century arcaded *almacén* (warehouse) on Plaza de la Constitución, which houses a cultural centre and one of the best tapas bars in town.

Beyond Baena, the mountains of the **Parque Natural de la Sierra Subbética** (32,000 hectares/124 square miles) beckon, and the A316 climbs up to the most picturesque village in the region. **Zuheros** is a cluster of beautiful whitewashed houses clinging to the cliffs, topped by a Moorish castle with spectacular views.

Nearby, **La Cueva de los Murciélagos** (Cave of the Bats) doesn't actually shelter any bats, but you'll see some incredible stalactites and stalagmites on the guided tour, which describes the neolithic paintings and human remains that were found here. The caves are approached via a hair-raisingly spectacular road up from Zuheros following the Canyon de Baillón to the rocky, wild scrub landscape that is a dominant feature of the Subbética.

Nearby **Luque** is also very pretty, with a castle dating back to the ninth century perched high above the town. From here, wind your way along the CV230 to Priego de Córdoba.

**Priego de Córdoba** is a fine town with a whiff of sophistication about it, and sits on a rocky outcrop looking south-west up to the highest mountain in the province, **La Tiñosa** (1,570 metres/5,150 feet). The town's glorious churches (all open 11am-1pm, 5-7pm daily) have earned Priego the sobriquet of capital of Córdoban baroque architecture. The main ones to check out are the church of **La Asunción** (on Plaza Abad Palomino), with its awesome sacristy and golden balcony, created in 1784, and the church of **La Aurora** (Carrera de Álvarez), which has a wedding-cake façade. The magnificence of Priego's churches was made possible by the boom in silk production in the town during the 18th century. The main monument to the industry is the **Fuente del Rey** on Calle Rio, a fountain with 139 water spouts surrounding a statue of Neptune.

Beyond the much-altered Moorish castle lies a maze of winding alleys that form the **Barrio de la Villa**, which dates back to Moorish times. The lanes are united by the Balcón de Aldarve, an elevated promenade with magnificent views. The Paseo de Colón, a quiet shady walkway and ornamental garden, shares the same view. For a better understanding of Priego's history, check out the local **Museo Histórico Municipal**, which displays local paleolithic, Roman and Moorish remains. In the Plaza de la Constitución is a monument to Niceto Alcalá Zamora, first president of the Spanish Republic (1931-36), who was born here. His home on Calle Rio doubles as the town tourist office and museum (same hours).

Heading west from Priego, the CV220 leads to the small village of **Carcabuey** with its Gothic-Renaissance church of **La Asunción** (open times of services). Further south you'll pass through some of the prettiest scenery in the Subbética en route to the small village of **Los Villares**, where there are lots of signposted walks to suit all abilities.

**Córdoba Province**

The castle at **Zuheros**. See p223.

### Cueva de los Murciélagos

*Zuheros (957 69 45 45/www.cuevadelos*
*murcielagos.com).* **Open** (Guided tours only)
*Apr-Sept* noon, 5.30pm Mon-Fri; 11am, 12.30pm,
2pm, 5.30pm, 6.30pm Sat, Sun. *Oct-Mar* noon,
5.30pm Mon-Fri; 11am, 12.30pm, 2pm, 4pm, 5.30pm
Sat, Sun. **Admission** €4.40. **No credit cards.**
Call a day in advance to book.

### Museo Arqueológico

*Mirador, Zuheros (957 69 45 45).* **Open** *Apr-Sept*
10am-2pm, 5-7pm daily. *Oct-May* 10am-2pm; 4-6pm
daily. **Tours** noon, 5.30pm Mon-Fri; 11am, 12.30pm,
2pm, 5.30pm, 6.30pm Sat, Sun. *Oct-May* noon, 4.30pm
Mon-Fri; 11am, 12.30pm, 2pm, 4.30pm, 5.30pm Sat,
Sun. **Admission** €1.80 (includes guided tour of
castle). **No credit cards.**

### Museo Arqueológico & Museo de Semana Santa

*Casa de la Tercia, C/Santo Domingo de*
*Henares 5, just off Plaza de la Constitución,*
*Baena (957 67 19 46).* **Open** 11am-2pm, 6-8pm
Mon-Sun. **Admission** €2; €1.50 concessions.
**No credit cards.**

### Museo Histórico Municipal

*Carrera de las Monjas 16, Priego de Córdoba*
*(957 54 09 47).* **Open** 10am-1pm, 6-8.30pm Tue-Fri;
10am-1.30pm, 5-7.30pm Sat; 10am-1.30pm Sun.
**Admission** free.

### Nuñez de Prado

*Avenida de Cervantes 15, Baena (957 67 01 41).*
**Open** *July-Sept* 8am-3pm Mon-Fri. *Oct-June* 9am-
2pm, 4-6.30pm. Phone 3-4 days ahead to arrange a
tour. **Admission** free.

## Where to stay & eat

The best hotel in Baena is **La Casa del
Grande** (Avenida de Cervantes 35, 957 67 19
05, double €80-€103, restaurant €€), a grand,
faintly Gothic pile, with large, airy rooms and
a very good restaurant. For a gastronomic treat,

eat under the stone-vaulted ceiling at **Mesón
Casa del Monte** (Plaza de la Constitución s/n,
957 67 16 75, closed Mon, €€). Try the *habas
'mata' con jamón* (beans, ham and eggs).

In Zuheros, the modern **Hotel Zuhayra**
(C/Mirador 10, 957 69 46 93, www.zuheros.com,
double €48, restaurant €€) is reasonably priced
and well situated, with a good restaurant.

Three kilometres (two miles) north-west
of Priego is **Hotel Huerta de las Palomas**
(CP99, km3, 957 72 03 05, www.zerca
hoteles.com, double €78-€96), a tranquil spot
in the heart of the Sierra, with a pool, sauna
and first-class restaurant (€€); it's an ideal
base for hiking.

In Priego itself there are some basic hotels,
including the good-value **Hostal Rafi** (C/Isabel
la Católica 4, 957 54 07 49, www.hostalrafi.net,
double €32-€38), which has clean, air-
conditioned rooms and a restaurant/bar.
The best restaurant in town is **Restaurante
Río** (C/Rio 7, 957 54 00 74, closed every other
Tuesday, €€), where the speciality is *collejas*
(a type of chard) and the English translation of
the menu is one of the funniest you'll ever see
(numerous dishes feature 'scum'); below it is a
lively bar. Another top spot for food is **Balcón
de Adarve** (Paseo de Colombia 36, 957 54 70
75, closed Mon, €€), which has a tapas bar and
terrace restaurant with great views.

South-west of Priego de Córdoba on the
CV220 is the **Posada la Niña Margarita**
(Aldea Los Villares, 5km from Carcabuey, 957
70 40 54, www.casasdelasubbetica.com, double
€40, cottage for 4 €50), a delightful old house
with a pool, surrounded by self-catering cottages;
it makes another great base for walking.

## Resources

### Tourist information

**Parque Natural de la Sierra Subbética** *Centro
de Visitantes, A340, km57, Cabra (957 33 40 34).*
**Open** 6-8pm Fri; 10am-2pm, 6-8pm Sat, Sun.
**Priego de Córdoba** *C/Rio 33 (957 70 06 25/
www.aytopriegodecordoba.es).* **Open** 10am-1.30pm,
5-7.30pm Tue-Sat; 10am-1.30pm Sun.
**Zuheros** *C/Nueva 1 (957 69 45 45).* **Open** 10am-
2pm, 5-8pm Mon-Fri; 10am-3pm Sat, Sun.

## Getting there

### By bus

Several bus companies run services between the
main towns, mainly during the morning. For info,
call the bus station in Córdoba (957 40 40 40).

### By train

The only rail line in the area runs south from
Córdoba twice a day via Montilla (40mins), Aguilar
de la Frontera (45mins) and Puente-Genil (1hr).

Córdoba Province

# Jaén Province

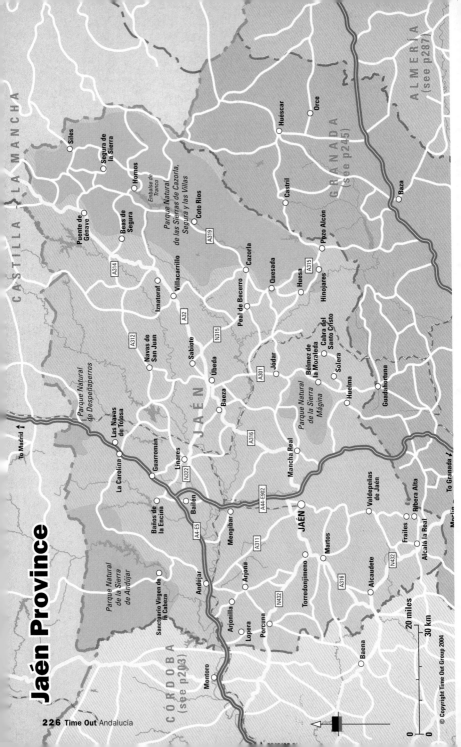

# Jaén Province

© Copyright Time Out Group 2004

# Jaén Province

Two perfect Renaissance towns, wild mountains and an awful lot of olives.

Despite being the traditional entry point into
Andalucía from Castilla (via the Despeñaperros
pass), the north-eastern province of Jaén is one
of the least known parts of the region. As its
surfeit of castles testifies, this was the front
line between Christian and Moorish forces for
centuries. Defined to the north by the brooding
Sierra Morena, and to the east by the more
appealing Sierra de Segura, the majority of the
province is a hypnotic rolling expanse of olive
fields. The precariously monocultural economy
depends almost solely on olive cultivation,
and nowhere in Andalucía is the distinction
between the wealthy minority and the poor
majority so stark. Few tourists come to Jaén,
and most of those who do stop only at the
spectacular Renaissance towns of Úbeda
and Baeza. Yet, for those who care to look, the
province offers a wealth of historical, cultural
and natural attractions.

### JAÉN CITY
The provincial capital, though largely modern
and not immediately engaging, is a lively
town with a distinctive character. Backed by
a dramatically sited castle, Jaén has a Moorish
core of winding streets, classic tapas bars,
and a couple of excellent museums.

Jaén City.
See p228.

## The best...

### Architecture
**Baeza** (*p236*); **Jaén City** (*p228-30*);
**Úbeda** (*p238*).

### Castles
**Alcalá La Real** (*p231*); **Baños de la Encina**
(*p234*); **Jaén City** (*p228*); **Segura de la
Sierra** (*p243*).

### Food & drink
**Cazorla** (*p242*); **Úbeda** (*p238*).

### Mountains
**Sierras de Cazorla, Segura y las Villas**
(*p242*); **Sierra Mágina** (*p232*).

### Villages
**Cazorla** (*p242*); **Hornos** (*p244*);
**Iznatoraf** (*p240*); **Sabiote** (*p240*);
**Segura de la Sierra** (*p243*).

### SOUTH OF JAÉN
The southern part of Jaén province is a land
of many olives and few visitors, with the hills
of the Sierra Sur de Jaén and the Sierra Mágina
providing the major scenic draws.

### NORTH OF JAÉN
A monotonous yet weirdly intoxicating eternity
of undulating olive fields stretches west into
Córdoba province and north to the foothills
of the Sierra Morena. Its uniform appearance
belies the fact that this is a region of immense
archaeological richness and diversity, and was
a key battleground – both in the early stages
of the *reconquista* and in the Spanish Civil War.

### EAST OF JAÉN
The neighbouring frozen-in-time Renaissance
towns of Baeza and Úbeda are deservedly
the biggest draw in the province. Their
embarrassment of 16th-century architectural
riches makes them two of the most charming
and unique towns in the whole of Spain. Not far
away lies the huge extent of the mountainous
Parque Natural de las Sierras de Cazorla,
Segura y Las Villas, a wonderfully diverse
natural playground.

# Jaén City

Picturesque it is not, but Jaén does have some impressive monuments.

The regional capital doesn't get much positive press from guidebooks. And, approaching through its tatty, depressed suburbs, it's not hard to see why. Unemployment here, as in much of the rest of the province, is high, and 20th-century development has done Jaén few aesthetic favours. Yet the city rewards those who aren't put off by first impressions, and has attractions enough to occupy a day.

The hulking mass of the outsize cathedral and the impressive form of the Castillo de Santa Catalina dominate Jaén, while all around stretches an endless ocean of olive trees. Jaén's economy has been intimately connected with *aceitunas* (olives) since Roman times. Under the Moors this was a key staging post between Castilla and the rest of Andalucía (the name derives from *Geen*, meaning 'caravan route'), but, when the city fell to Fernando III in 1246, its Moorish ruler was forced to flee to Granada (where he founded the Nasrid dynasty), and a long period of decline followed.

Jaén has yet to recover, and a faint air of desperation can be sensed in many parts of the city. Sadly, things are unlikely to improve in the near future now that the European Commission has slashed subsidies for olive oil production. At least the opening of a university in the 1990s has livened up the nightlife.

## Sightseeing

In a nutshell, Jaén's must-see sights are the cathedral, the castle, the Arab baths and the Iberian sculptures in the Museo Provincial.

The **Catedral de Jaén**, built on the site of the town mosque, dwarfs the surrounding buildings. Construction began in the mid 16th century under Andrés de Vandelvira, though it was not completed until the late 18th century. The exuberant west façade (incorporating superb statuary by Sevillian master Pedro Roldán) dates from the late 17th century, and contrasts with the dark and somewhat forbidding atmosphere within. Don't miss the fine late-baroque carvings in the choir.

The streets leading from the cathedral towards the church of **San Ildefonso** (953 19 03 46, open 8.30am-noon daily) are some of Jaén's liveliest at night. The church, founded in the 13th century, but rebuilt and altered many times since, is dedicated to Jaén's patron saint.

Just north-west of here is Jaén's main square, the unimpressive, incoherent Plaza de la Constitución, from which the wide Paseo de la Estación heads straight north towards the train station. On the Paseo's western side, just after a hideous monument to the battles of Las Navas de Tolosa and Bailén, is the **Museo Provincial**. Built in 1920 into the 16th-century remains of an old granary and the church of San Miguel, the museum's ground floor is devoted to archaeological finds from the surrounding area. Upstairs is the **Museo de Bellas Artes**, containing an amusing collection of 19th- and 20th-century works, which veer from the titillating to the ridiculous. In a separate room there's a Picasso drawing, surrounded by works by his near contemporary, Jaén-born Manuel Ángeles Ortiz. However, the real reason to visit the Museo Provincial is to admire the best collection of fifth-century BC Iberian sculptures in Spain. These luminous, vivacious, yet exquisitely controlled pieces were discovered in 1975 at Obulco, outside the town of Porcuna in the west of the province. The sculptures can be found in the basement of the Sala de Exposiciones Grabado, to the right of the main building.

North-west of the cathedral, the winding streets of the old Moorish town climb the lower slopes of Santa Catalina hill – this is the most pleasant area for strolling. Here you'll find the **Palacio de Villadompardo**, a late-16th-century building encompassing the superb 11th-century **Baños Árabes** (Arab Baths – the largest to survive in Spain), the enjoyable **Museo Internacional de Arte Naïf** (International Museum of Naïve Art) and the **Museo de Artes y Costumbres Populares** (Museum of Popular Arts and Customs).

A little further up the street is the **Real Monasterio de Santo Domingo** (953 23 85 00, open 8.30am-2pm Mon-Fri, 5-7.15pm Wed, Thur), a 14th-century monastery built over a Moorish palace, which has one of the loveliest cloisters in the city. The building has had a number of incarnations, and now houses the town's archives.

Just north-west, in the Plaza de la Magdalena, is the church of **La Magdalena** (953 19 03 09, open 9am-12.30pm, 5-8pm daily), again, built over a mosque and reputedly the oldest church in the city. The bell tower was the minaret and you can still see the courtyard where the faithful performed their ablutions.

It is possible to climb from the old town up to the **Castillo de Santa Catalina**, but it's a long and arduous haul. More realistic is to drive up to enjoy the memorable views. There's been a castle here since the 13th century, though it has been remodelled many times since. Even when the castle is closed, you can park in the *parador* car park and walk beside the walls to the end of the ridge, which is dominated by a huge cross. Part of the castle is now Jaén's premier hotel – stop in for a drink and a gawp.

### Castillo de Santa Catalina

*953 12 07 33.* **Open** *May-Sept* 10am-2pm, 5-9pm Tue-Sun. *Oct-Apr* 10am-2pm, 3.30-7.30pm Tue-Sun. **Admission** €3; €1-€2 concessions. **No credit cards. Map** p229 A1.

### Catedral de Jaén

*Plaza Santa María (953 23 42 33).* **Open** Cathedral *May-June* 8.30am-1pm, 5-8pm Mon-Sat; 9am-1pm, 6-8pm Sun. *July-Sept* 8.30am-1pm, 5-8pm Mon-Sat; 9am-1pm Sun. *Oct-Apr* 8.30am-1pm, 4-7pm Mon-Sat; 9am-1pm, 5-7pm Sun. Museum 10am-1pm, 5-8pm Tue-Sun. **Admission** €3. **No credit cards. Map** p229 A1/2.

### Museo Provincial & Museo de Bellas Artes

*Paseo de la Estación 27 (953 25 06 00).* **Open** 2.30-8.30pm Tue; 9am-8.30pm Wed-Sat; 9am-2.30pm Sun. **Admission** €1.50; free with EU passport. **Map** p229 off B2.

### Palacio de Villadompardo

*Plaza María Luisa de Marillac s/n (953 23 62 92).* **Open** 9am-8pm Tue-Fri; 9.30am-2.30pm Sat, Sun. **Admission** free. **Map** p229 B1.

## Where to eat & drink

The main areas to head for are the streets north of the cathedral (particularly Calle de Arco de Consuelo) and the parallel streets running east from the cathedral to the church of San Ildefonso. The nicest spot for sitting outside in the centre is **Bar El Pósito** on the lively Plaza del Pósito.

### Casa Vicente

*C/Francisco Martín Mora s/n (953 23 28 16).* **Open** varies. **Average** €€. **No credit cards. Map** p229 A1. Located in a fine mansion close to the cathedral, this attractive old restaurant specialises in trad local dishes, such as *pastel de carne de caza* (game pie).

### Cerveceria Daniel

*C/Nueva 9 (953 24 20 41).* **Open** 10am-midnight Mon-Thur; 10am-1am Fri, Sat. Closed Aug. **Average** €. **No credit cards. Map** p229 A2. A modern bar with an impressive selection of tapas.

### La Gamba de Oro

*C/Nueva 5 (953 24 17 46).* **Open** 11am-4pm, 8pm-midnight daily. **Average** €€. **Credit** V. **Map** p229 A2. It's not much to look at, but the locals flock here for the best seafood in town.

### El Gorrión

*C/Arco de Consuelo 7 (953 23 20 00).* **Open** noon-4pm, 8pm-2am Tue-Sun. Closed 4wks July-Aug. **No credit cards. Map** p229 A1. This famous old bar opened in 1888 and looks as though it hasn't changed since. If you ask the bartender, he'll be pleased to take you down to the cellar to view the splendidly gruesome remains of a leg of *jamón*, put into a glass case after World War I.

**Jaén Province**

Viewpoint near Jaén's **Castillo**. *See p229.*

### Pub Iroquai

*C/Adarves Bajos 41 (mobile 680 43 45 90/www.*
*salairoquai.com).* **Open** 4pm-6am daily. **Admission**
free-€5. **No credit cards. Map** p229 A2.
One of the hipper, more youthful bars in town, with
live gigs most Thursdays.

### Taberna La Manchega

*C/Bernardo López 8 (953 23 21 92).* **Open** 10am-
4pm, 8pm-midnight Mon, Wed, Thur; 10am-2pm,
8pm-midnight Fri-Sun. Closed Aug. **No credit**
**cards. Map** p229 A1.
A lively tapas bar that's been around for over a century. The first-rate, ultra-cheap food includes great
baked potatoes and a huge range of *bocadillos*.

### Taberna Pepón

*C/Doctor Eduardo Arroyo 12 (953 23 63 68).*
**Open** 11am-3pm, 8pm-midnight Mon-Sat. Closed
July. **No credit cards. Map** p229 A1.
Another reliable, characterful old bar, with *jamones*
hanging from the ceiling and strip lighting.

## Where to stay

There's scant accommodation in Jaén, and
what there is – with the notable exception of
the *parador* – tends to be characterless. At the
bottom end of the scale there are a number of
*pensiones*, including **Hostal Renfe** (Paseo de
la Estación s/n, 953 27 47 04, double €41, map
A/B2), which is in the train station, and **Carlos**
**V** (Avenida Madrid 4, 953 22 20 91, double €32,
map B2), near the bus station.

### Hostal La Española

*C/Bernardo López 9 (953 23 02 54).*
**Rates** €17-€22 single; €32-€41 double; €43-€54
triple. **No credit cards. Map** p229 A1.
This creaky, crumbling but characterful *hostal* is the
only place to stay in the old town. It's within staggering distance of some of Jaén's best tapas bars.

### Hotel Condestable Iranzo

*Paseo de la Estación 32 (953 22 28 00/www.*
*condestable.com).* **Rates** €53-€66 single; €67-€97
double; €119-€149 suite. **Credit** AmEx, MC, V.
**Map** p229 B2.
This three-star near the Museo Provincial has a big
flashy lobby, comfortable rooms and, er, bingo.

### Hotel Europa

*Plaza de Belén 1 (953 22 27 00/902 10 07 10/*
*www.gremiodehospedaje.com).* **Rates** €45 single;
€55 double; €68 triple. **Credit** AmEx, DC, MC, V.
**Map** p229 B2.
Part of the Husa chain, this three-star offers plenty
of comfort and smart communal facilities.

### Parador Castillo de Santa Catalina

*953 23 00 00/www.parador.es.* **Rates** €98 single; €122
double. **Credit** AmEx, DC, MC, V. **Map** p229 A1.
By far the best place to stay in town, with stone
corridors, massive vaulted ceilings, suits of armour,
vast fireplaces and hanging tapestries in the public
rooms. All the usual *parador* comfort, plus rooms
with terraces and some of the most spectacular
views you'll ever enjoy. A restaurant and pool too.

### Hotel Xauen

*Plaza Deán Mazas 3 (953 24 07 89/www.hotel*
*xauenjaen.com).* **Rates** €43 single; €59-€65 double.
**Credit** AmEx, MC, V. **Map** p229 A2.
This three-star is the most central of Jaén's hotels
(just off Plaza de la Constitución), though it has
little else to recommend it. Rooms are smallish and
no better than functional.

## Resources

### Internet

*Cyber Cu@k, Adarves Bajos 24 (953 19 06 16).*
**Open** *Mid June-mid Sept* 6pm-midnight daily. *Mid*
*Sept-mid June* 5.30-11.30pm Mon-Fri; 6pm-midnight
Sat, Sun. **Map** p229 A2.

### Police station

*C/Arquitecto Berges 11 (953 29 51 17).* **Map** p229 B2.

### Post office

*Plaza de los Jardinillos (953 24 78 00).* **Open** 8.30am-
8.30pm Mon-Fri; 9.30am-2pm Sat. **Map** p229 A/B1.

### Tourist information

*C/Maestra 13 bajo (953 24 26 24/19 04 55).*
**Open** *Mid June-mid Sept* 10am-8pm Mon-Fri; 10am-
1pm Sat, Sun. *Mid Sept-mid June* 10am-7pm Mon-Fri;
10am-1pm Sat, Sun. **Map** p229 A1.

## Getting there

### By bus

The bus station is at Plaza Coca de la Piñera 6 (953
25 01 06, map B2). There are around 3 buses a day
to Sevilla (5hrs), 2 to Almeria (4hrs 30mins), 8 to
Córdoba (2hrs), 14 to Granada (2hrs), 6 to Madrid
(6hrs), 4 to Málaga (4hrs), 14 to Úbeda and Baeza
(1hr 30mins/1hr) and 2 to Cazorla (2hrs).

### By train

The railway station is on Plaza de Jaén de la Paz
(also known as Paseo de la Estación, 902 24 02 02) on
the northern side of the town (map off B2) – a couple
of kilometres from the centre. There is 1 direct train
a day to Córdoba (1hr 35mins), 1 to Sevilla (3hrs) and
2 to Madrid (4hrs 10mins).

# South of Jaén

Discover an Andalucía untouched by tourism.

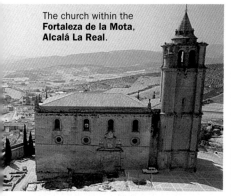

The church within the **Fortaleza de la Mota, Alcalá La Real.**

Few visitors stop in southern Jaén. At first glance is seems little more than one vast expanse of olive fields, cut through by a couple of speedy roads designed to take you somewhere more interesting. Yet it's an area that rewards the curious and offers plentiful insight into the real Andalucía, a world away from the *costas* and other tourist centres.

Its urban hub is **Alcalá La Real**, 50 kilometres (31 miles) north-west of Granada, and around 70 kilometres (44 miles) south of Jaén. The escarpment from which the modern town descends has been inhabited since prehistoric times and was a strategically key Moorish stronghold, protecting the northern approaches to Granada. Christian forces took the town in 1341 (from which time the 'Real' – Royal – of its name dates). The citadel, known as the **Fortaleza de la Mota**, is well worth a visit, and contains a mélange of ruins and structures from the 12th century to the 16th. At the highest level, the Moorish keep contains a museum of local archaeological finds. The Golden Age sculptor Juan Martínez Montañés was born in Alcalá in 1568, and is commemorated by a statue in the attractive old town square.

Around 28 kilometres (18 miles) north-west of here is **Alcaudete**, topped by another Moorish castle (closed for restoration). Like many places in Jaén, it's an uneasy mix of wealth (for the few) and poverty (for the many). From November to February – the time of the olive harvest – there's work for all; the rest of the year there's chronic unemployment, and flat-capped men hang around listlessly outside the shuttered mansions of the olive oil barons. Doña Jimena, the manufacturer of some of the best traditional Andalucian lard- and almond-based biscuits (*mantecados*), is based here.

North of Alcaudete, and 24 kilometres (15 miles) west of Jaén city, **Martos** is another centre of olive oil production, backed by a ruined castle atop a huge outcrop of rock. In the first week of December, the olive harvest is celebrated by the four-day **Fiesta de la Aceituna**.

Between Alcalá La Real and Jaén city lies the beautiful but little-visited **Sierra Sur de Jaén**, a wild yet intimate expanse of wooded hills and valleys (one containing an isolated hideaway used by superstar *matadores* such as Jesulín de Ubrique). In recent years, the pristine scenery has been marred somewhat by the erection of huge power-generating windmills.

The workaday, friendly village of **Frailes**, 15 kilometres (nine miles) east of Alcalá, is part-time home to the British writer Michael Jacobs, author of *Andalucía*, the best general book on the region. Jacobs' wonderful book, *The Factory of Light*, tells the story of Frailes, its inhabitants and a remarkable cinematic event that he masterminded here in 2001, when the village's abandoned but perfectly preserved cinema was reopened for one final performance, attracting the ageing Spanish film star Sara Montiel and the national press. It also became the subject of a short film entitled *Rewind: El último cuplé*.

North of Frailes a long, slow road winds through stunning virgin hills to Jaén city via the sizeable village of **Valdepeñas de Jaén**. At the latter, don't miss a wonderful short walk up the **Paraje de las Chorreras** – a cool, verdant rocky gorge through which a crystal stream descends. It's not much more than half-an-hour's stroll to the top and back again (look for the sign on the south side of Valdepeñas next to the Meubles Almendra furniture shop).

The Sierra Sur has a strong local tradition of mysticism and faith-healing (documented as far back as the 15th century), which continues today. The most distinctive of the area's healers are the so-called *santones* or 'saints', who are thought of as intermediaries between the earthly and supernatural realms. Unrecognised by the Catholic Church, but famous locally for having worked countless miracles, they have powers that are said to be hereditary.

**Jaén Province**

The most revered of all the local saints is the 'Santo Custodio', who, though he died in 1961, is still the object of a huge (if partially secretive) cult. He lived all his life in the now-prosperous hamlet of **La Hoya del Salobral** – to reach it turn right four kilometres (2.5 miles) north of Frailes on the Noalejo road. Follow the sign marked 'Ermita' to the top of a rocky outcrop that has spectacular views of the Sierra Nevada. In recent years the Catholic Church has built a sanctuary to the Virgen de la Cabeza here, which, on the last Sunday of April, attracts up to 10,000 pilgrims. The pilgrimage is really a disguised homage to the Santo Custodio, who came up here to pray in a small rock shelter. This shelter, marked by a cross garlanded with flowers, is reached by steps to the right of the sanctuary, and is filled with offerings. The Santo Custodio's house stands in the main square of La Hoya del Salobral, and is technically open to visitors every morning; it's a fascinating example of an almost unchanged rural dwelling from around 1900.

Just east of Jaén city is the rugged **Parque Natural de la Sierra Mágina**. Though easily accessible, this mountainous park sees few visitors, and its 19,985 hectares (77 square miles) provide wonderful walking territory without much chance of bumping into anyone else. The town of **Huelma** is a possible base, and there are a number of other interesting places worthy of a visit, such as **Solera** (which offers fabulous views of the Sierra), **Bélmez de la Moraleda** and handsome **Cabra del Santo Cristo**. The latter is named after a much venerated image of Christ that was being transported from Burgos to Guadix when it was intercepted by the locals of Cabra, who decided they liked the image so much that they wouldn't let it go any further. Bélmez has a ruined Renaissance castle.

### Fortaleza de la Mota

*Alcalá La Real (953 58 20 77/mobile 639 64 77 96). **Open** June-Sept 10.30am-1.30pm, 5-8pm daily. Oct-May 10.30am-1.30pm, 3.30-6.30pm daily. **Admission** €1.50; €1 concessions; free under-12s. **No credit cards**. This is also the town's tourist office.*

## Where to stay & eat

The area is so far off the tourist trail that accommodation options are few. In Alcalá, the best choice is the new two-star **Hospedería Zacatin** (C/Pradillo 2, 953 58 05 68, www.hospederiazacatin.com, double €36-€40), which has a decent restaurant (€).

In Frailes, the somewhat eccentric **Hostal Ardales** (C/Avenida 18, 953 59 35 08, double €33) is above the Aztec-inspired village disco, though the owner Paqui (who features in Michael Jacobs' *The Factory of Light, see p231*) says it's not open when she's got guests. Wonderful,

simple home cooking (particularly goat, as the name implies) is available in **El Choto** (C/Deán Mudarra 24, 953 59 32 85, closed Thur and 1wk early Sept, €), while the atmospheric bar **La Cueva** (C/Cuevas 5, 953 59 31 02) is, logically, in a cave. The biggest culinary surprise in the whole of Jaén is the **Rey de Copas** in the village of Ribera Alta, next to Frailes (Carretera de Frailes 27, 953 59 33 05, closed Tue, €€€). An unassuming frontage leads into an elegant dining room where chef Juan Matias del Moral Garrido serves up startlingly innovative cuisine using quality local ingredients. No wonder that it's *Driving Over Lemons* author Chris Stewart's favourite restaurant in Andalucía. Opening hours aren't reliable; phone to check.

In Huelma, the **Angel** (Carretera La Cerradura-Huelma s/n, 953 39 08 70, closed 1wk Sept, double €27) has 27 decent rooms. In Cabra del Santo Cristo, **Casa Herminia** (C/Moya 12, 953 39 75 06, closed 1st 2wks Sept, €), located in a converted cinema, does an excellent home-made partridge pâté and a good lunch menu.

## Resources

### Tourist information

**Parque Natural de la Sierra Mágina** *Centro de Visitantes 'Castillo de Jódar', A301, km24, Jódar (953 78 76 56)*. **Open** *May-Sept* 10am-2pm Thur, Fri; 10am-2pm, 6-8pm Sat, Sun. *Oct-Mar* 10am-2pm Thur, Fri; 10am-2pm, 4-6pm Sat, Sun.

## Getting there

### By bus

Alsina Graells (www.alsinagraells.es) runs 10 buses a day (fewer at weekends) between Granada and Alcalá (45mins-1hr), 2 a day to Alcaudete (1 hr) and 1 a day to Cabra (1hr). There are 4 a day Mon-Fri and 1 on Sat & Sun (Autocares Contreras, www.autocares contreras.com) between Jaén and Alcalá. Alcalá's bus station (953 58 27 32) is at Avenida de Andalucia 48.

The **Paraje de las Chorreras**. *See p231*.

# North of Jaén

History casts a long shadow on the gateway to Andalucía.

At first glance it doesn't look much, but the friendly little town of **Porcuna**, close to the border with Córdoba province (just off the A306) has hidden depths. In Iberian times it was known as Obulco, and just north of the town at Cerrillo Blanco a funeral site was uncovered that contained possibly the finest Iberian-era sculptures yet found in Spain; it is now open as the **Parque Arqueológico de Cerrillo Blanco**. Although the original sculptures are housed in the Museo Provincial in Jaén (*see p228*), a couple of replicas can be seen in a small museum in Porcuna's *Ayuntamiento* (Town Hall), and there are further interesting archaeological finds in the recently restored 15th-century **Torre de Boabdil**. The tower was once part of Porcuna's all-but-vanished fortifications, and, in 1485, acted as prison for the last Moorish king of Granada, Boabdil, following his capture after the Battle of Lucena.

Porcuna's other points of interest include the late 19th-century church of **Nuestra Señora de la Asunción** (open hours of services), which contains paintings by the much-loved Córdoban peddler of kitsch, Julio Romero de Torres (*see p210* **Cliché**), and what is probably the region's oddest attraction, the **Casa de Piedra** (House of Stone), designed and built entirely by hand in self-quarried stone between 1931 and 1960 by the frankly unhinged Antonio Aguilera, who embodied the Francoist ideals of iron will and unbending hard work.

Ten kilometres (six miles) north of Porcuna is the smaller town of **Lopera**, centred around a Moorish castle (closed to the public) and enjoying fine views over olive groves. At one time there were ten *bodegas* in Lopera – only

one remains: the atmospherically cobwebby **Bodega Herruzo** (C/Doctor Fleming), which does tastings of the local sweet wines. The town is chiefly of interest, however, as a key Civil War site – it was here that the English writers John Cornford and Ralph Fox were killed; bunkers and trenches still scar the surrounding country (*see p234* **Echoes of war**).

The largest settlement in this north-western corner of Jaén is **Andújar**, 45 kilometres (28 miles) from the provincial capital. It's a busy, likeable, if not particularly picturesque town of Roman origin, sitting at the foot of the Sierra Morena. A much-restored bridge over the Guadalquivir river dates back to the time of Trajan. On the Plaza Santa Maria a medieval bell tower now houses the tourist office, while opposite is the 13th-century church of **Santa María**. Inside – surprisingly – is an outstanding painting by El Greco, *Christ on the Mount of Olives*, as well as an *Immaculate Conception* by Pacheco, Velázquez's teacher.

North of Andújar, the remote and little-visited **Parque Natural de la Sierra de Andújar** (73,976 hectares/285 square miles) stretches into the Sierra Morena mountains. Hunting, cattle farming, beekeeping and the production of cork are the area's traditional activities, while its inaccessibility provides sanctuary for the like of lynx and Imperial eagles. Once a year (in April) the peace is broken by the **Romería de la Virgen de la Cabeza** (*see p46*), one of Andalucía's largest pilgrimages, when thousands travel to the Sanctuario Virgen de la Cabeza, 31 kilometres (19 miles) north of Andújar. The mountain setting is superb, though the original shrine (founded in the 13th

**Baños de la Encina.**
*See p234.*

Jaén Province

# Echoes of war

A border zone during the Civil War between Republican and Nationalist Spain, the area around **Lopera** is today movingly evocative of this war, and of the death here of two of the most prominent British intellectuals fighting for the International Brigade, **Ralph Fox** and **John Cornford**.

On 26 December 1936, nearly six months after the outbreak of the war, Lopera became one of the first towns in the province of Jaén to be taken by the Nationalists. Over the next three days the Republicans attempted to recapture the town in a battle that proved to be one of the bloodiest in Andalucía of the whole war. Fox, Cornford and 17 other British and Irish members of the 121st Battalion (a division of the XIV International Brigade) were among the hundreds of losses incurred by the Republicans, who, while never retaking Lopera, managed to retain the greater part of Jaén for a long time afterwards.

The Halifax-born Ralph Fox, though thought of in Lopera today as a poet, was a writer of varied literary output who had ambitions primarily as a novelist and travel writer. Enlisting with the International Brigade in Paris soon after the outbreak of the Civil War, he ended up early in December 1936 in the bleak Castillian town of Albacete, where he was responsible for the political education of other British volunteers. On Christmas Day 1936, when the Nationalists were advancing on Lopera, he and the newly formed 121st Battalion were sent to the Republican barracks in the northern Jaén town of Andújar, from where they set off two days later to the front.

John Cornford, who was travelling with them, celebrated his 21st birthday on that very day, 27 December. The son of a well-known Cambridge professor of ancient philosophy, Cornford was a truly Byronic figure who started writing poetry at the age of 15, and was already known as a political activist by the time he was 18. Earning an immediate reputation in the Civil War for his bravery and daring, he also wrote some of his finest poems in Spain, including one addressed to his lover Margot Heinemann, in which he seems to have a premonition of his death:

*'And if bad luck should lay my strength*
*Into the shallow grave,*
*Remember all the good you can;*
*Don't forget my love.'*

There are different opinions as to how exactly the two British writers died. An elderly Lopera man recently claimed that he was driving Fox, Cornford and many other British soldiers from Andújar when they came under heavy machine-gun fire. The official account of Fox's death is that he perished on 27 December while running across open ground to try and outflank the enemy; Cornford meanwhile seems to have been shot the following day while rushing to the aid of a wounded companion. At all events the rough location of their deaths can be identified as halfway along the side road linking Lopera to the former main road between Madrid and Cádiz (now the J203).

Republican trenches can still be seen on the hill to the west, while to the east is the Cerro del Calvario (which was referred to as 'English Crest'), where the Nationalist forces were initially based. The most easily accessible of the area's surviving vestiges of the Civil War is a complex of trenches and gun emplacements on the banks of the Río Salayo, next to the rebuilt bridge on the Lopera–Bujalance road. In Lopera itself, in a small garden now known as the Jardín de los Poetas Ingleses, is a 1999 concrete memorial to Fox and Cornford. Remarkably, this is the only monument in Spain to the Republican war effort.

century) is long gone and the current sanctuary is a bleak Franco-era structure. This was the site of a famous siege during the Civil War, when 250 Nationalist Guardia Civil held out for nine months in 1936-37 against a Republican army that eventually numbered 20,000.

From Andújar, the motorway to Madrid skirts the foothills of the Sierra Morena, passing the town of **Bailén**, famed as the site of a battle in 1808, when Spanish troops under General Castaños inflicted a surprise defeat on a French army, causing a key setback for Napoleon during the Peninsular War.

A more appealing place to stop, though, is the village of **Baños de la Encina**, just to the north, which is dominated by one of the best preserved Moorish castles in Andalucia, the **Castillo de Burgalimar**. Completed in 968 (though the large keep was added in the 13th and 14th centuries), the castle is entered through a double-horseshoe arch, and the battlements that link its 14 square towers can be climbed. The village itself is a charming spot for a wander, and contains a number of fine *palacios* and churches.

Another 20 or so kilometres along the motorway is the curious, small, grid-plan town of **La Carolina**. It was founded in 1768 by the enlightened Carlos III and his minister Pablo de Olavide. The aim was to encourage foreigners to settle the lawless lands around the Madrid–Sevilla road (so as not to depopulate other parts of the country). La Carolina was one of 12 colonies established by largely German, French and Flemish settlers, but it didn't flourish. Olavide was brought down by his political enemies, and many of the northern European settlers couldn't cope with the climate. Within a few generations there was little evidence that outsiders had ever lived here.

On the road heading north-east out of La Carolina is a hideous modern monument to one of the most important battles ever to take place on Andalucían soil. On 16 July 1212, Christian forces inflicted a crushing defeat on a Moorish army at Las Navas de Tolosa, marking the start of the *reconquista*. The Moors are said to have fled north through a mountain pass, which was henceforth known as the **Desfiladero de Despeñaperros** ('pass of the overthrow of the dogs'). For centuries, this stunning pass was the only natural point of entry into Andalucía from Castilla. The wild area around the pass forms the **Parque Natural de Despeñaperros** (7,502 hectares/29 square miles), home to lynx, golden eagles and even wolves.

### Casa de Piedra
*Paseo de Jesús s/n, Porcuna (953 54 41 77).* **Open** *Mid June-mid Sept* 9am-2pm, 4-9pm daily. *Mid Sept-mid June* 9am-2pm, 3-6pm daily. **Admission** €2; €1 concessions. **No credit cards**.

### Castillo de Burgalimar
*Baños de la Encina (953 61 32 00).* **Open** (by appointment only) 9am-8pm daily. **Admission** free.

### Parque Arqueológico de Cerrillo Blanco
*Porcuna.* **Open** (by appointment) *July-Sept* 9am-noon daily. *Oct-June* 10am-noon daily. To arrange a visit, call the *Ayuntamiento* (953 54 40 04/mobile 625 90 45 35).

### Torre de Boabdil
*C/José Moreno Torres s/n, Porcuna (www.museode obulco.com).* **Open** *June-Aug* noon-2pm, 7-9pm Sat. *Sept-May* noon-1pm Tue-Thur; noon-2pm Fri, Sun; noon-2pm, 4-7pm Sat. Outside of official opening hours make an appointment to visit by calling the *Ayuntamiento* on 953 54 40 04 or mobile 625 904 535.

## Where to stay & eat

In Porcuna, squeeze yourself into **Epi** (C/Ramon y Cajal 5, no phone), one of the smallest bars in Andalucía and in the same family for more than a century (there's no

sign outside). The only place to stay here is **El Triunfo** (C/Carrera de Jesús 19, 953 54 47 71, www.restauranteeltriunfo.com, double €36), which also has a good restaurant (€-€€).

In Andújar, the two-star **Don Pedro** (C/Gabriel Zamora 5, 953 50 12 74, double €41-€43) is the one of the best places to stay in the centre. The best-known restaurant in town is **Restaurante Madrid–Sevilla** (Plaza del Sol 4, 953 50 05 94, closed dinner Wed and last 2wks Sept, €€), named after its position on the old road between the cities, and purveyor of some classic meaty dishes (the game is particularly good); it has an enormous wine cellar. For cheaper but equally hearty fare, try **Las Perolas** (C/Serpiente 6, 953 50 67 26, €).

In Baños de la Encina, the newish three-star **Hotel Restaurante Baños** (C/Cerro Llamada s/n, 953 61 40 68, www.hotelbanos.com, double €56-€62, restaurant €-€€) is a great place to stay, with a big terrace and many rooms enjoying fine views of the castle.

A classic hotel near La Carolina, **La Perdiz** (A4-E5, km268, 953 66 03 00, www.nh-hoteles. com, double €85) is popular with hunters and has a restaurant specialising in game (€€).

## Resources

### Tourist information

**Andújar** *Torre de Reloj, Plaza de Santa María (953 50 49 59/www.ayto-andujar.es).* **Open** *July-Sept* 8am-2pm Tue-Sat. *Oct-June* 10am-2pm, 5-8pm Mon-Sat.

**La Carolina** *A4-E5, km269 (953 68 08 82).* **Open** *July, Aug* 10am-2pm, 4-7pm Mon-Fri. *Sept-June* 10am-2pm, 4-7pm Mon-Fri; 10am-1pm some Sats.

**Parque Natural de Despeñaperros** *Centro de Visitantes 'Puerta de Andalucía', A4-E5, km257 Santa Elena (953 66 43 07).* **Open** *Apr-Sept* 10am-2pm, 4-8pm daily. *Oct-Mar* 10am-2pm, 3-7pm daily.

**Parque Natural de la Sierra de Andújar** *Centro de Visitantes, J5010, km12 (953 54 90 30).* **Open** *May-Sept* 9am-1pm Thur, Sun; 9am-1pm, 6-8pm Fri, Sat. *Oct-Apr* 9am-1pm Thur; 9am-1pm, 6-8pm Fri-Sun.

**Porcuna** *Ayuntamiento, Plaza de Andalucía s/n (953 54 40 04).* **Open** 8am-3pm Mon-Fri.

## Getting there

### By bus

Andújar bus station (953 51 30 72/www.infonegocio. com/estacionbusandujar) is at Sector Sevilla 27. Around 18 buses (fewer at weekends) run daily from Andújar to Jaén, 3 go to Écija, Carmona and on to Sevilla, 6 to Córdoba (3 on weekends), 2 to Baeza and Úbeda, and 2 on weekdays to Lopera and Porcuna.

### By train

There is 1 daily direct train from Andújar station (902 24 02 02) to Jaén (45mins), 4 to Linares-Baeza (30mins), 5 to Córdoba (50mins), 2 to Sevilla (2hrs 15mins) and 1 to Cádiz (4hrs).

**Jaén Province**

# East of Jaén

A brace of perfect 16th-century towns and vast expanses of raw nature.

## Baeza

Although Jaén province is one of the lesser-known corners of Andalucía, it contains what are undoubtedly two of the region's (and the country's) Renaissance jewels – the glorious neighbouring towns of Baeza and Úbeda. **Baeza**, the smaller of the two (and the less affected by unsympathetic 20th-century development), lies 48 kilometres (30 miles) north-east of Jaén city. It was a significant centre in Roman and Visigothic times, and the capital of a sizeable city state under the Moors. When it fell to Christian forces in 1227 the incoming nobles proceeded to indulge in centuries of violent bickering with each other before the town enjoyed its golden age (like Úbeda) in the 16th century. It was during this brief time that Baeza's nobles commissioned the wealth of buildings that distinguish this compact, sleepy town today.

Tourism is not novel in Baeza, but the coach parties rarely stay the night, and evenings are often the loveliest times to wander the streets and look out over the surrounding countryside, echoing the words of one-time resident, the poet Antonio Machado: 'Fields of Baeza, I shall dream of you when I can no longer see you.'

### Sightseeing

The town's focal point is the coffin-shaped, bar-specked Paseo de la Constitución, which joins with the smaller Plaza de España at its northern end. The outstanding building on the *paseo*'s eastern side is the 16th-century **La Alhóndiga**, an elegant arcaded corn exchange, while the 17th-century **Casas Consistoriales Bajas** (Lower Town Hall) is the pick of the buildings on the opposite side. Overlooking Plaza de España is the **Torre de los Aliatares**, one of the few remnants of Baeza's Moorish fortifications.

The southern end of the Paseo de la Constitución leads into the tiny, exquisite Plaza del Pópulo, with the Fuente de los Leones (Fountain of the Lions) at its centre. Here you can pick up a town map from the tourist office, which is housed within the **Casa del Pópulo**. The other building of note on the square is the **Antigua Carnicería** (Old Slaughterhouse), bearing the two-headed eagle of Emperor Carlos V. On the square's southern side are

two arches: the **Puerta de Jaén** (Jaén Gate), and the **Arco de Villalar**, erected by Carlos to commemorate the crushing of the Castilian revolt of the Comuneros (1520-21).

Uphill, east of the *plaza*, lies the peaceful heart of Renaissance Baeza. From behind the tourist office, follow Cuesta San Gil and then turn left up Calle Obispo Mengibar to reach stunning Plaza Santa María. Its eastern side is formed by two conjoined buildings: the **Casas Consistoriales Altas** (Upper Town Hall; currently being renovated) and the **Santa Iglesia Catedral**. The latter was built on the site of a mosque in the 13th century and given a fine nave in the mid 16th century by Andrés de Vandelvira, though the late-Gothic chancel remains. The greatest surprise within the airy interior comes if you put a one euro coin in a box marked 'Custodia' at the end of the aisle (on the side of the main door). A painting slides back to reveal an astonishingly ornate revolving 18th-century silver custodia (by Córdoban Nuñez de Castro). The church tower can be climbed, though the views from the top are disappointing; the bells are fenced off, meaning you can't get to the edge of the tower overlooking the town. On the opposite side of the *plaza* is the severe 17th-century **Seminario Conciliar de San Felipe Neri**, now home to the International University of Andalucia.

From here, Calle San Felipe Neri leads to the arresting **Palacio de Jabalquinto** (currently being renovated), the most unusually decorated building in Baeza. Built for the Benavides family in the 15th century, its façade is a riot of Isabelline-plateresque ornamentation. In stark contrast, the *palacio* is faced by the engagingly simple 13th-century church of **Santa Cruz**.

Continuing along the street brings you to the huge **Universidad**, the former university, where poet Antonio Machado (*see p37*) taught French for eight years until 1919 (after it had been converted into a school). The interior patio is open to the public, as is Machado's classroom (953 74 01 54, closed Wed, Machado's classroom by appointment only), which has been kept much as it was in his day and contains various artefacts related to his time in Baeza.

There is a further clutch of fine buildings west of the Paseo de la Constitución. Taking Calle Gaspar Becerra, you soon reach the **Ayuntamiento** (Town Hall; originally the law courts and a prison), a stunning exercise in plateresque exuberance, completed in 1569. Opposite, at the corner of the street, is the house where Machado resided during most of his stay in the town. At the other end of Pasaje Cardenal Benavides is the church of **La Purísima Concepción**, while just south of here on Calle de San Francisco are the partially restored remains of Vandelvira's **Convento de San Francisco**, which was badly damaged by an earthquake and then by marauding French troops in the early 19th century.

From Plaza de España, Calle de San Pablo leads northwards past a series of fine 16th-century Renaissance mansions, the star of which is **Casa Cabrera**. A little further up is the 15th-century Gothic church of **San Pablo**.

## Where to eat & drink

The **Hospedería Fuentenueva** (*see below*) has a good restaurant, as does the **Hotel Palacete Santa Ana** (*see p238*), located close to the hotel at Escopeteros 12.

### Bar-Cafeteria Mercantil
*Plaza de España s/n (no phone).* **Open** 8am-midnight daily. **Average** €. **No credit cards**. **Map** p237 A1.
Machado was a regular at this atmospheric place with a large terrace. It's the most popular spot in town and features a huge menu of tapas and *raciones*.

### Casa Juanito
*Paseo Arca de Agua s/n (953 74 00 40/www.juanito baeza.com).* **Open** 1.30-4pm Mon, Sun; 1.30pm-4pm, 8.30pm-11pm Tue-Sat. Closed 1st 3wks July. **Average** €€. **Credit** MC, V.
The most celebrated restaurant in the area – despite its location next to a petrol station – but overrated.

### Restaurante Sali
*Pasaje Cardenal Benavides 15 (953 74 13 65/ www.restaurantesali.com).* **Open** 1-5pm, 8.30pm-12.30am Mon, Tue, Thur-Sun. Closed 2wks Sept. **Average** €€. **Credit** AmEx, MC, V. **Map** p237 A2.

This eaterie has a good range of fish, shellfish and meat dishes, plus outside tables from which to gaze at the wonderful town hall opposite.

### El Sarmiento
*Plaza del Arcediano 10 (953 74 03 23).* **Open** 1.30-4.30pm, 8.30-11.30pm Tue-Sat; 1.30-4.30pm Sun. Closed 1st 2wks July. **Average** €€€. **Credit** MC, V. **Map** p237 off B2.
In the streets behind the cathedral, this upmarket eaterie is famed for its local fare, such as *perdiz* (partridge). It has a pleasant *terraza*.

### Vandelvira
*C/San Francisco 14 (953 74 81 72/www.vandelvira.es).* **Open** 1.30-4pm, 8.30-11pm Tue-Sat; 1.30-4pm Sun. **Average** €€. **Credit** V. **Map** p237 A2.
The premier dining choice in town, with fine renditions of local and regional dishes, located within in a restored part of Vandelvira's 16th-century Convento de San Francisco.

## Where to stay

### Hospedería Fuentenueva
*Paseo Arco del Agua s/n (www.hospederia fuentenueva.com).* **Rates** €46 single; €71-€90 double. **Credit** AmEx, DC, MC, V.
Just north of the bus station, this little hotel, with its own pool and 12 good-sized rooms, is set within a former women's prison. It was due to change ownership at the time of writing (call 953 75 72 87 for details).

**Jaén Province**

The **Ayuntamiento** in **Baeza**. *See p236.*

**Plaza de Vázquez de Molina, Úbeda** (*p239*).

### Hotel Palacete Santa Ana

*C/Santa Ana Vieja 9 (953 74 16 57/www.palacete santaana.com).* **Rates** €49-€52 single; €58-€90 double; €130-€150 suite. **Credit** AmEx, MC, V. **Map** p237 A2.
This beautifully restored 16th-century *palacio* has 28 exquisite bedrooms filled with antiques and paintings, plus patios for guests to enjoy, a restaurant with *tablao* flamenco and a roof terrace.

### Hotel Puerta de la Luna

*C/Canónigo Melgares Raya s/n (953 74 70 19/ www.hotelpuertadelaluna.es).* **Rates** €102-€136 single/double; €178-€193 suite. **Credit** AmEx, DC, MC, V. **Map** p237 B2.
This recently opened four-star gem is the best place to stay in town. A former home for the canons of the cathedral, the original 16th-century building has been lovingly restored, with 44 boutique-style rooms, some with *terrazas*, ranged round a pretty courtyard with a small pool in the centre. There is also a spa, Turkish baths, garage and an excellent restaurant. Ask about special offers on rates.

### Hotel TRH Baeza

*C/Concepción 3 (953 74 81 30/www.trhhoteles.com).* **Rates** €60-€75 single; €73-€88 double; €121-€136 suite. **Credit** AmEx, MC, V. **Map** p237 A1.
This hotel, within the unsympathetically modernised Renaissance Hospital de la Inmaculad Concepción, has functional rooms in a peaceful location.

### Pensión El Patio

*C/Conde Romanones 13 (953 74 02 00).* **Rates** €12-€15 single; €22-€28 double. **No credit cards**. **Map** p237 B2.
A very cheap *pensión* in a wonderfully crumbling 17th-century *palacio*.

## Resources

### Internet

*Speed Informática, Plaza de la Constitución 2 (953 74 70 05/www.speed.com.es).* **Open** *Mid June-mid Sept* 10am-2pm, 5.30-9.30pm Mon-Fri; 10am-2pm Sat. *Mid Sept-mid June* 10am-2pm, 5-9pm Mon-Fri; 10am-2pm Sat. **Map** p237 A/B2.

### Tourist information

*Plaza del Pópulo s/n (953 74 04 44).* **Open** *June-Sept* 9am-2.30pm, 5-7pm Mon-Fri; 10am-1pm Sat; 10am-2pm Sun. *Oct-May* 9am-2.30pm, 4-6pm Mon-Fri; 10am-1pm Sat; 10am-2pm Sun. **Map** p237 B2.

## Úbeda

**Úbeda**, nine kilometres (six miles) east of Baeza and 57 kilometres (36 miles) north-east of Jaén, is one of the most extraordinary towns in Andalucía, and Spain – not that you'd know it from its scruffy outskirts. Cradled within an arc of unappealing modern development lies a historical centre of remarkable coherence and architectural richness.

Úbeda's origins are ancient, but it only developed into a centre of importance after the arrival of the Moors. When the town fell to Fernando III in 1234, the king established a number of noble families to oversee the area, who, following generations of in-fighting, had settled most of their differences by the time of Úbeda's greatest period of prosperity in the 16th century. The most significant figures of the time were Francisco de los Cobos y

Molina – who, as secretary to Emperor Carlos V, amassed phenomenal wealth and power – and his nephew, Juan Vázquez de Molina, who replaced his uncle when Carlos decided that Francisco's ambitions were getting out of hand, and later served Felipe II. Between them they commissioned many of the Renaissance mansions and churches that grace Úbeda today, a large number of which are the work of the city's greatest architect, Andrés de Vandelvira.

The fortunes of the town's nobility and textile trade declined rapidly in the early 17th century, and few significant building projects were undertaken after this time, giving the old centre its unique, preserved-in-amber Renaissance cast.

## Sightseeing

The centrepiece of Úbeda's Zona Monumental is undoubtedly the astonishing, elongated **Plaza de Vázquez de Molina**, lined on every side by remarkable buildings. At its eastern end stands the **Sacra Capilla del Salvador del Mundo**, loosely based on designs by Diego de Siloé but built by Vandelvira. The chapel, commissioned by Francisco de los Cobos y Molina (who is buried within) is a masterpiece of the Spanish Renaissance; it was completed in just over 20 years (1536-59), and has been little altered since. Inside, the church is dominated by a glittering polychrome *retablo* of the Transfiguration over the high altar. The figure of Christ is by Alonso Berruguete; the rest of the scene is a modern restoration following Civil War damage.

Immediately east of the chapel is the former old-folks' home, the **Hospital de los Honrados y Venerables Viejos del Salvador**, with a Vandelvira façade. It marks the abrupt edge of town, with fine views over olive fields towards the mountains.

Back on the *plaza*, to the west of the church, is the **Palacio del Condestable Dávalos**, now home to one of the most elegant hotels in the state-owned *parador* chain (*see p241*). Opposite is the **Antiguo Pósito**, the old granary, attached to the **Palacio del Marqués de Mancera**, a solid, somewhat retro structure when it was built at the turn of the 16th century.

At right angles to the *palacio*, and fronting a statue to Vandelvira and a tourist information booth, is the **Cárcel del Obispo** (Bishop's Prison; now a police station), which adjoins the **Colegiata de Santa María de los Reales Alacazares**. This church, consecrated in the 1230s, stands on the site of Úbeda's main mosque. It displays a range of Gothic, Mudéjar, Renaissance, baroque and neo-Gothic styles.

Across the square is the vast yet neatly proportioned **Palacio de Juan Vázquez de Molina**, popularly known at the **Palacio de las Cadenas** (after the chains that once decorated its façade ). Construction was started by Vandelvira in 1540, but Vázquez de Molina never lived here, deciding even before its completion that the building should be used as a Dominican convent (953 75 04 40, open 10am-2pm, 5-9pm daily, free).

Wandering the narrow streets north and west of the Plaza de Vázquez de Molina reveals countless other examples of superb Renaissance architecture. Heading west along Calles Afán de Rivera and Ventanas brings you to Plaza San Lorenzo, where the church of **San Lorenzo** is built into the old city wall (its ivy-clad bell tower provides a picturesque photo opportunity). On the same square is the **Casa de las Torres** (953 75 05 18, open 8am-2.15pm, 4-6pm Mon-Fri, free), named after its two hefty towers. Built in the first two decades of the 16th century, this was the first plateresque mansion in Úbeda, and contains one of the town's first Renaissance patios; it now houses a school of arts and crafts.

North of here, the 16th-century **Palacio del Marqués de la Rambla**, on Plaza del Marqués, is now an upmarket hotel (*see p241*). Just to the east, facing each other across Calle Juan Pascuau, are the church of **San Pedro** (built at the end of the 14th century, with a façade from 1605) and the **Convento de Santa Clara**, founded in 1290 as the first Franciscan convent in Andalucía, altered many times up until the 18th century and currently undergoing more restoration work. The nuns sell a range of baked goodies to the public. Further along the street is the **Palacio de los Condes de Guadiana**.

From here, Calle Real – the main shopping street of the old town – leads down to Plaza del Ayuntamiento, flanked to the south by one side of the Palacio de las Cadenas, and with the fine **Palacio Vela de los Cobos** by Vandelvira at its north-west corner.

North-east of the square is Plaza Primero de Mayo, home to the vast late-Gothic church of **San Pablo** (13th-14th centuries) and, at its south-west corner, the graceful, arcaded 16th-century **Ayuntamiento** (the old Town Hall).

Calle Juan de la Cruz is where the saint-poet John of the Cross died of gangrene in 1591. Little of the 16th-century building remains, though a small museum dedicated to the saint – the **Museo Biblioteca San Juan de la Cruz** – includes the cell in which he died and artefacts relating to his life. A chapel, the **Oratorio de San Juan de la Cruz**, was built in 1627 to house his tomb, but his remains were subsequently moved to Segovia.

North of here is a superb double horseshoe-arched 14th-century Mudéjar gate, the **Puerta de Losal**, from which Calle de la Merced runs to Calle de Valencia and into the heart of Úbeda's pottery quarter. The town's traditional green-glazed ceramics make great souvenirs.

At the north-west edge of the old town, the partially arcaded Plaza de Andalucia is overlooked by the (unusually for Úbeda) largely baroque 18th-century church and convent of **Santisima Trinidad** and the **Torre del Reloj**, a 16th-century clock tower atop a hunk of 13th-century city wall. Shopping streets stretch out from the square; Calle Mesones leads into Carrera del Obispo Cobos and down to the bullring, bus station and Vandelvira's austere **Hospital de Santiago**, sometimes known as the 'Andalucían Escorial'.

North of here, Avenida Ramón y Cajal is the locale of much of Úbeda's cheap places to stay and has the greatest concentration of bars and restaurants in the town.

If you are heading towards the Cazorla Natural Park from Úbeda it's worth making brief detours to see a couple of fine villages. **Sabiote** (nine kilometres/five-and-a-half miles north-east of Úbeda) is a place almost comparable in artistic and historical importance to Úbeda and Baeza, but virtually unvisited. Its heyday was the 16th century, when Carlos V's secretary Francisco de los Cobos y Molina made it the capital of his fiefdom; it has extensively preserved medieval walls and a ruined Renaissance castle (one of the most impressive in Andalucía; a policeman from the town hall will accompany you there). The 16th-century architect Vandelvira was born in the village. **Iznatoraf**, a further 30 kilometres (19 miles) north-east towards Albacete, enjoys an eyrie of a location, with remarkable 360-degree views of the surrounding countryside.

### Museo Biblioteca San Juan de la Cruz

C/Carmen 13 (953 75 06 15). **Open** 11am-1pm, 5-7pm Tue-Sun. **Admission** €1.20; 60¢ concessions. **No credit cards. Map** p241 C1.

### Sacra Capilla del Salvador del Mundo

C/Baja del Salvador s/n (953 75 81 50). **Open** Mid June-mid Sept 10am-2pm, 5-7.30pm Mon-Sat; 10.45am-2pm, 4.30-7.30pm Sun. Mid Sept-mid June 10am-2pm, 4.30-7pm Mon-Sat; 10.45am-2pm, 4-7pm Sun. **Admission** €2.25; €1-€1.50 concessions. **No credit cards. Map** p241 C2.

## Where to eat & drink

The old town can be deathly quiet after dark, with only a scattering of eating and drinking options. There's more choice around Avenida Ramón y Cajal in the new town, particularly at the lower end of Calle Virgen de Guadalupe.

### El Gallo Rojo

Plaza Manuel Baraca 3 (953 75 20 38). **Open** 8am-midnight daily. Closed 2wks Oct. **Average** €. **Credit** MC, V. **Map** p241 A1.
At the new town end of C/Trinidad, this lively bar-restaurant has outside tables and good, solid food.

### Mesón Navarro

Plaza del Ayuntamiento 2 (953 79 06 38). **Open** 1-4pm, 8.30-11pm daily. **Average** €. **Credit** MC, V. **Map** p241 C2.
Still firmly in the hands of the locals despite its prime old town location, this is easily the best place for a tapa and a tipple in the area. Though it has a dining room at the back, most of Navarro's lively clientele stand at the bar or take one of the tables at the front (or on the plaza in good weather). Excellent tapas come with each drink. Try the navajas (razor-shell clams).

### El Porche

Redondo de Santiago 7 (953 75 72 87/ www.restauranteelporche.com). **Open** 1-4pm, 8.30-11.30pm daily. **Average** €€. **Credit** AmEx, DC, MC, V. **Map** p241 A3.
A classy place on the edge of the new town, close to the Hospital de Santiago, serving superior versions of the Spanish classics in a refined setting. The roof is open to the sky on temperate days.

### Restaurante Marqués

Plaza Marqués de la Rambla 2 (953 75 72 55/ www.hotel-maria-de-molina.com). **Open** 1.30-4pm Tue-Fri; 1.30-4pm, 8.30-11pm Sat, Sun. **Average** €-€€. **Credit** MC, V. **Map** p241 B2/3.
Located on a tiny plaza, opposite the monumental façade of the Palacio del Marqués de la Rambla, this excellent restaurant is owned by the Hotel María de Molina (see p241).

## Where to stay

All the classiest accommodation is in the old town, which is by far the nicest area to stay (though largely lifeless at night). All the budget places are in the new town, mostly along busy Avenida Ramón y Cajal, a ten-minute walk from the historic centre, and with lots of bars and restaurants nearby. There's little to choose between the hostels – try **Hostal Sevilla** (Avenida Ramón y Cajal 7, 953 75 06 12, closed Aug, double €33-€35) or **Hostal Castillo** (Avenida Ramón y Cajal 20, 953 75 04 30, double €35-€38), which has the advantage of a car park and a small restaurant. Quieter, and closer to the old town, is the **Hostal Victoria** (C/Alaminos 5, 953 75 29 52, double €33-€35).

### Álvar Fáñez

C/Juan Pasquau 5 (953 79 60 43). **Rates** (incl breakfast) €49-€86 single; €65-€129 double; €92-€153 triple; €152-€228 quad. **Credit** AmEx, MC, V. **Map** p241 B2.

Álvar Fáñez was a Christian knight who (apocryphally) strayed off into the nearby hills in pursuit of a Moorish girl, thereby missing a key battle against the Moors. His peregrinations gave rise to the popular expression 'to wander off on the hills of Úbeda', meaning 'to be distracted'. The 12-room hotel that bears his name is a classy, stylish affair, arrayed around a courtyard and well located in the old town. Its restaurant is in a 16th-century *bodega*.

### Hotel María de Molina

*Plaza del Ayuntamiento s/n (953 79 53 56/www.hotel-maria-de-molina.com).* **Rates** €50-€77 single; €77-€99 double. **Credit** AmEx, DC, MC, V. **Map** p241 C2. This delightful hotel, arrayed around an elegant courtyard, is excellent value for money and occupies a prime position, a minute's walk from glorious Plaza de Vázquez de Molina. Rooms are kitted out with rustic repro furniture and the bathrooms are first rate.

### Hotel La Paz

*C/Andalucía 1 (953 75 08 48/www.hotel-lapaz.com).* **Rates** €35 single; €54 double; €73 triple; €90 4-person apartment. **Credit** MC, V. **Map** p241 A1. This two-star hotel is the most upmarket option in the new town. It looks a bit grim from the outside, but some of its 45 rooms (all with air-con and TV) are a good size and unexpectedly stylish. A number have balconies, but bear in mind the traffic noise.

### Palacio de la Rambla

*Plaza del Marqués 1 (953 75 01 96/www.palacio rambla.terra.es).* Closed mid July-mid Aug. **Rates** (incl breakfast) €77 single; €107 double; €120 suite. **Credit** AmEx, DC, MC, V. **Map** p241 B2/3. Live like a *marquesa* in the Marquesa de la Rambla's 16th-century *palacio*. The eight wonderful rooms, many decorated with antiques, surround an atmosphere-rich courtyard.

### Parador Condestable Dávalos

*Plaza Vázquez de Molina s/n (953 75 03 45/www. parador.es).* **Rates** €92-€104 single; €115-€129 double; €193 suite. **Credit** AmEx, DC, MC, V. **Map** p241 C2. One of the loveliest of all the hotels in the *parador* chain, this 16th-century mansion, formerly home to the chaplain of the neighbouring church of San Salvador, is on Úbeda's grandest square. It's been sensitively modernised, and has all the usual *parador* luxury touches. Non-guests can enjoy the courtyard for the price of a drink.

### Rosaleda de Don Pedro

*C/Obispo Toral 2 (953 79 61 11/www.rosaledade donpedro.com).* **Rates** €60-€88 single; €75-€110 double. **Credit** DC, MC, V. **Map** p241 C2. A member of the Husa chain, this new hotel in the old town lacks the character of its rivals, but does boast the only hotel pool in Úbeda.

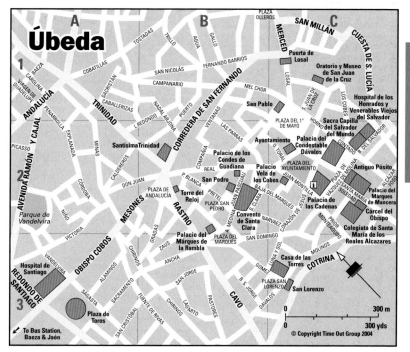

**Jaén Province**

# Walk Cazorla circuit

**Distance** 5.5km (3.5miles)
**Time required** 2hrs

This is a short, easy walk out from Cazorla that covers little distance but gives you a feel of the valley and the kind of terrain that awaits you should you choose to do a longer walk in the Parque Natural. It leaves the village from the beautiful Plaza de Santa María, then follows a dirt track gently up Cazorla's river valley before looping back to the village along a higher path.

The walk begins in front of the hotel Ciudad de Cazorla in the main square of Cazorla: Plaza de la Corredera. Cross the square and go down the street next to the Banesto bank. At the end of this street, bear left following signs for 'Ruinas de Santa María'. Pass by a fountain and emerge into the square of Santa María. Cross the square in front of the *hostal-restaurante* La Cueva and follow the street upwards, passing the ruined church of Santa María to your left.

Climb gradually and, at the first fork, bear left into Camino del Angel. The paved road soon becomes a track and you cross the bridge over the river. Pass by the Molino de la Farraga, just to one side of the track,

and continue to climb on a narrow path that soon meets with a track. Here, go right and head up a narrow path that follows the left bank of the river.

The paved section of path comes to an end and here there is a sign for Cazorla (2.5km). Swing hard round to the left and climb up a dirt road passing a small shed built into the rocks. The track comes up to an attractive house with a wooden terrace, where it veers right into a grove of olives and then bears round to the left again. You are now heading uphill towards a large cairn.

## Resources

### Internet

*Cyberworld, C/Picasso 8 (953 75 75 29).*
**Open** 11.15am-2.15pm, 5-10pm daily. **Map** p241 A2.

### Tourist information

*Palacio de Marqués de Contadero, C/Baja del Marqués (953 75 08 97).* **Open** *June-Sept* 9am-2.45pm, 5-8pm Mon-Fri; 10am-2pm Sat, Sun. *Oct-May* 9am-2.45pm, 4-7pm Mon-Fri; 10am-2pm Sat, Sun. **Map** p241 C2.

## Parque Natural de Cazorla

The one overwhelming natural draw in eastern Jaén is the huge and immensely varied **Parque Natural de las Sierras de Cazorla, Segura y las Villas**. Covering 209,418 hectares (809 square miles), it is one of Spain's largest Natural Parks and encompasses vast expanses of wooded mountains (a number of peaks top 2,000 metres/6,560 feet), flatlands, a 20-kilometre (12.5-mile) reservoir and a wide variety of flora and fauna. The vegetation

is some of the richest to be found in the Mediterranean basin, with 1,300 catalogued species (24 of which are exclusive to the area, including the Cazorla violet), and provides a home to Spanish ibex, wild boar and otters, golden eagles and Egyptian vultures, and such exclusive species as the wall lizard of Valverde.

The one major centre for the park is the town of Cazorla in the south; the northern part is far less touristed. Despite its size, the park can get very busy in summer and at weekends (only a few roads cross it). Out of season you'll have the roads and trails to yourself.

## Cazorla & around

Located 45 kilometres east of Úbeda, and 900 metres (3,000 feet) up on the edge of the Sierra de Cazorla, the little town of **Cazorla** is the main jumping-off point for the park, and an attractive destination in its own right. If you are just passing through you can easily leave with the impression that Cazorla is a lively,

On reaching a parking space beside another pretty house go left and zigzag up through the olive groves on a narrow footpath. Soon you reach a better-surfaced footpath. Turn left onto this path and head back towards Cazorla. The river is down to your left and there are wonderful views down and across the valley.

As you pass a water deposit on your right the path begins to descend. Pass a second water deposit and, just before reaching the first of the town's buildings, bear sharp left and drop down to meet Calle Paseo del Solar. Continue steeply downwards, passing Bar Torrecillas to your left, and then swing left into Calle del Solar Bajo. Continue down some steep steps and at the bottom turn right into Calle de la Torre. At the end of this street, bear left and then right into Calle de Mariano Estremera.

Turn left at the end of the street and then sharp right and follow the road along past the Agencia de la Seguridad Social. Turn left at the end, descend, and then bear right into Calle Gomes Calderón. You arrive back at Plaza de la Corredera.

*From* Walking in Andalucía *by Guy Hunter-Watts (Santana)*

largely modern town, yet there has, in fact, been a settlement here for well over 2,000 years. Beyond the lower town and the hectic Plaza de la Constitución (the tourist office is a minute's walk north of here on Paseo del Santo Cristo), a beguiling whitewashed settlement climbs up the valley.

Calle Doctor Muñoz leads from the square up to Plaza de la Corredera, the oval-shaped focus of this part of Cazorla, and then, through narrow streets to the lovely Plaza de Santa María. Here stand the remains of the ruined 16th-century church of **Santa María**, built by Andrés de Vandelvira and trashed by Napoleon's soldiers.

A short, steep walk up from the plaza brings you to the **Castillo de la Yedra**, which was largely built by the Moors on the site of a Roman fortification, and was restored in the 15th century. A kilometre outside town at the village of La Iruela there's an even more spectacularly sited ruined Moorish castle, up to which it's possible to scramble. From La Iruela, a road runs into the Sierra for

around 25 kilometres (16 miles) to Cañada de las Fuentes, the source of the Guadalquivir, where, according to the poet Antonio Machado, the river is born in 'a flash of clear water'.

The A315 runs through the southernmost tip of the park, crossing the Sierra and descending into the desert landscapes of Granada province. It's a fine drive, and passes the small town of **Quesada**. The works contained within the town's **Museo Rafael Zabaleta**, dedicated to the local painter, are of no great merit, but Zabaleta knew many of the great artistic names of his day, and there are lithographs dedicated to him by the likes of Picasso and Miro. Further on is the **Sanctuario de Tíscar**, a commandingly situated shrine (built over a Moorish fortress) containing an image of the Virgin and a painting by Zabaleta of the annual pilgrimage here.

The main road into the park from Cazorla goes past La Iruela, snakes over the Sierra de Cazorla and then heads north-east through the spectacular wooded Guadalquivir valley towards the long reservoir, the Embalse de Tranco. Just off this stretch of road are most of the park's hotels, campsites, picnic sites and visitor facilities. The Torre del Vinagre Centro de Visitantes (around 30 kilometres/19 miles from Cazorla) has information on all aspects of the park, including accommodation, and details of the many wonderful walks in the area.

### Castillo de la Yedra
*Cazorla (no phone).* **Open** 3-8pm Tue; 9am-8pm Wed-Sat; 9am-3pm Sun. **Admission** free.

### Museo Rafael Zabaleta
*C/Los Arcos de los Santos s/n, Quesada (info 953 73 31 33).* **Open** *May-Sept* 10am-2pm, 5-9pm Wed-Sun. *Oct-Apr* 10am-2pm, 4-8pm Wed-Sun. **Admission** €2. **No credit cards**.
The museum is due to move in spring/summer 2005 to Plaza Cesario Rodriguez Aguilera. The website www.cazorlasurrural.com has up-to-date information.

## Segura de la Sierra & around

Far fewer visitors come to the northern part of the park than the more easily accessible southern reaches, yet it's worth the journey just to gawp at the most stunningly sited village in the area: **Segura de la Sierra**. Clinging to the slopes of a hill beneath a (much restored) Moorish castle, this tiny place has as commanding a position – and yet it was one of the earliest fortresses in Andalucía to fall to the Christians (in 1214). The village's other main attraction is the mid 12th-century **Baño Moro** (Moorish bath), just off the Plaza Mayor. Both castle and bath are usually open all day every day. It's also worth taking a look at the strange, tiny, rectangular bullring on the way up to the castle.

**Jaén Province**

Around 20 kilometres (12.5 miles) south-west of Segura is **Hornos**, another pretty castle-topped village in a spectacular setting, with wonderful views out over the waters of the **Embalse de Tranco**. From here, it's a lovely meandering drive alongside the reservoir towards **Coto Rios**, an agreeable little village with plenty of accommodation options nearby.

Seven kilometres (four miles) north of Coto Rios is the **Parque Cinegético**, a modest wildlife park. There's a half-hour circular walk through the park with three viewpoints along the way, from which you've a good chance of seeing a few deer or ibex.

## Where to stay, eat & drink

There's plenty of accommodation in Cazorla. Of the cheaper options, the **Pensión Taxi** (Travesía de San Antón 7, 953 72 05 25, mobile 606 58 76 57, double €30) is handily located just off Plaza de la Constitución; **Pensión Betis** (Plaza Corredera 19, 953 72 05 40, double €22-€24) is another possibility. The **Villa Turística de Cazorla** (Ladera San Isicio s/n, 953 71 01 00, www.villacazorla.com, €58-€74 for 2 people) on the edge of town offers immaculate self-contained chalets, plus a pool and restaurant. In La Iruela, just outside Cazorla, the classy but good-value **Hotel Sierra de Cazorla** (Carretera de la Sierra s/n, 953 72 00 15, www.hotelsierradecazorla.com, double €52-€66) also has a pool and restaurant – be sure to ask for a room enjoying the spectacular view of the castle. The luxury **Parador El Adelantado** (953 72 70 75, www.parador.es, closed Jan, Dec, double €87-€104) is 25 kilometres (16 miles) from Cazorla in a beautiful, isolated position within the park – be warned, though, that most rooms do not have views. There's a pool in the grounds.

Cazorla is well equipped with good tapas bars, particularly around the main squares. Try **Bar Las Vegas** (Plaza de la Corredera 17, 953 72 02 77, closed Mon & dinner Sun, 2wks Jan & 2wks June, €), **Bar Rojas** (Plaza de la Constitución s/n, 953 72 19 36, €) or **Bar Sola** (C/Doctor Muñoz 30, 953 72 00 58, closed Sun & mid July-early Aug, €). For a quarter of a century the most upmarket dining option in town has been José and Rosa's outstanding, inventive **La Sarga** (Plaza del Mercado s/n, 953 72 15 07, closed Tue & Sept, €€€), where specialities include supreme of pheasant with grape sauce, artichokes with rosemary sauce.

In Segura, **La Mesa Segureña** (C/Postigo 2, 953 48 21 01, www.lamesadesegura.com, closed Mon & dinner Sun, €) is an eating option and rents out apartments (€54 for 2 people). If you want to stay in Hornos, try **Bar El Cruce**

(Puerta Nueva 27, 953 49 50 03, closed some Mons Oct-May, double €24), or **El Mirador** (Puerta Nueva 11, 953 49 50 19, double €27, restaurant €) – the latter, as the name implies, has rooms with lovely views.

If you want to stay out in the wilds, try the self-catering cottages at **El Mesoncillo** in La Platera, not far from Hornos (953 42 53 90, mobile 646 81 02 52, www.mesoncillo.com, cottage for 2 or 3 €42-€48, cottage for 4-6 €64-€73, cheaper weekly rates) or, for a bit more luxury (and a swimming pool), the **Hotel La Hortizuela** (Carretera del Tranco, km50.5, 953 71 31 50, www.lahortizuela.com, closed early Jan-late Feb, double €45-€59). In the area of Coto Rios, the **Hotel Paraíso de Bujaraiza** (Carretera del Tranco, km59, 953 12 41 14, www.paraisodebujaraiza.com, double €54-€65) enjoys a stunning position on the bank of the reservoir, and also has apartments and a pool.

## Resources

### Internet
**Cazorla** *Parra Multistore, Plaza de la Constitución 12 (953 72 08 75).* **Open** 10am-2pm, 4.30-9.30pm daily.

### Tourist information
**Cazorla** *Paseo del Santo Cristo 17 (953 71 01 02/ www.ayto-cazorla.es).* **Open** *Mid July-Aug* 10am-1pm, 6-8pm daily. *Sept-mid July* 10am-1pm, 5.30-8pm daily.

**Parque Natural de las Sierras de Cazorla, Segura y las Villas** *Centro de Visitantes 'Torre del Vinagre', Carretera del Tranco, km18, Santiago-Pontones (953 71 30 17/www.ayto-cazorla.es).* **Open** *Mid June-mid July* 11am-2pm, 5-8pm daily. *Mid July-Sept* 10.30am-2pm, 5-8.30pm daily. *Oct-mid June* 11am-2pm, 4-6pm daily.

## Getting there

### By bus
There are plentiful buses each day to Jaén and Úbeda. Úbeda's bus station is at C/San José s/n (953 75 21 57, 953 75 18 35) on the western side of town (close to the Hospital de Santiago), from where there are frequent services to Jaén, Córdoba, Granada, Málaga and Sevilla. Cazorla buses stop at Plaza del Pueblo (Alsina Graells 953 75 21 57, www.alsinagraells.com). There are several Alsina Graells services a day to/from Baeza and Úbeda (approx 25mins). Baeza bus station is at C/Alcalde Puche Pardo (953 74 04 68).

### By train
The nearest train station to Baeza and Úbeda is Linares-Baeza (902 24 02 02), 15km/9 miles from Baeza and 19km/12 miles from Úbeda. Buses to both towns connect with most trains. There are 3 direct daily trains from Jaén (40 mins), 4 from Córdoba (1hr 20mins), 1 from Sevilla (3hrs), 3 from Málaga (3hrs 30mins), 3 from Almería (3hrs 45mins), 4 from Granada (2hrs 15mins) and 7 from Madrid (3hrs 10mins).

# Granada Province

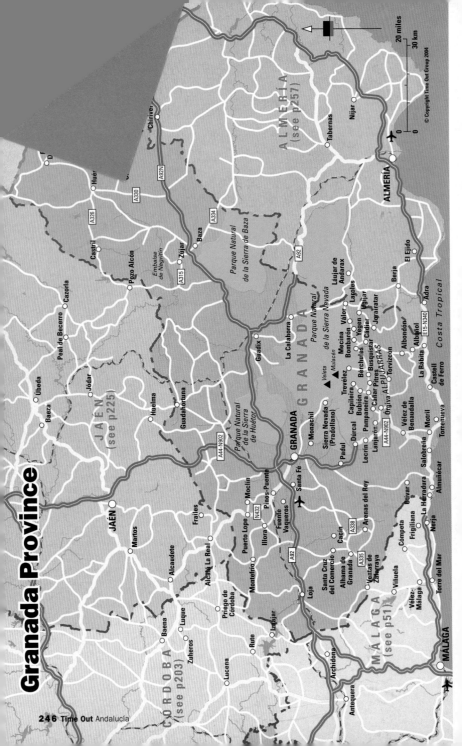

# Granada Province

# Granada Province

So much more than just the Alhambra…

Whatever you seek, you shall find it somewhere in this most varied of provinces – an outstanding palace overlooking a fascinating city, the tallest mountains in Spain, the solitude of wild desert landscapes, the bustle of lively seaside resorts; the list goes on…

### GRANADA CITY

The glorious, fêted Alhambra remains Granada's (and Andalucía's) prize attraction. But the mystique of this extraordinary palace should not detract from the city's many other draws: a fine Renaissance cathedral; an atmospheric Moorish quarter; gypsy cave dwellings; and an over-the-top baroque monastery – not to mention free tapas and a lively nightlife scene.

### WEST OF GRANADA

Beyond the flat expanse of the *vega* is a region of rolling hills and olive groves that formed a buffer zone between the Nasrid kingdom

and advancing Christian forces from the 13th to 15th centuries. The events of the *reconquista* are writ large in the numerous castles and churches that stud this area. Highlights include the spectacularly sited small towns of Moclín, Montefrío and Alhama de Granada.

### EAST OF GRANADA

Head east from the city and raw, arid, bleached landscapes open up. Amid the desert-like fastnesses are a handful of unique destinations – the town of Guadix with its extensive cave quarter and impressive cathedral, the remarkable Renaissance castle of La Calahorra, and even – perhaps – the cradle of European Man in Orce.

### THE SIERRA NEVADA AND THE ALPUJARRAS

South-east of Granada city rise the snowcapped Sierra Nevada – the highest peaks in Spain. The mountains provide the setting for the most southerly ski resort in Europe. On the southern slopes, the Alpujarras once sheltered Moorish exiles from Granada, and now attract increasing numbers of expat northern Europeans. This enclave of terraced river valleys and distinctive villages is one of the most picturesque in Andalucía, and makes perfect walking and hiking territory.

### COSTA TROPICAL

The coast of Granada province has been dubbed the Costa Tropical due to its balmy climate, which allows tropical fruits and sugar cane to thrive. It's less developed than the Costa del Sol and less intensively farmed than the Costa de Almería. The main resorts of Almuñécar and Salobreña, although developed, are the most attractive places to stay.

## The best...

### Architecture, Moorish heritage, tapas & nightlife
Granada City (*p248-69*).

### Castle
La Calahorra (*p272*).

### Cave dwellings
Guadix (*p272*); Sacromonte, Granada (*p258*).

### Mountains
Sierra Nevada (*p274-82*).

### Towns & villages
Alhama de Granada (*p270*); Castril (*p272*); Montefrío (*p270*) and the Alpujarras generally (*p274-82*).

### Views
The Alhambra from El Mirador de San Nicolás (*p258*); the Valle de Poqueira from Capileira (*p278*); the Sierra Nevada from Moclín (*p270*); the Axarquía from the Zafarraya pass (*p271*).

Granada Province

# Granada City

The Moors' last site – a city to make a grown man weep...

**The Alhambra**, from the Carrera del Darro.

During his stay at the Alhambra in 1829, Washington Irving was startled one evening by a 'turbaned Moor' sitting in the Patio of the Lions. To the romantically minded American diplomat, it seemed as if 'some ancient inhabitant of the Alhambra had broken the spell of the centuries and become visible', but the Moor assured him that he was merely a trinket seller who liked to visit the Alhambra because it reminded him of the old Muslim palaces of his homeland.

Nearly two centuries later, nowhere else in Spain can evoke past Islamic glories with such force; the Alhambra is, quite simply, a medieval Moor's idea of paradise, and the most complete surviving example of its kind in the world.

The Alhambra is the main draw to Granada still; indeed, many visitors stay near the monument, visit it and leave without even venturing into the centre of town. At first glance they think they're not missing much – Granada doesn't have Sevilla's obvious grandeur, or

Córdoba chocolate-box quaintness. Yet what it does have is the vibrancy and colour of a bustling town with a young population (the thousands of students at its university joined by a seemingly equal number of party-hungry backpackers), and its roughness, gruffness and edge will appeal to some – just as it will repel others. Its nightlife is probably the best and hippest in Andalucía. And despite the *granadino*'s dour, unfriendly reputation, the city remains one of the few places in Andalucía to maintain the generous tradition of free tapas with every drink in most bars.

Apart from the cathedral and some glorious baroque churches, the heart of the modern city isn't that pretty, but it is crowned by two jewels – the Alhambra and the Albaicín district, facing each other over the gorge of the Darro valley, with the (almost always) snow-capped peaks of the Sierra Nevada as a breathtaking backdrop. Both are important markers of the Moorish influence on Granada – an influence that can still be sensed in the Albaicín's whitewashed *carmen* villas, and which is undergoing something of a rebirth. A fashion for North African and Eastern exoticism means there are almost as many couscous houses and *teterías* as tapas bars on the main *tapeo* drags, and gaudily-tiled 'Arabian' bathhouses offer to indulge visitors like a sultan. A more authentic reflection of the renewed appreciation of Granada's Muslim past can be seen in the building of the major new mosque and Islamic studies centre in the Albaicín, the workshops and conferences promoted by the Legado Andalusi cultural education foundation and the 'Science in El Andalus' exhibition at the Parque de las Ciencias.

One tip: the city is a nightmare to negotiate by car (and has been deliberately made so). Finding a parking space in the centre is all but impossible, so head straight for a car park.

## HISTORY
The present city of Granada was the site of small Iberian, Roman and Visigothic settlements but did not achieve any significance until well after its initial takeover by Muslim invaders from Africa in 711. It was during the 11th century that the Berber tribe known as the Zirids established themselves in nearby Illiberis (Elvira), and then decided to move to the more easily defensible Garnatha. (The name eventually became

Granada; it is mere coincidence that this means 'pomegranate' in Spanish, although this fruit has become a much-loved symbol of the city.) They made their headquarters in the Albaicín (a pre-existing Jewish settlement, about which virtually nothing is known, was on the future Alhambra hill). The Zirids were responsible for the two oldest Islamic sites in Granada – the ruined bridge along the Darro and the adjoining Bañuelo (baths).

By the early 13th century, as the Castillians began to reclaim the *taifas* of Córdoba, Jaén and Sevilla, the population of Granada swelled with refugee Muslims, mostly concentrated in the Albaicín area. The Nasrid chieftain, known to history as Mohammed I, entered Granada in 1237 and soon annexed Almería and Málaga to form the last independent emirate, of which Granada was the capital. He was a canny politician, maintaining this last bastion of al-Andalus with the aid of North African Berber princes, while simultaneously paying tributes to Castilla. He even provided the Christian armies with military aid in campaigns against other Moorish *taifas*, most famously in the siege of Sevilla.

Over the next 250 years, Granada enjoyed relative peace and prosperity, which provided fertile ground for artistic and scientific progress. However, the Nasrids were always living on borrowed time and, by the 15th century, relations had become strained with the kingdoms of Aragón and Castilla, now powerfully united through the marriage of Fernando and Isabel. In 1481 Sultan Muley Hasen could no longer keep up with the escalating payments demanded by the Catholics and threw down the gauntlet to Fernando's messenger: 'Tell your king that Granada no longer mints coins to pay Christians. Now it forges swords and lances to fight them.' Legend has bestowed Fernando with an equally pithy reply: 'I'll pluck the seeds from this pomegranate one by one.'

It was not for nothing that Machiavelli praised Fernando's cunning and strategic genius in *The Prince*. Rather than launch a full-scale siege, Fernando sat back and let the internal feuds that plagued the Sultanate do their work. Harem quarrels over the accession had divided Granada into factions, one side backing Muley Hasen's wife and her son 'Boabdil' (a Spanish corruption of Abu-Abdullah), another side supporting the sons of the Sultan's Christian concubine, Zoraya, and still others in favour of his brother, El Zagal. The bloody soap opera finally concluded with Boabdil taking possession of Granada – but his rule was to be a short one. In 1491 over 150,000 Catholic troops sealed the city with a heavy blockade.

Boabdil, last Sultan of the Nasrid dynasty, finally surrendered on 2 January 1492 on the condition that Spanish Muslims be allowed to retain their religion, language, traditions and judicial system. Fernando and Isabel soon reneged on this promise; their brutal treatment of Granada's Jewish and Muslim citizenry resulted in rebellion and mass emigration. Drained of artisans and trade, the city fell into economic decline (though major monuments, such as the cathedral, were built in the Renaissance and baroque periods), which was further compounded by the later destruction and looting by Napoleon's troops.

The 1898 Baedeker guide described Granada as 'a living ruin'. Modernisation in the 20th century has not necessarily improved matters. The poet Ángel Ganivet decried the new 'love of the straight line' as contrary to Granada's dreamy, tranquil spirit, and many (including Lorca) mourned the covering over of the Río Darro; the waters that once irrigated the gardens of sultans now trickle under the traffic-choked boulevards of the city centre.

## The Alhambra

Since Washington Irving's 'rediscovery' of the Alhambra in the early 19th century, and the subsequent flood of panegyrics celebrating its wonders that issued from the pens of Romantic travellers, this remarkable palace has been one of the major tourist destinations not just in Andalucía, or Spain, but in the whole of Europe. And despite the often overwhelming hype surrounding it, the Alhambra remains one of the most extraordinary and rewarding collections of buildings and gardens on the continent.

The Alhambra complex started life in the 11th century as a basic structure of blush-coloured walls and fortified towers, which gave the site its name: *qa'lat al-Hamra* or the 'Red Castle'. Its strategic location on the inaccessible hill of al-Sabikah attracted Mohammed I, the founder of the Nasrid dynasty (1237-1492), who set up a hydraulic system of aqueducts and cisterns to support an independent township. The most spectacular period of Nasrid architecture came in the mid to late 14th century during the reigns of his successors, Yusuf I and Mohammed V, who built the Palacio de los Leones and the Palacio de Comares; 'Granada in those days was as a silver vase filled with emeralds and jacinths,' sighed one Moorish poet. The subsequent additions of Christian monarchs rankle with many visitors and certainly disrupt the aesthetic unity of the Alhambra, yet the Palacio de Carlos V and the Convento de San Francisco are undeniably beautiful in their own right and heighten the Alhambra's sense of history.

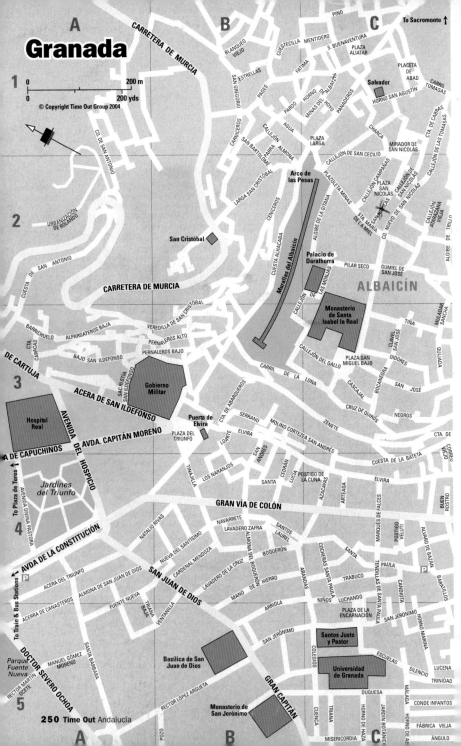

# Granada

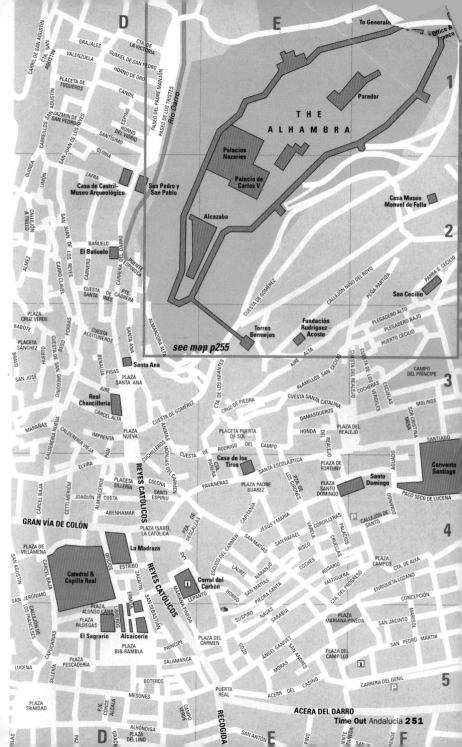

**D**

CARRIL DE SAN AGUSTIN
CTA. DE SAN AGUSTIN
GRAJALES
CTA DE LA VICTORIA
VALENZUELA
GUMIEL DE SAN PEDRO
PLACETA DE TOQUEROS
HORNO DE ORO
CANDIL
PASEO DEL PADRE MANJÓN
CARRELLOS SAN PEDRO
JAZMIN DE LOS REYES
ESPINO
SANTÍSIMO
HORNO DEL VIDRIO
GLORIA
ZAFRA
Casa de Castril–Museo Arqueológico
San Pedro y San Pablo
CALLEJÓN A TRILLO
GUINEA
LIMÓN
SAN JUAN DE LOS REYES
BAÑUELO
El Bañuelo
CARRERA DEL DARRO
CARNERO
PTE. ESPINOSA
ALMEZ
CARRO CLAVEL
SAN JUAN DE LOS REYES
CUESTA SANTA INÉS
DE CABRERA
PTE. DE CABRERA
PLAZA CRUZ VERDE
BABOTE
PORRAS
RESO SAN GREGORIO
CUESTA ACEITUNEROS
SANTA ANA
ALMANZORA ALTA
PLACETA SÁNCHEZ
BRAVO
HUERTO
BENALÚA
PISAS
Santa Ana
PLAZA SANTA ANA
SAN JOSÉ
AIRE
Real Chancillería
CÁRCEL ALTA
MARAÑAS
CALDERERÍA NUEVA
CALDERERÍA VIEJA
IMPRENTA
PAN
CUESTA DE GOMÉREZ
PLAZA NUEVA
ELVIRA
REYES CATÓLICOS
CUCHILLEROS
MONJAS DEL CARMEN
PLACETA SILLERÍA
COLCHA
CTA. PAPIÚ
CUESTA DE RODRIGO
CÁRCEL BAJA
CETTI-MERIÉM
JOAQUÍN
COSTA
ALMIRECEROS
SANTI ESPIRIÚ
PAVANERAS
ABENHAMAR
**GRAN VÍA DE COLÓN**
PLAZA DE VILLAMENA
PLAZA ISABEL LA CATÓLICA
**REYES CATÓLICOS**
La Madraza
OFICIOS
SAN AGUSTÍN
CÁRCEL BAJA
PLAZA DE LOS FRANCESES
Catedral & Capilla Real
ESTRIBO
ZACATÍN
MARIANA PINEDA
SAN SEBASTIÁN
Corral del Carbón
LEPANTO
HORNO
SAN JERÓNIMO
CALLEJÓN DE LOS FRANCESES
PLAZA ALONSO CANO
LIBREROS
ERMITA
PLAZA PASIEGAS
El Sagrario
Alcaicería
PRÍNCIPE
CAPUCHINAS
PLAZA BIB-RAMBLA
SALAMANCA
LUCENA
PLAZA PESCADERÍA
SILLERÍA
BOTEROS
PLAZA TRINIDAD
PJE. CONDE ALCALÁ
MESONES
CAMPO VERDE
PUERTA REAL
BLAS
PAZ
**D**
GRACIA
ALHÓNDIGA
PLAZA DEL LINO

**E**

To Generalife
Office & Entrance
To Generalin

**THE ALHAMBRA**

Parador

Palacios Nazaries

Palacio de Carlos V

Casa Museo Manuel de Falla

Alcazaba

San Pedro y San Pablo

CALLEJÓN NIÑO DEL ROYO

PARRA S. CECILIO

PEÑA PARTIDA

San Cecilio

PLEGADERO ALTO

PLEGADERO BAJO

HUERTO CECILIO

CUESTA DE GOMÉREZ

*see map p255*

Torres Bermejas

Fundación Rodríguez-Acosta

AIRE ALTA

CUESTA DEL REALEJO

CUESTA DE LOS COCHERAS

ESCALIAS

CAMPO DEL PRÍNCIPE

**3**

ALAMILLOS SAN CECILIO

CTA. DE LOS INFANTES

CRUZ DE PIEDRA

CUESTA SANTA CATALINA

ALAMILLOS SAN CECILIO

MOLINOS

SOR CRISTINA MESA

SANTIAGO

PLACETA PUERTA DE SOL

DAMASQUEROS

HONDA

DEL REALEJO

PLAZA DEL REALEJO

OIDAVÍO

**Convento Santiago**

CAMPO

Casa de los Tiros

SANTA ESCOLÁSTICA

PLAZA DE FORTUNY

PZA. DE LOS BIRONES

**Santo Domingo**

DOMINGO

PACO SECO DE LUCENA

PLAZA PADRE SUAREZ

PLAZA SANTO DOMINGO

CALLEJÓN DE SANTO

**4**

LAS DESCALZAS

ESCUDO DEL CARMEN

CAPITANÍA

JESÚS Y MARÍA

SAN MATÍAS

SAN RAFAEL

VARELA

CORDILLERAS

PALACIOS

CRUELLAS

PLAZA CAMPOS

CTA. DE AIXA

LAUREL

NARANJO

COCHES

RISCO

ROSARIO

FALTIGUERA

CTA. DEL PROGRESO

ENRIQUETA LOZANO

SAN MATÍAS

PIEDRA SANTA

SABRIA

CONCEPCIÓN

SUSPIRO

NAVAS

SARABIA

PLAZA MARIANA PINEDA

SAN JACINTO

MARISOL

GOZO

ÁNGEL GANIVET

SAN ANDRÉS

MORAS

PLAZA DEL CAMPILLO

SAN PEDRO MÁRTIR

PLAZA DEL CARMEN

CARRERA DEL GENIL

ACERA DEL CASINO

**ACERA DEL DARRO**

PUERTA REAL

SAN ANTÓN

**RECOGIDA**

CAMPO VERDE

**E**

PINO

**F**

**Time Out** Andalucía **251**

*Carmen Verde Du Luna* (handwritten)

# Alhambra essentials

The Alhambra's immense popularity – it is the most visited monument in Spain – has resulted in a strict admission policy that limits the daily number of visitors. This means that, effectively, tickets must be bought in advance (although it is possible to turn up on the day, it's not advised). The prime attraction, the Palacios Nazaríes, are easily log-jammed by crowds of tourists, and each visitor is subject to a strictly observed entrance system of half-hourly time slots, which are printed on the tickets. You must enter the Palacios during your allocated time, but, once inside, you are free to stay as long as you like. It's essential to arrive well before your appointed slot to give yourself time to pick up your ticket from the ticket office and make your way to the entrance of the Palacios.

Alternatively, you can visit just the complex's gardens with a garden ticket. For this, you buy either a morning (8.30am-2pm) or afternoon (2-8pm March-Oct; 2-6pm Nov-Feb) ticket and can enter at any time during these periods.

## WHERE TO BUY TICKETS

If at all possible, buy your tickets as far in advance as possible. You can do this (up to a year in advance) through the BBVA bank, either in branches or at cash machines (the closest branch to the Alhambra is at Plaza Isabel la Católica 1); on the phone (902 22 44 60 within Spain/ +34 915 37 91 78 from outside Spain); or online at www.alhambratickets.com. You pick up the tickets at the Alhambra ticket office on the day of your visit; you'll need your reference number, passport and the credit card used to buy the tickets.

The only place to buy tickets for entry the same day is at the Alhambra ticket office. But this can involve extremely lengthy queues and there may be no tickets left when you get to the front. If you have no alternative, arrive at the ticket office as early in the day as possible to have a chance of picking up a ticket for the same day.

Alternatively, your hotel can usually book Alhambra tickets for you. Make sure you're just getting a ticket and not a tour you may not want.

If you buy the Granada City Pass (Bono Turístico) (*see p269*), then your Alhambra entry slot and ticket are already part of the package.

## THE BEST TIME AND WAY TO VISIT

If at all possible, try to visit out of peak season. For the best, least crowded experience, we can't emphasise strongly enough that it's worth forcing yourself out of bed and pre-booking a ticket for the first slot of the day (8.30-9am). If you manage this, head straight for the Palacios Nazaríes on entering the complex, and then, when the doors open, zip through the first couple of rooms (you can always backtrack

After Carlos V left in the mid 16th century, the whole site gradually fell into ruin and went on to suffer terrible abuse at the hands of Napoleon's troops, who were stationed here in 1812. Twenty years later Washington Irving's bestselling book, *Tales of the Alhambra*, put Granada firmly on the tourist map and the Spanish government finally allotted funds to the site's restoration; it remains an ongoing project (though the recent directorship of Mateo Revilla was highly controversial, with more and more of the complex being closed to tourists).

The recommended route through the site allows a slow immersion in the historical contexts. It begins at the **Alcazaba** military fortress to the west, followed by the **Palacio de Carlos V**, the **Palacios Nazaríes** (the highlight of any visit), with a stroll through the **Generalife** gardens forming a sensual coda.

The tour of the entire complex takes at least three hours, and involves quite a lot of walking, so wear comfy shoes and bring something to eat and drink. The detailed audio guide is a good investment and is available in various languages on deposit of a passport or credit card.

## Entering the complex

To protect the monument, vehicle access is restricted to taxis and the **Alhambrabus** (numbers 30 and 32, every 10mins from the Plaza Nueva, 90¢). Cars follow a circuitous route to the car park just above the ticket offices.

On foot, the standard ascent is up Cuesta de Gómerez from Plaza Nueva: a steep 20-minute walk to the ticket offices. This narrow street, lined with *hostales* and souvenir shops, opens out into a shady avenue once you reach the **Puerta de las Granadas** (Gate of the Pomegranates), later) so that you can enjoy the later chambers and patios in solitude – an unforgettable experience.

Be sure to frequently sit on the ground when contemplating your surroundings – the Nasrids would have viewed their palaces from cushions and carpets on the floor. It has also been suggested that the rulers were largely absent during the day and that the architecture and decoration of the Alhambra was specifically designed to be appreciated by candle- and moonlight. Book for one of the magical night-time visits and you'll soon find yourself subscribing to the theory.

The Junta de Andalucía's website on the Alhambra can be found at www.alhambra-patronato.es.

**Note**: The details below may change without notice; be sure to check the Alhambra's website or call the phone numbers above beforehand.

### The Alhambra & Generalife

**Open** *Mar-Oct* 8.30am-8pm daily (ticket office 8am-7pm). Nighttime visit (Palacios Nazaríes only) 10-11.30pm Tue-Sat (ticket office 9-10.30pm). *Nov-Feb* 8.30am-6pm daily (ticket office 8am-5pm). Nighttime visit (Palacios Nazaríes only) 8-9.30pm Fri, Sat (ticket office 7.30-8.30pm). **Admission** €10; €7 concessions; under-7s free. *Gardens only* €5. **No credit cards** (at ticket office). **Map** p251 E1/2 & p255.

an imposing Renaissance arch built by Carlos V, with the eighth-century **Torres Bermejas** (Vermillion Towers) to the south. From here, the left-hand path takes you to a king-sized drinking fountain added by Carlos V and overlooked by the most impressive of the four Alhambra gateways, the **Puerta de la Justicia** (Gate of Justice), built by Yusuf I in 1348. As is the custom in defensive Arab gateways, the steep road makes four right-angled turns to slow down invading armies and make them sitting ducks for the defending forces. The marble keystone is decorated with a sculpted hand thought to represent the five precepts of Islam, while on an inner arch is a sculpture of the famous Nasrid key, only found on gateways in the kingdom of Granada. The key symbolises the opening to paradise and, more prosaically, indicated the entrance to a township or *medina*. The ticket office is a further ten minutes' uphill walk.

Beyond the ticket barriers, follow signs for the Palacios Nazaríes along a cypress-lined walk past the ruins of the old **medina**. This was once a thriving city, complete with houses, schools, baths, a tannery, a mosque and kilns. Cypress trees were planted here as symbols of mourning and eternity during the Alhambra's reconstruction to simulate fallen walls and trace the lines of the original buildings.

At the end of the walk is the **Convento de San Francisco** (now a luxury *parador*; *see p266*), where Isabel and Fernando were temporarily interred during the construction of the Capilla Real (*see p259*); a marble floor-slab by the tiny chapel commemorates their stay. From here, Calle Real runs west down the hill, past a strip of tacky tourist shops and the bulky Palacio de Carlos V to the **Puerta del Vino** (Wine Gate; this ruddy-coloured arch formed the toll-gate and principal access to the *medina*) and the Alcazaba.

## The Alcazaba

Through the Puerta del Vino is the **Plaza de los Aljibes**, where giant underground cisterns (*aljibes*) were built immediately after the Christian conquest. Look out for the small plaque on the left, just inside the gate, which commemorates the invalid soldier, José García, who risked his life to stay behind and defuse the explosives planted by Napoleon's troops when they left Granada in 1812.

Though much of the Moorish Alcazaba is ruined, its towers and walls are well preserved, and you can trace the foundations of what was once a fortified military zone, complete with barracks, dungeons, a mosque, a communal bath and the Plaza de Armas parade ground. Of the four towers, the best known is the **Torre de la Vela**, an imposing landmark and watch-tower that has featured in the city's official coat of arms since 1843. The tower is also a potent symbol of the Catholic victory over the Moors, as it was from here that Fernando and Isabel flew the victorious Christian flags on 2 January 1492; the event is still celebrated locally on the same date each year as **El Día de la Toma** (though to increasing protests).

## Palacio de Carlos V

East of the Alcazaba is the huge bulk of the Renaissance Palacio de Carlos V. The chance to build a palace in the very heart of the last Muslim stronghold in Europe was too loaded with symbolism for a Christian warlord like Emperor Carlos V to resist. It may hardly blend with the Palacios Nazaríes next door, but is nevertheless one of the finest expressions of

Tuscan Renaissance architecture outside Italy. Designed by Pedro Machuca, a student of Michelangelo, the centrepiece is a two-tiered circular courtyard, set inside a perfect square, with an octagonal chapel in the north-eastern corner. The carved reliefs show bloody battle scenes on the western side and mythological scenes to the south, representing the Emperor and the Empress respectively.

On the ground floor of the Palacio is the **Museo de la Alhambra,** home to the world's finest collection of Nasrid art, largely made up of findings from the Alhambra itself. The star exhibits are the huge carved door taken from the Sala de las dos Hermanas, the 132-centimetre-high (51-inch) 'Gazelle Jar', with lacy blue and gold decoration depicting Oriental-style gazelles (now the symbol of the Alhambra Foundation) and a magnificent fountain from the Caliphate period depicting lions attacking gazelles.

The less essential first-floor **Museo de Bellas Artes** (closed at the time of writing; due to re-open mid 2005), meanwhile, has nine chronologically ordered rooms containing art from the *reconquista* to the 20th century. Highlights are Florentino's emotionally charged *Burial of Christ*, a sensitive carving of the Virgin and Child by Diego de Siloé and a bizarre 'miracle' painting by Pedro de Raxi of a black man and a white man swapping their left legs. Local bigshots like Pedro de Mena, José de Mora and Alonso Cano all get a look-in, and, though the later sections are much weaker, there are some expressive portraits by Federico de Madrazo.

In various parts of the Alhambra complex you'll see carved the words 'Plus Ultra'. This was Carlos V's megalomaniacal family motto (literally, 'there is more'); an immodest riposte to Alexander the Great's supposed utterance of 'ne plus ultra', 'there is no more', implying he'd conquered all there was to conquer).

### Museo de la Alhambra

*Ground floor, Palacio de Carlos V (958 02 79 31).* **Open** 9am-2.30pm Tue-Sat. **Admission** free.

### Museo de Bellas Artes

*1st floor, Palacio de Carlos V (958 22 48 43).* **Open** *Apr-Sept* 2.30-6pm Tue; 9am-6pm Wed-Sat; 9am-2pm Sun. *Oct-Mar* 2.30-8pm Tue; 9am-8pm Wed-Sat; 9am-2.30pm Sun. **Admission** €1.50; free with EU passport.

## Palacios Nazaríes

The Alhambra's star attraction is undoubtedly the Palacios Nazaríes (Nasrid Palaces). Built in brick, wood and adobe, it's remarkable that this beautiful, light and fragile collection of stunningly decorated buildings and courtyards survives. It stands as easily the finest surviving example of Nasrid art and architecture.

The purpose of the art of this period was, by rhythmic symmetries and endless sequences of repetition, to express the infinite glory of Allah in finite terms. Linear mazes of cursive and Kufic script feature heavily in the decoration; mostly as poems eulogising the sultans and their palace or as repeated verses from the Koran, most frequently the Nasrid motto and war cry: *'Wa la ghalib ila Allah'* ('There is no conqueror but Allah'). The eight-pointed star is also a key feature, expressing the convergence of heaven and earth. Just when it seems that a pattern is sealed in perfection, there is a gap or irregularity. Builders and decorators included these on purpose – to aspire to create something perfect was forbidden as blasphemous by the Koran. The same humility (and the Nasrids' straightened circumstances) is implied in the choice of cheap and perishable materials, such as plaster, wood and clay.

The palace complex consists of three major sections, each set around a courtyard and each with its own function: the **Palacio de Mexuar,** where the sultans conducted their official business and saw to judicial matters; the **Palacio de Comares** (or Serallo), where they would receive emissaries and important guests, and the **Palacio de Leones** (or Harem), the private living quarters of the sultan and his family.

### PALACIO DE MEXUAR

The Mexuar is the first area of the palaces that visitors enter. Completed in 1365 (though greatly altered on many occasions since), it's thought to predate the other two surviving palace complexes. Its name possibly derives from the Arabic word *mashawari,* meaning 'place of counsel', and it seems to have been dedicated to judicial and bureaucratic business. The strange mixture of Islamic and Catholic decoration in the main chamber comes from the 16th-century conversion of the room into a chapel, complete with a choir in the upper balustrade. The adjoining **Cuarto Dorado** (Golden Room) was probably used as an antechamber to the Palacio de Comares, and was where the ruler, seated on a throne, held public audiences.

### PALACIO DE COMARES

The breathtaking stucco work, glazed tiles and carved wood of the Palacio de Comares (or Serallo) were largely created for Mohammed V in 1370. This area separated the administrative zone of the palace from the private royal quarters (though it should be noted that it's almost impossible to determine the function of many of the rooms in the Alhambra as this was likely to have been fluid). The Cuarto Dorado leads into the delicate stucco arcades of the **Patio de los Arrayanes** (Patio of the Myrtles), originally

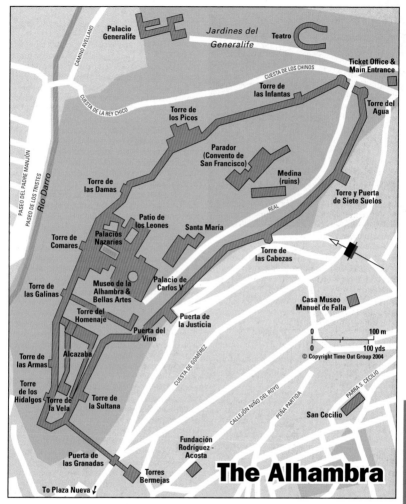

Palacio Generalife

CAMINO AVELLANO

*Jardines del Generalife*

Teatro

Ticket Office & Main Entrance

CUESTA DE LOS CHINOS

Torre de las Infantas

Torre del Agua

CUESTA DE LA REY CHICO

Torre de los Picos

Parador (Convento de San Francisco)

Medina (ruins)

PASEO DEL PADRE MANJÓN

Río Darro

PASEO DE LOS TRISTES

Torre de las Damas

Torre y Puerta de Siete Suelos

REAL

Patio de los Leones

Santa María

Torre de Comares

Palacios Nazaríes

Torre de las Cabezas

Torre de las Galinas

Museo de la Alhambra & Bellas Artes

Palacio de Carlos V

Casa Museo Manuel de Falla

Torre del Homenaje

Puerta de la Justicia

Puerta del Vino

Torre de las Armas

Alcazaba

CUESTA DE GOMÉREZ

Torre de los Hidalgos

Torre de la Vela

Torre de la Sultana

PARRA S. CECILIO

CALLEJÓN NIÑO DEL ROYO

PEÑA PARTIDA

San Cecilio

Puerta de las Granadas

Fundación Rodríguez - Acosta

Torres Bermejas

**The Alhambra**

To Plaza Nueva

0 — 100 m
0 — 100 yds
© Copyright Time Out Group 2004

built during the reign of Yusuf I (1333-54). For all its splendour it still adheres to the basic blueprint of Islamic domestic design: an enclosed space looking on to a patio with a central pool and perfumed plants (in this case, myrtle bushes, which originally would have been sunken so as to preserve views of the water from all directions). The four dwellings along the sides may possibly have housed the four wives allowed to each Muslim male.

Linking the patio to the 45-metre (148-foot) **Torre de Comares** (Comares Tower) is the **Sala de la Barca** (Hall of the Boat), which served as the antechamber to the throne room. Its name might derive from the hull-shaped wooden ceiling (a copy of the original that burned down in 1890), but is more likely to be a corruption of the Arabic phrase 'al-Baraka' (benediction or blessing), which is endlessly carved on the walls.

The throne room itself, also known as the **Sala de Comares** or the **Salón de Embajadores** (Hall of the Ambassadors), is one of the most spectacular and intimidating chambers in the Nasrid Palaces. The inclined planes of the inlaid cedarwood ceiling create a

**The Albaicín**. *See p257.*

dizzying three-dimensional effect and represent the seven heavens of Koranic paradise with Allah residing at its peak. Emblems of Fernando and Isabel were later worked into the dome and into the flooring beneath.

### BAÑOS REALES

From the Palacio de Comares, a passage leads to the **Baños Reales** (Royal Baths), probably built during the reign of Ismail I (1314-25). The first chamber you come to is the rest room, the **Sala de las Camas** (Hall of the Beds), with benches separated by horseshoe arches. There's a gallery from where it is said the Sultan would watch his naked wives, then throw an apple to the one with whom he'd chosen to spend the night. This room was subject to a much-criticised reconstruction in the 19th century. From here another passage leads to the other bathing rooms: the cold room, the warm room and then the hot room, which would have contained two large hot water basins in which to submerge oneself. The water and rooms were heated by a hypocaust, and the inner walls had vents to let the air out.

### PALACIO DE LEONES

Adjoining the Palacio de Comares, the Palacio de Leones (or Harem) was built during the reign of Mohammed V (1362-91) as private quarters for the ruler and his family. (In Nasrid times, the two palaces were entirely separate, with no direct access between them.) At its heart is the arcaded **Patio de los Leones**, one of the world's most breathtaking structures, which centres on a fountain surrounded by 12 lions; it's become the archetypal image of Moorish Granada. The original, not-very-realistic lions (the 19th-century

traveller Théophile Gautier thought that 'it would be hard to find anything less resembling lions') are now gradually being replaced by copies. The channels, which begin and end in the central fountain, are a representation of the four rivers of paradise, while the po-faced beasts may represent the 12 signs of the zodiac, the 12 hours of the clock or may be a gift from a Jewish tribe representing the 12 Tribes of Israel. The marble fountain is wreathed in verses by Ibn Zamrak that poetically describe its complicated hydraulic system. Although there's an ascetic beauty to the patio's warm-hued stone and stucco, this isn't what you would have seen in the 14th century; it was originally painted in vibrant tones and – like most of the rest of the complex – hung with colourful textiles.

At the east end of the patio is the **Sala de los Reyes** (Hall of the Kings), named after the painted sheepskin ceiling panels that some claim are a chronology of the ten Nasrid emirs, from Mohammed I to Mohammed V (though, as the latter was the eighth Nasrid ruler, the painting clearly can't date from his reign).

On the patio's south side is the **Sala de los Abencerrajes**, which has a stunning stalactite ceiling arranged within an eight-pointed star, and 16 windows that flood light over the milky stucco. It is reflected back on itself by the marble pool beneath, but this serenity belies the violent story that gives the room its name. It was here that Sultan Muley Hasen slaughtered the males of the Abencerraje family after one of them was suspected of having a fling with Zoraya, his favourite concubine; the rust stains on the floor are popularly supposed to be the victims' indelible blood. The lateral staircases led up to the harem, where the concubines were waited on by blind eunuchs and kept from view behind trellised wooden screens.

The **Sala de las dos Hermanas** (Hall of the Two Sisters) at the north end of the patio takes its name from twin marble floor-slabs. The *muqarnas* ceiling incorporates a cupola of over 5,000 tiny, hanging prisms refracting light from one central star, and the walls are decorated with a lengthy poem by Ibn Zamrak celebrating the circumcision of the Sultan's son. (The hall's original door is now in the Museo de la Alhambra.)

The Sala leads through to the **Sala de los Ajimeces** or **Mirador de Daraxa** (a corruption of the Arabic *'ayn dar Aixa'* or 'eyes of the house of Aixa'), whose mullioned windows were low-slung to allow inhabitants to enjoy the view from a lounging position. The richness of the colourful stucco, the stained-glass ceiling and the elaborate tiling have led many to claim it as the perfect example of the Nasrid baroque style.

A small passage from here takes you to the chambers built to accommodate Carlos V in 1528 while his nearby palace was under construction, and which were later inhabited by Washington Irving.

To the east lies the area known as the **Partal**, made up of gardens grouped around the five porticoed arches (today known as the **Torre de las Damas**) that remain from an older palace, constructed by Mohammed III (1302-09). From this area you can explore the towers and fortress walls, some of which retain their battlements and defensive trenches.

## The Generalife

An inspired pattern of walkways, fountains and garden patios covers the adjoining **Cerro del Sol** (Hill of the Sun) like a living Persian carpet. These are the pleasure gardens of the sultans, known as the Generalife (*yannat al-arif* or Garden of the Architect), where the imagination of the Islamic gardeners pushed the potential of their natural materials to new heights. In the **Patio de la Acequia** (Patio of the Conduit) water spouts in a jaunty criss-cross pattern down the length of two long pools, while the upper gardens the **Escalera de Agua** (Water Staircase) has balustrades topped by a gushing stream of water. The steps may originally have led to an oratory and were designed for the ablutions required before Muslim prayer. Just beneath is the high-walled **Patio de la Sultana**, where Zoraya met her Abencerraje lover (*see p256*) in the secret shade of a massive and ancient cypress tree.

The gardens are a wonderful place to rest after footslogging around the rest of the Alhambra. They enjoy stunning views over the complex and towards the Albaicín, and are impossibly romantic at night.

The **Palacio del Generalife** is currently being restored and is closed to visitors. It was originally built in the 14th century as a simple country retreat for the sultans and their wives.

The long promenade back to the palaces is densely canopied with oleander and passes an amphitheatre where concerts are sometimes held in the summer.

While on the Alhambra hill, art- and music-lovers might want to check out two small museums. Between 1916 and 1930 the painter José María Rodríguez-Acosta built for himself one of Andalucía's most notable 20th-century buildings, fusing modernist and historical styles. Located next to the Torres Bermejas, it is now home to the **Fundación Rodríguez-Acosta** and features a regularly changing programme of art exhibitions and events. The Cádiz-born composer Manuel de Falla lived in Granada

from 1919 until he emigrated to Argentina in 1939, and his home in the city has been restored as the **Casa Museo Manuel de Falla**.

### Casa Museo Manuel de Falla

*C/Antequeruela Alta 11 (958 22 21 88/ www.manueldefalla.org/museo)*. **Open** 10am-2pm Tue-Sat. **Admission** €2; €1 concessions. **No credit cards. Map** p251 F2 & p255.

### Fundación Rodriguez-Acosta

*Callejón Niños del Rollo 8 (958 22 74 97/ www.fundacionrodriguezacosta.com)*. **Open** 10am-2pm Wed-Sun; open by prior arrangement Tue. **Admission** €3; €1 concessions; free under-8s. **No credit cards. Map** p251 F2 & p255.

## The Albaicín

The hillside facing the Alhambra was one of the most densely populated and wealthy areas of Moorish Granada. Its typical *carmenes* (villa-like houses with terraced gardens and patios) and narrow cobbled streets are beautifully preserved. The name Albaicín derives from the name of the Muslims of Baeza who were expelled from the Christians and resettled here in 1227; at its zenith there were over 30 mosques in the district, most of which were converted to Christian churches after the *reconquista*. Today, the Muslim population of Granada is again increasing. A large new mosque (the **Mezquita de Granada**) has been built next to the Mirador de San Nicolás, along with an Islamic studies centre. The mosque's small, peaceful garden (with the same view as the Mirador) can be visited, and there's usually someone there to offer mint tea and information to the curious.

The best approach to the district is from Plaza Nueva, following the Carrera del Darro, a cobbled road that flanks the Rio Darro. At No.31, **El Bañuelo** (Arab Baths) is thought to date from the 11th century, making it the oldest civic building in the city, not to mention the most complete bathhouse preserved in Spain. The baths are accessed through a small house, where the attendant would have lived. Inside, shafts of light enter through star-shaped skylights that could be covered to control the temperature and humidity in the perfumed steam baths, which were heated from below by fires in giant pits.

For a hands-on experience, cross over the bridge to **Hammam Baños Arabes** (C/Santa Ana 16, 958 22 99 78, www.grupoalandalus.com) and the similar but slightly cheaper **Aljibe Baños Arabes** (C/San Miguel Alta 41, 958 52 28 67, www.aljibesanmiguel.es). Pre-booking is essential for both.

A little further along is the ornate façade of the **Casa de Castril**, a mansion once owned by the secretary to Fernando and Isabel. It was purposely built in the Islamic quarter as part of the attempt to Christianise the area after the *reconquista*. Since 1879 the mansion has served as the province's **Museo Arqueológico y Etnológico** (Archaeological and Ethnological Museum). Seven rooms display Granadan artefacts from the Palaeolithic period up until 1492. The labelling is in Spanish only, but the illustrations are clear and easy to follow.

Over the water, opposite the church of **San Pedro y San Pablo** (open hours of services), is the crumbling tower and amputated arch of **La Puerta de los Tableros**, a bridge and gateway connecting the Alhambra with the Albaicín.

Following the river under the Alhambra's battlements, the road opens out into the tree-shaded **Paseo de los Tristes**. Bullfights and tournaments used to be held here, but it is now full of restaurants and bars. At the end of the road, take the left turning along Cuesta del Chapiz to reach the heart of the Albaicín. Keep following this road as it bends to the left. Pass the church of **El Salvador** (Plaza de Abad 2, open 10am-1pm, 4-8.30pm Mon-Sat), which was built over a mosque and retains its original patio, to reach Calle Panaderos. This leads to the lively produce markets on Plaza Larga, overlooked by the **Arco de las Pesas** (Arch of Weights). There are two explanations for this name: either the severed hands of cheating market traders and thieves were dangled from here, or, less bloodthirstily, the faulty weights used by unscrupulous stallholders were confiscated and strung up on the archway.

The other major landmark in the Albaicín is the **Mirador de San Nicolás**. If you head up the slope from either Calle Elvira or Carrera del Darro you're likely to hit it eventually. (If you get lost just follow the sound of bongos, didgeridoos and the smell of fragrant tobacco.) It's a meeting point for leather-clad bikers, crusty buskers and souvenir-hawking gypsies, but don't let this put you off; the lookout offers the quintessential Alhambra view, especially at sunset when the opaline Sierra Nevada glows in the background.

**Note**: the Albaicín has an ongoing petty crime problem and you should be careful to keep to main routes and make sure your valuables are out of sight, particularly after dark. Don't be scared, but do be careful.

### El Bañuelo

*Carrera del Darro 31 (958 02 78 00)*. **Open** 10am-2pm Tue-Sat. **Admission** free. **Map** p251 D2.

### Mezquita de Granada

*Plaza San Nicolás (958 20 19 03/www.mezquita degranada.com)*. **Open** Garden *Apr-Sept* 11am-2pm, 6-9.30pm daily. *Oct-Mar* 10am-2pm, 4-7pm daily. **Admission** free. **Map** p250 C2.

### Museo Arqueológico y Etnológico

*Casa de Castril, Carrera del Darro 43 (958 22 56 40)*. **Open** 2.30-8pm Tue; 9am-8.30pm Wed-Sat; 9am-2.30pm Sun. **Admission** €1.50; free with EU passport. **No credit cards**. **Map** p251 D2.

## Sacromonte

Bordering the Albaicín to the north-east is Sacromonte, the heart of the gypsy (*gitano*) quarter. The *gitanos* originated from India and had appeared in Spain by the mid 15th century, with their own dress, customs and language (*caló*). They were deemed a threat to public order and their civil rights were severely restricted in the following centuries, leaving them marginalised on the edges of society. Today, the strongest residue of their ancient traditions – not to mention an important source of income – is the *zambra* (a generic name for *gitano* dances and music); many of Spain's finest flamenco artists come from gypsy families (*see p184* **Cliché**).

The gypsy cave quarters on Sacromonte hill were initially segregated from the Albaicín by a 14th-century Moorish rampart, but the influx of a poor, rural population at the end of the 19th century rapidly increased the need for cheap cave dwellings, and by 1950 there were over 3,500 inhabited caves in the district. Although many were abandoned after heavy floods in 1963, about 80 per cent of the Sacromonte population continues to live in converted caves, some of which are surprisingly luxurious.

For a better understanding of the community, visit the **Centro de Interpretación del Sacromonte**. This fascinating open-air centre, incorporating seven reconstructed cave dwellings, aims to explain the environmental and socio-cultural genesis of Sacromonte, and to preserve some of its dying local traditions. Call for information about live performances.

Also on the hill is the **Abadía del Sacromonte**, a little-visited abbey that contains a superb collection of religious art and treasures. It was founded in the 17th century after 25 leaden tablets inscribed in Arabic and other items concerning the martyrdom of Saint Cecilio (the city's patron saint) were miraculously discovered on the site. Unfortunately, later evidence suggested that the tablets were fakes. To reach the abbey, take the number 31 bus.

### Abadía del Sacromonte

*C/Abadía del Sacromonte s/n (958 22 14 45)*. **Open** (guided tours every 30mins) 11am-1pm, 4-6pm Tue-Sat; 4-6pm Sun. **Admission** €3; €2 concessions. **No credit cards**. **Map** p251 off D1.

### Centro de Interpretación del Sacromonte

*Barranco de los Negros (958 21 51 20/www.sacromonte granada.com).* **Open** *June-Oct* 10am-2pm, 5-9pm Tue-Fri; 10am-9pm Sat, Sun. *Nov-May* 10am-2pm, 4-7pm Tue-Fri; 10am-7pm Sat, Sun. **Admission** *Museum* €4; free under-4s. *Mirador & botanical route* €1; free under-4s. **No credit cards. Map** p250 off C1.

## The Catedral & around

West of the Alhambra hill and the Albaicín, modern Granada sprawls out across the plain. The backbone of the city is the traffic-choked Gran Vía, which stretches from the Jardines del Triunfo to Plaza Isabel la Católica. From the latter, Calle Reyes Católicos links Granada's two main squares, Plaza Nueva to the north-east, at the foot of the Alhambra hill and the Albaicín, and Puerta Real to the south-west. The major sightseeing focus in this part of town is immediately west of Plaza Isabel la Católica: the cathedral and the Capilla Real.

A few months before her death in 1504, Isabel commissioned Enrique de Egas to build the **Capilla Real** (Royal Chapel) as a mausoleum for herself and her husband, who wished to be buried in Granada, the scene of their most important victory. The late-Gothic chapel was completed in the following decades and is Granada's finest Christian building.

The royal coffins rest in the crypt; they are simple plain lead boxes, but sit beneath elaborate Renaissance sepulchres. The lower of the two sepulchres is by the Florentine sculptor Domenico Fancelli, and is covered in myriad symbols of Isabel and Fernando's reign: corpulent lions denoting royal status; gryphons representing paganism; and a pelican ripping open its own chest as a symbol of Christian sacrifice. The split pomegranate, a metaphor for defeated Granada, is depicted underneath the *Reyes Católicos'* unifying emblems of the yoke and sheaf of arrows. Isabel and Fernando themselves look peaceful, if a little jowly; the fact that Isabel wielded greater power is perhaps suggested by her head sinking more deeply into the pillow than her husband's.

Next to Fancelli's sepulchre is the tomb of Isabel and Fernando's daughter, Juana la Loca ('the Mad'), and her faithless husband, Felipe el Hermoso ('the Handsome'). This second tomb, carved by Bartolomé Ordóñez, is grander in dimension but lacks the fine expression of Fancelli's work.

In front of the tombs, the stunning altarpiece depicts the life of Christ and the tortures of John the Baptist and John the Evangelist in lingering detail, while, to the right, two massive carved wooden doors lead to the **Sacristía**.

The soaring **Catedral**. *See p259.*

This houses a priceless collection of crown jewels, including Isabel's crown and sceptre and Fernando's sword, which were traditionally paraded though Granada in the annual celebration of the conquest. There are also 15th-century Flemish paintings, including works by Rogier van der Weyden, Hans Memling and Dieric Bouts.

Almost immediately opposite the entrance to the Capilla Real, is **La Madraza** (C/Oficios 14), with a stunning original *mihrab* (prayer niche). This building is all that remains of the richly decorated Moorish university (*medressa* in Arabic) that was constructed on the orders of Yusuf I in 1349. One of the university's most famous students was the court poet of the Alhambra, Ibn Zamrak. It's now part of the modern university (you are free to look inside when it's open).

Built on to the Capilla Real is the **Santa Iglesia Catedral Metropolitana de Granada**, which replaced Granada's mosque as a final expression of the Catholic rehabilitation of the city. It was started in the 1520s by the Gothicist Enrique de Egas, and then taken over five years later by Renaissance-inclined Diego de Siloé. Though it wasn't finished until the 18th century, the interior was constructed much as de Siloé had intended and is one of the most sensational and original examples of Spanish Renaissance architecture. Highlights are the bright, lofty curves of Siloé's central chapel and Alonso Cano's melancholy Immaculate Virgin in the sacristy.

The cathedral's vertiginous main façade by Cano is designed to resemble a Roman triumphal arch – an allusion to the Christian victory over Islam – and is best viewed from the Plaza Alonso Cano, which also contains a statue of the architect (bearing an uncanny resemblance to the young Charlton Heston).

From here, the Alcaicería runs towards Calle Reyes Católicos. Once a bustling bazaar, which had existed since the days of the old *medina*, it's now a rather tacky tourist arcade. The original structures burned down in 1843 and were replaced with the gaudy stucco you see today.

Directly opposite the main arcade as it emerges onto Calle Reyes Católicos is the graceful brick archway that forms the entrance to the **Corral del Carbón** (closed for renovation, not reopening before 2006). Built at the beginning of the 14th century and situated in the streets that led from the city gates to the *medina*, this is the best surviving example of a typical eastern *caravanserai* in Spain. Merchants lodged and stored their goods on the upper floors while their animals were safely tethered in the courtyard below. Its present name derives from the coal merchants who used it 200 years later.

### Capilla Real

*C/Oficios 3 (958 22 92 39/www.capillareal granada.com)*. **Open** *Apr-Oct* 10.30am-1pm, 4-7pm Mon-Sat; 11am-1pm, 4-7pm Sun. *Nov-Mar* 10.30am-1pm, 3.30-6.30pm Mon-Sat; 11am-1pm, 3.30-6.30pm Sun. **Admission** €3; free under-10s. **No credit cards. Map** p251 D4.

### Santa Iglesia Catedral Metropolitana de Granada

*C/Gran Vía 5 (958 22 29 59)*. **Open** *Apr-Oct* 10.45am-1.30pm, 4-8pm Mon-Sat; 4-8pm Sun. *Nov-Mar* 10.45am-1.30pm, 4-7pm Mon-Sat; 4-7pm Sun. **Admission** €3; free under-10s. **No credit cards. Map** p251 D4.

## The University & the north

Five minutes' walk west of the cathedral is the **Universidad de Granada**, founded by Carlos V in 1531 in order to propagate the

---

# Federico García Lorca

Lorca, the most widely translated Spanish author of all time, was born in 1898 in the farming village of Fuente Vaqueros, just west of Granada; his birthplace now houses a small, but beautifully laid-out museum. Although the family moved to the city when Lorca was 11, the rural surroundings and folklore of his early childhood retained a strong hold on his adult imagination. Through his mother's influence, Lorca became a highly accomplished pianist, and his love of traditional music and flamenco lay at the very heart of his poetic vision. (Much to his father's irritation, it also distracted him from his law degree at the University of Granada.)

After some modest success with his play *Mariana Pineda*, he finally achieved major renown in 1928 with *El Romancero Gitano*, a poetic blend of gypsy ballads, mythology and surrealism. Overnight, he became seen as a champion of Andalucían subculture and Spain's 'Gypsy Poet' – a title he detested. After a miserable year spent studying English in New York 'where the sky does not exist', he returned to Spain and began a highly prolific period that established his reputation as a playwright. The 'rural' trilogy of *Bodas de Sangre* (*Blood Wedding*), *Yerma* and *La Casa de Bernada Alba* (*The House of Bernada Alba*) gained massive popularity in both Spain and Latin America.

In July 1936, with the country on the brink of civil war, Lorca made a fatal decision to postpone a trip to Mexico and spend the summer in Granada. The city quickly fell to the Falangists, who launched a crusade to hunt down and execute all Republican sympathisers. Although Lorca was not politically active, he was closely associated with the liberal left by dint of his homosexuality, the 'inflammatory' nature of his plays, and the fact that his sister, Concha, was married to Granada's newly elected Socialist mayor. Lorca sought refuge at the house of Luis Rosales (now the Hotel Reina Cristina), but was dragged out of hiding on 16 August and murdered three days later in the nearby village of Viznar. As Lorca eerily predicted in a poem, his body was never found.

Under the Franco administration any mention of the playwright's name was prohibited. Fortunately, the city has finally given Lorca the recognition he deserves; one of the family properties in Granada has been converted into a memorial park and museum (the **Huerta de San Vicente**), though, alas, the architects have also succeeded in almost entirely destroying the atmosphere of the place – the characterless modern park replaced a wonderful old orchard.

teaching of Christian doctrine, and now home to 60,000 students (a good number of whom are foreigners). The old university building (now the law faculty) has a baroque portal.

Also in Plaza de la Universidad, the sumptuous 18th-century church of **Santos Justo y Pastor** (open hours of services) stands on the site of the old mosque and Majadalbecy cistern; it's worth a peek inside for its frescoes and sacristy treasures.

The real gem of the quarter, however, is the **Monasterio de San Jerónimo**, which lies at the very end of Calle Duquesa. The monastery, founded by Fernando and Isabel, was originally sited in Santa Fé to the west of the city, but a plague of insects forced the Hieronymite order to move to Granada in 1521. One of the graceful courtyards is filled with fragrant orange trees and portals by Diego de Siloé, the other – only glimpsed through a grille – has Gothic gargoyles and Mudéjar wooden ceilings, and served as lodgings for Empress Isabel on her honeymoon. (Rather unromantically, Carlos V,

her new husband, stayed at the Alhambra.) The stunning frescoed church is a masterpiece of the Spanish Renaissance and the burial place of 'El Gran Capitán' Gonzalo Fernández de Córdoba, the swashbuckling commander of Isabel and Fernando's troops. His many victories are depicted in some of the church's frescoes, and his jewelled sword originally slotted into the painting to the left of the magnificent altarpiece, but was stolen in the 17th century and replaced with a wooden copy.

Gonzalo also provided the land for the **Monasterio de la Cartuja**, located on the northern outskirts of the city. This is Spain's most lavishly decorated 16th-century Carthusian monastery and houses some showstopping examples of Spanish baroque. After rooms full of grisly paintings depicting the torture of English monks under Henry VIII, the visitor is rewarded with the glorious splendours of the church itself, especially the blinding effect of the Virgin of the Assumption surrounded by mirror-encrusted golden pillars.

The other major Lorca sites are the **Museo-Casa Natal Federico García Lorca** in his native village of Fuente Vaqueros, around 16 kilometres (ten miles) north-west of Granada, and **Parque Federico García Lorca** in the village of Viznar, where he was shot.

### Huerta de San Vicente

*C/Virgen Blanca s/n (958 25 84 66/ www.huertadesanvicente.com).* **Open** (guided tours every 45 mins) *Apr-June, Sept* 10am-12.30pm, 5-7.30pm Tue-Sun. *July, Aug* 10am-2pm Tue-Sun. *Oct-Mar* 10am-1pm, 4-7pm Tue-Sun. **Admission** €1.80; free to all Wed. **No credit cards.**
Named after Lorca's mother, Vicenta, this house (west of the city centre) was the summer residence of the Lorca family from 1926 to 1936. It is now surrounded by a manicured park flanked by the Neptuno shopping mall, but when Lorca lived here it sat amid orchards, with views of the Sierra that filled Lorca with inspiration: 'It is there, in my Huerta de San Vicente, that I write my most tranquil theatre.' The downstairs rooms hold some original furniture, portraits and photographs of the Lorca family, plus material pertaining to a children's puppet show that Lorca staged at the house in 1923. Upstairs is a host of memorabilia, including a hand-painted poster for 'La

Barraca', Lorca's travelling theatre troupe, which took popular farces and tragedies to rural Spanish communities in 1933.
To reach Huerta de San Vicente, take bus number 4 heading west from Gran Vía or Plaza del Carmen towards the Palacio de Deportes.

### Museo-Casa Natal Federico García Lorca

*C/Poeta García Lorca 4, Fuente Vaqueros (958 51 64 53/www.museogarcialorca.org).* **Open** (guided tour only) *Apr-June, Sept* 10am-1pm, 5-7pm Tue-Sun. *July, Aug* 10am-2pm Tue-Sun. *Oct-Mar* 10am-1pm, 4-6pm Tue-Sun. **Admission** €1.80. **No credit cards.**
Lorca was born in this plain village house on 11 June 1898. Although the building has been extensively altered, the well-cared-for museum remains evocative. Downstairs, the family's living quarters have been recreated, while the top-floor granary has an extensive display of memorabilia, including costumes, posters and drafts of Lorca's plays. The guided tour (in Spanish only) is detailed and leaves plenty of time for fans to study the exhibits at leisure. Buses leave Granada for Fuente Vaqueros between 9am and 9pm hourly Monday to Friday, and every two hours on Saturday and Sunday.

**Granada Province**

Behind the presbytery is a tabernacle of polychrome marble, jasper and rare woods, which sits under a frescoed cupola by Palomino depicting Saint Bruno, the monastery's founding father. The whole extravaganza is topped off by the single-nave sacristy, where cataracts of white pillars, foaming with geometrical mouldings, shoot down from another frescoed cupola and an impossibly ornate vaulted ceiling. To reach the monastery, catch bus number 8 or letter 'C' from Gran Vía, heading away from Plaza Isabel la Católica.

### Monasterio de la Cartuja

*Paseo de la Cartuja s/n (958 16 19 32).* **Open** *Apr-Oct* 10am-1pm, 4-8pm Mon-Sat; 10am-noon, 4-8pm Sun. *Nov-Mar* 10am-1pm, 3.30-6pm Mon-Sat; 10am-noon, 3.30-6pm Sun. **Admission** €3; free under-8s. **No credit cards.**

### Monasterio de San Jerónimo

*C/Rector López Argueta 9 (958 27 93 37).* **Open** *Apr-Oct* 10am-1.30pm, 4-7.30pm daily. *Nov-Mar* 10am-1.30pm, 3-6.30pm daily. **Admission** €3. **No credit cards**. **Map** p250 B5.

## Parque de las Ciencias

In a city with so much history and art, it may seem strange to visit something as futuristic as a science park, but it's entirely appropriate. A fascinating exhibition here celebrates the philosophers, thinkers, engineers and artists of al-Andalus who made invaluable contributions to modern science in all its forms. The park extends over a huge site, with lots of outdoor installations – an astronomy garden, hydraulics exhibits, a maze, a 'mental gymnasium' (oversize puzzles), and lots of toys and gadgets demonstrating scientific principles, as well as a butterfly house. It is located on the south-western edge of the city. To reach it, take bus 4, 5, 10 or 11; if travelling by car, you'll see it from the A338 heading towards Alhama de Granada, or come off the A44-E902 Jaén–Motril motorway at 'Salida 131' (for Palacio de Congresos).

### Parque de las Ciencias

*Avenida del Mediterráneo (958 13 19 00/www.parque ciencias.com).* **Open** 10am-7pm Tue-Sat; 10am-3pm Sun. **Admission** *Museum* €4; €3 concessions. *Planetarium* €1.80; €1.50 concessions. **Credit** V.

## Where to eat & drink

The tourist breakfast hotspots are terrace tables on neighbouring Plazas Bib-Rambla, Pescadería and Pasiegas, behind the cathedral. For a cheaper *desayuno* with the locals, try **Cafe Opera** (C/Alvaró de Bazan, map D4), by the *mercado municipal*, **Cafeteria Carlos** (C/Molinos 2, map F3), near Campo del Príncipe, or the slick new

**Cafe Bar Sancho** (C/Tablas 16, map off D5), off Plaza Trinidad. This square also has a great little bread stall, **Kiosco Enriqueta**, with golden brioches and sugar-dusted *ensaimadas* (doughy pastries) for breakfast on the go.

Granada is one of the few places left in Spain where the free tapas tradition still thrives. Order a drink at a bar and, if the server shouts '*Un primero*' ('One first'), you know your first free tapas is on its way. Usually, the level of gastro delight rises with each drink (eg olives with first beer, ham with second, paella with third) but it varies from bar to bar (and hour to hour). The bars listed below generally give good *primero*. Top tapas hunting grounds are in and around Plaza Campo del Principe (map F3), Calle Navas (map E4) and Calle Elvira (map D3).

Calle Elvira and its environs are also home to the reverse *reconquista* of Granada's gastro landscape – with kebab shops and *teterías* (tea rooms) jostling for space. The *teterías* are popular with backpackers and young locals and are becoming vital stops on the nightlife trail, some offering live music along with infusions and hookahs. The best and most tranquil *teteria*, though, is near the Arab Baths: **La Tetería del Bañuelo** (C/Bañuelo 5, 958 22 41 97, closed Mon, map D2) has a peaceful leafy terrace and lush, ornate interior.

A new interest in Granada's Moorish past is also enlivening the normally staid offerings in the city's restaurants – especially in the **Albaícin**. Here you'll find a slew of *carmen* restaurants with beautiful terraces and gardens. Beware, though, that many are trading on their views, rather than the food and service.

It's easy to avoid the tourist traps – steer clear of laminated menus and touting waiters – which are predictably clustered around the Alhambra, Plaza Nueva and Plaza Bib-Rambla. To dine with the locals, head for the area above the Camino del Ronda around Plaza de Gracia (map off D5) or to the *pijo* (posh) bars and restaurants within the Plaza de Toros (map off A4), such as restaurant **La Ermita** (Plaza de Toros, 958 29 02 57) and tapas bar **Tendido Uno** (Plaza de Toros, 958 27 23 02, www.tendido1.com).

### Albahaca

*C/Varela 17 (958 22 49 23).* **Open** 1.30-3.30pm, 8.30-11pm Tue-Sat; 1.30-3.30pm Sun. Closed Aug. **Average** €-€€. **Credit** MC, V. **Map** p251 E4.
Near Santo Domingo church, this good-value restaurant has a genteel tearoom feel. The simple, strangely Brit-like dishes include roast lamb with duchess potatoes and salmon in hazel-nut sauce.

### Ajo Blanco

*C/Palacios 17 (958 22 81 28).* **Open** 1-3.30pm, 8pm-1am Mon-Sat. **Average** €. **No credit cards.** **Map** p251 E3.

Tucked away down some steps opposite Santo Domingo, this tiny wine bar is a real find. The charming owner, Nicolás Fernández Única, has an superb *bodega*, including some fantastic cavas that you won't find anywhere else is Granada. His small range of (free) tapas are gastronomic delights.

### Arrayanes

*Cuesta Marañas 4 (958 22 84 01/www.rest-arrayanes.com).* **Open** 1.30-4.30pm, 7.30-11.30pm Mon, Wed-Sun. **Average** €€. **Credit** MC, V. **Map** p251 D3.
Just off Caldería Nueva, this is far and away the best Moroccan restaurant in town. Specialities such as tagines, *bastela* or *kefta* are served up in ornate and luxurious surroundings. The friendly owner speaks seven languages. Unlicensed.

### Bodega Espadafor

*C/Tinajilla s/n (958 20 21 38).* **Open** *June-Sept* noon-4pm, 8pm-midnight Mon-Sat. *Oct-May* noon-4pm, 8pm-midnight daily. **Average** €. **No credit cards. Map** p250 B4.
A rough diamond, this historic (opened 1910) barn-like tapas bar doesn't need its beautiful old tiles, distinctive mural and old *fería* posters to attract attention – its delicious tapas and good service are more than enough reason to linger. If you're not given the wonderful *jamón asado* (roast pork) as your first tapas, don't wait – just buy some.

### Bodegas Castañeda

*C/Almiceros 1-3 (958 21 54 64).* Open 11.30am-4.30pm, 7.30pm-1am Mon-Thur; 11.30am-1am Fri-Sun. **Average** €. **Credit** MC, V. **Map** p251 D4.
This traditional stand-up bar (divided into two following a family dispute) is packed out at weekends with a mix of locals and tourists taking advantage of the excellent free tapas. The *verbena* (selection) of tapas is big enough for sharing.

### Botánico

*C/Málaga 3 (958 27 15 98).* **Open** noon-1am Mon-Thur, Sun; noon-2am Fri-Sat. **Average** €€. **Credit** MC, V. **Map** p250 C5.
With terrace tables opposite the botanical gardens, this oh-so-hip, cream and orange joint has lounge-style sounds, light simple dishes of the day and a more creative, fusion menu, including veggie options.

### La Brujidera – Casa del Vino

*C/Monjas del Carmen 2 (958 22 25 95).*
**Open** 12.30-4pm, 8.30pm-1am Mon-Thur, Sun; 12.30-4pm, 8.30pm-2am Fri-Sat. **Average** €-€€. **No credit cards. Map** p251 D3/4.
This small, smoky wine bar stocks an impressive array of Spanish wines, and serves up interesting tapas, such as *mollejas* (duck gizards) in orange sauce or marinated *lomo de orza* (pork loin).

### Carmen de Verde Luna

*Camino Nuevo de San Nicolás 16 (958 29 17 94/www.terra.es/personal2/carmenverdeluna).* **Open** *Mar-Nov* 8.30-11pm Wed-Sun. *Dec* 1.30-3.30pm, 8.30-11pm Sat-Sun. Closed Jan, Feb & 1wk July-Aug. **Average** €€€. **Credit** MC, V. **Map** p250 C2.

A young team runs this terrace restaurant – one of the more affordable dining-with-a-view options in the Albaicín. The monthly-changing menu is based on seasonal produce, featuring dishes such as artichokes with bean mousse, prawns and crisped ham.

### Casa Torcuato

*C/Pages 31 (958 20 28 18/www.casatorcuato.com).* **Open** *June-Sept* 11am-4pm, 8pm-midnight Mon-Sat. *Oct-May* 11am-4pm, 8pm-midnight Mon-Sat; 11am-4pm Sun. **Average** €-€€€. **Credit** DC, MC, V. **Map** p250 B1.
It seems the whole of the Albaicín, locals and tourists, descends on this famed bar-restaurant for the excellent fried fish tapas or dishes such as *solomillo* with foie gras and mushrooms, and pork loin with grapes. Terrace tables offer a more tranquil experience at the weekend.

### Los Diamantes

*C/Navas 26 (958 22 70 70).* **Open** *Mid June-July* 2.30-4pm, 8.30-10.30pm Mon-Fri. *Sept-mid June* 2.30-4pm Mon, Sat; 2.30-4pm, 8.30-10.30pm Tue-Fri. Closed Aug. **Average** €. **No credit cards. Map** p251 E4/5.
This tiny, bustling seafood tapas bar would be easy to miss were it not for the crowds of locals lapping up the perfect fried seafood (including wonderfully sweet prawns), which can be yours for the price of a beer. Its tiled walls and long zinc counter give it a trad feel but don't help the noise levels. Some of the best free tapas in Granada.

### Iberos y Patagónicos

*C/Escudo del Carmen 36 (958 22 07 72).* **Open** 1.30-4pm, 8.30-11pm Tue-Sat. Closed 2wks Jan. **Average** *lunch* €; *dinner* €€€€. **Credit** MC, V. **Map** p251 E4.
This recently opened restaurant takes Granadine dining into fresh territory by introducing the New Spanish cuisine that's already taken Barcelona and the Basque Country by storm. Its inventive dishes play with textures and use techniques such as foaming the ingredients. The modern, elegant dining room seems off-puttingly stark and bright, but don't let this put you off one of Granada's most interesting dining experiences.

### Kiki San Nicolás

*Plaza de San Nicolás 9 (958 27 67 15/mobile 639 02 16 87).* **Open** 8am-midnight Mon, Thur-Sun; 8am-6pm Tue. Closed 2wks July. **Average** €€. **No credit cards. Map** p250 C2.
Considering its location, this should be a tourist trap, but it's actually wonderful: sunny terrace tables (the locals eat inside), amazing tapas and *platos*, and an outstanding *bodega* of quality wines.

### Mesón El Trillo

*Callejón de Aljibe de Trillo 3 (958 22 51 82/www.granadainfo.com/trillo).* **Open** 1.30-4pm, 8pm-midnight Mon, Wed-Sun. **Average** €€-€€€. **Credit** DC, MC, V. **Map** p251 D2.
To gain admission, ring the bell at the gate of this tranquil, friendly garden restaurant deep in the Albaicín. The Basque chef/owner blends elements

**Palacio de Carlos V.** *See p253.*

of the superb cuisine of her homeland with distinctly Granadan touches in the large-portioned, large-flavoured dishes. Highlights include *bacalao al pil pil* (salt cod with garlic and chilli) and a creamy cheesecake-style raspberry tart. The lunchtime *menú* is a steal.

### Mirador de Aixa

*Carril San Agustín 2 (958 22 36 16/www.mirador deaixa.com).* **Open** 1.30-3.30pm, 8.30-11pm Tue-Sat; 1.30-3.30pm Sun. Closed 2wks end Jan-early Feb & 1st 2wks Nov. **Average** €€€€. **Credit** MC, V. **Map** p251 D1.

One of the best 'mirador' *carmen* restaurants looking across at the Alhambra from the Albaicín, Mirador de Aixa is a family concern, run by the charming Paco Pastor and his efficient staff. There's a small dining room and outside terrace, as well as terraced gardens dotted with fruit trees, jasmine and fragrant herbs. The cod poached in oil with prawns and peppers, and the chocolate dessert *lagrimas de Boabdil* ('the tears of Boabdil'), are recommended.

### El Pozo

*Cuesta de San Agustín 5 (958 22 53 98).* **Open** *May-mid Oct* noon-4pm Mon; noon-4pm, 7pm-1am Wed-Sun. *Mid Oct-Apr* noon-4pm Mon; noon-8pm Wed-Thur; noon-11pm Fri-Sun. **Average** €-€€. **No credit cards. Map** p251 D1.

Named after the old stone well in the garden, this tiny, family-run bar dishes up a good variety of well-prepared salads, *raciones* and *plato combinados* at reasonable prices. There are two excellent-value lunchtime *menús*.

### El Rincón de Michael Landon

*C/Rector García Duarte 2 (no phone).* **Open** noon-4pm, 8pm-1am Mon-Sat; 8pm-1am Sun. **Average** €. **No credit cards. Map** p250 off C5.

Near Plaza Gran Capitán, in the heart of the student nightlife quarter, this odd-but-great little bar is a friendly spot for a snack and a beer and for finding out where the best late-night clubs and bars of the moment are. The friendly couple that run it know all about the local night scene. And the name? Well, they're retro kitsch fans. Even the tapas sport names such as JR (*jamón* and roquefort) and Falcon Crest (chicken nuggets).

### La Sabanilla

*C/San Sebastián 14 (mobile 659 11 85 83).* **Open** 8.45pm-2am Tue-Sun. Closed 2wks late Aug. **No credit cards. Map** p251 D4/5.

One of the oldest, smallest and hardest-to-find bars in the city barrels out excellent local wines and sherries to a friendly crowd.

### Taberna La Opipara

*Campo del Príncipe 15 (958 22 70 83).* **Open** 12.30-4.30pm, 8.30pm-1am Tue-Sun; 8.30pm-1am Mon. **Average** €€. **No credit cards. Map** p251 F3.

There's a string of eateries on this square, but this recently-opened *taberna* adds something different. Its warm colours, candlelight and chilled tunes create a welcoming space – an atmosphere reinforced by its enthusiastic owner Manuel, who hand-picks quality produce for his salads, *tostadas* and *raciones*, such as French farmhouse cheeses and *mojama* (air-dried tuna) from Barbate on the Costa de la Luz.

### Las Tinajas

*C/Martínez Campos 17 (958 25 43 93).* **Open** noon-5pm, 8pm-midnight daily. Closed mid July-mid Aug. **Average** €€€-€€€€. **Credit** V. **Map** p251 off E5.

Always crowded, this reassuringly staid, traditionally decorated restaurant is roundly regarded as one of the best places to eat in town and it regularly participates in gastronomic events. The menu features traditional dishes with an Arabic hint, such as suckling lamb with honey and *Mozarabe*-style ham.

### Tragaluz

*C/Nevot 26 (958 22 29 24/mobile 687 32 27 04).* **Open** 1.30-4pm, 8.30pm-midnight Tue-Sat; 1.30-4pm Sun. Closed Aug. **Average** €€-€€€. **Credit** V. **Map** p251 off F2/3.

This intimate, very friendly and self-styled 'unconventional' restaurant, just east of the Campo del Príncipe, is a well-known meeting place for artists, writers and others fond of a hearty discussion over the excellent, uniquely special tagines, houmous (try to work out the secret ingredient) and other dishes with a Moorish or Sephardic flavour. The owner, writer and academic Mustafa Akalay Nasser, is a local celeb.

## Flamenco

There's plenty of flamenco to be found in Granada, but if someone tells you where to see real flamenco, chances are it won't be very real; it is, by nature a spontaneous phenomenon (*see p184* **Cliché**). If you hang out in an Albaicín or Sacromonte bar and you're very lucky, you may eavesdrop on a *gitano* knees-up. If you want something scheduled you'll have to compromise.

The *zambras* at the flamenco caves in the Sacromonte have a reputation as rip-off tourist traps, and it's true they're expensive and very touristy. Although the performers are usually fine, they're normally pretty bored, and the uninitiated audience can't give them the feedback they need for a special performance. Also, most hotels push pricey packages where you're ferried to and from the cave, given a walking tour and a free drink as well as the show. You may save a few quid just turning up and seeing what's on offer, but ask about prices before going in or ordering anything.

One place in the Albaicín that offers a better experience for the more knowledgeable flamenco fan (at a decent price) is the **Peña La Platería** (Placeta de Toqueros 7, 958 21 06 50, restaurant open noon-3pm Mon, Wed-Sun), the oldest flamenco *peña* (a kind of flamenco social/fan club) in Granada, which has shows open to the general public on Thursdays at 10pm (€6 incl drink, no shows July-Sept). An even cheaper option is a performance in one of the tearooms and bars around Calle Elvira, where a renewed interest in the possible Arabic roots of flamenco takes the form of 'flamenco-fusion' performances by young local musicians. Entry is normally free, though drinks prices may go up when there's live music. A good bet is the bar **Eshavira** (*see below*).

But if you really want to see top-class flamenco, time your visit to coincide with a performance by touring professional artists at venues like the Centro Internacional de Estudios Gitanos, more commonly known as **La Chumbera** (Camino del Monte s/n, 958 22 45 97, www.centroflamenco.org) or, better still, come during the international music and dance festival (**Festival Internacional de Música y Danza de Granada**) in June and July, which often attracts top national flamenco stars, and also offers lots of free shows.

## Nightlife

With a large student population augmented by waves of young travellers, Granada has plenty of life in its nightlife. The heart of Granada clubland is split by the Gran Vía – the university area below it features mostly small, fashion-conscious music venues and cheap-beer pubs. A good place to start the night here is **El Rincón de Michael Landon** (*see p264*). The lower reaches of the Albaicín (around Calle Elvira) generally hosts a grungier dope-led scene, where your politics (sexual as well as social) are more important than your labels. To mix with the beautiful people, head out to the Plaza de Toros (map off A4), or try along Calle Pedro Antonio de Alarcón (map off E5). The disco-caves in Sacromonte fill up in the summer with sweaty youth dancing to cheesy hits.

To get the lowdown on the gay/lesbian/mixed scene, start with tapas (great tortilla) at friendly, lesbian-leaning **La Tortuga** (C/Elvira 46, map C/D3), or **La Sal** (C/Santa Paula 11, mobile 651 89 54 34, map C4), the oldest *ambiente* bar in town. The pick-up parlour **Tic-Tac** (C/Horno de Haza 19, 958 29 63 66, map C5), with its busy dark room, is one for the boys (except for Kylie on the stereo). There's normally more guys than gals at swish disco **Six Colours** (C/Tendillas de Santa Paula 6, 958 20 39 95, open from 9pm daily, free, map C4/5) too – though straight women may be attracted by the claim that it pulls in the best-looking men in town. For information on the web about the city's gay scene, see http://granadainfo.com/pamela/gaygranada.htm.

**Afrodisia** (C/Almona del Boquerón, corner of C/Zafra, no phone, open from 11pm daily, free, map B4) is where Granada's b-boys and smokers come for 'undergroundblacksounds' – hip hop (Tuesday), ska and reggae (Wednesday), funk and afro-latino sounds (Thursday) and jazz (Sunday), and any of the above on Fridays and Saturdays.

**Enano Rojo** (C/Elvira 91, 958 20 30 84, open from 10pm daily, free, map D4) is a hot and sweaty bar that's always spilling out into the street; there's funk, soul and hip hop on the decks, with live music on Wednesday and Thursday nights.

Down the most unlikely looking alleyway off Calle Azacayas lurks **Eshavira** (C/Postigo de la Cuna 2, 958 29 08 29, open from 10.30pm daily, admission varies, map C4) a low-ceilinged, smoky bar, which serves up great live jazz on Wednesday and Thursday and flamenco on Sunday nights; veteran guitarist Emilio Maya is a regular.

Not far away is **Granada Diez** (C/Cárcel Baja 10, 958 22 40 01, club open from 12.30am daily, €6 incl one drink, map D4), a super-kitschy converted cinema that becomes a club after midnight (though it doesn't really kick-off until around 3am); the squidgy gold sofas hold dressed-up behinds when they're not shaking to Spanish Top 40 and cheesy tunes. No trainers.

In the university area, long-established **Planta Baja** (C/Horno de Abad 11, 958 22 23 75, www.planta-baja.com, gigs 10pm, club open from midnight Thur-Sat, closed July & Aug, €5 incl 1 drink Fri, Sat, free Thur, map C5) is still the place to go. The upper room has chilled-out tunes, while downstairs is a popular venue for live concerts by cult heroes of alternative rock, like Will Oldham, and hip DJs such as Ninja Tune's Vadim. After the gigs, there's dancing to lounge music on Thursdays, electroglam on Fridays and groove-funk on Saturdays, but the mood is always eclectic.

Granada's anglophile indie kids crowd in to the city's top power-pop stop **Sugar Pop** (C/Gran Capitán 25, no phone, map B5) for good vibes and reasonably priced drinks.

A young crowd heads out of town to the award-winning (best venue in Andalucía) warehouse-like **Industrial Copera** (Carretera de Armilla, C/Paz, Nave 7, 958 13 64 49, opening times and admission varies). Look out for flyers for details on the ever-changing club nights and gigs, covering everything from techno to hip hop to metal, including occasional appearances by international artists. Get a cab and get the company number for the return journey.

## Shopping

Granada's main shopping area is centred on the streets south of the cathedral. Department store **El Corte Inglés** (Carrera del Genil 22, 958 22 32 40, map F5) is a good one-stop shop. For food shopping, try the **mercado municipal** on C/San Agustín (map D4), off the Gran Vía, and the street stalls that run from here to Plaza Pescadería. For bric-a-brac and antiques head for the Calle Elvira and its surrounding streets.

Specialist food shops worth seeking out include **La Alacena** (C/San Jerónimo 3, 958 20 68 90, www.alacena.net, closed last 2wks Jan, map D4), run by a Spanish-British couple, which sells olive oils, hams and other regional produce; **La Oliva** (C/Rosario 9, 958 22 57 54, map E4), whose warm, knowledgeable owner Francisco offers tastings of his superb artisanal wines, cheeses, oils, preserves, honeys, chocolates and hams; and **Ora et Labora** (Plaza Pescadería 7, 958 25 81 67, map D5), which sells cakes, sweets, honeys, wines and cheeses made in Spanish monasteries and convents.

Other interesting specialist shops are **Cerámica Fabre** (Plaza Pescadería s/n, 958 28 81 92, closed 2wks Feb & 2wks Oct, map D5), with its typical local handmade blue-and-green-painted ceramics; the classical and flamenco guitar workshop **Guitarrería Germán Pérez Barranco** (C/Reyes Católicos 47, 958 22 70 33, www.guitarreria.com, map D4) – it's also a

reliable place for non-aficionados to make their first flamenco CD purchase; **Manuel Morillo Castillo** (Cuesta de Gomérez 8, 958 22 57 15, map D3) for Arab-style furniture and boxes from an on-site *taracea* workshop; and the city's only international book shop, **Metro Bookshop** (C/Gracia 31, 958 26 15 65, map D5).

## Where to stay

Hotel rooms fill quickly in Granada; always book ahead if possible, particularly in high season. If you turn up without a reservation, head for the streets around Plaza de la Trinidad (map D5), which are crammed with *hostales*, or contact the tourist office (*see p269*).

Hotels around Plaza Nueva are central but the streets are noisy; old buildings converted into boutique hotels in the Albaícin are more atmospheric but harder to find; places near the Alhambra are quieter at night and obviously benefit from easy access to the monument, but are isolated from the rest of the city at the top of a steep hill. If you're driving, check if your hotel is reachable by car, and where you should park – parking generally in the city is a nightmare.

**Note**: the hotels and *hostales* below are listed by price, with the most expensive places first.

### Parador San Francisco

*C/Real de la Alhambra s/n (958 22 14 40/ www.parador.es).* **Rates** €230 single/double; €270 triple; €310 triple adults; €268 suite. **Credit** AmEx, DC, MC, V. **Map** p251 F1 & p255.
If you can book far enough in advance, then an Albaícin-view room in this converted monastery in the grounds of the Alhambra is an unforgettable place to lay your head. Even if you don't stay here, you can still soak up the atmosphere by coming for a drink or the set-price lunch *menú* in the terrace bar-restaurant (smart-casual dress).

### Alhambra Palace

*Plaza Arquitecto García de Paredes 1 (958 22 14 68/ www.h-alhambrapalace.es).* **Rates** €139 single; €180 double; €264 junior suite. **Credit** AmEx, DC, MC, V. **Map** p251 F2 & p255.
Perfectly positioned for the Alhambra, this neo-Moorish four-star hotel was built in 1910. Almost all of its 126 gracious, if slightly worn, rooms (and the terrace bar) boast breathtaking views of the Sierra Nevada, city and the *vega*. Be warned that eating and drinking in the hotel can be very expensive.

### Hotel AC Palacio de Santa Paula

*Gran Vía de Colon 31 (958 80 57 40/www.ac-hotels.com).* **Rates** €158-€236 single/double; €245-€271 suite. **Credit** AmEx, MC, V. **Map** p251 D4.
The modern, business-like façade of Granada's only five-star hotel hides an enchanting historic interior. The luxurious rooms also mix sleek modern design and technology with antique charm. Nice touches

**Hotel Casa Morisca**. *See p268.*

include free newspapers, coffee in the 'library' and minibar (beer and soft drinks). There's a small sauna, steam room and gym, and a smart fusion restaurant in the beautiful cloisters. Ask about off-season and weekend deals.

### Casa de los Migueletes

*C/Benalúa 11 (958 21 07 00/www.casamigueletes. com).* **Rates** €139-€214 single/double; €247-€537 suite. **Credit** AmEx, DC, MC, V. **Map** p251 D3. Follow the signs from Plaza Nueva down winding cobbled alleys to this 17th-century mansion, beauti-fully converted into a boutique hotel. It's an oasis of calm, reserved elegance – an ambience reflected by the helpful staff (who can offer great restaurant recommendations). You don't get the full benefit of your historical surroundings in the lower-end rooms, so be prepared to fork out for an Alhambra view (at least €199) or the luxury Alhambra suite with a fabulous view, four-poster bed and jacuzzi.

### Catedral Suites

*Plaza de las Pasiegas s/n (958 53 51 30/ www.catedral-suites.com).* **Rates** €110 single; €137 double; €161 triple. **Credit** AmEx, DC, MC, V. **Map** p251 D5.

**Hostal Restaurante La Ninfa**.

The recently opened Catedral Suites are elegant self-catering apartments in an enviable position overlooking the *plaza* and the cathedral (no.12 has windows overlooking the plaza on two sides). The kitchenettes and bathrooms are well equipped and the decor is crisp and understated, with white walls, parquet floors and a muted colour scheme.

### Hotel Casa Morisca
*Cuesta de la Victoria 9 (958 22 11 00/www.hotel casamorisca.com).* **Rates** €98-€146 single; €123-€184 double; €211 suite. **Credit** AmEx, MC, V. **Map** p251 D1.
This restored 15th-century mansion preserves the patio, barrel-vaulted stable (now the breakfast room) and painted wooden ceilings of the original structure. Friendly staff, smart (if not always spacious) rooms and antique-filled corridors create an ambience of blissful luxury.

### Hotel Plaza Nueva
*C/Imprenta 2 (958 21 52 73/www.hotelplazanueva. com).* **Rates** €97-€119 single; €124-€162 double; €162-€189 suite. **Credit** MC, V. **Map** p251 D1.
This newish four-star hotel offers 25 bright, comfortable (if a possibly a bit staid) rooms in a great location. It's worth paying extra for views over the Alhambra and Plaza Nueva, especially during the Semana Santa processions. Staff are very polite and helpful.

### Hotel Casa del Capitel Nazarí
*C/Cuesta Aceituneros 6 (958 21 52 60/ www.hotelcasacapitel.com).* **Rates** €75 single; €98 double. **Credit** MC, V. **Map** p251 D3.

The fact that this is the cheapest of the Albaicín boutique hotels by no means reflects its quality. Seventeen rooms clad in wood beams and white linen (and with internet connections) cluster around galleries and cloisters chock-a-block with historic features. There's a cosy TV room, and an ornate patio where changing art exhibitions are displayed. Plaza Nueva is seconds away.

### Casa del Aljarife
*Placeta de la Cruz Verde 2 (958 22 24 25/www. granadainfo.com/most).* **Rates** €77 single; €96 double; €123-€134 triple. **Credit** MC, V. **Map** p251 D3.
Host with the most Christian Most has converted this 17th-century Albaicín house into a beautiful, warm, luxury B&B. Through the leafy patio you reach the four charming, individually decorated rooms through low-ceilinged, wood-beamed corridors and up wonky staircases. Room 4 is our favourite; it's the smallest but has incredible views and a wonderful bathroom. There's no better place to stay in Granada, so be sure to book ahead.

### Hotel Alixares
*Paseo de la Sabica 27 (958 22 55 75/www.hotelesporcel. com).* **Rates** €72 single; €96 double; €115 triple; €130 suite. **Credit** AmEx, DC, MC, V. **Map** p251 off F1.
If you want to stay near the Alhambra you could do a lot worse than the package-tour-style 171-room, three-star Alixares. Better value than both its luxury and budget neighbours, it has good facilities (including an outdoor pool) and views at a reasonable (and often negotiable) price. Some rooms have a small terrace and suite 510 has a corner jacuzzi bath and terrace with views over the *vega*.

### Santa Ana Apartamentos Turísticos
*Puente Espinosa 2 (958 22 81 30/mobile 670 52 41 82/www.apartamentos-santaana.com).* **Rates** (minimum stay 2 nights) €65 2 people; €90 3-4 people. **Credit** MC, V. **Map** p251 D2.
Overlooking the Darro river, these five apartments are light, modern and extremely spacious, with TV, bathroom, fully-equipped kitchen and some great views over the Albaicín. There's also a cave apartment set into the rockface under the Alhambra.

### Cuevas El Abanico
*Verea de Enmedio 89 (958 22 61 99/mobile 608 84 84 97/www.el-abanico.com).* **Rates** €58 cave for 1-2 people; €73 cave for 3 people; €88 2-bedroom cave for 1-4 people; €103 2-bedroom cave for 5 people. **Credit** MC, V. **Map** p251 off D1.
Express your inner troglodyte by staying in one of these cave houses at the edge of the Sacromonte, equipped with kitchens (a couple of electric rings, a sink), fireplaces and modern bathrooms. The five caves open onto a shared terrace with far-reaching views. Minimum stay is two nights.

### Hostal Restaurante La Ninfa
*Cocheras de San Cecilio 9 (958 22 79 85/ www.hostallaninfa.net).* **Rates** €45 single; €52 double; €65 twin. **Credit** MC, V. **Map** p251 F3.

The façade of this friendly *hostal* is almost too cute to be true, with hundreds of painted ceramic stars and plant pots covering the exterior. Inside, the kitsch factor goes through the roof but fortunately the 11 bedrooms are more restrained, with beamed ceilings, comfortable furnishings and en suite bathrooms.

### Hostal Marquez

*C/Fábrica Vieja 8 (958 27 50 13/hostal-marquez@ ozu.es.* **Rates** €17 single; €30-€36 double; €54 triple. **Credit** MC, V. **Map** p250 C5.
A well-cared-for and great-value *hostal* in the university area. Small but clean rooms have iron bedsteads, TVs and good bathrooms (get an en suite; the communal facilities are shared by up to three rooms). Those facing the interior can be quite dark; exterior rooms are brighter but a little noisier.

### Hostal Mesones

*C/Mesones 44 (958 26 32 44/hostalmesones@ hotmail.com).* **Rates** €18 single; €30-€36 double; €45 triple. **Credit** AmEx, MC, V. **Map** p251 D5.
Trinket-filled stairways lead to sparkling, well-furnished and -equipped rooms, with balconies overlooking the street. All rooms have private bathrooms, whether en suite or in the corridor. Corridors can be locked off to form 'apartments' for groups. Top marks for location, vibe and value.

### Hostal Venecia

*2nd floor, Cuesta de Gomérez 2 (958 22 39 87/ trevisovenecia@jazzfree.com).* **Rates** €15 single; €28-€39 double; €3 supplement per person (up to 5) in double room. **Credit** MC, V. **Map** p251 D3.
A basic but characterful *hostal*. The well-turned-out Mari Carmen is as particular about the appearance of her place as she is about her own. A good choice for backpacking groups of friends who want a quiet family atmosphere – scented candles burn in the kitsch corridors and guests are offered a herbal infusion in the morning. Room 1 is a bargain considering its view over Plaza Nueva.

### Hostal Meridiano

*C/Angulo 9 (958 25 05 44/www.hostalmeridiano. com).* **Rates** €17-€18 single; €28-€38 double; €45-€50 triple. **Credit** AmEx, MC, V. **Map** p250 C5.
An extremely friendly, peaceful, bargain-priced *hostal* near Plaza Trinidad. All the rooms are clean and appealing, but the best are on the first floor. Only four have double beds and some share a bathroom (at most between four people). There's internet access and a drinks machine in reception. The multilingual owners will shower you with info on Granada.

### Hostal Arteaga

*C/Arteaga 3 (958 20 88 41/hostalarteaga@hotmail. com).* **Rates** €22 single; €25-€36 double; €50 triple; €60 quad. **Credit** AmEx, DC, MC, V. **Map** p250 C4.
This basic but homely *hostal* just off the Gran Vía, at the bottom of the Albaicín, has a really friendly, relaxed vibe thanks to owner María Angeles. Rooms tend to be smallish and darkish but are jollied up with sunny bed linen.

## Resources

The **Granada City Pass (Bono Turístico)** costs €22.50 (from the Alhambra and Capilla Real ticket offices) or €24.50 (from Caja General de Ahorros de Granada in Plaza Isabel la Católica) and is valid for seven days. It can be used for nine rides on bus or mini-bus services in the city, one day's free pass on the tourist bus (www.granadatur.com), and admission to the Alhambra (pre-programmed entry agreed at time of booking), Parque de las Ciencias, Monasterio de la Cartuja, Monasterio de San Jerónimo, Catedral and Capilla Real. It may also entitle you to hotel and restaurant discounts. For details go to the website http://caja.caja-granada.es and click on 'entradas' and then 'bono turístico'.

### Internet

*Uninet, Plaza de la Encarnación 2 (958 20 83 82).* **Open** 9.30am-11pm Mon-Fri; 10.30am-11pm Sat, Sun. **Map** p250 C5.

### Police station

*Plaza de los Campos 3 (958 80 80 00).* **Map** p251 F4.

### Post office

*Puerta Real 2 (958 21 55 98).* **Map** p251 E5.

### Tourist information

*Turismo de Granada, Plaza Mariana Pineda 10 (958 24 71 28/www.turismodegranada.org).* **Open** 9am-8pm Mon-Fri; 10am-7pm Sat; 10am-3pm Sun. **Map** p251 D4.
Other offices are at C/Santa Ana 4 (958 22 59 90) and the Alhambra ticket office (958 22 95 75, *see p253*).

## Getting there

### By air

Granada's domestic airport is located 17km (11 miles) west of the city. *See p308.*

### By bus

Except for local buses to nearby towns, all services operate from the bus station on Carretera de Jaén (3km/2 miles north-west of the city centre, 958 18 54 80). The station is served by city bus numbers 3 and 33, which stop along Gran Vía. The largest company is Alsina Graells (958 18 54 80, www.alsinagraells.es), which has 9 daily services to Córdoba (2hrs 30mins), 9 to Sevilla (3-4hrs), 17 to Málaga (2hrs), 6 to the Alpujarras (1-3hrs) and 10 to Madrid (5hrs). Autedia (958 40 06 01, www.maestra-autedia.com) covers the north and east of Granada province, while Bonal (958 46 50 22) runs one bus daily to the Sierra Nevada (1hr) in summer and about four in winter.

### By train

Granada train station is at Avenida Andaluces s/n (902 24 02 02), a couple of kilometres west of the city centre. There are 4 trains daily to Sevilla (2hrs 30mins-3hrs), 4 to Almería (2hrs 30mins), 3 to Ronda (3hrs) and 2 to Madrid (6 hrs).

**Granada Province**

# West of Granada

Moors and Christians long fought over this now tranquil rural landscape.

The rolling landscapes of western Granada province, polka-dotted with countless olive trees, have more in common with south-eastern Córdoba than the Granadan *vega* or mountains to the east. Fortified Moorish castles and fine Renaissance churches speak of the importance of this region in the final years of the Nasrid Kingdom, when it formed a frontier between Granada and the encroaching Christian forces.

The village of **Moclín**, 35 kilometres/22 miles north-west of Granada, clusters below a craggy hill topped by an extensive castle. After the fall of Alcalá La Real in 1341 it became a key stronghold in the defence of Granada, before finally succumbing to the Christians in 1486. The lower part of the castle consists of a tower gateway, fortified wall, Renaissance granary and the church of **El Cristo del Paño** (open hours of services), donated to the town by Fernando and Isabel. The church houses a 16th-century canvas of Christ that is said to heal cataracts – a condition popularly known as *el paño*, or 'the cloth', because it veils the sight – and to improve female fertility. The *romería* to the church on 5 October is one of the most popular events in the province and is described in Lorca's tragedy *Yerma*. A steep, rocky climb upwards leads to the Moorish citadel, offering sublime views across olive-clad hills towards the Granadan *vega* and the Sierra Nevada.

Around Moclín are a number of watchtowers that provided a defensive network for the Nasrid state. There are also prehistoric remains in the area, including notable neolithic cave paintings and megalithic dolmens; ask at the *Ayuntamiento* for details of walking routes.

Thirty-two kilometres (20 miles) west of Moclín by road, and close to the Córdoban border, **Montefrío** enjoys a stunning setting between rocky hills and olive groves. A vast ledge of rock, looking like an impacted wisdom tooth, juts out of the earth at a jaunty angle above the town, topped by the 16th-century church of **La Villa** and the remains of the walled Moorish **Alcazaba**. The church, by Diego de Siloé, has a lovely vaulted interior. It is no longer used for services, because of the heart-stoppingly steep climb to reach it, but instead houses an interactive museum on the history of the region (opening times are erratic). At the centre of the town, the sloping Plaza de España is dominated by the bulging dome of

the Pantheon-like church of **La Encarnación** (open hours of services), built to the designs of Spain's leading neo-classical architect, Ventura Rodríguez; venture inside to admire its vast, womb-like cupola and peculiar acoustics. On the other side of the square is the 17th-century **Ayuntamiento** and the 16th-century **Casa de los Oficios**, which houses the tourist office.

Signposted off the GR222, a few kilometres east of Montefrío, is the extraordinary archaeological site of **Las Peñas de los Gitanos**. This extensive area flanked by limestone cliffs was occupied from the third millennium BC until the Middle Ages and incorporates cave dwellings, neolithic dolmens, a ruined Roman fort, a Visigothic burial ground and a medieval citadel. In the gorge below are the remains of six Roman water mills. Ask at the tourist office for directions to the site.

**Alhama de Granada** (53 kilometres/33 miles south-west of Granada) was an important spa town under the Moors, and its conquest by Christian forces in 1482 was one of the defining moments in the *reconquista*, as it blocked one of the Nasrid kingdom's routes to the coast. On the outskirts, a minor road leads past a Roman bridge to the spa that gives the town its name – *al hamma* means 'hot springs' in Arabic. Any illusions of finding a luxurious health resort are disabused by the sanatorium-style hotel building and the sight of elderly clients in towels. However, the setting in a wooded gorge is idyllic, and the naturally hot bathing pools (closed Nov-May) are enticing. The original Moorish baths no longer exist, but a magnificent cistern from around 1100, resembling a submerged mosque, does survive.

The town itself is situated on a rocky shelf above a cliff-lined *tajo* (ravine) formed by the Río Alhama. Winding streets lead to the capacious Plaza de la Constitución in the old town, where you'll find pleasant terrace cafés, with cool tiled interiors. At the far end is a privately owned Moorish castle with some unfortunate 19th-century embellishments. Past the tourist office on the east side of the square is the charming church of **El Carmen** (open hours of services), behind which is a *mirador* overlooking the gorge. Beyond the Plaza de la Constitución, narrow medieval streets twist around the Plaza des Presos and its 13th-century granary. Fronting the square

**Montefrío**. *See p270.*

is the 16th-century church of **La Encarnación** (open hours of services), whose Renaissance bell tower by Diego de Siloé dominates the skyline. Fernando and Isabel donated the church to Alhama shortly after the *reconquista*; the vestments in the sacristy may have been embroidered by the Queen herself.

South of Alhama the A355 emerges on to a wide fertile valley, backed to the west by the bare, elephant-hide bulk of the **Sierra de Loja**. From here it climbs to the edge of the **Sierra de Tejeda**, where the road drops away with a top-of-the-rollercoaster lurch through the **Zafarraya Pass** to reveal an awesome view across the Axarquía to the Med.

## Where to stay & eat

**El Rincón de Marcelo** (C/San José 25, 958 41 76 95, www.rincondemarcelo.com, double €42, restaurant €, hotel and restaurant closed 1wk July & 1wk Sept, restaurant closed Mon) is a comfortable rural *hostal* and restaurant in the village of Tózar, close to Moclín.

On the outskirts of Montefrío, the three-star **Hotel Enrea** (Paraje de la Enrea s/n, 958 33 66 62, www.hotel-laenrea.com, double €56-€63) has 19 spacious bedrooms in a converted olive mill, plus a bar and pleasant courtyard. In Montefrío, the ridiculously cheap **Mesón Pregonero** (Plaza de España 3, 958 33 61 17, closed Tue and 2wks early July, €), next to the tourist office, offers generous tapas and an authentic atmosphere. The tourist office can provide details of delightful *casas rurales* in the vicinity, including **El Castillo** (958 33 61 15,

www.granadainfo.com/castillo, sleeps up to 9 people, phone for prices), below La Villa church, and **Casa Paquita** (958 31 05 32, www.casasdepaquita.com, from €60 a day for 2 people), close to the Peñas de los Gitanos site.

On the outskirts of Alhama, the **Hotel Balneario de Alhama** (958 35 00 11, www.balnearioalhamadegranada.com, closed mid Nov-mid Mar, double €82-€88) offers spa facilities and all mod cons combined with a faintly institutional atmosphere. In the town itself there's the pleasant **Hostal San José** (Plaza de la Constitución 27, 958 35 01 56, double €31) and **La Seguiriya** (C/Las Peñas 12, 958 36 08 01, www.laseguiriya.com, double €50), owned by a flamenco singer who has named its characterful rooms after flamenco styles. Just outside Alhama, the **Hotel-Restaurante El Ventorro** (Carretera de Jatar, km2, 958 35 04 38, closed 2wks Jan, double €42, restaurant €, closed Mon), offers rooms, trad cuisine and walking and riding excursions.

Right by the western border with Málaga province, a little off the motorway, is the ultra-exclusive and luxurious five-star **Finca La Bobadilla** (Apartado 144, exit 175 from A92, 958 32 18 61, www.la-bobadilla.com, closed last 3wks Jan, double €284-€326, restaurant €€€), a favourite with celebs such as Brad Pitt and Placido Domingo. Set within a 400-hectare (1,000-acre) estate, the hotel looks like a small Moorish village, with a lovely main courtyard, a chapel and a labyrinth of pathways. All rooms are splendidly kitted out and have views of the pretty gardens or the estate. There are also two restaurants, an outdoor and an indoor pool, a jacuzzi and beauty treatments.

## Resources

### Tourist information

**Alhama de Granada** *Ayuntamiento, Paseo Montes Jovellar s/n (958 36 06 86/www.turismode alhama.org).* **Open** *July-mid Sept* 9.30am-2pm Mon-Fri; 10am-2pm Sat, Sun. *Mid Sept-June* 9.30am-3pm Mon-Fri; 10am-2pm Sat, Sun.

**Moclín** *Ayuntamiento, Plaza de España 1 (958 40 30 51).* **Open** 8am-2pm Mon-Fri.

**Montefrío** *Plaza de España 7 (958 33 60 04/ www.montefrio.org).* **Open** 10am-2pm, 4.30-6pm Mon-Fri; 10.30am-1.30pm Sat, Sun.

## Getting there

### By bus

Alsina-Graells (958 33 62 38, www.alsinagraells.es) runs 2 daily buses from Granada to Montefrio Mon-Sat, and 1 service on Sun (1hr 15mins). Autobuses Ronabus has 2 daily services to Moclin from outside the University of Granada. There are also daily services from Granada to Alhama.

# East of Granada

Troglodyte cities and a parched, lunar landscape.

Tourists may pour into the city of Granada by their thousands, but only a tiny fraction of these visitors venture into the vast open spaces to the east. It's their loss. Between the *sierras* that define the province's boundaries is a majestic landscape redolent of the American West, a tough land of parched, multihued soil and scrubby vegetation, punctuated by a couple of silvery reservoirs, its plains ripped and corrugated by countless twisting ravines.

Just east of Granada, the motorway passes through the small but spectacular **Parque Natural de la Sierra de Huétor** before skirting the largest, most interesting and strangest settlement in the eastern half of the province, **Guadix**. Located 55 kilometres (34 miles) east of Granada, this town is one of the oldest in Spain – it was an important Roman colony and one of the first Visigothic bishoprics in the country. Today, Guadix is chiefly famed for its cave dwellings. Wind-whipped pinnacles of tufa give the town a surreal backdrop and for centuries have provided an easily worked material for the construction of cave houses, which protect their occupants from the savage heat of summer. The caves were first inhabited during the Moorish period, and 2,000 are still in use, making up the largest inhabited cave complex in Europe. Wandering around the cave district, the **Barrio Santiago**, is a surreal and voyeuristic experience; you half expect a hobbit to come scuttling out of every round door. Be warned: any offer to see inside a cave will likely be followed by a demand for money. If you want to know more about the troglodyte life, visit the **Cueva-Museo**.

The old quarter of Guadix, extending south from Plaza de las Américas and the cathedral, makes for enjoyable wandering. Started in 1510, and not completed until 1796, the impressive **Catedral** is a melding of the original Gothic design, remodelling by Diego de Siloé and later baroque additions (including possibly Andalucía's most spectacular baroque façade). There is a small religious museum attached. An arch in front of the cathedral leads to the arcaded Renaissance Plaza de la Constitución (aka Plaza Mayor), which was badly damaged in the Civil War but has been restored. South of here, the Renaissance **Palacio de Peñaflor** stands next to the Gothic-Mudéjar church of **Santiago** and the originally 11th-century

Moorish **Alcazaba** (closed for restoration). In the nearby **Seminario de Torcuato** is the **Sala Alarconiano**, a re-creation of the home of the Guadix-born writer and politician Pedro Antonio de Alarcón (1833-91). His story *The Three-Cornered Hat* was made into a ballet with music by Manuel de Falla. The town's other famous son is Pedro de Mendoza, the *conquistador* who founded Buenos Aires.

Impressive though this castle is, it can't compare with that of **La Calahorra**, located on a small hill at the foot of the Sierra Nevada, around 20 kilometres (12 miles) south-east of Guadix. One of only a handful of new castles built by Christian forces after the fall of Granada in 1492, its austere rectangular plan with cylindrical, domed towers is in contrast to the elegant Italianate interior set around a two-storey arcaded marble courtyard.

The motorway from Guadix heads east through increasingly wild, desert-like scenery to the bustling but not especially interesting town of **Baza**. South of here extends the mountainous 52,237-hectare (202-square-mile) **Parque Natural de la Sierra de Baza**, an extension of Almería's Sierra de los Filabres.

To the north are the mountains of the **Sierra de Segura** and Jaén province (*see p242*). It's a tremendous drive from Baza on the A315 and A326, past the vast **Embalse de Negratín** reservoir and up into the hills via the hugely appealing village of **Castril**. Situated at the entrance to a mountainous nature reserve, and with panoramic views towards Baza and the Sierra Nevada, Castril is a well-preserved village built around a massive rock pinnacle. At its highest end is a homely Renaissance church, while far below is a spectacular modern footpath jutting above a gushing mountain torrent.

The A326 continues on to the town of **Huescar**, which had a turbulent history on the Arab-Christian frontline and was, due to a bizarre anomaly, officially at war with Denmark from 1809 until 1981. Today it's a mainly busy modern town, though not without interest – for instance, the decaying façade of the **Casa de los Peñalva** (on Paseo del Santo Cristo, just off the main square) is one of the very few examples of art nouveau in Andalucía.

Further to the north-east, Granada province shades into Murcia, while to the south is the isolated and dozy little town of **Orce**, which would be entirely unremarkable, were it not for its confident and startling claim to be the 'Cradle of European Humankind'. The parched and starkly beautiful flatlands that surround Orce were, for the best part of the last four million years, a vast lake, and many prehistoric animals watered at its edges. Large numbers of animal bones have been found in the area, but in 1976, in nearby Venta Micena, a fragment of bone was uncovered that its discoverers claimed was part of a human skull. If true, it would date the presence of early humans in the area from the previously accepted figure of 500,000 years ago to around a million years earlier. However, the identification of the bone fragment is the subject of some controversy, and many experts now believe that the 'Hombre de Orce' is, in fact, a goat. Unsurprisingly, the locals refuse to accept this, and you can learn their side of the story within the **Museo de Prehistoria y Paleontología**, housed within a restored Moorish tower in the village centre.

From Orce it's a 30-minute drive to Vélez Blanco and northern Almería (*see p303*).

### Castillo de la Calahorra

*La Calahorra (958 67 70 98).* **Open** 10am-1pm, 4-6pm Wed. **Admission** free. **No credit cards**.

### Catedral de Guadix & Museo

*Guadix (958 66 50 89).* **Open** 11am-1pm, 4-6pm Mon-Sat. **Admission** €2; €1 concessions. **No credit cards**.

### Cueva-Museo

*Plaza de la Ermita Nueva, off Plaza del Padre Poveda, Guadix (958 66 93 00).* **Open** 10am-2pm, 4-6pm Mon-Fri; 10am-noon Sun. **Admission** €1; 50¢ concessions. **No credit cards**.

### Museo de Prehistoria y Paleontología

*Palacio de los Segura, C/Tiendas, Orce (958 74 61 71).* **Open** 10am-1pm, 5-7pm daily. **Admission** €2; €1.50 concessions. **No credit cards**.

### Sala Alarconiano

*Seminario de San Torcuato, C/Barradas s/n, Guadix (958 66 93 00).* **Open** 10.30am-2pm, 4-6pm Tue-Sat; 10.30am-2pm Sun. **Admission** €1.75. **No credit cards**.

The castle of **La Calahorra**. *See p272*.

Tourism is rare in this part of the province, and accommodation scarce. In Guadix, the most central place to stay is the somewhat faded three-star **Hotel Comercio** (C/Mira de Amezcua 3, 958 66 05 00, www.hotelcomercio.com, double €63), which has a good restaurant (€€). If you fancy kipping in a cave, try **Cuevas Pedro Antonio de Alarcón** (Barriada San Torcuato s/n, 958 66 49 86, www.andalucia.com/cavehotel, cave for 2 €55-€66), with all mod cons and pool, or, a few kilometres north of Guadix near Benalúa, **Cuevas La Granja** (Camino de la Granja s/n, 958 67 60 00, mobile 666 55 80 30, www.cuevas.org, cave for 2 €63-€68), which are equally luxuriously appointed and can sleep up to 6 people; the complex also has a restaurant and pool. For eating in Guadix, try Plaza de la Constitución or the area around the Plaza de los Naranjos.

An fine spot to eat in La Calahorra is **Manjon** (C/Los Caños 20, 958 67 70 81), just off the main square, which specialises in fish and roast lamb, and also has an attached *hostal* (double €32).

In Castril, the 21-room two-star **La Fuente** (Avenida del Portillo s/n, 958 72 00 30, double €41) is a pleasant place to lay your head, while **El Café de Emilio** (C/Carmen 10, 958 72 00 05, €) is an endearing old bar and the best place in the area to try local specialities like *maimones* (a tomato and red pepper stew).

There are also cave dwellings around Orce. The **Cuevas de Orce** (A317, 958 74 62 81, www.cuevasdeorce.com, cave for 2 €64-€86) have cable TV, bathroom and kitchen.

### Tourist information

**Guadix** *Avenida Mariana Pineda s/n (958 66 26 65).* **Open** 9am-3pm Mon; 9am-6pm Tue-Fri; 10am-2pm Sat.
**Parque Natural de la Sierra de Baza** *Centro de Visitantes 'Narváez', Monte Narváez, A92, km324.* **Open** *Easter-Sept* 10am-2pm, 6-8pm Fri-Sun. *Oct-Easter* 10am-2pm, 4-6pm Fri-Sun.

### By bus

Maestra Autedia (958 66 06 57, www.maestra-autedia.com) runs most buses in the area. From Granada there are 11 daily to Guadix (1hr); 8 continue on to Baza (45 mins from Guadix), 4 go on to La Calahorra (55mins from Guadix) and 2 go on to Orce (55mins from Baza). There's 1 daily between Baza and Castril (1hr 40mins).

### By train

There are around 7 daily trains between Almería and Guadix (1hr 15mins), 4 daily from Guadix to Almería (1hr) and 3 daily to Linares-Baeza (1hr 50mins).

# Sierra Nevada & the Alpujarras

Soaring mountains and stunning valleys – welcome to a year-round playground.

Much of the visual appeal of the Alhambra is provided by its awesome backdrop – the snow-crowned peaks of the mighty Sierra Nevada, the highest mountain range in Spain. The two highest peaks **Mulhacén** (3,482 metres/11,424 feet) and **Veleta** (3,392 metres/11,128 feet) wear a white mantle almost year round, yet are barely an hour's drive from the coast, allowing *granadinos* to ski in the morning and hit the beach in the afternoon. The mountains are far more than a playground for city folk, however, providing a unique habitat for numerous animal and plant species that is protected as the 86,208-hectare (333-square mile) **Parque Nacional de la Sierra Nevada**.

For centuries the only people to labour up the Sierra Nevada's peaks were the *neveros* (icemen), who carried blocks of ice down from the high mountains to sell in the city. Today, though, the mountains draw ever-increasing numbers of visitors for a huge range of outdoor activities, from skiing (the season runs from November to May) and hiking to mountain-biking and paragliding.

Between the Sierra Nevada and the lower hills of the coastal ranges to the south lie the Alpujarras, described by British writer Gerald Brenan as 'a little country, shut in by its almost impassable mountains'. Access is considerably easier today, but the Alpujarras retains a distinctive feel. This fertile but traditionally

poor region, dotted with distinctive mountain villages, was first inhabited by the Visigoths and later by the Moors, who developed a unique system of irrigation and planted mulberry trees for the silk trade, which flourished here during the thirteenth century. After the Christian conquest of Granada, the Alpujarras became a final enclave of Moorish resistance. Boabdil, the last Nasrid Sultan, was initially exiled here, and the area remained beyond effective Catholic control until 1568. Even when Felipe III ordered the explusion of Muslims from Spain, two Moorish families were told to remain in each Alpujarran village to educate relocated peasants from the north about methods of irrigation. In the following centuries the Alpujarras remained poor, isolated and forgotten. It's only in recent years, with the influx of tourists and northern European expats, that this beautiful region has regained some prosperity and self-confidence.

There are around 70 villages in the Alpujarras today, distinguished by a style of architecture that's otherwise only found in the Moroccan Rif mountains. The low-lying dwellings have thick walls covered in local grey clay known as *launa* and are linked together by little bridge-like passageways known as *tinaos*. Their flat roofs double as terraces (*terrao*), and sport tall, distinctive chimneys; in silhouette they look like people wearing wide-brimmed hats.

On the piste in the **Sierra Nevada**.
*See p275*

# Sierra Nevada

The Sierra Nevada's environmental status vies for supremacy with its burgeoning ski industry. Around the resort of **Sierra Nevada** (aka **Solynieve** – 'sun and snow', aka **Pradollano**), on the western flank of Veleta, are 62 kilometres (39 miles) of slopes and 19 ski lifts. For more details, contact the **Sierra Nevada Club** (Plaza de Andalucía, 958 24 91 11, 902 70 80 90, www.sierranevada.es).

The resort, although well equipped, is a crass blot on the landscape, and spookily empty out of season. Increasingly, activities such as mountain biking, hiking and horse-trekking are being made available to entice visitors in the summer months. On the A395, north-west of the resort, the park information centre gives details on environmental issues and outdoor activities, and has a terrace café with spectacular views. Note that the road over the Sierra is closed to traffic above the Borreguiles ski station, but walkers can continue through the barren landscape up to the peak of Veleta (a reasonable three-hour hike) or even on to the village of Capileira, 30 kilometres (19 miles) to the south (*see p278*), passing the summit of Mulhacén on the way.

## Where to stay & eat

Many of the resort's hotels close at the end of the ski season, so always call ahead to check. One of the more attractive options is the **Hotel Rumaykiyya** (Urbanización Solynieve, 958 48 14 00, closed May-Nov, double €70-€210), where you can relax with a post-tundra sauna, jacuzzi or massage. It also has a buffet restaurant, **La Alquería** (dinner €€-€€€). A cheaper choice is **Hotel Monte Sol** (Edificio Acongra s/n, 958 48 10 00, www.hotelmontesolarttyco.com, phone in season for prices, closed May-late Nov), which offers en suite rooms and buffet-style meals. Or there's the great-value youth hostel: **Albergue Juvenil** (C/Peñones 22, 958 48 03 05, www.inturjoven.com, closed Aug, dorm bed €12-€18).

## Resources

### Tourist information

**Parque Nacional de la Sierra Nevada** *A395, km23, Güéjar Sierra (958 34 06 25/www.nna.es).* **Open** *July-Sept* 10am-2pm, 4.30-7pm daily. *Oct-June* 10am-2pm, 4-6pm daily.

# West Alpujarras

South of Granada the N323 climbs towards the **Puerto del Suspiro del Moro** (Pass of the Moor's Sigh). According to legend, this is where the banished Boabdil turned for one last look at his beloved Granada in 1492. His mother was not sympathetic: 'Weep like a woman, you, who have not defended your kingdom like a man.'

From the pass, the road descends into the **Valle de Lecrín**, a sweeping landscape of olive groves and citrus trees. To the east, where the valley meets the mass of the Sierra Nevada, is the spa town of **Lanjarón**, famed throughout Spain for its mineral water. The spa itself (Avenida de Constitución s/n, 958 77 01 37, www.aguasdelanjaron.es, closed Jan & Feb) is in an unprepossessing, institutional building at the west end of town, and attracts elderly clients for hydrotherapy and other treatments. Their presence gives Lanjarón a somewhat gloomy, geriatric atmosphere. Below the long main street is a ruined Moorish castle set atop a striking promontory – there's not much left of the original structure, but the views across the steep gorge to the mountains are extraordinary. You can explore the area on horseback with Sarah at **Caballo Blanco** (958 34 71 75, mobile 627 79 48 91, www.spanishhighs.com, 2hr trek €30).

Nine kilometres (six miles) east of Lanjarón is **Órgiva**, a gently sprawling market town set in a wide river basin at the foot of the mountains. During the Civil War it was evacuated and remained pretty much a no-go zone until the war ended in 1939. Fully recovered from those bloody days, today it is the commercial hub of the area, though it is most notable for its large New Age hippy colony, which occupies ancient camper vans and teepees on the edge of town. The New Agers are most conspicuous during the weekly outdoor market (Thursdays), where their crystals, herbs and tambourines provide a curious counterpoint to the local farmers' produce and the stalls selling cheap shoes and clothing. The area around the town has seen a huge increase in British residents in the last few years, partially as a result of Chris Stewart's bestseller *Driving Over Lemons* (*see p276* **Being Chris Stewart**) which is set in these parts.

Above Órgiva the road twists and turns towards the 'high' Alpujarras. The villages of **Cañar**, **Carataunas** and **Soportújar** have spectacular views south towards the bulk of the Sierra Lújar, and offer a first taste of the region's distinctive architecture.

A couple of kilometres further on (opposite the **Ermita del Padre Eterno** chapel), a rough gravel track leads up to the blissfully tranquil and awesomely situated **O Sel Ling Buddhist Centre** (958 34 31 34, open 3-6pm daily, admission free). This high mountain retreat, consisting of a scattered group of dwellings, a library, temple and *stupa*, was founded by the Tibetan monk Lama Yeshe and named the 'Place of Clear Light' by the Dalai Lama, who visited in 1982.

# Being Chris Stewart

'Don't say hello to him. That's Antonio the hunter, he's a shit!' Not quite the attitude one might expect from Chris Stewart, author of *Driving Over Lemons* and friend of all folk, even the dodgy ones. 'It's OK,' he adds reassuringly, 'He's supposed to be a shit.' Antonio, as it turns out, is an extremely life-like scarecrow wearing shades and clutching a rifle, who stands guard over the alfalfa crop in a field near the river.

Those who have read *Driving Over Lemons* will know all about the alfalfa crop that carpets the Stewarts' beloved valley, and the snake-tongued river that courses its way from the Sierra Nevada in shreds of silver past their home of almost two decades. Thanks to the book, and its sequel, *A Parrot in the Pepper Tree*, their house has become a pilgrimage for fans – a must-see on the Alpujarran circuit.

Though how on earth people find it is anyone's guess. The map in the book is utterly useless, yet incredibly, hoards of fans – as many as three or four a week in high season – manage to track down El Valero in the hope of a glimpse of Chris and his family. Doesn't it drive him mad?

'I realise I have a duty to my readers,' he explains cheerfully, 'Sometimes it gets a bit much, but mostly it's flattering. They are my public after all, and I owe my success to them. Of course, it's never anyone I fancy. Usually middle-aged women and ageing Swedes.'

In the flesh, Stewart is as charming, funny and laid-back as his books portray him to be; a joker, a talented wordsmith, a philosophiser and an itinerant philanthropist (the latest in the Alpujarran trilogy moves towards issues of immigration – a subject he is passionate about – and his nocturnal adventures illicitly helping frightened bands of North Africans towards a better life). He is a passionate historian, socialist and environmentalist. He loathes golf and TV and adores Barcelona for the sheer thrill of it, but his heart is very much at home with his wife and daughter and a parrot that detests him.

He's an unlikely celebrity; refreshingly modest and still somewhat bemused by the whole extraordinary caper:

'We made a lot of money out of the book, but I'm afraid to say that instead of blowing it and having a wild time like proper reprobates, we've been sensible and invested it in sure-fire property... Before, we never left the *cortijo* because we couldn't afford to go out.'

Stewart feels that the book's impact on the area has been mostly positive:

'A lot of people have come here after reading the book and so it has given a shot in the arm to the economy, which I'm very pleased about. Of course, a lot of foreigners will say, "bah, you're responsible for bringing all these foreigners down here." But it was a phenomenon that was happening anyway. I might have had an effect on accelerating it a little bit, that's about all.'

## Where to stay & eat

In the Valle de Lecrín there's comfortable accommodation and delicious breakfasts on offer at the British-run **Cortijo del Pino** (C/Fernán Nuñez 2, La Loma, 958 77 62 57, double €75) in Albuñuelas.

There are plenty of places to stay on the main drag in Lanjarón, none of them terribly inspiring. The most upmarket is the **Hotel Castillo Alcadima** (C/Francisco Tarrega 3, 958 77 08 09, www.castillo-alcadima.es, double €52), which is built around a series of gardens, patios and terraces. and has swimming pools and tennis courts. On a smaller scale, the **Hotel Albergue de Mecina** (C/La Fuente s/n, 958 76 62 54, www.ocioteca.com/hoteldemeccina, double €69, restaurant €€) has spacious, comfortable rooms and a rustic restaurant.

A cheaper option is to head for the super-friendly **Hotel Lanjarón** (C/Pérez Chaves 7, 958 77 00 94, abuxarra@yahoo.es, double €38). It's basic but clean and comfortable. By far the most pleasant option, and ideal if you want to use the area as a base for hiking, is to head two kilometres out of town to either **Cortijo El Arao** or **Cortijo La Fuente** (958 77 20 18, mobile 658 11 35 85, €15-€18 per person), rural cottages that sleep four or six people, with swimming pool, fireplaces and lots of privacy. Cafés and restaurants abound along Lanjarón's long main street.

Órgiva's best place to stay is the friendly **Hotel Taray** (A348, km18, 958 78 45 25, www.turgranada.com/hoteltaray, double €72, restaurant €€), surrounded by lush, secluded gardens, turtle ponds and an enormous swimming pool; its restaurant utilises home-

just as good a book – quite missing the point that they didn't and Stewart did.

'Inevitably, there is some anti-Chris Stewart feeling. There's this local magazine that asked me to write something about a quarry that they've been fighting to build on the other side of the hill for years. I thought, yes, that's useful and something I don't know enough about, so I did a whole lot of research and handed in about five pages worth of article. Then in the next issue, a letter appeared saying: "Nice to see that Chris Stewart can actually write something useful. Well done, Chris. But please, no more of that ghastly *Driving Over Lemons* rubbish." It was funny because I know the guy. He's an estate agent and he's actually making a killing out of all of the people that now come here.'

Not since Gerald Brenan's wonderful book, *South From Granada*, has the world paid so much attention to the Alpujarras. Indeed, the two writers have much in common, especially in terms of the personal and colourful insights they give into their lives, but Stewart is characteristically modest: 'Oh no, Brenan was erudite, a scholar, an academic. I'm a clown. Though clowning has its place,' he adds, 'I'm very happy if I can make people laugh.'

A clown Stewart may be, but he is a sympathetic and eloquent·clown with a big heart and a passion for the people and places around him. For this, *Driving Over Lemons* deserves its place among the classics of Spanish travel literature.

'Local Spanish people are thrilled about it,' he explains, 'to the extent that I was publicly embraced in the street one day by a local bar owner who told me I'd "made the fortunes" of his bar. He told me, "We're going to put up a monument to you. I've got it all worked out, you're going to have a stone colossus striding through the *plaza*." To which I replied, "Can't you run to something better than stone. Bronze would do the job."'

Expat friends and neighbours are either genuinely pleased for him, or grouchily envious. There are always those who will claim they could easily have written

grown produce and local trout. For unexpected seclusion in the heart of town, try the lovely **Casa Rural El Molíno** (C/González Robles 16, mobile 646 61 66 28, www.casaruralelmolino. com, double €48-€52), a former olive mill that's now a five-bedroomed hotel with a bath-jacuzzi on the patio. There are plenty of reasonable tapas bars and cafés in the town centre. The **Hostal Alma Alpujarreña** (C/González Robles 49, 958 78 40 85, double €30, restaurant €), with its pretty bougainvillea covered terrace, is hugely popular for home-cooked meals, while **Mesón Casa Santiago** (Plaza García Moreno 13, 958 78 42 29, closed Wed) is good for getting tanked up on local wines and cider.

A kilometre outside Órgiva, the **Puerta de la Alpujarra** (Las Barreras, 958 78 44 50, www.campings.net/puertadelaalpujarra, €) does a good-value menu, offering soups,

salads, roast chicken and fresh fish; it also has live flamenco, jazz and blues bands every weekend. The restaurant is part of a well-equipped campsite.

In keeping with Órgiva's reputation as a mecca for northern Europeans seeking an alternative lifestyle in the sun, **Cortijo Romero** (01494 782720 in the UK, www. cortijo-romero.co.uk) offers residential courses in yoga, shiatsu and other therapies.

## Resources

### Internet
**Lanjarón** *Cyberplay Internet, next to the Ermita de San Roque (no phone)*. **Open** 10am-1.30pm, 5.30-10pm Mon-Sat.
**Órgiva** *Ciber Ocio, Avenida González Robles, next to the Mirasol Hotel (no phone)*. **Open** 10am-1.30pm, 5.30-10pm Mon-Fri; 11am-2pm, 5.30-9.30pm Sat.

A copy of the Alhambra's famous lion fountain in **Yegen**. *See p281.*

### Tourist information

**Central de Reservas de Valle de Lecrín**
*C/Barrio Bajo 21, Dúrcal (958 78 15 71/mobile 619
94 30 63/www.elvalledelecrin.com).* **Open** 10am-
1.30pm, 5.30-8.30pm Mon-Fri; 10am-1.30pm Sat.

**Lanjarón** *Avenida de Andalucía s/n, opposite the
Balneario (958 77 04 62).* **Open** 10am-2pm, 5-8pm
Mon, Tue, Thur-Sat; 10am-2pm Sun.

## Central Alpujarras

Generally regarded as the most beautiful of
the Alpujarran valleys (and the most touristed
as a result), the **Valle de Poqueira** is a
steep-sided, verdant river gorge, flanked by
cultivated terraces and backed by snowy peaks.
In a picture-perfect location on its eastern side
are the villages of Pampaneira, Bubión and
Capileira; there are well-signposted walking
routes connecting all three.

The lowest of the three, **Pampaneira** has
a beautiful little central square opening out in
front of its ochre-coloured 16th-century church.
Here you'll find crafts shops, with traditional
rugs and ceramics on display, plus a couple
of bars and the Nevadensis information
centre (*see p280*). Above the square, typical
Alpujarran dwellings tumble down the hillside,
interlinked by a network of *tinaos* and steep
narrow streets. The *mantanzas* (pig-slaughter
festivities), held between the 5th and 8th
December, are among the best in Spain.

Higher up the valley, **Bubión** is more
sprawling than its neighbours, its houses
spilling down towards Plaza Iglesia. In

Moorish times, the church was both mosque
and watchtower, and offers a superb view
of the valley. Also on the square is the **Casa
Alpujarreña** folk museum, while nearby
is the **Taller del Telar** (C/Trinidad s/n,
958 76 31 71), where rugs, blankets and shawls
are woven on a hand-operated loom.

**Capileira** is the highest of the villages and
a good base for mountain walking and climbing.
Beyond here, the road (now permanently closed
to traffic) continues upwards close to the peaks
of Mulhacén and Veleta, before descending to the
Sierra Nevada ski resort (*see p275*). The **Museo
de Capileira** has displays of local crafts, plus
artefacts associated with the Guadix-born writer,
Pedro Antonio de Alarcón, who wrote a book
about the Alpujarras in the 19th century.

Elsewhere, seek out **El Horno de Luisa**,
a bakery that still uses its 500-year-old Moorish
oven. There are myriad walks from the villages,
including trails through the Poqueira gorge,
and east towards Pitres and Trevélez. For
serious and well-equipped climbers, the ascent
of Mulhacén takes two days from Capileira.
Horse treks (Cabalgar Rutas Alternativas,
958 76 31 35, www.ridingandalucia.com) and
paragliding (Horizonte Vertical, 958 76 34 08)
are also available.

Under the Moors, the settlements of **Pitres**,
**Pórtugos**, **Mecina Fondales**, **Ferreirola**
and **Busquístar** formed a league of villages
known as the 'Tahá', from the Arabic *tá*
meaning 'obedience'. Situated to the east
of Pampaneira, they are more tranquil than
their Poqueira neighbours, offering a taste

of mountain life little affected by tourism. The surrounding landscape is characterised by orchards and streams and provides plenty of opportunities for walking and exploring.

Beyond Buquístar, the road turns north into a dramatic, rugged valley towards **Trevélez** (meaning 'three villages'). Even today the *barrios bajo*, *medio* and *alto* each retain a distinctive flavour, and it's worth hiking to the higher parts to get a taste of old Trevélez (the *barrio bajo* is the most touristy, with innumerable shops hawking local artisans' wares). At 1,476 metres (4,842 feet) above sea level, this is the highest permanently occupied village in Spain, and is a starting point for ascents of the Sierra Nevada peaks. On 5 August each year, the villagers climb Mulhacén themselves to celebrate the festival of the **Virgen de los Nieves**. Trevélez is famed for its snow-cured *jamón serrano*; you'll see huge haunches of it hanging from every available inch of ceiling in the village's shops and restaurants.

### Casa Alpujarreña

*Plaza Iglesia 5, Bubión (958 76 30 32/ www.bubion.org).* **Open** 11am-2pm Mon, Wed, Thur, Sun; 11am-2pm, 5-7pm Fri, Sat. **Admission** €1.80. **No credit cards**.

### Museo de Capileira

*C/Mentidero 15, Capileira (958 76 30 51).* **Open** 11.30am-2.30pm Tue-Sun. **Admission** €1. **No credit cards**.

## Where to stay & eat

In Pampaneira, **Hostal Ruta del Mulhacén** (Avenida de la Alpujarra 6, 958 76 30 10, www.rutadelmulhacen.com, closed Jan-early Feb, double €33-€45) has en suite rooms strewn with colourful woven blankets and *jarapas* (rugs). Just below the village, the terrace at **Bar-Restaurante Guillermo** (Carretera Pampaneira, km46, 958 76 30 23, €-€€) is one of the most popular haunts, and great for drinks and complimentary tapas.

In Bubión, **Las Terrazas** (Placeta del Sol 7, 958 76 30 34, closed Jan, double from €29) is a friendly *pensión* with an extraordinary view; many rooms have terraces. For food, good options are **La Artesa** (C/Carretera 2, 958 76 30 82, closed 2wks early Jan & 2wks early July, €-€€) and **Restaurant Teide** (C/Carretera s/n, 958 76 30 37, closed mid June-early Jul, €-€€), on either side of the main road.

In Capileira, **Casa Ibero** (C/Parra 1, 958 76 32 56, €-€€) serves international food, including vegetarian dishes. There's a lively flamenco evening every Thursday at the **Cortijo Catifalarga** (800 metres up into the Sierra, 958 34 33 57, www.catifalarga.com,

double €55-€64, restaurant €), which has apartments, rooms, a restaurant and pool. For self-catering chalet-style accommodation try the **Cortijo Los Molinillos** (Carretera Bubión–Capileira, km1, 958 34 30 79, bigeasy@wanadoo.es, 2-4 people €60 a day, €400 a week), which is solar-powered and has views across to Morocco; book well in advance.

The excellent campsite **Balcón de Pitres** (958 76 61 11, €5 per person plus €5 per tent, €6 (caravan) nestles among trees just west of Pitres; it has self-catering cabins, a pool and a restaurant. On the other side of Pitres is the popular vegetarian restaurant **El Jardín** (C/Escuelas Viejas s/n, Parque El Mirador, mobile 689 63 35 29, closed Mon and Dec-Mar, €).

Book well in advance for a chance to stay at **Sierra y Mar** in Ferreirola (C/Albaycín 3, 958 76 61 71, double €50), a beautiful B&B with a heavenly walled garden. Another good option is the modern but cosy **Albergue de Mecina** in Mecina Fondales (C/La Fuente s/n, 958 76 62 54, double €70, restaurant €-€€).

There are numerous restaurants and hotels in Trevélez's *barrio bajo*. If you're after something a little special, the recently opened **Despensa de la Alpujarra** (958 85 87 57, €€-€€€) has been made to look old, with heavy antique doors, blackened beams and a gurgling spring in the entrance hall; it's unsurprisingly popular and the food is excellent, if not cheap. In the *barrio alto*, **La Sala Baja** (C/Cuesta Principal 44, 958 85 85 28, €) has a sweet terrace overlooking the town and a delightfully cosy dining room. **La Fragua I & II** (C/San Antonio 4, Barrio Alto, 958 85 86 26, 958 85 85 12, www.hotellafragua.com, closed mid Jan-mid Feb, double €35-€43, restaurant €) are the nicest places to stay in in the village, with fabulous views and a lovely restaurant.

The most upmarket place to stay in the area is the **Hotel Alcazaba de Buquístar** (GR421, km37, 958 85 86 87, www.alpujarralcazaba.com, double €77-€86), five kilometres (three miles) south of Trevélez. It has 44 suites arranged in terraces, plus a restaurant and an indoor pool. It's not to be confused with the more rustic **Alcazar de Busquístar** (Paraje de la Loma s/n, 958 85 74 70, jguardia@ujr.es, double €53), which is actually in the village. Rooms are very old-fashioned but the surrounds are stunning and it has a delightful restaurant with gingham table cloths and corn dollies, and a pool. For super-cheap, basic and out-of-the-way accommodation, head down the mountain to **Posada María** (Cástaras, 958 85 55 31, http:// es.geocities.com/castarasposada, double €22).

For local rental accommodation, contact the rural tourism agency **Rustic Blue** (*see p280*).

# Walk Ferreirola circuit

**Distance** 8km (5 miles)
**Time required** 3.5-4hrs

This walk begins and ends in the tiny village of Ferreirola (just east of Mecina Fondales). For most of the way it follows old muleteer tracks that twice cross the steep-sided *barranco* (gorge) of the Río Trevélez. Although there are two steep uphill sections, this is an easy half-day walk that you could stretch out by picnicking somewhere along the way – or by stopping for a coffee in Busquístar. There is a kilometre or so of road-walking but there's virtually no traffic and the views are excellent. Ferreirola and Busquístar are not in the least bit touristy and this would be a lovely first walk in the Alpujarras.

The walk begins in the main square of Ferreirola in front of the church. Pass in front of the four fountains and on past Villa Kiko and then descend between two stone walls. Continue past a house with two large earthenware pots outside. The street narrows, doglegs right and then left, and you walk beneath a *tinao* (a roof spanning the street). Pass a newly built section of high wall on your left and then pick up a path leading out from the village.

Pass by a spring, and then a second one, both just to the left of the path. Your path soon crosses a bridge, descends slightly and then reaches a fork. Here, branch left and climb gently upwards. You will see white and yellow waymarking. The *barranco* of the Río Trevélez is to your right.

The path divides again. Fork left and soon you reach a track. Here, bear right and descend slightly through an area of terraced fields beneath Busquístar. You reach a stand of poplars. Here, carry on uphill and then cross a bridge. The path becomes still steeper and you arrive at the outskirts of the village. You'll see a sign for 'Camino a Ferreirola'. Here, if you are planning to visit the village, turn left and climb up into the village, but remember that later you will need to retrace your footsteps back to this sign.

This path leads up past Casa de las Lillas, where you could have an early lunch (open 1-4pm daily). If you're not planning to visit the village, at the 'Camino a Ferreirola' sign turn right down the hill and then go left at a door with a painted arrow pointing your way.

Continue skirting round the bottom of the village until you reach a sign for 'Camino del Río'. Go right here and drop steeply down through the terraces. Soon you need to bear left round a house with a horseshoe above its entrance. As you proceed down to the river, you'll see wooden posts and red dots marking your way. A footbridge leads you across the river by a ruined mill and the path now zigzags steeply up the other side of the gorge. Prepare yourself for a long, steep climb. The path eventually levels and meets with a tarmac road just to the left of the Venta de Relleno.

Turn right on to the road in the direction of Almegíjar/Torvizcón. You should continue until you see a group of five buildings just to the right of the road. Turn right off the road at a marker post and climb up towards these buildings, watching out for a second marker post just to the right of the track. Here turn right, away from the track, and drop back down towards the Río Trevélez.

After five minutes or so of descending, the path runs just to the left of the overgrown ruins of some Arab baths; there is little to see now. Ferreirola is clearly visible on the other side of the valley. As you descend you'll occasionally spot marker posts. You cross the river once again. Swing left in front of a second ruined mill and climb up the northern side of the *barranco*.

You reach the fork where earlier in the walk you took the higher option to Busquístar. Here bear left and return to Ferreirola and retrace the path that you followed earlier in the day, all the way back to the square in front of the church.

*From* Walking in Andalucía *by Guy Hunter-Watts (Santana)*

## Resources

### Internet

**Bubión** *Café Morisco El Monfi, C/Alcalde Pérez Ramón 2 (958 76 30 53/www.cibermonfi.com).* **Open** 2pm-1am Mon, Wed-Sun.
This pleasant café also serves a menu of North African-influenced food.

## Tourist information

**Bubión** *Rustic Blue, Barrio La Ermita (958 76 33 81/www.rusticblue.com).* **Open** 10am-2pm, 5-7pm Mon-Fri; 11am-2pm Sat. An agency for rural holiday homes, tourism and guided treks (walking and riding).

**Pampaneira** *Nevadensis, Plaza de la Libertad (958 76 31 27/www.nevadensis.com ).* **Open** 10am-3pm Mon, Sun; 10am-2pm, 4-7pm Tue-Sat.

## East Alpujarras

Heading out of the Trevélez valley and east towards **Juviles** – famed for its silk in Moorish times – the landscape begins to open out, changing from the steep, wooded inclines of the western Alpujarras to drier, rockier terrain. **Bérchules** and **Alcútar** are surrounded by chestnut trees and offer splendid views over the Cádiar valley to the green and brown folds of the Sierra de la Contraviesa.

Continue through the increasingly arid sandstone landscape to reach the characteristic villages of **Mecina Bombarón** and **Yegen**. The latter is famous as the one-time home of the English writer Gerald Brenan, a peripheral member of the Bloomsbury Set, who moved here in 1920. During eight years' residence Brenan did some prodigious walking (including trekking from Granada to Yegen in one day) and became intimately acquainted with the landscape and people of his new home. He recorded his experiences in *South from Granada*, which remains the best account of life in the region and a must-read for any visitor to the Alpujarras. A plaque in the *barrio alto* marks the house where he lived. Many aspects of Brenan's description of Yegen in 1920 still hold true today:

'It was a poor village, standing high above the sea, with an immense view in front of it. With its grey box-shaped houses of a battered Corbusier style, all running down the hill and fusing into one another, and its flat clay roofs and small smoking chimneys, it suggested something that had been made out the earth by insects.'

The larger village of **Válor**, a couple of kilometres to the east, is incredibly pretty, and has its own soap and cheese factories. Here, the houses with pitched roofs mark a significant change from the dominant Alpujarran architecture. Válor's **Fiesta Patronales** in September is the best of the region's 'Moors and Christians' pageants (*see p48*), and celebrates the resistance of local-born *morisco* Aben Humaya to 16th-century Catholic persecution.

Beyond here the road splits, south to **Ugíjar** – the main town of the eastern Alpujarras, which years ago attracted innumerable fortune hunters seeking gold in its river, but is lacking in any real attractions today – and east to **Mairena** and **Laroles**, at the extremity of the Granadan Alpujarras. From the latter, you can enjoy the superb drive over the Sierra Nevada, via the **Puerto de la Ragua** pass, to reach the stunning castle of **La Calahorra** (*see p272*), or continue east to Laujar de Andarax and the Almerían Alpujarras (*see p304*).

## Where to stay & eat

In Bérchules, the recently opened **El Paraje de Matamoros** (GR421, km6, mobile 626 18 60 35, www.elparaje.com, double €35-€40) is an ecological hotel run by a Dutch couple. All rooms retain their original features but have been updated with the odd designer flourish. There's also a pleasant living and dining area for home-cooked, organic meals. Alternatively, you'll find good rooms, fine food and a warm welcome at **Hotel Los Bérchules** (Carretera de Bérchules 20, 958 85 25 30, www.hotelberchules.com, double €41, restaurant €€).

In Válor, the folks at **Cortijo La Cara** (Carretera Mairena s/n, mobile 646 73 56 37, 630 23 16 42, www.aspectsofandalucia.com, double €36-€48) have created a home-away-from-home in a lovingly converted *cortijo*, with comfortable, farmhouse-style bedrooms and communal areas. The owners also offer walking and photography holidays, and meals on request. For eats in town, the **Restaurante Aben Humeya** (C/Los Bolos s/n, 958 85 18 10, €-€€) serves free tapas with drinks and has a superb restaurant specialising in typical *alpujarreño* cuisine, particularly game birds.

Just up the road in Mairena, **Casa Las Chimeneas** (C/Amargua 6, 958 76 03 52, www.alpujarra-tours.com, dillsley@moebius.es, double €60) specialises in walking tours. Accommodation is in a lovingly restored *cortijo* with astonishing views; all seven spacious bedrooms have en suite bathrooms and a balcony or terrace. Homey communal areas have crackling fires and rocking chairs, and the terrace is a top spot for evening barbecues and a dip in the pool as the sun goes down.

The rooms at **El Rincón de Yegen** (Camino de Gerald Brenan, 958 85 12 70, elrincondeyegen@telefonica.net, closed 1st 2wks Feb, double €36, restaurant €€, closed

Trevélez. See p279.

VENDIMIA

Viña y sol de un camino,
vendimiadores en fila.
Cada canasta destila
la promesa de un buen vino.
¡Qué pasillo divino
hacia el lagar de la muerte!
Aquí el débil es el fuerte
y es un triunfo la derrota.
Hasta la última gota.
Y que Dios reparta suerte.

"Rafael Guillén"

Seclusion, fine food and priceless views mark out the **Alquería de Morayma**, near Cádiar.

Tue) are cosily decked out with woven rugs and blankets; the hotel also has a small pool. The restaurant is first-rate, set in pretty gardens, and offers interesting dishes such as onion and basil tart, stuffed pork loin and local partridge.

Another super place to stay is the **Alquería de Morayma** (A348, km20, 958 34 32 21, www.alqueriamorayma.com, double €59-€63, restaurant €€), based around an organic farm and vineyard. The farmhouse has a lovely dining room where you can feast on excellent local cuisine, while the outbuildings – including a converted chapel – house rooms and self-contained suites, stylishly decorated with Alpujarran and Moorish furnishings. There's a pool for use in high season.

## Getting there

### By bus

Alsina Graells (958 18 54 80/77 00 03/78 50 02) runs 2 buses daily between Granada and Alcútar, calling at Lanjarón (1hr), Órgiva (1hr 30mins), the Poqueira villages (2hrs 5mins) and Pitres (2hrs 45mins), with 2 services continuing to Trevélez (3hrs 15mins) and Alcútar (3hrs 50mins). Other buses travel from Granada to Ugíjar via Torvizcón (2hrs 20mins), Cádiar (3hrs), Yegen (3hrs 30mins) and Válor (3hrs 45mins). Ugijar and Bérchules are also served by buses from Almería. There are less frequent bus services between Lanjarón and Motril/Málaga. Autocares Bonal (958 46 50 22) runs 1 bus daily in summer from Granada to the Sierra Nevada ski resort (1hr); in winter there are 3 buses Mon-Fri and 4 buses on Sat, Sun.

# Costa Tropical

Granada's coastline has a distinctly laid-back vibe.

Granada province's stretch of coastline has been dubbed, somewhat optimistically, the Costa Tropical. Its section west of Almuñécar remains a beautiful and little-explored coast of craggy sandstone cliffs, herb-scented hills and tiny, secluded beaches broken only by the quiet fishing village turned watersports mecca of La Herradura. East of Almuñécar, however, monstrous plastic greenhouses are gradually gobbling up the plains, but there are still a couple of towns worth a stop; in particular Salobreña and the quiet, thoroughly Spanish resorts of Castell de Ferro and Calahonda.

## Almuñécar & around

Just over the Málaga-Granada border, the pleasant, sleepy resort of **La Herradura** is situated on a wide bay. The clear waters here have made the village a hub for watersports, particularly scuba-diving: try **Buceo Atlántida** (Paseo Andrés Segovia 58, Urbanización Castillo de Mar, 958 64 06 57, www.buceoatlantida.com/www.turingranada.com) for scuba diving, or **Windsurf La Herradura** (Paseo Marítimo 34, 958 64 01 43, www.windsurflaherradura.com) for sailing and windsurfing lessons and hire. A little further east is the **Marina del Este** yacht marina (958 64 08 01, www.marinasmediterraneo.com), the naturist **Playa del Muerte** and a small bay at **Cotobro**, from where a seafront *paseo* leads into the main resort of Almuñécar. The nicest beaches, however, are back towards Nerja, such as the nudist beach of **Cantariján**, just beyond the Cerro Gordo tunnel. Some are only accessible on foot.

From afar **Almuñécar** doesn't look like it has much to recommend it. The urban centre is a chaotic jumble of one-way streets and pile-'em-high-sell-'em-cheap apartment blocks and parking, even out of season, is nightmarish. On the upside, the lively Friday market attracts folks from miles around, there's a decent strand, and the old town of **Sexitano** is a delight, crammed with top-notch tapas bars and some good shops.

Founded as a fishing settlement by the Phoenicians in the first millennium BC, Almuñécar was developed by the Romans (when it was known as Sexi), and with the arrival of Abd al-Rahman in 755 became a significant

Moorish port. More recently, it was a centre of sugar cane production, and was immortalised as 'Castillo' in Laurie Lee's *As I Walked Out One Midsummer Morning* (there's a plaque dedicated to the writer on the promenade).

The two main beaches, the **Playa San Cristóbal** and the **Playa Puerto del Mar**, are separated by the rocky **Peñón del Santo** headland. (Climb up the steps here for a good view of the whole resort.) The beaches are shaley rather than sandy, and become absolutely packed in high season, but at other times you'll find acres of space on which to spread your towel. Further east, the **Aquatropic** water park marks the start of long, grey **Playa Velilla**, beyond which are the smaller rocky coves of **Playa Galería** and **Playa Cabria**.

The town's tourist office is in a lovely 19th-century, neo-Moorish mansion, a block inland from the Playa San Cristóbal. Just opposite is a small botanic garden, **Parque El Majuelo**, incorporating the curious remains of a Roman fish-curing factory (Factoría de Salzones) and a portion of the city walls. Nearby, the raucous squawking of 1,500 birds alerts you to the presence of the **Parque Ornitológico**.

From here it's a steep climb up to the **Castillo de San Miguel**, which crowns the old town. The original Phoenician fort was taken over by the Romans and later by the Moors, who used it as both a pleasure palace and a prison. On its surrender to the Christians in 1489 it was given its current name and underwent extensive remodelling, but this did not prevent it from being nearly destroyed by the British navy in 1808. For much of the 19th and 20th centuries the castle was used as the town cemetery. There are fine views from here, and a small museum showing the development of Almuñécar.

The ticket for the castle also allows entry to the atmospheric **Museo Arqueológico**, housed in the **Cueva de Siete Palacios** ('Cave of Seven Palaces'). This vaulted space was built into the side of the hill by the Romans in the first century AD. The museum's highlight is a unique Egyptian vase from the 17th century BC, inscribed with the oldest text ever found on the Iberian Peninsula. You can arrange to be shown around by an English-speaking guide by phoning the tourist office (958 63 11 25) in advance.

The narrow streets between the castle and the museum are a maze of whitewashed houses that transport you a long way from the tourist-thronged modernity of the coastal strip. Continue downhill from the museum to reach café-lined Plaza Ayuntamiento, the 17th-century church of **La Encarnación** (Puerta de Granada 1, 958 63 06 46, 8am-1pm, 7-9pm Mon-Fri, Sun; 8am-1pm Sat), and the busy Plaza Mayor, where excavation work has revealed remains of the town's Roman water system.

A prestigious **International Jazz Festival** is held in Almuñécar in July, and it's also a good place to join in the revelry honouring the Virgin of El Carmen on 16 July, when fishermen adorn their boats with flowers and ribbons

The tourist office can direct you to several impressive Roman aqueducts located inland around the village of **Torrecuevas**. From here there is also access to the **Peña Escrita** ecological park, a 400-hectare (1.5-square mile) mountain reserve that has been set aside for rural tourism. Beyond Torrecuevas the road snakes north along the Río Verde, towards the pleasant mountain villages of **Jete**, **Otívar** and **Lentegí** and into the Alpujarras (see p275).

### Aquatropic

*Paseo Reina Sofía s/n (958 63 20 81).* **Open** *June-Sept* 11am-7pm daily. Closed Oct-May. **Admission** €12; €5-€8 concessions; free under-4s. *After 3pm* €8; €4-€6 concessions; free under-4s. **Credit** AmEx, DC, MC, V.

### Castillo de San Miguel

*No phone.* **Open** *Apr-June* 10.30am-1.30pm, 5-7.30pm Tue-Sat; 10.30am-1.30pm Sun. *July-mid Sept* 10.30am-1.30pm, 6.30-9pm Tue-Sat; 10.30am-1.30pm Sun. *Mid Sept-Mar* 10.30am-1.30pm, 4-6.30pm Tue-Sat; 10.30am-2.30pm Sun. **Admission** (combined with Museo Arqueológico) €2; €1.40 concessions. *July-Sept* (also with Parque Ornitológico and tourist train) €5.50; €3.50 concessions. *Oct-June* (also with Parque Ornitológico) €3.20; €2.20 concessions. **No credit cards**.

### Museo Arqueológico 'Cueva de Siete Palacios'

*Barrio de San Miguel (no phone).* **Open/Admission** as for Castillo de San Miguel above.

### Parque Ornitológico

*Plaza de San Cristóbal (no phone).* **Open** *July-mid Sept* 11am-2pm, 6-9pm daily. *Mid Sept-June* 11am-2pm, 4-6pm daily. **Admission** €2.70; €1.40 concessions. *July-Sept* (combined with Castillo & Museo Arqueológico) €5.50; €3.50 concessions. **No credit cards**.

## Where to eat & drink

There are plenty of seafront restaurants and bars in Almuñécar, but better places can be found in the old town. Among them is the impressive **Horno de Candida**, the catering school's restaurant (C/Orovia 3, 958 63 46 07, closed lunch Sun, €), where you can dine on a pleasant rooftop terrace. The town has the reputation as the best place on the Costa Tropical for tapas. **Bodega Francisco** (C/Real 14, 958 63 01 68, closed Jan & Feb, €) is as authentic as they come, with barrels of *fino* behind the bar and shanks of *jamón* hanging from the ceiling. For entertainment, head for the **Taberna Flamenca Ricardo de la Juana** (C/Manila 4, 958 63 51 98, closed Mon & Tue, free), an authentic family-run *peña*, and the only place between Málaga and Almería to experience genuine flamenco.

Heading west from town, **Jacquy Cotobro** (Río Playa s/n, Playa Cotobro, 958 63 18 02, closed Mon mid Sept-mid June, €€€-€€€€) is the top dining destination in the area, serving superlative Belgo-Spanish cuisine. The staff can be a touch snooty.

In La Herradura, the restaurant at the **Hotel La Tartana** (*see p285*; closed lunch and all Sun June-Oct, Mon & Sun Nov-May, €€-€€€) is well on the way to becoming one of the region's best, with its menu of American-International fusion dishes (Asian fish cakes and stuffed *jalapeños*, baby back ribs and meat loaf, and sumptuous puds from their five-star pastry chef), in beautiful, romantic surrounds. Booking is crucial. Back on the beach, the **Restaurante Chiringuito Bueno** (Paseo Andrés Segovia, 958 64 08 43, closed Tue Jan-June, Mon & Sun Nov-May, €-€€) is a shade cheaper than the competition and has some interesting dishes such as cardoons (a member of the artichoke family) with clams and prawns. At the other end of the strand, **Restaurante El Chamboa de Joaquin** (Playa de la Herradura, Paseo Andrés Segovia s/n, 958 64 00 44, €€) is famed for its giant *paella* served every Saturday and Sunday from 2.30pm throughout the summer. The west end of the beach has several lively beach bars, or if you're after something more upmarket, **Bonache** (next door to the Hostal La Caleta) is as smooth as they come, with a wood and stone finish and elegant cocktails.

Inland, a number of roadside restaurants in Otívar offer mountain views to accompany the local delicacy, *pollo a la manzana* (chicken with apples). Towards Nerja, **La Barraca** (Cantarijan Playa, 958 34 92 87, €-€€) does decent food and has live Cuban music and dancing on Thursday nights from July to September.

## Where to stay

Among the hotels along Playa San Cristóbal in Almuñécar is the three-star **Hotel Helios** (Paseo de San Cristóbal s/n, 958 63 44 59, double

€65-€120), or, for a more personal touch try the **Hotel Casablanca** (Plaza San Cristóbal 4, 958 63 55 75, www.almunecar.info/casablanca, double €49-€70), a friendly two-star with an attractive Moorish interior. Next door is the budget **Hotel Playa San Cristóbal** (Plaza San Cristóbal 5, 958 63 11 12, www.almunecar. info/sancristobal, closed mid Oct-mid March, double €40-€56). In Sexitano, the **Hostal Altamar** (C/Alta del Mar 13, 958 63 03 46, closed Oct-Mar, double €39-€54) is a steal, with fresh, bright rooms and a cosy lounge and breakfast area. Alternatively, luxury suites are available at the **Hotel Albayzin del Mar** (Avenida Costa del Sol 23, 958 63 21 61, www.hotelalbayzindelmar.com, 2-bedroom suite €95-€210).

In La Herradura, despite being on the wrong side of the main road, the **Hotel Tartana** (A7-E15, exit 14, Urbanización San Nicolás, 958 64 05 35, www.hotellatartana.com, double €59-€85) can't be beat for boutique chic. It has six Moorish-accented rooms arranged around a central courtyard, with 16th-century fittings and huge double beds. Several pretty terraces at the front have sea views, but also suffer the rumble of traffic, and there's a comfortable, candle-lit bar and restaurant (*see p284*). Just a block from the beach, the recently opened **Hotel Almijara** (C/Acera del Pilar 6, 958 61 80 53, www.hotelalmijara.com, double €64-€115) has comfortable, Laura Ashley-esque rooms with plenty of facilities. The roof terrace bar and restaurant is a top spot on a moonlit night. On the beach itself, **Hostal La Caleta** (Paseo Andrés Segovia 11, 958 82 70 07, double €45-€50) is friendly, clean and has a cheap, decent restaurant beneath.

Inland, you'll find log cabins (€33-€59 for 2 people), simple *casas* (€33-€59 for 2 people), a campsite (€10-€13 per tent) and a restaurant in the **Peña Escrita** ecological park (mobile 615 32 14 62; *see p284*).

## Resources

### Internet

**Almuñécar** *Mundo Digital, C/Alta del Mar 8 (958 63 40 07).* **Open** *July-Sept* 11am-2pm, 6pm-midnight Mon-Sat. *Nov-June* 11am-2pm, 5pm-midnight Mon-Sat.

**La Herradura** *Panoramix Informática, C/Unidad 9 (958 64 01 49).* **Open** *July-Sept* 9.30am-2.30pm, 5.30-11.30pm daily. *Oct-June* 10am-2pm, 5-9.30pm daily.

### Tourist information

**Almuñécar** *Palacete de la Najarra, Avenida de Europa s/n (958 63 11 25/www.almunecar.info).* **Open** *Apr-June, mid Sept-Oct* 10am-2pm, 5-8pm daily. *July-mid Sept* 10am-2pm, 6-9pm daily. *Nov-Mar* 10am-2pm, 4.30-7pm daily.

The **Peñón del Santo, Almuñécar**. *See p283.*

**La Herradura** *Paseo Andrés Segovia (no phone).* *Apr-June, mid-Sept-Oct* 10am-1.30pm, 5-7pm Mon-Fri; 10am-1.30pm Sat, Sun. *July-mid Sept* 11am-1.30pm, 6-8.30pm Mon-Sat; 10am-2pm Sun. *Nov-Mar* 10am-1.30pm, 4-6pm Mon-Fri; 10am-1.30pm Sat, Sun.

## Salobreña & further east

From Almuñécar the A7-E15 continues eastwards on to a wide coastal plain, backed by the hills of the **Sierra de las Guájares**. There's a great view of **Salobreña** from the road: perched on a steep hill, surrounded by a sea of sugar cane, its whitewashed houses tumble down from the Moorish Alcazaba. Sadly, the impact of its location has been dulled in recent years by an encroaching tide of growers' plastic to the north and east, and increasing development, which has linked up the town to its resort. Two pebbly beaches are separated by **El Peñón**, a rocky headland, and backed by an increasing number of apartments and holiday complexes.

The old town is a pretty tangle of crooked streets and is still fairly untouristy; you can easily spend a morning getting pleasantly lost here. The ruined **Castillo Árabe** offers panoramic views of the plains, the snowy peaks of the Sierra Nevada and the coast. From here, follow a steep, flower-adorned *paseo* down to the 16th-century church of **Nuestra Señora del Rosario** (Plaza de la Iglesia, 958 61 03 14, open hours of services), built in Múdejar style on the site of the town's former mosque. Just below it is La Boveda, a medieval passageway into the fortified town. Close by in the Plaza Antigua Ayuntamiento, the old town hall houses the **Museo Histórico**, with artefacts from Salobreña's 6,000-year history. A flower-filled promenade, Paseo de las Flores, circumnavigates the hill's northern flank below the castle, with views of the town's 19th-century sugar-processing plant.

**Motril**, inland to the east, is an unappealing industrial centre, while the nearby resort of **Torrenueva** veers from hot and heaving in high summer to drab and deserted out of season. Beyond Torrenueva, spick-and-span **Calahonda** occupies a small corner of the coast with mile upon mile of pebble beach, a handful of *chiringuitos* and a decent hotel.

Continuing east, the road passes through dramatic scenery, with bare, rocky cliffs dropping into the sea, before emerging at **Castello de Ferro**, easily the most appealing resort along this eastern stretch of coast and popular among Spanish families in high season. The town, overlooked by the ruins of an *atalaya* (watchtower), has a couple of decent pebbly beaches and a pleasant seafront prom.

Towards Almería, as the plastic greenhouses get more prevalent, so too the resorts, such as **La Rábita**, become less appealing. From La Rábita, however, the magnificent Alpujarras (*see p275*) are less than an hour away across the **Sierra de la Contraviesa** via the wine-growing villages of **Albondón** and **Albuñol**.

### Castillo Árabe

*Salobreña (958 61 27 33)*. **Open** *July-mid Sept* 10.30am-1.30pm, 5-9pm daily. *Mid Sept-June* 10.30am-1.30pm, 4-7pm daily. **Admission** *Castillo Árabe only* €1.90. *Combined with Museo Histórico* €2.55. **No credit cards**.

### Museo Histórico

*Plaza Antigua Ayuntamiento, Salobreña (958 61 27 33)*. **Open** as Castillo Árabe above. **Admission** *Museo Historico only* €1.30. *Combined with Castillo Árabe* €2.55. **No credit cards**.

### Where to stay, eat & drink

The most luxurious place to stay in the area is the Italianate **Casa de los Bates** (A7-E15, km329.5, 958 34 94 95, www.casadelosbates.com, double €142) between Salobreña and Motril. Built at the turn of the 19th century,

it has been beautifully restored with period details, and is surrounded by a luscious tropical garden with pool. The three-star **Hotel Salobreña** (A7-E15, km323, www.hotelsalobrena.com, 958 61 02 61, double €57-€75) also has a pool and enjoys a lofty position on a headland just west of town. Nearby is the **Hotel Salambina** (A7-E15, km326, 958 61 00 37, www.hotel salambina.com, closed 10 Jan-10 Feb, double €39-€45, restaurant €€-€€€) has a good restaurant with a balcony. Budget options in Salobreña include **Pensión Marí Carmen** (C/Nueva 32, 958 61 09 06, double €20-€25) and, just below the *casco antiguo*, **Pensión San José** (C/Cristo 68, 958 61 03 54, double €22), with simple but pleasant rooms surrounding a charming, bougainvillea-filled courtyard; bathrooms are communal.

For food, **Bar Restaurante Pesetas** (C/Bóveda 11, 958 61 01 82, closed Mon Oct-June, €) sticks to the basics with an excellent and extensive range of fish and shellfish tapas; it has a pleasant roof terrace. Otherwise, there are plenty of restaurants serving seafood and steaks along the beach. **El Peñón** (Playa del Peñón, Paseo Marítimo, 958 61 05 38, closed Mon Sept-June) stands out for its remarkably pretty location on a rocky outcrop by the sea.

In Calahonda, **Hotel El Ancla** (Avenida Los Geráneos 1, 958 62 30 42, double €42-€60, restaurant €€) has basic but comfy rooms; the best have balconies and sea views. It also has a very good restaurant serving lobster, crab and *quisquilla de Motril* (local giant white prawns), and a handsome terrace.

Inland, on the southern slopes of the Sierra de Lújar, the **Cortijo Torrera** (Rambla de Lújar s/n, 958 34 91 39, www.torrera.com, double €48, cottage for 4 people €68) is a beautifully restored country house with a pool, and offers horse-riding holidays.

### Resources

### Tourist information

*Salobreña Plaza Goya s/n (958 61 03 14/ www.ayto-salobrena.org)*. **Open** *July-mid Sept* 11am-2pm, 6-9pm Mon, Sun; 10.30am-1.30pm, 4-7pm Tue-Sat. *Mid Sept-June* 9.30am-1.30pm, 4-7pm Tue-Sat.

### Getting there

#### By bus

The coast is served by regular Málaga–Almería buses, and local interconnecting services. Almuñécar bus station (Avenida Juan Carlos I/Avenida Fenicia) also has frequent buses to/from Granada.

# Almería Province

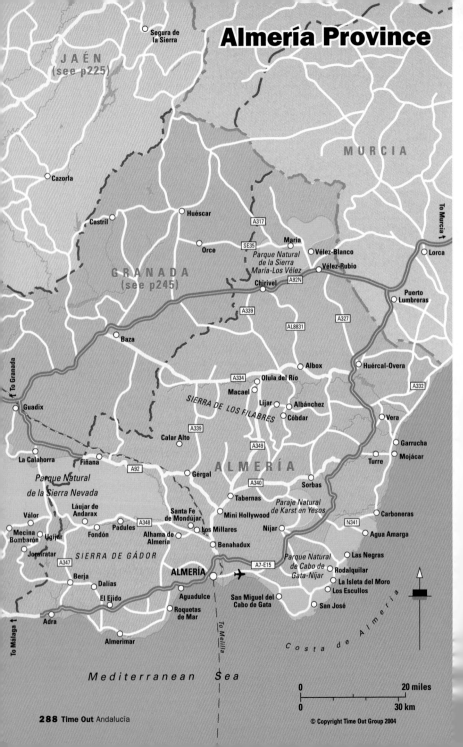

# Almería Province

JAÉN
(see p225)

Segura de
la Sierra

MURCIA

GRANADA
(see p245)

Cazorla

Castril

Huéscar

A317

SE35
Orce
María
Parque Natural
de la Sierra
María-Los Vélez
Vélez-Blanco
Vélez-Rubio
Lorca

To Murcia ↑

Chirivel
A92N

Puerto
Lumbreras

A339
AL8831

A327

Baza

Albox
Huércal-Overa
A332

A334
Olula del Río
Macael
Líjar
SIERRA DE LOS FILABRES
Albánchez
Cóbdar
Vera

Guadix
A339
Calar Alto
A349
ALMERÍA
Garrucha
Mojácar

La Calahorra
Fiñana
A92
Gérgal
A340
Sorbas
Turre

Parque Natural
de la Sierra Nevada
Tabernas
Paraje Natural
de Karst en Yesos

Válor
Láujar de
Andarax
Santa Fe
de Mondújar
Mini Hollywood
Carboneras

Mecina
Bombarón
Ugíjar
Padules
A348
Los Millares
Níjar
N341
Agua Amarga

Jorairatar
Fondón
Alhama de
Almería
Benahadux
Las Negras

A347
SIERRA DE GÁDOR
ALMERÍA
A7-E15
Parque Natural
de Cabo de
Gata-Níjar
Rodalquilar
La Isleta del Moro
Los Escullos

Berja
Dalías
Aguadulce

El Ejido
Roquetas
de Mar
San Miguel del
Cabo de Gata
San José

To Málaga ↑
Adra
Almerimar
To Melilla ↑

Costa de Almería

Mediterranean Sea

0 — 20 miles
0 — 30 km

© Copyright Time Out Group 2004

# Almería Province

Long Andalucía's forgotten corner, the sun-bleached south-east is virgin wilderness fringed (in part) by one of the region's few unblemished coastlines.

As the hottest, driest and sunniest corner of Europe, Almería province might seem to have long had it made as a holiday destination. Yet, before the development of intensive fruit- and vegetable-growing under plastic, this was one of the economically poorest corners of Spain. But, as the supermarket orders and package tourists have poured in over the past couple of decades, so has the economy of Almería turned around, and, alas, so has much of the coast become blighted by seas of plastic and holiday complexes. However, oases remain, and once you leave the coast, the wilderness of the interior comes as a surprising and welcome tonic.

### ALMERÍA CITY
The provincial capital is a city on the move. A key port in Moorish times, but something of a backwater ever since, Almería is finally starting to assert itself as the *plasticultura* wealth rolls in. It's a relaxed and eminently enjoyable little city, with enough attractions and distractions to take up a leisurely couple of days. The magnificent Moorish Alcazaba is the major draw, but there's also plenty of good wandering to be done in the old town, and no shortage of first-rate tapas bars in which to shelter from the sun.

### COSTA DE ALMERÍA
The coastline of Almería province splits neatly into three distinct segments. Closest to Granada province, and stretching all the way to Almería city, is the almost entirely unappealing stretch of plastic-tent-covered land, punctuated by the odd antiseptic resort. East of the capital, in utter contrast, is the magnificent and unspoiled Cabo de Gata – a wild and raw expanse of hills, tiny fishing villages and superb beaches. North of here is the wannabe Costa del Sol, centred around Mojácar – touristville, for sure, but good relaxed fun if you're in the mood.

### ALMERÍA INTERIOR
Few tourists venture away from Almería's coast, other than to visit the bizarre Western theme park of Mini Hollywood, which leaves the sparsely populated, livid-red desert landscapes and the obscure mountains of the Sierra de la Filabres to the adventuresome few. This is tremendous driving country, and in the far north there is more little-visited hill country in the area around the appealing town of Vélez Blanco.

The **Cabo de Gata**. *See p297.*

## The best...

**Beaches**
Cabo de Gata (*p297*).

**Castles**
Almería City (*p290*); Gérgal (*p304*); Tabernas (*p304*); Vélez Blanco (*p303*).

**Cowboys**
Mini Hollywood & Texas Hollywood (*p304*).

**Deserts**
Around Tabernas (*p304*).

**Moorish heritage**
Almería City (*p290-95*).

**Mountains**
Almerían Alpujarras (*p304*); Sierra de los Filabres (*p303*).

**Nightlife**
Mojácar Playa (*p301*).

**Prehistory**
Cueva de los Letreros (*p303*); Los Millares (*p304*).

**Resorts**
Agua Amarga (*p299*); Mojácar Playa (*p301*); San José (*p298*).

# Almería City

An impressive Moorish past and a low-key, relaxed present.

When you've got the likes of Sevilla, Granada, and Cádiz for rivals, it's perhaps no surprise that the city of Almería isn't on many tourists' itineraries. Yet this is one of the most laid-back and enjoyable cities in the region, and rewards a stay of a couple of days.

Today, the city is largely a bustling modern affair, yet it has a long and – at one distant point at least – important history. Its peak of influence came a thousand years ago, when the Caliph of Córdoba decided to build an arsenal and fort (Alcazaba) here, transforming the town into the foremost port in al-Andalus. Almerians will proudly recite to you the old saying that 'When Almería was Almería, Granada was but its farm'. Silk and ceramics, poetry and philosophy flourished, but not for long. By the mid 12th century the city had started to decline, helped on its way by a series of earthquakes. Recently, however, it has started to shake off its centuries-old feeling of decay and neglect. As agri-business and tourism euros flow in, and as it prepares for the 2005 Mediterranean Games (*see p294* **Almería 2005**), the future of Almería is looking brighter than it has for 800 years.

The fortress-like **Catedral**. See p291.

## Sightseeing

The main area of interest for visitors is the old town, sandwiched between the Alcazaba in the west and the Rambla de Belén in the east (also known as the Avenida de Federico García Lorca – once a dry riverbed, now a pleasant, wide, tree-lined boulevard). The port marks the southern boundary of the old city, while the Puerta de Purchena (the original gate is long gone) is as far north as most visitors venture.

Almería is dominated by one sight above all: the mighty **Alcazaba** – one of the greatest surviving examples of Almohad military architecture. Its crenellated walls (1,430 metres/ 4,692 feet long), commanding the hill on the west side of the city and overlooking the harbour, still impress today; their impact, when first erected on the orders of the Caliph of Córdoba, Abd al-Rahman III in 995, can only be imagined. The fortress was later altered and extended by Fernando and Isabel.

The Alcazaba, reached via a zigzagging path from Calle Almanzor, is divided into three distinct sections – two of Moorish origin, one of later Christian construction. The entrance, via

the **Puerta de la Justicia** (Gate of Justice), brings you into the first Moorish section, now filled with gardens. Originally, a small town occupied the site, complete with houses, public baths, water cisterns and other civic facilities.

Dividing this area from the second Moorish section of the Alcazaba is a wall that continues down into the valley to the north and up to the **Cerro de San Cristóbal** (St Christopher's Hill; complete with an oversize statue of Christ) in a great and highly photogenic sweep. The wall was an extension of the original fortifications, ordered by the *taifa* king Jayran in 1014-28. (It can be reached along Calle Antonio Vico from the Puerta de Purchena.) Behind the wall, surprisingly, are pens of gazelles, antelopes and other endangered Saharan species – this is the **Instituto de Aclimatación de Fauna Sahariana**, a research and rescue centre.

The second compound of the Alcazaba once contained a range of buildings, including a palace said to rival the Alhambra. Alas, all that remains are the remains, though they make for fascinating archaeology. A Moorish house has been recreated here, and it is possible to make out the ground plan of a bathhouse.

Another wall divides this area from the smallest of the three sections, the castle constructed by Fernando and Isabel on the taking of the city in 1489. Massive walls and circular towers – which were needed following the invention of effective artillery – distinguish this area. The **Torre de Homenaje** (Tower of Homage) contains a small photographic exhibition organised by the Centro Andaluz de la Fotografía, which also has a gallery in town (*see p292*). From the western **Torre de Pólvora** (Gunpowder Tower) there are fine views to the former cave dwellings of the poor Barrio Chanca district.

After the obligatory visit to the Alcazaba, the best way to get to know Almería is simply to wander the streets of the old town. Start, perhaps, at the tourist office close to the port on Parque de Nicolás Salmerón, pick up a city map, and then head north-west towards the 16th-century **Catedral**. Its formidably rugged construction was never intended to be a style statement; rather, it was designed to be part

church, part stronghold, since the city at this time was constantly being harassed by pirates and disaffected *moriscos*.

The cathedral was founded in 1524 on the site of Almería's main mosque, which had been converted into a church but destroyed in an earthquake two years earlier. The initially Isabelline-Gothic style employed was modified to a Renaissance model when Juan de Orea took over its construction in 1550. Inside, the church has three naves with Gothic vaulting, and is surprisingly graceful and unadorned. The best paintings hang in the **Capilla de la Piedad** (behind the altar), and include three works by Alonso Cano and an *Immaculate Conception* by Murillo. The unusually spacious cloister was added in the 18th century in neo-classical style.

On the cathedral's east side is Plaza Bendicho, which contains, in its south-west corner, the city's oldest house, known as the **Casa de los Puche**. It dates from the 18th century – and looks like it hasn't been maintained since – and now belongs to the brotherhood of the Cofradía del Prendimiento. In the centre of the square is a memorial to the poet Celia Viñas, who penned the lines:

# Let me take you down, cause I'm going to Almería

Not a lot of people know it, but **John Lennon** wrote *Strawberry Fields Forever* in Almería. During 1966 the Beatle was staying in the city for six weeks during the filming of Richard Lester's anti-war black comedy *How I Won the War*, about a group of British soldiers dropped behind enemy lines to create a cricket pitch to impress a visiting VIP.

Lennon starred as Private Digweed alongside a distinguished cast that included Michael Crawford, Michael Hordern, Sheila Hancock, Roy Kinnear and Robert Hardy. The wild arid landscapes around Carboneras, Tabernas and Cabo de Gata stood in for Egypt in the film.

Initially, John stayed in a small apartment called El Delfín Verde near the city beach of El Zapillo. It was here that he started strumming the initial chords of *Strawberry Fields*. Later, his wife Cynthia and Ringo came out to celebrate John's 26th birthday at the nearby La Manzanilla restaurant (no longer in existence).

At Cynthia's request John then moved to a bigger house, Santa Isabel (on Camino de

Romero, on the north-eastern edge of the city), where he completed the song and recorded a number of demo versions of it. The house had been abandoned for 30 years before local journalist and Beatles fan Adolfo Iglesias uncovered its story (www.upv.es/~ecabrera/letme/almeria.html). It is now being converted into a cultural centre by the city council, though, sadly, there are no plans to acknowledge the Lennon connection, or the fact that Sam Spiegel used the building as his production centre for *Lawrence of Arabia*.

Information on John's sojourn in Almería is frustratingly scant. Iglesias has uncovered what he can: this includes such facts as that 'like many English visitors' Lennon got sunburnt, that few Spaniards asked for his autograph (though 'one group of children did it four times. Ringo was the mediator') and that John's Rolls-Royce broke down, forcing him and Cynthia to travel around by taxi. Years later the relevant cab driver 'had no memories whatsoever' of his famous passengers.

*Almería! Almería!*
*On the white terrace roof*
*The breeze forms into crystal droplets.*
*A light sea wind*
*Sun and lime.*

North-west of the cathedral, and closed to traffic, is the 17th-century arcaded Plaza de la Constitución (also known as the Plaza Vieja), containing the pastel-shaded *Ayuntamiento* (Town Hall) and a gleaming white marble memorial to 24 liberals who landed at Almería in 1831 to proclaim liberty from the rule of Ferdinand VII, only to be captured and shot.

Further north, the ancient Calle de las Tiendas contains one of Almería's most interesting churches, the church of **Santiago** (open hours of services), designed (like the cathedral) by Juan de Orea, and erected in the 1550s. The streets around here contain many of the city's best bars, restaurants and shops. Calle Real is one such street: here you'll find the minor charms of the new **Museo del Aceite de Oliva** (Olive Oil Museum), where you can stop in for a drink and excellent tapas. Close by, on Calle Tenor Iribarne, are the Moorish water cisterns, the **Aljibes Arabes**.

Further south is the headquarters of the first-rate **Centro Andaluz de la Fotografía** (Andalucían Centre for Photography), which regularly puts on interesting exhibitions. Close by is the long Paseo de Almería, the city's principal artery. Here, at No.56, stands the grand late 19th-century **Círculo Mercantil e Industrial y Teatro Cervantes**, which now contains the incongruously named but agreeable Molly Malone bar (*see p294*).

West of here you may well come across crowds of North and sub-Saharan Africans queuing outside government agencies – Almería is, after Tarifa, one of the main ports of entry for migrant workers, most of whom are destined for the stifling *plasticultura* tents that scar the coastline west of the city (*see p297* **Tent city**).

Across the Paseo, and further north, is the two-level covered **mercado** (market), built in the 1890s, while east of the Rambla is the **Centro de Arte** (Arts Centre), which puts on art exhibitions. Not far away is the **Museo Arqueológico**, which should be the city's most impressive museum, but has been under reconstruction for years with no sign yet of a completion date. In the meantime, a few of its exhibits – including those from the Chalcolithic site of Los Millares (*see p304*) – can be seen at the Biblioteca Pública Francisco Villaespesa.

### Alcazaba

*C/Almanzor s/n (950 27 16 17).* **Open** *July-Sept* 9am-8.30pm Tue-Sun. *Oct-June* 9am-6.30pm Tue-Sun. **Admission** €1.50; free with EU passport. **No credit cards. Map** p293 A2.

### Alijbes Arabes

*C/Tenor Iribarne (950 27 30 39).* **Open** 10am-2pm Mon-Fri. **Admission** free. **Map** p293 B1.

### Catedral de Almería

*Entrance on C/Velasquez (mobile 609 57 58 02).* **Open** 10am-4.30pm Mon-Fri; 10am-1pm Sat. **Admission** €2; €1.50 concessions. **No credit cards. Map** B2.

### Centro Andaluz de la Fotografía

*C/Martínez Campos 20, 1st Floor; exhibition entrance on C/Pablo Cazard 1 (950 00 27 00/caf.ccul@junta deandalucia.es).* **Open** 9am-2pm, 7-10pm Mon-Fri; 7-10pm Sat. **Admission** free. **Map** p293 C2.

### Centro de Arte

*Plaza Barcelona (950 26 96 80).* **Open** 11am-2pm, 6-9pm Mon-Fri; 11am-2pm Sat; 6-9pm Sun. **Admission** free. **Map** p293 off B1.

### Museo del Aceite de Oliva

*C/Real 15 (950 62 00 02/www.castillodetabernas.com).* **Open** 11am-3pm, 6.30-10pm Mon-Fri; 11am-3pm Sat. **Admission** free. **Map** p293 B2.

### Museo Arqueológico

*Biblioteca Pública Francisco Villaespesa, C/Hermanos Machado s/n (950 23 03 75).* **Open** 9am-2pm Mon-Fri; 9.30am-1.30pm Sat. **Admission** free. **Map** p293 off C2.

## Where to eat & drink

The streets immediately south of the Puerta de Purchena and those between the cathedral and the Paseo de Almería are the best places to head for a drink or meal. The quality of the tapas bars is generally higher than that of the restaurants.

### Casa Puga

*C/Jovellanos 7 (950 23 15 30).* **Open** 11am-4pm, 8pm-midnight Mon-Sat. **Average** €€. **Credit** AmEx, MC, V. **Map** p293 A2.
One of Almería's classic tapas bars. Stand by the counter with the regulars or take a table at the side beneath dangling hams and wines racked upside down (the wine list is astonishing). The bar has been under the ownership of the same family since 1870.

### El Quinto Toro

*C/Juan Leal 6 (950 23 91 35).* **Open** noon-4pm, 7pm-midnight daily. **Average** €. **No credit cards. Map** p293 B1.
On the street leading south from the market, this superb tiled tapas bar (named after the fifth – supposedly best – bull of the *corrida*) has bags of charm.

### Restaurante Sol de Almería

*C/Ulpiano Diaz 7 (950 26 29 60/mobile 670 67 23 12).* **Open** noon-4pm, 8-11pm daily. **Average** €. **No credit cards. Map** p293 B1.
On the street leading around the market, this small place offers the twin charms of a cheap *menú* and a pleasant patio at the back.

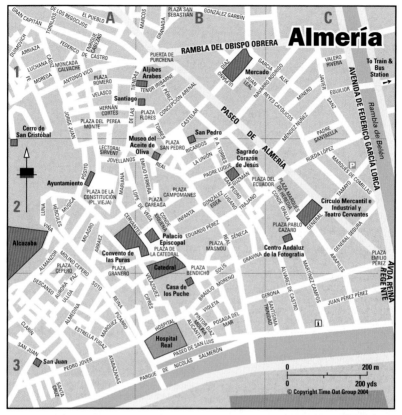

Almería

### Restaurante Valentín

*C/Tenor Iribarne 19 (950 26 44 75).* **Open** 1-4pm, 8pm-midnight Tue-Sun. **Average** €€€€. **Credit** AmEx, DC, MC, V. **Map** p293 B1.

There are a number of good restaurants in this street. This classy but pricey place specialises in seafood, and has an excellent *menú degustación* at €32.

### Tetería Almedina

*C/Aurora Paz 2 (mobile 629 27 78 27).* **Open** 1-11pm Wed-Sun. **Average** €€. **No credit cards**. **Map** p293 A3.

At the foot of the Alcazaba, this Moroccan-style tea-house serves traditional teas, sweet cakes, and more substantial dishes such as couscous with lamb.

## Nightlife

The city doesn't have many dance clubs and late-night bars – those that exist can be found within a few streets of each other, west of the Paseo de Almería, just south of Calle Padre

Luque, or along the Parque de Nicolás Salmerón, where the city youth congregates outside with shop-bought bottles of spirits and cola on Friday and Saturday nights.

Most of Almería's summer nightlife is in the beach resorts west of the city. Almería's top flamenco club, located in the atmospheric Aljibes Árabes, is the thoroughly authentic **Peña El Taranto** (C/Tenor Iribarne 20, 950 23 50 57, bar closed last 2wks Sept and no shows July-mid Oct, admission €14, map B1), which has shows every couple of weeks between October and July. Though, strictly speaking, you need to be a member here, sometimes you can walk in off the street. Outside of show times it's a bar with a pleasant roof terrace.

### Amarga Sound Café

*Plaza Marques de Heredia 8 (950 08 39 59).* **Open** 7am-late daily. **No credit cards**. **Map** p293 C2.

New, hip *bar de copas*/café in a *plaza* just north of the old Teatro.

# Almería 2005

Not so long ago Almería was one of the poorest and most neglected regions of Spain. A measure of quite how far this parched corner of Iberia has come – thanks to the proceeds of tourism and *plasticultura* (*see p297* **Tent city**) – is that the province was chosen to host the 15th **Mediterranean Games**. Between 24 June and 3 July 2005 athletes from 21 countries (and three continents) bordering the Med will compete in 24 sports.

The Games were the idea of a Turk, Mohammed Taher Pasha, who, in a post-World War II spirit of togetherness, revived the ancient Roman idea of '*mare nostrum*' ('our sea') as a unifying symbol for the diverse countries around its edges. Sport was to provide the forum for friendly competition between these nations. The first Games were held in Alexandria in Egypt in 1951 and they've been taking place every four years ever since.

The majority of events will be based in Almería city, where a major improvement in the regional capital's infrastructure is underway to cope with the expected influx of visitors, including a huge investment in new sports facilities – the centrepiece will be the Mediterranean Stadium.

The people of Almería have embraced the Games as a sign of how far they have risen from the poverty and obscurity of only a few decades earlier. Not since the times of the Moors has the future for Almería looked so bright.

For information on the Games, see www.almeria2005.es.

### La Dolce Vita

*Parque de Nicolás Salmerón 11 (950 28 05 49)*.
**Open** 11pm-7am Mon, Tue, Thur-Sat. **No credit cards**. **Map** p293 B3.
This is one of a number of Dolce Vitas around the city: a dark, loud and crowded disco-bar.

### The Irish Tavern

*C/González Egea 4 (no phone)*. **Open** varies.
**No credit cards**. **Map** p293 B2.
Apart from the faux-Irish decor and Guinness on tap, this popular bar is about as un-Irish as you can get, with loud music, a hip crowd and an outside *terraza*.

### Mae West

*Parque de Nicolás Salmerón 9 (950 25 35 20)*.
**Open** 7pm-6am Mon-Sat. **Credit** AmEx, DC, MC, V. **Map** p293 B3.
Cavernous bar/pub full of 'authentic' Irish memorabilia that really gets going at weekends.

### Molly Malone

*Teatro Cervantes, Paseo de Almería 56 (950 24 62 83)*. **Open** 7am-3am Mon-Sat; noon-3am Sun.
**Credit** AmEx, DC, MC, V. **Map** p293 C2.
Towards the bottom end of the Paseo, this excellent café has outside seating during the day and a bar in the evening that plays very loud Spanish music.

## Shopping

The city isn't particularly notable for its shops. Most of its commerical activity is concentrated on the streets radiating out from the Puerta de Purchena, and particularly in those between here and Plaza San Pedro to the south. For guides, maps and English language books, try Libreria Cajal (C/Navarro Rodrigo 14, 950 23 61 48, map B/C1) or **Picasso** (C/Reyes Católicos 17, 950 23 56 00, map C1), both just south of the market. For clothes and shoes try Paseo de Almeria; staples **Zara** (950 27 44 20) and **Mango** (950 23 00 60) are at numbers 79 and 47 respectively (map B1/C2).

## Where to stay

Almería is not blessed with a huge range of characterful accommodation; set your sights on clean-and-adequate.

### AM Torreluz

*Plaza Flores 5 (950 23 49 99/www.amtorreluz.com)*.
**Rates** €71-€79 single; €135-€204 double.
**Credit** AmEx, DC, MC, V. **Map** p293 B1.
There are three hotels bearing the name Torreluz around the Plaza Flores. This four-star is the top option, with a gym and a small rooftop pool.

### Gran Hotel Almería

*Avenida Reina Regente 8 (950 23 80 11/www.granhotelalmeria.com)*. **Rates** €116 single; €144 double; €171 junior suite; €268 suite.
**Credit** AmEx, DC, MC, V. **Map** p293 C3.
The flashest option in town, this four-star has a pool and a private garage (a definite boon – parking in the centre is very limited), and a location close to the port.

### Hostal Bristol

*Plaza San Sebastian 8 (950 23 15 95)*. **Rates** €30 single; €40 double; €50 triple. **Credit** MC, V.
**Map** p293 B1.
Decent, no-frills rooms in a good location for shopping, eating and nightlife.

### Hostal Nixar

*C/Antonio Vico 24 (950 23 72 55).* **Rates** €24-
€29 single; €40-€47 double; €48-€57 triple.
**Credit** DC, MC, V. **Map** p293 A1.
Unremarkable but adequate *hostal*, well located just
west of the Puerta de Purchena.

### Hotel Costasol

*Paseo de Almería 58 (950 23 40 11/www.hotel
costasol.com).* **Rates** €60 single; €76-€87 double;
€96 triple. **Credit** AmEx, DC, MC, V. **Map** p293 C2.
The Costasol is old-fashioned, but not offensively so,
and it's good value, considering the central location.

### Hotel Sevilla

*C/Granada 25 (950 23 02 09).* **Rates** €30-€33 single;
€43-€48 double. **Credit** DC, MC, V. **Map** p293 B1.
You won't find a better one-star place in the city. And
the location, just off the Puerta de Purchena, is prime.

### Hotel Torreluz II

*Plaza Flores 6 (950 23 43 99/www.torreluz.com).*
**Rates** €35-€41 single; €57-€70 double; €88 triple.
**Credit** AmEx, DC, MC, V. **Map** p293 B1.
Another notch down from its posher namesakes in
terms of facilities, but the rooms are fine, and you're
right in the heart of the bar and restaurant district.

### Hotel Torreluz III

*Plaza Flores 3 (950 23 43 99/www.torreluz.com).*
**Rates** €46-€59 single; €74-€91 double; €114 triple.
**Credit** AmEx, DC, MC, V. **Map** p293 B1.
The middle of the three Torreluz hotels. Three-star
facilities, 122 rooms, inoffensive if unexciting decor
and a great central location, with a surprisingly good
*taberna* attached.

### NH Ciudad de Almería

*Jardín de Medina s/n (950 18 25 00/www.nh-hotels.
com).* **Rates** €80-€140 double. **Credit** AmEx, DC,
MC, V. **Map** p293 off C1.
Located by the railway station, this member of the
classy NH chain offers plenty of creature comforts
and a decent helping of style.

## Resources

### Internet

*Ciber Indalnet, Edificio Cadena Ser, Avenida del
Mediterráneo 159 (950 15 18 04).* **Open** 10am-
10pm daily.

### Police station

*C/Santos Zarate 15 (950 62 12 06/21 00 19).*
**Map** p293 off B2.

### Post office

*Plaza Casanello 1 (950 24 02 31).*

### Tourist information

*Parque de Nicolás Salmarón s/n, corner of C/Martínez
Campos (950 27 43 55/www.andalucia.org).* **Open**
9am-7pm Mon-Fri; 10am-2pm Sat, Sun. **Map** p293 C3.

## Getting there

### By air

Almería's airport is 10km (6 miles) east of the city.
*See p308.*

### By boat

Trasmediterranea (950 23 61 55/6/www.tras
mediterranea.es) has 1 sailing most days (more in
summer) to the Melilla in Morocco (6hrs by standard
boat, 3hrs 30mins by the summer fast boat).
Ferrimaroc (950 27 48 00) runs a similar service to
the Moroccan town of Nador, south of Melilla (7hrs).

### By bus

A number of companies run services out of Almería's
bus station (950 26 20 98), located just north of the rail
station on Plaza Barcelona. Each day Alsina Graells
(950 23 51 68) operates buses to and from Adra
(1hr 15mins; every hr), 2 buses to Cádiz (9hrs), 1 to
Córdoba (5hrs 15mins), 5 to Granada (2hrs 15mins), 4
to Málaga (3hrs 30mins) and 3 to Sevilla (5hrs 30mins).
Bernardo (950 25 04 22) has 2-3 daily buses to San José
(1hr). There are also 2-3 daily buses from Madrid via
Guadix (4hrs 15mins) to Almería (7hrs 45mins).

### By train

Almería's railway station is located a kilometre east
of the centre at Plaza de la Estación. For ticket sales/
reservations, call 902 24 02 02; for international info,
phone 903 24 34 02. Almería is at the end of the line
that runs to Sevilla via Granada. There are 3 daily
trains to Sevilla (just over 5hrs), all of which call at
Granada (2hr 15mins) and Antequera (3hrs 30mins),
and 1 additional daily service between Almería and
Granada. Before it reaches Granada, a fork from this
line heads north towards Madrid (2 trains daily/6hrs
45mins). To reach Almería from Cádiz or Huelva
you'll need to change at Sevilla; to get there from
Córdoba or Málaga, change at Bobadilla.

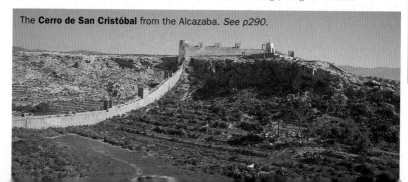

The **Cerro de San Cristóbal** from the Alcazaba. *See p290.*

**Almería Province**

# Costa de Almería

The good, the bad and the ugly.

The beach at **Aguadulce**.

## Adra to Aguadulce

Heading into Almería province along the coast road from Granada's optimistically named 'Costa Tropical' (*see p283-85*), you'll already have become familiar with the huge, hideous plastic tents (*invernaderos*) that are squeezed onto whatever level land is available. Yet nothing will have prepared you for what awaits along the stretch of coast from Adra to Almería city. From the foot of the Sierra de Gádor mountains to the coastline, an overwhelming sea of pale green and grey plastic shimmers beneath a blast-furnace sun. Under here grows much of the fruit and vegetables bought in supermarkets across northern Europe. This is *plasticultura*, the Almerían miracle – an economic gold-mine, a social time bomb and an aesthetic nightmare (*see p297* **Tent city**).

This dispiriting sight does nothing to encourage the visitor to linger in the area, and the local towns and resorts are largely characterless, dull and overdeveloped. From west to east, the workaday port of **Adra** is the spot where Boabdil, last king of the Moors, was finally hounded out of Europe to Africa (*see p17*). The next major settlement to the east, **El Ejido**, is the boomtown of *plasticultura* – 25 years ago it wasn't much more than a village; today its population is around 50,000. When those who made their fortunes on the plains want to kick off their shoes they head due south from El Ejido for six kilometres (four miles) to the resort of **Almerimar**, a spookily artificial confection of landscaped roundabouts, pristine holiday complexes and a concrete yacht marina.

The next resort of any size is **Roquetas de Mar**, which, once upon a time, was an appealing fishing village; its character has long since been submerged under a rash of holiday developments and hotels. **Aguadulce**, ten kilometres (six miles) from Almería city, is the oldest resort on this part of the coast and probably the most attractive (though this isn't saying much), with a long, inviting beach.

But Almería province has far better to offer. If you crave sand and sea, but want to avoid the usual Costa atmosphere, overdevelopment and crowds, head straight onwards to the Cabo de Gata (*see p297*).

## Where to stay

If you find yourself in need of a room in Aguadulce, the four-star **Portomagno** (Paseo Maritimo s/n, 950 34 22 16, www.hvsl.es, double €97-€162) is well located close to the beach, while the **Hostal Juan de Austria II** (Avenida de Carlos III 150, 950 34 01 63, www.infonegocio.com/juandeaustria, double €40-€52) is a good-value budget option. In Roquetas de Mar the very reasonably priced four-star **Mediterráneo Park** (Pez Espada s/n, 950 33 32 50, www.mediterraneo-park.com, double €93-€110) has tons of facilities (including a good pool). If that's beyond your budget, try the **Hostal El Faro** (Avenida Sabinal 190, 950 32 10 15, double €30-€42).

## Resources

### Tourist information

*Avenida Mediterráneo 2 (950 33 32 03/www.roquetas digital.com).* **Open** *July-mid Sept* 9.30am-2pm, 5.30-8.30pm Mon-Sat; 10am-1pm Sun. *Mid Sept-June* 9.30am-2pm, 4.30-8.30pm Mon-Fri; 10am-1pm Sat, Sun.

## Cabo de Gata

After you've butted your way through the sea of plastic west of Almería city, nothing could come as a more delightful contrast than the Cabo de Gata. This wild, mountainous peninsula, a mere 20-minute drive from the regional capital, has been largely protected from encroaching *plasticultura* by its designation since 1987 as a Parque Natural.

The Cabo de Gata massif is part of a huge volcanic region that continues under the Mediterranean and emerges in North Africa. It's a unique environment, with the lowest annual rainfall in Europe (around 200 millimetres/eight inches), whose dramatic topography encompasses basalt and gypsum formations, towering cliffs and undulating red plains, reefs and islands and scores of secluded coves and sandy beaches. More than 1,000 plant species and over 50 types of vertebrate can be found in the semi-desert landscape, including the natterjack toad, the troglodyte bat, the hoopoe and the flamingo. Such is the Cabo de Gata's variety of flora and fauna that UNESCO designated it a Biosphere Reserve in 1997.

Unlike the wildlife, humans have found it less easy to survive on the Cabo de Gata. The high temperatures, sparse rainfall and scarcity of spring water made agriculture difficult. What's more, following the expulsion of the Moors from Spain, this coast was under constant threat of harassment from North African pirates. Over the following centuries a series of defensive fortifications were constructed – 14 survive today within the boundaries of the park.

Times are changing, though, and not all the development is positive. The march of the plastic tents has reached the very edges of the park and even encroached into it in certain areas. The biggest threat to the Cabo de Gata's protected status is a new development strategy that has allowed the growth of urban centres within the park, abolished height and size restrictions for new buildings and approved 80 new plastic tent sites within the park itself.

Coming from Almería city, a suitable place to begin a tour of the Cabo de Gata is the **Centro de Visitantes de las Amoladeros**, just off the road from Retamar to the cape itself. This is a good spot to pick up maps and guides, before continuing on to the village properly known as **San Miguel del Cabo de Gata** (though more

## Tent city

Almería has always had the sun (320 days a year of it); what it's lacked is the water. The invention of drip-feed irrigation and the tapping of deep water sources, however, has transformed what was once parched wilderness into some of the most valuable agricultural land in the world. With additional advances in biological engineering, Almería's *plasticultura* bigwigs became able to force-grow fruit and veg to order – any size, any shape, any colour, any time of year.

Quite apart from fears about the depletion of water reserves, the thoroughly unorganic nature of the business and objections about the emphasis on appearance over taste, the meteoric expansion of *plasticultura* has brought with it a variety of social problems. A shortage of local labour meant that large numbers of workers from all over Spain and from North and sub-Saharan Africa were drawn to the region to work in the usually stifling, back-breaking environments inside the tents (known as *invernaderos*). The conditions they lived in were frequently appalling, and local resentment of the newcomers simmered away before exploding into a major riot in 2000.

Since then, the government has taken some measures to improve the lot of the workers, and put in place a better health and social infrastructure. Their lives, however, remain unenviably tough, and the spectre of racism still haunts the coast.

**Almería Province**

usually called simply Cabo de Gata). There's been a settlement on this site for several hundred years, though, beyond the 18th-century watchtower at the southern edge of the village and the 19th-century parish church, you wouldn't know it. There's an air of artificiality about the place, but the decent beach pulls in the youth of Almería city on hot days, and there are a handful of bars and cafés along the front.

The road continues along the coast towards the haunting silhouette of the **Iglesia de las Salinas** – an isolated, weirdly ravaged church built in 1907, and looking like a relic from one of the Westerns filmed around Tabernas (*see p304*). The church stands sentinel over the economically and ecologically significant salt pans (*salinas*). Salt is said to have first been produced on this site by the Phoenicians, though there's no documentary evidence of such activity here before the end of the 15th century. It's still a long pedigree, and one that continues to this day. This also happens to be one of the most notable micro-ecosystems in Andalucía. The salt pools are rich in halophilous plants, providing food for more than 80 types of bird that pass through, and reed beds for nesting and resting. The most famous residents and visitors are pink flamingoes. A hide is provided for twitchers.

The road continues on past a couple of tiny villages, then starts to climb and wind (and becomes perilously narrow in parts) before arriving at a dead end at a lighthouse – the **Faro de Cabo de Gata**. The first lighthouse on this site was built in 1863, warning ships of the treacherous rocks of the **Arrecife de la Sirenas** (Reef of the Sirens), located just below. The views from here are superb, and there's a tapas bar just before you reach the lighthouse to assuage hunger and thirst. Boat trips ply these treacherous waters from April to September (up to eight a day); call ahead to make a reservation (mobile 637 44 91 70, www.elcaboafondo.com, €15, €12 children).

Around eight kilometres (five miles) east along the coast is the Cabo de Gata's main resort, **San José**. There's no through road for cars here, but there is a well-marked trail for walkers, which passes through some stunning scenery and by a number of pristine beaches, such as the **Playa del Mónsul** (which featured in *Indiana Jones and the Last Crusade*).

Drivers need to backtrack to around four kilometres (2.5 miles) before the village of Cabo de Gata and take the road to San José from there. The resort is a friendly, relaxed place to hang out for a few days, with a reasonable beach (though a better one, the **Playa de Genoveses**, is just around the headland to the south-west). However, holiday developments are breaking out all around San José at an alarming rate and starting to sprawl along the coast. They're all low-rise, but their number and architectural banality are threatening to irreversibly swamp the character of the village.

You can sample some good diving off the coast with **Indalosub** (Avenida Cabo de Gata 187, 950 24 31 96) and **Alpha** (Puerto, 950 38 03 21, www.alphabuceo.com), both in San José.

One of the most attractive features of the Cabo de Gata is that roads run along very little of its coastline, allowing for undisturbed walks and swimming in isolated coves. Just such a blissful trek of seven kilometres (four miles) from San José east and northwards brings you to the next coastal settlement, tiny **Los Escullos** (drivers need to head inland from San José and take the first road on the right). There's little here bar a couple of places to stay and eat, some picturesquely ruined buildings and the impressive **Castillo de San Felipe**, which sits atop a curious outcrop of fossilised sand dune. The fort dates from 1765 – one of nine four-cannon batteries built at the time along the coast of the Kingdom of Granada.

A kilometre further on lies the diminutive fishing village of **La Isleta del Moro**. Some fishing still takes place here, but the cranes have descended, and the holiday flats are rising. For the moment, though, it retains a quirky low-key charm and has a good place to stay and eat right on the seafront (and a good beach immediately to the north).

From Isleta, the road climbs, affording fine views, and then turns inland towards **Rodalquilar**. Just before it turns inland you can make your way down to the palm-fringed beach **Cala de los Toros**. The sizeable village of Rodalquilar has a strangely disconcerting atmosphere, due largely to the number of derelict and crumbling houses on its outskirts and the abandoned mine workings above it. Mining has been big in the area for centuries and probably dates back to before Roman times. Alum – used in printing, dyeing, papermaking and tanning – was mined here in the 16th century, and, in the early 20th century, significant quantities of gold were found. Production continued until the mines were finally closed in 1966, devastating the economy and population of the village.

The main road continues north. A kilometre further on, a rough road leads down to the impressive sweep of sand at El Playazo, north of which broods the 18th-century **Batería de San Ramón**, now converted into a private residence. The road to the beach passes an even older structure – a decrepit, squat little tower that is actually the oldest fortification on the coast, the **Torre de los Alumbres**, built around 1510 to protect the alum mines.

The next settlement along the coast is **Las Negras**, which, like La Isleta, is changing character rapidly as it is developed for tourism. The beach is not very appealing, but there are a couple of decent places to eat and drink.

The road stops here, but walkers can continue for around ten kilometres (six miles) to **Agua Amarga** through more stupendous scenery and past yet more idyllic beaches, as well as the **Castillo de San Pedro**, which once guarded a small bay with the only constant fresh water spring along the whole Cabo de Gata coast.

It's worth persevering – either on foot or by car (drive back to the motorway or take the newly-tarmaced ten-kilometre/six-mile road from Fernán Pérez) – to reach the delightful little resort of **Agua Amarga** (meaning 'bitter water'), which marks the northernmost reaches of the park. This thoroughly chilled-out place is possibly the most appealing spot to stay on the peninsula, with a few excellent accommodation and eating and drinking options.

Inland from the coast, the onward creep of plastic tents has breached the park boundaries. There's plenty of evidence, amid the new wealth, of how hard life has long been in this arid region, with many abandoned and disintegrating buildings spotting the landscape. One such is the once grand **Cortijo del Fraile**, reached along a four-kilometre (2.5-mile) unpaved road from the village of **Los Albaricoques**. This remote farmstead was one of the key locations in a passionate crime that was to be elaborated upon and immortalised by Federico García Lorca in his play *Blood Wedding*. In 1928 Francisca Cañadas Morales, engaged for two years to Casimiro Pérez Pino, eloped with her lover Curro Montes Cañadas. They had got about eight kilometres (five miles) away when Casimiro's brother caught up with them and shot Curro dead. The brother was convicted of the murder, Casimiro was haunted by the shame of the incident all his life and Francisca never married, living as a recluse until her death. A more desiccated, red-raw location for such an incident is hard to imagine. (Both the *cortijo* and Los Albaricoques featured in *For A Few Dollars More*.)

A few kilometres inland from the Cabo de Gata, across the motorway, is the pretty town of **Níjar**. Despite being geographically separate, it is also, somewhat inexplicably, part of the Natural Park (the official name of which is the Parque Natural de Cabo de Gata-Níjar). Its main claim to fame, however, is its pottery. The best of it is bold, bright and colourful – as is the worst of it. The long, steep main street is lined with shops displaying pottery and *jarapas* (rag-made bedspreads and rugs), for which Níjar is also known. Be warned that the town is very much on the tourist trail, and there's a fair amount of tat on display, though pickings are richer on Calle Las Eras in the Barrio Alfarero, which forks off the main street. The most charming part of Níjar is the area above the church, a maze of whitewashed alleys, many of which are decorated with plants in home-thrown pots.

Lovers of deserts should take the AL102 north from Níjar, through the fabulously eroded canyonland of the **Paraje Natural de Karst en Yesos**, and continue on to **Sorbas**, which hangs spectacularly on the edge of a gorge. It lends its name to the magnificent caves, the **Cuevas de Sorbas**, in the Paraje Natural,

San Miguel del Cabo de Gata. *See p297.*

The 18th-century fort at **Los Escullos**. *See p298.*

**Almería Province**

**Los Escullos.** See p298.

which can be visited on guided tours (950 36 47 04, www.cuevasdesorbas.com, tours €10.50, €6.50 concessions, call ahead to book).

## Where to stay, eat & drink

Along the beachfront in the village of Cabo de Gata, pretty **La Goleta** (950 37 02 15, closed Mon Oct-June and all Nov, €€) is the best bet for a meal, though the more basic **Bar Playa** (C/Barrio Nuevo 78, mobile 659 08 49 64, closed Mon, €) does good tapas and *raciones*. For en suite rooms try the **Hostal Las Dunas** (Barrio Nuevo 58, 950 37 00 72, closed Dec, double €42-€51), a couple of minutes' walk from the beach.

San José has the widest range of accommodation in the park (note that prices tend to drop dramatically out of season). The best high-end choice is the **Cortijo El Sotillo** (950 61 11 00, double €97-€132), on the edge of town. This sympathetically designed ranch-like complex (horse riding can be arranged) has spacious rooms, each with its own little terrace, and a pool. The same management have opened a new upmarket place in town, **Doña Pakyta** (C/Correos s/n, 950 61 11 75, www.hotel pakyta.com, double €110-€162), which has wonderful views of the bay from its *terrazas*, but no pool. Right by the beach is the ugly but

well-equipped four-star **Hotel Don Ignacio** (Paseo Marítimo s/n, 950 61 10 80, double €70-€180). The hotel also runs the new **Hostal San José** near the port (C/Las Olas s/n, 950 61 10 80, double €56-€144). Cheaper places include the highly recommended 26-room **Hotel Atalaya** (C/Correos s/n, 950 38 00 85, www.atalaya delsur.com, double €45-€96), a keenly priced, tasteful place where the good-sized rooms all have little terraces. There's also the **Hostal Costa Rica** (C/Correos s/n, 950 38 01 03, double €50-€70) and the **Hostal Bahía** (C/Correos 16, 950 38 03 07, double €35-€60). Both are in the centre of the village, near the beach.

There are a number of places to eat on the main road into San José, but by far the most attractive nosh spot is the cute little strip of eight restaurant-bars between the beach and the harbour. There's also a more upmarket restaurant in the **Cortijo El Sotillo** (*see above*), while **La Gallineta** (Carretera San José s/n, 950 38 05 01, closed Mon and 2wks Jan & all Feb, €€€), in the little village of Pozo de los Frailes just outside San José, is the most refined choice in the area. For later drinking, there are a clutch of places off the main square, but the best is **Maimono El Pirata** (C/Correos s/n, 950 38 05 47, closed Tue), on the road leading west out of town towards the Doña Pakyta.

The place to stay and eat in La Isleta del Moro is the superbly located beachside **Hostal Isleta del Moro** (C/Areiz s/n, 950 38 97 13, double €22-€51).

In Agua Amarga, the best accommodation – and perhaps the finest in the whole Cabo de Gata – is to be found at the super-stylish **El Tío Kiko** (C/Embarque s/n, 950 13 80 80, www.eltiokiko.com, closed Dec or Jan, double €144-€161), at the top of town; the whitewashed rooms have terraces and marble bathrooms with jacuzzis, and are ranged round a pool area and an excellent restaurant.

The **Hostal Restaurante La Palmera** (C/Aguadea s/n, 950 13 82 08, double €70-€80), at the northern end of the beach (ask for a room with a sea view), has a good restaurant attached (€€). Other options are the friendly French-owned **Hotel Family** (C/La Lomilla s/n, 950 13 80 14, closed Nov & first 2wks Dec, double €45-€100) and the two-star **Hotel Las Calas** (C/Desagüe s/n, 950 13 80 16, www.hotellas calas.com, double €62-€111) at the other end of the beach. The beachfront **Bar Restaurante Playa** (Playa Agua Amarga, 950 13 81 67, closed Oct-Apr, €€) serves up enormous plates of *calamares a la plancha*, while just beyond is another good restaurant, **Costamarga** (Playa Agua Amarga, 950 13 80 35, closed Oct-Easter, €€), with a wide selection of fresh fish. Behind the front, **Café Bar La Plaza** (C/Ferrocarril

Minero s/n, 950 13 82 14, closed Nov & Dec, €)
is a locals' favourite. There are a number of
campsites in the area. Contact the tourist office
in San José for details.

## Resources

### Internet
**San José** *Blablabla, Pasaje del Curry s/n (950 61 10
44/www.parquenatural.com/blablabla).* **Open** 9am-
midnight Mon, Tue, Thur-Sun (also Wed in Aug).
On a small street beside the Cajamar bank.

### Tourist information
**Parque Natural de Cabo de Gata-Níjar**
*Centro de Visitantes de las Amoladeros, Carretera
Cabo de Gata–Almería, km 7 (950 16 04 35/
www.cabodegata-nijar.com).* **Open** *July-Sept* 10am-
2pm, 5.30-9pm daily. *Oct-June* 10am-3pm daily.
**San José/Níjar** *C/Correos s/n, San José (950 38 02
99/www.cabodegata-nijar.com).* **Open** *Easter-Oct*
10am-2pm, 5-9.30pm daily. *Nov-Easter* 10am-2pm,
5-9.30pm Mon-Sat; 10am-2pm Sun.

## Mojácar & around

While the stretch of the Almería coast from
Agra to Aguadulce is largely given over to
agriculture, and the Cabo de Gata is chiefly
left to nature, the most easterly part of the
Andalucían coastline is rapidly becoming the
province of hardcore tourism. When the Costa
del Sol was being pumped with development
money and concrete in the 1960s, a community
of writers and artists settled in the hilltop
village of **Mojácar**, in what was then a sparsely
populated and impoverished part of the coast.
In the last decade or so Mojácar has made up
for lost time, developing at an ever-increasing
rate – it's now Almería's major resort.

There are, in fact, two Mojácars. The original
*pueblo* – enjoying an eagle's nest of a location a
kilometre inland – and the newer *playa* (beach),
essentially a six-kilometre (four-mile) strip of
hotels, restaurants and bars lining a beachside
road. It's still easy to see what drew all those
artistic types to the *pueblo* 40 years ago; its
setting is impossibly picturesque, its flower-
clad white houses and labyrinthine alleys
remain irresistibly photogenic. Yet there's no
location in the world that can't be ruined by one
coach party too many. It's at its most appealing
in the evening when the daytime crowds have
left and you can watch the sun set over the hills
from one of the cafés in the town square.

While the *pueblo* might still make some
pretence of being a 'traditional' Almerian village,
the *playa* knows exactly what it is – a sun, sea
and sand service station. Here's where to come if
you long to swig bitter at Snoopy's British Bar
Diner before a good fry-up at The Codfather.

As intensive holiday development goes, it's
actually not too tacky, and the beach is certainly
attractive. The beachfront is currently being
spruced up, with the first phase of a beachside
promenade completed in the south of the strip,
and a new pavement and fancy streetlights
on the road from the *playa* to the *pueblo*.

The sprawl of Mojácar ends abruptly in the
south, and the road winds along some lovely
coastline, with the odd decent (and usually
not too crowded) beach, before arriving at the
unprepossessing town of **Carboneras**.

The same road heading north passes
endless holiday complexes before coming to the
nondescript fishing town of **Garrucha**. There's
little incentive to stay here, but it is worth
stopping to sample the excellent fresh fish.

If you're travelling with kids, you may wish
to head inland for ten kilometres (six miles) to
cool off at the **Parque Acuático Vera**.

### Parque Acuático Vera
*C3327 (902 36 12 94/www.aquavera.com).*
**Open** *Mid May-June, 1st 2wks Sept* 11am-6pm
daily. *July, Aug* 11am-7.30pm daily. **Admission**
€13.50; €8 under-12s; 40% discounts after 3pm.
**Credit** AmEx, MC, V.

## Where to stay, eat & drink

The pick of the places to stay and eat in
Mojácar Pueblo is the long-established
**Mamabel's** (C/Embajadores 5, 950 47 24 48,
www.mamabels.com, closed early Jan-early
Feb, double €64-€86, ), which has eight
individually decorated rooms and a terrace
with stunning views. A more recent addition
is the big, ugly three-star **Hotel El Moresco**
(Avenida de en Camp s/n, 950 47 80 25, closed
Oct, double €62-€109), which does have the
advantage of a rooftop pool and great views
from most rooms. Cheaper options include the
five-room **Pensión El Torreón** (C/Jazmín 4-6,
950 47 52 59, mobile 639 16 17 29, double €36-
€50), which has a beautiful patio-reception and
flower-filled balcony with stunning views, and
the 19-room **Pensión Casa Justa** (C/Morote 7,
950 47 83 72, double €35-€42).

There are a lot of overpriced restaurants in
Mójacar Pueblo. **Palacio** (Plaza del Caño 3, 950
47 28 46, €€€) and **Mamabel's** (*see above*; €€,
closed lunch and all Jan & Feb) are the pick
of the bunch, or go for one of the tapas bars
around the main square. It's worth climbing
to the top of the village to admire the views and
sip a drink in one of the bars on the **Mirador
del Castillo** square, while contemplating the
(alas, now disproved) legend that Walt Disney
was born in Mojácar, subsequently orphaned
and adopted by a Californian family. (Though it
does seem that he did have family connections

**Almería Province**

here.) If you are after a late-night drink in the *pueblo*, your best bet is **Budú** (C/Estación Nueva, no phone), right at the top of town. By far the weirdest, kitschiest and most characterful place in the area for a drink is the rambling bar-cum-art-gallery **Delfos de Mojácar** (AL151, km3, mobile 678 94 30 24, open evenings daily), just off the road to Turre.

There are countless hotels and *hostales* in Mojácar Playa. The top option is the modern **Parador** (Paseo del Mediterráneo s/n, 950 47 82 50, www.parador.es, double €90-€104). One of the few places on the beach side of the main road is the two-star **Hotel Playa** (Paseo del Mediterráneo 30, 950 47 88 51, double €39-€77). The **Hotel Virgen del Mar** (Paseo del Mediterráneo 245, 950 47 22 22, www.hotel virgendelmar.com, double €48-€80, restaurant €€) is another good two-star option, with a better-than-average restaurant.

Food in Mojácar Playa is generally of a pretty low standard, though there's no shortage of choice (particularly at the southern end of the beach, where you'll also find most of the bars). Your best bet is probably **Tito's** (Mojácar Playa, 950 61 50 30, €), which serves an eclectic range of dishes (such as Thai beef salad and tuna sashimi) in a relaxed beachside atmosphere. The restaurant in the **Parador** (*see above*) is as upmarket as you'll find. In season, the beach is heaving with alfresco bars and discos.

## Resources

### Internet
**Mojácar Playa** *Indaltur, Paseo Mediterráneo 293 (950 61 51 56).* **Open** 10am-2pm, 5-8pm Mon-Fri; 10am-2pm Sat.

### Tourist information
**Mojácar Pueblo** *C/Glorieta 1 (950 61 50 25/ www.mojacar.es).* **Open** 10am-2pm, 5-8pm Mon-Fri; 10.30am-1.30pm Sat.
There's also an info point by the beach in Mojácar Playa, close to the *parador* (hours same as above).

## Getting there

### By bus
Alsina Graells (950 23 51 68) runs hourly daily services between Adra and Almería, all of which call at Aguadulce, and there are also half-hourly buses between Almería and Roquetas de Mar. Alsa Enatcar (info 902 42 22 42, tickets 950 61 70 25/71 36) runs about 3 buses daily from Almería to Mojácar, and hourly buses run between Mojácar Playa and Pueblo. Public transport is scarce in the Cabo de Gata. Autocares Bernardo (954 25 04 22) runs 3 buses daily to San José from Almeria, and 4 from San José to Almeria, except Sundays when there are 2 either way. One bus runs between Isleta del Moro and Almeria on Mondays and Saturdays.

**Mojácar** old and new. *See p301.*

# Almería Interior

Lose yourself in the tourist-free desert landscapes of Andalucía's Wild East.

Most visitors to Almería province stick closely to the coastline, losing sight of the sea only for such standard tourist forays as trips to Mini Hollywood and Nijar. Yet this is all to the benefit of those with a little more initiative. It's true that much of the province's interior is wilderness, but it's a magnificent wilderness, veering from forested mountain peaks to lunar canyonscapes.

## Vélez Blanco & around

In the north of Almería province lies the **Parque Natural de la Sierra María-Los Vélez** (22,600 hectares/87 square miles), a mountainous, multi-hued expanse of trees, rock and dust. There's plenty of rugged walking in the area – for details, ask at the park visitors' centre.

There are two main towns in the area: **Vélez Rubio**, the larger of the two, which is chiefly of note for its superb, outsize, mid 18th-century church; and the more appealing **Vélez Blanco**. The latter is a close-knit, relaxed place, clustered under one of the most striking castles in Andalucía. This was originally a simple Moorish structure, but was embellished and extended in the early 16th century by an Italian architect called Florentini. He also installed a superb Renaissance bronze door and fitted out the courtyard entirely in marble. To appreciate this, alas, you will need to visit the Metropolitan Museum of Art in New York, for the castle's impoverished owner sold off almost all the internal decoration in the early 19th century; the courtyard was eventually acquired and reconstructed by the US museum. Still, although it may be a shell, the castle is atmospheric, and the views from its towers are quite superb.

A kilometre south of Vélez Blanco on the road to Vélez Rubio is a sign (close to a petrol station) to the **Cueva de los Letreros**. The cave is actually more of a shallow depression in a wall of rock, but it contains the faint remains of 6,000-year-old cave paintings depicting animals, birds, symbols and human figures. It was here that the '*indalo*' (a stick figure holding an arc over its head) was first seen – it's since been adopted as the symbol of Almería province. To see the cave, go first to the Natural Park visitors' centre in Vélez Blanco (*see below*) to get the key to the gate (the *cueva* is fenced off); you'll need to leave your passport as a deposit.

You can take your car a certain distance along the rough road towards the cave, but there's still a steep 15-minute walk up to the cave itself.

### Castillo de Vélez Blanco

*950 41 50 27.* **Open** 11am-1pm, 5-6pm Mon, Tue, Thur, Fri; 11am-6pm Sat, Sun. **Admission** €1. **No credit cards**.

## Where to stay & eat

The best place to stay in Vélez Blanco is undoubtedly the three-star **Casa de los Arcos** (C/San Francisco 2, 950 61 48 05, www.casa delosarcos.net, closed June, double €45-€54), a beautifully converted 18th/19th-century mansion, and surprisingly good value. Second choice would be the newer **Hotel Velad Al-Abyadh** (C/Balsa Parra 28, 950 41 51 09, www. hotelvelad.com, double €58-€64), where many of the bedrooms have magnificent views (ask for an exterior room). If you're on a tighter budget, try the **Hostal Restaurante La Sociedad** (C/Corredera 14, 950 41 50 27, double €30-€40), which has decent rooms. Its bar is a focus of local life, and serves good tapas and *raciones*. There are a couple of more upmarket places to eat, including **El Molino** (C/Curtidores s/n, 950 41 50 70, closed dinner Thur and 1st wk July), with its lovely terrace.

## Resources

### Tourist information

**Parque Natural de la Sierra de María-Los Vélez** *Centro de Visitantes 'Almacén del Trigo', Avenida del Marqués de los Vélez s/n, Vélez Blanco (950 41 53 54).* **Open** 10am-2pm Mon-Thur, Sun; 10am-2pm, 6-8pm Sat.

## The Sierra de los Filabres to the Almerían Alpujarras

The centre of Almería province is dominated by the mountains of the **Sierra de los Filabres**, essentially a continuation of the Sierra Nevada. The region is thinly populated, and few tourists venture this far inland, making it all the more enjoyable for lovers of wild and dramatic scenery.

In the area around the neat villages of **Cóbdar** and **Albánchez**, wooded slopes and narrow valleys create a more intimate landscape, broken occasionally by great white scars cut by marble quarriers. One such quarry dominates the hillside above Cóbdar, and the rough road west of the village leads past another, with massive blocks of marble piled by the roadside.

Andalucían villages have a bizarre tendency to unilateral declarations of war. Huescar in Granada province took against the Danes (*see p272*), while **Lijar**, a few kilometres west of Albánchez, was officially at war with France from 1883 until 1983, supposedly sparked by an insult hurled at Alfonso XII as he passed through Paris.

South of the Sierra, the mountains give way to desert. Romantically desolate, this bone-bleachingly dry area has long drawn in filmmakers, who see in the majestic scale of its canyons and ravines, its polychromatic geology and weirdly eroded topography similarities with the American West.

Close to where the A7 meets the C3326 to Guadix is **Mini Hollywood**, a film set turned tourist attraction. This was the original location for many classic Westerns, as well as for scores of other films that made use of the wild, lunar landscapes and crystalline air. It was here that Sergio Leone built the set for *A Fistful of Dollars*, which was later also used in *For a Few Dollars More* and *The Good, the Bad and the Ugly*. The set was subsequently bought by the local extras and run as a Western theme park. Now owned by the Playa Hoteles group, the site has been heavily commercialised (and is comparatively expensive), but is still fun, particularly if you time your visit to coincide with the Western show – a hammy but enjoyable 're-creation' of the demise of the James brothers. The most frustrating aspect of Mini Hollywood is the lack of information about the cinematic classics filmed here – the potentially interesting 'Museum of Cinema' is no more than a load of old film cameras and posters. Tacked to the back of the park, incongruously, is a sizeable zoo. It's not badly done, but many of the cages and pens are very small, and how many of the animals cope with the blistering summer heat can only be imagined.

Mini Hollywood is not the only Western-themed tourist attraction in the area. Closer to **Tabernas** (which is overlooked by a romantically ruined castle) is **Texas Hollywood,** which isn't as commercialised as its better-publicised neighbour. The enjoyable English of its brochure proudly boasts the local filming of classics like '*One Dolar for the Deads*', '*The Long Way of the Revenge*' and '*The Seven Magnificients*'. Here you'll find a fly-blown Western town, an Indian settlement, a Mexican village, 'Fort Bravo' and

the usual range of 'shows', plus bison, camels and 'the biggest horses in the world'. A third location, **Western Leone**, contains the ranch from the opening scene of *Once Upon a Time in the West* among its attractions.

From Mini Hollywood, the main road towards Guadix and Granada brings you after 17 kilometres (11 miles) to **Gérgal**, with its fine castle. Behind here towers a mountain topped by the very *X-Files* **Observatorio de Calor Alto**, a further 23 kilometres (14 miles) by road. It's actually a series of German-Spanish observatories (home of the Max Planck Astronomy Institute) where, supposedly, stars can be seen more clearly than anywhere else in Europe. Cloud-free skies are assured for around 200 nights a year (four times what could be expected in northern Europe).

Back at Mini Hollywood, the main road heads south towards Almería city. Leading off it, the A348 winds westwards along the course of the River Andarax into the **Almerían Alpujarras**. A few kilometres along the road you'll see a sign to **Los Millares**, the largest Bronze Age settlement in Europe. Located on a spur-shaped plateau by the Andarax river (which was then navigable up to this point), the 19-hectare (47-acre) site was occupied between about 2700 and 1800 BC and consists of a necropolis containing 80 megalithic passage graves and a village protected by a complex defensive system.

West of Los Millares, the Sierra Nevada rises to the north and the Sierra de Gádor to the south as the main road leads from the harsher, barer landscapes of the Almerian Alpujarras towards the higher, more heavily wooded Granadan Alpujarras (*see p274-82*).

Few of the villages along the route merit more than a quick refreshment stop (though **Canjáyar** is pretty and has a fine inn; *see p305*), but the drive is spectacular. If you fancy exploring the area, the best base is **Laujar de Andarax**. The deposed Boabdil fled to Laujar after leaving Granada in 1492, but Fernando and Isabel reneged on the deal by which he was to rule an Alpujarran kingdom from the town, and within a year he was exiled to Africa. The source of the Andarax is just outside the town (follow the signs to '*nacimiento*') – a leafy spot inundated with picnicking locals at weekends.

### Los Millares

*Santa Fe de Mondújar (mobile 677 90 34 04).* **Open** 10am-2pm Wed-Sun. **Admission** free. Phone ahead if you want to join one of the free tours of the site, which begin at 10am and noon.

### Mini Hollywood

*A7, km464, Tabernas (950 36 52 36).* **Open** *Apr-Oct* 10am-9pm daily. *Nov-Mar* 10am-7pm Sat, Sun. *Wild West show* noon, 5pm (extra show

8pm in summer). *Can-can show* 1pm, 4pm (extra show 7pm in summer). *Parrot show* 11am, 3pm, 6pm. **Admission** €17; €9 concessions. **Credit** DC, MC, V.

### Texas Hollywood

*A7, km468, Paraje de Lunhay, Tabernas (950 16 54 58/www.texashollywood.topactive.com).* **Open** (phone in advance) 9am-7.30pm daily. *Shows* May-Nov 12.30pm, 2pm, 5.30pm, 7.30pm daily. **Admission** €12.50; €7.50 concessions. **Credit** MC, V.

### Western Leone

*C3326, Tabernas (950 16 54 05/www.western leone.com).* **Open** *Apr-Oct* 10am-dusk daily. *Nov-Mar* 10am-dusk Sat, Sun. *Shows* 12.30pm, 2.30pm, 5.30pm, 7.30pm. **Admission** €9; €4.50 concessions. **No credit cards.**

## Where to stay & eat

Tourists are very rare in the Sierra de los Filabres, and, consequently, places to stay are few. The **Hostal Amanecer** in the village of Albánchez (Avenida Los Molinos s/n, 950 12 23 23, www.hostalamanecer.com, double €30-€36) is the best bet, with a lovely communal terrace.

In Laujar, try the **Hostal Nuevo Andarax** (C/Canalejas 27, 950 51 31 13, closed mid Dec-1st wk Jan, double €35) above a bar-restaurant, or the **Hostal Fernández** (C/General Mola 4, 950 51 31 28, double €33), with a terrace. For more luxury, there's the **Villa Turística de Laujar** (Cortijo de la Villa s/n, 950 51 30 27, closed early-mid Jan, double studio €68-€82, villa for 4 €137-€165, villa for 6 €160-€190), which has bungalows set in gardens with a pool. For tapas, try **Bar Rodríguez** (Plaza Moajor de la Alpujarras 1, 950 51 31 10, €).

In Canjáyar, **La Posada de Eustaquio** (Plaza de la Iglesia 15, 950 51 01 77, www.posadaeustaquio.com, double €40) is a real village inn; warm, inviting and stuffed with antiques; the best room is the suite with exposed beams and a balcony over the *plaza*. A cheaper option is at top of the hill at the **Hotel Restaurante La Piscina** (C/General González 86, 950 511 050, double €27-€30), which does indeed have a swimming pool.

## Getting there

### By bus

Bus services in the interior are scant. There's one daily bus from Almería to Láujar (Alsina Graells 950 22 18 88) and a couple each day from Almería to Vélez Blanco (Enatcar general info 902 42 22 42, Almería info 950 28 16 60; Autobuses Giménez Garcia 968 44 19 61) and a few local services, but a car is really necessary to get around with any ease.

### By train

The only rail line in the province goes from Almería to Guadix, but doesn't stop anywhere of great interest.

**Mini Hollywood.** *See p304.*

**Vélez Blanco** castle. *See p303.*

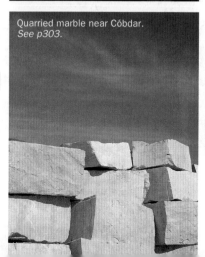

Quarried marble near Cóbdar. *See p303.*

# Directory

## Features

# Directory

## Getting There & Around

### By air

Log on to www.aena.es for info on all Spanish airports and live departure and arrival details.

### Airlines

A vast number of airlines fly from the UK to Andalucía, and particularly to Málaga. Below is a list of the main scheduled operators. In addition, many charter companies offer flights to southern Spain. From North America, you'll need to connect in Madrid (or London).

**Aer Lingus** *(from the UK Ireland 0818 36 50 00/from Spain 952 10 54 38/88/ www.aerlingus.com).* Dublin and Cork to Málaga.

**bmibaby** *(from the UK 0870 264 2229/from Spain 902 10 07 37/ www.bmibaby.com).* Cardiff, Manchester, Nottingham East Midlands and Teeside to Málaga.

**Britannia** *(from the UK 0870 607 6757/from Spain call Thomson's 24hr helpline 971 70 62 25/ www.britanniaairways.com).* Seasonal flights from most UK airports to Málaga.

**British Airways** *(from the UK 0870 850 9850/from Spain 902 11 13 33/www.ba.com).* Gatwick, Heathrow, Stansted, Birmingham and Manchester to Gibraltar, Málaga and Sevilla.

**easyJet** *(from the UK 0871 750 0100/from Spain 902 29 99 92/ www.easyjet.com).* Luton, Gatwick, Stansted, Belfast, Bristol, Liverpool, Nottingham East Midlands and Newcastle to Málaga.

**Flybe** *(from the UK 0871 700 0123/from Spain 00 44 139 226 8529/www.flybe.com).* From Exeter and Southampton to Málaga.

**GB Airways** *(from the UK 0870 850 9850/from Spain 902 111 333/www.gbairways.com).* This BA franchise operator flies from Gatwick and Heathrow to Almería, Gibraltar, Málaga and Sevilla.

**Iberia** *(from the UK 0845 601 2854/from Spain 952 13 61 66/ www.iberia.com).* Gatwick and Heathrow to Málaga and Sevilla.

**JMC** *(from the UK 0870 010 0434/ www.jmc.com).* Seasonal flights from most UK airports to Málaga, and Gatwick, Birmingham, Glasgow and Manchester to Almería.

**Monarch Airlines** *(from the UK 0870 040 5040/from Gibraltar 350 47 477, flight info 350 73 026/from Spain 952 04 83 47, flight info 952 04 82 03/www.monarch-airlines. com).* Gatwick, Luton and Manchester to Málaga, and Luton and Manchester to Gibraltar.

**MyTravelLite** *(from the UK 08701 564 564/from Spain 902 02 01 91/ www.mytravellite.com).* Birmingham to Almería and Málaga.

**Ryanair** *(from the UK 0871 246 0000/from Ireland 0818 30 30 30/ from Spain 807 22 00 22/ www.ryanair.com).* Stansted to Jerez, and Dublin to Málaga.

**Thomsonfly** *(from the UK 0870 190 0737/from Spain 914 14 14 81/ www.thomsonfly.com).* Coventry to Málaga.

### Airports

#### Almería

*AL12, km9, Almería (950 21 37 00/ flight info 950 21 37 90/97).*
Almeria airport is 10km (6 miles) east of the city. There are regular flights to and from Madrid and Barcelona, but the only international scheduled flights are twice weekly from London with GB Airways. However, in high season, Almería airport is used by many charter companies. Local bus no.20 runs to and from the airport and C/Doctor Gregorio Marañon, at the north-eastern edge of Almería city centre, every half hour on weekdays and every hour on weekends and holidays, from around 6.30am to about 10.30pm (for information, call 950 62 47 35). One-way tickets cost 80¢. The journey time is approximately 30mins. Taxis are also available: a fare to the centre costs approximately €9.

#### Gibraltar

*956 77 30 26.*
Gibraltar airport, which is run by the Royal Air Force, is a couple of kilometres from the town centre, near the frontier. British Airways flies to Gibraltar from Gatwick, and Monarch from Luton and Manchester. There are also regular flights to/from Tangiers, Casablanca and Marrakesh. There is a bus service every 15-20mins from around 6.30am to 8pm. A single costs 60p and the journey takes 5mins. A taxi into town will cost about £5.

#### Granada

*A329, Granada (958 24 52 00/Iberia flight info 958 24 52 37/38).*
Granada airport is located about 16km (10 miles) west of the city. It is served by domestic flights only. The airport bus (958 24 52 00, €3 single) is scheduled to coincide with flights and takes about 25mins from the airport to the city centre. A taxi to the centre costs about €18-€20.

#### Jerez

*A4-E5, km631, Jerez de la Frontera (956 15 00 00).*
Jerez airport is 7km (4 miles) north-east of the city. There are about 5 flights a day to Madrid, Barcelona and Gatwick and Stansted. There's no public transport into Jerez – you'll need to take a taxi (about €11).

#### Málaga

*Avenida García Morato, Málaga (952 04 84 84/flight arrivals 952 04 88 38/44/flight departures 952 04 88 04/42).*
By far the region's busiest point of entry, Málaga's Pablo Picasso airport is 6km (4 miles) south-west of the city, just off the A7. A train service (902 24 02 02) runs from outside the international terminal to Málaga every 30mins (airport to Málaga/ Málaga to airport 7am-10.40pm, journey time 12mins, €1-€1.10 single) and south-west to Fuengirola every 30mins (airport to Fuengirola 6.45am-10.40pm, Fuengirola to airport 5.50am-11.40pm, journey time 10mins, €1 single). There's a half hourly bus service (No.19, 902 52 72 00) between the Paseo del Parque in the centre of Málaga and the airport (airport to Málaga 7am-11pm, Málaga to airport 6.30am-11pm, journey time 20mins, €1 single). Ten daily buses (more July-Sept) run between the airport and Marbella (902 14 31 44, airport to Marbella 6.15am-11pm, Marbella to airport 5.30am-10.30pm, journey time 45mins, €3.68 single). A taxi from the airport should cost around €8-€9 to Málaga or Torremolinos, €22 to Fuengirola and €45 to Marbella.

## Sevilla

*A4-E5, km532, Sevilla (954 44 90 00/tickets 954 67 52 10).*
Sevilla's San Pablo airport is 5km (3 miles) east of the city. From the airport, a bus service operated by Los Amarillos (902 21 03 17) – look for an 'Aeropuerto de Sevilla' sign on the front of the bus – runs every half hour on weekdays and every hour on weekends and holidays between the airport and C/Palos de la Frontera, via Santa Justa train station and C/San Francisco Javier (6.45am-11.30pm Mon-Fri, less frequently at weekends, journey time 20-25mins). It costs €2.30 for a single ticket. A taxi to the town centre from the airport will cost a flat fee of €17 on weekdays and €21 on weekends and holidays.

## By bicycle

Despite their love of the car, the Spanish are cycling fanatics; every weekend you'll see smaller roads clogged with stern-faced lycra-clad peddlers. Out of high season, cycling is a lovely way to see the back routes of the region, and you'll be shown a surprising amount of consideration by drivers. You can take your bike on to most trains. Tip: don't even think about cycling around Andalucía in the summer – the heat is too fierce.

For further information and route maps contact the **Spanish Cycling Federation** (Real Federación Española de Ciclismo, 915 40 08 41, www.rfec.com). For information on mountain biking holidays, *see p315*.

## By boat

There are no direct ferries from the UK to Andalucía, but there are two services to the northern Spanish coast: Portsmouth to Bilbao and Plymouth to Santander.

The **Portsmouth–Bilbao** service is operated by **P&O Ferries** (from the UK 08705 20 20 20, from Spain 944 23 44 77, www.poferries.com) and runs twice weekly (less frequently Jan-Mar); the 35-hour outward crossing involves two nights on board, while the 29-hour return means one night aboard.

The **Plymouth–Santander** service is run by **Brittany Ferries** (from the UK 08705 360 360, from Spain 942 36 06 11, www.brittanyferries.com), with twice weekly sailings (three a week from late June to early September) and takes 24 hours.

If you fancy taking the boat and then the train, there's one daily direct service from Bilbao to Córdoba (11hrs 30mins) and Málaga (14hrs 40mins), although it's quicker to take one of the three daily trains to Madrid (7hrs 30mins) and to change to the high-speed AVE there (*see p311*). No direct trains run from Santander to Andalucía, though there are three daily services to Madrid (5hrs 35mins-8hrs 35mins). For info, see www.renfe.es/ingles.

## By bus

**Eurolines** (from the UK 020 7730 8235, www.euro lines.co.uk) runs several services from London to destinations in Andalucía, including Algeciras, Málaga, Sevilla, Granada and Córdoba, with a journey time of around 35 hours. For services from other European countries, see www.eurolines.com.

Andalucía's bus services are generally excellent and probably the best way to get around the region if you don't have a car. Most buses are comfortable, clean and air-conditioned and they connect almost every obscure village as well as all the major cities. There are dozens of companies providing services (see the 'Getting There' section at the end of each chapter). You can buy tickets at the station or sometimes on board.

## By car & motorbike

From the UK you can take one of the two car ferries to Spain (*see above*), and drive down from Bilbao or Santander, or cross the Channel and drive down through France.

Driving around the south of Spain is usually easy and stress-free. The main roads are generally well maintained and pretty empty outside the cities. You are highly unlikely to find

# Drive time

Approximate driving times within Andalucía (hours: minutes)

| | Almería | Cádiz | Córdoba | Granada | Huelva | Jaén | Málaga | Sevilla |
|---|---|---|---|---|---|---|---|---|
| **Almería** | | 5:30 | 3:50 | 1:50 | 5:10 | 2:30 | 2:20 | 4:20 |
| **Cádiz** | 5:30 | | 2:40 | 3:30 | 2:10 | 4:00 | 3:00 | 1:20 |
| **Córdoba** | 3:50 | 2:40 | | 2:10 | 2:30 | 1:30 | 2:10 | 1:30 |
| **Granada** | 1:50 | 3:30 | 2:10 | | 3:30 | 1:00 | 1:20 | 2:30 |
| **Huelva** | 5:10 | 2:10 | 2:30 | 3:30 | | 3:40 | 3:00 | 1:00 |
| **Jaén** | 2:30 | 4:00 | 1:30 | 1:00 | 3:40 | | 2:00 | 2:50 |
| **Málaga** | 2:20 | 3:00 | 2:10 | 1:20 | 3:00 | 2:00 | | 2:20 |
| **Sevilla** | 4:20 | 1:20 | 1:30 | 2:30 | 1:00 | 2:50 | 2:20 | |

**Directory**

a traffic jam on a motorway (*autopista*). Having said that, the narrow, twisting roads in many small towns and villages can make driving pretty hairy.

## MOTORBIKES AND SCOOTERS

This is a great way of seeing the region, especially inland, where you'll have many roads almost to yourself. If you plan on doing some serious touring, you will need a decent-sized bike to get up the steep hills, but for a few days pottering along the coast, a scooter is fine. Most resorts will rent scooters and there's also a good network of major-name franchises. Be sure to take out full insurance cover.

Helmets are compulsory. Speed limits are enforced on an ad hoc basis. The police are hot on headlights, which should be set on half-beam at all times.

## Legal requirements

● In order to drive in Spain, you'll need a valid driving licence and third-party motor insurance. Theoretically, all valid UK driving licences should be accepted, but older all-green licences and Northern Ireland licences issued prior to 1 January 1991 do not conform to the EU model and may cause confusion. Photo driving licences from other European countries and North America are usually accepted, though you might like to obtain an International Driving Permit as a further guarantee.
● The minimum age at which you may drive a temporarily imported car and/or motorcycle (over 75cc) is 18. Most rental companies require the driver to be at least 25 years old.
● Severe penalties, including fines and the withdrawal of your driving licence, may be enforced if the level of alcohol in your bloodstream is found to be 0.05 per cent or above.

● Fines are issued on the spot and can be steep: always ask for an official receipt. A 20 per cent reduction is usually available for foreigners.
● Seat belts are compulsory for front and rear seat occupants, if fitted.
● Children under 12 cannot travel as front-seat passengers unless a suitable restraint system is used.
● By law you must carry a fluorescent warning triangle, which must be set up on the hard shoulder some way behind the car if you break down. You must also carry a spare set of headlight bulbs.

## Speed limits

On major roads and motorways the speed limit is 120kmph (75mph); in built-up areas it is 50kmph (31mph); on other roads it is either 90kmph (55mph) or 100kmph (62.5mph).

## Roads & tolls

Map reading in Spain can be something of an endurance test. Roads are frequently reclassified and reappear in different forms, sometimes in different places, and, confusingly, many of the major routes have two different classifications. A recent reclassification has left most Spaniards (even cartographers) perplexed. All *carreteras nacionales* (N-roads) have been renamed to begin with an A (standing for *autopista* – motorway), or AP if it's a *peaje* (toll road); in some cases the road number has changed too (*see below*).

The most reliable map is Michelin's Andalucía (map 578).

### ROAD CLASSIFICATIONS

**E = European route.** Major highways that, in theory, connect Spain with the rest of the continent. The E1 runs from Sevilla almost to the border with Portugal; the E5 runs from Cádiz, through Sevilla, and on to Madrid, Burgos and beyond; the E15 runs west from Estepona and

then north to Barcelona and the border with France. They are all very fast, good-surface toll roads.

**A/AP = Autopista.** These are inter-region highways (often toll roads – *peaje* – prefixed AP), which are of the same standard as the E roads. In fact, E and A roads are often the same thing and will be signposted accordingly. Toll roads are often very quiet.

**A/C = provincial roads.** You can usually work out the standard of these roads by the number of digits that follow their letter prefixes (the fewer, the better). C roads usually have two lanes.

**AL/CA/CO/GR/HU/JA/MA/SE = local roads.** The two-letter prefix relates to the province (SE = Sevilla, CO = Córdoba, etc.). These roads are generally narrow (sometimes only a single track) and vary in quality.

## RECENT ROAD CHANGES

**A4** Sevilla–Cádiz toll motorway is now **AP4**
**A7** Málaga–Guardiaro toll motorway is now **AP7**
**NIV** Madrid–Sevilla motorway (and Jerez A48) is now **A4**
**N332** Bailén–Linares motorway becomes **A32**
**N340** Barcelona–Algeciras motorway is now **A7**
**N323** Bailén-Motril motorway becomes **A44**
**A44/N331** Variante Aguilar/Antequera–Málaga becomes **A45**
**N340/A4** San Fernando–Algeciras is now **A48**
**N344** eastern access road to Almería becomes **AL12**
**N432** northern access road to Córdoba changes to **CO31**
**H49** access road Huelva is now **H31**
**N340** eastern access road to Málaga via La Araña becomes **MA24**
**N351** access road to Gibraltar changes to **CA34**
**NIV** San Fernando–Cádiz highway becomes **CA33**
**N354** access road to the Málaga port is now **MA22**

## Breakdown services

If you are taking your car to Spain, you should take out breakdown cover at home before setting out. For UK drivers, the AA (0800 085 2721, www.theaa.co.uk) and the RAC (0800 828 282, www.rac.co.uk) both offer good policies.

## Driving tips

● Don't expect drivers to allow you into a lane in heavy traffic. Instead, wait for a gap or simply barge your way in.
● Do not hold back from using your horn – it is not regarded as offensive in Spain.
● Look out for cars tailgating you at 120kmph on the *autopista* before overtaking with hardly any space before the oncoming vehicle.

## Signs & terms

● *cede el paso* – give way
● *usted no tiene la prioridad* – you don't have the right of way
● *único sentido* – one way
● *cambio de sentido* – indicates a junction that allows you to change direction
● *recuerde* – remember
● *ronda de circunnavegación* – ring road (around cities)

## Fuel

The majority of fuel stations employ attendants to fill your car for you (tipping is not expected). Only unleaded petrol (*sin plomo*) and diesel (*gasoil*) are available; both are much cheaper than in the UK.

## Parking

Parking is often a nightmare. In the smaller villages, park on the outskirts rather than trying to navigate the tortuously narrow roads. In towns, head for the nearest *aparcamiento* (car park; they're never very expensive). If a parking space is blocked, you can often push the offending car out of the way – many Spanish drivers leave the handbrake off for this reason – or simply sit on your horn until the culprit turns up.

## Car rental

Renting a car is cheap in Andalucía compared to the rest of Europe. There's lots of competition so it pays to shop around. The local firms are usually cheaper than the big international names, but make sure you check about hidden extras before signing up. At Málaga airport, in particular, there's a huge choice of companies, and you should be able to find the cheapest compact car for around €130 for a week all inclusive. It's worth checking whether your airline has a special arrangement with any rental company. Most companies require drivers to be 25 or over and to have held a valid licence for at least one year. You'll need to present your licence and a credit card when you hire the car.

As well as the companies below, **Holiday Autos** (0870 400 4447/www.holiday autos.co.uk) offers very competitive rates.

### Avis
www.avis.com
**From the UK** 08700 100 287.
**Almería airport** 950 29 82 21.
**Granada airport** 958 44 64 55.
**Jerez airport** 956 15 00 05.
**Málaga airport** 952 04 84 83.
**Sevilla airport** 954 44 91 21.

### Budget
www.budget.co.uk
**From the UK** 08701 539 170.
**Almería airport** 950 29 82 21.
**Jerez city** 956 33 80 54.

### Europcar
www.europcar.com
**From the UK** 0870 607 5000.
**Almería airport** 950 29 29 34.
**Granada airport** 958 24 52 75.
**Jerez airport** 956 15 00 98.
**Málaga airport** 952 04 85 18.
**Sevilla airport** 954 25 42 98.

### Hertz
www.hertz.com
**From the UK** 0870 844 8844.
**Almería airport** 950 29 27 83.
**Gibraltar airport** 956 74 27 37.
**Granada airport** 958 24 52 77.
**Jerez airport** 956 31 00 15.
**Málaga airport** 952 23 30 86.
**Sevilla airport** 954 51 47 20.

### Local companies
**Almericar** Almería airport 950 23 49 66/www.almericar.com.
**Autopro** Málaga airport 952 17 60 30/www.autopro.es.
**Dany Car** Málaga a 80/www.andalucia.com
**Helle Hollis** Málaga airpor 55 44/www.hellehollis.com.

## By train

There are no direct trains from other European countries (except Portugal) to Andalucía. If you want to arrive by train, your best bet is to get to Madrid, and then take one of the 21 daily high-speed AVE services from there to Córdoba (1hr 42mins) and Sevilla (2hrs 30mins).

For Eurostar tickets between London and Paris, call (from the UK) 08705 186 186 or see www.eurostar.co.uk. For European rail tickets, contact Rail Europe (from the UK 08705 848 848, www.rail europe.co.uk).

Andalucía relies upon a fairly comprehensive and generally reliable, though complicated, train system. Fares are cheap by UK standards. The network is operated by **RENFE** (information and reservations 902 24 02 02; some staff speak English). For information (in English) on train times, route planning and fares, consult RENFE's superb website **www.renfe.es/ingles**. You can also book tickets online via the site for many services.

The pride of the network is the **AVE** (Altitud Velocidad España – 'high speed Spain'), which connects Sevilla to Madrid via Córdoba in less than two hours 30 minutes. (The line is currently being extended to Málaga; due to be completed in 2007.) The rest of the region is criss-crossed by a variety of different train types, the best of which are the **Talgo** and the **TER** services, which are smart and speedy and connect the major cities. Slower but more picturesque are the (misleadingly named) **expreso** and **rapido** services, which tend to stop everywhere.

**Directory**

accom... ...iful
and good va... ...ou
shouldn't have di...ulty
finding a room except during
specific high-profile events,
such as Carnaval in Cádiz,
Semana Santa and the Fería
de Abril in Sevilla. Resorts are
likely to be packed in July and
August, but should have rooms
available at other times of year.

Prices vary a great deal
depending on the season, and
it's possible to get some real
bargains off peak. In most
places in Andalucía, and
certainly in the resorts, high
season is from 15 June to 15
September. You may pay even
more during Semana Santa,
when rooms are at a premium
throughout Andalucía, and
during major festivals. The
rest of the year generally
counts as low season, although
some places may have mid-
season rates. Some hotels –
particularly those in resorts –
close between late November
and January. Note, however,
that July and August are
regarded as low season for
inland cities such as Sevilla,
Jerez and Córdoba.

Prices are generally cheaper
than in much of the rest of
Europe, except in the major
cities, in particular Sevilla.
Most places will display the
tariff at reception and behind
the door of your room. It
is unlikely you will ever be
ripped off, but there is always
a *libro de reclamaciones*
(complaints book) 'at your
disposal' at reception.

Value-added tax, known as
**IVA**, will be added to your final
bill at the rate of **seven per
cent**, though it may or may
not be included in the prices
you are quoted – always check.

Breakfast (*desayuno*) may or
may not be included in the rate.

**In this guide we have
added IVA to prices for
accommodation where
relevant, so the price listed
should be the price you pay**
(at the time of going to press).

## Hotels

Most of the hotel chains in
Andalucía are Spanish. They
include the upmarket **AC** (902
29 22 93, www.ac-hoteles.com)
with nine hotels, and **Sol
Meliá** (902 14 44 40, from
the UK 0800 962 720, from the
US 1888 55 MELIA, www.sol
melia.com) with 31 hotels;
mid-market **NH** (902 11 51 16,
www.nh-hotels.com) with ten
hotels, and **Husa** (902 10 07 10,
www.husa.es) with 20 hotels.

There are five grades of
hotels, from one star to five
stars; the apellation 'GL' beside
the five stars means that the
hotel is 'Gran Lujo' ('grand
luxury'), which is even posher
than five stars. The stars
correspond to facilities, size
of room, and so on, and are
regularly inspected, but don't
reflect quality of services,
atmosphere or location.

At the one-star level expect
a simple room, usually with
en suite shower, and little
else. At this level there is little
difference to a decent *hostal*,
and often you may pay more
simply for a phone in the room.
At two stars you are likely
to find all rooms en suite
with certain facilities such as
TV, minibar and perhaps air-
conditioning. From three stars
up you can expect all mod
cons, maid service, often a
café or restaurant and perhaps
even a swimming pool. Four-
and five-star hotels are as you
would expect worldwide, with
prices to match, although it's
worth noting that four stars
does not guarantee a pool.

'HA' denotes Apartment-
Hotels, which are graded one to
four stars and offer self-catering
facilities such as a kitchen.

### PARADORES

The 86-strong *parador* chain
(915 16 66 66, from the UK:
Keytel International 020 7616
0300, from the US: Marketing
Ahead 212 686 9213 or 1-800
223 1356, www.parador.es)
was founded in 1928
and consists of state-run,
subsidised hotels that are,
for the most part, located in
converted historical buildings
such as monasteries, castles,
palaces or stately homes.
They range from three to
four stars, and, despite their
often fabulous locations, are
always much cheaper than the
commercial equivalent. The
idea behind the scheme was
to generate tourism in places
people did not generally visit.
Hence, you will find them in
mountain villages and market
towns and not, for example, in
Sevilla or Marbella. There are
16 *paradores* in Andalucía.

Although *paradores* have
many advantages, they are
part of a chain, so you may
not get the level of character
and personal service you
might find in the best privately
owned hotels; also, their
restaurants tend to be formal,
pricey and of variable quality.

All *paradores* in Andalucía
are individually listed under
the relevant chapter. Check the
website for details of discount
schemes and loyalty cards.

## Hostales & pensiones

*Hostales* (and *hostal-residencias*)
are graded in the same way
as hotels, with one or two stars.
Most offer simple rooms with
en suite facilities at reasonable
prices. Some have a restaurant

or café attached, and most are family-run. *Residencia* simply means that no other meal than breakfast is served.

There is little difference between a *hostal* and a *pensión*, although *hostales* perhaps have the edge in terms of quality. At the lowest level a *pensión* is going to be pretty basic. *Pensiones* are also graded with one or two stars, but there's little difference between the categories.

## Casas Huespedes, Fondas & Camas

You don't often see the letters 'CH' (*casa huespedes*), but they signify basic accommodation, often not much more than a room in someone's house. You'll be lucky to have a sink and are likely to be sharing the bathroom with the owners. *Fondas*, denoted by 'F', are of a similar quality. '*Camas*' indicates that the homeowner rents beds for the night.

## Villas turisticas

*Villas turisticas* are self-catering apartments in rural areas run by the regional government. They usually have a reception and all the facilities you would expect at three- or four-star level, with prices to match. Despite their unpromising name, they are often very tastefully appointed. For a list of all *villas turisticas* in the region, contact the **Centro Internacional de Turismo de Andalucía** at C/Compañía 40, 29008 Málaga, 902 20 00 37, www.andalucia.org).

## Turismo rural & villa hire

*Turismo rural* is the Junta de Andalucía's way of getting more tourists away from the coast and into the countryside. There has been significant growth in this area, with many

UK tour operators offering rural dwellings for rent. In high season you will probably have a minimum-stay requirement of a week, but out of this period you can usually negotiate the length of your stay.

A *casa particular* (guesthouse) is the equivalent of British B&B-style accommodation. You'll stay in someone's farmhouse or country cottage, with the advantages of home cooking and a distinct lack of tourists. A full list is available from the **Red Andaluza de Alojamientos Rurales** (Apartado de correo 2035, 4080 Almería, 950 26 50 18, 902 44 22 33, www.raar.es).

Other organisations that can book characterful rural accommodation are the **Asociación de Hoteles Rurales de Andalucía** (C/Ramal Hoyo, Edificio El Congreso 1, Local 82, 29620 Torremolinos, Málaga, 952 37 87 75, www.ahra.es), **Rural Andalus** (C/Montes de Oca 18, 29007 Málaga, 952 27 62 29, www.ruralandalus.es) and **Rustic Blue** (958 76 33 81, www.rusticblue.com).

**Casa Andaluza** (956 45 60 53, www.casa-andaluza.com) specialises in villas in western Andalucía, while **Anda-Luzia-Reisen** (956 44 62 75, mobile 676 87 42 81, www.anda-luzia-reisen.com) focuses purely on the Costa de la Luz. For the eastern Costa del Sol around Nerja, try **James Villa Holidays** (from the UK 01622 655 900, www.jamesvillas.co.uk).

## Youth hostels

There are 20 *albergues juveniles* in Andalucía and one in Gibraltar, open to anyone with an IYHF (International Youth Hostel Federation) card. They are well maintained and many have pools. In rural areas they offer an excellent cheap accommodation option,

and in July and August you can also camp in the grounds for a few euros a night. In city areas, however, youth hostels are often a bus ride from the city centre, so you be may be better off in a *pensión*.

**Inturjoven** manages the network of hostels and seasonal camping grounds across Andalucía. Bookings can be made either with the hostel direct, from the central booking number (902 51 00 00) or online at www.inturjoven.com.

## Camping

There are around 130 official campsites in Andalucía, the majority of which are along the coast. You can camp elsewhere, but use your discretion: urban areas, private farmland and tourist beaches are off-limits; if you camp here you are liable for a fine.

Most campsites are well maintained with showers and functioning toilets; many also have bars attached or are within walking distance of restaurants. They won't cost you much more than €4 per person per night, plus €4 per night for the tent and the same for a caravan. The Junta de Andalucía publishes an official *Guía de Camping*, available from many tourist offices, which details all the officially recognised sites and prices.

## Refugios

Mountain refuges, or *refugios*, are dormitory huts with washing and cooking facilities situated on popular hiking or climbing routes. You will find them dotted around the sierras, particularly in the Sierra Nevada (where there are 12). They are usually indicated on maps, but for a full list contact the **Federación Andaluza de Montañismo** in Granada (Camino de Roda 101, Edificio Atalaya, piso°1 Oficina 7G, 958 29 13 40, www.fedamon.com).

**Directory**

# Sport, Activities & Special Interests

## Sport

### Bullfighting

Despite widespread international opposition, bullfighting remains popular in Spain, and particularly in Andalucía. The region has around 70 permanent bullrings and many village *ferías* climax with a *corrida*. The most renowned venues are the beautiful old ring in Ronda (built in 1785), which is regarded as the birthplace of bullfighting, and Sevilla's famed Maestranza, dating from 1761, which attracts the country's top matadors. The bullfighting season runs from April to October. For information on what to expect at a *corrida see p174* **Cliché**. The website www.mundo-taurino.org is packed with *toro*-related information.

### Football

Football (*fútbol*) is an obsession in Spain and by far the country's best-loved sport. You'll see it on TV in every bar in every town and village during the season, which lasts from September to June. The big three Andalucían teams are **Sevilla**, its (traditionally working-class) city rival **Betis** and **Málaga**, all of which have maintained solid mid-table form in the first division over the past few seasons. The best of the rest is probably **Recreativo Huelva** (Spain's oldest club), while other regional teams in the second division are **Cádiz**, **Córdoba**, **Polideportivo Ejido**, **Xerez** and **Almería**. Unless it's a big match, tickets are available on the gate until kick-off and start from as little as €15. Trouble is rare and the atmosphere is generally friendly.

## Activities

### Aerial sports

For details of where to take part in skydiving, parachuting, paragliding and other aerial sports, contact the **Federación Andaluza de Deportes Aereos** (Avenida San José 5, 41012 Sevilla, 954 23 58 64, www.feada.org). One recommended paragliding school is **Fly Spain** (contact: Rob Mansley, mobile 651 73 67 18, info@flyspain.co.uk), based in Algodonales in north-eastern Cádiz province, which offers a range of flights and courses for beginners.

### Birdwatching

Andalucia is one of Europe's premier spots for twitchers. For some prime birdwatching sites, *see p89* **Top five**.

### Climbing

Serious mountaineers head to the Sierra Nevada, the highest mountains in Spain (*see p274*), which offer some of the best climbing outside the Alps. Its peaks (topped at 3,482m/11,424ft by Mulhacén) are snow-capped for most of the year. For information, contact the **Federación Andaluza de Montañismo** in Granada (Camino de Roda 101, Edificio Atalaya, piso°1 Oficina 7G, 958 29 13 40, www.fedamon.com).

### Cycling & mountain biking

For information on getting around Andalucia by bike, see *p309*. Mountain biking in the region's rugged terrain is becoming increasingly popular. For mountain biking holidays, *see p315*.

## Diving & snorkelling

Diving off the Andalucían coast is not spectacular, but it does offer a few surprises. Perhaps the most exciting dives are to be had around Gibraltar (*see p144*), where the water is clogged with sunken warships. If you are after clear waters and an abundance of marine life, head to the Cabo de Gata nature reserve in Almería. There are a number of good dive schools here offering courses and shore and boat dives (*see p298*). For a full list of dive centres consult the local tourist office.

## Fishing

Sea fishermen head to the Andalucían coast for spectacular swordfish fishing from July to September; another draw is open-sea tuna fishing. Marinas up and down the coast can supply information. Freshwater fishermen are attracted primarily by the excellent trout fishing. One of the best (year-round) spots is Río Frío, near Loja in western Granada province; trout have been caught here since at least the 17th century. For information and permits, contact the **Alberge de Pescadores de Río Frío** (Riviera de Rio Frío s/n, 18300 Loja, 958 32 31 77). Look out for Turismo Andaluz's useful booklet *Sport Fishing* in tourist offices.

## Golf

Andalucia's warm climate means that you can play golf year-round. Here you'll find more than 60 golf courses (a third of all the golf courses in Spain), around 40 of which are on the Costa del Sol. The choice of Valderrama in Sotogrande as the venue for the 1997 Rider Cup sealed the reputation of the 'Costa del Golf' as one of Europe's premier golfing destinations. There are so many courses, in fact, that prices are fairly keen and you can get a round at some of the smaller ones for as little as €30. Many resort hotels even have their own courses. For companies offering golfing holidays, see *below*. For more information on the courses, see www.andalucia.com/golf/home.htm.

## Horse riding

Andalucians love horses and breed some of the finest in the world. The varied landscapes lend themselves perfectly to riding. For horse-riding holidays, *see below*.

## Sailing

There are marinas all along the coast, and sailing is big business in this part of the world. Most of the boats you'll see berthed along the Costa del Sol are for pleasure purposes only but there are plenty of sailing clubs too. Consult the website www.andalucia.com/sailing for details. General information is also available from the **Royal Spanish Sailing Federation** (Luis de Salazar 9, 28008 Madrid, 915 19 50 08, www.rfev.es).

## Skiing

Skiing is confined to the Sierra Nevada ski resort (Pradollano; *see p274*), about an hour's drive from Granada city. The resort is the most southerly in Europe and is small by Alpine standards. However, there are more than enough runs of varying standards (4 green, 18 blue, 18 red) to keep you entertained for a weekend, which is about the length of time most people spend here in season. For details, see www.tuspain.com/travel/sierra.htm.

## Surfing, kitesurfing & windsurfing

All three of the above are hugely popular activities on the windy Costa de la Luz in Cádiz province. The beach of El Palmar near Conil de la Frontera is favoured by surfers, while kite- and windsurfers flock to the beaches north of Tarifa. For more information, see www.tarifainfo.com/en/surfing.html.

## Walking

Andalucia's varied and often spectacular landscapes make for wonderful walking and hiking. In this guide we have detailed five fine walks, but the possibilities are limitless. For other ideas, get a copy of Guy Hunter-Watts' book *Walking in Andalucía*. For general information about hiking in Andalucía (and Spain) contact the Barcelona-based **Federación Español de Deportes de Montaña** (Federation of Mountain Sports, 934 26 42 67, www.fedme.es). For hiking maps, *see p319* **Maps**. For companies running walking holidays, *see below*.

## Specialist interest holidays

### Archaeology
**Earthwatch International** *(from the US 1-800 776 0188/ 978 461 0081/www.earthwatch.org/ expeditions/gibert.html).*

### Birdwatching
**Limosa Holidays** *(from the UK 01263 578143/www.limosa holidays.co.uk).*

### Cookery
**Buenvino Cookery Courses** *(from Spain 959 12 40 34/ www.fincabuenvino.com).*
**Madrid and Beyond** *(from Spain 917 58 00 63/www.madridand beyond.com).*

### Culture
**ACE** *(from the UK 01223 835055/ www.study-tours.org).*

**Martin Randall Travel** *(from the UK 020 8742 3355/www.martin randall.com).*

### Dance
**Dance Holiday Company** *(from the UK 01293 527722/www.dance holidays.com).*

### Golf
For information tailored to the golfing visitor see www.golf holidays.net.
**Tee G Golf Holidays** *(from Spain 952 93 92 38/www.teeggolf.com).*
**Executive Golf Marbella** *(from Spain 952 83 85 56/from the UK 0871 871 4905/www.executive golfholidays.com).*

### Horse riding
**Natural Horse Riding in Spain** *(from Spain 952 72 02 71/ www.naturalhorseridinginspain.com).*
**Rancho Los Lobos** *(from Spain 956 64 04 29/www.rancholos lobos.com).*
**Rustic Blue** *see p280.*
**Rutas Alternativas Cabalgar** *(from Spain 958 76 31 35/ www.ridingandalucia.com).*
**Spirit of Andalucia** *(from the UK 0845 230 1220/www.spirit-of-andalucia.co.uk).*

### Mountain biking
**Mountain Biking España** *(from the UK 01494 870486/ www.mountbik-espana.co.uk).*

### Painting
**Andalucian Adventures** *(from the UK 01453 834137/ www.andalucian-adventures.co.uk).*
**Andalucian Painting Holidays** *(from the UK 01382 553736/ www.langeart.co.uk).*

### Walking/trekking
**Andalucian Adventures** see above.
**Explore Worldwide** *(from the UK 01252 760000/www.explore.co.uk).*
**Headwater Holidays** *(from the UK 01606 720099/720033/ www.headwater.com).*
**Ramblers Holidays** *(from the UK 01707 331133/www.ramblers holidays.co.uk).*
**Rustic Blue** *see p280.*
**Sherpa Expeditions** *(from the UK 020 8577 2717/www.sherpa-walking-holidays.co.uk).*
**Waymark Holidays** *(from the UK 01753 516477/www.waymark holidays.co.uk).*

### Wine
**Winetrails** *(from the UK 01306 712111/www.winetrails.co.uk).*

**Directory**

# Resources A-Z

## Addresses

These are written street first, number second. In other words: C/Andalucía 7. Flat addresses are written according to the floor and which side of the block the flat is on: dcha = derecha (right); izda = izquierda (left); cto = centro (centre). Piso 1° dcha would therefore translate as first-floor flat on the right. The odd moniker s/n means *sin número* ('no number'). *Código postal* is the five-figure postcode and should always be included. Most Spanish street names are preceded by 'Calle', often abbreviated to 'C/' and not marked on many street maps.

## Age restrictions

The minimum legal age for smoking and drinking is 16, but this is not strictly enforced. The age of consent for both hetero- and homosexuals is 13, one of the lowest in Europe. Due to the fact that many young Spaniards live at home until they marry, casual sex and teenage pregnancy are relatively rare. To drive a car you need to be 18.

## Attitude & etiquette

The Spanish are far more tactile than northern Europeans; the common greeting between members of the opposite sex is a kiss on both cheeks. Personal space is much less guarded than in the UK or USA so do not be fazed if you find someone crowding you or bumping into you without apologising. It's the same with queuing, which is a largely alien concept in Spain.

Noise levels are also much higher than you may be used to – the first time you go into a bar you'll notice the TV, radio, coffee-maker and numerous high-volume conversations all going on simultaneously.

## Children

The Spanish love children – so much so that they take them with them wherever they go at almost any time of day or night. The Spanish are also much less strict about keeping control of their kids than northern Europeans.

Bars and restaurants will bend over backwards to look after children or babies, even if they have no special facilities, and most hotels accommodate kids at reduced rates.

In terms of facilities and amusements, the best place is the Costa del Sol, which has water parks, theme parks, aquariums and other child-oriented attractions.

## Consulates

### Australia
C/Federico Rubio 14, Sevilla (954 22 09 71). **Open** 10am-noon Mon-Fri.

### Canada
Edificio Horizonte, Plaza Malagueta 2, 1°, Málaga (952 22 33 46). **Open** 10am-1pm Mon-Fri.

### Ireland
Plaza de Santa Cruz 6, bajo A, Sevilla (954 21 63 61). **Open** 10am-2pm Mon-Fri.

### UK
Edificio Eurocom, bloque Sur, C/Mauricio Moro Pareto 2, 2°, Málaga (952 35 23 00/www.ukspain.com). **Open** Summer 9am-2pm Mon-Fri. Winter 9am-2.30pm Mon-Fri.

### USA
Edificio Lucía 1°C, Avenida Juan Gómez 'Juanito' 8, Fuengirola (952 47 48 91). **Open** 10am-1pm Mon-Fri. Paseo de las Delicias 7, Sevilla (954 23 18 85). **Open** 8.30am-1pm Mon-Fri.

## Consumer

Each municipality in Spain has its own 'OMIC' (Oficina Municipal de Información al Consumidor) office that aims to keep consumers informed of their rights and responsibilities. Ask at the local town hall for details.

## Customs

There are no restrictions on the import/export of duty-paid goods into Spain from any other EU country, provided the goods are for personal consumption only. Amounts

---

# Travel advice

For up-to-date information on travel to a specific country – including the latest news on safety and security, health issues, local laws and customs – contact your home country government's department of foreign affairs. Most have websites packed with useful advice for would-be travellers.

**Australia**
www.dfat.gov.au/travel

**Canada**
www.voyage.gc.ca

**New Zealand**
www.mft.govt.nz/travel

**Republic of Ireland**
www.irlgov.ie/iveagh

**UK**
www.fco.gov.uk/travel

**USA**
www.state.gov/travel

qualifying as personal consumption are as follows. (If you import more than these amounts, you may be asked to prove that the goods are solely for your use.)

● up to 800 cigarettes, 400 small cigars, 200 cigars or 1kg loose tobacco.

● 10 litres of spirits (over 22 per cent alcohol), 90 litres of wine (under 22 per cent alcohol) or 110 litres of beer.

If you are travelling into Spain from outside the EU, the limits are as follows. You are advised not to break these or you will risk a very heavy fine.

● 200 cigarettes or 100 small cigars, 50 cigars or 250g loose tobacco.

● 1 litre of spirits (over 22 per cent alcohol) or 2 litres of wine and beer (under 22 per cent alcohol).

● 50g perfume.

● 500g coffee; 100g tea.

These limits also apply if you are entering mainland Spain by boat from the Canary Islands or the Spanish protectorates of Melilla and Ceuta in Morocco, or from Gibraltar.

When you enter Spain from Gibraltar, expect to be stopped and searched at the border for illegally imported goods. You may also find yourself subject to a search if you are coming back from Morocco into Algeciras, Tarifa or Gibraltar. You are likely to be offered hashish in Morocco: do not try and bring it into Spain – although attitudes to personal possession within Spain are fairly relaxed (*see below* **Drugs**), smuggling is regarded as a serious offence and you're likely to face jail or a huge fine.

## Disabled

Andalucia is not very well geared up for disabled travellers and you will not find many facilities, particularly on public transport. Trains are better than buses in this respect, with wheelchairs usually available at most stations. Some car-hire companies offer specially adapted cars for hire. Disabled parking bays are denoted by a blue wheelchair sign.

Most public buildings and monuments, certainly in the cities, have disabled access and facilities by law. This also applies to larger hotels, including most *paradores*. Youth hostels in Andalucia also tend to have adapted access and accommodation, but smaller hotels and *pensiones* are unlikely to be equipped for disabled visitors. Larger restaurants and service stations in tourist areas will have disabled access, but away from the main routes, facilities are scarce.

In terms of accommodation, it's worth getting hold of the *Guía de Hoteles y Pensiones de Andalucía* from tourist offices; all wheelchair-accessible accommodation is marked with a wheelchair symbol.

### Organisations

Get a list of wheelchair-friendly accommodation and useful disabled tips about Andalucía before you go from the Spanish National Tourist Offices around the world (*see p324* **Tourist information**).

#### Access Travel
*6 The Hillock, Astley, M29 7GW (01942 888844/www.access-travel.co.uk).*
Tour operator that organises holidays for disabled people.

#### Holiday Care
*2nd floor, Imperial Building, Victoria Road, Horley, RH6 9HW (0845 124 9971/www.holidaycare.org.uk).*
Can provide a guide to accessible accommodation and other facilities for the disabled in Spain.

#### RADAR
*250 City Road, London EC1V 8AF (020 7250 3222/Minicom 020 7250 4119).*
The Royal Association for Disability and Rehabilitation has useful travel tips and information.

## Drugs

Andalucía's proximity to Morocco means it is the main gateway for drugs coming into Spain and Europe from North Africa. Cannabis (known as *chocolate*) is plentiful and cheap in the south and you may well find yourself offered it as you walk around. Tolerance towards soft drugs has become stricter since the heady days of the late '80s when it was perfectly acceptable to smoke in parks and public spaces and in many bars and cafés. Today, you might see people smoking joints (*porros*) in certain areas, but it's not as commonplace.

Cannabis possession is illegal in Spain but if it's a matter of just a few grams the police are unlikely to be concerned. Much more than that and you'll get a fine and a possible court appearance. If you are found in possession of any other drugs, you are looking at big fines and a prison sentence.

## Electricity

Spain operates on a 220V, 50-cycle AC grid and uses two-pin plugs. You will need an adaptor if you are bringing British electrical appliances with you. Visitors from the USA will need to bring an adaptor and a transformer if they intend to use appliances from home.

## Gay & lesbian

Homosexuality was illegal in Spain under Franco, and it's taken some time for attitudes to same-sex relationships to relax. Attitudes to gays and lesbians in Andalucia have markedly improved in the last few years. You'll find big scenes in Sevilla, Granada, Málaga, Marbella and, particularly, in Torremolinos, where there's a good drag scene and at least 20 gay bars. In rural villages, however, it's an entirely different matter; as a gay visitor you may be met with outright hostility, particularly if you are trying to get a room with your partner.

For advice contact one of the local gay and lesbian groups. These include **COLEGA** (www.colega web.net, Almería 950 27 65 40, Cádiz 956 22 62 62, Córdoba 957 49 27 79, Granada 958 26 38 53, Huelva 959 28 49 55, Jaén 953 27 12 84, Málaga 952 21 71 99, Sevilla 954 50 13 77) and **NOS** in Granada (958 20 06 02). Information on the gay scene is available in the following publications: *Spartacus España* and *Guía Gay Visado*.

## Health

Travellers from the EU should obtain an E111 form before they travel (or have one sent or faxed over within four days of treatment), which entitles them to free basic medical and hospital treatment from any doctor or hospital within the Spanish health system (you may still have to pay for many medicines, however). The form is available from post offices in the UK. Note that the European Commission is planning to issue a European Health Insurance Card (due to be launched in late 2004), which would replace the E111 form and is intended to speed up the paperwork.

However, all travellers are strongly advised to take out comprehensive travel health insurance that will cover medical costs and repatriation, if required.

In a non-emergency, be aware that pharmacists are very well-informed and can often offer advice for minor complaints and injuries (*see below*).

**In a medical emergency, call 112.**

## Contraception

Condoms (*condones* or *preservativos*) can be bought from pharmacies and from vending machines inside the toilets of some bars. The female contraceptive pill (*la píldora*) can be bought at most pharmacies without prescription, but female travellers are advised to bring their own supply with them. Local doctors are also able to write prescriptions for the pill, although you'll have to pay for the consultation. If you need a pregnancy-test kit, ask in a pharmacy for *un test de embarazo*; for the morning-after pill, ask for *una píldora del día siguiente*.

## Doctors & dentists

Medical treatment covered by the E111 reciprocal health agreement is only provided by practitioners within the Spanish national health service, and in some parts of rural Andalucía you may have to travel some distance to attend a participating surgery (*consultorio*), health centre (*centro sanitario*) or hospital clinic (*ambulatorio*). If you require treatment, you will need to have a photocopy of your E111 form available to give to the doctor. Anyone without an E111 form who gets medical treatment in Spain (including all non-EU visitors) will need a doctor's signature in order to make an insurance claim. Dental treatment is not usually free of charge and you are unlikely to be able to claim back the costs unless you have comprehensive travel health insurance.

In Spain, doctors, health centres and hospitals have separate surgery times for private patients. If you are asked to pay for treatment, be aware that you are not being treated under the health service and that your E111

will not be accepted. If you need to call out a doctor in an emergency, make it clear that you have an E111 and you want to be treated under the EU arrangements.

## Hospitals

Urgent medical treatment is free at a public hospital for EU citizens who can present a valid E111 form. Other patients will be charged. For addresses of hospitals in major towns and cities in Andalucía, see under 'Resources' at the ends of the relevant chapters of this guide.

## Opticians

You can get a replacement pair of spectacles or order new contact lenses at any opticians (*optica*) as long as you bring along your prescription.

## Pharmacies

*Farmacias*, denoted by an illuminated green cross, can be found in most villages and all towns and cities. Pharmacists are highly knowledgeable and will often be able to save you a trip to the doctor. Pharmacies are usually open 10am to 2pm and 5pm to 8pm Monday to Saturday, but also operate a rota system so there is always one in the vicinity that is open 24 hours, as listed at the back of the local paper under '*Farmacias de guardia*'.

## Prescriptions

Holders of an E111 will be expected to pay up to 40 per cent of the cost of a prescription unless they are a pensioner, in which case it is free. All other visitors have to pay full prescription charges.

## STDs, HIV & AIDS

Spain has the highest number of AIDS cases and deaths in the EU, according to UN statistics. Most cases are caused by the use of infected needles by drug abusers, rather than by sexual contact. The national AIDS helpline can provide further information in English (freephone 900 11 10 00). There is also an Andalucía helpline (freephone 900 85 01 00, Spanish only, calls taken 10am-2pm Mon-Fri).

## Helplines

These are official lines run by the Junta de Andalucía and are likely to be in Spanish only. Numbers prefixed with 900 can be dialled free of charge.

**Child abuse** 900 21 09 66.
**Drug addiction** 900 16 15 15.
**Drugs** 900 84 50 40.
**Elderly** 900 22 22 23.
**General emergencies** 902 50 50 61.
**Teenage/juvenile** 900 23 22 32.
**Women** 900 20 09 99.

## ID

You are meant to carry some form of ID with you at all times in Spain; the Spanish have identity cards but a passport is ideal for most foreign visitors. If you are stopped by the police and are not carrying valid ID, you will probably get a warning, although you may be liable to an on-the-spot fine. Valid ID (passport) is essential when checking into a hotel, hiring a car, exchanging, or paying with, travellers' cheques and collecting poste restante.

## Insurance

All travellers should take out personal travel insurance to cover trip cancellation, emergency medical costs and

loss or theft of baggage, money or travellers' cheques. If you're planning on taking part in horse riding, skiing, scuba diving, moutaineering or paragliding, for example, you should also consider additional 'dangerous sports' cover. Keep a record of your policy number and the emergency telephone number with you.

## Internet

You'll have little difficulty finding an internet café; often even small villages have web facilities. The bigger towns and cities are full of them, so prices tend to be reasonable. See the 'Resources' section at the end of relevant chapters in this guide. Many hotels and even *hostales* have a web page, often with online booking facilities, but only the bigger establishments are likely to have online computers for guest use and the prices will be high.

Many ISPs (such as Wanadoo, 902 01 19 02, www.wanadoo.es) offer free basic access, while others (like Auna, 902 50 00 60, www.auna.com) give a slightly better service for a monthly fee.

For useful websites on Andalucía, *see p329*.

## Left luggage

*Consignas* are available at most bus and train stations and airports for a few euros a day.

## Legal help

Consulates (*see p316*) can assist tourists in emergencies, and provide a list of English-speaking lawyers/interpreters.

## Libraries

Municipal libraries are open 9am to 9pm Monday to Friday and 9am to 2pm on Saturday.

### Almería
**Biblioteca Pública del Estado Francisco Villaespesa**
*C/Hermanos Machado s/n (950 23 03 75).*

### Cádiz
**Biblioteca Pública Municipal**
*Avenida San Severiano s/n (956 25 18 94).*

**Biblioteca Pública Municipal José Celestino Mutis** *C/San Miguel 17 (956 22 61 56).*

### Córdoba
**Biblioteca Pública Municipal**
*C/Amador de los Ríos s/n (957 47 55 56).*

### Granada
**Biblioteca de Andalucía**
*C/Profesor Sainz Cantero 6 (958 02 69 00).*

**Biblioteca Pública Municipal**
*C/Profesor Cantero 6 (958 27 28 93).*

### Huelva
**Biblioteca Pública Municipal**
*Avenida Martin Alonso Pinzón 16 (959 28 35 29).*

### Jaén
**Biblioteca Pública del Estado**
*C/Santo Reino 1 (953 22 39 50).*

### Málaga
**Biblioteca Pública del Estado**
*Avenida Europa 49 (952 34 49 44).*

### Sevilla
**Biblioteca Pública Municipal**
*Avenida de Maria Luisa 8 (954 62 20 29).*

## Lost property

If you lose something in your hotel, report it to the concierge. There are lost property offices at most train or bus stations and at airports. If you lose something outside these areas, go to your nearest police station (see 'Resources' at the end of the relevant chapter in this guide).

## Maps

All *turismos* (tourist offices) supply free city-centre maps that list the main sights.

# Emergencies

In any emergency situation, call the **Servicios de Urgencias** on **112**; multi-lingual operators will connect you to the police, fire or ambulance services, as required.

**Directory**

Regional *turismos* stock maps of the province. If you plan on driving, get the Michelin Andalucía map (no.578) (though make sure it's the most recent edition as many major roads were renumbered in 2004; *see p310*). Walkers should consult the website www.barrabes.com, which sells walking and hiking maps for specific areas. Of the topographical maps available, the most reliable are those produced by SGE (Servicio Geográfico del Ejército). The Spanish Cycling Federation publishes cycling route maps on its website (www.rfec.com).

## Media

### Newspapers & magazines

In Spain newspapers and magazines are sold from *kioscos* – kiosks on the street. The Spanish press is generally serious and pretty dry; you won't find anything equivalent to the British tabloids. This may well account for the low circulations of most newspapers and for the fact that Spaniards tend to rely on the radio for their news.

The biggest seller on a national level, with a circulation of about 400,000, is the left-of-centre *El País*, which has the best foreign coverage and political analysis. The regional edition has a daily Andalucía supplement inside. *El Mundo* and *Diario 16* are both good centrist alternatives, while *ABC* is solidly conservative and reactionary.

The cities each have their own newspaper: *Diario de Sevilla*, *Diario de Cádiz*, *Diario de Córdoba*, *Ideal* (Granada) and *Sur* (Málaga). All of these have excellent listings and are particularly useful during big festivals, when they run supplements that include route maps and details of the events.

*Sur* also publishes a good English edition with local news, which is useful for classifieds.

There are numerous expat-orientated newspapers and magazines along the Costa del Sol, which carry little news but lots of property ads. Among them are *The Entertainer*, *Lookout* and *Marbella Life*. Many British newspapers also print a Spanish edition, which is distributed in the resorts of the Costa del Sol. Otherwise, many British and US newspapers are available the same day in the larger cities, and the following day in smaller towns.

Celebrity gossip is confined to the magazines – in fact, Spain pioneered the genre with the sycophantic glitz of *¡HOLA!*. Parents should note that Spain's laissez-faire attitude towards pornography means that you will find hard-core porn magazines next to *National Geographic* and within easy reach of children.

## Radio

The Spanish are avid radio fans; you'll hear radios blaring out in bars, cafés, buses and taxis. **Radio Nacional de España** is the main public broadcaster, with four stations. The main commercial broadcaster is **SER** (Sociedad Española de Radiofusión), which controls four networks: SER, a news network, and music channels. There are an enormous number of talk radio-style stations with endless discussions about current affairs.

For music, by far the best station is, surprisingly, state-owned **Radio 3** on 99.0 FM, which plays a fantastically eclectic range of rock, pop, jazz, hip hop, blues and world music. Otherwise, for pop there are **Onda Cero** and **Cadena Cuarenta**, which play about two Spanish songs to every three English-language ones

and are full of ad breaks. **Radio Olé** is fun for flamenco, and **Radio Clasical** is a relaxing alternative. The official local radio station in Andalucía is **Canal Sur**.

Along the Costa del Sol you'll also find a few English channels, and as you approach Gibraltar you will be able to pick up British forces radio and **Radio Gibraltar** – each as dire as the other. US forces radio can be picked up further west, around Rota.

## Television

Spanish television is shockingly poor, but you'll find it dominating almost every bar or café you visit. There are five main channels, which pump out an endless diet of tacky game shows, talk shows, really bad imported *telenovelas* (soaps) from South America and badly dubbed American movies. Just about the only redeeming feature is the news, while **Canal 2** does show some good documentaries and films. Andalucía also has its own regional channel, **Canal Sur**, which shows plenty of bullfighting action during the season.

In most three-star-or-above hotels you should be able to get BBC World and CNN. Cable channel Canal Plus offers premium sport and music.

## Money

Spain is part of the euro zone. Each euro (€) is divided into 100 cents (¢), known as *centimos* in Spain. Notes come in denominations of €500, €200, €100, €50, €20, €10 and €5. Coins come in denominations of €2, €1, 50 cents, 20 cents, 10 cents, 5 cents, 2 cents and 1 cent. Euro travellers' cheques are widely accepted. In Gibraltar the pound is still legal tender but you will find that most tourist outlets also accept the euro.

**Directory**

## ATMs

Almost every bank has an ATM (Automated Teller Machine) that can be used to withdraw cash. ATMs accept most credit cards as well as debit cards that display the Cirrus symbol and they are usually the most convenient way to get hold of local currency. For both credit and debit cards you will need a valid PIN number in order to withdraw money. Your card issuer is likely to charge you a fee for using an ATM abroad.

## Banks

You will find a bank in even the tiniest rural community, usually with an ATM. Banks invariably offer better rates of exchange than bureaux de change. For opening hours, *see below*.

## Credit cards

Credit cards, especially MasterCard and Visa, will be accepted in all major hotels and many upmarket restaurants in Andalucía, as well as in supermarkets and petrol stations. Note that, restaurants excepted, you may be asked to show your passport or driving licence when paying by credit card. However, smaller shops, bars, *hostales* and restaurants in rural areas are unlikely to have credit card facilities. If your card has a Maestro symbol, you can use it as payment in shops and hotels.

## Tax

Value-added tax (IVA) at seven per cent is included in the price of all consumer goods and will be added on to the total bill in hotels and restaurants. (Be aware that it is often not included in initial quotes for rates in hotels.) IVA is non-recoverable for EU citizens. Visitors residing outside the EU should pick up a form at the airport and keep all receipts in order to get an IVA refund.

## Natural hazards

● In summer beware the strength of the sun and temperatures that can reach 50°C (122°F) inland.
● In the mountains, watch out for rockfalls, flash flooding and avalanches in the winter.
● If you are swimming, beware the strong currents in the Strait of Gibraltar.
● Take extreme care not to walk through a field of *toros bravos* (fighting bulls), especially during mating season. Look out for signs reading *¡Peligro!* (danger) or *¡No Pasar!* (no entry).
● Beware semi-wild dogs in rougher parts of the cities, in small villages and on farmland.
● Mosquitoes can be a problem in low-lying areas, especially in the Doñana National Park, and around inland reservoirs when it's warm or muggy.

## Opening hours

### Banks

Opening hours are 9am to 2pm Monday to Friday. Banks in towns and cities are also open 9am to 1pm on Saturdays from October to April.

### Bars & cafés

Bars and cafés usually open at about lunchtime and stay open until midnight or 1am. Some cafés may open as early as 5.30am or 6am, depending on their clientele. *Bares de copas*, where the emphasis is more on drinking, rarely open before 7pm and may continue serving until 4am. *Discoteca*-bars start later still and do not close until after dawn at 6/7am.

### Museums & monuments

Opening hours vary, although a siesta period in the afternoon is not uncommon. Most sights are also closed on a Monday.

### Post offices

*Correos* are open from 8am to noon and again from 5pm to 7.30pm, although the ones in big cities do not close in the afternoon. Some offices are also open on Saturdays.

## Restaurants

Restaurants are generally open from 1/2pm until 4/5pm and again from 8/9pm until midnight/1am at weekends. In tourist areas along the coast UK opening hours will apply. Note: most restaurants have a *día de descanso* (rest day), usually Monday or Wednesday and sometimes Sunday evening. Away from the coast they may close for the holidays in August (*cerrado por vacaciones*).

## Shops

Most shops are open from about 9.30/10am until 1/2pm, when they close for a siesta until 5pm. In the evening they stay open until 8pm. Some smaller shops such as bakers (*panadería*) and greengrocers (*frutería*) will open much earlier, at 7/8am, and big department stores and supermarkets stay open all day, sometimes until 10pm.

## Police & crime

There are three types of police in Spain: the *policía municipal* operate on a city or town level, directing traffic and dealing with intra-urban crime; the *policía nacional*, who wear brown uniforms, patrol the areas outside the cities; while the *Guardia Civil* spend most of their time on highway patrol handing out speeding tickets. The *Guardia Civil* were once the most feared men in uniform in Spain, acting as Franco's private police force, but they're not so scary these days.

## Postal services

For opening hours, *see above*. There is usually just one post office per urban area, often characterised by endless queues, so if you are only after stamps (*sellos*) you are better off going to a tobacconist (*estanco*), which is recognisable by its brown and yellow *tabacos* sign.

Stamps for letters and postcards up to 20g (1oz) cost 27¢ within Spain, 52¢ within the EU and 77¢ for other international destinations. For items between 20g and 50g (2oz) the costs rise to 40¢, €1.18 and €1.66 respectively.

**Directory**

Post can take days just to go to the next town. Airmail within Europe takes at least five days, but often longer; to a destination outside Europe it takes at least ten days.

## Poste restante

Poste restante is available at any post office. Letters should be addressed to the recipient at '*Lista de correos*'. You will need your passport to collect your post. American Express offers the same service.

## Religion

Andalucía is a strongly Catholic region – certainly the strongest in Spain – and Sunday church services are well attended. However, as elsewhere in Europe, church-going is dominated by the older generation.

It is also worth noting that religious festivals, such as Semana Santa and the *romerías*, are almost pagan in their idol worship, with the emphasis more on ritual than on the actual tenets of Catholicism.

Having said that, some aspects of the Catholic doctrine are still quite closely adhered to in Andalucía, including no sex before marriage or, in the Spanish variation, sex only with the person you are going to marry.

## Safety & security

Serious crime is rare in Andalucía, although drug-related crime is on the increase. Petty crimes such as bag-snatching, pickpocketing and opportunistic theft are also on the rise, particularly in Sevilla and Granada cities. For this reason you should take reasonable precautions when you're out and about:

● Don't flash around wads of cash or indeed carry a lot of cash on your person; lock it in your hotel safe instead.

● Conceal cameras and other valuables.
● Keep a tight grip on your handbag, both when walking and when sitting in a café or restaurant. (A good tip is to slip the strap of your bag under your chair leg.)

Theft from hotel rooms is more common in cities in the lower-end establishments. Again, it generally tends to be opportunistic, so don't leave mobiles or wallets lying around when you leave your room. Either put them in the safe or give them to the hotel reception for safe-keeping.

Cars are vulnerable when parked, or in stationary traffic with the window open, when scooter riders can snatch belongings from the passenger seat. Overnight, try and park in a hotel garage or a patrolled public garage.

If you are the victim of a theft, report it at the nearest police station. You're unlikely to ever see your bag or camera again, but you'll need the police report in order to make an insurance claim. Be warned: the police rarely speak English, especially in rural areas, and the form-filling (which is likely to be in Spanish) takes ages.

If you have your passport and/or all your cash and credit cards stolen, contact your nearest consulate (*see p316*).

## Smoking

Cigarettes in Spain – both international and local brands – are extremely cheap by UK standards and attitudes towards lighting up are relaxed. The only places you'll find no-smoking areas are on public transport and in parts of the airports. If you are a non-smoker, some hotels have no-smoking floors and some smarter restaurants have designated areas. If you ask for a no-smoking room, it might mean no more than that the staff remove the ashtray.

## Study

If you want to learn Spanish in Spain, check out the **Instituto Cervantes** website (eee.cervantes.es). This provides a full list of the courses on offer in Spain. You'll also find links to language schools at www.andalucia. com/language/schools.htm.

## Universities

The Erasmus student exchange scheme and Lingua project are the main parts of the EU's Socrates programme to help students move between member states. Interested students should contact the Erasmus co-ordinator at their home college. Information is available in the UK from the **UK Socrates-Erasmus Council**, R&D Building, Kent University, Canterbury, Kent, CT2 7PD (01227 762712/ erasmus@ukc.ac.uk).

**Universidad de Almería** *Carretera Sacramento s/n, La Cañada de San Urbano, Almería (950 01 50 00/www.ual.es).*
**Universidad de Cádiz** *C/Ancha 16, Cádiz (956 01 50 00/www.uca.es).*
**Universidad de Córdoba** *C/Alfonso XIII 13, Córdoba (957 21 80 36/www.uco.es).*
**Universidad de Granada** *C/Cuesta del Hospicio s/n, Hospital Real, Granada (958 24 30 03/ www.ugr.es).*
**Universidad de Huelva** *C/Doctor Cantero Cuadrado 6, Huelva (959 01 81 02/www.uhu.es).*
**Universidad de Jaén** *Campus Las Lagunillas s/n, Jaén (953 01 21 21/ www.ujaen.es).*
**Universidad de Málaga** *Avenida de Cervantes 2, Málaga (952 13 10 00/www.uma.es).*
**Universidad de Sevilla** *C/San Fernando 4, Sevilla (954 55 10 00/ www.us.es).*
**Universidad Pablo de Olavide** *A376, km1, Sevilla (954 34 92 00/ www.upo.es).*

## Telephones

The Spanish phone network (Telefónica) is efficient and fairly cheap.

## Dialling & codes

Telephone numbers in Andalucía consist of nine numerals, divided into the three-figure area code and then six numbers. When calling a number in Spain you always need to dial the area code, even if you are phoning from within that region.

### To phone Spain from abroad

Dial the international access code (0011 from Australia; 00 from Ireland, New Zealand and the UK; 011 from the USA and Canada), followed by the country code for Spain (34), followed by the area code and the number.

### To make international calls from Spain

To call abroad from Spain, dial '00' plus the international country code (Australia 61, Ireland 353, New Zealand 64, UK 44, USA & Canada 1), area code and number. Remember to omit the initial '0' from the area code.

To phone Gibraltar from anywhere in Andalucía except Cádiz province dial 956 7; from Cádiz province dial just 7.

## Public phones

It's much cheaper to make a call from a phone box than from a hotel. There are plenty of phone boxes in towns and villages; most will take coins (you'll need a fistful) and phonecards (*tarjeta telefónica*). Phonecards are the simplest option and can be bought at most *kioscos* (kiosks) and *estancos* (tobacconists) as well as from phone shops. Many bars also have pay phones.

To make a call from a public phone, lift the receiver, insert the card or coins, then dial the number (including the area code). If you wish to make another call and you have change left, press the 'R' button and dial again rather than hanging up.

You can also make calls from *locutorios*, which are small rooms full of phone booths where you sit down to talk and pay at the end. These often double as internet cafés and you can also send a fax from here. Faxes may also be sent from hotels and stationery shops (*papelerías*).

## Operator services

In most phone boxes operator services will be denoted by little buttons with signs on the main phone panel. You will usually have to insert a coin even to make a free call, although it will be returned when you hang up. English is not commonly spoken or understood by Spanish phone operators, although English is spoken by international operators and international directory enquiries.

### Useful numbers

**National operator** 1009.
**National directory enquiries** 1003.
**Operator for calls to EU** 1008.
**International operator** 1005 (call for international reverse-charge/collect calls, other than to Europe and North Africa, in which case you call 1008).
**International directory enquiries** 11825.
**Weather reports** 807 17 03 65.
**Speaking clock** 093.

## Telephone directories

These can occasionally be found in phone boxes but more often you will find them in *locutorios* or post offices.

## Mobile phones

Most European mobile phones (*moviles*) work in Spain but be warned that even if you are making a local call you will be charged at international roaming rates. You will also be charged for incoming calls. Contact your service provider for details. US handsets are not GSM compatible and will not work in Europe.

If you plan on being in Andalucía for more than a few weeks, you might be better off buying a pay-as-you-go package when you arrive for around €80 and then top-up cards. Spanish service providers include Vodafone (607 123 000), Amena (1474) and Movistar (1485).

## Time

Spain is an hour ahead of Greenwich Mean Time and six hours ahead of Eastern Standard Time. The clocks go back in the last week of October and forward in the last week of March.

## Tipping

Waiter service is generally charged at ten per cent and is rarely included in the bill except in smarter restaurants. The service charge is not obligatory, however, and if you have had poor service don't feel you have to pay. Many Spaniards do no more than round bills up.

You are not expected to tip at the bar but you might wish to if the same barman has served you all evening. Taxi drivers expect a small tip for longer journeys. Hotel staff don't rely on tips to supplement their wage and will not expect them. Having said that, it is perfectly acceptable to reward particularly good service.

## Toilets

In bars and restaurants toilets can be pretty basic, though often they're perfectly acceptable. They tend to be less private than in the UK or USA, with sometimes just one door rather than two giving on to the facilities. In rural areas women are advised to bring their own toilet paper with

**Directory**

them. Public toilets are rare and generally not well maintained, but most bars are happy to let you use their facilities.

Toilets are known as *servicios, aseos, baños* or *lavabos*, and are usually denoted by 'S' or 'D' for ladies (*señoras* or *damas*) and 'C' for gentlemen (*caballeros*). Sometimes, however, you'll find an S on both doors, denoting *señoras* and *señores*.

## Tourist information

Andalucía is well geared up for tourists and has an excellent network of tourist offices (*turismos*) run by the Junta de Andalucía, even in the smallest places (for details, see the end of relevant area chapters under 'Resources').

Tourist office staff are usually helpful, though, out of the main tourist areas, they may only speak a little English. As well as supplying (usually free) maps and pamphlets with information on the local area, they can also help you find accommodation and provide lists of hotels and restaurants.

In towns and cities *turismos* open throughout the day and at weekends. In villages they often close for siesta and at weekends. Out of season, village and resort *turismos* may operate a winter timetable with reduced hours.

If there is no actual tourist office in the place you are visiting, try the *Ayuntamiento* (town hall), which should be able to supply you with basic information and maps.

For tourist information before you leave your own country, contact your local Spanish National Tourist Office (SNTO).

### Spanish tourist offices abroad

**Australia** *Spanish Tourism Promotions, Level 1, 178 Collins Street, Melbourne (03 9650 7377).*

**Canada** *SNTO, 2 Bloor Street West, 34th floor, Toronto, Ontario M4W 3E2 (1-416 961 3131).*
**UK** *SNTO, 22-3 Manchester Square Gardens, London W1M 5AP (020 7486 8077).*
**USA** *OK Spain, 8383 Wilshire Boulevard, Suite 960, Beverley Hills, CA 90211 (1-323 658 7188/ www.okspain.org); Water Tower Place, Suite 915 East, 845 North Michigan Avenue, Chicago, IL 60611 (312 642 1992); 1211 Brickell Avenue, Miami, FL 33131 (305 358 1992); 666 Fifth Avenue, New York, NY 10103 (212 265 8822).*

## Visas & immigration

If you are a citizen of an EU country, the USA, Canada, Australia or New Zealand, you do not need a visa to enter the country and for stays of up to 90 days. For longer stays, citizens of EU countries no longer require a residency permit, but it is advisable to register with your local *Ayuntamiento* (town hall).

Visa requirements are subject to change, so check the latest information with your country's Spanish embassy before leaving home.

## Weights & measures

Spain uses the metric system.

### Conversions

1 kilometre (km) = 0.62 miles
1 metre (m) = 3.28 feet
1 litre (l) = 1.76 UK pints/
2.12 US pints
10 grams (g) = 0.35 ounces
1 kilogram (kg) = 2.2 pounds
(9/5 Celsius temperature) +32 =
temperature in Fahrenheit

## What to take

There's likely to be very little you need to bring from home that you can't get in Andalucía.

## When to go

The best time to visit Andalucía is in the spring when the blossom is out, the sun is not too fierce and the fiesta season is just beginning. At this time, prices (except during Semana Santa and the Feria de Abril) are still low but the weather is often warm enough to enjoy a beach holiday. Inland, however, it can still be a bit damp and chilly, so come prepared.

From mid June prices and temperatures rise steeply and by July and August Andalucía is a furnace. Villages empty as people head for the coast, which becomes packed. If you are touring inland at this time, you may find many places closed as Spaniards tend to take their main holiday in August.

By mid September high season is officially over and prices and temperatures start to fall. This is a good time to visit as the fine, mild weather often stretches into late October.

November to February is officially Andalucía's winter but on the coast it's often more like a mild English summer. Inland it's a different matter, though, especially in the hills where sub-zero temperatures are not uncommon. This is also the rainy season and sudden downpours after months of near drought can lead to flash floods. The Sierra Nevada gets its snow at this time and the ski season begins.

## Climate

Andalucía enjoys one of the mildest climates in Europe with a year-round average temperature of 18-20°C (64-68°F) on the coast and an average of over 300 days sunshine throughout the year. For average monthly temperatures around the region, *see p325* **Weather**.

## Public holidays

The Spanish enjoy more public holidays than any other country in Europe. In Andalucía there are also holidays specific to the region and, of course, local fiestas. If a holiday falls midweek, the Spanish will often take the following day(s) as holiday, too, turning it into a long weekend. On national and regional holidays banks, post offices and public buildings close down and many museums and monuments operate Sunday opening times. Note, too, that many Spaniards take off the whole of August as holiday and that many restaurants and shops away from the resorts will close for the whole month. Gibraltar follows the UK holidays with a couple more thrown in for good measure.

## Public holidays
### ... in Andalucía
**1 Jan** *Año Nuevo* (New Year's Day)
**6 Jan** *Epifanía* (Epiphany)
**28 Feb** *Día de Andalucía* (Andalucía Day)
**Mar/Apr** *Jueves Santo* (Maundy Thursday; 24 Mar 2005; 13 Apr 2006)
**Mar/Apr** *Viernes Santo* (Good Friday; 25 Mar 2005; 14 Apr 2006)
**1 May** *Día del Trabajo* (Labour Day)
**25 July** *Día de Santiago* (St James's Day)
**15 Aug** *Asunción* (Assumption)
**12 Oct** *Día de la Hispanidad* (Columbus Day)
**1 Nov** *Todos los Santos* (All Saints' Day)
**6 Dec** *Día de la Constitución* (Constitution Day)
**8 Dec** *Inmaculada Concepción* (Immaculate Conception)
**25 Dec** *Navidad* (Christmas Day)

### ... in Gibraltar
**1 Jan** New Year's Day
**2nd Mon in Mar** Commonwealth Day (14 Mar 2005; 13 Mar 2006)
**Mar/Apr** Good Friday (25 Mar 2005; 14 Apr 2006)
**Mar/Apr** Easter Monday (28 Mar 2005; 17 Apr 2006)
**1st Mon in May** May Day Bank Holiday (2 May 2005; 1 May 2006)
**Last Mon in May** Late Spring Bank Holiday (30 May 2005; 29 May 2006)
**11 June** Queen's Birthday
**Last Mon in Aug** Late Summer Bank Holiday (29 Aug 2005; 28 Aug 2006)
**10 Sept** Gibraltar Day
**25-26 Dec** Christmas Day & Boxing Day

## Women

Attitudes towards women in the south of Spain would probably be considered fairly macho compared to the rest of Europe. However, as a tourist you are unlikely to encounter any more harassment than you would at home. The most irritating thing is probably the staring, especially if you are tall and/or blonde. Women encounter few problems travelling solo; you may be approached if you are on your own in a bar or café, but if you make it clear you are not interested, you are likely to be left alone. Sex crimes are very rare compared to the UK and the USA, but use your common

sense. As in the res[...] some areas of major c[...] as ports or red-light dis[...] are best avoided at night.[...]

## Working in Andalucía

Citizens of EU countries have the right to live, work and study in Spain for an indefinite period without having to apply for residency. If you want to make a voluntary application for a *tarjeta de residencia* (residency permit) for any reason, you should be able to do so at any police station.

People from countries outside the EU, however, will need to get a special visa from a Spanish consulate in your home country; this can be a lengthy process. Contact the consulate for further information.

By far the easiest and most usual way of finding work in Andalucía is as an English teacher. The smallest town will often have an *academia de Inglés* and the cities each have numerous language schools. You do not even have to speak Spanish to become an English teacher (many schools prefer it, in fact, if you don't) but most want you to have a TEFL qualification (Teaching English as a Foreign Language).

# Weather

Average daytime temperatures (minimum/maximum in °C)

|       | Almería | Cádiz | Córdoba | Granada | Huelva | Jaén  | Málaga | Sevilla |
|-------|---------|-------|---------|---------|--------|-------|--------|---------|
| Jan   | 8/16    | 8/15  | 4/14    | 1/12    | 6/16   | 5/12  | 8/16   | 6/15    |
| Feb   | 8/16    | 9/16  | 5/16    | 2/14    | 7/18   | 5/14  | 8/17   | 6/17    |
| Mar   | 10/18   | 11/18 | 8/19    | 5/18    | 9/20   | 8/17  | 10/19  | 9/20    |
| Apr   | 12/20   | 12/21 | 10/23   | 7/20    | 11/22  | 10/20 | 11/21  | 11/23   |
| May   | 15/22   | 14/23 | 13/26   | 9/24    | 13/25  | 13/24 | 14/24  | 13/26   |
| June  | 18/26   | 18/27 | 17/32   | 14/30   | 16/29  | 17/30 | 17/28  | 17/32   |
| July  | 21/29   | 20/29 | 19/36   | 17/34   | 18/32  | 21/34 | 20/30  | 20/36   |
| Aug   | 22/29   | 20/30 | 20/36   | 17/34   | 18/32  | 21/34 | 20/30  | 20/36   |
| Sept  | 20/27   | 19/27 | 17/31   | 14/29   | 17/29  | 18/29 | 18/28  | 18/32   |
| Oct   | 16/23   | 16/23 | 13/24   | 9/22    | 14/25  | 13/22 | 15/24  | 14/26   |
| Nov   | 12/19   | 12/19 | 8/19    | 5/17    | 10/21  | 9/16  | 12/20  | 10/20   |
| Dec   | 9/17    | 9/16  | 5/14    | 2/12    | 7/17   | 5/12  | 9/17   | 7/16    |

...he time, but, as
a foreigner it's wise to use the
more polite *usted* with people
you do not know, and certainly
with anyone over 50. In the
phrases listed here all verbs
are given in the *usted* form.

For help with a Spanish
menu, *see p40* **Menu glossary**.

## Pronunciation

**c**, before an **i** or an **e**, and **z** are like
th in **thin** (though in Andalucia, it is
more commonly pronounced as an 's')
**c** in all other cases is as in **cat**
**g**, before an **i** or an **e**, and **j** are
pronounced with a guttural **h**-sound
that does not exist in English – like
ch in Scottish lo**ch**, but much harder
**g** in all other cases is pronounced
as in **get**
**h** at the beginning of a word is
normally silent
**ll** is pronounced almost like a **y**
**ñ** is like **ny** in ca**ny**on
a single **r** at the beginning of a word
and **rr** elsewhere are heavily rolled

### STRESS RULES

In words ending with a vowel, **n** or **s**,
the penultimate syllable is stressed:
eg ba**ra**to, **vi**ven.

In words ending with any other
consonant, the last syllable is
stressed: eg exte**rior**, universi**dad**.

An accent marks the stressed
syllable in words that depart from
these rules: eg esta**ción**, **tó**nica.

## Basics

**hello** *hola*; **hello** (on the phone)
*hola, diga*
**good morning, good day**
*buenos días*; **good afternoon,**
**good evening** *buenas tardes*; **good**
**evening** (after dark), **good night**
*buenas noches*; **goodbye/see you**
**later** *adiós/hasta luego*
**please** *por favor*; **thank you**
**(very much)** *(muchas) gracias*
**you're welcome** *de nada*
**do you speak English?** *¿habla*
*inglés?*; **I don't speak Spanish**
*no hablo español*
**I don't understand** *no entiendo*
**what's your name?** *¿cómo se llama?*
**speak more slowly, please** *hable*
*más despacio, por favor*

**wait a moment** *espere un momento*
**Sir/Mr** *señor (sr)*; **Madam/Mrs**
*señora (sra)*; **Miss** *señorita (srta)*
**excuse me/sorry** *perdón*
**excuse me, please** *oiga* (the
standard way to attract someone's
attention, politely; literally 'hear me')
**OK/fine/**(or to a waiter) **that's**
**enough** *vale*
**where is...?** *¿dónde está...?*
**why?** *¿porqué?*; **when?** *¿cuándo?*;
**who?** *¿quién?*; **what?** *¿qué?*;
**where?** *¿dónde?*; **how?** *¿cómo?*
**is/are there any...?** *¿hay...?*
**very** *muy*; **and** *y*; **or** *o*; **with** *con*;
**without** *sin*
**open** *abierto*; **closed** *cerrado*
**what time does it open/close?**
*¿a qué hora abre/cierra?*
**pull** (on signs) *tirar*; **push** *empujar*
**I would like...** *quiero...* (literally,
'I want...'); **how many would**
**you like?** *¿cuántos quiere?*
**I like** *me gusta*; **I don't like** *no*
*me gusta*
**good** *bueno/a*; **bad** *malo/a*;
**well/badly** *bien/mal*; **small**
*pequeño/a*; **big** *gran, grande*;
**expensive** *caro/a*; **cheap** *barato/a*;
**hot** (food, drink) *caliente*; **cold** *frío/a*
**something** *algo*; **nothing** *nada*
**more/less** *más/menos*
**the bill/check, please** *la cuenta,*
*por favor*
**how much is it?** *¿cuánto es?*
**do you have change?** *¿tiene cambio?*
**price** *precio*; **free** *gratis*; **discount**
*descuento*; **bank** *banco*; **to rent**
*alquilar*; **(for) rent, rental** *(en)*
*alquiler*; **post office** *correos*;
**stamp** *sello*; **postcard** *postal*;
**toilet** *los servicios*

## Getting around

**airport** *aeropuerto*; **railway station**
*estación de ferrocarril/estación de*
*RENFE* (Spanish Railways)
**entrance** *entrada*; **exit** *salida*;
**car** *coche*; **bus** *autobús*; **train** *tren*;
**a ticket** *un billete*; **return** *de ida y*
*vuelta*; **bus stop** *parada de autobús*;
**the next stop** *la próxima parada*
**excuse me, do you know the**
**way to...?** *¿oiga, señor/señora,*
*sabe como llegar a...?*
**left** *izquierda*; **right** *derecha*; **here**
*aquí*; **there** *allí*; **straight on** *recto*;
**to the end of the street** *al final*
*de la calle*; **as far as** *hasta*; **towards**
*hacia*; **near** *cerca*; **far** *lejos*

## Accommodation

**do you have a double (single)**
**room for tonight (one week)?**
*¿tiene una habitación doble (para*
*una persona) para esta noche*
*(una semana)?*

**where is the car park?** *¿dónde*
*está el parking?*
**we have a reservation**
*tenemos reserva*
**an inside/outside room**
*una habitación interior/exterior*;
**with/without bathroom** *con/sin*
*baño*; **shower** *ducha*; **double bed**
*cama de matrimonio*; **with twin**
**beds** *con dos camas*; **breakfast**
**included** *desayuno incluido*;
**air-conditioning** *aire*
*acondicionado*; **lift** *ascensor*;
**swimming pool** *piscina*

## Time

**morning** *la mañana*; **midday**
*mediodía*; **afternoon/evening**
*la tarde*; **night** *la noche*; **late**
**night/early morning** (roughly
1-6am) *la madrugada*; **now** *ahora*;
**later** *más tarde*; **yesterday** *ayer*;
**today** *hoy*; **tomorrow** *mañana*;
**tomorrow morning** *mañana por la*
*mañana*; **early** *temprano*; **late** *tarde*;
**delay** *retraso*; **delayed** *retrasado*
**at what time...?** *¿a qué hora...?*
**in an hour** *en una hora*; **the bus**
**will take 2 hours** (to get there) *el*
*autobús tardará dos horas (en llegar)*;
**at 2** *a las dos*; **at 8pm** *a las ocho de*
*la tarde*; **at 1.30** *a la una y media*;
**at 5.15** *a las cinco y cuarto*; **at**
**22.30** *a veintidós treinta*

## Numbers

**0** *cero*; **1** *un, uno, una*; **2** *dos*; **3** *tres*;
**4** *cuatro*; **5** *cinco*; **6** *seis*; **7** *siete*; **8**
*ocho*; **9** *nueve*; **10** *diez*; **11** *once*;
**12** *doce*; **13** *trece*; **14** *catorce*;
**15** *quince*; **16** *dieciséis*; **17** *diecisiete*;
**18** *dieciocho*; **19** *diecinueve*; **20**
*veinte*; **21** *veintiuno*; **22** *veintidós*;
**30** *treinta*; **40** *cuarenta*;
**50** *cincuenta*; **60** *sesenta*; **70** *setenta*;
**80** *ochenta*; **90** *noventa*; **100** *cien*;
**1,000** *mil*; **1,000,000** *un millón*

## Days, months & seasons

**Monday** *lunes*; **Tuesday** *martes*;
**Wednesday** *miércoles*; **Thursday**
*jueves*; **Friday** *viernes*; **Saturday**
*sábado*; **Sunday** *domingo*
**January** *enero*; **February** *febrero*;
**March** *marzo*; **April** *abril*;
**May** *mayo*; **June** *junio*; **July** *julio*;
**August** *agosto*; **September**
*septiembre*; **October** *octubre*;
**November** *noviembre*; **December**
*diciembre*
**spring** *primavera*; **summer** *verano*;
**autumn/fall** *otoño*; **winter** *invierno*

# Glossary

## Architecture

**artesonado** wooden inlaid ceiling of Moorish design
**atalaya** watchtower
**azulejo** glazed ceramic tile
**Churrigueresque** elaborate 17th-/18th-century baroque style named after the Churriguera family of architects and artists
**coro** central part of a church, built for the choir
**Isabelline** ornamental late Gothic style, named after Queen Isabel I.
**mihrab** prayer niche facing towards Mecca in a mosque
**Mozarabic** Christian style developed under Moorish rule
**Mudéjar** Muslim-style of decoration and architecture in Christian buildings
**muqarna** Moorish ceiling ornamentation resembling stalactites
**patio** inner courtyard
**plateresque** ornate, decorative late 15th- and early 16th-century architectural style reminiscent of silverwork (platería)
**puerta** gateway
**reja** window grille
**retablo** carved altarpiece
**rococo** light, florid late-baroque decorative style.
**sacristía/sagrario** sacristy

## Around town

**alameda** tree-lined promenade
**alcazaba** Moorish castle
**alcázar** fortified Moorish palace
**ayuntamiento** town hall
**bar de copas** night-time bar (unlikely to serve tapas)
**barrio** quarter or district
**bodega** wine bar/cellar
**calle** street
**capilla** chapel
**carmen** villa with a garden (used only in Granada)
**cartuja** Carthusian monastery
**casa particular** guesthouse
**castillo** castle

**chiringuito** beachfront seafood eaterie
**colegiata** collegiate church
**convento** convent/monastery
**correos** post office
**ermita** hermitage
**hammam** Moorish bathhouse
**iglesia** church
**judería** Jewish quarter
**medina** Moorish town
**mercado** market
**mezquita** mosque
**monasterio** monastery/convent
**palacio** mansion
**parador** a member of the government-owned chain of luxury hotels
**parroquia** parish church
**paseo** promenade
**peña** semi-private flamenco club
**plaza** square
**plaza de toros** bullring
**plaza mayor** main square
**posada** inn
**puente** bridge
**puerto** port
**turismo** tourist office
**urbanización** housing development

## Culture

**cante jondo** 'deep song'; the most emotionally charged form of flamenco
**corrida de toros** bullfight
**duende** the soul/passion of flamenco
**fería** annual fair
**gitano** gypsy
**juerga** gypsy party
**Junta de Andalucía** regional government
**mantilla** traditional scarf or shawl worn by women to cover the head and shoulders
**matador** principal bullfighter
**matanza** traditional pig slaughter
**paso** float for carrying holy images during Semana Santa processions
**romería** religious procession/pilgrimage
**Semana Santa** Holy Week

**solera** method of blending sherry and brandy
**tablao** flamenco show

## History

**Almohads** Berber Muslims who ruled Andalucía in the late 12th/early 13th centuries
**Almoravids** Berber Muslims who ruled Andalucía in the 11th and 12th centuries
**converso** Jew who converted to Christianity
**Falange** Spanish fascist party
**morisco** baptised Muslim Spaniard who was subject to Christian rule
**mozarabe** Christian Spaniard subject to Moorish rule
**Mudéjar** practising Muslim Spaniard under Christian rule
**reconquista** Christian conquest of southern Spain in the 13th-15th centuries
**los Reyes Católicos** 'The Catholic Kings': Isabel I of Castilla and Fernando V of Aragón
**taifa** small Moorish kingdoms that developed after the fall of the Córdoban Caliphate

## Landscapes

**arroyo** stream
**autovía/autopista** motorway
**barranco** steep gorge
**campiña** flat countryside
**carretera** main road
**cerro** mountain, hill or peak
**ciudad** town or city
**cortijo** rural farmhouse
**coto de caza** hunting reserve
**cuesta** slope/hill
**cueva** cave
**dehesa** partially cleared area of forest
**embalse** reservoir
**latifundio** large estate
**marisma** marshland
**mirador** viewpoint
**pueblo** village
**puerta** mountain pass
**río** river
**sierra** mountain range
**vega** cultivated fertile plain

# Further Reference

## Books

### Fiction

**Alarcón, Pedro de** *The Three-Cornered Hat & Other Stories*
Tales of 18th-century Spanish life by a 19th-century writer born in Guadix, Granada.

**Ali, Tariq** *Shadows of the Pomegranate Tree*
A Granadan family saga set in the last years of the Nasrid Kingdom.

**Barea, Arturo** *The Forging of a Rebel Trilogy (The Forge, The Track, The Clash)*
Covering the war in Morocco and the Civil War.

**Cervantes, Miguel de**
*Don Quijote*
The quintessential Spanish novel.

**Day, Douglas** *Journey of the Wolf*
The experiences of a Civil War fighter who returns 40 years later to his home in the Alpujarras.

**Hemingway, Ernest**
*For Whom the Bell Tolls*
The experiences of a young American volunteer fighting in the Civil War.

**Hewson, David** *Semana Santa*
The Easter celebrations form a vivid backdrop for this crime novel.

**Irving, Washington**
*Tales of the Alhambra*
Fanciful but influential stories and anecdotes inspired by the writer's residence in the Alhambra in the early 19th century.

**Jiménez, Juan Ramon**
*Platero & I*
Lyrical novel by the Nobel Prize-winning poet, which takes the form of conversations between the narrator and his donkey, Platero.

**Maalouf, Amin** *Leo the African*
Evocative historical novel based on the eventful life of a 15th-century Moorish traveller and diplomat, starting with the fall of Granada in 1492.

**Machado, Antonio**
*Juan de Mairena*
Based on the writer's experiences of teaching in Baeza, Jaén.

**Pérez Reverte, Arturo**
*The Seville Communion*
Superior crime tale involving priests and politicians, set in Sevilla.

**Rushdie, Salman**
*The Moor's Last Sigh*
Complex epic that uses the fall of Moorish Granada as the starting point for a multi-faceted account of modern India.

### Food & wine

**Casas, Penelope** *The Foods & Wine of Spain/Tapas: The Little Dishes of Spain*
Comprehensive, readable overviews of Spanish and Andalucian cuisine.

**Jeffs, Julian** *Sherry*
All you need to know about Andalucia's famous drink.

**Luard, Elizabeth**
*Flavours of Andalucia*
Recipes for all the local favourites.

### General reference

**Baird, David** *Inside Andalusia*
A fascinating and perceptive introduction to the region.

**Elms, Roberts** *Spain: A Portrait After the General*
Unromantic, witty look at modern-day Spain.

**Gibson, Ian** *Federico García Lorca/The Assassination of Federico Garcia Lorca/Lorca's Granada*
An in-depth biography; an account of the forces that led to the poet's murder; and an exploration of the city through a series of detailed walks.

**Hooper, John** *The Spaniards*
Authoritative survey of contemporary Spanish life.

**Jacobs, Michael** *Andalucia*
An exemplary overview that reaches far beyond the usual clichés in its entertaining coverage of Andalucía's cultural, historical and sociological background. A useful gazetteer is included.

### History & architecture

**Brenan, Gerald**
*The Spanish Labyrinth*
Study of the background to the Civil War: politics and social history with a personal slant.

**Burckhardt, Titus**
*Moorish Culture in Spain*

A classic study of the 700 years of Moorish dominance in southern Spain.

**Elliot, JH**
*Imperial Spain 1469-1716*
Entertaining, well-written study of the Golden Age Spain.

**Fletcher, Richard**
*Moorish Spain*
Entertaining and provocative introduction to the history of the Moors in Spain.

**Fraser, Ronald** *Blood of Spain*
Oral accounts form the basis of this impressive book on the Civil War.

**Fraser, Ronald** *In Hiding*
Account of the Republican mayor of Mijas, who spent 30 years in hiding following the Civil War.

**Fraser, Ronald** *The Pueblo*
Follows the trials and tribulations of a mountain village on the Costa del Sol in the early 1970s.

**Goodwin, Godfrey** *Islamic Spain*
An architectural guide to the most significant Moorish buildings in Spain.

**Irving, Washington**
*The Conquest of Granada*
The last days of the Nasrid Kingdom as described by the 19th-century American diplomat.

**Irwin, Robert** *The Alhambra*
Arabist Irwin's take on Granada's palace on the hill.

**Jacobs, Michael** *Alhambra*
Beautiful photos and authoritative text in a guide to the most iconic of Andalucia's monuments.

**Preston, Paul** *Concise History of the Spanish Civil War*
Reader-friendly text and striking illustrations provide an excellent guide to Spain's darkest days.

**Watt, WH & Cachia, PA**
*History of Islamic Spain*
The lowdown on al-Andalus.

### Plays & poetry

**Arberry AJ** *Moorish Poetry*
Translations of classic Hispano-Arab verse.

**García Lorca, Federico**
*Romancero Gitano/Three Tragedies/Selected Poems/Poem of the Deep Song*
Works by Andalucia's greatest playwright and poet.

**Directory**

**Machado, Antonio**
*Eighty Poems*
His best-known works, in English.

## Travelogues

**Borrow, George**
*The Bible in Spain*
The amusing, idiosyncratic travels and travails of an unconventional 19th-century salesman.

**Boyd, Alastair** *The Sierras of the South/The Road from Ronda*
Boyd lived in Ronda during the 1960s; these two titles record landscapes and life in the Serranía de Ronda during that time.

**Brenan, Gerald**
*The Face of Spain*
Travels through Franco's Spain in 1949.

**Brenan, Gerald**
*South from Granada*
Superb depiction of the author's isolated life in a small village in the Alpujarras during the 1930s.

**Ford, Richard**
*A Handbook for Travellers in Spain & Readers at Home*
The classic 19th-century guide and travelogue: entertaining, opinionated and erudite.

**Gautier, Théophile**
*A Romantic in Spain*
Lucid and elegant account of a French traveller in 1840s Spain.

**Hemingway, Ernest**
*Death in the Afternoon*
The American's depiction of Spanish bullfighting.

**Hewson, Gerald**
*The Flamencos of Cádiz Bay*
Detailed and unrivalled account of an Englishman learning the flamenco lifestyle.

**Jacobs, Michael**
*The Factory of Light*
Affectionate and perceptive hymn to an obscure yet remarkable village in southern Jaén province.

**Lee, Laurie** *As I Walked Out One Midsummer Morning*
Well-observed trek through Spain on foot just before the Civil War.

**Lee, Laurie** *A Rose for Winter*
Fifteen years on, Lee returns to many of his old 1930s Andalucía haunts in this vivid though slight and sometimes cloying travelogue.

**Stewart, Chris**
*Driving Over Lemons/A Parrot in the Pepper Tree*
Enjoyable good-life-abroad tales of one-time Genesis drummer Stewart's attempt to set up a farm and a new life in the Alpujarras.

**Webster Jason**
*Duende: A Journey in Search of Flamenco/Andalus: Unlocking the Secrets of Moorish Spain*
A rites-of-passage tale following the author from Alicante to Madrid to Granada, and a quest to trace the influence of the Moors in modern Spain.

## Walking & nature

**Garcia, Ernest & Paterson, Andrew** *Where to Watch Birds in Southern Spain*
Essential guide for twitchers in one of Europe's richest regions for birdwatching.

**Grunfeld, Frederic & Farino, Teresa** *Wild Spain*
There's a chapter on Andalucía in this summary of Spain's national parks and wildlife.

**Hunter-Watts, Guy**
*Walking in Andalucia*
Excellent guide to more than 30 walks across the region.

**Oldfield, John & Christine**
*Andalucía & the Costa del Sol*
Twenty-three detailed walks for all abilities.

## Websites

### General reference

**www.andalucia.com**
Comprehensive site with subsections for each province, plus general information on customs and culture.

**www.andalucia.org**
Official tourist website for the region, with useful information on just about every significant village and town in Andalucía.

**www.andalucia2.com**
Amateur-looking, but with wide-ranging, useful links to other sites.

**www.idealspain.com**
Thinking of relocating to Spain? This site has all you need to know.

**www.junta-andalucia.es**
Regional government website.

**www.livinginspain.co.uk**
Info for the English-speaking expat community.

**www.okspain.org**
Spanish tourist board in the USA.

**www.parador.es**
Official guide to Spain's state-run *parador* hotel chain.

**www.red2000.com**
Useful tourist guide to Spain.

**www.renfe.es/ingles**
Official Spanish rail website.

**www.spainalive.com**
Lively magazine-style site with plenty of cultural and tourist information.

**www.tourspain.es**
Official website of the Spanish tourist board.

### Leisure & culture

**www.arrakis.es/%7Ejols/tapas/indexin.html**
Comprehensive guide to Spanish tapas.

**www.asoliva.com**
All you need to know about Spanish olive oil.

**www.flamenco-world.com**
Details of this quintessential Andalucian art form all over the globe.

**www.mundo-taurino.org**
Links to bull-fighting websites.

**www.parquesnaturales.com**
Information about Spain's Natural Parks.

**www.sherry.org**
Lowdown on Andalucía's favourite tipple.

### Towns & cities

**www.aboutgranada.com**
City guide to Granada.

**www.almeria-turismo.org**
Tourist guide to Almeria.

**www.aboutsevilla.com**
City guide to Sevilla.

**www.cadiznet.com**
Provincial guide to Cádiz.

**www.costasol.com**
Tourist info for the Costa del Sol.

**www.gibraltar.gi**
Best internet resource for the Rock.

**www.guiadehuelva.com**
Provincial guide to Huelva.

**www.malaga.com**
City guide to Málaga.

**www.marbella.com/eng/**
Hotels, golf courses, real estate and restaurants.

**www.sol.com**
Sevilla city and its province.

**www.turiscordoba.es**
Tourist guide to Córdoba.

**Directory**

# Index

**Note**: Page numbers in **bold** indicate section(s) giving key information on a topic; *italics* indicate photographs.
  Note also that there are individual city indexes within the main index for **Granada** and **Sevilla**.

## a

Abd al-Malik 15
Abd al-Rahman I **15**, 23, 206, 208
Abd al-Rahman III **15**, 23, 28, **206**, **207**, 208, 290
Aben Humaya 48, 281
Abencerraje family **256**, 257
Abu al-Mansur **15**, 206, 207
accommodation 312-313
Acero, Vicente **32**, 106, 114
Acinipo *see* Ronda La Vieja
activity holidays 314-315
Adamuz 219
addresses 316
Adra 13, **296**
adventure sports 80, 129, 274, **314**
aerial sports 314
age restrictions 316
Agua Amarga 289, **299**, 300
Aguadulce **296**, *296*, 297
Aguilar de la Frontera 221-222
AIDS 318-319
airlines 308
airports 308
al-Hakam II 206, 207, 208
al-Mutamid 34
al-Qaeda 17
al-Zahrawi (Abulcasis) 208
Alájar 149, *156*, **157-162**
Alarcón, Pedro Antonio de **37**, 272
Albánchez **303**, 305
Albaricoques, Los 299
Albondón 286
Albuñol 286
Alcalá de los Gazules 128
Alcalá La Real 49, 227, **231**, *231*, 232
Alcaudete 231
Alcázar, Balthasar del 35
Alcornocales, Parque Natural de los 101, 105, **128**
Alcútar 281
Aldehuela, Martín de **91**, 92
Alfarnate 76
Alfonso VI, King **15**, 23
Alfonso VII, King 29
Alfonso VIII, King **15**, 23
Alfonso X 'the Wise', King 30, 124, 17, 178
Alfonso XI, King 170, 208
Alfonso XII, King 211, 304
Alfonso XIII, King **19**, 88
Algeciras 20, 48, **140-141**
Alhama de Granada 247, **270**, 271
Alhambra, the 17, 23, **28-29**, 247, 248, *248*, **249-257**, 267
Alhaurín de la Torre 48
Ali, Tariq 37
Almanzor *see* Abu al-Mansur
Almería airport 308
Almería
  City 17, 20, 28, 29, 31, 48, 289, **290-295**
  Province 287-306
Almerimar 296
Almodóvar del Río 205, **218-219**
Almohads, the **15**, 23, 28, 29, 166, 170
Almonaster La Real 29, 46, 149, **156**, 157
Almoravids, the **15**, 23, 28
Almuñécar 13, 27, 247, **283-285**, *285*
Alpujarras, the 17, 23, 247, **274-282**, 289, 304
Andersen, Hans Christian 54, 55
Andújar 14, 46, **233**, 235
*anis* 222
Antequera 13, 27, 48, 53, **84-87**, *84*, *87*, 88
Aquatropic 283
Aracena 47, 49, 149, **158**, 162, *162*
archaeology holidays 315
Árchez 82
Archidona 85, **88**
architecture 27-33
  books 328
Arcos de la Frontera 105, **126-128**, *129*
Arganthonius, King 13
Aroche 48, 149, **156**, 157
Arrecife de la Sirenas 298
Arroyomolinos 129
Athanagild, King 14
ATMs 321
attitudes 316
*Atún y Chocolate* 132
AVE (high-speed train) 22, 26, **311**
Averroës 15, 16
Axarquía, the 53, *74*, **75-79**, *77*, *247*
Ayamonte 151-153
Aznar, José María **22**, 26

## b

Baelo Claudia 14, 27, 29, **133**, 134, 138
Baena 46, 205, **223-224**
Baetica **14**, 23
Baeza 17, 29, 30, 31-32, 47, 227, **236-238**, *238*
Bailén 234
Bailén (1808), Battle of **19**, 234
Bailén (208 BC), Battle of 13
Banderas, Antonio 55, 58, 59
bandits 75, 76, 91, **98**
banks 321
Baños de la Encina 227, *233*, **234**, 235
bar and café opening times 321
Barbate 14, **132**, 138
baroque architecture 29, **32**
Baza 272
Bécquer, Gustavo Adolfo 36
Belalcázar 220
Bélmez 220
Bélmez de la Moraleda 232
Benahavis 60, **70**
Benalmádena Costa **62**, 65, 66
Benalmádena Pueblo 53, **62**, 63, *63*
Benaoján **94**, 101, 102
Bércules 281
Berruguete, Alonso 31, 239
bicycle *see* cycling
birdwatching &
  birdwatching holidays **152-153**, **314-315**
  birding spots, top five 89
Bizet 178
*Blood Wedding* 299
Boabdil **17**, 222, 223, 249, 274, 275, 296, 304
boat, getting to Andalucía by 309
Bobastro 88
Bolonia **134**, 137
Bomberg, David 91
Bonaparte, Joseph **19**, 23
Bonaparte, Napoleon *see* Napoleon
books on Andalucía 328-329
  *see also* literary Andalucía
Borge, El **75**, 76
Borrow, George 36
Bosque, El **128**, 130
Bowles, Paul 134, 135
Boyd, Alistair 91
brandy 118-119
breakdown services 310
Breña y Marismas del Barbate, Parque Natural de la 132

Brenan, Gerald **37**, 274, **281**
Bubión **278**, 279
Buddhist Centre, O Sel Ling 275
bullfighting 90, **91**, **174-175**, 216, 314
Burroughs, Williams 134
bus, getting to and around Andalucía by 309
Busquistar **278**, 279, 280

## c

Cabalgata de los Reyes Magos 47
Caballero, Fernán 36-37
Cabo de Gata 289, *289*, 296, **297-299**
Cabo de Gata (village) *see* San Miguel del Cabo de Gata
Cabra 205, **221**
Cabra del Santo Cristo 232
Cádiar 282
Cádiz
  City 13, 17, 18, 19, 20, 23, 27, 32, 47, 105, **106-112**
  Province 103-146
Caesar, Julius 71, 106
Calahonda 286
Calahorra, La 32, 247, **272**, 273, *273*, 281
Calatrava, Santiago 33, 179
Calderón, Serafín Estébanez 36
Caliphal style architecture 27-28
Caliphate, the **15**, 23
Camarón de la Isla, El 184
*camas* 313
Campaña, Pedro de 178
Campiña, La 165
camping 313
Cañada de las Fuentes 243
Cañar 275
Candelas de San Juan 47
Canillas 83
Canjáyar **304**, 305
Cano, Alonso **32**, 107, 116, 177, 254, 259-260, 291
Cano, Miguel 178
Caños de Meca, Los 105, 131, **132**, 136
Cantaraján (beach) 80
Cantariján 283
*Canterbury Tales, The* 118
Capileira 247, **278**, 279
car
  getting around by 309-311
  rental 311
Caracol, Manolo 184

# Advertisers' Index

Please refer to the relevant sections for full details